The Biltmore Nursery

8/21/08
With Best Wishes!
Bill Alexander

THE BILTMORE NURSERY

A BOTANICAL LEGACY

FEATURING

THE 1912 BILTMORE NURSERY CATALOG

REPRODUCED IN ITS ENTIRETY

BILL ALEXANDER
LANDSCAPE AND FOREST HISTORIAN

Published by Natural History Press
A Division of The History Press
Charleston, SC 29403
www.historypress.net

The first retail Biltmore Nursery Catalog was originally published in 1907 by the Biltmore Nursery. The 1912 edition is reprinted here in its entirety, though the original order form has been removed.

Front Cover: Image of the leaves and fruit clusters of the flowering dogwood (*Cornus florida*) from original illustration on the back cover of the 1912 edition of the Biltmore Nursery catalog.

First published 2007

Manufactured in the United Kingdom

ISBN 978.1.59629.238.3

Library of Congress Cataloging-in-Publication Data

Alexander, Bill, 1950-
The Biltmore Nursery : a botanical legacy / Bill Alexander.
p. cm.
ISBN 978-1-59629-238-3 (alk. paper)
1. Biltmore Nursery (Biltmore, N.C.)--History. 2. Landscape plants--North Carolina--History.
3. Germplasm resources, Plant--North Carolina--History.
I. Title.
SB118.74.N82A44 2007
580.73'75688--dc22

2007001415

Notice: The information in this book is true and complete to the best of our knowledge. It is offered without guarantee on the part of the author or The History Press. The author and The History Press disclaim all liability in connection with the use of this book.

For my wife, Jackie,
Who has graciously supported me with love, patience and understanding
while I have pursued my career at Biltmore.

Contents

Part I

The Biltmore Nursery

A Botanical Legacy

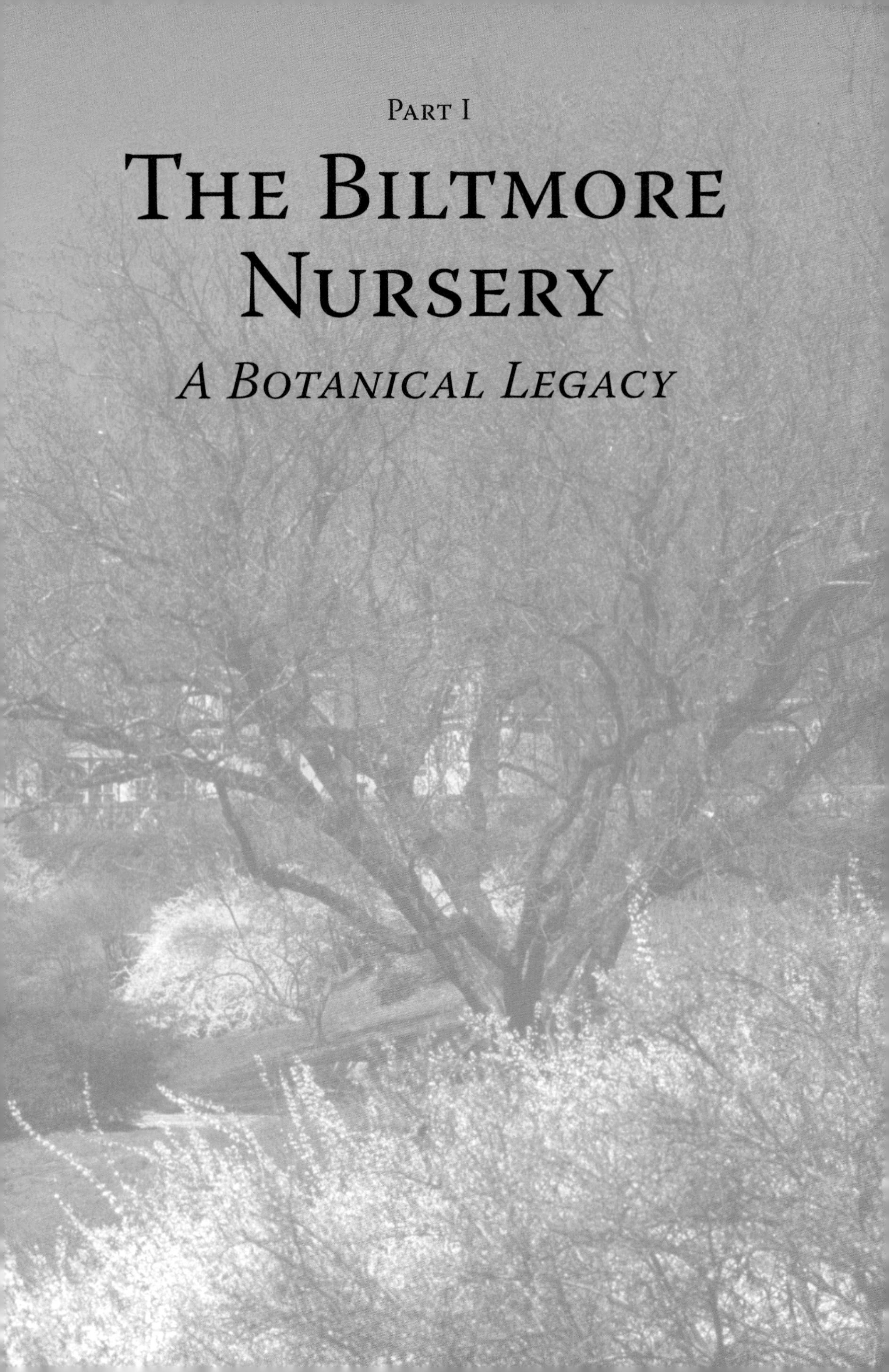

Preface

THE STORY OF THE BILTMORE Nursery is fascinating to say the least. From the date of its establishment in 1889 and through the years of its existence, it was ranked among the top nurseries not only in North America, but also in the world in terms of scale and offerings of plant varieties and numbers. As a commercial nursery, it produced and sold one of the broadest selections of hardy, temperate, ornamental plants available anywhere. The Biltmore Nursery was unique in many ways because it was more than just a nursery. It was the cornerstone of an enterprise, a grand undertaking the likes of which had never been seen. The Nursery played more than just a supporting role on the vast estate of its founder and entrepreneur, George Washington Vanderbilt. Guided by the vision and creative genius of his planner and advisor, landscape architect Frederick Law Olmsted, Vanderbilt put into effect an extraordinary and unprecedented experiment in forestry, agriculture and horticulture in the southern Appalachian region of Western North Carolina. An experiment? Yes, because no one had ever attempted to do what he accomplished on such a large scale at his Biltmore Estate.

Totaling some 125,000 acres or 195 square miles at its peak, the Estate was the site of America's first systematically managed forest of such proportions that was designed to return a profit to the landowner while reclaiming thousands of acres of land that had been denuded by a century of exploitive over-cutting and poor farming practices. The forestry operations led to the establishment of the Biltmore Forest School, the country's first. The Estate's agricultural operations included one of the largest premier dairies in America and Vanderbilt's experts introduced the latest agricultural technology and innovative farming methods into the region.

Olmsted recommended the establishment of a Nursery to serve multiple purposes. First, as there were no large commercial nurseries within a reasonable shipping distance from Biltmore, Olmsted knew that the cost of importing the quantities of plants needed to carry out his plans would be prohibitive. Secondly, many of the tree, shrub and other plant varieties that would be desirable to plant either weren't available from nurseries or weren't available in large enough quantities. A nursery would facilitate the propagation and growing of the millions of trees, shrubs and other plants that would be needed for several ambitious projects: landscaping the extensive Home Grounds and gardens near Mr. Vanderbilt's residence; planting a 250-acre pastoral English-style park with groves of trees; planting the picturesque borders of the 3-mile Approach Road and many miles of other pleasure drives; reforesting a vast acreage of abandoned pastures and cut-over woodland; and planting Olmsted's proposed arboretum on both sides of 12 miles of roads. The Biltmore Arboretum would be designed as "a museum of trees" to provide opportunities for research as well as for viewing pleasure. It would include an extensive scientific herbarium and a comprehensive botanical library. The Biltmore Arboretum, in Olmsted's thinking, would be "finer and more instructive than any other...to which naturalists would resort from all parts of the world."

This account is not intended to be a definitive treatise of the Biltmore Nursery or the many aspects of Biltmore Estate's horticultural and forestry legacies. Rather, it is an introduction and glimpse into the grand integrated scheme that Olmsted planned for Vanderbilt's Estate and a little sketch of how portions of it played out. The Biltmore Company Archives contain tens of thousands of documents, including correspondence, reports, journal entries, invoices and receipts, maps and drawings and photographic images, relating to the above subjects. Additionally, the special collections at the Frederick Law Olmsted National Historic Site, the Olmsted and Pinchot Papers at the Library of Congress and other repositories contain many other documents concerning the forestry and landscape developments at Biltmore. Volumes could be written based on research of these collections about Biltmore's landscape, forestry operations, the Herbarium collections and the Nursery's plant acquisitions and distributions.

It is hoped that this reproduction of the complete 1912 edition of the Biltmore Nursery's "descriptive catalog" will be a valuable resource for horticulturists and gardeners, botanists and dendrologists, landscape architects and students, historians and anyone else who wants to learn more about the wealth of plants described herein. According to the introduction of the catalog, the stock offered in the present season (1912) "embraces one of the largest and most complete collections of ornamentals in the world." Included are conifers, deciduous trees, broad-leaved evergreen trees and shrubs, deciduous shrubs, roses, vines, ornamental grasses and bamboos, hardy ferns, aquatic and bog plants and herbaceous perennials. The catalog should be a useful reference in planning the restoration of period landscapes and gardens or equally in designing contemporary ones with heirloom varieties. As many plant names have changed over time, an appendix is included at the end of part I with notes on nomenclature and a list of plant genera. Lastly, it is hoped that the reader will simply enjoy reading and learning about the many wonderful plants included in this beautifully illustrated edition of the Biltmore Nursery catalog.

Acknowledgements

In most works, authors research and draw from information from a wide range of resources and owe gratitude to others who have worked to organize and make available historic documents and other materials relevant to particular subjects. There are too many people to mention individually and some that I have never even met, who in the course of their own work have contributed to the collective knowledge of the history of Biltmore Estate's creation and evolution. I am indebted to many who have served on the staff of the Frederick Law Olmsted National Historic Site for conserving and making available for research the many various documents of "Project No. 0170—Property of George W. Vanderbilt (Biltmore Estate)." I would like to acknowledge all who have laboriously worked over the years in the organization and publication of the Olmsted Papers at the Library of Congress—what an awesome job! I particularly want to thank Dr. Charles Beveridge, series editor of the Frederick Law Olmsted Papers, Washington, D.C., for his inspiration and support over the more than twenty-five years that we have been acquainted. Dr. Beveridge is, in my opinion, the greatest living Olmsted scholar.

I want to personally acknowledge my director, Ellen Rickman, and all of my colleagues in the Museum Services Department at Biltmore Estate who have supported me in this and other projects. I would like to thank Suzanne Durham, special collections manager, and the staff, past and present, who have diligently labored behind the scenes to organize and process the many thousands of documents in the Biltmore Company Archives to make them easier to research.

Lastly, I owe my sincere respect and gratitude to George W. Vanderbilt's grandson, Mr. William A.V. Cecil Sr.; Vanderbilt's great-grandson, Mr. William A.V. Cecil Jr., current president and CEO of The Biltmore Company; and other Cecil family members for their dedication and perseverance in maintaining and preserving Biltmore Estate, a National Historic Landmark, and its horticultural, agricultural and forestry legacies. Most of all, I would like to thank them for letting me be a part of it all for the past twenty-eight years. Perhaps it was fate that brought me here, I don't know. I do know, however, that I agree with Frederick Law Olmsted when he wrote many years ago as work on the forest, Arboretum and grounds of Biltmore Estate progressed, "It is a great work of Peace that we are engaged in, and one of these days we will all be proud of our parts in it."

Introduction

In the spring of 1888, George Washington Vanderbilt started buying old farms and sparsely wooded tracts of land in the Blue Ridge Mountains near Asheville, North Carolina, where he had vacationed with his mother. Then twenty-six, George was the youngest son of William Henry Vanderbilt and grandson of "the Commodore" Cornelius Vanderbilt, who had made the family fortune in shipping and railroads. At the time, the area was a new "winter resort" for Northerners who were attracted by its healthful and comparatively moderate winter climate, as well as its scenic beauty. For nearly a century after its establishment, Asheville's location in the heart of the mountains kept it largely isolated from more populous areas. Although accessible only by horse and wagon roads, the village became popularly known as the "Land of the Sky." Asheville's fame as both a vacation and health resort quickly spread far and wide after the first railroad penetrated the rugged Blue Ridge topography in 1880. By 1885, the village had become a town, more than doubling its year-round population to five thousand, and continued to grow at a rapid pace. Annually, additional thousands of "summer people" from Charleston and other Southern cities flocked to Asheville and nearby resorts like Flat Rock and Highlands to escape the heat. Besides numerous hotels and inns, many boardinghouses flourished, some operated solely as sanitaria for tuberculosis patients. Asheville's prominence as a health resort was the primary reason that George Vanderbilt and his mother, Mrs. W.H. Vanderbilt, who suffered from a lingering case of malaria, came to visit.

While staying in Asheville, Vanderbilt found the air mild and invigorating and he enjoyed the distant scenery and views of the mountain peaks. In one of his rambles, Vanderbilt came to a particular spot overlooking the French Broad River and thought the prospect finer than any he had seen. It occurred to him that he might like to have a house there. Although the immediate surroundings had frequently been slashed, burned and overgrazed, Vanderbilt imagined that the land could be improved over time. Through his agent, he quietly started purchasing vacant tracts of land that had been on the market for a considerable time and were "beyond the field of speculation." Parcel by parcel he quickly acquired several thousand acres along both sides of the French Broad. Not sure of what he would do with all of his land, Vanderbilt then invited two of America's preeminent designers—noted architect Richard Morris Hunt, an expert in the Beaux Arts style of architecture, and landscape architect Frederick Law Olmsted, America's leading park maker—to design his house and help him plan the extensive grounds on his Estate, which he would call Biltmore. Being brought together to collaborate on a project of such grand scale, these two creative geniuses drew from their collective years of talents and experiences to design an unparalleled country estate for their client. Biltmore, in essence, became the crowning jewel for both men at the pinnacles of their careers.

Olmsted, at Vanderbilt's invitation, made a site inspection of Vanderbilt's recently acquired holdings in North Carolina in the fall of 1888 and took notes on his observations and the conditions he found. He additionally arranged for a local civil engineer, J.G. Aster, to make a survey of the acreage and to report any information on the local features that he could pick up incidental to the survey. Olmsted was interested in finding out as much as he could about the character of the soils, geological aspects, presence of any ledges that could possibly supply stone for building or quarrying, the location of streams and springs and the quality of any existing timber. He informed Mr. Aster that, "You will understand confidentially that Mr. V. wants as the result of your preliminary survey to be able to thoroughly consider a proposition to build a winter and spring residence for himself and certain members of his family circle to whom the climate of New York is too harsh or the winters too long, and that a part of the question is how he could turn the larger part of the property to good account, as a matter of business, in a manner that would allow him to take some pleasure in its management and that would make the scenery and advantages for a pleasant out-of-door life not less agreeable than at present." Olmsted also solicited the assistance of Robert Douglas from Waukegan, Illinois, a nurseryman and authority on forest tree species, in inspecting Vanderbilt's lands with respect to their adaptability to the growth of forest trees.

During the ensuing months, Olmsted began to outline his initial thoughts and formulate his preliminary recommendations to Vanderbilt. He corresponded with Richard M. Hunt in the late winter and early spring concerning Hunt's plans for the residence and suggestions as to position, while discussing his own ideas for various considerations and amenities in the immediate vicinity of the chateau. On July 12, 1889, Olmsted addressed a thirty-six-page report to his client in the form of a letter, in which his ideas and suggestions were separated under nine headings. The subjects included his suggestions for positioning the residence, greenhouse and service garden, his views on the condition and treatment of the forest, agricultural considerations, the approach drive to the residence, a park, a proposed Arboretum and Nursery. A few months later, Olmsted recounted his conversations with Vanderbilt in a letter to his friend, Fred Kingsbury.

> *I take pretty nearly your view of the Vanderbilt property. It is in itself (i.e. regardless of the outlooks) a generally poor and vagabondish region but there are potentialities in parts of it, especially in the valleys, of which we can make something. Knowing that within fifty miles there is grand local scenery and almost the finest deciduous forest in the world, I was at my first visit greatly disappointed with its apparent barrenness and the miserable character of its woods. Standing at what is now the house site, Mr. Vanderbilt said to me, "I came to Asheville with my mother. We found the air mild and invigorating and I thought well of the climate. I enjoyed the distant scenery. I took long rambles and found pleasure in doing so. In one of them I came to this spot under favorable circumstances and thought the prospect finer than any other I had seen. It occurred to me that I would like to have a house here. The land was beyond the field of speculation and I bought a piece of it at a low rate…and step-by-step, without any very definite end in view, I have acquired about 2,000 acres. Now I have brought you here to examine it and tell me if I have been doing anything very foolish." "What do you imagine you will do with all this land?" I asked. "Make a park of it, I suppose."*

> *"You bought the place then simply because you thought it had a good air and because, from this point, it had a good distant outlook. If this was what you wanted you have made no mistake. There is no question about the air and none about the prospect. But the soil seems to be generally poor. The woods are miserable, all the good trees having again and again been culled out and only runts left. The topography is most unsuitable for anything that can properly be called park scenery. It's no place for a park. You could only get very poor results at great cost in attempting it." "What could be done with it?"*
>
> *"Such land in Europe would be made a forest; partly, if it belonged to a gentleman of large means, as a preserve for game, mainly with a view to crops of timber. That would be a suitable and dignified business for you to engage in; it would, in the long run, be probably a fair investment of capital and it would be of great value to the country to have a thoroughly well organized and systematically conducted attempt in forestry made on a large scale. My advice would be to make a small park into which to look from your house; make a small pleasure ground and garden, farm your river bottom chiefly to keep and fatten live stock with view to manure; and make the rest a forest, improving the existing woods and planting the old fields."*

Although Olmsted's recommendations called for surrounding Biltmore House with a park and landscape of pleasure grounds and gardens and miles of carriage drives, his plans went beyond mere aesthetics. Olmsted advised reforesting the abandoned hillside pastures and improving the existing woodlands to create a systematically managed forest as a much-needed model for the country. He envisioned a major arboretum on the Estate as an outdoor museum of trees, complete with a botanical library and Herbarium, where dendrologists, botanists and landscape gardeners from around the world could study and learn. He also advised Vanderbilt on the agricultural possibilities for his land. To accomplish these grand schemes, however, millions of trees, shrubs and other plants would be needed. Even Vanderbilt could ill afford to import such vast quantities of plants to fulfill Olmsted's vision for the Estate. A Nursery for propagating and growing great quantities of plants of every desirable variety would prove to be the answer. In January 1891 Olmsted reported:

> *This advice struck him* [Vanderbilt] *favorably and after thinking it over several months he told me that he was prepared to adopt it. Since then I have been giving it practical form and have each division of the scheme in operation. Having a commercial forest in view, he has since added to the property, piece after piece, until now it amounts to quite 6000 acres. We have been forming a nursery for the estate in which we already have growing 40,000 trees and shrubs and are propagating a much larger number; these for the borders of the roads and for the home grounds. We have planted on the "old fields" 300 acres of white pine and are preparing schedules of stock for the forest planting and are instructing and breaking in two foremen with small gangs for taking out the poor and dilapidated trees of the existing woods.*

As has been stated, the greater part of the Estate's landscape was to be a "forest" with a "small" park, and a pleasure ground and garden taken out near the residence. Olmsted's Arboretum scheme was intended, also, to be part of the forest, a special part for displaying an extensive variety of trees and shrubs. Likewise, the landscape along the three-mile Approach Road to Biltmore House was intended to create a "sensation of passing through the remote depths of a natural forest." The Nursery was established to grow countless numbers of trees to reforest much of the land; to plant the proposed Arboretum and park, which was really a type of "open forest"; and to provide the ornamental plantations for the gardens and drives. This story, then, would not be complete without an understanding of Olmsted's vision for how the forest and the other various aspects of his master plan were intertwined. The first section provides an insight into the prior history and treatment of the Estate's acreage and Olmsted's philosophies on forestry, and is intended to help the reader gain an understanding of what led him to make certain recommendations concerning the forest and why he felt forestry at Biltmore would be so important. Additional sections are devoted to some of the more important features of the Estate's landscape design in order to illustrate the role of the Biltmore Nursery as the cornerstone of Olmsted's grand scheme for the Estate. Included are discussions on the Deer Park, the Ramble or Shrub Garden, the Glen, the Approach Road, the Biltmore Arboretum and Herbarium, all of which were dependent upon the plant collections and production of the Nursery. Lastly, the significance of the Biltmore Nursery as a commercial enterprise is presented to illustrate its botanical and horticultural influences on the country's varied landscapes, public parks, institutional and private grounds and the nursery industry.

Part II is devoted to a reproduction of the entire 1912 edition of the descriptive Biltmore Nursery catalog that includes more than 1,700 varieties of plants. With its detailed descriptions and numerous photographic illustrations, the catalog is a virtual encyclopedia of ornamental plants being grown in the early part of the twentieth century. The catalog is one of the most comprehensive guides to horticultural plant varieties for that period and should be a useful reference and resource for those seeking to further their knowledge of historic varieties of trees, shrubs and many other kinds of plants.

A Model Forest

At a time when the country was still relentlessly devastating its forests, Frederick Law Olmsted was considering how to stop the thoughtless destruction and demonstrate how the long-term, scientific management of forests could be a wise investment for landowners. He was one of several prominent individuals in North America advocating the need for managing forests for the future. Olmsted—along with men like Professor Charles Sprague Sargent, director of the Arnold Arboretum; Franklin B. Hough from New York; Prussian forester Bernard Fernow; noted landscape architect Horace W.S. Cleveland; and numerous others—was part of a growing movement to establish forestry in the United States and Canada. Their views and concerns were published in periodicals like *Garden and Forest* (established by Sargent in 1888) and Fernow's *Forestry Bulletin*, in papers presented at the American Forestry Association meetings and forestry congresses and in the USDA's Division of Forestry annual reports.

Although Olmsted had tried unsuccessfully to get other clients to implement systematic forestry management, it wasn't until young George Vanderbilt invited the elder Olmsted to Asheville in the fall of 1888 that Olmsted's dreams of a model forest started to take shape. In his thirty-six-page report to Vanderbilt in July 1889, Olmsted devoted sixteen pages to the section titled "The Forest." The fact that he devoted so much time and space to the subject suggests that the treatment of the forest was of the highest priority in Olmsted's overall master plan for the Estate's landscape. His report consisted of a detailed discussion of the conditions of the existing woodlands, his theories of how those conditions had occurred and some of his recommendations for managing the forest. He began by stating, "Knowing that at no great distance from the Estate and under conditions of climate as far as I could judge, less favorable at least to southern forms of vegetation, there was the finest natural forest and the most varied in its constituents, to be found in the United States, or possibly in the temperate regions of the world, I was last year greatly disappointed to find your property so deficient in respect both to variety of trees and to local beauty of trees in mass. Exploring the narrow valleys I have found, this impression a little relieved." It is obvious from Olmsted's observations that the existing forest cover on Mr. Vanderbilt's land stood out in contrast to the natural forest conditions of the surrounding areas of Western North Carolina. He must have thought that there was hope for recovery of the forest when he stated that, based on his studies of the circumstances, aided by Mr. Douglas, he was led to think that the defects to which he referred had been of comparatively recent occurrence and that "there had been once and might be again…a much greater variety of trees and shrubs than are found at present on the Estate." Prior to writing this report, Olmsted had asked Robert Douglas, a nurseryman from Waukegan, Illinois, and an authority on forest tree species, to do an assessment of Vanderbilt's land and advise him on recommended tree species for reforestation.

The historic land use patterns in the century before Vanderbilt purchased his land had certainly had an impact on the area and its forests. The first permanent settlement in the region west of the continental divide of the Blue Ridge Mountains had been established in 1785 along the Swannanoa River a few miles east of its confluence with the French Broad River. By 1792, when Buncombe County was founded, more than two hundred families had settled in the area, many of them establishing farms on the fertile bottomlands adjacent to the French Broad River that later became part of Biltmore Estate. Others had settled on the thickly wooded uplands to carve out their farms and a living. Thus began a century of changes and exploitation of the virgin, indigenous forest that ultimately became Biltmore Estate. The forest was cleared at first, little by little, to open up land needed to raise crops and pasturage for livestock, to produce timber for building cabins, barns and fences and for firewood. Thousands of trees were simply girdled to die in place in order to allow light for crops planted around them. Because much of the cleared land was steep and the soil highly erodible, many of the farms became worn out very quickly. The practices of allowing livestock, particularly hogs, to graze in the woodlands and setting intentional, periodic wildfires to beat the forest back were particularly devastating. Many of the landowners were forced to begin cutting all of their best remaining timber to sell to sawmills in order to supplement their income and feed their families. Eventually, as the land grew poorer, many sold out and moved on. By the late 1880s when George Vanderbilt began purchasing tracts of land, many parcels had changed ownership several times and had ended up in the hands of real estate speculators rather than resident owners. The exceptions were a few of the larger, more prosperous farms in the bottomlands along the river and a scattering of small tracts on the hills above.

Upon exploring and surveying the land, particularly the patchwork of existing woodland, Olmsted later expressed his opinions to Vanderbilt as to why much of the Estate's forested areas were in such an unnatural and poor condition.

> *As to the way in which the present conditions have been brought about it appears probable that although there have been no permanent residents on the greater part of the Estate it has been occupied for generations past by a succession of campers, squatters and transient settlers in such numbers that the final effect of their operations has been not unlike what would be expected from those of a much denser population. I saw what remains of four saw mills on the Estate, three of which must have been at work a good number of years; there have been others, probably, on the Estate, for all that were within much less than half its entire space, and yet others near it, drawing from it. Almost certainly, also, shingles and boards have been worked on it in large quantity without mill saws. For these purposes and those of the mills, every tree desirable for any sort of salable lumber has been felled. What is now seen is the refuse. As always the case, to get out the best trees, many a little less choice have been felled or broken down and ruined. Of what remained the settlers have taken great numbers for their cabins, fences and fuel. Big fires are the one luxury of the pioneer cabins. Then more have been taken to feed Asheville hearths than you can readily imagine. With many, when anything was wanted from a store, the readiest* [sic] *way to get it was*

> *to take a load of fire-wood to town. You may often see distant settlers, even now, drawing jags of hickory cordwood with a runty bull before a creaking cart into Asheville for the same purpose, and, undoubtedly, similar expeditions have been made from the region of the Estate constantly for many years past.*

Vanderbilt had purchased numerous tracts of land from absentee landowners. With no one watching over many of these vacant ownerships, there apparently had been a lot of unchecked removal of wood from the area. Besides the past cutting and removal of most of the valuable trees, Olmsted's observations and study accounted for two other factors that contributed to the extreme poverty of the woodlands and the paucity of good regeneration of tree species (other than oaks) and understory plants in general. First, he stated, "The woods have been a range for stock and stock has been often hard pressed, forcing the hogs to root searchingly for seeds of trees in the soil and the horned cattle to close browsing. Oak sprouts are comparatively tough and astringent and sprouts of other trees have been selected by the cattle in preference to them." Secondly, Olmsted noted that there had been the destruction by fires. He supposed young oaks had been better able to resist fire than young trees of other indigenous species. Fires had been of two classes: first, there had been "comparatively light fires, generally started intentionally in the spring, to clear the surface of dead leaves and stubs so that a better growth of annual grasses and other herbage might spring up for the pasturage of cattle and hogs." It was commonly accepted that the practice had been a custom of the Indians inhabiting the region and had been taken up by the earliest white settlers and perpetuated by successive landowners. There had also been occurrences of more intense and devastating fires started accidentally during drought periods in the slash and brush left from timbering. Olmsted suspected that those fires had destroyed the seed previously existing in the surface soil, and the younger crop of oaks had grown from seed falling from the older trees that were still standing. He also blamed the fires for the absence of undergrowth and of superficial leaf-mould and the sterile appearance of the surface of the ground in many places.

Olmsted's assessment of the existing condition of the land and its past history of treatment was not limited to just the woodland areas, but also to the mosaic of clearings on the property. He judged that there was an aggregate of some two thousand acres on the Estate, consisting of many small patches where the forest had been cleared for crops. He noted that the ground had been cultivated in a very shallow way, "the plow often being a mere prong drawn by one small bullock and its operation a scratch but three or four inches deep." With such tillage, crops of corn, grain and tobacco had been grown year after year until the land was "worn out." Olmsted observed that when the land was thoroughly exhausted, it had been "turned out," and then, as a rule, after a few years, a growth of several species of pines "peculiar to barren lands" had sprung up, and the most common one, known as the scrub pine, was generally recognized as a badge of poverty.

Having described the existing conditions and past use (or abuse) of the patchwork of woodlands on the Estate, Olmsted turned to making some general suggestions to Mr. Vanderbilt concerning forestry. Olmsted's idea of considering the aesthetics or landscape effects along with the economical or utilitarian aspects of forestry was ahead of its time. He related to Vanderbilt,

> *Considering that you were likely to use the Estate as a winter resort I suggested last year that there would be a considerable advantage in having considerable portions of it planted with White Pines, having in view, first a contrast to prevailing Oaks; second, winter verdure; third, the pleasant footing that is always found under a White Pine wood; fourth, the agreeable balsamic odor of the tree; and, lastly, its probable future value. As to the feasibility of growing it thriftily on the Estate I more particularly sought Mr. Douglas's opinion. This was entirely favorable, and I have asked a proposition from him, looking to the immediate planting on the old fields of several hundred acres of White Pines, by contract. Other suggestions as to general planting and the management of the forest I reserve for the present. I will simply say, at this point, that I am inclined to advise you to have in view the establishment and maintenance of an unbroken forest from the north to the south end of the Estate, to extend from the east border, as a general rule, to the edge of the river bottom on the west, but with a "Park" to be taken out near the residence as to be hereafter proposed. Perhaps with certain fields to be also taken out for agricultural purposes. Your property on the left bank of the river to be also maintained in forest condition and improved.*

It is readily apparent from these statements that Olmsted intended that the forest would be the largest, and perhaps the most important, part of his plan for the Estate. He recommended that the overgrown, ill-formed oaks be gradually eliminated and replaced with more valuable and pleasing trees. The younger oaks and other trees should be thinned so that they could develop more fully, and in desirable localities an "underwood" should be established.

Olmsted observed that under the old remnant oaks, the younger oaks weren't growing very well, partly because the older oaks shaded many of them and partly because the roots of the older oaks were taking "the lion's share of the moisture and a certain part of the remaining constituents of the soil needed for their nourishment." Further, the younger oaks weren't yet stunted, or so cramped by crowding that, if "judiciously thinned," they would soon acquire "fine, characteristic, stalwart and umbrageous forms, such as you have seen oaks taking in Windsor Forest, for example." Olmsted suggested removing all oaks that were not of "exceptional and admirable character," selectively thinning the thickets of the younger oaks and giving the other trees—such as hickories, chestnuts, limes, tupelos, beeches, maples, tulips and birches—that were sparsely growing with them a fair chance. He asserted that if supplemental planting of other trees, natural to the circumstances, was done in the occasional vacant spaces and a growth of understory shrubs, young trees and other plants was encouraged, "a forest would result that would easily come in time to be the finest in the country."

In the rest of the section of his report dealing with forestry, Olmsted offered various reasons to Mr. Vanderbilt as to why forestry at Biltmore would be a wise and justifiable use of his land.

> *You may ask, if forest undertakings are desirable in this country why are there no notable examples of them other than those recently entered upon by Railway Corporations in the treeless regions of the far West? Simply because no considerable "investment" in forests can be made with the large* <u>*early*</u> *profits that necessity, and custom growing out of general necessity, lead our people beyond all others to be passionately eager to secure. For the harvest of a forest crop one must look more years ahead than he does months for the harvest of other crops. But, so*

looking ahead, a well managed forest is likely to be as good a property, all things considered as any other. Mean time, the management of it; the oversight of its development and improvement from year to year, would be a most interesting rural occupation; far more interesting, I am sure, to a man of poetic temperament than any of those commonly considered appropriate to a country-seat life. Certainly there can be no prospect of success, of profit or pleasure from year to year, in any other use to be made of your ridge lands to compare with it. You cannot find an upland farm in all the mountain region that has a thoroughly pleasant aspect; hardly one that does not make a doleful impression. But where the native forest has not been wholly ruined in the manner I have described it to be; wherever it has been but moderately injured, its beauty, its mystery, its solem[n]ity, are really fascinating. Years ago I rode alone for a full month through the North Carolina forests, and it was with great regret that last I emerged from them. There is no experience of my life to which I could return with more satisfaction.

Olmsted's arguments for forest management covered the bases from the practical, economical, aesthetic and spiritual viewpoints, and he was obviously trying to persuade Vanderbilt that it would be a most worthy occupation for him. In his last paragraph, he makes his final case for convincing Mr. Vanderbilt that forest management would be his best option for the greater part of the Estate.

I have written in a too desultory way but you will see that in what I have said there is the substance of a proposition, which is much the most important of all that I have to submit to your consideration. That the subject may be more completely and intelligently brought before you, I advise you to read the pamphlet by my friend Mr. Cleveland that I send herewith. Reading it you will see what I meant, when I said last year, that adopting the suggestion, as then less fully presented, you would not only make the best use of the property for the direct satisfaction of yourself and friends but would be doing the country an inestimable service and thus from the start give the Estate a rank like that which Blair Athol has among the great British estates.

Again, it seems obvious from the above that Olmsted considered forestry, out of all his propositions to Mr. Vanderbilt, to be without question the most important. To make sure that Vanderbilt had more thorough and detailed information on the subject and value of forestry, Olmsted had included a copy of the publication "The Cultivation and Management of Our Native Forests for Development as Timber or Ornamental Wood" by Horace W.S. Cleveland, a landscape designer, land manager and planner and longtime friend of Olmsted's. Like Cleveland, Olmsted advocated the wise management of existing forests as valuable and renewable natural resources. Both men also promoted the establishment of artificially planted forests as experiments for studying the adaptability and growth potential of economically valuable species and for arousing public interest in forestry. Olmsted knew that his proposed forestry program at Biltmore was on the cutting edge of forestry in America and would not only provide Mr. Vanderbilt satisfaction himself, but would also be a most valuable contribution to the country.

An undated and unsigned eleven-page document titled "Project Of Operations For Improving The Forest Of Biltmore" provided certain principles and guidelines to be followed in the treatment of the Estate's woodlands. Although the document, assumed to have been written by Olmsted, doesn't take into account such technical measures as volumes and yield, it may very well be the first "working" forest management plan for a large acreage in the country. The details within provide an insight to the degraded condition of the Estate woodlands existing at the time, the probable causes and the specific steps needed for improvement of the forest's health, vigor and landscape aesthetics.

> *What is to be here considered as the Forest, is that part of the upland region of the Biltmore Estate that is now wooded, except so much of it as shall be taken for the Park, Garden and Pleasure Grounds attached to the House. Various tracts of this region that have been lately cleared and in cultivation are to be planted and when planted will be part of the Forest. But in the present Memorandum only the existing wooded land is to be considered, the extent of this being, it is estimated, something more than 4,000 acres.*
>
> *The management of forests is soon to be a subject of great national, economic importance, and as the undertaking now to be entered upon at Biltmore will be the first of the kind in the country to be carried on methodically, upon an extensive scale, it is even more desirable than it would otherwise be that it should, from the first, be directed systematically and with clearly defined purposes, and that instructive records of it should be kept.*

Olmsted was very much aware of the political discussions concerning forestry at the time, and certainly recognized the need to reclaim the vast acreage of America's exploited forests. But as no one had yet practiced forestry on the ground to any extent, he was anxious to make Biltmore the country's first example. The report expounded upon his earlier account of the existing conditions of the forest and reiterated what brought them about. "As soon as it began to be profitable to market any kind of wood from this region, saw-mills were established to work it into merchantable form and the forest was culled of its largest and most valuable trees to supply these mills." Over time the forest had been culled again and again. With the arrival of railroads, the establishment of "manufactories" at Asheville and the resulting local need for common building materials and firewood,

> *the demand at last came to be such that nearly every sound tree of the territory now forming the Biltmore Estate, that would measure a foot in diameter at the butt, could be felled and its trunk drawn to a mill with profit. The present older and taller growth of the Biltmore Forest is thus the refuse of the refuse of repeated cullings of the original forest...After each culling, most of the trunks of the felled trees were drawn to the mills and a few, with some of the larger limbs, were taken for fencing and firewood. All the fallen wood not thus disposed of, being very large in amount, was left on the ground where, when dry, it was consumed by accidental fires, which were made so intense by it as to do much more injury than they otherwise would, not only by scorching the living trees remaining on the ground, but by consuming the leaf mould that otherwise* [would] *have kept the soil moist and furnished the best of tree food.*

It is clear by this description that the existing forest on the Estate had been extensively exploited. In his wisdom, Olmsted knew that by applying good methods of forestry, the degraded forest conditions could be reversed. Olmsted's management prescription for improving the forest addressed not only the health and growth of the forest, but also such issues as aesthetics and biodiversity. The report instructed,

> *The entire Biltmore Forest is to be gradually gone over, removing the superfluous trees, and as this will take several years, by the time the work is done it will be time to thin it a second time. Therefore it is not necessary that the first cutting out of old trees should be exhaustive, and whenever there is reason for doubt whether the forest would be improved by the immediate removal of a tree, it may for the present be left.*

Instructions were also outlined for thinning the low growth of saplings to not only provide them with more room and moisture but also "to secure as even a distribution as is practicable of the choicest trees, so that, after a few years, there will be growing on the land nearly the largest amount of valuable timber that it can bear." The practical objectives of thinning to induce better growth and form were to occasionally "yield to that of retaining and promoting the growth and exhibition of particularly interesting single trees, and that of securing passages of more agreeable sylvan scenery than would result from a strict adherence to motives of purely commercial profit." There would occasionally be found young trees and groups of young trees, which, because of their beauty, would "desirably be allowed to stand until from natural decay they are of no value for timber." Opportunities were to be given "such chosen trees and groups to spread freely and attain majestic, or further develop picturesque forms," and the surrounding trees were to be cut away as needed to give them room to do so.

Thus, the plan advocated not only thinning for selection and improvements in the growth, form and vigor of the young trees as timber, but it also encouraged that consideration be given to retaining character trees and improving the scenery or aesthetics of the forest, even if it would sacrifice some future profit. Additionally, specifications were given as to which species of trees should be favored and which should not.

The last part of the document is devoted to instructions for the superintendent (James Gall, known as the "Resident Landscape Architect and Forester") to train foremen for the process of thinning and some very specific details on making decisions on which trees to take out and which to leave depending on the particular situation. Because there were no workers yet trained in America to do the kind of selective cutting that he desired to be done, Olmsted instructed that the superintendent should not give absolute freedom for decisions to his foreman until he fully understood the principles involved. Olmsted knew he was breaking new ground in this forestry program and felt it was critical that it be done to his specifications. He directed that "all engaged in this work are to be instructed and trained to be cautious and skillful when felling trees, to avoid letting them fall so as to mutilate others" and that the superintendent should look for "opportunities of forming points of special landscape interest by the development and exhibition of particular trees and groups, particularly those immediately about springs, brooks and notable outcrops of rock...An occasional glade or small open space in the Forest, with unusually promising trees on its borders, is desirable." Olmsted looked well beyond just the practical needs for trees to grow and develop. He was introducing a new, innovative concept of incorporating landscape effect, or aesthetics, into forestry management, rather than managing only for the maximum production of timber, with trees occupying every inch of available space.

After this initial forest management scheme was in place and three hundred acres of old fields had been planted to white pine by Robert Douglas, Olmsted realized that the long-term success of the forestry program would be dependent upon professional guidance by a trained forester. He wrote to George Vanderbilt on November 27, 1891, recommending that he consider hiring Gifford Pinchot as his consulting forester. Pinchot, at the time, was just beginning a career that would lead him to national acclaim as the first chief of the federal agency that came to be known as the U.S. Forest Service. Pinchot, if Vanderbilt desired, "would make an initial study of the Estate's woodlands, noting the species of trees, growth conditions, densities, quantities of board feet per acre, condition of the soil and forest floor, and silvicultural requirements, etc., and then block out a scheme or permanent plan of operations." Olmsted advised,

> *If you are to have the benefit of Mr. Pinchot's service in any way, it would undoubtedly be desirable with respect to the forest proper that nothing be done except under his advice. I say this the more confidently because I am satisfied that he would be glad to be identified with the undertaking, look to make his reputation upon it, and serve you with a degree of zeal that you could not expect to obtain from anyone else.*

Vanderbilt was agreeable to Olmsted's recommendation and Pinchot began his work at Biltmore on February 3, 1892. In a report describing what was meant by the term forestry and how forestry applications could be applied to benefit both the forest and the landowner, Pinchot stated that the "Biltmore Working Plan" would draw "attention to the fact that there is such a thing in America as forest management...As the first attempt of its kind in the United States, the experiment at Biltmore will have, it is hoped, a distinct national bearing and importance."

The greater part of Pinchot's efforts as Biltmore's forester were devoted to cruising the forests, gathering data, devising the management plan and supervising improvement cuttings and timber harvests. He divided the Estate property into ninety-two manageable compartments averaging forty-two acres each. The boundary lines were natural features such as ridges, streams and hollows supplemented by woods roads. He planned to manage the forest on the east side of the French Broad River under the "Regular High Forest System," a system in which there would be as many subdivisions as there were years in the rotation. According to Pinchot, "The trees of each sub-division would be of equal age and would differ from those of the next sub-division by one year." Once the oldest subdivision reached maturity and was "ready for the axe," it would be harvested (and reforested) and then the others in succession until the first subdivision was again mature and the rotation started over again. The system was perfect for managing the plantations being established on the old farm fields.

On the west side of the river, Pinchot planned to use the "Selection System," in which the woodland "has trees of all ages mixed together everywhere instead of being separated into groups of uniform age." The annual yield would be based on a twenty-five-year harvest rotation under what Pinchot termed the "Localized Selection System," with some trees to be taken each year from one-fifth of the area during each period of five years. Selective harvesting would return to the same section once every twenty-five years. His plan also included the continuation of the program initiated by Olmsted of converting old farm fields into forest plantations. In 1893, he reported that "after the subtraction of all land occupied for any definite purpose, there remains considerably more than 1,000 acres lying waste, but which is to be used later on for planting forest trees...The list of seedlings now being raised in the Nursery for forest planting includes twenty species, with an estimated total of 1,867,000 individuals."

Pinchot described these and other components of his management schemes in a booklet entitled "Biltmore Forest, An Account of its Treatment, and the Results of the First Year's Work," which was published and distributed at the 1893 Columbian Exposition in Chicago. The forty-nine-page account describes the history and the poor conditions prevalent in the Biltmore woodlands when the program was begun and outlines his management objectives and methods to achieve them. Pinchot stated that the working plan had three primary objectives: profitable production, a nearly constant annual yield and an improvement in the condition of the forest. Even under trying conditions, his working plan would prove that forestry could be profitable while improving the overall health and condition of the forest. Another significant contribution Pinchot made to Biltmore was his assessment of some large tracts of forested mountain land near and beyond Mount Pisgah, which led to their purchase by Vanderbilt for forestry purposes. The purchases increased his land holdings to approximately 125,000 acres, or nearly 195 square miles.

In 1895, Dr. Carl Alwin Schenck succeeded Pinchot, who left Biltmore to pursue his career as a consulting forester and by 1898 as the chief of the federal government's Division of Forestry. Schenck was a young forester from Darmstadt, Germany, who had been recommended by Sir Dietrich Brandis, an internationally renowned forestry expert and Pinchot's mentor. In January 1895 Schenck received a cable from George Vanderbilt asking him if he was "willing to come to America and to take charge of my forestry interests in western North Carolina?" Years later in his retirement, Schenck pondered this invitation and wondered why Vanderbilt wanted him, "a young German forester, for the pioneer task of establishing forestry on privately owned lands in the United States." He had never been to the country, knew almost nothing of its forests, people, language, customs or economy, nor did he feel properly prepared to answer the call.

Apparently the prospect, even with its numerous challenges and unknowns, was intriguing enough for Schenck to accept the proposition. During his fourteen-year tenure as a respected forester at Biltmore, Schenck devised a plan and implemented selective harvest systems and experiments in Vanderbilt's extensive Pisgah Forest tracts as well as continuing the management and improvement of Biltmore Forest that was begun by Olmsted and Pinchot. Schenck devoted a great deal of time and effort to the reforestation of hundreds of acres of old, abandoned farm fields on the Estate. Through his many experiments (successes and failures) with plantations of both conifers and hardwoods, much of the previously abused and exhausted farmland was transformed into productive forests. From experiments with nearly forty species of trees, the white pine and shortleaf most readily adapted to the poor, worn-out soils. Only on scattered sites with the best soil and moisture did hardwoods succeed as plantations.

With Vanderbilt's blessings, Schenck founded the Biltmore Forest School in September 1898. The idea of a forestry school at Biltmore had been discussed by Olmsted and Pinchot, but had not been pursued. Partly because of frustrations with the lack of trained assistants to help him with his work and partly in response to the needs of his apprentices, Schenck became convinced that the time was right to begin a school. During its existence (1898–1913), the Biltmore Forest School graduated 300 of the more than 350 attendees of the school. The course was designed to give the students all of the practical knowledge and experience needed to prepare them for the various duties required of foresters in a variety of situations, particularly in private industry. Many of the graduates became prominent and successful foresters for both federal and state agencies as well as private forest industries.

In November 1908, the twentieth anniversary of forestry at Biltmore was celebrated with the Biltmore Forest Fair. Invitations to the festival were sent by Schenck to governors, senators, congressmen, foresters from state and federal divisions, lumber company owners and anyone else who had an interest in forestry, even President Taft, who declined. Fifty guests participated in the informative and festive three-day event. On foot and in carriages, the attendees viewed the progress of the various plantations, results of improvement cuttings and other projects of the Forest Department. Despite the apparent success of the fair, Schenck would spend his last months at Biltmore in 1909. Due in part to a misunderstanding with Vanderbilt and a dispute with another of Vanderbilt's managers, Schenck sadly resigned as forester at Biltmore in the summer of 1909. As chief forester at Biltmore for fourteen years, head of the country's first forestry school and as a consultant, Schenck left his mark as one of the pioneers of American forestry. His correspondence and other papers number in the tens of thousands of documents and attest to the fact that his advice and opinions on forest management, forest policies, regulations and related issues were widely sought by state and federal agencies, universities, timber companies and other large landowners, field foresters and students.

After Schenck's departure from Biltmore, Estate nurseryman and superintendent Chauncey D. Beadle assumed the responsibility of overseeing the Estate's forestry interests. Between 1910 and 1912, Vanderbilt, in an effort to generate revenues to help alleviate his worsening financial situation, had sold some "timber rights" on nearly 90,000 acres of Pisgah Forest to two different companies. One of the tracts of 20,000 acres included an option for assuming ownership after the tenth annual and final lease payment. Under the provisions of the 1911 Weeks Act, George and Edith Vanderbilt granted an option to the federal government to purchase "86,000" acres of Pisgah Forest for the creation of a national forest. Edith Vanderbilt finalized the transfer of some 83,398 acres within a few months after the death of her husband in 1914. Vanderbilt's Pisgah Forest tract became the nucleus of Pisgah National Forest, the first national forest east of the Mississippi. Mrs. Vanderbilt retained nearly 500 acres around the Estate's Buck Spring Lodge near Mount Pisgah and some 12,000 acres surrounding Biltmore House that were not part of the Pisgah Forest tract.

Upon Beadle's recommendation, Mrs. Vanderbilt endorsed a cooperative project with the U.S. Forest Service begun in 1916 to conduct a number of experiments on some of the early plantations. The Southeastern Forest Experiment Station, established in 1921, continued the research, consisting primarily of conducting periodic thinning of white pine and studying the resulting effects on growth rates and yield. Some of the knowledge learned from several decades of research in Biltmore's forest plantations was incorporated into forestry management and silviculture textbooks in the country's forestry schools.

Olmsted's vision for a model forest at Biltmore was fulfilled in that it demonstrated the value of systematic and progressive forest management for American forests, both private and public.

A Model Forest

George Vanderbilt embraced and invested in the idea of sustainable forestry at a time when it was not yet an accepted practice for large landowners. Through his forestry experiments, he quietly set an example for others in good stewardship of the land and its resources. In her letter to the secretary of agriculture on May 1, 1914, negotiating the sale of the Pisgah Forest tract, Edith Vanderbilt paid tribute to her late husband.

> *Mr. Vanderbilt was the first of the large forest owners in America to adopt the practice of forestry. He has conserved Pisgah Forest from the time he bought it up to his death, a period of nearly twenty-five years, under the firm conviction that every forest owner owes it to those who follow him, to hand down his forest property to them unimpaired by wasteful use. I keenly sympathize with his belief that the private ownership of forestland is a public trust, and I probably realize more keenly than anyone else can do, how firm was his resolve never to permit injury to the permanent value and usefulness of Pisgah Forest to the Government for National Forest purposes…I make this contribution towards the public ownership of Pisgah Forest with the earnest hope that in this way I may help to perpetuate my husband's pioneer work in forest conservation, and to insure* [sic] *the protection and the use of enjoyment of Pisgah Forest as National Forest, by the American people for all time.*

"A Small Park and a Small Pleasure Ground and Garden"

Although Olmsted recommended that the majority of the Estate be turned into a "systematically managed forest," he advised Mr. Vanderbilt to "make a small park into which to look from your house...and a small pleasure ground and garden."

Concerning the park, Olmsted stated, "There is no park-like land on the Estate. None in which park-like scenery of a notably pleasing character, could be gained in a lifetime. Plenty of land in which agreeable, wild, woodland scenery can be had in a few years." The "park-like scenery" that he was referring to was reminiscent of the pastoral parks of England's great country estates that both he and Vanderbilt had seen in their travels. Since Olmsted knew that Vanderbilt had expressed great interest in having a park, he determined the best location for this important landscape feature for his client. He advised that "the best place in which to keep deer or other animals where they may be seen to advantage, and which will, as far as practicable, have what is otherwise to be desired in a private park, will be on the west side of the residence where it can be looked into from its windows and terrace. So situated, the inconvenience of having gates wherever transit is to be made in any direction toward or from the residence on the entrance front will be avoided."

If anyone knew how to design parks and park-like scenery, it was certainly Olmsted, as he had been doing so for his entire career as a landscape architect. Olmsted's name was, to most who recognized it, instantly associated with places like New York's Central Park or Prospect Park, the parks in Boston, Buffalo, Louisville and numerous others in which expanses of pastoral meadows with scattered tree groves were pleasant and peaceful areas to relax. Olmsted told Vanderbilt,

> *The park would differ from the forest in having a much larger proportion of un-wooded ground; in having a larger proportion of its trees standing singly and in groups; in being more free from underwood and in having a turf surface, forming a fine pasture and giving a pleasant footing for riding or walking freely in all directions. It might be grazed and the turf kept moderately close by herds of the native fallow deer, of the Antelope of the Rocky Mountains and of South Downs or some other herd of small, choice mutton sheep. The latter would probably have to be folded at night on account of dogs.*

Olmsted suggested the size and limits of the proposed park:

A park that would answer every desirable purpose would not, I think, exceed two hundred and fifty acres. If much larger it would be a worrisome business to take care of it and the needed fences, gates and other requirements of keeping would be inconvenient. The central parts of it would be nearly midway between the residence and the river. It would include the valley next north of the residence; extend southwardly to the neighborhood of the Alexander place and would take in the lower hill, at present nearly covered with scrub-pine, which is very prominent in the view westward from the scaffolds...Also, probably, the hill on the north of this, beyond the conspicuous road. This road will desirably be demolished and in place of it a road carried on the edge of the bottom land at least as far as the next opening of the hills, where there is now a tolerable farm road.

In reference to some wooden towers or platforms that Olmsted had erected to show Vanderbilt and his architect, Richard Morris Hunt, how the views would look from the residence, he noted, "You will observe, when looking from the scaffolds, that by the removal of a few trees a considerably larger space of the river will be brought under view from the windows of the Residence."

In November 1893, Olmsted wrote to the Estate's general manager, Charles McNamee, that

preparations may be made at Mr. Gall's discretion, for laying down to grass all that portion of the Deer-Park south of the house and garden. In this work care [is] *to be taken to still further obliterate the old hill-side road and to so modify all abrupt and rugged surfaces, as to secure long and graceful undulations. The poorer trees, especially where they have been growing in straight fence-rows, are to be removed. Some groups of trees are to be planted on this hill-side, with care to maintain long vistas between them. The removal of any trees, as to which Mr. Gall is at all in doubt, may be left until the complete planting plan for the hill-side and lake border has been worked out.*

Olmsted wrote again in December 1894 with further instructions concerning the improvement of the plantations west of the house.

The few small trees that have been blazed are to be taken out by the roots. Trees are prepared to be transplanted to the various positions where stakes have been set with the names of the trees on them. Pits ten feet across and three feet deep are to be made ready for these, and enough good soil and compost is to be placed near them to refill the pits. This work is to be under the direction of Mr. Beadle [the Estate's nurseryman] *who will use his discretion as to which of the prepared trees can be desirably moved during the Winter. Some, it will be best probably, to leave where they are another year, in order that their new roots in the prepared ground may be tougher. It is presumed that most of them can be moved by the frozen-ball process, on a stone-boat, but as to this, also, Mr. Beadle will decide, attempting nothing that cannot surely be well done. He may think it better that all the trees should stand where they are another year. In each case he will decide. If any accident occurs injuring a tree, that tree is to be rejected. The utmost care should be used and the best results possible had in view. Mr. Beadle should personally see to the quality of the soil, manure, etc., and spare no pains to secure the highest*

> *success for this very important planting. Only good garden soil is to be used and it is to be well enriched with leaf mold and rotten cow-yard dung. All pains should be taken to guard the trees from rough treatment and preserve them from jar.*

Olmsted's highly detailed instructions illustrate several important points: the "Deer-Park" was undoubtedly considered an important part of Olmsted's overall plan, as shown by his personal involvement in staking out tree locations and his instructions given with such a high level of detail; Olmsted's apparent knowledge of sound tree planting techniques and horticultural methods in general; and his obvious confidence in the ability and judgment of Mr. Beadle in the implementation of his plans. Olmsted's park at Biltmore came to be known as the Deer Park, and although decisions were made not to enclose it with a fence, the native whitetail deer were stocked on the Estate and were free to roam through the park at will. Olmsted further designed the Lagoon, a six-acre lake in the lower end of the Deer Park, as a reflecting body of water to add another element of peacefulness to this pastoral setting.

Olmsted wrote to architect Richard M. Hunt on March 2, complimenting him on his "new plan" and his suggestions "as to position." However, Olmsted immediately made several suggestions of his own relating to the site, position of the house and added features, including a terrace and stable. This letter, which is very early in the project, is important in that it begins to frame Olmsted's vision and creative genius for Biltmore and it establishes (for better or worse) his working relationship with Hunt. The bulk of the letter deals with making the best advantage of the site and the views by the creation of a terrace or "prominade" [*sic*] "thrown out southwardly from the house." The proposed terrace would provide a place for "a short stroll or a prominade... from which while walking, the great view westward—the valley and the distance with its far-away snow-capped hills—can be enjoyed." It would not, however, be suitable during harsh winter weather, as Olmsted explained:

> *But no prominade south of the house with a western outlook would be available for use with an icy northwester sweeping down the valley doubled in force as it would by the current deflected and concentrated by the walls of the house. Hence a place out-of-doors is wanted which attractive at all times in different way from the terrace, will be available for a ramble even during a northwester and in the depth of the winter. This would be a glen-like place with narrow winding paths between steepish slopes with evergreen shrubbery, in the lee of the house on the southeast. Look at the map and you will see that the topography favors the suggestion. You will see also that a terrace thrown out southwardly from the house, a little but not much lower than the floor of the house, would still further fend off the cold winds from such a place and make it more secluded and genial.*

This is the earliest known documentation of Olmsted's conceptual plans for the area that came to be called the Ramble or Shrub Garden. It is apparent that, although Olmsted intended for this "glen-like place" to have year-round beauty and be "attractive at all times," he was at this point thinking of the space as being usable even during winter weather. This becomes more evident with the statement,

> *I think that a good place for glass (a greenhouse) can be made east of my winter garden at an elevation about 30' below that of the plateau, the nearest point of it being about 350 ft. southeast of the library window, the roof ridge being well below the line of the eye of those passing along the approaching road and easily planted wholly out of view from the house and the entire entrance plateau, if that is desirable.*

So it would seem that Olmsted intended that the "winter garden" or Ramble plantings would also function to screen any views of the greenhouses in the valley below.

In a document titled "Notes of a conversation with F.L.O., concerning Biltmore" sent to the Estate in November 1892, the design intent of the Shrub Garden was summarized.

> *The Ramble, as Mr. Olmsted calls the shrub garden, is to have a considerable amount of turf between the walk and plantations. In this turf is to be dotted a variety of individual trees and shrubs breaking out from the main bodies of planting. The main bodies of planting will be made up of large shrubs near the upper parts, which can be looked over by any one standing on the terrace. There may also be in this part of the Ramble, plantations of Rhododendrons to make a foreground for the most important views. This will be made up of large native plants in the center, and cultivated plants on the outside, and could probably be planted next Spring with plants thinned out from the edges of the lower approach road.*

It is noted, however, that "the use of Rhododendrons in this place is not fully determined." It is believed that rhododendrons were probably never planted in the Ramble after consideration was given to the fact that the slope had a southwest aspect, making it hot and dry, and thus unfavorable to rhododendrons.

> *Farther down the slope the Judas Tree, Thorns, and Flowering Dogwood will predominate in the center of the masses. These masses will be made up of more garden-like shrubs and small trees. Flowering Cherries, Flowering Apples, etc., would be used. In the lower part of the ramble more trees would be used, perhaps the English White Birch which would not materially obstruct the view on account of its spire-like top.*

Even while construction of Biltmore House was progressing, the Ramble and other garden areas were being graded and prepared for planting. Nurseryman Beadle prepared "A List of Plants Available for Planting" in September 1892, which he sent to the Olmsted firm. Other lists included specifically those "Plants used in the Upper Approach Road and Ramble, Fall 1892, with number [of] available plants and quantity used" and "Additional Plants to be Added in Ramble Planting Spring 1893." The Olmsted firm prepared yet another specific planting list for the Ramble from a Biltmore Nursery inventory of "Available Nursery Stock for the Planting during the Autumn 1893 and Spring 1894" that was included on the finished and very detailed "Planting Plan for the Shrub Garden." Altogether, the Biltmore Nursery provided the needed quantities of more than five hundred varieties of trees, shrubs, vines, groundcovers and perennial flowers for the four-acre Shrub Garden. Although somewhat natural and informal in design, the garden is distinctly different from the "wildness" of the thick plantings of the woodland Ramble

Olmsted created in Central Park or the naturalistic woodland plantings along the borders of Biltmore's Approach Road. While some "native" plant materials were used, the extensive planting list consisted of many exotic trees and shrubs from various regions of the world, especially Japan and China, as well as many cultivated hybrids.

Sheltered in a valley between two ridges and situated below the south end of the Ramble is the one space that fit Olmsted's definition of a "garden." It is surrounded by a massive stone wall with arched entry gates that visually separate it from the general landscape scenery surrounding it. This area was not intended to be part of the scenic progression leading away from the house. Olmsted intended to devote this garden to growing choice fruits, vegetables and "decorative flowers" for use in the house. He especially wanted to demonstrate the art of growing espaliered fruit trees along the walls, which would have educational value, since few Americans did that sort of gardening.

The preliminary design by Olmsted in 1892 was for a functional garden, in that it included many kinds of fruits and vegetables as well as flowers—typical of "kitchen" gardens on the English estates. However, George Vanderbilt noted that he could obtain fruits and vegetables from his farm and wanted "a garden of ornament rather than utility." This garden was transformed over time into primarily a flower garden. The four-acre garden is square and symmetrical in design and is divided centrally by "vine clad" grape arbors. Various beds and borders throughout the garden were planned for an array of ornamental flowers for color through the seasons including annuals, perennials, ornamental grasses, herbs and roses. Flanking the south wall of the garden is the Conservatory and greenhouses, a collaborative design by the Olmsted and Hunt firms.

Other elements of the "Home Grounds" included the tree-lined entry Esplanade with an inclined vista to the east of the mansion; a formal terrace garden with basins for aquatic plants and fish; and a "Vernal" or "Spring Garden," in which a cool grassy glade between steep slopes planted with flowering shrubs was surrounded by a woodland. Olmsted additionally planned a woodland "Glen" in the valley below the Conservatory and Spring Garden with paths leading to a lake with a rustic boathouse and waterfall that spilled into a picturesque ravine below.

The proposed Glen took in a valley of some twenty acres that was bordered on the east side by the Glen Road, which continued the carriage drive southward from the residence; on the west by the Deer Park; and on the south end by the Lake (Bass Pond). While Olmsted had a rudimentary design in mind for the Glen, he did not advance his ideas enough for a finished planting plan while developing plans for other areas. In his planting instructions for the fall and winter of 1894–95, he specified,

> *The planting of the steep slopes at the south end of the bridge, the pond on the east side of the road is not to be done at present as these slopes are likely to be changed. At the dam Hemlocks are to be planted at the edge of the water above the dam at the east end. At the west end of the dam the space back of the Rhododendrons and below the Hemlocks, running down towards the level land on the south side, is to be planted with Pines. Similar planting is to be made north of the dam on this end which will come down to the water's edge and cover the point of land above the dam for about seventy-five feet in a north-westerly direction. This last plantation will extend up the hill about one hundred feet. A narrow connecting plantation will be made between these two Pine plantings.*

In December 1894, Olmsted wrote the Estate manager, Charles McNamee.

> *We expect to visit the Estate in February, when, after an inspection of the results of what has been done in the meantime, instructions for refinements may be added. We hope that by that time all the rougher blocking-out work required may have been accomplished, so that a review with reference to details and finishing operations can then be made to better advantage...Stakes have been set and verbal directions given under which Mr. Gall can sub-grade a walk six feet wide, as staked, between the head of the Lake and the Spring Garden, with branches to the hot-house and to the gardener's cottage. This walk is to cross the stream passing through the Glen where it enters the Lake; thence be led to a boat-house which is to be built at a point designated by stakes on the east shore of the north end of the Lake, and thence, upon a course which has been staked, to a point on the Glen Road. A short staircase will be required on the steep slope sustaining Glen Road. Neither the boat-house, the bridge, nor the staircase need to be constructed for permanence this Winter.*

A letter from the Olmsted firm to James Gall on November 1, 1895, pointed out that "some revision of the brook where it is blasted through the ledge above the bridge, to which attention was called by Mr. Vanderbilt and for which instructions were given you verbally on the ground, should be completed as soon as possible, if not already done, as the adjoining banks are to be planted at once." It is not clear what the revision entailed or why it was necessary, but apparently it concerned Mr. Vanderbilt. By this time, Olmsted had been forced to step down from the firm due to his failing health and memory lapses. His stepson, John C. Olmsted, and son, F.L.O. Jr., took charge of the Biltmore project.

On November 2, 1895, the firm sent a lengthy twenty-four-page letter to Beadle with instructions and thoughts for plantings in a number of different locations that was a follow-up to verbal instructions given during a previous site visit.

> *We will set down in writing some of the ideas which we discussed with you with reference to planting operations for this Fall and next Spring, and wish merely to call attention to certain other planting matters discussed with you last Spring...At various points along the Glen road low-growing shrubs and creepers should be substituted for the tall shrubs, in order to keep open glimpses of the Glen, the pond and the brook below the pond. A few trees, chiefly oaks, should be added for shade...The native trees are to be gradually thinned out from year to year and their places taken by choicer garden varieties, such as the Magnolias, Horse chestnuts, red and white flowered,* Cladrastis tinctoria, *flowering apples and thorns and a great variety of other trees, but avoiding such as would make very strong contrasts with the surrounding native forest as seen from the Esplanade and Glen road. The less natural-looking trees should be placed in the least conspicuous positions and presumably where they would be seen from the glen walk on the side toward the green houses, so that their artificiallity* [sic] *would be associated insensibly in the mind with the exotic gardening centring* [sic] *in the green houses and garden. The spruces, firs and other spire-topped trees should also be hidden among other trees or planted at the base of the bank below the green houses. Most of the Glen is to be kept in nice turf and as the ground is now in very rough and poor condition and cannot be improved*

properly without large quantities of manure, probably the finishing of this ground will have to be deferred for some time. Advantage should be taken of the brooks to grow collections of iris, choice water-lilies and other water-loving plants. The moist places adjoining the brook in some localities could be made shady by the use of pines and hemlocks, so that when sufficiently grown the ground below them could be covered with ferns and other interesting shade-loving plants. In fact, a considerable portion of this ground may be used for special effect to be examined leisurely and as matters of horticultural interest rather than as a landscape…It is not necessary to go into the matter in detail at this time except as a guide to such improvements of the ground, the banks of the brook, etc. as may seem desirable to undertake at once. No tall-growing trees are to be planted in the Glen where they would hide the pond in the view from the Glen road near the Esplanade.

It is clearly evident from the above statements that the intent was to take advantage of the brooks and associated moist places for collections of plants suited to such areas and arranged for horticultural interest rather than as a naturalistic setting.

Another document titled "Notes on Planting" was received from the firm a few days later, on November 6, stating,

The planting of the Glen has not been studied in sufficient detail as yet and operations may be confined to cleaning it up, getting rid of weeds, etc. If the plants are ready, the swampy places may be planted with Iris, Sarracenium [Sarracenia] *and other marsh plants as discussed with Mr. Beadle and Mr. Bottomley* [Robert Bottomley, the head gardener], *and sufficient stock of such plants should be procured, if they are not already on the ground.*

The Olmsted firm wrote to George Vanderbilt the following April with follow-up comments from their recent inspection of the work at Biltmore and considerations on various matters of design to bring to his attention. The first three pages were devoted to a discussion on the design intent and relationship between forested and agricultural lands on the Estate in general and with some specific suggestions for the River Bend Peninsula. The rest of the document was devoted to recommendations for additional work and/or changes for the completion or improvement of various areas under six main headings: Biltmore Village, Railroad, Roads, Arboretum, Pond and Vicinity and Planting. Under the heading "Pond and Vicinity" was a short discussion concerning the surface of the walks in the Glen, Spring Garden and Shrub Garden, which were "still far from satisfactory." It was pointed out that "in the Garden the surface has at points been considerably improved by the use of sand, but even this will prove unsatisfactory." Crushed stone from the quarry was being used in the construction of the garden paths and roads. Apparently the material used in these areas was too coarse and sand had been added. Olmsted Sr. was never quite satisfied with the surface of the garden paths. Coarser material, without a bonding agent, was necessary on the sloping paths to prevent washing, because a finer crushed stone with a more pleasing appearance would erode away with every rain. Under the heading "Planting" was a single statement concerning the Glen: "A thick growth of pines has been planted in the Glen and additional planting can be done this season, but it is not expected to entirely finish the work here at present."

Little, if any, correspondence concerning the Glen exists after April 1896 from the Olmsted firm until early October 1900. In a "Memo. For Mr. McNamee" from C.D. Beadle on November 27, 1900, Beadle was responding to questions that McNamee apparently had regarding his budget.

> *Answering your letter of the 26th inst. referring to items in the Landscape Department budget, I beg to reply to them in the sequence presented…You have slightly misconstrued my meaning as to the amount of plants required in the Glen. It was my intention to impress you that a sum ranging between four and five thousand dollars would represent the value of plants (other than those which could be collected) needed to execute all of the items of planting shown under heading "Planting." Please notice that the work in the Glen is but one of the many items there enumerated. I do not understand Mr. Vanderbilt's meaning in the sentence you quote from his letter as follows: "For instance in the Glen planting, after deducting the number of plants to be bought outside, the expense for plants bought from nursery seems disproportionate to the total returns from nursery sales in nursery account." Please let me quote the instructions I received from the Olmsteds and trace each step of my calculations which are presented in the budget. Extract from letter of Olmsted Brothers, October 18th, 1900. "It is probable that four thousand lineal feet of carefully constructed dirt paths averaging two to three feet in width, will be needed in this tract. These paths will cross the brook at many points and you may estimate on ten or twelve small rustic bridges or stepping stone crossings. The bridges will be very simple in design and it is unlikely that any cut stone work will be required upon them. (Provided for in Construction and Grading, in budget). Ten thousand shrubs and small trees will be needed of which number it might be well to assume that one-fifth will be purchased outside the estate. Two hundred and twenty-five specimen trees will be needed, averaging two to three inches in caliper. It will also be well to make allowances of five hundred dollars for herbaceous plants not including planting. Probably fifty existing small trees will need to be uprooted and there are also a considerable number of stumps which must be grubbed." Looking up my original notes, I find that the items under planting have been considered as follows:*

Grass seed and labor for seeding	*110.00*
225 specimen trees 2–3 inches in caliper, collected from woods or by judicious thinning from existing plantations, including the planting and restoration of conditions at existing sites, $5.00 each	*1125.00*
8000 small trees and shrubs from nursery, estimated at $50.00 per thousand	*400.00*
2000 plants to be purchased outside of nursery, estimated at $75.00 per thousand	*150.00*
Herbaceous plants as per allowance of Olmsted Bros.	*500.00*
Labor planting domestic and purchased plants	*245.00*
Removing stumps and refilling bales	*100.00*
Fertilizers and cost of applying	*250.00*
Total cost of estimate	*$2880.00*

My figures show, and I think conclusively, that I have given the Glen planting the advantage in the matter of plants from the Nursery. Please note that there is $25. per thousand difference between plants purchased outside and those from the nursery. In the absence of any planting lists or plans, it was impossible for me to apply any catalogue rates to stock that might be drawn from the Biltmore Nursery and as I was most careful not to take advantage of the estate demands to further the nursery interests, being both nurseryman and planter, I feel that the figures shown are more to the advantage of the planting than to the nursery. The specimen trees two to three inches in caliper are not on the nursery—and for that matter, are not procurable in any nursery—and consequently "Nursery" can receive no part of the money there shown, and, as shown in the estimate nursery cannot receive more than $400.00 for 8000 plants, unless the final plans demand more plants, or more expensive plants, from the nursery. I make this explanation to show that I have not taken advantage of the situation to further the interests of the nursery, which is endeavoring to stand on its own feet. The inventory of the present year shows an amount of stock valued at $9200.00, the exact amount of which is reflected in the budget as running expenses and as credits by cash sales. It will be impossible, therefore, for me to realize this sum unless the estate pays market prices for the plants which we may require.

The above account of an estimated planting budget for the Glen was prepared by Beadle based on the Olmsted firm's estimates of the numbers and types of plants that would be needed for the upcoming project, even though the final plans and plant lists had not been fully developed at this point. The numbers would have been "guestimates" based on the overall square footage of the Glen area. The actual numbers and varieties of plants that ultimately would be needed would have been determined after a detailed scale drawing with plant list was completed.

The Olmsted Brothers, as they now called the firm, did send the "LIST OF PLANTS FOR THE GLEN" in early February 1901. It was an extensive and comprehensive fourteen-page list of trees, shrubs, groundcovers, herbaceous wildflowers and ferns to accompany the planting plan for the Glen. The list included a mix of both native plants and exotic ornamentals. It is of interest to note that no conifers are included in the list. Several varieties of azaleas, both natives and exotic types, were included, as were other members of the heath family, such as rhododendrons, kalmia, leucothoe, rhodora, etc. The quantities of most trees and shrubs were shown, but not for herbaceous plants.

Another undated document titled "NOTES ON THE GLEN" contained fifty-one instructional notes that apparently corresponded with a map showing locations of the stakes numbered one through fifty-one. The words "GARDEN PATH ENTRANCE" at the head of the list probably mean that the numbered stakes began at the garden's entrance. Judging by the contents, these notes seem to indicate that the garden was a "work in progress" or in a stage where some plantings had been in place for a while already and others were yet to go in. It has not been determined whether these notes preceded the finished plan for the Glen or were intended to go with the plan. Some of the notes specify taking plants out for various reasons: because they were overgrowing something else or were scraggly, to open up views or to substitute something else in their place. (E.g., "[4] Cut out scraggly rose. [10] Take out roses, symphoricarpos and other coarse growth and show up Althaea if it is good, by making a bay. [11] Open view through, under locusts into valley. [13] Take out most of roses and take out ribes and other plants that interfere with *Neillia opulifolia*. Take out Hypericum between Stephanandra. [25] Replace damaged willow oak with canoe birch.") Other notes indicate that some trees and other plants were present naturally or were remnants from the old farm that had existed prior to Vanderbilt's purchase. (E.g., "[27] Replace sprout hickory by Halesia tetraptera. [30] Within the area marked by these 6 stakes remove oaks and plant magnolias and rather thickly. If necessary, prepare soil. [33] Between these 2 stakes remove all dogwoods, alders, etc., leaving Nyssa, and plant a mass of Tradescantia and Podophyllum, and perhaps Anemone japonica, and extending to within about 10' of the walk. [49] Remove apple tree.") It is fairly clear that the design of the Glen was to be one of little or no formality, but rather one that was generally natural in appearance—suggestive of a woodland setting with intermittent meadow-like openings with ferns and herbaceous wildflowers, backed by thickets of shrubs or bordered by a swamp or brook. (E.g., "[18] Cut birch, cut small oaks at the [back] of meadow as well as birches, leaving all oaks over 4" in diameter. Plough up the meadow, cultivate it thoroughly, removing roots as much as possible and seed down to grass. [31] In the bay behind these two [2] stakes plant ferns and mints, in large masses around the bases of the shrubs and low branching trees which form the outline of the little meadow. Clear out center more. Between the upper of these two stakes marked 31 and stake 29 plant ferns near the brook. The belt of ferns should be from 20–35 feet wide and 50–75 feet long, and upon its western side it should follow the brook. [36] Behind this mass of maple starting at stake #36, plant a mass of marsh mallow extending down to the border of the swamp to stake 37.") Although the setting was natural in appearance and many native plants were specified, the Glen was by no means intended to only showcase native plants, but rather a mix of both native and exotic plants were blended to create an otherwise naturally appearing "garden." (E.g., "[21] Between these 9 stakes plant Jasminum nudiflorum. [35] Between these 3 stakes plant Acer monspessulanum [some other form will do—FLO Jr.] [40] Between these two stakes plant mullein in mass. [41] Between these two stakes plant tansy in mass, carefully blending off edges and ends.")

It is interesting to note that a large area (two acres) was intended to be planted with conifers, which is somewhat unusual since the planting plan and accompanying plant list prepared by the Olmsted Brothers in 1901 contains no reference to coniferous plants of any kind. (E.g., "[38] Within the large tract [2 acres?] bounded by these many stakes, plant Conifer. The portion of the brook included [see map] is to be devoted to moisture loving conifers and particularly those loving shade. The vegetation along the brook should, therefore, be removed gradually to allow the new trees proper light and to prevent a scar in the valley. It is to be noted that the meadow behind the mass of marsh mallow is to be kept in bushes and willows to hide the coniferae. The same purpose is to be served higher up on the glen path by the open groves of oak and the crest of the hill. A separate path is to traverse the coniferae. The bushes, etc. cannot hide the coniferae after the latter are over 12' high.") A handwritten note to the left of the above states, "This idea has been omitted." The recommended treatment of the borders of the Glen where it verged with the Deer Park is explained in notes 47 and 48. ("[47] It will be best to keep the deer off the knob because they will tear the turf. Put fence back of it. Call fence 20' from walk all along. If the deer are to be fenced to drink in the pond, they will, perhaps, present a prettier picture. Plant a dozen prostrate junipers. [48] At and behind upper stake #48 put mass of azalea calendulaceum. For the sake of shade and for interest, plant [something else] all along here [200] feet along walk to give shade. Mass the trees heavily above and below, and leave a little more in the middle to give view of deer park. Gradually remove other trees.") The last three pages of the document include a list of plants preceded by this statement: "Only a few of the notes including #38 are on map."

On May 2, 1901, Beadle wrote to George Vanderbilt, then in Paris, a seven-page letter in which Beadle acknowledged receipt of instructions from Vanderbilt in regard to several projects and a general report outlining the status of progress on numerous projects under the current 1900–01 budget. Under the heading "Maintenance of Planted Areas" he reported, "Besides the ordinary routine, the cutting, thinning and improvement of plantings bordering the Service, Glen and Approach Roads has been completed." Under the heading "Planting," item number 14, "The Glen," he reports, "Bulk of planting as per plan of Olmsted Brothers, completed. In this connection I beg to say that it will require more than this season to perfect all of the plantings suggested in the plan referred to, as the conditions of soil and exposure for some of the plants is dependent upon the success of the planting now indicated." Beadle was most likely referring to plants that required some shade and higher moisture to be successfully established, which would only come about with the growth of the other plantings.

Thus, it can be seen that the Glen became the last of the garden areas conceived by Olmsted to be planted. It is believed that his sons, the Olmsted Brothers, completed it in a manner befitting their father's vision of what it should become.

The Approach Road

Both public and private roads, some of which had existed for a century, traversed the many tracts and parcels of land that George Vanderbilt had purchased to make up his Estate. Many of the roads, particularly farm and woods roads, were crude and rutty from poor maintenance or improper construction grades. Olmsted felt that these preexisting roads of the Estate had been located "on the ridge lands, where they could be made and kept passable at the least cost. Near them the timber has been naturally poorer and has been worse used than elsewhere and the local scenery is mountainous and forlorn. It is in the valleys or gulches between the ridges that the most interesting foliage is to be seen; where there is the greatest moisture and all conditions are the more picturesque." These observations strongly influenced his recommendations for routing the Approach Road to the residence through "Ram Branch valley" to take advantage of the brook and existing springs to create water features as well as opportunities for varied types of planting effects. The ascent of nearly 250 feet in elevation from the entrance to the residence gave additional opportunities for interesting topographical changes. In July 1889, Olmsted wrote to Vanderbilt with his thoughts on numerous topics, including the Approach Road:

> *I suggest that the most striking and pleasing impression of the Estate will be obtained if an approach can be made that shall have throughout a natural and comparatively wild and secluded character; its borders rich with varied forms of vegetation, with incidents growing out of the vicinity of springs and streams and pools, steep banks and rocks, all consistent with the sensation of passing through the remote depths of a natural forest. Such scenery* [is] *to be maintained with no distant outlook and no open spaces spreading from the road; with nothing showing obvious art, until the visitor passes with an abrupt transition into the enclosure of the trim, level, open, airy, spacious, thoroughly artificial court, and the Residence, with its orderly dependencies, breaks suddenly and fully upon him. Then, after passing through the building, the grandeur of the mountains, the beauty of the valley, the openness and tranquility of the park would be most effectively and even surprisingly presented, from the windows, balconies and terrace.*

It is fairly clear that Olmsted intended that the Approach Road become an experience in itself for those traveling along its path. He explained in the letter that a sketch map showing the proposed route would be sent and that it would be "approximately indicated by stakes on the ground" for Mr. Vanderbilt to see when he went to the Estate. After giving a general description of the route, Olmsted expressed that he believed that fairly easy grades with occasional levels could be had on all of this line, "without heavy construction and without curves that would be inconvenient for four-in-hand driving." He pointed out that he would be able to advise Vanderbilt on this point and others much better after Mr. Thompson (his civil engineer) made the survey that Olmsted had requested of him.

In the following months, Olmsted wrote numerous times to James Gall, who was in charge of the grading and construction of the roads, stone bridges, parapet walls and water features. In early February 1890 Olmsted sent a letter outlining detailed instructions dealing primarily with modifying, deepening and forming the course of "the water channel"(Ram Branch), which needed to be done before other work could advance. Olmsted advised Gall to

> *please get these well fixed in your mind and use your best judgment in the matter having it in your mind from the start that there is nothing in Landscape Gardening that oftener fails of wholly satisfactory results, more especially in respects to naturalness, than an undertaking of this kind...I shall presently lay down a few simple general principles for your guidance and give you certain figures of measurement. Within the limits thus fixed you must exercise your artistic taste and judgment...In order to admit drain tile to pass at sufficient depth under the road and discharge into the water course, the bottom of the water course will need to be generally at least four feet below the level of the finished grade of the road, and in order to avoid crumbling banks, to obtain variety of graceful, dimpled slopes, and to give footing for occasional large shrubs, the middle line of the water course will need to be generally at least 12 feet from the gutter of the road...At certain points, however, near bridges and where the road passes at the greatest elevation above the water, it will be well to lay out the water course as near as practicable to the road, the middle of it being say, six feet from the gutter, but in such cases, the road must be sustained by a strong wall with a parapet at least two feet high, the roadside of which parapet would be one foot from the outer edge of the gutter.*

Olmsted advised that it would be "very desirable to have the top and roadside face of parapets and all that shows in the masonry of bridges formed of fitting rock with natural weathered face, carrying moss or lichens or at any rate not of raw color." He encouraged Gall to "be on the lookout for specially good bits of rock." Considering limits, "The course of the revised stream will generally follow the course of the present stream but the widening and deepening of it will sometimes be on one side sometimes on the other so that the revised course will be more meandering...More commonly it will best be at a distance from the road varying from 12 to 20 feet." It may sometimes

> *be momentarily lost sight of from the road...The water should appear sometimes in still, broad pools with low, nearly flat immediate banks; sometimes in rapids of varying breadth and more or less obstructed by rocks or pebbly shoals and with bold banks, and sometimes in small cascades with yet bolder banks buttressed with rock. The localities where the larger loops in the course of the stream can best be made and those in which it will be desirable to introduce a retaining wall, will be obvious in the natural circumstances on the ground; the*

> *pools will come in naturally where you find the ground nearest level and bottom broadest; the rapids where the valley is narrowest and the fall of the present stream most rapid.*

Olmsted noted that there would be places where it would be difficult to get the bottom as much as four feet below the road and provisions would need to be made to take under drainage through conduits below ground to a lower point of discharge. Rough grading to establish the general course and grade of the bottom of the stream should be done first, and

> *the detailed modeling of the banks and shores to be taken up as a work of itself. This will mainly follow local suggestions, the surface being "humored" to the best trees and shrubs and to conditions of soil; grade of the slope being studied and a pleasing play with another. Avoid all petty effects; aim to maintain a large scale and broad lights and shadows. Let one character of bank contrast with another, high banks with low, concave with convex surfaces, low shelves with high. Always of course, keeping in view the methods of nature.*

Olmsted wrote numerous letters and memoranda to both Gall and Mr. Beadle over the course of the ensuing years of the Estate's construction with instructions and suggestions for carrying out his plans for the Approach and other roads on the property. Sometimes the letters outlined work to be accomplished before his next visit or reiterated verbal instructions that had been given on the ground. He wrote in March 1891,

> *The purpose of the greater part of the planting that has just been done between the quarry and the first ledge above the pools has been that of establishing masses and groups of plants in suitable relation one to another. In all this planting, a little adjustment of plants along the edge of most of the patches is now required, mainly with the object of overcoming any clean and direct lines of division and to secure a soft dovetailing of one patch into those adjoining it, and where the men in rapid planting have been allowed to get the plants along the edges too nearly in rows, of breaking up such rows and securing more natural outlines to the groups.*

In reply to an inquiry from the Olmsted firm in January 1893 regarding the planting of native rhododendrons on the upper part of the Lower Approach Road, Beadle reported, "Very extensive collections of the native Rhododendrons and Kalmias have been made, and are still in progress, for this planting." He further reported that the plantings from the quarry to the third bridge were generally in a thriving and prosperous condition and that "the nursery grown plants are somewhat brighter in color than the collected broad leaved evergreens and coniferous plants, owing to the greater root vigor and consequent foothold in the soil."

Olmsted wrote on the last of November 1893 with instructions for various works to be accomplished before his next visit in February. "The middle Approach Road is to be completed including some low border planting, as to which instructions have been given to Mr. Bottomley [the head gardener]…Mr. Bottomley is also to be employed, under Mr. Gall's orders, in improving the planting all along the Approach Road." Olmsted felt that there needed to be more dovetailing together of groups on the Upper Approach Road and that "a larger number of brambles, briers, chinquapins and other native shrubs" needed to be introduced to "better disguise the fact that the plantations are artificial, and to make them appear more nearly spontaneous and wild." Mr. Gall was to see to it that Mr. Bottomley was not timid in that respect and that he had "a sufficient supply of native plants for the purpose stated."

In a memorandum in June 1895, Olmsted sent instructions for the section of the entry drive coming in from Biltmore Village. "Most visitors will get their first decided impression of the local scenery while passing over this road. Hence in laying it out and forming its borders, the aim will be (1) to present available passages of scenery to the best advantage; (2) to secure strong and effective foregrounds for the views over it." In July, he sent Beadle an eight-page letter of intense discussion concerning the revision of details of the plantings on the Lower Approach Road to achieve the feel of "sub-tropical luxuriance." The document is perhaps one of the most important in defining Olmsted's design intent for the finished plantings of the Lower Approach Road. Olmsted felt that the results thus far had not achieved the intended effect that he had envisioned for this area. He had obviously spent considerable time on the subject and wanted to impress his thoughts upon Beadle so that his ideas would be successfully implemented on the ground. He apologetically begins by saying,

> *Excuse me if this letter turns out to be a reiteration of reminders of various items on which I have verbally and, in successive previous letters, asked you to be studying this summer, in order to make progress in planning a revision of details of the plantations on the borders of the Lower Approach Road. There is nothing that we are now so immediately anxious about at Biltmore as that these borders should more fully acquire the general aspect originally intended to be given them, and which is broadly suggested by saying that it is an aspect more nearly of sub-tropical luxuriance than would occur spontaneously at Biltmore, or than is now fully promised, or than has, as yet, been as fully provided...The subject is one of so much interest that I may be pressing advice upon you more than is reasonable. But I am impressed with the reflection that just now, after the early growth of this present summer has reached its limit, is a good time for further and more accurate study of ways and means to the end in question than it can have yet received, and that it is for you to make such study of it, in respect to detailed particulars, as can only be made on the ground by a trained horticulturist.*

Olmsted was once again, as he had numerous other times, relying on the expertise of Beadle to take his concepts and craft them into the finished landscape he was envisioning. Olmsted attempts to define what this vision was:

> *The term "sub-tropical luxuriance" is, of course, used only suggestively. The result desired is to be brought about largely by a profuse use of plants that simply, in certain respects, are calculated to produce a distant, broad, general resemblance to the landscape qualities of sub-tropical scenery; more so, at least, than we are accustomed to see, or than would be practicable with such slight contraction of opportunity as we should have, for example, about New York, or even Washington, but that will form compositions more nearly approaching in general landscape character such as are to be seen further south than any that are the result of spontaneous growth near Biltmore. Absolute luxuriance is mainly provided for by manure, but only here and there is much manure now wanted. The special effort aimed at is to be obtained*

chiefly by giving a preponderance to certain plants and by the exclusion of others. Still do not neglect what I have before said about manure at special points. Much depends on the rapid luxuriant growth of some, and the suppression of other plants. Upon the very rich feeding of grape-vines, for example, on the upper hillside, grape-vines and other vines and creepers that have to grow eventually up the larger trees and to hang from them in the manner of the great climbers of a tropical forest.

After this elaborate description of how he meant to achieve the effect of subtropical scenery, Olmsted downplayed the importance of bloom as part of the overall result.

Coincidently with, but subordinately to, the end so defined, a richer and more profuse display of bloom early in the Spring will be provided for, but this end is to be made wholly subordinate to that which has above been stated...Bear in mind, on this point, that Mr. Vanderbilt and his guests nearly always miss the best of <u>*the bloom*</u> *and that they will continue to do so. It is, therefore, the distant, lasting and constant semi-tropical effect of bodies of foliage that we must here and now have in view. Everything else must give way to what will make for this purpose. It is the result that will be constant through the year that we must care most for.*

Olmsted cautioned that in attaining the desired effect,

We should have to sacrifice too much of the landscape value of that <u>*of which we are sure,*</u> *if we tried to do more than we are planning to do for this purpose. The result of our work would be wanting in character if we aimed at anything less. People coming from New York to Biltmore in the Winter or Spring must be made to feel that they are decidedly nearer the sun. We must aim, then, to gain as much of sub-tropical general* <u>*character of scenery*</u> *as we can without a large sacrifice of existing elements of the woodland beauty of the Southern temperate region.*

The fact that the process of construction and the implementation of the landscape took place over a period of several years gave Olmsted and Beadle a chance to experiment and observe the results. The things learned from these experiences provided confidence and opportunities for making revisions and improving upon the ultimate design and results. Olmsted expressed this to Beadle. "You have now been making experiments for several years by means of which we have been hoping that you would prove whatever is available for all details of this purpose. From this time on, therefore, we should be able to proceed with much more confidence as to details than we could earlier."

Olmsted knew that if Beadle had ownership in the project, he would utilize his experience and expertise to produce the best possible results. "Looking critically upon what is now to be seen on the ground, and upon what is to be seen in your nursery, with reference to this general purpose, we wish you to make this general purpose your own to the fullest degree that, with careful study of your local experience down to this time, you can think practicable."

The idea of creating a landscape effect that closely approached the look of subtropical scenery seemed to possess Olmsted's thinking, as he continued,

In going over the Lower Approach Road I have felt that, on its immediate borders, there is not now as much promise of luxuriance and profusion of vegetation as it is possible to establish in the situation, and that there is a great deal too much yet to be overcome that is raw, barren and rude, comparatively with the standard that we may not unreasonably have before us. There is too little that is permanent that we might not find in the more Northern temperate regions. We are not gaining as much as possible from our little advantage of climate. That is to say, people coming from the North will not realize, from what we have yet prepared, that they are gaining as much advantage of climate as it is desirable that they should, and we ought to provide, with all the art we can bring to bear upon the point, for the appearance of much more difference of climate than can actually be realized. This only makes it more important that we now move in the direction thus indicated to the last point that, after these three years of experience and study, we are justified in thinking that, by any skill we can, at best, make practicable. With the knowledge which you have been earning in these years, you should be able to gauge, with a close approach to accuracy, the limit of our resources for reaching the last possible point in this respect; the last point, that is to say, of semi-sub-tropicality [sic].

Trusting Beadle's ability, Olmsted encouraged him to exercise his judgment.

Do not hesitate to transplant the old plants where, with this later acquired knowledge, you can see opportunity to better accomplish what we want, and do not limit your calculation of effect in this respect to what can be gained quickly. Keep using a strongly cultivated, specially imaginative forecast of what is to be attained in the future by progress in growth. This question can be studied now much more closely than it could when we began the Biltmore work. We may hope that anything that has barely survived after recent transplanting in your low, bleak nursery will, with more mature growth, do better in the sheltered valley.

Olmsted specifically outlined what was needed to achieve the desired effect for the lower sections of the Approach Road in these following statements.

What I find most plainly wanting in this Ram Branch district, at present, is a more conspicuous and more consistent profusion of the smaller and more refined smooth-leaved evergreens. With reference to these, especially much of these as are less easily obtained otherwise, you have constantly, from the first, been urged to push your propagations. I mean that we need more especially a profusion of this class of low, smooth-leaved evergreen plants near the edges of the road and down upon the shores of the brook. That is to say, upon ground that one looks down upon when passing in carriages along the road. The shores of the brook so looked closely down upon are yet nearly everywhere of a much more coarse, crude and commonplace character than we have meant them to be. Use every resource and all the ingenuity that you can to refine and enrich the low vegetation, by which the edge of the water in the brook will be covered. Nearly every foot of the water's edge needs to be verdantly covered more perfectly, and to be more delicately covered verdantly, than it is. A larger amount and a greater variety of low delicate vegetation is needed, also close upon the roadside as well

> *as on the banks of the brook, room being made for it. All the foreground surface needs to be better covered and with a greater variety of low foreground plants; with Ivy, for instance, and other evergreen creepers of the more delicate sorts. You can judge much better than we began what will succeed in accomplishing what is needed in these respects. The knowledge which, meantime, you have been gaining in the nursery should be of value for the purpose. I should say, without going into further detail, that the immediate foreground from the road is to be improved by liberal additions, sometimes substitutions, for instance, of Abelia rupestris; Mahonia aquifolia prostrata, and, possibly, in some cases, with some of the lower growing Mountain Rhododendrons, if there are any that can yet be hoped to succeed, and with the small sorts of Kalmias, etc. An increased breadth of low evergreen planting is plainly needed on the borders of the road, and some things now planted there are to be taken out to make place for this lower creeping foliage. I mean there needs to be a greater breadth here and there of Ivy and smaller Japanese sorts of evergreen Euonymus, and a choice of all those things, more particularly, that Mr. Boynton was to collect for you, and which you were to develop and give trial to in the nursery, especially with a view to gaining a greater variety for this particular purpose. All these low evergreens growing close upon the ground are needed to be planted profusely in front of the larger ones, or making them apparently sit on cushions and platforms of low plots of foliage.*

The above instructions very clearly define the intended look or finished appearance of the foreground plantings Olmsted desired, even if specific plant selections were left to Beadle. There was enough detail, yet leeway was also given to achieve the results of a layered, stepped up effect that was suggestive of the natural edge of a forest with a preponderance of broad-leaved evergreens. Olmsted further gave Beadle the freedom to make decisions to remove plants that were doing poorly or were in the way of the additions specified.

> *Some things now on the ground must be set back to make places for these smaller growing plants, and, occasionally some of the larger must be removed entirely in order to increase the breadth of those of low growth. It is a question for you to determine whether some of the larger Rhododendrons, especially some of those which have suffered in transplanting, making them stemmy* [sic] *and thin in foliage, should not be given up, so as to make the foreground broader, more varied, richer and more luxuriant in detail, than it otherwise will ever come to be. Bear in mind that you have to make good foreground places, also, for the finer flowering budded Rhododendrons that you have been propagating and bringing forward in the nursery, and this must be done by excision and setting back some of those that now occupy the ground.*

Olmsted obviously had much faith in Beadle's knowledge and judgment in such matters, as he states,

> *Do not hesitate to act boldly and improve on these suggestions, where you see occasion, always having regard more to the spirit than to the letter of them. You are more likely to be over-cautious than over-bold in all this work. The revisions required were all, in a tentative and nebulous way, intended to be made from the first, as the result of experience and enlargement*

of our safe resources should make them expedient. I feel sure that after this experience we can run to much greater refinements than we could at first.

The remainder of this letter, one of Olmsted Sr.'s last concerning the Approach Road, was devoted to emphasizing his sense of urgency about getting this stage of work completed. He wanted to know if Beadle needed anything further for accomplishing the work, and wrote to Mr. McNamee as a way of encouraging him to supply Beadle with anything he might need.

In December 1894, Olmsted had written to Charles McNamee, the Estate's general manager, concerning the work on Ram Branch and expressed the difficulty of obtaining satisfactory results in trying to achieve a natural aspect while artificially making brooks and brook sides. Although more work needed to be done, he felt that even in its rough condition, the brook and its banks made an impression of nearly as much "unsophisticated naturalness" as in their former state, and in some ways had an even "more interesting character." It was Olmsted's desire that ultimately the brook and pools, as well as the road and bridges, did not appear to be of "artificial" construction. The value of having the Nursery and planting supervision both under Chauncey Beadle proved to be advantageous, and Olmsted felt they were making headway in achieving the finished landscape in the "comparatively wild and natural character" that he wanted. Olmsted expressed to Beadle that with all of the knowledge and experience he had been gaining in the Nursery along with other additional resources on hand, Olmsted could see no reason why they couldn't have "a perfect realization, a few years later, of our ideas in all the Ram Branch valley." Considering the extraordinary amount of time and detailed attention that Olmsted gave to the Approach Road, it was apparent that he placed extreme importance on that part of the project. As work on the Approach Road was still progressing, Richard Morris Hunt had elaborated early on about Olmsted's success with it:

Hasn't Olmsted done wonders with the approach road? It alone will give him lasting fame... If only Burnett, Pinchot, and I succeed as well, what a blissful time is ahead for George, in the fulfillment of his ideas; may he live to a ripe old age to enjoy his and our work.

The Biltmore Arboretum

In the years since Olmsted had collaborated with Professor Charles Sprague Sargent to plan and design the Arnold Arboretum at Harvard in the 1870s, he had contemplated a yet greater scheme for an arboretum, but had been frustrated and unsuccessful in finding the right situation and client to develop his ideas. At Vanderbilt's Biltmore Estate, which came at the culmination of his career, he came closer to fulfilling his dream of creating an arboretum that would be "by far finer and more instructive than any other in the world." He presented his preliminary thoughts in a lengthy report to Vanderbilt in July 1889.

> *As to the suggested Arboretum, I have conceived the outline of a plan for it the general nature of which I will try to indicate, but before offering any final recommendation, even as to its general scope, I should want to give the matter more study.*
>
> *This plan would be to lay out a road starting from the residence in such a manner that, bending to the valley southward, it would follow up Four Mile Creek to the meadow above the second dam, cross from the meadow near (if I recollect aright) the Hart place, and so to the valley of the next creek south; down this valley to the French Broad bottom-land, then back to the point of departure by the Four Mile valley. A dam could be built on the site of the present lower dam of Four Mile Creek and ten feet higher, which would form a lake, extending up the north valley of the creek to a point a little above where the steam saw mill stood. This lake would probably be visible from the residence garden and perhaps from the terrace. In a branch of the Four Mile valley, where there is now a vacant house a little north east of what would be the head of the lake, is probably the best place for your service gardens, propagating houses, etc.*
>
> *Such a road as I have thus indicated would make convenient sub-divisions of the forest and in connection with the streams, which it would follow, would be a guard against the spread of fires. It would be a very picturesque road, and on its borders there would be situations of great variety in respect to soil and exposure and generally of the highest fertility to be found on the Estate. Some would be rocky; some marshy; some meadowy; the most, fair upland. My idea in a word, is to form the Arboretum by cutting back and thinning out the present standing wood on the borders of this road, leaving the best trees and bushes, but making place for the planting of the collection, choosing for each rep*[re]*sentative tree a position adapted to develop its highest character and exhibit it, in several specimens, to the best advantage. Water-side trees by the lake; Ash, on the fertile well-drained meadow; Magnolias in the dingles opening southward; Oaks on the higher upland, and so on.*

Without doubt an arboretum could be formed in this way by far finer and more instructive than any other in the world, an arboretum to which naturalists would resort from all parts of the world. It would, of course, be backed at all points by the main forest of the Estate and the trees would group with those of the forest.

Olmsted had visited Dropmore, an arboretum in England, during July of 1892. What he saw excited him greatly about the prospects for the Biltmore Arboretum. Summarizing his feelings, he wrote, "It is so comparatively wild. It comes near to being a model of what we want in the arboretum at Biltmore, I mean in a general effect. Our plan will be much more complete and valuable."

As Olmsted was still sorting out his thoughts for the Arboretum scheme, Vanderbilt was apparently not yet committed to the idea of a scientific Arboretum at Biltmore. Olmsted wrote on December 19, 1893, asking Vanderbilt to give him a little more time to study into the matter and seek some counsel from others.

I want you for a little further time to consider the problem of the Arboretum an open one, and you must not believe that I am plotting anything which I do not think that you will find reason to approve when I am fully prepared to fairly present it to you. The Arboretum is a problem to which it is difficult to do justice. I am disposed to regard it as nearly the most important and most difficult problem with which I have, in all my professional life, had to do. I want to pursue it deliberately; I want to proceed with the best counsel that I can obtain, and particularly at this stage to give it my best patient, personal study. I will soon write you at length upon it.

In less than two weeks, on December 30, Olmsted sent to Vanderbilt a detailed sixteen-page letter entirely about the Arboretum scheme.

We have for several years been making progress, as if against head winds through complex channels, in the development and better definition of what we have been calling the Arboretum scheme. The fact is that a good deal is involved in, or dependent on, the plan for carrying out this scheme which the word arboretum does not at once suggest. No existing arboretum has been planned with the same motives; none has been planned to fit parallel circumstances, and in none has the accomplishment of the objects in view required that a plan should be prepared on as large a scale or with as much study and contrivance. I suppose that more work may have been already given to the development of the scheme than to everything else that we have been planning for you…Much that remains to be determined in the advice that we are to give you about the laying out of other parts of the Estate is in some way dependent on the shape which the Arboretum scheme will finally take.

Olmsted informed Vanderbilt that he was preparing his thoughts for a more definite consultation and discussion, first with his partners, then with Mr. Pinchot, Mr. Manning and Mr. Beadle and lastly with Professor Sargent. All of this discussion was "preparatory to the maturing of a more fully digested scheme to be submitted for your consideration." In early February

1894, Olmsted wrote that for some time they had not known whether Vanderbilt favored the "Arboretum scheme," but after speaking with him during the previous week, they now knew that he did favor the plan.

Excerpts from Olmsted's successive correspondence and reports to George Vanderbilt clearly demonstrate the magnitude of his vision for the Biltmore Arboretum, which would serve to complement his equally significant landscape, Nursery and scientific forestry programs. He explained:

> *What we propose for the borders of the long southern main circuit road of the Estate, east of the river, is a treatment, which to superficial observation would not appear very different in artistic motive from that. It would differ from it, however, in this important respect, that the trees to be planted should be so chosen and arranged that they would constitute a museum of living trees…It will cost but little when preparing and planting the border of this road with a view to variety of character in the foliage displayed, to provide also that the plantations for that purpose shall be of a finer, more beautiful, more distinguished and more useful museum of living trees than any now existing in the world.*
>
> *Such a museum would have great, even critical and eventful, practical national value. It would serve much more to advance the science of dendrology, the business of forestry, and the art of landscape improvement, than any and all things which have been done for these purposes or that have thus far been projected, or even suggested, to be done by the national government or by any public institution of the country. Such a museum will be conveniently designated the Biltmore Arboretum.*

This statement of Olmsted's vision of the Biltmore Arboretum is especially significant, as he had designed, along with Charles Sprague Sargent, the Arnold Arboretum at Harvard University, which was the country's premier arboretum at that time. Yet, the Arnold did little to address "the business of forestry," which Olmsted emphasized as one of the unique features of the proposed Biltmore Arboretum. Olmsted also knew that the Estate's more southern latitude and its position in the southern Appalachians' zone of flora (some of the richest in the world) would allow for greater opportunities than any other yet done or planned. Olmsted saw at Biltmore yet another opportunity to make it the most unique and nationally significant landscape of his career.

"The Arboretum is proposed to be planned more particularly as a field, in which the value may be studied of a large variety of trees and shrubs for extensive planting, whether with a view to landscape improvement or to the commercial profits of forestry in the eastern part of the continent." Expanding his idea that the primary purpose of the Arboretum plantings would be to study their value in reference to landscape improvement or to the commercial profits of forestry, Olmsted detailed his scheme:

> *As to the Arboretum considered as a museum of living woody vegetation, not less than four specimens are to be planted, near the road, of each species of trees to be exhibited. Before these four trees come to crowd one another, two of them are designed to be removed, leaving the two which promise to best represent the character of trees of their species, when grown*

> *with room for their* [sic] *to spread, at least on two opposite sides, to the greatest distances that they would be likely to spread if wholly unimpeded by other trees. At a suitable distance behind such spreading specimen trees others are to be planted, with a view to the exhibition of the character of trees of the same species when grown in groups. And back of these, chiefly on existing clearings, it is proposed (at the suggestion of Mr. Pinchot) to plant plots of about an acre of each of a certain number of the more valuable forest trees. The general object of these "Forest Acres" is to present examples growing in forest form and under forest conditions of all trees valuable for their wood which are likely to prosper at Biltmore, in order to obtain from them a variety of information which could not be afforded by the single trees or groups of the same species planted in the body of the Arboretum. To provide for the specimen trees and groups at least ten specimens of nearly all the trees to be planted in the Arboretum are now being propagated or are growing in the nursery of the Estate. The larger number is already grown to a size suitable for planting out.*

In a booklet on the "Biltmore Forest" that was exhibited at the 1893 Columbian Exposition in Chicago, Gifford Pinchot wrote,

> *Under the direction of Mr. Frederick Law Olmsted a collection of trees and shrubs has been made with the intention of planting them out, when they have attained a proper size, along the line of a road called the Arboretum Drive. This road, about five miles in length, will run through some of the most beautiful portions of the Estate, and will be lined for a hundred feet on either side by the plants of the collection. It is the intention to make this Arboretum one of the finest in existence. There are already in the Nursery more kinds of trees and shrubs than there are in the Botanical Gardens at Kew, near London, and the number is being steadily increased.*

An article titled "Mr. Vanderbilt's Forest," published by Professor C.S. Sargent in *Garden and Forest* on December 4, 1895, states,

> *A third feature of Biltmore is the arboretum, which is expected to contain a collection of the trees and shrubs hardy in Biltmore, gathered from all over the world. Such a collection, even if it is not arranged or managed in the most rigidly scientific way, will be of great importance to all planters who can here see individuals and groups of trees and shrubs which are available for us in the northeastern United States. The dendrologist will here be enabled to study the entire forest flora of the north temperate regions of the earth, and the forester will find information as to the character and growth of important forest trees not elsewhere to be obtained. The usefulness of the arboretum will be greatly aided by the Forest Acres, a tract of some three hundred acres of land on which something like a hundred of the most valuable forest species which are hardy at Biltmore will be planted in forest form, so as to furnish information about their silvicultural character and needs, and, in the more important instances, it will show their quality in mixture with other trees. The arboretum as a whole will cover some eight hundred acres, and the collection proper will be distributed along both sides of a road twelve miles in length.*

Taken all together, this work at Biltmore is an unprecedented attempt, in this country at least, to gather information which will be of use in forestry and illustrate its practical operation. There is no other place in the United States at present where practical forest management can be studied, and we are glad to know that Dr. Schenck, the resident forester, is already collecting around him a small body of American forest students. This is an appropriate beginning for a real forest school, and if it develops into the first fully equipped school of forestry in America it will be a natural and normal growth. Biltmore would be an ideal home for such an institution and for a forest experiment station, and a result like this would be a happy culmination of a broadly conceived and wisely conducted enterprise.

Chauncey Beadle, the superintendent of the Biltmore Nursery, wrote an article titled "Biltmore Nursery and Arboretum" for T.K. Bruner, secretary of North Carolina's State Board of Agriculture, to be included in their 1896 publication of "North Carolina and its Resources." In the article, Beadle reported,

Although the list of species and varieties in cultivation on the nursery is a large one, it is not complete. Many kinds of plants known to science have never been cultivated, and are, consequently, only procurable through the agency of collectors or botanical exchanges…The nursery, through its paid collectors and generous contributors, is constantly adding rare or little known plants to its collection.

He referred specifically to two extremely rare plants from North Carolina recently introduced into cultivation at Biltmore, the dwarf sumac (*Rhus michauxi*, Sargent) and the deciduous kalmia (*Kalmia cuneata*, Michaux). Beadle had previously reported in the *Reports of the Nurseryman* on August 3, 1895, that "One of the few remaining species of woody plants indigenous to North Carolina which we have been unable to find or represent in our collection, and which, according to Dr. Chapman, 'must be considered one of the rarest plants on the American Continent,' has unexpectedly been located in Davie County. This is the *Rhus pumila* of Michaux." By the end of that month, Beadle reported that the Department of Botany of Columbia College had confirmed their determination of the *Rhus pumila* of Michaux and that it had been introduced into the Biltmore Nursery—the first attempt ever made to cultivate this species, which is regarded as "one of the rarest plants of the American flora."

The question was posed in Beadle's article "as to the intrinsic value of many of the plants thus neglected or not in cultivation." The response was,

A direct answer could not be given at the present time, but their value in pleasing combinations of foliage or flower in landscape planting or home decoration is possible. To the student of certain branches of natural history they have an added charm, and when it is considered that the efforts of the nursery in this respect are preliminary steps towards the establishment of a vast museum of living trees and shrubs, to be called the Biltmore Arboretum, in which will be illustrated examples of every species and sub-species of woody vegetation that will thrive unprotected in the soil and climate of the locality, its future object will be better understood.

Beadle summarized the status and intent of the Biltmore Arboretum:

> *Although no planting has yet been done on the arboretum, active work has been in progress for some time; the energy being expended in laying out the line and making the necessary clearings. In effect, the arboretum will appear as a line of road traversing the valleys and slopes for a total distance, including several loop roads, of about twelve miles. On either side, and extending back for two hundred feet or more, will be planted the trees and shrubs it is intended to exhibit, first, in isolated specimens, second, in small masses, and third, in bulk. To plant this vast area with suitable specimens and to provide a living blanket to protect and cover the intervening ground and space beneath the spread of the greater trees, it will require possibly more than ten million plants.*
>
> *Beginning with the first species coming within the classification to be adopted, one may pass along the line and view the ligneous plants of many temperate countries in botanical sequence, at least so far as the peculiarities of soil and exposure will admit of such an arrangement. When the progress of the nursery and arboretum has sufficiently advanced and the proposed plantings have reached characteristic peculiarities, it is expected that the student and lover of plants may find ample field for study and recreation; the planter, the types of beauty appealing to his senses, and the artist, the shades and tints of Flora in her seasons.*

Charles Sprague Sargent, director of the Arnold Arboretum, had advised Olmsted that if the Biltmore Arboretum was to be successful and ensured of upkeep, it should be separated from the main Estate, generously endowed and operated by scientific men under the direction of a board of trustees. Sargent, who had seemed supportive of Olmsted's initial plans, doubted that Vanderbilt would consider such an arrangement, and encouraged Olmsted to abandon his idea for a scientific arboretum and design one with more ornamental and picturesque character. This change of advice and support from Sargent was frustrating and troubling to Olmsted. The Arboretum, perhaps as much as forestry, had become for Olmsted the most important and cherished part of the Biltmore project, and he was not willing to compromise its scientific aspect.

Out of all of Olmsted's grand visions for Biltmore Estate, the Arboretum was the only major one that was never fully developed. The Arboretum Road was constructed and some areas cleared and even prepared for planting. Tens of thousands of trees and shrubs, scheduled for the Arboretum, were growing in the Biltmore Nursery. Olmsted's vision for the Biltmore Arboretum was perhaps unparalleled anywhere in the world then, and maybe even to this day. The Estate's general manager, Charles McNamee, summed up Olmsted's passion for the Arboretum when he wrote to an acquaintance in February 1895 that "Olmsted looks upon it [the proposed arboretum] as the greatest work he has ever done…how great it will be as a museum." After Olmsted's failing health forced his retirement by late 1895, his son, Frederick Law Olmsted Jr., and Chauncey D. Beadle, supervisor of the Biltmore Nursery, carried the Biltmore Arboretum project forward. In a letter to his son in December 1895, Olmsted encouraged him to personally "get the direction of the Biltmore Arboretum into his own hands." Over the course of the next few years, George Vanderbilt's interest in the Arboretum continued to be more as a "pleasure ground" rather than the scientific arboretum that Olmsted envisioned, and in early 1901 he made the decision to abandon the scheme of a scientific arboretum. Beadle wrote a memorandum to the Estate manager's office on February 7:

> *I am requested by Mr. Vanderbilt in a letter, which I received a few days ago, to announce that the scheme which he has entertained for some time of planting and establishing on Biltmore Estate an Arboretum, is abandoned…Mr. Vanderbilt's decision in regard to the Arboretum is evidently not intended to effect the Herbarium, as you know he has approved the appropriation for maintenance during the present fiscal year, and in the same letter noting the abandonment of the former scheme; he approves of the publication of the little journal about which I spoke a few days ago to emanate from the Biltmore Herbarium and to be titled "Biltmore Botanical Studies." I am preparing the manuscript and plates for this publication and will send them at the earliest opportunity to the printer.*

The Biltmore Herbarium

In a memorandum from Frederick Law Olmsted concerning "Scientific Collections at Biltmore," he advised, "All holding positions of trust or authority on the Biltmore Estate are requested to have in view the intention of the proprietor to form collections representative of the Geology and Mineralogy of the Estate and its neighborhood, its vegetation, its animal life, and the condition of its ancient human inhabitants." The memorandum lists specific types of collections desired: "Geology and Mineralogy, Archaeology, Botany, Dendrology, Entomology and Zoology." Under "Botany," it is stated,

> *A complete collection of such flowering plants (including grasses and sedges) native and introduced, as were on the grounds before recent operations upon it began, is desirable to be secured as soon as practicable. It is not likely that many new sorts have as yet been established, but the seeds of some are sure to have been introduced with the packing of foreign trees and other things brought in, and it is desirable that, before any plants growing from them have become common, records should be made of their first observed appearance; the probable method of their introduction, and afterward of the rapidity of their distribution, etc. Some newly introduced plants spread very rapidly and sometime become weeds difficult and expensive to keep in subjection.*

Additional specifications were listed under "Dendrology."

> *In addition to Herbarium collections, there will be a special collection illustrative of the woody growth of the region. This will include sections of trunks showing bark, grain of wood, illustrations of the value of the wood in various forms, rude and finished; seeds, nuts and malformations of growth produced by insects or disease.*

Olmsted's vision for the Biltmore Nursery and Arboretum included provisions for a scientific Herbarium and botanical library. A directive from the Olmsted firm titled "Preliminary Instructions as to the Biltmore Herbarium" stated,

> *A complete, and in every way excellent, Herbarium, is from the first to be had in view... That the Herbarium may be of the highest scientific value several specimens of each plant should be collected. Of flowering plants, each specimen should be of a size sufficient to represent as fairly as possible, the flower, fruit, leaves, root-leaves, roots and underground*

> *stems. In dioecious plants, each specimen should represent both forms of flowers. Care should be taken that specimens of Sedges are well ripened. Specimens are required of all flowering plants, such as Ferns, Mosses, Lichens, Fungi and Algae, with mature frutification* [sic], *when distinguishable.*

The purpose for "The Scientific Collections at Biltmore" was initially to establish a record of the existing geological, archaeological and natural resources of the Estate before grading and construction permanently altered or destroyed their evidence. The botanical and dendrological collections would provide a record of all preexisting flora before new introductions of plants or seeds became part of the mix. Olmsted stated that "books giving general directions for forming an Herbarium of permanent scientific value, and all materials necessary for the treatment of specimens in accordance with the instructions, will be provided herewith." Olmsted further intended that the Biltmore Herbarium, along with a botanical library, would not only complement his proposed arboretum but also would have immense value in providing opportunities for research of a wide range of temperate flora. The Olmsted firm was preparing lists of reference books for the Nursery and botanical library as well as ordering supplies for the "scientific" and "natural history" collections in the summer and fall of 1890 soon after the Nursery was formally established and Chauncey D. Beadle was hired to direct it. In December 1891, the firm sent "about 12,000 paper slips for Beadle to record observations of plants." Estate manager Charles McNamee wrote to botanist Frank E. Boynton on December 4, 1893, offering him a one-year position in the Nursery, on Boynton's terms, if he could start immediately. Boynton, who had been recommended by Professor Charles S. Sargent, arrived at Biltmore a few days later to commence work collecting plants for both the Nursery and Herbarium. Olmsted wrote to Beadle at the same time urging him to take the time to study the proper and "standardized" scientific plant names for preparing the list of plants for the Arboretum. He reported that Frank E. Boynton was hired to do the collecting, which Beadle no longer had the time to conduct.

The botanical library for the Arboretum and Herbarium was being compiled as a necessary reference resource for helping with identification and classification of plants and specimens. Successive letters over the next few years discussed the "Second, Third, and even Fourth Adjusted Lists of Books for the Biltmore Arboretum Library." Invoices in the Biltmore Archives reflect numerous purchases from sources in America and abroad. It was reported in November 1895 that a number of books had been purchased from noted botanist Dr. A.W. Chapman and quotations had been received from Dr. A.E. Foote of Philadelphia and William Wesley & Son of London. Beadle prepared several extensive lists of books that he recommended to be purchased from both Foote and Wesley. Receipts show that Wesley sold George Vanderbilt nine cases of books in early 1896. By March, Beadle presented the Estate manager's office with an "A" and "B" list of books and also a "Sixth Adjusted Book List for the Arboretum Library." Botanical and forestry books were purchased from botanical book dealer A. Bergstraesser's Buchhandlung of Darmstadt. Beadle had written to Secretary of Agriculture J. Sterling Morton, inquiring how to secure all publications of the Department of Agriculture pertaining to botany and horticulture.

In an article, "The Biltmore Nursery and Arboretum," that Beadle submitted for the book *North Carolina and Its Resources*, published by the North Carolina State Board of Agriculture in 1896, he wrote, "To facilitate the compilation of the list of plants to be represented, their identification and subsequent classification necessary for their distribution in the arboretum, a magnificent library and several herbaria (collections of dried plants) have been installed in the nursery buildings as a nucleus for the great undertaking." He reported that the library already contained a large number of "masterpieces in botanical literature" and additions were to be made as rapidly as suitable works could be procured. He emphasized that among the herbaria represented was the "type collection" of Dr. A.W. Chapman, upon which he based his work, *The Flora of the Southern States*. Vanderbilt had purchased Chapman's collection at Beadle's recommendation. He added, "The botanical collectors are now engaged in preparing thousands of botanical specimens illustrating the flora of Western North Carolina, and it is expected to offer these specimens and many others from our vast country, either living or dried, in exchange for material not represented in the present collection." Less than three weeks earlier, on May 6, Beadle had written the Estate's manager informing him that by the coming fall and early winter it was his intention to have ready for exchange and distribution "in the neighborhood of one hundred thousand botanical specimens."

Exchanges of herbarium specimens had been going on prior to this time. In January 1896, Beadle had written to F.L.O. Jr. discussing the compilation of a plant specimen exchange list between the Biltmore Arboretum and Kew Arboretum. In February, Beadle wrote to Dr. Benjamin Robinson with Gray Herbarium, sending him a specimen of the rare *Rhus pumila* of Michaux that Biltmore plant collectors had recently located. At the same time, Beadle corresponded with Dr. A.W. Chapman and listed plant specimens he hoped Chapman could furnish to the Herbarium. In late February, Beadle reported to the Estate manager on the need to collect extensively for the Arboretum, Herbarium and for the "exchange catalog" and employ an additional collector. Beadle acknowledged George Vanderbilt's approval of the "Arboretum collecting project" in March and recommended the hiring of Frank Boynton's brother, C.L. Boynton, for the collector's position. In the next few weeks, Beadle wrote to Professor Sargent discussing *Torreya taxifolia* and *Taxus floridana*, which he had obtained from a correspondent in Bristol, Florida, and sent a box of requested plants to J.G. Jack at the Arnold Arboretum. By that summer, Beadle was off on a collecting trip to the Rocky Mountains, leaving an assistant, John Perry, to take care of business in the Nursery. Beadle solicited the assistance of his father, D.W. Beadle, to begin collecting and shipping plants from Ontario to Biltmore. Near the end of the year, Frank Boynton reported that his brother, C.L. Boynton, had a successful collecting trip to Virginia where he "secured over five hundred plants of the rare Pachystima which will be worth at least fifty cents to us in exchange."

In January 1897, Beadle ordered five thousand copies of the "Biltmore Herbarium exchange pamphlets" from the Citizen Company. Beadle corresponded with Mrs. H.W. Ravenel concerning further details on the materials for sale from the H.W. Ravenel Herbarium and sent a box of *Shortia galacifolia* seed to G.W. Oliver at the U.S. Botanic Gardens designated for William Thompson & Co. in Ipswich, England. He wrote to Professor W.W. Rowlee in March and enclosed an "exchange list of woody plants and seeds between Biltmore Nursery and Cornell University" and again in early April enclosing a list of plants shipped to Rowlee from the Biltmore Herbarium. Beadle also corresponded with Dr. Henry Kraemer at Northwestern University Pharmacy School to discuss botanical nomenclature. Beadle began searching for "certain agents in England and the Continent who would assist in the shipping of herbarium specimens to patrons." A year later, Beadle reported that four boxes of botanical specimens were sent via Wesley & Son in London to Russia, Austria, London and Australia.

Both the Herbarium and library continued to grow at a rapid pace. Boynton and his assistants made numerous collecting trips to various regions of North Carolina, from the mountains to the coast, as well as to other states, from South Carolina and Tennessee to Georgia, Florida, Missouri, Colorado and others. Beadle made arrangements with botanists and nurserymen throughout the Southeast and from Texas, Missouri, Nebraska, Montana and Wyoming to Washington, Oregon, California and Arizona to acquire indigenous plants of those regions. In February 1896, Beadle had written a draft report on the "Western Collecting Project." George Vanderbilt showed great interest in the Herbarium and botanical library. Beadle notified Mrs. H.W. Ravenel in March 1897 verifying Vanderbilt's decision to purchase her late husband's book collection. Shortly after, Beadle was making plans to order "a complete set of southern mosses for the Biltmore Herbarium" from Dr. John K. Small at Columbia University. Even while Mr. Vanderbilt was abroad, Beadle wrote reports concerning the welfare of the Herbarium and Arboretum and such issues as the exchange list, news of the collectors and collecting fields, the library and finances. In April 1897, Beadle copied a letter he had received from Dr. A.W. Chapman, who was in financial distress and requested that Vanderbilt assist Chapman "as it would add to the Biltmore Herbarium and Arboretum's collections." Two weeks later Beadle wrote to Dr. Chapman informing him that Vanderbilt "will advance him 850 dollars to be applied to his debt" and discussed Chapman becoming an exclusive collector for the Biltmore Herbarium. Soon after, Vanderbilt's financial support allowed Chapman to cancel the debt incurred in the publication of his third edition of *Southern Flora*. Vanderbilt also approved the promotion of Frank E. Boynton to his new position as "Guardian of the Biltmore Herbarium" and C.L. Boynton as "chief collector." Botanist T.G. Harbison was hired to fill a new assistant collector position. In June 1897, Beadle wrote to Gilbert H. Hicks of the *Asa Gray Bulletin*, stating he would "submit an article and photographs of the Biltmore Herbarium at a future date when the new buildings were completed."

Like other enterprises on the Estate however, the Herbarium was also subject to the will and discretion of the proprietor or affected by the financial situation at the time. Beadle wrote to his father in December 1897 that the Herbarium was in abeyance until Mr. Vanderbilt "sees fit to continue the undertaking." A month later, writing to Gifford Pinchot concerning plans for the Arboretum, Beadle stated his "spirits are at the lowest ebb in regard to its welfare in the future." At the same time, he wrote to F.L. Olmsted Jr. discussing the reason for no extensive exchange with Kew Gardens, stating that Vanderbilt had "restricted me from making requests for living material to be received at Biltmore for a time." He mentioned, though, that Vanderbilt had budgeted $1,200 for continuance of the Herbarium work, but restricting such work as sending the force "far afield" to collect materials. The situation apparently improved, as Beadle was back to receiving and shipping plants and specimens soon thereafter, including five crates of botanical specimens to William Wesley & Son in London to distribute to various institutions abroad. In early February 1901, Beadle announced that Vanderbilt had abandoned the project of establishing an Arboretum at Biltmore, but that the Herbarium would be maintained for the present year. Beadle wrote to the Olmsted brothers in late May about the major flooding that had caused a lot of damage to the Estate's roads, bridges, buildings and plantings; the Nursery had suffered severely. In spite of this setback, repairs were made, and later in the fall Beadle reported to his staff about Vanderbilt's plans to continue the Biltmore Herbarium and endow a "sum sufficient to provide a revenue of five or six thousand dollars" and to enlarge the Nursery office. In October, Beadle and Vanderbilt discussed the cost estimates for the extension of the Nursery building and the arrangement of the proposed Herbarium building.

On November 9, 1901, another setback occurred. Beadle wrote to Vanderbilt informing him of a fire in the storeroom of the Nursery office building and stated that the loss of the building was considerable. The library and Herbarium were not seriously damaged and the important records were intact, although about 90 percent of the duplicate herbarium materials were lost. The fire was due to spontaneous combustion of botanical specimens. Later in December, Beadle reported to Dr. John K. Small that Vanderbilt approved plans for a larger herbarium and an endowment to maintain the collection.

As the size and operations of the Herbarium grew, so did its reputation as a serious botanical collection. Extensive records in the Biltmore Company Archives attest to the prominence of both the Herbarium and its trusted director and chief botanist C.D. Beadle, through the exchange of information and plant specimens with hundreds of individuals and institutions. A few examples include: Dr. Benjamin L. Robinson, curator of the Gray Herbarium at Harvard University; William T. Thistleton-Dyer and G. Nicholson, both directors of the Royal Gardens at Kew; Joseph Crawford of the Academy of Natural Sciences; Charles Copineau of the Botanical Society of France; M.L. de Vilmorin, ref. Michaux Herbarium in Paris; Dr. John K. Small, director of the New York Botanical Garden; Dr. J.H. Maiden, director of the Sydney Botanic Gardens; J. Medley Wood, curator of the Natal Botanic Gardens; Charles Louis Pollard, assistant curator of the U.S. National Herbarium; Professor Charles S. Sargent, director of the Arnold Arboretum; Professor William Trelease, director of the Missouri Botanical Garden; G. Bolling of the Botanisches Institute at the University of Heidelburg; Professor Charles Flahault in the Botany Department at Montpellier University in France; Professor Nikolai von Kusnezow of the Botanic Gardens at the University Jurjew; Dr. J.N. Rose and others with the USDA, Division of Botany; and William W. Ashe and Dr. Charles T. Mohr, both noted botanists and forest specialists with the USDA Forest Service. Mohr, in fact, eventually moved to Asheville, where he spent his final months, at times in the Biltmore Herbarium, until his death on July 17, 1901. Beadle wrote and published numerous articles for botanical journals, including a series of articles relating to flora of the Southeastern United States for the *Botanical Gazette*, University of Chicago Press. He submitted a paper on the "Bamboos" for Professor L.H. Bailey's *Cyclopedia of American Horticulture*. Beadle became known and respected as an authority for his knowledge and publications on the genus *Crataegus* (hawthorns) and, with his collectors, discovered and described several new species of hawthorns as well as numerous other plants. Reprints of his articles for the *Botanical Gazette* and his publications of the "Biltmore Botanical Studies" were in great demand. Additionally, Beadle was called on to review and proof manuscripts of others, including Alice Lounsberry's *A Guide to the Wild Flowers*, *A Guide to the Trees* and *Southern Wild Flowers and Trees*. In June 1900, Beadle wrote to Dr. John K. Small stating he would "proof Small's publication on Southern flora."

The Biltmore Herbarium at its peak contained more than 100,000 specimens representing flora from across the Southeastern United States, various regions of North America from coast to coast and other countries as well. As previously mentioned, Biltmore had acquired the second herbarium collection of noted botanist Dr. Alvin W. Chapman from Apalachicola, Florida, who had assembled it for his book, *The Flora of the Southern United States*. Dr. Chapman considered his collection of more than 3,000 specimens to be his "gem" and gave his personal assurance that it was the only collection that contained every plant mentioned in his book. Other lesser-known herbaria had been purchased from various botanists and collectors, including portions of the Russell-Wilson and H.W. Ravenel herbaria. The combined collections formed what was believed to be the most complete herbarium of Southeastern plants in existence at that time. A considerable number of new species and subspecies of flora had been discovered and first described by the botanists and plant collectors of the Biltmore Nursery and Herbarium.

After the untimely death of George Vanderbilt on March 6, 1914, Mrs. Vanderbilt was considering donating the Biltmore Herbarium to a small educational institution as the nucleus of a working collection to make it more accessible to botany students. Unfortunately, before that happened, a devastating flood on July 16, 1916, effectively closed the doors on Biltmore Estate's great botanical era. It not only ended the Biltmore Nursery's large-scale commercial production and sale of nursery stock, but the flood waters also destroyed approximately three-fourths of the Biltmore Herbarium and much of the botanical library of several hundred volumes, many of which were rare, that was housed in a special wing of the Biltmore Nursery office building. Beadle wrote to a local botanist, Mary L. Wilson, in August confirming her fears about the Herbarium. He reported that the Herbarium building and contents "suffered heavily" and everything was being done to salvage the Nursery and the books and treasures in the buildings. He wrote Miss Wilson again in early October to inform her that the Russell-Wilson Herbarium along with the Chapman, Ravenel and Biltmore Herbaria suffered heavily in the flood. He described the sand and silt that covered them, the resulting effects of decomposition and stated that some of the brick buildings had collapsed. Beadle had ascertained that about a third of the Russell-Wilson Herbarium and about a fourth of the Biltmore Herbarium were salvageable, along with about a quarter of the book collection.

After visiting the Estate in October after the flood, William W. Ashe, forest inspector with the U.S. Forest Service, wrote to W.R. Maxon, associate curator at the National Museum (Smithsonian Institution), encouraging him to write to Mrs. Vanderbilt requesting that she give the remaining herbarium specimens and books to the museum. He stated,

> *The July flood worked irreparable ruin on this collection, which represented the flora of the Southeastern states far more fully than any other herbarium. Of the twelve tiers of shelves in the herbarium room the nine lower ones were covered by water and the contents of these nine, except for a few which contained type material and which were rescued, were destroyed. Consequently the remnant consists of only one-fourth of the original collection... The excellent working library which was in the room adjoining the herbarium stacks, while two-thirds submerged in water, has received such careful attention that most of the books except those printed on sized paper are in good useable condition.*

Associate curator Maxon in turn drafted a memorandum to Frederick V. Coville, former chief botanist for the USDA and honorary curator of the National Museum, recommending that immediate steps should be taken to bring about the acquisition of the remaining portions of this "extremely rich herbarium" that would "fill a very important niche in the National Herbarium." He pointed out to Mr. Coville that he had brought up the possibility a year or two ago of "securing the Biltmore Herbarium for the National Museum and that the plan, though extremely desirable, seemed doubtful at the time." Coville instructed Secretary Charles D. Walcott to write Mrs. Vanderbilt to see if she would be willing to consider placing the remainder of the Herbarium and the library connected with it in the U.S. National Museum. In his letter to Mrs. Vanderbilt, Walcott stated, "The Biltmore collection would be of great practical importance and value to the National Museum, as representing the very rich flora of a region relatively not well represented in that herbarium." He further stressed that even in its incompleteness, "The large number of types in critical genera alone renders it extremely desirable that the collection be centrally located, so that it would be readily available to the greatest number of students."

The following April, Beadle wrote Secretary Walcott on behalf of Mrs. Vanderbilt that "whenever you can conveniently do so, we would welcome the transfer of the material to a safe and available place, such as you can bestow, as the damaged buildings are to be torn down." In his prompt response, Walcott wrote,

> *No one realizes more fully than I what the destruction of the greater part of this notable collection has meant to the science of botany, especially as the loss is irreparable. We shall be extremely glad to receive what remains of the specimens and books and give them the care and protection they deserve in the National Herbarium, which is housed under excellent fireproof conditions. Thus a part of your extensive labors on the collection may be preserved perpetually.*

Walcott told Beadle that he would send someone from the Institution to "pick out and prepare the material for handling." Beadle replied,

> *At any time to suit your convenience, and on our part preferably at the earliest opportunity, we will welcome and assist your representative in getting the remaining specimens and books of the Biltmore Herbarium ready for the transfer to the Smithsonian Institution. I shall hope that the specimens and books that were rescued from the flood, which are only a small part of the former Biltmore Herbarium, will in some measure, at least, enrich the National Herbarium.*

In June, associate curator Maxon wrote to Richard Rathbun, who was the "Assistant Secretary in charge of the National Museum," detailing his trip to Biltmore in May for "sorting, packing, and shipping the books and plants of the Biltmore Herbarium." Of the approximate 100,000 specimens, Maxon reported that the number saved and brought to Washington was approximately 25,000, including a large portion of the Chapman Herbarium. He also stated that about 1,500 specimens of the "difficult genus Crataegus" were left temporarily with Beadle for identification.

On June 19, 1917, Secretary Walcott wrote,

> *My dear Mrs. Vanderbilt: It gives me much pleasure to announce the receipt of the valuable botanical specimens and library, and the microscopes, which formed part of the Biltmore*

Herbarium, and I beg to assure you of my deep appreciation of your generous action in donating this material to the National Museum, where its importance is fully recognized.

Because so many duplicate Biltmore Herbarium specimens were collected and exchanged with other collectors and institutions in the years before the flood, countless numbers of the Biltmore Herbarium's botanical treasures still exist in various universities and herbaria across the United States and abroad.

1. Biltmore House, Esplanade and formal Garden Terrace, circa 1910. The design of the formal parts of the "Home Grounds" immediately surrounding the house was a collaborative effort between Frederick Law Olmsted and architect Richard Morris Hunt. The simplicity of the Esplanade's trim expanse of turf and the double allée of tulip trees was designed intentionally to present the ornate features of the chateau. *Courtesy of The Biltmore Company.*

2. Future site of Biltmore House, 1889. This ridge top farm pasture and surrounding cutover woodland was typical of the 597 tracts of land totaling 55,000 acres that George W. Vanderbilt purchased in Buncombe County to create Biltmore Estate. His total landholdings in four counties eventually encompassed 125,000 acres, most of it managed as a working forest. *Courtesy of The Biltmore Company.*

3. View of Biltmore House on March 26, 1895, eight months before its scheduled completion. Olmsted's plans included reforesting former pastures with white pines and other native trees, as seen in the foreground. The Ramble or Shrub Garden below the formal terraces was designed for strolling through plantings of trees, shrubs and other plants produced by the Biltmore Nursery. *Courtesy of The Biltmore Company.*

4. Croquet on the Garden Terrace (Italian Garden), May 1906. The Biltmore Nursery propagated many thousands of English ivy plants for "festooning" the stone walls in this garden, the South Terrace, the Walled Garden and Conservatory, various bridges and other areas around the Estate. *Courtesy of The Biltmore Company.*

5. West elevation of Biltmore House mirrored on the tranquil surface of the Lagoon, situated at the lower end of the Deer Park, circa 1900. Olmsted advised Vanderbilt to "make a small park into which to look from your house; make a small pleasure ground and garden, farm your river bottom…and make the rest a forest." *Courtesy of The Biltmore Company.*

6. Bridge on Approach Road, circa 1890. Olmsted intended that the Estate's three-mile drive to Biltmore House be a pleasurable experience for visitors. His design included "rest areas" with rustic stone seats to provide opportunities for travelers to pause and enjoy the beauty and serenity of the naturalistic setting while their horses watered at a nearby pool. *Courtesy of The Biltmore Company.*

7. Lower Approach Road, March 4, 1891. A bearded Olmsted is standing between nurseryman Chauncey Beadle and George Vanderbilt on the right with work crew supervised by James G. Gall. The Biltmore Nursery initially collected and grew forty thousand native rhododendrons, mountain laurels and leucothoes that were planted along the woodland borders of this naturalistically designed three-mile road, considered to be one of Olmsted's design masterpieces. *Courtesy of The Biltmore Company.*

8. Upper Approach Road, September 8, 1891. Olmsted's vision was to transform the cutover woodland and overgrazed farms into a landscape that would mimic the natural beauty of the surrounding Blue Ridge Mountains. For the Approach Road, he intended to create a setting with a "natural and comparatively wild and secluded character; its borders rich with varied forms of vegetation." *Courtesy of The Biltmore Company.*

9. Scene near the junction of the Service and Approach Roads, March 1896. Traces of the historic Long Shoals Road, one of the first public roads built when Buncombe County was established in April 1792, can be seen in the left side of this view. The Biltmore Nursery, located nearby, produced millions of tree seedlings to reforest hundreds of acres of abandoned pastures. *Courtesy of The Biltmore Company.*

10. Chauncey Delos Beadle in the Shrub Garden, 1906. Beadle studied botany at Ontario Agricultural College and Cornell University before being hired by Olmsted in 1890 to assist James Gall with managing the Estate's newly established nursery. By early 1894, Beadle became superintendent of the Biltmore Nursery and Herbarium and in time Estate superintendent, remaining at Biltmore until his death in 1950. *Courtesy of The Biltmore Company.*

11. Gardener's Cottage and the Walled Garden during construction, February 25, 1893. The stone cottage with terra cotta tile roof newly built for the head gardener stands in sharp contrast with the pre-existing settler's cabin and barns on one of many farms purchased by Vanderbilt. Olmsted's plans included transforming the pasture below the cottage into a woodland Glen. *Courtesy of The Biltmore Company.*

12. The Walled Garden, circa 1895. Olmsted's design intent for this four-acre "vegetable and flower garden," as he initially called it, was to be functional, supplying Biltmore House with "fine" fruits and vegetables, as well as flowers and herbs in the tradition of European country houses. Vanderbilt decided that since he was planting vegetable gardens and orchards on his farm, he wanted a garden of "ornament, not utility." *Courtesy of The Biltmore Company.*

13. Portion of the Home Grounds nearing completion in 1895. Olmsted's intent was that, in time, the plantings in the Ramble or Shrub Garden would screen the view of the formal and symmetrical layout of the walled "vegetable and flower garden" and Conservatory from the South Terrace. *Courtesy of The Biltmore Company.*

14. The Lake, circa 1895. Surrounded by a picturesque woodland landscape, the Lake, designed by Olmsted, came to be known as the Bass Pond and was situated at the terminus of the path through the Glen. The rustic boathouse provided a quiet retreat for observing nesting waterfowl on the adjacent islands and could be accessed by the stone steps leading from adjacent Glen Road. *Courtesy of The Biltmore Company.*

15. Early farms on both banks of the French Broad River purchased by George Vanderbilt in 1888 and 1889. The rugged topography of the steep, sparsely wooded parcels with worn-out pastures prompted Olmsted to advise Vanderbilt to make most of his estate a "systematically managed forest" rather than a "park." *Courtesy of The Biltmore Company.*

16. The Truck Farm or Market Garden, 1900. Situated in the fertile bottomland adjacent to the Swannanoa River, the Truck Farm produced a variety of fruits and vegetables such as melons, berries, lettuce, potatoes and cabbage for the Estate and for sale in the local markets. Chauncey Beadle, superintendent of the Biltmore Nursery on the opposite bank of the river, assumed responsibility for its operation in 1905. *Courtesy of The Biltmore Company.*

17. All Souls Crescent in Biltmore Village, 1906. Plans for Biltmore included a “model village” near the entrance to the Estate. The Biltmore Nursery provided the trees for lining the streets and the landscape plantings for the rental cottages and business establishments as planned by the Olmsted firm. *Courtesy of The Biltmore Company.*

18, 19, 20. *Left, above and below:* These circa 1930 views of the Rose Garden show a well-kept and professionally maintained garden. The Estate grew and displayed extensive varieties of roses in various classes, including hybrid perpetual roses, teas and hybrid teas, scotch and moss roses, bourbons, old-fashioned roses, briers, polyanthas, pillars, ramblers and climbers and species roses. *Courtesy of The Biltmore Company.*

21. Flood waters, as seen in May 1901, caused considerable damage to roads, bridges, plantings and buildings. Situated near the confluence of the Swannanoa and French Broad Rivers, both the Truck Farm and the Biltmore Nursery were vulnerable to repeated flooding. Western North Carolina's largest flood of the twentieth century occurred in July 1916, destroying the greenhouses in this photograph and permanently ending Biltmore's commercial nursery operations. *Courtesy of The Biltmore*

22. The violet racemes of wisteria adorn the pergola near the entrance to the Shrub Garden below Biltmore House. The orange and scarlet flowers of the trumpet vine (*Campsis radicans*) that is interplanted with the wisteria will continue the show after the wisteria has ended its display. *Courtesy of The Biltmore Company.*

23. The Olmsted firm produced this guide map for guests to find their way around the vast acreage of the Estate. The main headquarters and offices of the Biltmore Nursery were located on the north side of the Swannanoa adjacent to Southern Railroad for convenient shipping. The route of Olmsted's Arboretum Road began on the south side of the Bass Pond in the valley below the Biltmore House. *Courtesy of The Biltmore Company.*

AP
ESTATE
1/2
1MILE
1500
2000 METRES
DT, LANDSCAPE ARCHITECTS
SS.
Westover Hill
Dairy Farm
RIVERBEND
PENINSULA
Woodcote
Ferry Farm
Farmcote
Long Ridge
Long Bottom
Truck Farm
Nursery
Vernon Hill
Swannanoa
Brick House
Deer Park
BILTMORE HOUSE
The Glen
Lone Pine Hill
Biltmore Lodge
BILTMORE VILLAGE
RIVER ROAD
SERVICE
APPROACH ROAD
OVERLOOK ROAD
BUSBEE ROAD
HENDERSONVILLE ROAD
WENDOVER ROAD
SWANNANOA
VICTORIA ROAD
VERNON ROAD
SOUTHERN RY.
N
S

24. In July 1889, Olmsted recommended the "establishment and maintenance of an unbroken forest from the north to the south end of the Estate...with a Park to be taken out near the residence...Perhaps with certain fields to be also taken out for agricultural purposes. Your property on the left bank of the river [French Broad] to be also maintained in forest condition and improved." *Courtesy of The Biltmore Company.*

25. Splashes of golden daffodils and forsythia and pink-tinged petals of magnolias in early spring begin a procession of color that changes weekly through spring and early summer in the Estate's four-acre Shrub Garden. The Biltmore Nursery supplied thousands of plants in more than five hundred varieties of trees, shrubs, groundcovers and hardy perennials for this garden alone. *Bill Alexander photograph.*

26. The Biltmore Nursery procured and propagated an intensive collection of conifers, including the graceful weeping hemlock (*Tsuga canadensis* 'Pendula'), also known as the Sargent's weeping hemlock, and the dwarf, conical form of Eastern hemlock (*Tsuga Canadensis* 'Compacta'), shown here on the Estate's Home Grounds. *Bill Alexander photograph.*

27. Early spring brings a bright splash of forsythia's golden sunshine to the slopes of the Spring Garden. Olmsted designed this "Vernal Garden," as he sometimes referred to it, to display masses of flowering shrubs on the steep slopes above a verdant grassy glade. Towering white pines and hemlocks shelter a shady strolling path around the garden's perimeter. *Bill Alexander photograph.*

28. Extensive symmetrical beds of annual flowers, borders of hardy perennials and herbs hundreds of feet long and an acre and a half of roses provide a full three seasons of color in the Estate's ever-popular Walled Garden. Ornamental grasses, espaliered fruit trees and shrubs and central "vine-clad arbors" complete this "garden of ornament" that George Vanderbilt desired. *Courtesy of The Biltmore Company.*

29. The fifteen-acre Azalea Garden was formerly designed by the Olmsted firm as the Glen, with many varieties of flowering trees and shrubs, including azaleas. Estate nurseryman and botanist Chauncey Beadle donated his collection of native azaleas (his favorites) to the Estate in 1940. To honor Beadle's fifty years of faithful service at that time, Edith Vanderbilt Gerry renamed the Glen as the Azalea Garden. *Courtesy of The Biltmore Company.*

30. Flowering dogwoods brighten this sylvan scene along Biltmore Estate's Old Ferry Road, which illustrates the far-sighted vision of Frederick Law Olmsted. He planned for the reforestation of hundreds of acres of worn-out farmland such as this former pasture site more than a century ago. *Bill Alexander photograph.*

31. The pinxter flower (*Rhododendron periclymenoides*), a native azalea shown here in the Estate's Azalea Garden, was one of many varieties of deciduous azaleas grown by the Biltmore Nursery. The catalog described it as "a handsome free-flowering shrub...the extreme earliness and beauty of the flowers commend this shrub to the planters." *Bill Alexander photograph.*

32. The many hundreds of varieties of flowering shrubs produced by the Biltmore Nursery included such perennial favorites as old-fashioned weigelas (*Weigela*) and mock oranges (*Philadelphus*), shown in this grouping in the Estate's Shrub Garden. *Bill Alexander photograph.*

33. The prolific, honey-scented flowers of dwarf fothergilla (*Fothergilla gardenii*), a member of the witch hazel family, appear in early spring in Biltmore's Azalea Garden. Now more commonly grown in gardens and landscapes, fothergillas were grown at the Biltmore Nursery when they "were rarely seen in cultivation." *Courtesy of The Biltmore Company.*

34. A "colony" of bottlebrush or dwarf buckeye (*Aesculus parviflora*) is shown in flower near the Estate's Lagoon in early July. The Biltmore Nursery described it as "one of the handsomest of ornamentals" and if "planted in groups on the lawn, or in connection with other shrubbery, magnificent floral results may be obtained." *Bill Alexander photograph.*

35. The pink-tinted buds and blossoms of the indigenous rosebay rhododendron (*Rhododendron maximum*) appear after the flush of new growth in mid- to late June along Biltmore's Approach Road. Nurseryman Chauncey Beadle reported to Olmsted in January 1893, "Very extensive collections of native Rhododendrons and Kalmias have been made and are still in progress for the planting." *Bill Alexander photograph.*

36, 37. In July 1889, Olmsted advised Vanderbilt concerning the three-mile Approach Road to Biltmore House: "I suggest that the most striking and pleasing impression of the Estate will be obtained if an approach can be made that shall have throughout a natural and comparatively wild and secluded character; its borders rich with varied forms of vegetation, with incidents growing out of the vicinity of springs and streams and pools, steep banks and rocks, all consistent with the sensation of going through the remote depths of a natural forest." *Courtesy of The Biltmore Company.*

38. Notes from a conversation with Olmsted in November 1892. "The Ramble, as Mr. Olmsted calls the shrub garden, is to have a considerable amount of turf between the walk and plantations. In this turf is to be dotted a variety of individual trees and shrubs breaking out from the main bodies of planting." *Courtesy of The Biltmore Company.*

39. Water spills over the Bass Pond's stone dam into a picturesque ravine. Olmsted intended that the landscape surrounding the pond create "an effect of intricacy and mystery." Concerning the slopes above the road on the east side of the pond he wrote, "The effect to be produced is that of a 'hanging wood,' increasing the apparent height and steepness of the hill." *Courtesy of The Biltmore Company.*

40. Masses of showy hybrid azaleas adorn the rustic granite steps at the entrance to the Azalea Garden near the Conservatory. The dark green needles of the Oriental spruce (*Picea orientalis*) and the white, bell-shaped flowers of the two-winged silverbell or snowdrop tree (*Halesia diptera*) make a fitting backdrop for the dazzling display. *Courtesy of The Biltmore Company.*

41. Masses of golden forsythia and white spirea in March begin the procession of color that makes the Estate's four-acre Shrub Garden such a pleasant place for a "ramble," as intended by Frederick Law Olmsted more than a century ago. *Courtesy of The Biltmore Company.*

42. Olmsted drew from his vast storehouse of life experiences and travels in devising his philosophies for designing the various features of his landscapes. He wrote to Vanderbilt: "Years ago I rode alone for a month through the North Carolina forests, and it was with great regret that last I emerged from them. There is no experience of my life to which I could return with more satisfaction." *Courtesy of The Biltmore Company.*

43, 44. In a June 1895 memorandum outlining instructions for sections of the entry drive, Olmsted emphasized, "Most visitors will get their first decided impression of the local scenery while passing over this road." Following up with more detailed instructions to Chauncey Beadle, he wrote, "People coming from New York to Biltmore in the Winter or Spring must be made to feel that they are decidedly nearer the sun. We must aim, then, to gain as much of sub-tropical general character of scenery as we can without a large sacrifice of existing elements of the woodland beauty of the Southern temperate region…it is the result that will be constant through the year that we must care most for." *Courtesy of The Biltmore Company.*

45. George W. Vanderbilt commissioned noted artist John Singer Sargent to paint portraits of both Richard Morris Hunt, his architect, and Frederick Law Olmsted Sr., his landscape architect, in the summer of 1895. Olmsted is appropriately depicted amidst his Approach Road landscape of native mountain laurels, rhododendrons and dogwoods that characterized his naturalistic style of design. *Courtesy of The Biltmore Company.*

The Biltmore Nursery

As previously mentioned, Olmsted's recommendations to Vanderbilt were to transform the majority of his Estate into a "systematically managed forest" as a much-needed model for the country; to surround Biltmore House with a park and landscape of pleasure grounds and gardens; and to lay out miles of carriage drives through the various portions of his property. Additionally, he saw an opportunity to create a major Arboretum on the Estate as an outdoor museum of trees, complete with a botanical library and Herbarium, where dendrologists, botanists and landscape gardeners could study and learn. Olmsted knew that to accomplish these grand schemes, millions of trees, shrubs and other plants would be needed. Given the fact that there were no large commercial nurseries within a reasonable distance from Biltmore, he knew that the cost of importing the vast quantities and varieties of plants that would be desired would be prohibitive, even for Vanderbilt.

Early in the project, Olmsted advised Vanderbilt that

> *many of the trees, shrubs and vines that you will find it desirable to plant in considerable quantity cannot be found at the commercial nurseries; certainly cannot except in small numbers and at the price of rarities. To obtain them in quantity of a desirable planting size will take several years. Some can best be propagated on the ground; some obtained as small seedlings in Europe or from Japan and advanced on the Estate. There are numerous plants that may well be used that are not quite rare but for which there is no demand at the North because of their tenderness and not sufficient demand at the South to have led to their being grown for sale except at the price of rarities and in very small numbers.*

Olmsted mentioned that he had seen several smooth-leaved evergreens such as "Magnolia, the American Holly and Rhododendron Maximum" in Asheville gardens and a few on the Estate, proving that they were hardy in that area. He knew of others from trials in Washington that would endure the Asheville climate, and which Vanderbilt should have near his residence and in sheltered places along his roads. Larger quantities would be needed, however, than could "be obtained at this time from all the nurseries in the country or, as to some of them, in all the nurseries of Europe." Olmsted advised that "propagating and rearing them on a scale large enough to warrant the employment of a good gardener with a suitable plant for the purpose, they would cost you not a quarter as much as the commercial price." One can sense Olmsted's enthusiasm for the prospects of establishing a nursery at Biltmore as he convincingly tells Vanderbilt,

> *Taking such measures there are shrubs which are yet luxuries, seen only as "specimens," and many of these in New York only under glass, which you could easily have as profusely on the borders of your roads as you see rock ferns and "huckleberries" growing on the roads of Mt. Desert. You can have a stretch of bamboos, at a little less cost than one of blackberries, have it a quarter of a mile long if you like, provided you make preparations for it three or four years in advance. The nursery price of Rhododendron Maximum in New York, three feet high, has been $2.00 a plant. You can have plants gathered for you within twenty miles of your residence, by the thousand, probably at ten cents a plant, and after two years in nursery they will be better plants than I have been able to get from any nurseryman in Europe or America.*
>
> *Plant 10,000 of them along your road, as a background, and in front of them 5,000 of the most splendid hybrid Rhododendrons (such as they exhibit under tents at the Horticultural Gardens in London) and of the Himalayan and Alpine Rhododendrons; scatter among them clusters of Kalmias, the native and Japanese Andromedas, the Japanese Euonymus of which there are a dozen sorts that will surely be hardy with you, though they cannot live out in Philadelphia; the Japanese Aucubas, the refined little* Abelia ruprestris *with a cloud of most delicate bloom (I have had a hundred of them growing fully exposed for several years in Washington, though I have never seen a specimen elsewhere except in a hot house);* Mahonia aquifolia *which must be guarded here and is often scorched and sometimes killed, but would be at home with you; the Japanese Mahonia, still less hardy but safe with you; all these are smooth-leaved, laurel-like evergreen shrubs, which can be had, under a well organized system, in a few years, by the thousand, costing no more than people generally pay for the commonest deciduous bushes of our northern woods. I suppose you could naturalize in your woods more than five times as many sorts of fine, smooth-leaved evergreens as can be grown in the open air near New York.*

Olmsted told Vanderbilt, "These are hints of the capabilities of the Estate. Making good use of them, where would there be anything to compare with it? You would have people crossing the Atlantic to see it." Olmsted explained that to take advantage of having varieties of plants that were unavailable commercially, "the early starting of a propagating house, nursery and trial garden, will recommend itself to your consideration."

Vanderbilt was apparently sold on the idea of establishing a nursery on the Estate, as Olmsted wrote to James Gall, the firm's representative at Biltmore, in November 1889, explaining "the original idea was to employee a nurseryman and propagator on the Estate to collect and raise plants for use on the Estate for years to come." His first choice for the job had declined the offer, but Robert Douglas, the owner of a nursery in Waukegan, Illinois, offered to collect smooth-leaved evergreens to grow on the Estate. He went on to explain that "now Mr. Douglas wants a contract since collecting is harder than he had thought, increasing the cost considerably." Olmsted counseled Gall on working with Mr. Douglas to stock the Nursery and mentioned several plants to collect, including *Cornus florida*, hemlock, rhododendrons and *Kalmia latifolia*. In subsequent letters, Olmsted discussed specifications per Mr. Douglas's contract and pricing of the plants that he was stocking the Nursery with. In December Olmsted again wrote Gall to discuss options of either hiring Mr. Douglas to work under Gall or to put him in charge of the Estate's Nursery.

In a letter to Gall on December 11, 1889, Olmsted discussed the location and plans for a nursery and referred to land on both the north and south sides of the railroad. He asked Gall to write a plan and to "take into consideration the location of a road, a nurseryman's house for night duty, and access, drainage and exposure issues for the location." Olmsted advised that from his distance, he couldn't address these details. He further suggested that "propagation houses be built up under the bluff for shelter" and that a public road be run along the foot of the bluff. Packing sheds for small and delicate plants would be needed and the "nursery should have a neat, orderly, organized aspect." He suggested that four to six acres would accommodate all of this and would like for Gall to ascertain whether the area was in danger of flooding. Olmsted was expecting Gall to make meteorological reports in order to reach conclusions about the potential of the Estate. Apparently, Olmsted and his partners placed confidence in Gall's ability to plan the Nursery on the site. He wrote to the Estate's general manager, Charles McNamee, expressing, "We had expected, as you say, to prepare a plan for the nursery until our last visit to the ground, when going there with Mr. Gall and debating the matter with him, Mr. Codman and I were so well satisfied with his suggestions that we thought it best to leave the matter in his hands. The plan will be a very simple one."

Olmsted continued to write successive letters to Gall almost daily through the end of December with various instructions and suggestions. Olmsted wrote regarding a nurseryman named Harlan P. Kelsey in Highlands, North Carolina, who had offered to sell various shrubs to the Estate at prices much better than Douglas's. Olmsted favored using Kelsey, as his prices were better and he offered native plants. He asked Gall for a list of quantities of plants already collected for the Nursery before ordering more from Kelsey. Olmsted wrote that he wasn't prepared to make final arrangements concerning Kelsey and Douglas, as he was waiting for Vanderbilt to respond from Europe. On February 20, 1890, Olmsted wrote to Kelsey with terms of an agreement "to supply the following plants to Biltmore Nursery for planting in fall 1891: *Rhododendron maximum*, *Rhododendron catawbiense*, *Rhododendron punctatum*, *Leucothoe catesbaei*, *Leiophyllum buxifolium*; for planting in 1892: *Ilex opaca*, *Ilex dahoon*, *Ilex cassine*, *Ilex myrtifolium* and *Gaylussacia brachycera*." Besides contracts with Douglas, Kelsey and others, plant collectors were hired to collect seedlings and seeds of indigenous plants from around the region. Commercial quantities of many native plants were generally unavailable from nurseries, so collecting was the only means of building up stock. Collecting was done on various private tracts after arrangements were made with the landowners. A lot of collecting was done on the large forested tracts of land that Vanderbilt later acquired in the region surrounding Mount Pisgah. The Nursery and Forest departments also purchased tree seeds, such as oaks, chestnuts, white pines and hollies, from local people who were looking to make extra money.

When Olmsted hired Gall, who had been a foreman for Olmsted with the Central Park project, to come to Biltmore, he had given him the directorship "of operations of Agriculture, Horticulture, Forestry and Gardening." With time, this became too much responsibility for one man and as other experts were hired to manage areas like forestry and agriculture, those departments were transferred. As Gall's duties increased with the extraordinary amount of grading and construction of roads, building lakes and ponds, grading and preparing grounds for planting and various other things, he indicated the need for an assistant in the Nursery.

Olmsted agreed and started searching for the right candidate. Olmsted wrote to Gall on March 25, 1890, about someone that had been referred to him.

> *As a result of our correspondence and enquiry for a man to assist you in the nursery work and plant records, we have had brought to our attention, since the last letter to you, a young man who seems to have peculiar qualifications for the position. He was five years with a Canadian nursery firm, then in the Arboretum at Guelph, Ontario; then three years at Cornell University, under Professors Prentice and Bailey, which ought to be a most valuable experience in connection with records; then one year with one of the largest nursery firms in the West, and two years with B.A. Elliot & Co. of Pittsburg, one of the largest growers of hardy plants. He is now with John N. May, the New Jersey rose-grower.*
>
> *Mr. May unhesitatingly endorses him as a propagator of hardy plants, as well versed in horticultural matters and in botany, and says, "I am sorry to part with him..."*
>
> *We want zealous and intelligent observation and good orderly records as to the condition of the plants on arrival, and if they fail to flourish, as to whether they were poor plants, or badly packed or if there appears reason to conclude that they were distinctly not hardy, or for any reason, not desirable for Biltmore. Is your man capable of looking after this, following the matter up, forming a trustworthy judgment and making due records and reports?*
>
> *We have examined several other men besides the one whose letter we send; one of them another Englishman who we think would do, if this man would not, but we want to hear more of the man you have and to know your mind about the matter more fully before we go further.*

The man referred to in the letter was Chauncey Delos Beadle, a young Canadian trained in botany and horticulture. The F.L. Olmsted & Company reported on March 28, 1890, that the firm "has engaged an excellent man for the position. Our Mr. Codman yesterday engaged Mr. C.D. Beadle to go to Biltmore to take charge of the nurseries...Mr. Beadle is to leave New York for Biltmore on Monday next." Warren H. Manning, who worked with the Olmsted firm, wrote to Gall on behalf of Olmsted on March 31, 1890, informing him about Beadle. He reported,

> *Mr. F.L. Olmsted, who has just returned from New York, did not see Mr. Beadle, but Mr. Codman, who was there at the time and who made the arrangement with him, stated to Mr. Olmsted that he was the most desirable of several applicants before us, but quite young. I have met Mr. D.W. Beadle, the father, from whom there is a letter, and know of him by reputation. He is prominent in nursery and pomological circles and an able man. The son of such a man as I judge Mr. Beadle, Sr. to be, will be able to make a success of the work you will have for him to do, I believe.*

In an article Olmsted wrote for the Asheville *Lyceum* in December 1891 on "George Vanderbilt's Nursery," it is clear that the Nursery was a serious and large-scale operation from the beginning. He began the article by stating that anyone interested in botany and dendrology or wishing other information could seek it of the nurseryman in charge, Mr. C.D. Beadle. Olmsted then outlined the various projects that the Nursery's output of plants would be used for. The Nursery was part of an overall scheme for the Estate, on which a "systematically managed forest" would occupy the greater part of the acreage, some four thousand acres of the total at that time. He generally discussed the plans for the proposed Arboretum, which he described as an "Experiment Station and Museum of living trees," as well as an area of Glens in which it was intended to form "passages of local scenery occurring in many similar regions of North Carolina." This was most likely a reference to the borders of the three-mile Approach Road to the residence that he was designing. He listed several lustrous smooth-leaved evergreens such as rhododendrons (mountain laurel) and kalmias (ivy), ilexes (holly) and the leucothoe (locally called hemlock) as being the more notable constituents of the local flora that he had in mind. He described the marshy areas that occurred in some of the glens as "occasional partly flooded or water-soaked areas, in or on the edges of which grow cane, bulrushes, sagittarias and other aquatic forms of vegetation, mostly herbaceous." In addition to the indigenous plants, he planned to introduce a small number of foreign plantings of a generally similar, glossy, evergreen character to create a "greater variety and grace of form and vivacity of tint." It was intended at certain points to "produce a more complex intricacy of effect" than could be obtained if only native plants were used. Additionally, Olmsted noted that an attempt would be made to naturalize a few foreign plants such as "certain Bamboos, Nelumbiums and Nymphaeas," each having qualities that differed from those of the native aquatic and waterside plants, but would make a pleasing association with them.

The Nursery contained plantings for the various areas of the Estate, including "the Forest, the Arboretum Road, and the Glen areas." Olmsted stated that there were two or more samples each of 4,200 species and varieties for the Arboretum. Additionally, there were about 20,000 of the different species of "Rhododendron, Kalmia, Leucothoe, Andromeda, Ilex, Laurus, Osmanthus, Aucuba, Abelia and other smooth-leaved evergreens" that had been collected or obtained otherwise that were either in the Nursery or already planted on the banks of Ram Branch on the Lower Approach Road. Another 10,000 plants such as "Ivies, Evergreen Loniceras and Running Roses, Hypericum, Periwinkle, etc." were intended to be used as groundcovers. There were two samples each of 400 hybrid varieties of rhododendrons being tested on a trial basis. The intent for all of these plantings was to create a natural aspect and blend with the surroundings or to stand in "harmonious and modest subordinate relations with the general landscape of this region of the country."

Olmsted's plans included a small area of "kept grounds" near the residence, which were to be laid out formally for the most part, with "a view to domestic convenience and correspondence with the buildings, consequently, with a clearly defined demarcation from the natural landscape." It was intended to give little attention to plants that were commonly called "ornamentals," especially in regard to the "exhibition of mere curiosities, eccentricities or rarities of vegetation."

Altogether, Olmsted reported in the article that the stock of trees and bushes of merchantable size numbered about 100,000 and the total of seedlings and cuttings propagated on the grounds during the last year equaled about 500,000. Some of the stock plants had been obtained from as far away as southern Europe and Japan.

Biltmore Nursery listed orders in the spring of 1892 from the following nurserymen and seeds men:

Backhouse, J. & Sons, York, England
Bassett & Son, Hammonton, N.J.
Berckman, P.J., Augusta, Ga.
Berger, H.H. & Co., San Francisco, Cal.
Dicksons, Chester, England
Elliott, B.A. & Sons, Pittsburg, Pa.
Ellwanger & Barry, Rochester, N.Y.
Hoopes Bros. & Thomas, West Chester, Pa.
Kelsey, Harlan P., Linville, N.C.
Little, Wm. S., Rochester, N.Y.
Manning, J.W., Reading, Mass.
Meehan, Thos. & Sons, Germantown, Phila., Pa.
Meyer, H., Passaic, N.J.
Moon, S.C., Morrisville, Bucks Co., Pa.
Parker, G.A., Halifax, Mass.
Parsons & Sons, Flushing, N.Y.
Saul, John, Washington, D.C.
Thorburn, Jas. M. & Co., New York, N.Y.
Veitch J. & Sons, Chelsea, England

The inventory of plants in the Nursery continued to grow each year in spite of the quantities being planted in various areas of the Estate each season. By the end of 1893, when the walls of Biltmore House had reached the second floor, Beadle reported that his department had received 209,925 plants, had propagated another 2,935,615, had collected locally another 366,527 and had permanently planted on the Estate 2,870,628. It is not known whether this inventory account included seedlings being grown exclusively for the forestry department planting. Gifford Pinchot, in his 1893 booklet "Biltmore Forest: An Account of its Treatment, and the Results of the First Year's Work," reported that there was "considerably more than 1,000 acres at present lying waste, but which is to be used later on for planting forest trees...The list of seedlings now being raised in the Nursery for forest planting includes twenty species, with an estimated total of 1,867,000 individuals." He further stated that these were largely the "standard kinds" and that the "great majority of species for this work have not been planted."

A memorandum prepared by the Olmsted firm in February 1894 stated that

> *in the catalogue of plants now (Spring 1894) growing in the Biltmore Nursery there are represented, 92 orders, 353 genera, 4430 species and varieties. Of woody plants there are represented, 78 orders, 281 genera, 3645 species and hybrids (about 1000 of these are named varieties of rhododendrons, roses, weigelias* [sic], *altheas, tree paeonies and lilacs.) Of the kinds included in the "List of available nursery stock for the planting during the Autumn of 1893 and Spring of 1894" there were of woody plants, 61 orders, 175 genera, 907 species and varieties. Of these species and varieties, 577 were represented by from 10 to 100 plants, 211 were represented by from 100 to 500 plants, 119 were represented by 500 or more plants. Of the remaining 2738 species and varieties (of most of which two to twelve*

specimens were purchased) there have been propagated not less than ten of nearly all those varieties that are difficult to propagate or are of slow growth.

An article in *The American Architect and Building News* on May 5, 1894, reported, "Most of readers have probably heard of the great experimental forestry station and nursery which Mr. George W. Vanderbilt, of New York, is laying out on his country estate in North Carolina; but few of them, probably, are aware that Mr. Vanderbilt has already growing more varieties of trees and shrubs than are to be found in the Royal Botanic Gardens at Kew."

In May 1896, Mr. Beadle sent to the Estate manager, Charles McNamee, a sketch of "Biltmore Nursery and Arboretum" for Mr. Bruner's book, *North Carolina and its Resources*. T.K. Bruner was secretary of North Carolina's State Board of Agriculture, which produced the book in 1896. The "sketch" that Beadle wrote and submitted stated that

a little more than six years ago a nursery was established on the alluvial deposits of the Swannanoa River, at Biltmore, for propagating large numbers of native and hardy exotic forest trees and shrubs, and, as this industry has developed into one of the largest and most complete and consistent establishments of its kind, an outline of progress and results obtained, together with the future plans, may be of general interest.

The article further stated that "up to the time of the founding of the nursery very little was known regarding the capabilities of the soil and climate of the locality. Barring the tangible evidence of the indigenous species and a few foreign plants that were sparingly used about the homes of the residents, the plan of procedure was largely based upon the available meteorological data." Due to the lack of information regarding the kinds of plants that might thrive in the climate of the region, "considerable freedom was exercised in ordering the first consignments of stock plants." Orders were placed with the leading nurseries of the world for woody plants that were likely to thrive in the area.

It was clearly admitted that "the first season's work was one of experiment." The best cultural methods were employed to make sure that the plants were conditioned to "withstand the effects of winter." The first winter was not too severe and the majority of the species survived and "entered their second season with increased vigor." The article reported,

On the event of the second winter the stock could not have been in better condition to withstand the hardships which followed. The winter was very severe, accompanied by several remarkable depressions of the thermometer. With such a test it is evident that the surviving plants will serve as an invaluable criterion to the planter in the mountain district. Having thus gained the key to success, the employees are kept busy propagating the desirable species and varieties, and a glance at the great range of glass, frames and land leads one to believe that the annual output might reach vast and astonishing numbers. Since the erection of the first propagating house, between three and four millions of forest trees and shrubs have been turned over to the planters. In addition to this, at the present writing, nearly two millions of plants are in course of development, and the annual output may now be estimated at something over two millions of plants.

As the demand for nursery stock increased for use in planting of the various gardens and grounds areas, the 3-mile Approach Road borders and those along many miles of other carriage roads, the 250-acre Deer Park and for reforestation, the Nursery expanded accordingly. The April 14, 1894 entry in "The Reports of the Nurseryman" stated that the "new greenhouses are ready for occupancy." Later, in July, the Hunt firm supplied plans for additional greenhouses and received the construction bids in late October. The new greenhouses were completed by fall of the next year. The field space required for growing stock expanded also. Although the main Nursery headquarters was on the north side of the Swannanoa, the Nursery utilized vacant fields on other parts of the Estate for growing trees and shrubs.

For several years after its establishment, the bulk of the Nursery's output was utilized on the Estate grounds for landscaping and reforestation and for landscaping the streets, businesses and rental cottages in Biltmore Village and Vernon Hill. As the Nursery's fame spread, the office started getting a steady stream of inquiries about the availability of plants for sale. As early as December 1893, Charles McNamee wrote to the Olmsted firm to discuss the Nursery becoming a separate department with Mr. Beadle at the head, as it had been Vanderbilt's intention to have the Nursery become a commercial enterprise. McNamee stated that he had already received Vanderbilt's approval for this change. Some sales were randomly made depending on the availability of excess stock. Orders were filled locally for planting at residences and businesses as well as out-of-state orders to various botanists, plant collectors, other nurseries and places like the Arnold Arboretum, Cornell University and Washington Botanic Gardens. The Olmsted firm started ordering plants for other clients and projects like Cherokee Park in Louisville.

In December 1898, Beadle sent the Olmsted Brothers a list of plants at Biltmore Nursery that was in excess of planting demands and informed the firm that Mr. Vanderbilt was starting the Nursery as a commercial business. A series of ads were placed in gardening and other publications announcing the opening of the Biltmore Nursery to the public and including a price list and catalog. The response was immediate and orders began to pour in. Because of Biltmore Estate's reputation for quality and referrals by the Olmsted firm and others, Biltmore plants were sought by landscape architects, park superintendents, universities and other nurseries for resale. When Beadle sent his manuscript for the nursery trade list for the 1900–01 season to J.H. McFarland Company in Harrisburg, Pennsylvania, he ordered six thousand copies and instructed them to mail the trade lists to landscape architects and nurserymen. For several years only an unillustrated trade list was produced for wholesale or professional orders. In March 1907, Beadle corresponded with McFarland Company to discuss the publication of the first Biltmore Nursery descriptive retail catalog and indicated that he had a mailing list of about seven thousand names. In early August, Beadle ordered for the Nursery "an edition of ten thousand (10,000) copies of our descriptive catalog." In March of the following year, Beadle wrote to McFarland Publicity Services complimenting them on the new Biltmore Nursery booklet, "Flowering Trees and Shrubs," and ordered one thousand copies to be printed on heavier paper stock. Beadle worked with McFarland to produce successive specialty catalogs, including "Hardy Garden Flowers" in 1910, "The Iris Catalog" in 1911 and "Biltmore Roses" in 1913. The catalogs were apparently in great demand because when Beadle ordered an edition of ten thousand of "The Iris Catalog," he ordered five thousand reprints each of the "Descriptive" or general catalog, "Flowering Trees and Shrubs" and "Hardy Garden Flowers." In March 1913, a letter from Biltmore Nursery to

Longwood Nursery and Gardens stated, "The achievement of our 'Iris Catalog' has been one of the epoch marking features of our business, and the general interest displayed by the public in Iris plants was perhaps never at a higher crest."

The introduction of the 1907 edition of the descriptive catalog states,

> *Biltmore Nursery was established in 1889. For ten years almost the entire output was used on Biltmore Estate in the extensive and world-famous landscape and forest plantations. In 1898 we entered the commercial field, supplying stock to planters, dealers, landscape architects and park superintendents in the principal centers of the United States. The demand for Biltmore trees and shrubs has been unparalleled; so great, indeed, that we have been compelled to more than double our plantations. In this, our illustrated and descriptive catalog, is offered stock of the present season, which embraces one of the largest and most complete collections of ornamentals in the world. We have no connection whatever with any other nursery, and employ no agents, our entire business being transacted from our office at Biltmore, North Carolina.*

The extent and capacity of the Nursery is described as having

> *nearly three hundred acres devoted to the cultivation of trees and shrubs. Our greenhouses and coldframes cover an area of seventy-five thousand square feet, which, in connection with seed-beds to the extent of more than three acres, a large force of trained men and many varieties of carefully tilled soils, give us especial facilities for growing choice trees and plants on an extensive scale both in numbers and kinds.*

The Biltmore Nursery also offered a variety of services to customers, including drafting planting plans and answering horticultural questions on what to plant, how to plant and when to plant.

> *Our experience is at your command. Not only are we prepared to give advice, supply names of trees, shrubs and plants, either cultivated or wild, or to prescribe for plant diseases or attacks of insects, but we will gladly undertake, at small cost, to prepare plans for beautifying the home surroundings, showing a pleasing arrangement of paths and drives combined with an artistic grouping of trees and shrubs.*

The Biltmore Company Archives contain many thousands of documents relating to the Biltmore Nursery and Herbarium, including requests for quotes and availability of plants, orders, shipping invoices and related correspondence from all over the country and overseas as well. The Biltmore Nursery grew rapidly as a commercial supplier of plants for large planting projects. As the list of noted individuals and organizations that corresponded with or received plants from the Nursery is so extensive, only a few are included here.

In January 1898, George Vanderbilt made a gift of plants to beautify Executive Mansion Square, the public grounds surrounding the governor's mansion in Raleigh. Estate manager Charles McNamee wrote to Governor Russell describing the gift and suggesting that Biltmore send its head gardener, Mr. Bottomley, to oversee installation of the plants according to a plan.

> *Dear Sir:*
>
> *The Biltmore Nursery sends you with its compliments a number of shrubs and plants to be set out around the Governor's mansion at Raleigh. You were good enough to say when I saw you in Raleigh that you would be pleased to have these. If you will kindly have the plants when received taken charge of by someone who knows how to heel them in the ground for a few days, with your permission we will send one of our men here and we should be pleased if you would permit us to prepare a plan for the setting out of the plants after submitting it to you, and actually put them in the ground ourselves. This is landscape work of which so few people know anything that we should like to know that our little remembrance is used to the utmost possible advantage.*

A postscript included a list of the plants sent and the height to which they would grow. An article titled "Beautify the City" in the *Raleigh Morning Post* on March 23, 1898, praised McNamee, Vanderbilt and the Estate for the act of generosity:

> *That was a very graceful act on the part of Mr. Charles McNamee, manager of the Vanderbilt estates, to furnish shrubbery, etc., from the Biltmore gardens for the Executive Mansion Square, the work of arranging and planting to be done under the supervision of one of the best landscape gardeners employed on the great estate, all free of cost to the State. Mr. Bottomley is a distinguished expert in his art, and all know that the Biltmore possesses the best of everything that money can buy, in the New or the Old World; and the very best selections, suitable to this climate, will be transplanted and made to beautify our chief public square, the grounds of the home of the Chief Executive of the State. Mr. Vanderbilt's enterprise has already been worth a vast deal to the State as well as the immediate locality of his estate, the result of his experiments and developments. The products of the farm, the dairy and the stock yard exhibited at our State Fair have given some idea of the excellence of the work carried on in these departments, and indicate the character of that which is done in every department. In this act of properly beautifying our Mansion grounds is shown an interest in the State beyond the confines of his private possessions, which we are sure all the people will appreciate.*

In 1908, the Nursery shipped to Dr. Booker T. Washington at the Tuskegee Normal and Industrial Institute (today's Tuskegee University) the following: seventy-five Marie Pavil roses and three sequoia trees (one *Sequoia gigantea*, one *Sequoia Gigantea pendula* and one *Sequoia sempervirens*). In 1911, George Washington Carver, the pioneering director of agricultural research at Tuskegee, wrote requesting a Nursery catalog. He explained, "Individually, I do not need any trees, plants, or shrubs, but…as I lecture on agriculture more or less all over the South, [and also consult] on the beautifying of home grounds, and tell where they can get these trees, plants, shrubs, etc.; so a catalog is of great service."

In the months following George Vanderbilt's untimely death on March 6, 1914, Edith Vanderbilt, his widow, had to make a lot of management decisions regarding the Estate, its operations and financial security. Before his death, George had offered the Department of Agriculture an option to purchase approximately ninety thousand acres of Pisgah Forest as a national forest. Faced with tax burdens, Edith finalized the transaction within a few months following her husband's passing. She was in discussions with Beadle concerning the scaling down of various Estate operations and reducing the workforce. The Biltmore Nursery was faced with becoming one of the casualties. In 1916, numerous letters were written to various individuals informing them, "Since the death of the founder of our horticultural and forest interests two years ago, we have been in the process of liquidation." In response to requests for catalogs, a letter informed that "the last editions are out of print; it is not likely, in view of death of the founder two years prior, that revised editions will be printed."

If the Biltmore Nursery seemed to be already doomed to go out of business commercially, Mother Nature sealed its fate on July 16, 1916, when Asheville and the surrounding region woke up to a devastating flood of the French Broad River and its tributaries. Located on the banks of the Swannanoa River, a short distance from its junction with the French Broad, the Nursery headquarters—including the glass greenhouses, boiler plant, propagation frames, the offices and Herbarium wing—were all under more than seven feet of water. In the next weeks, requests for catalogs, orders for plants and other correspondence were answered with similar responses as in these examples:

> *Regretting to advise our nursery interests are now necessarily in abeyance and our community is putting forth every effort to recover from the losses occasioned by the recent flood.*
>
> *Replacement orders will be accepted on condition the plants will be in merchantable condition. We have been seriously damaged by the recent flood, but are unable to say at this time to what extent.*
>
> *Our nursery interests are now necessarily in abeyance while the community recovers from recent disastrous flood; our future program of operation is, at this time, an indefinite one.*
>
> *The nursery has been in liquidation since George Vanderbilt's death and the flood then nearly wiped out remaining stock with only a few acres unaffected. Will dispose of plants not destroyed by the flood as soon as possible.*
>
> *Apologizing for lack of nursery stock; many labels of plants were destroyed and will have to wait until plants bloom to ascertain what they are.*

Beadle wrote to his acquaintance and nurseryman Harlan P. Kelsey on October 23, 1916: "We are heavy losers, something like 85% of our nursery stock having been destroyed; but the material losses are nothing to the loss of life which occurred right in our midst. It was so appalling." He was referring to Captain J.C. Lipe, a former employee of the Estate who was one of the casualties. The "Great Flood" accounted for more than twenty-nine lives lost in Western

North Carolina, at least six in Asheville alone. Just before the Smith Bridge across the French Broad collapsed with the flood gauge on it, the river had risen to a stage of 18.6 feet; flood level was 4 feet. A later report by the Southern Railway Company, which was nearby the Biltmore Nursery, estimated that the water level in the French Broad rose 20 feet.

Beadle was devastated, no doubt, by the disastrous end to the enterprise that he had worked so diligently to make a success. He wrote to Robert L. Lewis on November 24, 1916, describing his Florida grove venture and the Biltmore Nursery affairs. He reported that the Nursery was almost completely out of existence and "were it not for the fact that I have on our farm an opportunity to grow a large number of plants and trees, I would have lost my hobby completely. I tell you a farm is a fine thing—especially to spend money on." Beadle had his own personal nursery on his farm just east of Asheville. It fortunately was on ground high above the floodwaters.

Although the grand era of the Biltmore Nursery was over, the forested and landscaped grounds on Biltmore Estate are living testimonies to the botanical legacies of Frederick Law Olmsted, Chauncey D. Beadle and the Estate's plant collectors who saw value in experimenting with new plants and in propagating them commercially. It is not known how many millions of Biltmore plants were shipped and distributed to destinations far and wide, but the Biltmore Nursery had a far-reaching impact on landscape gardening and horticultural trends from coast to coast. Many surviving trees, shrubs and other plants from Biltmore can still be found growing in botanical gardens, public parks and other landscapes across America and abroad. The botanical diversity of George Vanderbilt's Pisgah Forest is preserved in Pisgah National Forest, the first in the eastern United States. Designated by Congress in 1968 as a national historic site, the Cradle of Forestry in America preserves the "birthplace of forestry and forestry education" in America and the legacies of the Biltmore Forest School, the country's first. Many of the principles of scientific forest management and silviculture established at Biltmore by Gifford Pinchot and Dr. Carl A. Schenck are still taught in our universities. The North Carolina Arboretum, although not on the same scale as the one planned by Olmsted, is a public institution located "a stone's throw" across the river from the site of the ill-fated Biltmore Arboretum and continues to pay tribute to Olmsted's vision more than a century later.

The Biltmore Ash (*Fraxinus biltmoreana*), listed by some as a variety of white ash, is but one of numerous plant varieties discovered and named by or for Biltmore's botanists. On April 16, 1914, the New York Botanical Garden issued a resolution deploring the loss of George Vanderbilt and tendering its sympathies to his family. Reference was made to the publication in 1901 and 1902 of the *Biltmore Botanical Studies*. The naming of the genus *Biltia* in 1903 by Dr. John K. Small of Columbia University had marked Vanderbilt's services to botany. *Biltia vaseyi*, was found growing wild in the Pisgah Forest region of the Estate and is now known as *Rhododendron vaseyi*, the Pink-shell Azalea. Thus, the story of Biltmore Nursery is the story of a botanical legacy.

Primary Research Sources

The Biltmore Company Archives

Beadle, Chauncey D., correspondence.

Forestry Department letter press books (outgoing correspondence), volumes 1–80, 1895–1908, Forestry Department Records.

Gall, James G., correspondence, Biltmore Estate Landscape Department Records.

Incoming correspondence, Biltmore Nursery Department Records.

Nurseryman letter press books (outgoing correspondence), volumes 1–54, 1896–1916, Biltmore Nursery Department Records.

Olmsted, Frederick Law, correspondence, memoranda and reports, Superintendent's Office Records.

Pinchot, Gifford, and Carl A. Schenck, correspondence, memoranda and reports, Forestry Department Records.

Reports of Landscape Department, 1890–97, Biltmore Estate Landscape Department Records.

Reports of nurseryman, 1890–96, Biltmore Nursery Department Records.

Superintendent's Office records—correspondence and memoranda books.

Vanderbilt, George W., correspondence.

The Biltmore Company History Files

Miscellaneous records.

The Frederick Law Olmsted National Historic Site

Maps, drawings and miscellaneous records for Project 0170 (property of George W. Vanderbilt, Biltmore Estate).

Library of Congress—Manuscript Division

Frederick Law Olmsted Papers.

Olmsted Associates Records.

North Carolina Collection, Pack Memorial Public Library, Asheville, North Carolina

Miscellaneous articles relating to regional history.

D.H. Ramsey Library Special Collections, University of North Carolina at Asheville

Correspondence relating to Biltmore Estate's history.

Appendix A

The Biltmore Nursery Plant Distributions

THE FOLLOWING LISTS ARE ONLY a partial accounting of the countless organizations, institutions, businesses, properties and individuals that ordered planting stock from the Biltmore Nursery between 1889 and 1916. The bulk of sales began in 1898 after the Nursery published and distributed wholesale trade lists of available stock. There were, however, numerous exchanges, sales and shipments of "surplus" inventory during the years preceding the Nursery's official entry into the commercial field. The lists are arranged under several categories in an effort to group similar organizations, businesses and individuals and are in no way complete. They are intended only as a random sampling to show the range of the Biltmore Nursery's distribution and its far-reaching influence on the horticultural and botanical diversity of landscapes in the United States and many beyond its borders. Included are botanical gardens and arboretums, universities, municipalities, parks, cemeteries, private estates, hospitals, schools and other institutions, nurseries, landscape architects and others that conducted business with the Biltmore Nursery. More exhaustive research would add tremendously to the list, which for the purpose of this publication is not intended to be all-inclusive. Readers will undoubtedly know or learn of many others in their own cities or regions. The lists do not include the hundreds of botanists, plant collectors and institutions only receiving or exchanging plant specimens with the Biltmore Herbarium, which was located in a special wing of the Nursery complex. The last list includes a selection of nurseries and other suppliers that sold stock plants, seeds and bulbs to the Biltmore Nursery.

Botanical Gardens, Arboretums, Universities and Experiment Stations that Received or Exchanged Plants with the Biltmore Nursery

Alabama Polytechnic Institute and Experiment Station, Auburn, Alabama

Arnold Arboretum, Harvard University (Professor Charles Sprague Sargent, director, and John G. Jack)

Brooklyn Botanic Garden, New York

Buffalo Botanic Garden (J.F. Cowell, director)

Cornell University (Professor W.W. Rowlee)

Missouri Botanical Garden (Professor William Trelease)

New York Botanic Garden (Nathaniel Lord Britton, director)

New York State College of Forestry
Northwestern University (Dr. Henry Kraemer)
Royal Gardens at Kew (William T. Thisleton-Dyer, director, and G. Nicholson)
State University of Kentucky, College of Agriculture and Experiment Station, Lexington, Kentucky
University of Alabama, Tuscaloosa, Alabama
University of Michigan, Ann Arbor, Michigan
University of Minnesota
University of Tennessee, Experiment Station, Knoxville, Tennessee
University of Wyoming (Aven Nelson), Laramie, Wyoming
Utah Agricultural College, Logan, Utah
Washington [U.S.] Botanic Gardens (Superintendent W.R. Smith and G.W. Oliver)

Estates, Residences, Subdivisions

J.E. Annis, Chattanooga, Tennessee
Chester A. Congdon, Duluth, Minnesota
F.A. Constable, Mamaroneck, Westchester County, New York (Olmsted Brothers)
J.B. Dumont, Plainfield, New Jersey
Governor's Mansion, Raleigh, North Carolina (Governor Russell)
F.W.W. Graham, Asheville, North Carolina (Olmsted Brothers)
Frank Hibbard, Lake Forest, Illinois
H.M. Lane, Cincinnati, for property in Norwood, Ohio (Olmsted Brothers)
Clarence H. Mackay, Esquire, Roslyn, Long Island, New York
J.G. Merrimon, Asheville, North Carolina
Misses Norton, Chanteloup, Hendersonville, North Carolina
J.H. Patterson, Dayton, Ohio (Olmsted Brothers)
Thomas E. Proctor, Topsfield, Massachusetts
G. Reinberg, Lake Hopatcong, New Jersey
Mrs. R.J. Reynolds, Reynolda House, Winston-Salem, North Carolina
Mrs. M.R. Richardson, "Wedgewood," Aiken, South Carolina
Roland Park Co., Baltimore, Maryland (Olmsted designs)
R.H. Treman, Ithaca, New York (W.H. Manning design)

Hospitals/Institutions

Arlington Heights Sanitarium, Fort Worth, Texas
East Mississippi Insane Hospital, Meridian, Mississippi
Georgia State Sanitarium, Milledgeville, Georgia
High Oaks Sanatorium, Lexington, Kentucky
The Presidio (U.S. Army General Hospital), San Francisco, California
The Winyah Sanitarium, Asheville, North Carolina

Hotels, Inns, Clubs and Resorts

Automobile Club of Puerto Rico, San Juan, Puerto Rico
Cape Fear Club, Wilmington, North Carolina

Grand Pacific Hotel, Missoula, Montana
Lookout Mountain House, Lookout Mountain, Tennessee

Landscape Architects and Landscape Gardeners

Henry E. Burr, landscape architect, East Orange, New Jersey
Marian C. Coffin, landscape architect (National Arts Club, Gramercy Park), New York
J.W. Coolidge Jr., landscape architect (Howland's Estate)
J.W. Elliott, landscape architect, Boston, Massachusetts
Jenny & Jenny, landscape architects, Cleveland, Ohio
Beatrix Jones, landscape gardener, New York, New York
Daniel W. Langdon, landscape architect, Baltimore, Maryland (a founding member of the ASLA)
H.V. Lawrence, landscape gardener, Falmouth, Massachusetts
Arthur C. Leedle, landscape architect, Springfield, Ohio
Charles N. Lowrie, landscape architect, New York, New York (a founding member of the ASLA)
Warren H. Manning, landscape architect, Boston, Massachusetts
Charles Merryman, landscape contractor, Washington, D.C.
George H. Miller, landscape architect, Boston, Massachusetts
Paul Oglesby, landscape gardener
Olmsted Brothers, landscape architects
Olmsted, Olmsted and Elliot, landscape architects
Sibley C. Smith, landscape architect, Providence, Rhode Island

Nurseries and Nurserymen

American Nursery Co., Flushing, New York, and Springfield, New Jersey
Andorra Nurseries, Philadelphia, Pennsylvania
Arnsby Nurseries, Madisonville, Ohio
Ashford Park Nurseries, Atlanta, Georgia
Bay State Nurseries, North Abington, Massachusetts
The Bayside Nurseries, North Abington, Massachusetts
Beaverton Nursery, Oregon
Bloodgood Nurseries, Flushing, New York
A.T. Boener, nurseryman, Cedarburg, Wisconsin
Breck-Robinson Nursery Co., Lexington, Massachusetts
Campbell County Nurseries, Lynchburg, Virginia
L.W. Carr, nurseryman, Lakewood, Ohio
Chattanooga Nurseries, Tennessee
Claremont Nurseries, California
Clingman Nursery & Orchard Co., Keithville, Louisiana
Eastern Nurseries, Jamaica Plain, Massachusetts
F&F Nurseries, Springfield, New Jersey
Franklin Davis Nurseries, Baltimore, Maryland
Gainesville Nurseries, Florida
G.H. Miller & Son Nurseries, Rome, Georgia

Glen Saint Mary Nurseries Co., Glen Saint Mary, Florida
Greenville Nursery Co., Greenville, South Carolina
The Hawks Nursery Co., Wauwatosa, Wisconsin
H.F. Hillenmeyer & Sons, Blue Grass Nurseries, Lexington, Kentucky
H.J. Weber & Sons Nursery Co., Missouri
Idlewild Greenhouses, Asheville, North Carolina
Jackson & Perkins, Newark, New Jersey
Jay Hubbard, Nursery Farm, Magnolia Beach, Texas
J. Van Lindley Nursery, Pomona, North Carolina
Hiram T. Jones, Elizabeth, New Jersey
Kaleden Nursery Co., Limited, Kaleden, British Columbia
Martin Kohankie Nurseries, Painesville, Ohio
Maywood Nursery Co., Maywood, Illinois
Messrs. Stephen Hoyt's Sons, New Canaan, Connecticut
Montarisso Nursery, Santa Barbara, California
Morrisville Nursery (Samuel C. Moon), Morrisville, Pennsylvania
Mount Hope Nurseries, Lawrence, Kansas
Mount Hope Nurseries (Ellwanger & Berry), Rochester, New York
New England Nurseries (Chase Bros. Co.), Rochester, New York
Old Colony Nurseries, Plymouth, Massachusetts
Old Dominion Nurseries (W.T. Hood & Co.), Richmond, Virginia
Otto Katzenstein & Co., Tree Seedsmen, Atlanta, Georgia
Painesville Nurseries, The Storrs & Harrison Co., Painesville, Ohio
Piedmont Plant Co., Greenville, South Carolina
Pinehurst Nurseries, Pinehurst, North Carolina
Pleasant Run Nurseries, Pleasant Run, Hamilton County, Ohio
P.S. Peterson & Son, Chicago, Illinois
Red Towers Greenhouses, Hackensack, New Jersey
Rockmount Nursery, Boulder, Colorado
Rothenheber's Nurseries, Clayton, Missouri
Ryerson-Hutchinson Nursery
Scotch Grove Nursery, Scotch Grove, Iowa
Shady Hill Nursery Co., Boston, Massachusetts
Siebrecht & Son, nurseries, New Rochelle, New York
Silver Leaf Nurseries, Rose Hill, Virginia
Southern Nursery Company, Winchester, Tennessee
Spokane Nursery (Seed Co.), Washington
Spring Hill Nurseries, Tippecanoe City, Ohio
Swain Nelson & Sons Co., nurserymen, Chicago, Illinois
Texas Nursery Company, Sherman, Texas
Thomas Meehan & Sons, Philadelphia, Pennsylvania
Virginia Wholesale Nurseries, Staunton, Virginia
Winfield Nursery Co., Winfield, Kansas

PARKS, PARK DEPARTMENTS, MUNICIPALITIES, CEMETERIES

Albemarle Park (Thomas W. Raoul, president), Asheville, North Carolina

Audubon Park (E. Baker, superintendent), New Orleans, Louisiana

Boston Metropolitan Water Board, Boston, Massachusetts

Branch Brook Park, Clark's Pond, Essex County Park Commission, Newark, New Jersey

Buffalo City Cemetery (Forest Lawn), Buffalo, New York

Cave Hill Cemetery Co., Louisville, Kentucky

Chattanooga, City of, Department of Public Utilities, Grounds and Buildings (R.A. Stegall, superintendent of parks), Chattanooga, Tennessee

Cherokee Park, Louisville, Kentucky (Park Thomas, C.F. Warren, superintendent)

Cincinnati, City of, Board of Park Commissioners, Cincinnati, Ohio

Cleveland, City of, Park Commission (J. Bowditch), Cleveland, Ohio

Detroit, City of, Parks and Boulevards, Palmer Arboretum (F.J. Coryell, superintendent)

Forest Hill Cemetery (William Taylor, superintendent), Chattanooga, Tennessee

Graceland Cemetery, Sidney, Ohio

Greenwood Cemetery Co., Knoxville, Tennessee

Grove Park (W.F. Randolph), Asheville, North Carolina

Hartford Public Parks (Theodore Wirth), Hartford, Connecticut

Haverhill Parks Department (Henry Frost, superintendent), Haverhill, Massachusetts

Ithaca, New York, City of

Third Street Playground, Louisville, Kentucky (Olmsted Brothers)

Metropolitan Parks Commission, Blue Hills Reservation (Frank Dings, superintendent), Milton, Massachusetts

Metropolitan Water Board, Glenwood, Massachusetts (Olmsted Brothers)

Mount Vernon, New York

New York, City of, Department of Parks, the Arsenal, Central Park

Portland, City of, Department of Parks (E.T. Mishe, superintendent), Portland, Oregon

Queens, New York (C.W. Ward)

Quincy Boulevard and Park Association, Quincy, Illinois

Regina, Saskatchewan

Schenley Park (G.W. Wilson, director, Department of Public Works)

Weequahic Reservation, Newark, New Jersey (Olmsted Brothers)

Wichita, Kansas, City of

Woodland Cemetery Association, Dayton, Ohio

SCHOOLS AND INSTITUTES

College of the Holy Names, Oakland, California

Deaf and Dumb School, Morganton, North Carolina

Dr. Lawrence Normal and Industrial School

Hampton Normal and Agricultural Institute, Hampton, Virginia

Lawrence Scientific School (at Harvard University)

Massachusetts Institute of Technology, Boston, Massachusetts

Massey Business College, Birmingham, Alabama
Nampa Public Schools, Nampa, Idaho
National Arts Club, Gramercy Park, New York, New York
N.C. State Normal and Industrial College, Greensboro, North Carolina
New York School of Philanthropy, New York, New York
San Jose Normal School, San Jose, California
Statesville Public School (D. Mathew Thompson, superintendent)
St. Edith Academy, Bristow, Virginia
St. Genevieve's College, Asheville, North Carolina
Tuskegee Normal and Industrial School, Tuskegee, Alabama
Western State Normal School, Kalamazoo, Michigan
Westminster School (Olmsted Brothers)
West Texas Military Academy, San Antonio, Texas

Miscellaneous

Columbian Exposition, Chicago, Illinois
Ladies' Home Journal, Philadelphia, Pennsylvania
S.C. Interstate and West Indian Exposition (A. Fiche, superintendent), Charleston, South Carolina

Nurseries That Sold Plants or Seeds to the Biltmore Nursery

Alabama Nursery Co., Huntsville, Alabama
B.A. Elliott & Co., Pittsburgh, Pennsylvania
Bellvue Nursery—Bulbs, Ferns, Aquatics, Etc. (William F. Bassett & Son), Hammonton, New Jersey
Bissell & Co., Richmond, Virginia
B. Latour Marliac, Temple-sur-Lot, Lot-et-Garonne, France
Bloemhof Nurseries (E.H. Krelage & Son), Haarlem, Holland
Blue Hills Nursery
Charles E. Penock—nurseryman and fruit grower, Fort Collins, Colorado
John Lewis Childs—seeds, bulbs and plants, Floral Park, New York
Commercial Nurseries (W.S. Little & Co.), Rochester, New York
C. Petrick, Ghent, Belgium
Crete Nurseries (C.F. Stevens), Crete, Nebraska
Dickson's, Chester, England
Henry A. Dreer, seed, plant and bulb growers and merchants, Philadelphia, Pennsylvania
D.S. Grimes & Son (nurserymen, florists, seedsmen), Denver, Colorado
E.G. Hill Co., wholesale florists, Richmond, Indiana
Elysian Gardens and Nursery (Lyon & Cobbe), Los Angeles, California
Elizabeth Nursery Co., Elizabeth, New Jersey
Elm City Nursery, New Haven, Connecticut
F.J. Ulbricht—fruit and ornamental trees, Anniston, Alabama
Forest Nursery & Seed Co., McMinnville, Tennessee
Fromow & Sons, England (through August Rolker & Sons, New York)
F.R. Pierson Co., Tarrytown-on-Hudson, New York

Fruitland Nurseries (P.J. Berckmens Co.), Augusta, Georgia
G.A. Parker, Halifax, Massachusetts
Geneva Nurseries, Geneva, Nebraska
Gillet & Horsford, Southwick, Massachusetts
Highlands Nursery (Kelsey, Harlan P.) Kawana, North Carolina
H.H. Berger & Co., San Francisco, California
H. Waterer—importer and dealer in plants, seeds and bulbs, Philadelphia, Pennsylvania
James M. Thorburn & Co., New York, New York
J. Backhouse & Sons, York, England
Kissena Nurseries (Parsons & Sons Co.), Flushing, New York
Maple Avenue Nurseries (Hoopes Bros. & Thomas), Westchester, Pennsylvania
John N. May, rose grower, Summit, New Jersey
Meehans Nurseries (Thomas Meehan & Sons), Germantown, Philadelphia, Pennsylvania
Messrs. Nathan Smith & Son, Adrian, Michigan
H. Meyer, Passaic, New Jersey
S.C. Moon, Morrisville, Bucks County, Pennsylvania
Mount Hope Nurseries (Ellwanger & Barry), Rochester, New York
Multnomah Nurseries (Seth Winquist & Co.), Russellville, Oregon
Myomanock Nurseries & Orchards (William H. Harrison & Sons), Lebanon Springs, North Carolina
Painesville Nurseries (The Storrs & Harrison Co.), Painesville, Ohio
Penrose Nurseries (Robert Scott & Son), Philadelphia, Pennsylvania
Peter Henderson & Co., New York
Pike & Ellsworth (seedsmen and florists), Jessamine, Florida
Pilkington & Co., Portland, Oregon
P. Ouwerkerk, Holland
F.J. Pratt, Concord, Massachusetts
Reading Nursery (Jacob W. Manning), Reading, Massachusetts
Reasoner Bros., Manatee, Florida
R.D. Hoyt, Bayview, Florida
R & J Farquhar & Co., Boston, Massachusetts
Royal Exotic Nursery (J. Veitch & Sons), Chelsea, England
John Saul, nurseryman and florist, Washington, D.C.
Seattle Nursery (John Lietha)
Shady Hill Nursery Co., Cambridge, Massachusetts
Dr. John H. Smith, Southport, North Carolina
Southwick Nurseries (Dr. Edward Gillett), Southwick, New Jersey
Stark Bros. Nurseries & Orchards Company, Louisiana, Missouri
Theodore Bechtel, Staunton, Illinois
The Water Gardens (Wm. Tricker & Co.), Clifton, New Jersey
T. Smith, Newry, Ireland
United States Nurseries (Pitcher & Manda)—nurserymen, seedsmen and florists, Short Hills, New Jersey
W. Atlee Burpee & Company, Philadelphia, Pennsylvania
Waukegan Nurseries (Robert Douglas' Sons), Waukegan, Illinois

Appendix A

William S. Little, Rochester, New York

W.P. Peacock, dahlia specialist, Atco, New Jersey

Young & Elliott, New York

Youngers & Co., Geneva, Nebraska

Appendix B

Notes on Plant Nomenclature and Invasive Plants

Like all sciences, botany has evolved and will continue to evolve as new research and studies add to the collective knowledge base of the field. Within this very complex science is an equally complex area of study—taxonomy, or the systematic classification of plants according to their physiological characteristics. Although the binomial system of nomenclature developed by Swedish botanist Carl Linnaeus in the eighteenth century simplified and somewhat standardized the task of plant classification, it has not proved to be the cure-all for the system. Linnaeus couldn't have anticipated the plethora of hybrids, varieties and cultivars of ornamental plants that plant breeders, nurserymen and horticulturists, both professional and amateur, would develop or discover over the next couple of centuries. Plant explorations by botanists to the far corners of the world intensified during the nineteenth and early twentieth centuries. Thousands of new species and varieties were imported to European and American arboretums, nurseries and gardens as a result of these botanical expeditions. Nurserymen and horticulturists eagerly sought out the newly discovered plants to add to their collections and to trial in their nurseries or gardens. From both natural and intentional hybridization, countless new varieties or cultivars were and are still being selected, adding to the profusion of cultivated plants available and to the confusion of naming and classification. Countless plants have been given names as new varieties based on minute details including such subtleties as the forms and color shades of flowers, flowering season, leaf forms and degrees of variegation, dissection or pubescence, plant forms and habits, fruit colors, fall coloration and bark characteristics. Plants have often been given names based on who discovered or selected them or in someone else's honor, or named after the region in which they were found. One can readily see how confusion can develop over time.

In the decades since the Biltmore Nursery published its descriptive catalog, many plants have been reclassified or names have been changed as various panels of botanists and taxonomists have worked to sort out the complexities of botanical taxonomy following the guidelines of the *International Code of Botanical Nomenclature.* A large part of the problem relating to plant classification has been that various authors of the nomenclature and classification for given species have just not agreed. In some cases, old generic names have simply been discarded in favor of others [e.g.: A former genus designation for hickories, *Hicoria*, was changed to *Carya* and a former genus epithet for sweetshrubs, *Butneria*, was changed to *Calycanthus*]. Other plants have been given new species epithets [e.g.: redosier dogwood—*Cornus stolonifera* to *Cornus sericea*] or have been placed in entirely different genera [e.g.: spicebush—*Benzoin benzoin* to *Lindera benzoin*]. Some plants that were once thought to deserve species ranking have since been determined to be subspecies, forms or varieties of other species [e.g.: climbing hydrangea—*Hydrangea petiolaris* to *Hydrangea anomala* subspecies *petiolaris*; double file viburnum—*Viburnum tomentosum* to *Viburnum plicatum* Forma. *tomentosum*; Japanese plum yew—*Cephalotaxus drupacea* to *Cephalotaxus harringtonia*, var. *drupacea*]. Additionally, some forms or variations that were formerly included as part of the specific epithet are now more correctly listed as "cultivars," or cultivated varieties, and set aside by single quote marks [e.g.: golden-thread sawara falsecypress—*Chamecyparis pisifera filifera aurea* to *Chamaecyparis pisifera* 'Filifera Aurea']. In some cases, only the ending of the specific epithet has been changed from a masculine to feminine ending or vice versa [e.g.: Kentucky coffee tree—*Gymnocladus dioicus* to *G. dioica*]. Then there are the ever-growing lists of thousands of named varieties of popular garden plants like azaleas, rhododendrons, roses, chrysanthemums, dahlias, daylilies and irises. Additionally, common names, colloquial or regional, cause much confusion. For any given plant, there may be several different common names [e.g.: the fringe tree (*Chionanthus virginicus*) has been known as "White Fringe," "Grancy Gray-beard" or "Old Man's Beard"; the black gum (*Nyssa sylvatica*) is known variously as "Tupelo," "Sour Gum," "Bee Gum" or "Pepperidge"]. Conversely, sometimes the same common name is applied to different and totally unrelated plants [e.g.: the name "ironwood" has been applied to many different trees with dense, heavy and usually strong wood].

Space in this publication simply does not allow for a thorough and complete reference to changes of plant names since the 1912 edition of the Biltmore Nursery catalog due to the sheer number of plants listed. This appendix will only attempt to list some of the generic names that have changed and to identify their generally accepted synonyms as a starting point. If the most currently accepted nomenclature of a plant or plants needs to be determined, it is suggested that the reader consult the most recent editions of references such as *Hortus Third* (1976 by Cornell University), *Manual of Cultivated Plants* (L.H. Bailey) and *Standardized Plant Names* (Kelsey and Dayton). Numerous other resources exist that could be helpful in cross-referencing plant names. Various organizations and societies that are formed around particular groups of plants such as azaleas and rhododendrons, magnolias, roses, hollies, daylilies and irises are some of the best sources for up-to-date information for particular genera. Journals and other publications by various arboretums and botanical gardens, nursery associations and the U.S. Department of Agriculture can also be invaluable for researching plant names. Finally, there is probably not a single source in existence with all of the answers. Nomenclature is one of the intriguing aspects of horticulture and gardening or plant collecting. The following list represents the primary genera of plants in the Biltmore Nursery catalog that have been changed or moved into other genera.

Partial List of Generic Names and Their Synonyms

Adelia: *Forestiera*—forestieras

Ampelopsis (in part): *Parthenocissus*—woodbines

Asplenium (in part): *Athyrium*—lady ferns

Azalea: *Rhododendron*—azaleas

Bambusa (in part): *Arundinaria* and *Sasa*—various bamboos
Benzoin: *Lindera*—spice bushes
Bocconia (in part): *Macleaya*—plume poppies
Brauneria: *Echinacea*—coneflowers
Butneria: *Calycanthus*—sweetshrubs
Cerasus: *Prunus*—cherries
Cladrastis (in part): *Maackia*—Chinese yellowwood
Cydonia: *Chaenomeles*—flowering quinces
Dendrium: *Leiophyllum*—sand myrtle
Diervilla (in part): *Weigela*—weigelas
Dicksonia (in part): *Dennstaedtia*—hay-scented ferns
Dryopteris (in part): *Thelypteris*—New York ferns
Gemmingia: *Belamcanda*—blackberry lilies
Gynerium: *Cortaderia*—pampas grass
Hicoria: *Carya*—hickories
Laurocerasus: *Prunus*—cherry laurels
Libocedrus: *Calocedrus*—incense cedars
Limnanthemum: *Nymphoides*—floating hearts
Nelumbium: *Nelumbo*—lotus
Onoclea (in part): *Matteuccia*—ostrich ferns
Opulaster: *Physocarpus*—ninebarks
Persica: *Prunus*—flowering peaches
Pieris (in part): *Lyonia*—staggerbushes
Polycodium: *Vaccinium*—deerberries
Pteris (in part): *Pteridium*—bracken ferns
Rhodora: *Rhododendron*—rhodora
Rhus (in part): *Cotinus*—smoke trees
Sterculia: *Firmiana*—Chinese parasol trees
Stuartia: *Stewartia*—stewartias
Tecoma (in part): *Campsis*—trumpet vines
Thuya: *Thuja*—arborvitaes
Thuyopsis: *Thujopsis*—false arborvitaes
Toxylon: *Maclura*—Osage orange
Ulmaria: *Filipendula*—meadowsweets
Uniola (in part): *Chasmanthium*—spike grass or wild oats
Xanthoxylum: *Zanthoxylum*—prickly ash tree

Notes on Invasive Plants

The problems and adverse impacts caused by invasive species of plants are a major and growing concern of environmentalists, forest, park and refuge managers, farmers, wildlife biologists and virtually anyone else who deals with land and wildlife management. The problem plants are mostly, but not always, introduced species. Some indigenous species can be invasive as well, particularly if there has been a dramatic change in a landscape or if they are introduced outside their normal natural range. The earliest invasives in America came perhaps with the settlers as familiar plants from their mother countries. Some may have included varieties intended for food production for people and livestock and herbs for medicines and tonics, as well as for ornamental use. Still others may have escaped as weed seeds in various products that were imported. Plants like dandelions, plantains, pigweeds, daisies, chicory, Queen Anne's lace, nettles, thistles and others spread like wildfire across North America as settlers moved west. During the eighteenth, nineteenth and early twentieth centuries, many new plants were being collected on botanical expeditions around the world and imported to gardens, nurseries and arboretums scattered from coast to coast. Little was known about how the plants would respond to their new environments. Some plants are opportunistic by their nature and are able to survive under even the harshest of conditions. Species that seemed to stay in bounds in the North proved otherwise in the Southeast or the Southwest. Hardy and quick-growing trees and shrubs were sought for windbreaks on the prairies. As farmlands became worn out, other plants were recommended by agricultural and conservation agencies for erosion control or for food and cover for wildlife. A number of those plants, while performing their intended purposes, adapted to their new environments too well and quickly naturalized in surrounding areas. Nurserymen and horticulturists continued to grow and experiment with new varieties and distributed them to other regions.

The Biltmore Nursery existed during that exciting era of growing and experimenting with a tremendous variety of plants, including some that have since proved to be invasive. Virtually all of the top nurseries and botanical gardens in America and Europe were producing and cultivating plants that were potentially invasive in one region or another. The unique thing about history is that it can never be changed. The old adage, "Hindsight is better than foresight," can teach us all a lesson, though. It is my intention to advise readers to use caution in the selection and use of certain plants that are known to be invasive or in other cases to avoid them altogether. It is recommended to check locally with extension agents, botanical gardens staff or conservation agencies to learn about plants that may be invasive and avoid planting them. In some cases, federal or state laws now prohibit the growing or distribution of certain plants due to their invasiveness. Following is a partial list of historic plants in this catalog that are known to be problematic and invasive in certain regions, if not carefully managed. The purist may consider some of them necessary for accurate historic restoration; however, it is advised to seek suitable substitutions for some wherever possible.

Plants with Invasive Potential (by alphabetical order)

Ailanthus altissima (*A. glandulosa*)—tree of heaven
Akebia quinata—five-leaf akebia
Amorpha fruticosa—indigo bush or lead plant
Ampelopsis brevipedunculata (*A. heterophylla*)—porcelain ampelopsis
Berberis thunbergii—Japanese barberry
Celastrus orbiculatus—Oriental bittersweet
Cytissus scoparius (*Genista scoparia*)—Scotch or common broom
Elaeagnus umbellata—autumn olive
Ligustrum vulgare—common privet
Lonicera fragrantissima—fragrant or winter honeysuckle
Lonicera japonica—Japanese honeysuckle
Miscanthus sinensis (*M. japonicus*)—eulalia grass
Paulownia tomentosa (*P. imperialis*)—empress tree or princess tree

Phragmites australis (*P. communis*)—common reed
Rhamnus cathartica—common buckthorn
Rhamnus frangula—alder buckthorn
Rosa multiflora—Japanese or multiflora rose
Tamarix ramosissima (*T. odessana, T. pentandra*)—Caspian or five-stamen tamarix
Wisteria sinensis (*W. chinensis*)—Chinese wisteria

Related species to some of the listed plants may also have potential for being invasive, particularly the barberries, brooms, buckthorns, honeysuckles, olives and privets. Bamboos as a group were intentionally not included in the list because, with careful site selection and management and providing artificial or natural barriers for control of spreading by the underground rhizomes, bamboos can be effectively used in a garden or landscape setting without problems. There are certainly other plants with varying degrees of invasive tendencies that could be added to the list, but the author merely wanted to call attention to some of the ones with a high potential and to encourage thorough research of historic plants before specifying or planting them in a landscape.

Part II

The 1912 Biltmore Nursery Catalog

REPRODUCED IN ITS ENTIRETY

BILTMORE NURSERY
BILTMORE, N.C.

All illustrations in this catalog are from photographs made at Biltmore, and are the exclusive property of Biltmore Nursery

Biltmore Nursery

Biltmore, N. C.

Betula nigra. Example of a many-stemmed tree (See page 22)

NURSERY BUILDINGS

Introduction

BILTMORE NURSERY was established in 1889. For ten years almost the entire output was used on the Biltmore Estate in the extensive and world-famous landscape and forest plantations. In 1898 we entered the commercial field, supplying stock to planters, dealers, landscape architects and park superintendents in the principal centers of the United States. The demand for Biltmore trees and plants has been unparalleled; so great, indeed, that we have been compelled to more than double our plantations. In this, our illustrated and descriptive catalog, is offered the stock of the present season, which embraces one of the largest and most complete collections of ornamentals in the world. We have no connection whatever with any other nursery, and employ no agents, our entire business being transacted from our office at Biltmore, North Carolina.

OUR LOCATION is in the heart of the mountains of Western North Carolina, at elevations between two and three thousand feet above sea-level, where the temperature ranges from ninety degrees above to, in the instance of our higher fields, twenty degrees below zero. The main nursery is located on the northerly bank of the Swannanoa River, near its confluence with the French Broad and between the corporate limits of Biltmore and Asheville. The manager's office is in Biltmore, three minutes' walk from the terminus of the Asheville–Biltmore electric railway, and diagonally opposite the Southern Railway passenger depot. The superintendent's office is at the greenhouses, ten minutes' walk from the end of the trolley line. We invite inspection of our grounds any day except Sunday.

EXTENT AND CAPACITY. Nearly three hundred acres are devoted to the cultivation of trees and shrubs. Our greenhouses and coldframes cover an area of seventy-five thousand square feet, which, in connection with seed-beds to the extent of more than three acres, a large force of trained men and many varieties of carefully tilled soils, give us especial facilities for growing choice trees and plants on an extensive scale both in numbers and kinds.

QUALITY OF STOCK. The variations in temperature peculiar to the Southern Alleghany region, its evenly distributed and bountiful rainfall, and rich but shallow soil, combine to produce a quality of stock remarkably superior in root-formation, thriftiness and hardiness. Biltmore Nursery is inspected annually by the State Entomologist and a certificate pronouncing the stock free from all insects designated as dangerous pests, and apparently healthy in every respect, will be attached to every shipment. We are prepared to fumigate with hydrocyanic gas all or any nursery stock when state laws or customers require such treatment.

PLANTING PLANS AND HORTICULTURAL QUESTIONS. We are pleased to answer inquiries from friends or patrons concerning what to plant, how to plant, and when to plant. Our experience is at your command. Not only are we prepared to

Main office

give advice, supply names of trees, shrubs and plants, either cultivated or wild, or to prescribe for plant diseases or attacks of insects, but we will gladly undertake, at small cost, to prepare plans for beautifying the home surroundings, showing a pleasing arrangement of paths and drives combined with an artistic grouping of trees and shrubs.

ILLUSTRATIONS. The engravings in this catalog have been exclusively prepared for us and are, without exception, made from photographs of objects on our own grounds or those of Biltmore Estate.

BILTMORE TREES AND PLANTS are growing from Maine to California and from Canada to Mexico, besides several countries across the seas. In our comprehensive collection may be found plants adapted to the local conditions of the average planter, whether it be a locality where severe cold reigns in winter, or one where warmer sun prevails.

BY EXPRESS OR FREIGHT. We have suitable plants of all of the species and varieties for sending by express or freight. Such plants have been frequently transplanted, are shapely and select specimens, and represent honest values. They may be sent safely to any point having transportation facilities.

BY MAIL POSTPAID. Mailing-size plants are, of necessity, smaller than those usually sent by express or freight, but invariably they are robust, well-established field-grown plants and satisfactory where the inconvenience or expense of heavier shipments is a deterrent. If you have experimented with mailing-size plants from tiny pots or greenhouse benches and been disappointed, we know you have not tried Biltmore plants, for they are especially strong and well grown to insure success.

PACKING. The utmost care will be used in digging and preparing the plants for shipment. There are no charges for packing or packing-cases, or for delivery to our freight or express depots, except in the instance of shipments to foreign countries, where the preparation is often an important item of expense.

DIRECTIONS FOR SHIPPING. Please state how you wish goods sent. In the absence of explicit directions for mode of shipping, we will forward consignments according to our best judgment.

OUR RESPONSIBILITY. We refer you to any bank or bankers in Asheville, N. C. We guarantee safe arrival and satisfactory condition of all shipments, unless, from the lateness of the season or extreme causes, we write for consent to waive responsibility. We are most careful to have all plants correctly labeled, and hold ourselves prepared to replace, on proper proof, all that may prove untrue to label, or to refund the amount paid therefor; but it is understood that, in case of error on our part, we shall at no time be held responsible for a greater amount than the original price of such plants.

RATES AND PRICES. The price-list accompanying this catalog will be found on the last few pages of the book. The prices there shown supersede all previous rates and apply to quantities specified; but two hundred and fifty will be furnished at the thousand rate, twenty-five at the hundred rate, and six at the dozen rate. A schedule of freight and express rates appears in connection with the price-list.

TERMS CASH on or before delivery to forwarding agents, except that we extend credit to patrons by agreement, subject to the following limitations:—Invoices executed during the autumn are due and payable on or before December 31, following; those covering spring shipments are due and payable on or before June 1, following. We prefer not to open accounts for amounts less than one hundred dollars.

PACKING SEASON. We ship from October 1 to May 1, with the usual interruptions during winter.

Mail-order box

CARE OF STOCK ON ARRIVAL. Promptly on arrival the trees or plants should be unpacked and planted, or else the roots should be protected from sun or air by covering with moist earth. If the ground is frozen outside, or the packing material in the cases frozen, store the original package in a cool, moist cellar until the conditions are favorable for handling. Care should be taken in choosing soil and environment to the end that success may reasonably follow your labors in planting.

CATALOGUES SENT UPON REQUEST. We will gladly mail Catalogues to any one interested in plants, or to friends into whose hands you would care to place a copy.

HARDY PLANTS AS ANNIVERSARY PRESENTS. Orders are frequently received from patrons to send plants to special addresses as gifts or anniversary presents, with requests to convey to the recipients the proper form of acknowledgment, and in due time the items of stock selected. All such orders will be most carefully handled, and the plants definitely reserved for forwarding during the planting season.

BILTMORE NURSERY
Biltmore, North Carolina

CONE-BEARERS OR EVERGREENS

THIS group embraces some of the most beautiful trees and shrubs in cultivation, from which it is possible to select varieties adapted to almost any soil or climate. Evergreen trees are stately and majestic as individuals and strikingly effective and imposing in masses. They are invaluable as screens against objectionable objects, wind-breaks and hedges. Planted in informal masses, forming a background against which the showy flowers of spring-blooming shrubs may be contrasted, or the bright winter-colors of the twigs and bark of small trees and bushes intensified, evergreens make possible some of the most enchanting results in ornamental planting. Our evergreens have been frequently transplanted, and the larger sizes are shipped with compact balls of roots wrapped in burlap. This method of handling insures the plants against loss. We have a large collection of evergreens, perhaps the most extensive in the country, and we solicit orders, whether large or small, feeling assured that our plants will prove their superior qualities.

Abies · The Firs

Pyramidal trees, often attaining great height, combining symmetry of habit, adaptability and hardiness. During the period of early life, an interval varying from twenty-five to forty years, they are justly ranked among the most ornamental subjects available for the embellishment of lawn or landscape.

Abies amabilis. LOVELY SILVER FIR. A lofty tree and one of the most beautiful of the Firs, from the mountains of Oregon, Washington and British Columbia. Leaves dark green and lustrous, silvery white beneath. Cones 4 to 6 inches long, deep rich purple. Grows slowly in cultivation, but has not been sufficiently tested to demonstrate its value in our plantations.

A. apollinis. PARNASSUS FIR. A handsome tree of medium size, closely related to *Abies cephalonica*, from which it differs by its more slender habit, shorter branches and longer leaves. Native of Greece. Foliage dark green and lustrous, pale beneath. Cones 5 to 6 inches long, with protruding, reflexed bracts. A valuable ornamental tree.

A. arizonica. SILVER CORK FIR. A tall and slender tree closely related to *Abies lasiocarpa*. Native of the mountains of Arizona, at elevations of 8,000 to 10,000 feet, where it is often exposed to very severe cold. Foliage silvery green, of surpassing beauty. The bark of the trunk is very remarkable, being cream-colored and of a corky nature.

A. balsamea. BALSAM FIR. A slender tree, possessing qualities of extreme hardiness and rapid growth, of wide distribution. Occurs naturally from Labrador and the Virginia mountains to Minnesota and the North West Territory. Foliage fragrant in drying, dark green above, silvery beneath. Cones violet or purple, 2 to 4 inches long.

A. cephalonica. CEPHALONIAN FIR. A beautiful and stately tree with widely spreading branches. Native of Greece. Foliage dark shining green, pale beneath, broad and rigid, tapering to a sharp point. Cones 5 to 6 inches long, grayish brown, with reflexed bracts.

A. cilicica. CILICIAN FIR. A slender tree from the mountains of Asia Minor, very hardy and satisfactory in cultivation. Foliage dark green, silvery white beneath. Cones large, orange-brown, 6 to 8 inches long. A picturesque and desirable Fir, but comparatively rare in gardens.

A. concolor. WHITE FIR. A majestic tree and the most dependable Fir in cultivation. It is a native of the mountains from Oregon and California to Utah, Colorado and New Mexico. Perfectly hardy and a rapid grower. Leaves light glaucous green. Cones 3 to 5 inches long, green or grayish green. Cannot be too highly recommended.

A. concolor violacea. PURPLE-CONED WHITE FIR. Similar to the last except in the color of the cones, which are dark purple.

A. firma. JAPANESE SILVER FIR. The largest and most beautiful of the Japanese Firs. Gigantic dimensions are frequent among the trees planted in gardens and temple enclosures in its native country, but it has not been universally satisfactory in cultivation in America. Foliage dark shining green, pale and slightly glaucous beneath. Cones 4 to 6 inches long, with ascending bracts.

A. fraseri. FRASER'S BALSAM FIR. This is the "She Balsam" of the Southern Alleghanies, and, in cultivation, possesses great beauty in infancy. A slender, rather short-lived tree of extreme hardiness. Foliage fragrant in drying, dark green and shining, with pale bands beneath. Cones 2 inches long, dark purple, with yellow-green reflexed bracts.

A. grandis (*A. gordoniana*). TALL SILVER FIR. This, the tallest of the Firs, occurs from Northern California and Vancouver to the western slopes of the mountains of Montana. A fast-growing tree, rarely seen in cultivation. It does not always thrive in the Eastern States. Leaves dark green above, silvery white beneath. Cones 3 to 4 inches long, bright green.

For grades and prices of above, see page 131

Abies, continued

Abies homolepis (*A. brachyphylla*). NIKKO FIR. A large tree, native of the mountains of Central Japan, possessing great hardiness and beauty. One of the most desirable and rapid-growing of the Firs. Leaves dark green and shining on the upper surface, silvery white beneath. Cones 3 to 4 inches long, at first violet-purple, eventually dark brown.

A. lasiocarpa (*A. subalpina*) WESTERN BALSAM FIR. A tall tree with a dense slender spire-like top, found on the high mountains from Alaska to Arizona. Branches short and crowded, usually pendulous near the base of the tree. Leaves dark green, densely disposed, with two whitish bands on the lower surface. Cones dark purple, 3 to 4 inches long. Very hardy and ornamental, but grows rather slowly.

A. magnifica. RED FIR. The largest of the Firs. In the colder regions not so hardy as *Abies nobilis*. Native of the Sierra Nevada of California. Leaves glaucous green. Cones 6 to 9 inches long, violet-purple when young, dark brown at maturity. Of slow growth in cultivation, but a very beautiful evergreen.

A. magnifica glauca. GLAUCOUS RED FIR. A form with very glaucous foliage. Beautiful as specimen plants. Our strain has been very carefully selected from the bluest trees.

A. nobilis. NOBLE FIR. A majestic tree, and, in cultivation, among the best of the Firs. The famous avenue at Madresfield Court, England, is of this species. Leaves bluish green, sometimes glaucous, whiter beneath. Cones 4 to 6 inches long, beautifully arranged with pale green, reflexed bracts. Very highly recommended.

A. nobilis glauca. GLAUCOUS NOBLE FIR. An extremely blue form selected from the brightest colored trees. Our plants are superb.

A. nordmanniana. NORDMANN'S FIR. A very hardy and stately tree, and one of the most desirable Firs in cultivation. Native of the mountains contiguous to the Black Sea and the western spurs of the Caucasus. Foliage dark green and lustrous above, silvery beneath. Cones 4 to 6 in. long, dark brown. Late in starting into growth, consequently escaping injury from spring frosts.

A. numidica. ALGERIAN FIR. A slender tree with a dense gothic crown. From the Atlas Mountains of Algeria. Foliage bright green, with two white bands on the lower surface. Cones 5 to 6 inches long, nearly 2 inches in diameter. A beautiful and distinct tree, possessing the same relative hardiness as the Mount Atlas Cedar. Rare in cultivation.

A. pectinata. SILVER FIR. A tall tree and one of the oldest in cultivation, growing naturally in the mountains of Central and Southern Europe. Leaves dark green, shining above, silvery gray beneath. Cones 5 to 6 inches long, the bracts projecting beyond the scales into sharp reflexed points. Valuable as a park or garden tree.

A. pectinata pendula. WEEPING SILVER FIR. A graceful form with drooping branches, much admired as a specimen tree.

A. pectinata pyramidalis. PYRAMIDAL SILVER FIR. A distinct form of pyramidal outline frequently used to produce formal effects.

A. pindrow. HIMALAYAN FIR. A tall tree of great beauty, growing naturally at high elevations in the Kumaon and Kashmir Himalayas. Foliage dark, lustrous green, pale beneath, with faint silvery bands. Cones 4 to 5 inches long, violet-purple when young, or in age dark brown. Needs protection from piercing, cold winds.

A. pinsapo. SPANISH FIR. A medium-sized tapering tree from the mountains of Central and Southern Spain. One of the most ornamental of the European Firs. Should not be planted north of the Middle States. Leaves spreading from all sides of the stiff branches, bright green above, whitened beneath. Cones 4 to 5 inches long, grayish brown.

A. pinsapo glauca. GLAUCOUS SPANISH FIR. An attractive variety with glaucous foliage, said to be hardier than the typical form.

A. sachalinensis. SAGHALIEN FIR. A lofty tree of pyramidal outline, possessing great hardiness. Native of the Islands of Saghalien and Yesso. Leaves bright green and lustrous above, with a white band on each side of the midrib beneath. Cones about 3 inches long, with projecting, reflexed bracts. A handsome Fir and one likely to give satisfaction in the colder parts of the country.

A. sibirica (*A. pichta*). SIBERIAN FIR. A medium-sized, spire-like tree of great hardiness. Native of Russia, Siberia and the Amur region. More valuable in the North than in the South, where it is likely to become thin in habit. Leaves grass-green above, silvery whitened beneath. Cones 2 to 3 inches long, deep violet-blue when young, eventually brown.

A. veitchii. VEITCH'S FIR. A very hardy and beautiful Fir, of slender habit and average height, from the higher mountains of Central Japan. Foliage bright green, silvery white below. Cones freely produced, 2 to 2½ inches long, dark violet-blue, changing to brown at maturity. An ornamental tree of great value.

A. venusta (*A. bracteata*). SANTA LUCIA FIR. A stately tree with a slender trunk and spire-like head. Grows naturally on the Santa Lucia Mountains of California. Foliage massive, dark yellow-green and lustrous, silvery white beneath. Cones 3 to 4 inches long, purple-brown, the remarkably long pale brownish yellow bracts spreading in all directions. Rare in cultivation in America, but of great promise in the milder portions of the country.

Evergreens prepared for packing

Araucaria · The Araucarias

Massive evergreen trees belonging to the flora of the Southern Hemisphere. The genus includes about a dozen species, one of which, described below, possesses sufficient hardiness to withstand the winters in many places in the Southern States. The soil in which Araucarias are planted should have thorough drainage, and it is recommended to place them in full exposure to sun and air. Where the climate is severe they may be grown in pots or tubs and protected from cold. They are beautiful objects and invariably attract much attention.

Araucaria imbricata. CHILE PINE; MONKEY PUZZLE. A distinct and remarkable tree, strangely imposing as an isolated specimen and extremely impressive and effective when planted in avenues. Native of the western slopes of the Chilian Andes. Leaves broadly lanceolate, rigid and bristling, bright shining green, densely clothing the branches. Cones 4 to 6 inches in diameter, resembling a hedgehog. A rare and beautiful plant for jardinières.

For grades and prices of above, see pages 131 and 132

Cedrus · The Cedars

The true Cedars are justly classed among the most stately and beautiful trees, and in the South may be relied upon in the composition of park and garden effects. They thrive best in porous, well-drained soils, fully exposed to the sun.

Cedrus atlantica. MT. ATLAS CEDAR. A large and stately tree and the hardiest of the true Cedars, thriving in sheltered situations in Southern New York. Native of the Atlas Mountains. Of pyramidal, but loosely formal outline. Foliage silvery green, disposed in tufts and fascicles and contrasting strongly with the greenery of other trees. Cones 2 to 3 inches long, light brown. A rapid-growing tree with a wide range of adaptability.

C. atlantica glauca. MT. ATLAS SILVER CEDAR. A remarkable form with almost silvery white foliage. A very beautiful and vigorous tree. The blue forms of evergreens are hardier than the green ones, and this handsome tree is no exception to the rule.

C. deodara. DEODAR, OR INDIAN CEDAR. A majestic tree of pyramidal outline from the Himalaya Mountains. Along the seaboard from Washington, and especially in the Southern States and California, the Deodar is usually very satisfactory. Leaves in tufts or fascicles, bluish green. Cones 3 to 5 inches long, reddish brown. A magnificent lawn tree.

C. libani. CEDAR OF LEBANON. This venerable tree appeals to us with greater interest than perhaps any of the other conifers. Its associations with antiquity and the Sacred Writings and its great size and beauty commend it. More hardy than the Deodar. Foliage dark green and lustrous, sometimes bluish. Cones 3 to 4 inches long, brown at maturity.

Chamæcyparis · The Cypress and White Cedars

A group of beautiful evergreens, including some of the most interesting trees and shrubs in Nature. They are valuable as garden and park ornaments, and, in the smaller sizes, are widely used in window-boxes, jardinières and tubs. Adapted to a very wide range of soils and climate.

Chamaecyparis lawsoniana (*Cupressus lawsoniana*). LAWSON'S CYPRESS. A tall and graceful tree with horizontal and mostly pendulous branches, occurring in a wild state from Oregon to California. Foliage bright grayish green, disposed in fern-like expansions. Should not be planted north of the Middle States. One of the most beautiful evergreens in cultivation.

C. lawsoniana bowleri. WEEPING LAWSON'S CYPRESS. The branches of this graceful form are more slender and pendulous than those of the typical trees, of a darker green and of more dense and compact habit.

C. lawsoniana glauca. BLUE LAWSON'S CYPRESS. One of the hardier forms. Branchlets and foliage with a most pronounced metallic glaucous tint. Very beautiful and desirable.

C. nutkaensis (*Cupressus nutkænsis; Thuyopsis borealis*). NOOTKA SOUND CYPRESS. A handsome tree occurring from Sitka to Oregon. Broadly conical in outline, the ascending branches drooping at the tips. Foliage deep glaucous green, very dense. Fully as hardy as the Japanese species and very satisfactory. Highly recommended.

C. nutkaensis compacta. COMPACT NOOTKA SOUND CYPRESS. Of dwarf dense habit, forming a compact shrub of deepest green.

C. nutkaensis glauca. NOOTKA SOUND BLUE CYPRESS. A form with a pronounced glaucous color. Our stock has been carefully selected from the bluest specimens.

C. nutkaensis pendula. NOOTKA SOUND WEEPING CYPRESS. A graceful form with slender, pendulous branches, densely clothed with lustrous green foliage.

C. obtusa (*Retinospora obtusa*). JAPANESE CYPRESS. A handsome tree from Japan, where it has been cultivated from time immemorial. The famous miniature trees, produced by clipping and contorting and often trained into picturesque or ideal shapes, are largely of this species. Many of these dwarfed plants are of great age and high value. A strong, vigorous tree with horizontal fern-like branches, more or less pendulous. Foliage bright green and shining, somewhat whitened beneath. A satisfactory and desirable tree.

Chamæcyparis lawsoniana

C. obtusa aurea. GOLDEN JAPANESE CYPRESS. A smaller and more slender tree than the type. Foliage bright golden yellow, more intense during the growing period.

C. obtusa nana. DWARF JAPANESE CYPRESS. The smallest of the Japanese Cypress, rarely exceeding a foot or so in height. Very dense, bright green sprays of foliage. Curious and ornamental. Valuable for miniatures in jardinières.

C. obtusa nana aurea. DWARF GOLDEN JAPANESE CYPRESS. Similar to the last but of a pleasing golden yellow color. Very unique.

C. pisifera (*Retinospora pisifera*). SAWARA, OR PEA-FRUITED CYPRESS. A Japanese evergreen of great hardiness and vigor. All of the forms are extremely valuable and are widely cultivated. This is one of the trees which the Japanese produce in miniature by clipping, pruning and contorting. Foliage bright green, borne on somewhat pendulous branches. A beautiful tree but not so common in cultivation as its numerous varieties.

C. pisifera aurea. GOLDEN PEA-FRUITED CYPRESS. The new growth is rich golden yellow, eventually changing to greener hues. Very distinct and showy.

C. pisifera filifera. THREAD-BRANCHED CYPRESS. A remarkably decorative tree, the branches thread-like, gracefully pendulous and much elongated. Foliage bright green. Isolated specimens, when well established, command attention and admiration wherever seen.

C. pisifera filifera aurea. GOLDEN THREAD-BRANCHED CYPRESS. Similar to the last, but of a bright golden yellow color.

C. pisifera plumosa. PLUME-LIKE CYPRESS. A small dense tree of conical outline. Foliage bright green, disposed in numerous feathery branchlets. One of the most popular varieties.

For grades and prices of above, see page 132

Chamæcyparis, continued

Chamaecyparis pisifera plumosa argentea. SILVER-PLUMED CYPRESS. Young shoots creamy white, contrasting strongly with the other greenery of the tree.

C. pisifera plumosa aurea. GOLDEN-PLUMED CYPRESS. Terminal growths and foliage bright golden yellow. Decidedly the best of the variegated forms.

C. pisifera squarrosa. VEITCH'S SILVER CYPRESS. A low, densely branched tree with feathery spreading branches. Foliage silvery blue, soft and dense. Very distinct and perhaps the most beautiful Japanese Cypress.

C. thyoides (*Cupressus thyoides*). WHITE CEDAR. A very hardy slender tree, growing naturally in low lands from New England to the Gulf States. Foliage fragrant, green or glaucous, closely imbricated on the spreading, irregular branches. Cones very numerous, bluish purple with a glaucous bloom. Valuable in low or wet situations.

C. thyoides andelyensis. ANDELY'S WHITE CEDAR. A low tree of erect growth and the most valuable of the forms of the White Cedar. Foliage of a bluish green color, in cold climates showing tints of reddish brown during winter. Splendid for jardinières.

C. thyoides variegata. VARIEGATED WHITE CEDAR. A tree of more dense habit than the type, conspicuous by the golden variegation of its new growth and shoots. Attractive as a specimen tree.

Cryptomeria · The Japanese Cedar

A genus of but a single species, representing a type of vegetation of great antiquity. The famous avenue of Cryptomerias in Japan, some thirty miles in length, leading to the shrines at Nikko, is the admiration and wonder of every visitor. A deep, well-drained soil with abundant moisture should be selected as a planting site.

Cryptomeria japonica. JAPANESE CEDAR. A stately tree in its native country, China and Japan, although in cultivation of small or medium size. Young and thrifty plants possess remarkable grace and beauty. Will endure temperatures below zero, but thrives best in sheltered situations. Leaves short and scale-like, bluish green, or in winter tinged with brown. Cones reddish brown, an inch or less in length. When protected from cold winds the tree takes on the beauty which has made it so noteworthy in Japan.

C. japonica elegans. ELEGANT JAPANESE CEDAR. A smaller tree than the above, although of robust habit. Branches horizontal, drooping at the tips, clothed with bright green foliage which changes in early autumn to a bronzy crimson hue.

Cunninghamia

The only representative of this genus, a remnant of antiquity, is the species described. The Cunninghamia requires a moist, well-drained soil, and should be planted in positions where there is protection from piercing cold winds. Will withstand considerable cold, but more adapted to the South.

Cunninghamia sinensis. CUNNINGHAMIA. A tree of medium size with spreading branches disposed in more or less distinct whorls. Native of China. Leaves 1 to 2 inches long, pale lustrous green above, glaucous beneath. Cones about an inch in diameter, persisting on the branches for several years. A distinct and interesting evergreen.

Cupressus · The True Cypress Trees

A group of beautiful trees closely related to the genus *Chamæcyparis*, and differing chiefly in the time of maturity of the cones. Cypress trees are valuable in the milder portions of the country, California and the Gulf States. They thrive in moist, well-drained loamy soils.

Evergreens prepared for packing

Cupressus arizonica. ARIZONA CYPRESS. A small or medium-sized tree with horizontal branches, forming a narrow pyramidal head. Mountains of Arizona, at elevations of 5,000 to 6,000 feet. Foliage pale glaucous green, fading to brown and persisting two or three years. Rare in cultivation.

C. funebris. FUNERAL CYPRESS. A singular tree with wide-spreading pendulous branches, forming a pyramidal crown. Native of China. Foliage bright green, closely clothing the drooping branchlets. Frequently planted in the Orient in the temple courts, and originally associated with "The Vale of Tombs" in the north of China.

C. goveniana. GOWEN'S CYPRESS. A tree with slender, erect or spreading branches, forming a handsome crown. Grows naturally in the coast region of California. Foliage dark green, fading reddish brown and persisting for two or three years. A graceful and attractive evergreen.

C. knightiana. GLAUCOUS CYPRESS. A graceful tree of rapid growth, probably from the high mountains of Mexico. Foliage glaucous green, contrasting well with other greenery.

C. macnabiana. MENDOCINO CYPRESS. A bushy tree rarely exceeding 30 feet in height, forming a dense, pyramidal head. Native of California, in Mendocino and adjacent counties. Has the reputation of being the hardiest of the Cypress trees. Foliage deep green, often with a glaucous tint.

C. macrocarpa. MONTEREY CYPRESS. A picturesque tree with a graceful head, or, in old age, with a broad flat-topped crown. Occurs naturally in an extremely restricted area south of the Bay of Monterey in California. Foliage dark green. Extensively planted in the Pacific States, where it is often used for hedges and wind-breaks. In cultivation in the South it grows rapidly, forming a fine tree sometimes 30 feet tall.

C. macrocarpa lutea. GOLDEN MONTEREY CYPRESS. A form of garden origin of the preceding species with spreading plumose leaves. All of the current season's growth is suffused with light yellow, the color-tone gradually changing in the second year to the normal green. Very attractive.

For grades and prices of above, see page 132

Juniperus nana and Pinus strobus

Cupressus, continued

Cupressus sempervirens (*C. fastigiata*). PYRAMIDAL OR ROMAN CYPRESS. A tree common to the Mediterranean region and often a conspicuous feature of the landscape. Thrives in the South Atlantic and Pacific States, where it is often planted to enhance architectural effects. Of pyramidal or conical outline, the appressed branches clothed with verdant foliage.

C. torulosa (*C. majestica*). MAJESTIC CYPRESS. A tall tree of pyramidal outline, with slender, drooping branches, densely clothed with grayish green foliage. A handsome, vigorous-growing species from the Himalayas.

Fitzroya · The Fitzroyas

Evergreen trees and shrubs, of which one species, described below, possesses sufficient hardiness to withstand the winters in the South. Interesting in a collection, but its value in cultivation in the United States has not been fully proven. Requires a well-drained soil.

Fitzroya patagonica. PATAGONIAN FITZROYA. A tree of variable dimensions, native of the Andes, from Chile to the Straits of Magellan. Leaves dark green above, with two white lines beneath. Has been in cultivation over fifty years in Europe, but is rarely seen in this country.

Juniperus · The Junipers, Savin and Red Cedar

A group of evergreen trees and shrubs of great beauty and adaptability. They are largely used in garden and landscape planting and embrace species of great hardiness. The arborescent forms make beautiful specimens, while the prostrate varieties are widely used as a ground cover. In formal gardening, the pyramidal and columnar forms are very effective, giving an architectural emphasis that is often very desirable. A free exposure to sun and air is beneficial, combined with a well-drained substratum.

Juniperus chinensis. CHINESE JUNIPER. A very hardy and ornamental tree, perhaps the most ornamental of the Junipers for the lawn or garden. Pyramidal or columnar in outline, the foliage of a pleasing grayish green color. Possesses wonderful adaptability to extremes of temperature and kinds of soils.

J. chinensis aurea. GOLDEN CHINESE JUNIPER. The growth of the season is diffused with yellow, becoming more brilliant in full sunlight. This is a very attractive tree.

J. chinensis procumbens. PROCUMBENT CHINESE JUNIPER. A dense but robust, procumbent shrub with elongated stems and numerous short branchlets. A most charming plant for rock-gardens. Foliage grayish green.

J. chinensis procumbens aurea. GOLDEN PROCUMBENT CHINESE JUNIPER. Similar to the last, but with the growth of the season tinged with golden yellow.

J. communis. COMMON JUNIPER. Usually a shrub with spreading, sometimes prostrate branches which curve upwards near the ends; widely distributed throughout the colder regions and mountains of the Northern Hemisphere. Foliage grayish green, very dense. A beautiful shrub and valuable in rockeries or as a ground cover.

J. communis aurea. GOLDEN COMMON JUNIPER. Like the former, but with the growth of the current year suffused with bright golden yellow. Very ornamental and beautiful, especially at the beginning of the growing season.

For grades and prices of above, see page 132

Juniperus, continued

Juniperus communis hibernica. IRISH JUNIPER. A slender columnar form with numerous upright branches very closely appressed. Very formal in outline and invaluable in Italian gardens and where architectural features are desired. Foliage glaucous green.

J. communis oblongo-pendula. GRACEFUL JUNIPER. A columnar tree reaching a height of fifteen or twenty feet. Native of China. Leaves bearing two white lines above, bright green beneath, thickly clothing the closely ascending branches which droop perceptibly at the tips. Quite hardy and of great value in formal gardens.

J. communis suecica. SWEDISH JUNIPER. A slender but tall, fastigiate tree, with numerous closely appressed upright branches. Where formal effects are required the tall, columnar habit of this tree lends striking results. Foliage glaucous green.

J. drupacea. SYRIAN JUNIPER. A densely columnar tree with relatively short branches. Native of the mountains of Syria and the Cilician Taurus. Leaves rigid, spiny pointed, relatively broad, grayish white above, light green beneath. Forms an attractive object on account of the peculiar shade of green of its foliage. Withstands the cold at Biltmore, but its range of hardiness is not fully known.

Juniperus communis hibernica

J. excelsa. GREEK JUNIPER. A very ornamental tree of columnar or conical outline, from Greece and Asia. Leaves grayish white above, dark green beneath, freely borne on the ascending branches. A distinct species of great beauty. Valuable in the South.

J. excelsa stricta. SLENDER GREEK JUNIPER. A form of the last, of garden origin, possessing a more slender outline. The foliage is decidedly glaucous, lending a distinct grayish aspect.

J. macrocarpa (*J. neaboriensis*). LARGE-FRUITED JUNIPER. A dense shrub or small pyramidal outline, from the Mediterranean region. Foliage grayish green, the leaves spiny, pointed and spreading. Very valuable in the Southern States and California.

J. nana. PROSTRATE JUNIPER. A depressed or prostrate shrub growing naturally from Labrador and British Columbia to the Southern Rockies and Alleghanies. Foliage grayish green, densely disposed. Most beautiful as a ground cover or carpet, either under the shade of evergreen trees or exposed to full sun. Grand effects from the mat-like plants can be secured. Indispensable in rock-gardens where evergreens are used.

J. prostrata. DWARF SAVIN. A prostrate shrub with long trailing branches, the American form of the Savin. Foliage dark green, sometimes in exposed places of a bronze hue. Valuable in rock-gardens.

J. rigida. STIFF JUNIPER. A small tree or large shrub with spreading, somewhat pendulous branches. Very graceful and hardy, growing vigorously in most soils and exposures. Native of Japan. Foliage yellowish green.

J. sabina. SAVIN JUNIPER. A spreading shrub of variable habit, widely distributed in the mountains of Central and Southern Europe. Foliage dense, very dark green, exhaling a strong odor when bruised. Splendid for rock-gardens.

J. sabina tamariscifolia. TAMARIX-LEAVED SAVIN. A procumbent shrub of great beauty, from the mountains of Southern Europe. Leaves on the older parts of the branchlets needle-shaped, bluish or gray-green; on the younger growths, scale-like and bright green.

J. sabina variegata. VARIEGATED SAVIN. A garden form of the Savin Juniper with the branches conspicuously variegated with creamy white. It may be most successfully used wherever lively effects are desired, especially in formal gardens.

J. sphaerica (*J. fortunei*). ROUND-FRUITED JUNIPER. A bushy tree with close-set, upright branches, the youngest shoots slender and four-angled, clothed with dark green foliage. A hardy and desirable species, native of Northern China.

J. squamata. SCALY-LEAVED JUNIPER. A prostrate shrub with long and trailing branches. Foliage bluish green or glaucous. Valuable in rock-gardens.

J. virginiana. RED CEDAR. A tall tree of great beauty and hardiness, occurring from Canada to the Rocky Mountains, southward to the Gulf States. Of variable habit, but usually much branched and densely clothed with green or bronze-green foliage. From this tree the spicy fragrant pencil wood is obtained.

J. virginiana elegantissima. LEE'S GOLDEN CEDAR. Similar to the type, but with the tips of the young branches of a beautiful yellow color, eventually changing to a golden bronze.

J. virginiana glauca. BLUE VIRGINIA CEDAR. A very vigorous variety with silvery blue foliage. This is one of the most beautiful forms of the Red Cedar, and makes a splendid specimen tree.

J. virginiana pendula. WEEPING RED CEDAR. The branches of this fine tree are slender, elongated and very pendulous, lending a very striking and pleasing effect not obtained by any other evergreen.

Libocedrus · The Incense Cedars

A group of evergreen trees, in effect resembling somewhat the American Arborvitæ. One species is generally satisfactory in cultivation, forming a stately, columnar tree that thrives in a moist, well-drained soil, especially when freely exposed to sun and air. On account of the great difficulty experienced in transplanting, we grow the trees in pots, thereby insuring our purchasers against loss in moving them to their permanent positions.

Libocedrus decurrens. INCENSE CEDAR. A tall stately tree with a narrow, feathery crown, native of the mountain ranges from Oregon to California and Nevada. Thrives well except in the colder portions of the Northern States. Foliage dark glossy green, of a tint peculiar to the species. A grand tree and one of the most beautiful and distinct of the American evergreens.

Juniperus virginiana

For grades and prices of above, see pages 132 and 133

Picea · The Spruces

Evergreen trees of conical or pyramidal outline, many of them of great hardiness and adaptability. In appearance similar to the Firs, but easily distinguished by the drooping (not erect) cones and the four-angled spine-tipped leaves. The spire-like crowns of the Spruces lend a peculiar charm in garden and landscape, and several of the species are admirably adapted for avenue planting and wind-breaks. They thrive in well-drained soils, freely exposed to sun and air, and are particularly suited to the climatic conditions of the Middle, Western and Northern States.

Picea ajanensis. YESSO SPRUCE. A tall, pyramidal tree with ascending or horizontal branches. Native of Northern Japan and Eastern Siberia. Leaves dark green and shining, silvery white on the reverse side. Cones crimson when young, eventually light brown, 2 to 3 inches long. Flowers at a comparatively early age, and in spring, when loaded with young cones, is a most beautiful object.

P. alcockiana. SIR ALCOCK'S SPRUCE. A rare and local species from the mountains of Central Japan. A tree of medium size, with slender spreading branches. Leaves dark green, marked with bluish lines beneath. Cones 3 to 4 inches long, purple when young, at maturity light brown. A handsome, rapid-growing tree.

P. canadensis (*P. alba*). WHITE SPRUCE. A native tree of dense habit, ranging from Labrador to Alaska, and south to Montana and New York. Foliage light bluish green, exhaling a strong aromatic odor when bruised. Cones 1 to 2 inches long, glossy brown. Attractive and shapely.

P. engelmanni. ENGELMANN'S SPRUCE. A tall tree with slender, spreading branches, native of the Rocky Mountains from Alberta and British Columbia to Colorado and New Mexico. Young branches pubescent, thickly clothed with bluish green foliage, which, when bruised, emits a strong, aromatic odor. Cones light brown, 2 to 3 inches long. A very ornamental and hardy tree for lawn or landscape.

P. excelsa. NORWAY SPRUCE. A tall and picturesque tree and the most widely cultivated of all the Spruces. Native of Northern and Middle Europe. Extensively planted as an ornamental tree and for shelters and wind-breaks. Handsome and hardy, graceful and green, of rapid growth and great adaptability, this grand tree commends itself. Cones 5 to 7 inches long, light brown. Branches spreading, usually pendulous.

P. excelsa inversa. WEEPING NORWAY SPRUCE. A remarkable pendulous variety with drooping branches which are closely appressed to the stem of the tree. Leaves larger and lighter green than in the type.

P. excelsa pygmaea. DWARF NORWAY SPRUCE. A low dense bush in which the branches are much shortened and crowded. A peculiar and interesting form.

P. excelsa pyramidalis. PYRAMIDAL NORWAY SPRUCE. A spire-like form with the branches more erect and compact. Formal and effective.

P. mariana (*P. nigra*). BLACK SPRUCE. A small or medium-sized tree with slender, usually pendulous branches. Occurs from Canada to Virginia and British Columbia. Of great hardiness and value in the extreme Northern States. Foliage dark or bluish green, pale beneath. Cones about an inch long, grayish brown. From this tree spruce gum is collected, an article well known to those familiar to the regions within the home limits of the species.

P. obovata. SIBERIAN SPRUCE. A tree resembling somewhat the Norway Spruce in habit and aspect. Of slender outline, and with sub-pendulous branches, it affords a pleasing addition to the hardiest of the Spruces. Cones about 3 inches long, reddish brown. Native of Siberia.

P. omorika. SERVIAN SPRUCE. A remarkably distinct and ornamental species, of dense and narrow outline. Native of the mountains of Servia, in South-eastern Europe. Leaves dark green and shining, with white lines above. Cones about 2 inches long, bluish black when young, dark brown at maturity. A very hardy tree, with conspicuous purple flowers.

P. orientalis. ORIENTAL SPRUCE. A graceful middle-sized tree from Western Asia and the Caucasus. Foliage dark, glossy green, densely appressed to the branches on all but the lower sides. Cones 3 to 4 inches long, dull violet-purple, eventually changing to brown. One of the most ornamental Spruces and quite hardy.

P. polita. TIGER'S TAIL SPRUCE. A medium-sized tree of broadly conical outline. One of the most attractive and distinct of the Japanese Spruces. Foliage light green, rigid and spiny, spreading on all sides of the stout and numerous branches. Cones 4 to 5 inches long, glossy brown. A beautiful and desirable tree for lawn or landscape.

P. pungens. COLORADO SPRUCE. A beautiful and very hardy tree from the Rocky Mountains. Regularly branched in distinct whorls, which diminish in size upwards, forming a very symmetrical tree of narrow pyramidal or conical outline. Leaves glaucous green, rigid and spine-pointed. Cones 3 to 4 inches long, glossy brown. Cannot be too highly recommended.

P. pungens glauca. COLORADO, OR KOSTER'S BLUE SPRUCE. Unquestionably the most beautiful of the Spruces for garden or lawn. Foliage silvery blue, densely disposed on the numerous branchlets. Our stock is uniformly blue, the bluest strain that can be selected, grafted from the famous Koster variety.

Cones of Picea excelsa

P. pungens glauca pendula. WEEPING BLUE SPRUCE. A form with silvery blue foliage and drooping or pendulous branches. An interesting and striking object.

P. rubra. RED SPRUCE. A medium-sized handsome tree occurring in the Alleghanies from Canada to North Carolina. Leaves bright green and shining. Cones glossy brown, 1 to 2 inches long. Plant in cool situations, as it does not resist heat and drought very well.

P. sitchensis (*Abies menziesi*). SITKA SPRUCE. A beautiful tree from the Pacific Coast, ranging from Alaska to California. Leaves bright green and lustrous, silvery white on the reverse. Cones 3 to 4 inches long, brown. Broadly pyramidal in outline, the branches spreading horizontally.

For grades and prices of above, see page 133

Pinus · The Pines

A large group of evergreen trees with remarkably distinct characters. Among them may be found species adapted to the requirements of almost every section of the country, from the coldest to the warmest. They are indispensable in the composition of landscape effects, for wind-breaks and screens against objectionable tall objects. Many of the species are valuable as ornaments on the lawn, and, when given ample space, develop into majestic specimens.

Pinus austriaca. AUSTRIAN PINE. A tall tree with a broad, ovate crown, from Austria and Dalmatia. Leaves in pairs, about 4 inches long, rigid, very dark green. Cones 2 to 3 inches long, of a glossy yellowish brown color. A fast-growing, dense tree of wonderful adaptability.

P. cembra. SWISS STONE PINE. A large tree of broadly conical outline, the top eventually becoming enlarged, open and rounded. Very picturesque when old, and at all times a beautiful hardy tree. Leaves in fives, 3 to 4 inches long, dark green, bluish white on the reverse side. Cones 2 to 3 inches long, light brown.

P. contorta. OREGON PINE. A tree with relatively stout branches, forming a compact, round head. Occurs from Alaska to Colorado and California. A dense and shapely tree of slow growth, not requiring much room. Leaves twisted, dark green, 2 to 3 inches long.

P. densiflora. JAPANESE RED PINE. A rapid-growing and very ornamental hardy Pine. In Japan, where it is native, many curious and fantastic shapes are obtained by distorting and training. Leaves in pairs, bright bluish green, 3 to 4 inches long. Cones grayish brown, about 2 inches long. In age, the broad open crown presents a charming picture.

P. echinata. YELLOW PINE. A tall, handsome tree with slender, often pendulous branches, forming a broad oval crown. Grows naturally from New York and Illinois to the Gulf States. Leaves in twos and threes, dark green, 3 to 4 in. long. Cones about 2 in. long, dull brown. Splendid for lawn and landscape.

Pinus excelsa. BHOTAN PINE. A magnificent tree from the Himalayas. Branches spreading, the uppermost ascending, forming a broad, irregular pyramid. Leaves in fives, slender and drooping, grayish or bluish green, 5 to 7 inches long. Cones pendulous, 7 to 9 inches long. As a specimen plant on a broad lawn or park it is superb. Requires a sheltered position in the colder sections.

P. flexilis. LIMBER PINE. A tree of medium size, with stout, horizontal branches, forming a narrow pyramidal, or, in old age, a round-topped crown. Grows naturally from Alberta to California and New Mexico. Leaves dark green, 2 to 3 inches long. An ornamental hardy species of slow growth, recommended for planting on rocky slopes.

P. jeffreyi. JEFFREY'S PINE. A tree with spreading, often pendulous branches, forming a narrow, spire-like crown. Leaves 6 to 8 inches long, pale bluish green. Grows from Oregon to California, and

Pinus echinata

Pinus strobus on driveway

For grades and prices of above, see page 133

Pinus mughus and Tsuga canadensis

Pinus, continued

is hardy in Massachusetts. The young branches are fragrant when bruised or broken.

P. koraiensis. COREAN PINE. A handsome hardy Pine of relatively slow growth. Native of Corea. Of dense pyramidal outline. Leaves dark green and glossy on the convex side, bluish white on the flat sides. Where large trees are unsuitable, this comparatively small Pine is often used.

P. lambertiana. SUGAR PINE. This, the tallest of all the Pines, is a handsome tree with a wide flat-topped crown. Grows naturally from Oregon to Mexico. Leaves dark bluish green, 3 to 4 inches long. A majestic species, and, on account of its alpine habitat, possesses a considerable degree of hardiness.

P. laricio. CORSICAN PINE. A tall tree with stout spreading branches disposed in regular whorls, forming a symmetrical, pyramidal crown; or in old age broad and flat-topped. Leaves in pairs, 4 to 6 inches long, dark green. Cones 2 to 3 inches long, yellowish brown, glossy. A tree with a strong constitution and of very rapid growth, native of Southern Europe and Western Asia.

P. montana. SWISS MOUNTAIN PINE. Usually of dwarf habit. This hardy and attractive Pine is most attractive when planted in a rock-garden. The ascending branches are densely clothed with bright green leaves from 1 to 2 inches long. From the mountains of Middle Europe.

P. monticola. MOUNTAIN WHITE PINE. A tall and graceful tree with slender somewhat pendulous branches, forming a narrow pyramidal crown. Mountains of British Columbia and Idaho to California. Similar to *Pinus strobus*, but more slender. Leaves in fives, 2 to 4 inches long, bluish green and usually glaucous. Cones pendent, 7 to 9 inches long, yellow-brown.

P. mughus. DWARF PINE. Usually a low, handsome shrub with numerous ascending branches. Leaves in pairs, bright green, often twisted, 1 to 2 inches long. Cones 1 to 2 inches long, grayish brown. Native of the mountains of Middle Europe. Very valuable in rock-gardens or for covering rocky slopes.

Pinus parviflora. JAPANESE SHORT-LEAVED PINE. One of the most ornamental hardy Pines, thriving in many situations. A tree of dense pyramidal habit, with horizontal branches. Native of Japan. Leaves bright green, the flat sides with several silvery lines. Bears flowers and cones very freely even when young.

Cones of Pinus echinata

For grades and prices of above, see page 134

Pinus, continued

Pinus peuce. Macedonian Pine. A medium-sized tree of dense habit, forming a narrow, pyramidal crown. Native of the high mountains of Macedonia, in Southeastern Europe. Leaves bluish green, 3 to 4 inches long. A useful and hardy ornamental tree of comparatively slow growth.

P. pinaster. Cluster Pine. A pyramidal tree with spreading slightly pendulous branches, of very rapid growth. Native of Southern Europe. Leaves 6 to 9 inches long, twisted, bright glossy green. A handsome tree suitable for planting near the seacoast in the Southern States.

P. ponderosa. Bull Pine. A very large tree, perhaps the largest of the Pines, growing naturally from British Columbia to Nebraska and Mexico. Branches stout and spreading, sometimes pendulous, forming a narrow, conical crown. Leaves in threes, dark green, 6 to 10 inches long. Cones glossy brown, 3 to 6 inches long. Quite hardy and an important tree.

P. pungens. Table Mountain Pine. A medium-sized tree with stout horizontal branches, forming a broad, open, often flat-topped crown. A native of the Appalachian Mountains of the Eastern States. Leaves in pairs, stout and usually twisted, dark green, 1½ to 3 inches long. Cones about 3 inches long, light brown. Hardy and attractive.

P. resinosa. Red, or Norway Pine. A tall tree with stout, horizontal, sometimes pendulous branches forming a broad conical head, or, in age, an open round-topped crown. Grows naturally from Newfoundland to Minnesota, south to Pennsylvania. Leaves in pairs, dark green and shining, 4 to 6 inches long. Cones about 2 inches long, light brown. Very ornamental and of great value in park and landscape.

Cones of Pinus virginiana

P. rigida. Pitch Pine. A medium-sized tree with regular whorls of stiff, horizontally spreading branches, forming a conical or oval crown. Occurs naturally from Ontario and New Brunswick to Georgia and Kentucky. Leaves in threes, dark green, 3 to 5 inches long. Cones 2 to 3 inches long, light brown. An adaptable and rapid-growing tree.

P. strobus. White Pine. A tall and most beautiful tree with regular whorls of horizontal branches, forming a symmetrical pyramidal crown, or in age with a broad and open, very picturesque head. Indigenous from Newfoundland and Manitoba to Iowa and Georgia. Leaves in fives, soft bluish green, 3 to 4 inches long. Cones pendent, 5 to 6 inches long. The most valuable Pine, with a wide range of usefulness and adaptability, both for commercial and ornamental purposes.

Cones of Pinus rigida

P. sylvestris. Scotch Pine. A large tree with horizontal, sometimes pendulous branches, of pyramidal outline, or in age with a broad rounded top. Native of Europe and Asia. Leaves in pairs, twisted, bluish green, 2 to 3 inches long. Cones about 2 inches long, reddish brown. This is one of the chief timber trees of Europe. It is frequently planted as a screen and in sand-dune regions to prevent drifting.

P. thunbergi. Japanese Black Pine. A large and handsome tree of Japanese origin. Widely planted in the land of the Mikado for every conceivable purpose, and often trained and pruned into fantastic shapes. In America it is very hardy and appreciative of even the poorest of soils. Leaves in pairs, bright green, 3 to 4 inches long. Cones 3 to 4 inches long, grayish brown.

P. virginiana (*P. inops*). Jersey Pine. Mostly a small tree with slender, horizontal, sometimes pendulous branches, forming a pyramidal or flat-topped head. Grows naturally from Long Island to South Carolina and Indiana. Leaves in pairs, spreading and usually twisted, bright green, 2 to 3 inches long. Cones about 2 inches long, reddish brown.

Cones of Pinus pungens

Pseudotsuga · The Douglas Spruce

Generically separated from the true Spruces by botanists on account of aberrant characters. The Douglas Spruce seems to combine features of both the Spruces and Hemlocks. For its best development, trees should be planted in deep, thoroughly drained soils. Under such conditions the beauty and hardiness which has crowned it in many plantations will be apparent.

Pseudotsuga mucronata (*Abies douglasi*). Douglas Spruce. A tall, pyramidal tree with horizontal, pendulous branches. From the mountains of British Columbia and Montana to Colorado and Mexico. Foliage dark or bluish green, spreading from all sides of the subpendent branchlets. Cones pendulous, 3 to 4 inches long, with long exserted bracts. A beautiful tree of great hardiness.

For grades and prices of above, see page 134

Pseudotsuga mucronata

Pseudotsuga, continued

Pseudotsuga mucronata glauca. BLUE DOUGLAS SPRUCE. A smaller tree than the above, with shorter and stouter branches. The leaves vary from bluish green to almost silvery white. Generally considered hardier than the type, but of much slower growth. Our plants are grown from the most highly colored specimens and have their origin in Colorado. Recommended for the colder portions of the North.

P. mucronata pendula. WEEPING DOUGLAS SPRUCE. A form with pendulous branches and drooping branchlets. The foliage is usually more blue than in the typical form. This remarkable tree is much admired as a specimen plant.

Sciadopitys · The Umbrella Pine

The remoteness of relationship of the Umbrella Pine to any other species imparts to it a singular interest that few evergreens possess. The genus consists of a single species, a tree of considerable hardiness and of great beauty. Requires a moist but well-drained soil.

Sciadopitys verticillata. UMBRELLA PINE. A remarkable and beautiful Japanese tree with compact ascending branches, forming a narrow pyramidal head, or, in age, the branches spreading or pendulous. Foliage in whorls of 15 to 30 stiff, broad needles of a lustrous deep green color, 3 to 5 inches long. This beautiful tree thrives over a wide range of country, enduring temperatures much below zero. A gem for any garden.

Pinus strobus

Sequoia · California Redwood and Big Trees

This genus includes, seemingly, the climax of vegetation—the largest and oldest trees in the world. It is estimated that, early in the Christian Era, the largest of the Big Trees, now standing, were swaying in the Pacific breezes. Trees three hundred or more feet tall, with trunks twenty or thirty feet in diameter, have been recorded. It is interesting to cultivate these monarch trees, even though the proportions are vastly different. The Big Tree is hardy in New York, but the Redwood is more tender and adapted only to the South Atlantic, Gulf and Pacific States. A deep sandy loam should be chosen, and if protected from cold, piercing winds, the results are likely to be much better.

Sequoia gigantea. BIG TREE; MAMMOTH TREE. The largest and oldest of all trees. Native of the Sierra Nevada range of California. Foliage green or bluish green, completely clothing the branchlets. Cones 2 to 2½ inches long. This is the hardier species, and the one most often seen in cultivation.

S. gigantea pendula. WEEPING BIG TREE. A remarkable form of the foregoing species with very pendulous branches, which often hang so close as to hide the trunk.

S. sempervirens. CALIFORNIA REDWOOD. A gigantic evergreen tree, ranking second in size and age of the world's greatest trees. Grows naturally from Oregon to Southern California, near the coast. Leaves dark green, with two pale bands beneath. A fast-growing pyramidal tree, thriving best in the neighborhood of the sea.

Thuya occidentalis filicoides

Thuya · The Arborvitæs

A group of most useful hardy evergreens, thriving in a wide variety of soils and exposures. In general, a moist soil with a porous substratum is to be preferred. In the extreme North the American varieties are to be preferred, on account of greater hardiness, while in the South the Oriental varieties are best adapted to the conditions of climate and environment. Many of the formal varieties are successfully used in producing architectural effects and in geometric gardens. As tub plants, they are very durable and attractive.

Thuya gigantea (*T. plicata; T. lobbi*). WESTERN ARBORVITÆ. A tall and stately tree with short, often pendulous branches, of narrow pyramidal outline. Occurs naturally from Alaska to Montana and California. Foliage fragrant, bright glossy green, with silver spots beneath. Most beautiful and rapid-growing, and worthy of extensive cultivation.

T. japonica (*Thuyopsis standishi*). JAPANESE ARBORVITÆ. A small conical tree with short horizontal branches and bright green foliage. In moist soil it develops into a beautiful and attractive specimen. Much cultivated in Japan, its native country, but not often seen in American gardens.

T. occidentalis. AMERICAN ARBORVITÆ. A tree of variable height and pyramidal outline, especially beautiful when young. Grows naturally from Nova Scotia and Manitoba to North Carolina and Illinois. Foliage bright green, yellow-green beneath, or in winter assuming tones of brown and bronze. Both this species and the several varieties following are used in tubs, vases or jardinières for winter decoration of porches, vesti-

For grades and prices of above, see page 134

Thuya, continued

bules, etc. As garden plants they are very pleasing, some of the formal varieties lending striking effects.

T. occidentalis alba. WHITE-TIPPED ARBORVITÆ. In this form the tips of the young branches are white, contrasting strongly with the other greenery. A low tree of broadly pyramidal outline.

T. occidentalis aurea. GEORGE PEABODY'S GOLDEN ARBORVITÆ. A broadly pyramidal low tree, with the growth of the season diffused with yellow. Holds its color throughout the year.

T. occidentalis filicoides. FERN-LIKE ARBORVITÆ. Foliage bright rich green, fern-like and crested; very beautiful. A small tree of broadly pyramidal outline.

Thuya occidentalis globosa

T. occidentalis globosa. GLOBE ARBORVITÆ. A low, compact form with bright green foliage. In outline a symmetrical globe. A formal and very striking variety.

T. occidentalis plicata. SIBERIAN ARBORVITÆ. A small pyramidal tree of dense habit. Foliage very dark green, with a brownish tint, bluish green below. Branches short and rigid. Distinct and of extreme hardiness.

T. occidentalis pyramidalis. PYRAMIDAL ARBORVITÆ. A compact and narrowly pyramidal tree. Branches short and densely clothed with bright green foliage. Very formal and attractive, and the narrowest and most columnar of the Arborvitæs.

T. occidentalis spaethi. SPATH'S ARBORVITÆ. A peculiar form in which two kinds of foliage appear, the lower branches with spreading leaves, the upper branches with appressed leaves. Very singular and extraordinary in appearance.

T. orientalis (*Biota orientalis*). ORIENTAL ARBORVITÆ. A low, bushy tree of columnar or pyramidal habit, native of Asia. Foliage bright green in summer, assuming tones of bronze and brown in winter. Both the typical form and the varieties following are very useful as garden plants, and, in tubs or vases, as porch plants. Very hardy and beautiful.

T. orientalis aurea. GOLDEN ORIENTAL ARBORVITÆ. A low and compact shrub in which the foliage assumes a beautiful golden yellow color at the beginning of the growing season.

T. orientalis aurea nana. BERCKMAN'S GOLDEN ARBORVITÆ. A very dwarf, compact shrub, with golden yellow foliage. A very popular variety and one of the best of dwarf hardy evergreens.

T. orientalis compacta. COMPACT ORIENTAL ARBORVITÆ. A low and very compact form, with bright green foliage. Very formal and attractive, and a favorite everywhere.

T. orientalis pendula (*T. filiformis*). WEEPING, OR THREAD-BRANCHED ORIENTAL ARBORVITÆ. A remarkable variety and the most extreme of all the forms. The thread-like pendulous branches are much elongated and sparsely clothed with foliage. Attracts attention wherever seen.

Thuya orientalis pyramidalis. PYRAMIDAL ORIENTAL ARBORVITÆ. One of the tallest and hardiest varieties, of pyramidal outline.

T. orientalis semperaurescens. EVER-GOLDEN ORIENTAL ARBORVITÆ. Dwarf and compact, the foliage of a pleasing golden hue, retaining this color at all times.

Thuyopsis · The Japanese Thuya

A genus of a single species, closely related to Thuya, and differing mainly in the number of seeds under the cone scales. While quite hardy, thriving in New England, the plant requires for its best development a sheltered situation in moist, loamy soil.

Thuyopsis dolobrata. JAPANESE THUYA. A dense shrub or small tree with spreading or horizontal branches, of pyramidal outline. Foliage bright lustrous green, whitened beneath. A very beautiful Japanese evergreen, capable of withstanding much cold, but requires a moist soil and protection from piercing winds. In such situations it is an ornament to any garden.

Tsuga · The Hemlocks

A beautiful and extremely graceful group of trees, chiefly characterized by their slender, drooping shoots. Whether standing alone, in groups, or in contrast with other trees, Hemlocks are among the most effective subjects for lawn or landscape. They thrive in well-drained soils fully exposed to sun and air. As an evergreen hedge plant, either clipped or informal, they are satisfactory and desirable. Few evergreens that we handle are so confidently recommended.

Tsuga canadensis. CANADIAN HEMLOCK. A tall and graceful tree with spreading or drooping branches, forming a pyramidal crown. Grows naturally from Nova Scotia and Wisconsin to Georgia and Alabama. Foliage dark green and glossy. Cones half an inch or more long. A beautiful tree and indispensable for park or landscape. Makes a grand hedge, either clipped to formal lines, or untrimmed.

T. canadensis compacta. COMPACT CANADIAN HEMLOCK. A low conical or pyramidal form with numerous branches and small leaves. A very attractive variety.

T. canadensis pendula. WEEPING HEMLOCK. A low form with short, pendent branches, forming a dense flat-topped head. Extremely distinct and beautiful.

T. caroliniana. CAROLINA HEMLOCK. A stately tree, with grace and beauty seldom excelled. Of more compact habit and with larger cones than the last species. Native of the Alleghany Mountains from Virginia to South Carolina and Georgia. Leaves dark green and glossy, with two white lines beneath. Cones an

Thuya orientalis compacta

For grades and prices of above, see pages 134 and 135

Tsuga, continued

inch or more long, very much larger than those of the Canadian Hemlock. Very hardy and one of the most desirable evergreens.

T. hookeriana. WESTERN HEMLOCK. A beautiful tree with slender pendulous branches, growing naturally from British Columbia and Montana to California. Foliage bluish green, spirally arranged around the branchlets. Cones 2 to 3 inches long, violet-purple, changing to brown at maturity. A grand species.

T. mertensiana. WESTERN MOUNTAIN HEMLOCK. The largest of the Hemlocks, occurring naturally from Alaska to California and Montana. Branches spreading, their tips slender and pendulous, forming a narrow pyramidal crown. Leaves dark green, with two narrow bands of white beneath. Cones about an inch long. Very graceful and effective.

T. sieboldi. JAPANESE HEMLOCK. A stately tree with slender spreading branches, native of Japan. Leaves dark glossy green, marked by two white lines beneath. Cones about an inch long. A rare tree in American gardens.

Drupe-Fruited Evergreens and the Ginkgo

Trees and shrubs with plum- or berry-like fruits, evergreen with the exception of the Ginkgo. They are interesting subjects in any collection, and in several instances valuable factors in securing landscape and garden effects. The plants embraced in this group are of geological antiquity and represent types of vegetation that existed in earlier ages over wide areas of country. Our plants have been carefully selected and in most instances are sent out with compact balls of roots protected in burlap.

Tsuga canadensis (see page 16)

Cephalotaxus · The False Yews

These interesting plants should be grown in shade and sheltered from cold winds by surrounding trees or vegetation. They thrive in moist soils which are thoroughly drained. Under such conditions the foliage remains bright and glossy throughout the season. The species resemble somewhat the Yews, but are more graceful. They should be grown only in very sheltered situations in the North, as they are not altogether hardy in severe climates.

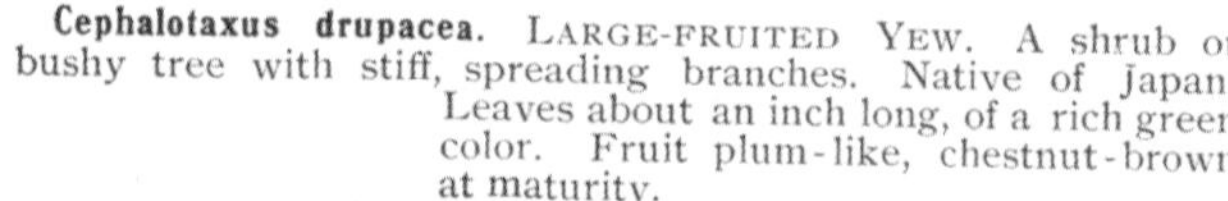

Cephalotaxus drupacea. LARGE-FRUITED YEW. A shrub or bushy tree with stiff, spreading branches. Native of Japan. Leaves about an inch long, of a rich green color. Fruit plum-like, chestnut-brown at maturity.

C. fortunei. FORTUNE'S YEW. A dense shrub or bushy tree from Northern China and Japan. A distinct and graceful species with long and slender branches. Leaves 2 to 3 inches long, dark green and lustrous. Fruit resembling a plum, about an inch long, greenish brown. Valuable for planting in shade.

C. pedunculata. STEM-FRUITED YEW. A bushy shrub with spreading, sometimes pendulous branches. Native of China and Japan. Leaves 1 to 2 inches long, dark green and shining above, paler and marked with dark lines beneath. Fruit about an inch long, resembling a plum.

C. pedunculata fastigiata (*Podocarpus koraiana*). KOREAN YEW. A columnar shrub with upright, somewhat appressed branches, resembling an Irish Yew. Leaves 1 to 2 inches long, spreading or spirally arranged, dark green and shining. The most valuable of the forms in cultivation, thriving in partly shaded situations. It withstands the cold at Biltmore better than any other of the species, growing at the rate of a foot or more each year.

Tsuga caroliniana (see page 16)

For grades and prices of above, see page 135

Ginkgo · The Maidenhair Tree

This strange species, the only representative of its genus, is of great antiquity. It is successfully cultivated in moist loamy soil as far north as Michigan and parts of Canada.

Ginkgo biloba (*Salisburia adiantifolia*). MAIDENHAIR TREE. A tall and very hardy tree with horizontal branches. Native of China. Leaves deciduous, borne in fascicles of three, five or more; dull green, striate with many parallel veins. Fruit plum-like, about an inch in diameter. Very picturesque, its curious maidenhair-like leaves imparting a pleasing aspect. Has proven most successful in Washington City as a street and avenue tree.

Taxus · The Yews

Attractive ornamental evergreen trees and shrubs with showy berry-like red fruits. They are valuable for planting in shade or sunshine, and especially on cool northern exposures. Several of the species are used for hedges, and the English Yew has been extensively used in fantastic topiary work. They thrive best in a moist but well-drained sandy loam.

Taxus baccata. ENGLISH YEW. A low tree of variable habit, everywhere seen in English gardens and often clipped into formal and fantastic shapes. The topiary gardens at Levens Hall and Elvaston Castle are famous examples of this fashion. Foliage dark green, pale beneath, an inch or less in length. Fruit bright scarlet, berry-like. The trees attain venerable, almost fabulous ages.

T. baccata fastigiata. IRISH YEW. A shrub of remarkably compact, upright habit; the dark glossy green leaves spirally arranged on the closely appressed branches. Very formal.

Taxus canadensis. CANADIAN YEW. A procumbent shrub with ascending branches, rarely exceeding 2 to 3 feet in height, the slender branches clothed with bright or yellowish green foliage. Occurs naturally from Newfoundland to Virginia, and westward to Manitoba and Iowa. Splendid for rock-gardens, especially in cold sections.

T. cuspidata. JAPANESE YEW. In cultivation usually a dense shrub with several stems. Foliage dark shining green, tawny yellow beneath. Fruit bright scarlet, berry-like. In Japan this beautiful and hardy species has been grown from time immemorial.

Torreya · The Nutmeg Cedars

Evergreen trees of yew-like aspect. The several species are undoubtedly the survivors of a vegetation at one time widely distributed over Europe and North America. The species are not altogether hardy in the North, although the one from Florida withstands the winters in sheltered situations near Boston. The Japanese species is, perhaps, the hardiest, but has not been sufficiently tested to determine its range of usefulness.

Torreya californica (*T. myristica*). CALIFORNIA NUTMEG. A tree with spreading somewhat pendulous slender branches, forming a pyramidal crown. Leaves dark green and lustrous, 1 to 3 inches long. Fruit oval, green striped with purple, about an inch long. Native of California. An interesting tree for southern gardens.

T. nucifera. JAPANESE NUTMEG CEDAR. A tree with spreading branches, forming a compact, pyramidal crown. Native of Japan. Leaves about an inch long, very dark green above, with two white lines beneath. Fruit plum-like, less than an inch in length. The bark is bright red, contrasting strongly with the foliage.

Deciduous Cone-Bearers

These interesting trees admit of striking landscape results on account of the graceful feathery foliage with its soft tones of green. Contrasted against the somber green of taller evergreens they are remarkably beautiful.

Larix · The Larches

Deciduous trees of pyramidal outline of great hardiness. They grow in almost any kind of soil, but prefer a moist well-drained situation, exposed to full sun and air. They are among the first trees to start into growth in the spring and on this account are preferably transplanted in autumn or in earliest spring. All of the species are highly recommended.

Larix americana. TAMARACK. A slender deciduous tree occurring from Labrador and the Yukon region to New Jersey and Minnesota. Branches horizontal, forming a narrow, pyramidal head. Leaves pale green, numerous in tufts or fascicles, fading and falling in autumn with tones of yellow and bronze. Cones globular, two-thirds of an inch long. Will grow in wet or swampy land.

L. europaea. EUROPEAN LARCH. A tall tree with a conical head, native of Middle Europe, where it is esteemed both as a timber tree and as a graceful object in park and landscape. Leaves deciduous, soft, light green, in tufts or fascicles of thirty to fifty, fading in autumn with beautiful yellow tones. Cones ovoid, about an inch in diameter. Only suitable for well-drained soils.

L. leptolepis. JAPANESE LARCH. A slender pyramidal tree with horizontal branches. A native of Japan. Foliage deciduous, very light green, contrasting strongly with the greenery of other vegetation, fading in autumn with a rich golden hue. A beautiful tree, which should be planted in moist soil.

Taxodium · The Deciduous Cypress

A handsome tree, hardy in the Middle States and New England. Thrives best in moist alluvial soil, but will grow on clay uplands. The habit of the tree depends to a certain extent upon the soil in which it grows, the drier positions tending to narrow the outline of the crown.

Taxodium distichum BALD CYPRESS. A tall tree with feathery deciduous foliage, of narrow pyramidal outline. Grows naturally in or near water from Delaware to Florida and Texas. In cultivation, makes a large and beautiful specimen. Foliage of the softest green, light and airy, fading and falling in autumn with tones of yellow and orange. A grand park tree.

Pseudolarix · The False Larch

A genus of a single species requiring a sunny exposure in well-drained moist soil. Should be given ample space. Closely related to the true Larches, and differing mainly by the pendulous, stalked flower-clusters. Quite hardy.

Pseudolarix kaempferi. GOLDEN LARCH. A tall pyramidal tree with spreading, whorled branches, pendulous at their extremities. Native of China. Leaves deciduous, soft, light green, glaucous beneath, fading in autumn with tones of clear yellow. Cones 2 to 3 inches long, reddish brown. A beautiful tree.

For grades and prices of above, see page 135

DECIDUOUS TREES

THE wide range in selection afforded the planter in choosing from the ranks of deciduous trees constitutes one of the charms of this very important group. Not only are the numerical factors extensive, but the characters of outline and habit, color tones of foliage and floral values, are almost equally diversified. No garden or landscape is complete without them, and their proper spacing and arrangement should constitute the basis or foundation upon which all other planting is made. Our trees are select, straight specimens, frequently transplanted, and are, so far as it is possible to control the selection, the offspring of noteworthy and desirable parents.

Acer · The Maples

Among the most valuable of ornamental trees for street or landscape planting, the Maples stand out prominently. The glorious autumnal colors which characterize so many of the species add greatly to their effectiveness. The leaf outlines are pleasing and symmetrical, and in the Japanese varieties assume a veritable flower-garden aspect. A moist, porous soil is best for them.

Acer campestre. European Cork Maple. A small dense tree with corky ridges on the branches, native of Europe and Western Asia. Leaves 3- to 5-lobed, dark dull green, fading in autumn to yellow and brown. Makes a neat specimen, especially if branched to the ground.

A. circinatum. Vine Maple. A small tree or shrub, native of the region from British Columbia to California, and hardy in the East as far north as Eastern Massachusetts. Leaves almost circular in outline, 7- to 9-lobed, the divisions irregularly serrate, bright green above, paler beneath, fading in autumn with gorgeous tones of orange and scarlet. Fruit rose-color.

A ginnala. Siberian Maple. A graceful small tree or shrub, native of China and Japan. Leaves 3-lobed, the middle division much elongated, their edges serrate, bright green, turning to a brilliant red in autumn. Handsome and desirable. Has been recommended as a substitute for the Japanese Maples when these are not hardy.

A. japonicum. Japanese Maple. A shrub or small tree of great beauty. Native of Japan. Leaves 7- to 11-lobed, the divisions doubly serrate, light green. This species and its forms, and *Acer palmatum*, are known as Japanese Maples. They are beautiful objects with extremely pretty foliage.

A. japonicum aureum. Golden Japanese Maple. Leaves of a beautiful golden yellow color, 7- to 11-lobed, their edges sharply toothed.

A. japonicum filicifolium. Fern-leaved Japanese Maple. Leaves large, divided nearly to the base into 9 to 11 segments, the divisions still further cut and toothed, of a beautiful bright green color.

A. japonicum purpureum. Purple Japanese Maple. Leaves purplish red, 7- to 11-lobed, the divisions doubly serrate.

Acer laetum. Colchicum Maple. A handsome tree with light green foliage, the spreading branches forming a symmetrical oval crown. Native of the Orient. Leaves 5- to 7-lobed, quite smooth, fading in autumn with tones of yellow and orange. Flowers yellow-green in spring.

A. laetum rubrum (*A. colchicum rubrum*). Red Colchicum Maple. Similar to the last, but with foliage of a dark blood-red color at the time of unfolding. It seldom attains a large size, but on account of its vernal color it is much used in connection with shrub plantations.

A. macrophyllum. Oregon Maple. A large tree, with stout, often pendulous branches, forming a compact, round head. Grows naturally from British Columbia and Oregon to California. Leaves 3- to 5-cleft, dark green and lustrous, pale beneath, turning in autumn to bright orange and red. Often cultivated in the West, and hardy in the East as far north as Eastern Pennsylvania.

A. monspessulanum. Montpelier Maple. A low tree or large shrub of relatively slow growth. Native of Southern Europe. Leaves 3-lobed, remaining green until frost. Flowers pale yellow in spring. An interesting tree with a dense round head, thriving even on poor, dry soils.

A. negundo (*Negundo aceroides*). Ash-leaved Maple. Box Elder. A rapid-growing tree with wide-spreading branches, occurring from New England to Florida, and westward to the Rocky Mountains. Twigs pale green and shining, or sometimes purple with a glaucous bloom. Leaves compound, with 3 to 5 leaflets, bright green, paler beneath, turning yellow in autumn. Frequently planted as an ornamental, and in the Middle West for wind-breaks and timber, where it withstands cold and drought.

A. nigrum. Black Sugar Maple. A large tree with dark-colored bark and spreading branches. Occurs

For grades and prices of above, see page 136

Acer, continued

naturally from New England and Ontario to Dakota, south to Virginia and Kentucky. Leaves 3- to 5-lobed, dark green and smooth above, paler and softly pubescent beneath, turning bright yellow in autumn. Differs chiefly from the common Sugar Maple by the heavy, drooping leaves, and by the yellowish or orange-colored twigs.

A. palmatum. JAPANESE MAPLE. A handsome shrub or small tree of dense and graceful habit. Native of Japan. Leaves 5- to 9-lobed or divided, the edges incised. This species and its several varieties, as well as *Acer japonicum*, are known as Japanese Maples. They are beautiful shrubs, especially in spring and autumn, on account of the varied shades of red, green and gold, and of the wonderful outline of their leaves. No garden or lawn is complete without them. The following are some of the best forms:

A. palmatum atropurpureum. BLOOD-LEAVED JAPANESE MAPLE. Leaves dark red in spring, eventually purplish red, doubly serrate, deeply divided. A compact, beautiful variety.

A. palmatum aureum. GOLDEN JAPANESE MAPLE. Leaves broad, sparingly incised, light yellow.

A. palmatum dissectum. CUT-LEAVED JAPANESE MAPLE. Leaves divided to the base into 5 to 9 pinnatifid lobes, of a beautiful rich green color. Very attractive and graceful.

A palmatum ornatum. DISSECTED BLOOD-LEAVED JAPANESE MAPLE. Leaves very deeply cut, with 5 to 7 pinnatifid lobes, of a deep red color. Beautiful and attractive.

Maple leaves

A. palmatum septemlobum. SEVEN-LOBED JAPANESE MAPLE. Leaves mostly 7-lobed, the divisions broad and serrate, of a glossy green color.

A. pennsylvanicum. MOOSEWOOD. STRIPED MAPLE. A small or medium-sized tree of dense, upright habit. Native of the region from Quebec and the Great Lakes to Georgia and Tennessee. Leaves 3-lobed at the apex, pale rose-color at the time of unfolding, eventually bright green, turning clear yellow in autumn. Bark of the trunk and larger branches striped with broad, pale lines.

A. platanoides. NORWAY MAPLE. A large and handsome tree with spreading branches and a compact round head. Native of Europe. Leaves 5-lobed, remotely toothed, bright green, paler beneath, smooth on both surfaces, fading with tones of yellow and gold. A splendid street tree and equally desirable for lawn or landscape.

A. platanoides cucullatum. CRIMP-LEAVED NORWAY MAPLE. An interesting and beautiful form with rich green leaves, the blades of which are prominently ridged and crimped. The lobes are remarkably short, the points forming the crests of the ridges.

A. platanoides globosum. ROUND-HEADED NORWAY MAPLE. A variety with a remarkably globose, dense head. A vigorous-growing tree. Leaves deep green, pale beneath.

A. platanoides reitenbachi. REITENBACH'S PURPLE MAPLE. A beautiful tree, remarkable for the changing colors of its leaves. In spring the foliage is of a delicate reddish green, in summer a decided dark purple, and in autumn fades with tints of red and purple.

A. platanoides schwedleri. SCHWEDLER'S PURPLE MAPLE. Another handsome tree with color-changing foliage. The vernal leaves are bright purplish and crimson, the summer foliage dark green, fading in autumn with tones of purple, red and brown. A general favorite.

Acer pseudoplatanus. SYCAMORE MAPLE. A large tree of vigorous growth with spreading branches, forming a large oval crown. Native of Europe. Leaves 5-lobed, coarsely toothed, deep green above, glaucous beneath. A handsome species of great hardiness.

A. pseudoplatanus purpurascens. PURPLE SYCAMORE MAPLE. Leaves deep green above, and of a beautiful purplish red color on the lower side. A vigorous and desirable form.

A. rubrum. RED, OR SCARLET MAPLE. A large tree with upright or spreading branches, forming a comparatively narrow, round head. Occurs in a wild state from Quebec and Ontario to Wisconsin and Florida. Leaves 3- to 5-lobed, sharply serrate, light green on the upper, white and more or less pubescent on the lower surface, turning in autumn to brilliant shades of scarlet and orange. Flowers in earliest spring or late winter, bright scarlet or red. Highly valued, and one of the most beautiful trees on account of its early and brilliant flowers, the showiness of its bright red fruit, and finally its gorgeous tints in autumn.

A. rubrum tridens. SMALL-FRUITED RED MAPLE. A more widely branched tree than the type, and usually with a larger crown. Occurs from New Jersey to Texas. Leaves 3-lobed, remotely serrate, dark green above, glaucous and usually pubescent beneath, fading with intense tones of scarlet and gold. Flowers very brilliant, followed by ample clusters of rich, often glowing red fruit, which is smaller and even more highly colored than in the species.

A. saccharinum (*A. dasycarpum*). SILVER MAPLE. A large tree with wide spreading branches and pendulous branchlets. Of wide range, occurring from Canada and Dakota to the Indian Territory and Florida. Leaves deeply 5-lobed, the divisions again lobed and toothed, bright green above, silvery white beneath, turning pale yellow in autumn. The fruit ripens usually before the leaves appear. Widely cultivated and a grand tree.

Maple leaves

A. saccharinum wieri. WIER'S CUT-LEAVED SILVER MAPLE. A beautiful form with deeply cleft and divided leaves. Branches pendulous, often sweeping the ground. A great favorite and of deserved popularity.

A. saccharum. SUGAR, OR ROCK MAPLE. A large stately tree of upright, dense habit, thriving in almost any soil. Grows naturally from Newfoundland and Manitoba to Florida and Texas. Leaves 3- to 5-lobed, dark green on the upper, pale on the lower surface, turning in autumn to brilliant shades of scarlet, orange and yellow. A grand street and lawn tree. This is the tree from which maple sugar is principally made.

A. spicatum. MOUNTAIN MAPLE. A shrub or bushy tree with upright branches. Occurs naturally from the St. Lawrence River to the Saskatchewan, and southward along the Appalachian Mountains to Georgia. Twigs bright red in winter. Leaves 3-lobed, bright green, turning in autumn to shades of orange and scarlet. Fruit bright red in summer. A beautiful Maple.

A. tataricum. TARTARIAN MAPLE. A shrub or small tree with a close round head. Indigenous to Europe and the Orient. Leaves broadly oval, mostly without lobes, the borders serrate. Very distinct.

A. velutinum. VELVETY-LEAVED MAPLE. A handsome tree from the Caucasus. Leaves large, deeply 5-lobed, bright green, soft velvety beneath by the presence of a dense coat of downy hair. Flowers in large erect panicles. One of the rare good trees, and especially valuable in the milder sections.

For grades and prices of above, see pages 136 and 137

Æsculus · The Horse-Chestnuts and Buckeyes

Hardy trees with handsome flowers. The larger species are widely used as shade and street trees, being extremely adaptable to the conditions afforded them They thrive best in moist, loamy soils.

AEsculus glabra. OHIO BUCKEYE. Usually a large tree with spreading branches, occurring from Pennsylvania, Iowa and Kansas, southward to Alabama and Tennessee. Leaves with 5 to 7, usually five leaflets, light green above, paler beneath, turning yellow in autumn. Flowers yellowish, in clusters 5 to 6 inches long. Fruit prickly, enclosing the large seed, or "Buckeye."

AE. hippocastanum. EUROPEAN, OR COMMON HORSE-CHESTNUT. A large tree, usually planted for shade on streets and lawns; native of Europe. Leaves with 5 to 7 leaflets, dark green, turning yellow and brown in autumn. Flowers white, tinged with red, in showy panicles 8 to 12 inches long. Fruit prickly, enclosing the large, attractive seeds. A handsome and hardy tree of great adaptability. Very showy in flower.

AE. hippocastanum flore pleno. DOUBLE-FLOWERED HORSE-CHESTNUT. A form with double flowers of surpassing beauty. Bears no fruit. The flowers are more durable than the single ones, thereby extending the blooming period for several days.

AE. octandra. YELLOW BUCKEYE. A large tree with spreading, sometimes drooping branches, occurring in the mountains from Pennsylvania to Georgia, and westward to Iowa and Texas. Leaves with 5 to 7 leaflets, bright green, turning yellow in autumn. Flowers yellow, borne in panicles 5 to 7 inches long, enclosing the large seeds. A beautiful tree.

AE. parviflora (*A. macrostachya*). LONG-RACEMED HORSE-CHESTNUT. A shrub of great beauty, growing wild from South Carolina and Alabama to Florida. Endures a great deal of cold and is often cultivated in the North. Leaflets 5 to 7, deep green above, tomentose beneath, fading with yellow tones. Flowers creamy white, borne in panicles 10 to 15 inches long. Fruit without prickles; the seeds large. A handsome species when in flower, presenting a charming aspect.

AE. pavia. SMOOTH-FRUITED BUCKEYE. A shrub or small tree growing naturally from Virginia to Missouri, Florida and Texas. Leaflets 5 to 7, deep green, turning yellow in autumn. Flowers purplish red, borne in panicles 4 to 6 inches long; fruit without prickles. Very ornamental and attractive.

AE. rubicunda. RED-FLOWERING HORSE-CHESTNUT. A handsome tree of garden origin. Leaflets mostly five, dark green, fading with tones of yellow; flowers varying in tone from scarlet to red, borne in panicles 6 to 8 inches long. Commonly planted and a great favorite.

Ailanthus · Tree of Heaven

Few trees have the ability to withstand the smoke and gases of towns and cities as well as the Ailanthus. The cramped space often allotted to curb trees is but a slight deterrent to this vigorous species. The fertile plants are quite free from any disagreeable odor at flowering time—an objection sometimes raised against the pollen-bearing or staminate form.

Ailanthus glandulosa. TREE OF HEAVEN. A rapid-growing tree from China. Leaves odd-pinnate, with 13 to 25 leaflets, bright green. Flowers in large panicles, succeeded by dense fruit-clusters which are often very highly colored. Much used for street planting where smoke or dust affects other species.

Albizzia · The Mimosa Tree

The hardiest member of this genus, described below, will stand considerable cold, being hardy as far north as Washington and Memphis. Very ornamental tree with feathery, graceful foliage and showy acacia-like flowers. Thrives in any well-drained soil.

Albizzia julibrissin (*Acacia nemu*). MIMOSA TREE. A tree with spreading branches, forming a low, flat-topped crown. Native of Asia. Leaves compound, consisting of many leaflets, rich green. Flowers borne at the tips of the branches in large heads, pink or light yellow and pink. Everywhere associated with Southern gardens, and, in blossom, remarkably beautiful.

Alnus · The Alders

Hardy, rapid-growing trees, thriving in moist land. They are extremely valuable and ornamental for waterside planting, and, in early spring, the abundant staminate catkins are much admired. The shrubby forms will be found in their respective places under "Deciduous Shrubs."

Alnus glutinosa. EUROPEAN, OR BLACK ALDER. A vigorous and rapid-growing tree, native of Europe and Asia. Leaves dull, dark green, the borders irregularly toothed, turning yellow in autumn. Of great value for planting in cold, damp ground.

A. glutinosa imperialis. CUT-LEAVED ALDER. Leaves deeply cut, the lobes long and narrow. A handsome tree.

A. incana. SPECKLED, OR HOARY ALDER. A large shrub or small tree, depending upon the environment, growing in damp or wet ground. Widely distributed in the Northern Hemisphere; occurring in America from Newfoundland and the Northwest Territory to Pennsylvania and Nebraska. Leaves oval or ovate, finely toothed, dark green above, pale or glaucous and pubescent beneath. Valuable for waterside planting.

A. rugosa. SMOOTH ALDER. A shrub or small tree occurring from Maine to Minnesota, Florida and Texas. Very valuable for planting in low, damp ground, and for waterside planting. Leaves green on both sides, oval in outline, minutely toothed. Flowers in earliest spring or late winter, the staminate ones drooping in long, slender catkins.

Amelanchier · The Service Trees

Ornamental trees of extreme hardiness and floral beauty. They thrive in almost any well-drained fertile soil, and are perhaps seen at their best in small scattered groups with an undergrowth of shrubs. Steep hillsides and banks of streams may be effectively planted with these early-flowering subjects. The shrubby species will be found in their respective places under "Deciduous Shrubs."

Amelanchier botryapium. SERVICE BERRY. A tree with upright or spreading branches, distributed from New Brunswick to Manitoba, southward to Florida and Louisiana. Leaves densely coated with white tomentum at the time of unfolding, dark green at maturity, turning yellow in autumn. Flowers appearing with the leaves, borne on erect or nodding racemes, pure white. Fruit edible, glaucous purple when ripe.

A. canadensis. SHADBUSH. A tree with small spreading branches and slender branchlets, growing from New England to the Gulf States, westward to Missouri. Leaves reddish brown at the time of unfolding, eventually dark green, turning bright yellow in autumn. Flowers appearing with the leaves, in erect or nodding racemes, pure white. Fruit edible, bright red when fully grown, becoming dark purple and glaucous when ripe. A beautiful tree and one of the earliest to bloom.

For grades and prices of above, see page 137

Fruit and flowers of Aralia spinosa

Aralia · The Angelica Trees

Small trees or bushes with handsome compound leaves. Relatively hardy, but require protection from piercing winds in the colder sections of the country. They impart a tropical aspect and are seen at their best in connection with plantations of shrubs or small trees. The larger or tree-like stems are ordinarily surrounded by smaller unbranched shoots which spring up from the ground. A moist fertile soil is best adapted to their requirements. The shrubby species of this genus will be found in their respective places under "Deciduous Shrubs."

Aralia chinensis (*A. mandchurica* and *A. japonica*). CHINESE ANGELICA TREE. A small tree or large shrub with mammoth compound leaves. Native of China and Japan. Flowers creamy white, disposed in numerous umbels, in a large compound panicle. Very ornamental. Generally regarded as the more robust and hardier of the two species here described.

A. spinosa. ANGELICA TREE. HERCULES' CLUB. A small tree or large shrub with stout, prickly stems and compound leaves often 3 to 4 feet long. Grows naturally from Pennsylvania and Missouri to Florida and Texas. Flowers creamy white, in huge panicles, followed by a wealth of dark purple berries.

Asimina · The Pawpaw

This interesting tree is rarely seen in cultivation, although it possesses ornamental qualities. The large leaves and flowers are very attractive. Grows best in moist, rich soil, and is quite hardy. Our stock has been carefully and frequently transplanted.

Asimina triloba. PAWPAW. A low tree or large shrub with spreading branches. Distributed naturally from Ontario to Florida, westward to Michigan and Texas. Leaves ovate, the borders entire, light green on the upper surface, pale beneath, 10 to 12 inches long. Flowers brown or reddish brown, about 2 inches wide, appearing when the leaves are unfolding. Fruit oblong, greenish yellow when fully grown, at maturity dark brown, the flesh sweet and luscious.

Betula · The Birches

Hardy trees of great value. The picturesque trunks, clothed with papery bark, are very ornamental. The white-barked species are remarkably attractive and conspicuous objects, and, by contrast against somber evergreens, the effect may be greatly intensified. They are trees of graceful habit, with slender, often pendulous branches, and grow rapidly in moist, loamy soils.

Betula alba. EUROPEAN WHITE BIRCH. A beautiful tree with white bark and, in age, spreading and pendulous branches. Native of Europe. Leaves ovate, deep green, hanging from slender petioles, fading in autumn with tones of yellow. A graceful and hardy species of drooping habit.

B. alba atropurpurea. PURPLE BIRCH. Leaves dark purple, contrasting strongly with the beautiful white bark.

B. alba fastigiata. PYRAMIDAL WHITE BIRCH. A remarkable form of upright, columnar habit, on the order of the well-known Lombardy Poplar. Tall and formal.

B. alba laciniata pendula. CUT-LEAVED WEEPING BIRCH. A tall tree with gracefully pendulous branches and deeply cut foliage. Bark white when several years old. A superb lawn tree and one universally admired. Highly recommended.

B. alba youngi. YOUNG'S WEEPING BIRCH. A picturesque form of naturally trailing habit, grafted on straight, upright stems. Forms an irregular weeping head of great density.

B. lenta. CHERRY, SWEET or BLACK BIRCH. A tree with aromatic bark, the slender branches eventually spreading and drooping at the tips. Occurs naturally from Canada to the Gulf States, and westward to Illinois and Missouri. Leaves dark green, ovate in outline, the borders sharply serrate, turning bright yellow in autumn. A fragrant oil is distilled from this species, and a beverage known as birch beer made from the sap. A very handsome tree for lawn or landscape.

B. lutea. YELLOW BIRCH. A handsome tree with paper silvery gray, lustrous bark, growing in a wild state from Canada and Northern Minnesota to North Carolina. Branches spreading and pendulous, forming a broad, round head. Leaves ovate, red or bronze at the time of unfolding, at maturity dark green, turning bright yellow in autumn. Splendid as a specimen tree.

B. nigra. RIVER, OR RED BIRCH. A tall tree with a single, or more frequently a divided, trunk, clothed with light reddish brown papery bark. Grows from New England to Florida, and westward to Texas and Wisconsin. Leaves ovate, sharply serrate, deep green and lustrous, turning dull yellow in autumn. Frequently cultivated, and as a picturesque lawn tree, especially those with several stems, most highly esteemed and admired.

B. papyrifera. PAPER, OR CANOE BIRCH. A handsome and very ornamental tree with pendulous branches and creamy white papery bark. Grows from Labrador and the Northwest Territory to New York,

Betula, continued

Michigan and Montana. Leaves ovate, sharply serrate, dark green, turning yellow in autumn. A beautiful tree and one that is freely planted in the North.

B. populifolia. AMERICAN WHITE BIRCH. A small or medium-sized tree with papery, white bark and slender, pendulous branches. Distributed from Nova Scotia and Ontario, southward through New England to Delaware and New York. Leaves nearly triangular, the borders serrate, dark green and lustrous, turning pale yellow in autumn. A graceful but comparatively short-lived tree, thriving in dry, poor soil.

Broussonetia · The Paper Mulberry

A rapid-growing ornamental tree that is cultivated in Asia for paper-making. Thrives best when planted in moist rich soil in sheltered positions. A tree capable of withstanding the deleterious effects of smoke or gases, consequently well adapted to the conditions of smoky towns and cities.

Broussonetia papyrifera. PAPER MULBERRY. A tree with a broad round head commonly cultivated in the Southern States, and capable of withstanding depressions a few degrees below zero. Native of China. Leaves heart-shaped, long-petioled, the borders coarsely toothed, or often deeply lobed. Bark grayish green, blotched with brown.

Carpinus · The Hornbeams

Hardy ornamental trees that thrive in almost any soil or situation. They bear severe pruning without detriment, and both species are remarkably free from the attacks of insects. As specimen trees they are perhaps seen at their best in proximity to water.

Carpinus betulus. EUROPEAN HORNBEAM. A hardy and very ornamental tree with a dense round head. Native of Europe. Leaves ovate-oblong, sharply serrate with impressed veins, fading in autumn with tones of yellow and brown, and remaining on through the winter. Stands clipping remarkably well, and for this reason is often used for tall hedges or pillars to a formal entrance.

C. caroliniana. AMERICAN HORNBEAM. BLUE BEECH. A bushy tree with a dense round head. Distributed from Ontario and Georgian Bay to Florida, and westward to Texas and Minnesota. Leaves ovate-oblong, sharply serrate, dull bluish green above, yellow-green below, turning orange and scarlet in autumn. Makes an attractive specimen tree. Splendid for tall hedges and for clipping to sharp lines. The bark of the trunk strongly resembles that of the Beech.

Castanea

The Chestnuts and Chinquapin

Hardy ornamental trees with pleasing foliage and attractive flowers. In addition to their ornamental qualities, all of the species are more or less valuable for their edible nuts. They grow best in well-drained soils with sunny exposures. The named varieties of the Spanish Chestnut are grafted.

Castanea dentata (*C. americana*). AMERICAN CHESTNUT. A large and beautiful tree with stout, spreading branches, forming a broad, round-topped head. Distributed from New England and the Great Lakes to Georgia and Mississippi. Leaves broadly lanceolate, coarsely serrate, bright green, turning yellow in autumn. Flowers showy, opening in June or July. Nuts sweeter than those of any other variety. A noble shade tree.

C. japonica. JAPANESE CHESTNUT. A small tree with a dense oval crown. Native of China and Japan. Leaves glossy green, long pointed, the margins serrate with bristle-tipped teeth. Fruit very large, the individual nuts over an inch wide. Begins to bear fruit when six or eight years old. The nuts are not so sweet as those of the American Chestnut.

C. pumila. CHINQUAPIN. A large shrub or small round-topped tree, distributed from Pennsylvania to Florida, westward to Arkansas and Texas. Leaves oblong-oval, coarsely serrate, bright green, turning dull yellow in autumn. Flowers showy, appearing in May or June. Fruit usually solitary. Valuable for dry, poor soils.

C. sativa. SPANISH CHESTNUT. A vigorous-growing tree with a broad round head. Native of Europe and Asia. Leaves broadly lanceolate, coarsely serrate, bright green, fading with tones of yellow. Flowers showy, appearing in June. Nuts very large, but inferior in flavor to those of the American Chestnut. A number of horticultural forms are often planted for their profuse crop of large nuts. We have the varieties Paragon and Ridgley, which may be selected if preferred.

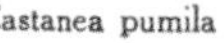

Castanea pumila

Catalpa · The Catalpas

Several of the species of this interesting group have been extensively planted in the Middle and Western States for the durable qualities of their wood, which is used for fence posts and cross ties. As ornamental trees they are very attractive, both on account of the large showy flowers and the long, slender seed-pods. Catalpas thrive in almost any soil which is moist.

Catalpa bignonioides. CATALPA, OR INDIAN BEAN. A tree with showy flowers and stout, brittle branches, forming a broad crown. Native of the Southern States. Leaves large, the borders usually entire, broadly ovate, light green, falling with the first frosts. Flowers, which open in June and July, in large, many-flowered panicles, white with yellow and purple spots, nearly two inches broad. Fruit 10 to 18 inches long, pendent.

C. bignonioides aurea. GOLDEN CATALPA. A form of the last with yellow foliage, contrasting strongly with the greenery of other trees.

C. bignonioides nana (*C. bungei*). ROUND-HEADED CATALPA. A dense round-headed bush, grafted high on a straight, upright stem. Very hardy and effective; much used in formal gardens, having the outlines of the standard Bay Trees.

C. ovata (*C. kæmpferi*). JAPANESE CATALPA. A small tree of great hardiness from China. Leaves heart-shaped, often slightly lobed, bright green, falling after the first frosts. Flowers in large panicles, fragrant, white, with internal spots. Seed-pods long and slender.

C. speciosa. WESTERN CATALPA. A large or medium-sized tree of great hardiness. Distributed from Illinois to Tennessee and Missouri. Naturalized farther South. Leaves oval, mostly entire, dark green, falling after the first frosts. Flowers in May or June, borne in large, comparatively few-flowered panicles, white, with yellow and purple spots, two inches or more broad. Fruit 10 to 18 inches long. Widely planted, both as a timber tree and as an ornamental.

For grades and prices of above, see page 138

Cedrela · The Cedrela Tree

A rapid-growing tree with handsome feathery foliage, introduced in comparatively recent years from China. Thrives best in rich loamy soil.

Cedrela sinensis. CHINESE CEDRELA. A tree with large compound leaves, similar to the Ailanthus, and of equal hardiness. Leaves long-stalked, abruptly pinnate, with 10 to 22 leaflets. Flowers white, in very long pendulous racemes, without odor. An ornamental tree with decidedly tropical aspect, frequently used as a street tree in narrow or smoky thoroughfares.

Celtis · The Nettle Trees

Hardy ornamental trees that thrive in a wide range of soils, but reach their greatest development in moist, loamy situations. In the Middle and Southern States they are successfully used as shade trees, the wide-spreading crowns affording protection to considerable space. They are valuable as specimen trees for the lawn on account of the pleasing color tone of the foliage.

Celtis crassifolia. HACKBERRY. A tree with a graceful broad crown and pubescent twigs, occurring naturally from New York and Kansas to South Carolina and Tennessee. Leaves ovate, rough on the upper surface, the edges serrate, light green, turning yellow in autumn. Fruit reddish purple or nearly black at maturity, resembling a small black cherry.

Pods of Cercis canadensis

C. mississippiensis. SOUTHERN HACKBERRY. A graceful tree with spreading, sometimes pendulous branches, forming a broad, round head. Grows naturally from Illinois to Florida, and westward to Texas and Missouri. Leaves oblong-lanceolate, oblique and long-pointed, mostly entire, dark green. Fruit resembling a diminutive cherry, bright orange-red, with thin dry flesh.

C. occidentalis. NETTLE TREE, OR SUGARBERRY. A handsome tree with stout, spreading, sometimes pendulous branches and glabrous twigs, forming a round-topped crown. Distributed from Quebec and Manitoba, southward to North Carolina and westward to Kansas. Leaves ovate, smooth or nearly so above, the borders sharply serrate, light green and lustrous, fading to tones of yellow in autumn. Fruit nearly black at maturity, like a small cherry.

Cerasus · The Cherry Trees

The bright, cheerful aspect of the Flowering Cherries, which are literally covered with blossoms in early spring, is well known to those who have planted them. No garden is quite complete without these beautiful trees. Besides their ornamental qualities they have the added advantage of attracting birds which feed upon the fruits. Cherries thrive in any fertile soil.

Cerasus avium flore pleno. EUROPEAN DOUBLE-FLOWERING CHERRY. A small tree of garden origin, with double white flowers, produced in spring in great profusion. The flowers are very beautiful, more lasting than any single-flowered Cherry, consequently of great service as cut-flowers. Makes a charming garden tree.

C. hortensis. JAPANESE FLOWERING CHERRY. The famous Flowering Cherry of Japan, so beautifully portrayed in many Japanese scenes. The flowers are very large, pink or blush, opening just as the leaves begin to expand, borne on elongated, often much-branched peduncles. The single forms have a charm not surpassed by the double flowers, and both should be in every garden.

C. hortensis flore pleno. JAPANESE DOUBLE-FLOWERING CHERRY. Similar to the last, with double flowers, resembling little roses. Splendid for cut-flowers, and a great acquisition to any garden.

C. padus. EUROPEAN BIRD CHERRY. A shrub or small tree resembling the Choke Cherry. Native of Europe. Leaves oval, sharply serrate, deep green, fading with tones of yellow and bronze. Flowers in dense drooping racemes, white, appearing in late spring. Fruit the size of a pea, red or purple-black. Very showy.

C. pendula. JAPANESE WEEPING, OR ROSE-BUD CHERRY. A small tree with drooping, crooked branches. Native of Japan. Leaves ovate, very sharply serrate, bright green, fading with tones of yellow. Flowers literally covering the branches, rose-pink, in small clusters, appearing when the leaves begin to unfold. One of the handsomest and perhaps the most picturesque of early-flowering trees. A beautiful and graceful object.

C. pennsylvanica. WILD RED CHERRY. A shapely tree with slender spreading branches, forming a narrow round head. Distributed naturally from Hudson's Bay to North Carolina, and westward to the Rocky Mountains. Leaves oblong-lanceolate, bronze-green at the time of unfolding, eventually bright green and lustrous, turning bright clear yellow in autumn. Flowers appearing with the leaves, white, in 4- to 5-flowered clusters. Fruit light red.

C. serotina. WILD BLACK CHERRY. A graceful tree, the small horizontal branches forming a narrow, oblong head. Occurs from Nova Scotia to Lake Superior, southward to Florida and Texas. Leaves oval, dark green and shining, turning bright yellow before falling. Flowers appearing when the leaves are nearly grown, white, disposed in many-flowered racemes. Fruit almost black when ripe. Excellent for lawn or landscape. As an attraction to birds, the fruits of this species seem unsurpassed, and continue to ripen over a period of several weeks.

C. virginiana. CHOKE CHERRY. A shrub or small tree distributed from Newfoundland to British Columbia, and southward to Georgia and Colorado. Leaves broadly oval or obovate, dark green, turning yellow before falling. Fruit dark purple or nearly black. Handsome when in flower.

Cercidiphyllum · The Kadsura Tree

A genus with a single species, representing one of the most distinct and desirable of the newer acquisitions in ornamental trees. Thrives in a fertile, moist soil. A rapid-growing hardy tree, possessing great beauty, both of outline and foliage.

Cercidiphyllum japonicum. KADSURA TREE. A hardy, compact tree of pyramidal outline, the branches fastigiately disposed, forming a dense mass of foliage. Native of Japan. Leaves purplish at the time of unfolding, eventually light green, fading with tones of yellow and scarlet. A beautiful tree.

For grades and prices of above, see pages 138 and 139

Cercis · The Judas Trees

These beautiful hardy trees are among the showiest of ornamentals, being literally covered with handsome flowers in early spring. They are seen at their best in small groups or colonies with an underplanting of shrubs, although as single specimens on the lawn they are effective and desirable. A moist loamy soil is to be preferred.

Cercis canadensis. RED BUD, OR JUDAS TREE. A small tree with a wealth of floral beauty. Distributed naturally from Ontario to Minnesota and Nebraska, southward to New Jersey, Florida and Texas. Leaves heart-shaped, deep rich green, fading with tones of bright, clear yellow. Flowers produced in early spring, almost concealing the branches, borne in clusters of four to eight, of a beautiful rose-pink color. One of the best of the flowering trees.

C. chinensis (*C. japonica*). ORIENTAL JUDAS TREE. In cultivation, a shrub of great beauty. Native of China and Japan. Leaves heart-shaped, deep green and lustrous, turning yellow in autumn. Flowers in great profusion, in clusters of 5 to 8, rose-pink with a purple cast: pods 3 to 4 inches long. A grand shrub, with beautiful flowers expanding in earliest spring.

C. siliquastrum. EUROPEAN JUDAS TREE. A handsome low tree with a flat spreading crown. Native of Europe. Strikingly beautiful in spring when covered with its numerous bright purplish pink flowers, which appear before the leaves. Leaves heart-shaped, bluish green.

C. siliquastrum album. WHITE-FLOWERING JUDAS TREE. A form with whitish or very light-colored flowers.

Chionanthus · The Fringe Tree

A handsome free-flowering tree that thrives in moist loamy soil. It is relatively hardy, but requires a sheltered position in the colder portions of the country. With a background of evergreens or dark-leaved trees the effect of the showy flowers is much intensified.

Chionanthus virginica. WHITE FRINGE. A shrub or low tree, the stout branches forming an oblong, narrow head. Occurs from Pennsylvania to Florida, westward to Arkansas and Texas. Leaves ovate, dark green, turning yellow early in autumn. Flowers appearing when the leaves are almost grown, white, in loose drooping panicles. Fruit blue, resembling a small plum. The flowers are exceedingly feathery and graceful.

Citrus · The Hardy Orange

The species described below is remarkably hardy, enduring the winters as far north as New York. It thrives best in moist, loamy soil, and in the colder sections should be protected from piercing winds. As specimen plants they are very attractive and invariably incite interest when seen north of the Orange belt. It is a valuable hedge plant for the South and stands clipping remarkably well.

Citrus trifoliata. TRIFOLIATE ORANGE. A small tree with green bark and numerous stout branches armed with strong, sharp thorns. Native of Japan. Flowers white, fragrant, resembling those of the true Orange. Fruit golden yellow, about as large as a walnut. A remarkably attractive ornamental.

Cladrastis · The Yellow-wood Trees

Hardy ornamental trees of graceful habit, with showy flowers and handsome foliage. As specimen trees for the lawn they are invaluable, on account of their flowers and the bright autumnal colors of the foliage. They thrive in almost any soil, reaching their greatest development in moist loam.

Cladrastis amurense (*Maackia amurensis*). MANCHURIAN YELLOW-WOOD A low-spreading tree with compound leaves, native of Manchuria. Leaflets 7 to 11, bright green, turning golden yellow in autumn. Flowers white, borne in long, erect racemes in summer.

C. lutea (*Virgilia lutea*). YELLOW-WOOD. A tree, usually with a divided trunk and numerous widespreading, somewhat pendulous branches, forming a symmetrical, rounded head. Occurs from Kentucky and Tennessee to Alabama and North Carolina; rare and local. Hardy as far north as the Great Lakes and in New England. Leaves compound, with 7 to 9 leaflets, bright green, turning golden yellow in autumn. Flowers white, appearing in early summer, disposed in loose drooping panicles. Wood bright yellow, changing to light brown on exposure. A beautiful lawn tree.

Citrus trifoliata

Cornus · The Dogwoods

Small trees of great hardiness and floral beauty, thriving in almost any soil or exposure. The white-flowering Dogwood, especially, is recommended as one of the showiest of flowering trees. Some of the most enchanting results in ornamental planting are attained by the liberal use of these valuable subjects.

Cornus alternifolia. ALTERNATE-LEAVED DOGWOOD. A shrub or small flat-topped tree, growing naturally from New Brunswick and Minnesota to Georgia. Leaves oval, bright yellow-green, turning yellow and scarlet in autumn. Flowers cream-color, expanding in late spring or early summer, disposed in terminal flat cymes. Fruit bluish black. Very ornamental.

C. florida. WHITE-FLOWERING DOGWOOD. One of the most beautiful flowering trees. A small bushy tree with upright or spreading branches, distributed from New England and Ontario to Florida and Texas. Leaves oval, bright green, turning red or scarlet in autumn. Flowers expanding in spring, the large white petal-like bracts often diffused with pink. Fruit bright scarlet. Indispensable for lawn or landscape.

C. florida pendula. WEEPING DOGWOOD. This graceful form has the same beautiful flowers and fruit as the type, but the branches are pendulous.

C. florida rubra. RED-FLOWERING DOGWOOD. A strikingly beautiful form, especially when planted in contrast with the white-flowered or typical forms. The floral bracts are of a bright pink color.

For grades and prices of above, see page 139

Cratægus punctata
(see page 27)

Cratægus · The Hawthorns

Small trees of great hardiness, thriving in almost any kind of soil. They are extremely ornamental objects, both in flower and fruit, and are successfully used in combination with shrubs, or, in the instance of the larger-growing species, as specimen trees for lawn or landscape. The double-flowered forms are most valuable for cut-flowers and floral decorations.

Crataegus apiifolia. PARSLEY-LEAVED THORN. One of the most distinct of the Thorns. A shrub or small tree distributed from Virginia to Florida, westward to Missouri and Texas. Leaves cleft and deeply incised, bright green, fading with lively tones of yellow and orange. Flowers white, disposed in compound corymbs. Fruit bright scarlet, long persistent.

C. boyntoni. BOYNTON'S THORN. A shrub or small tree with ascending or spreading branches. Native of the mountains of North Carolina and Tennessee. Leaves ovate or oval, the borders serrate and incised, bright green, fading with tones of yellow and bronze. Flowers white, with yellow anthers, disposed in 4- to 10-flowered corymbs. Fruit yellow-green, flushed with red.

C. buckleyi. BUCKLEY'S THORN. A shrub or small tree similar to the last. Flowers white with purple anthers, borne in 3- to 7-flowered corymbs. Fruit red or russet.

C. collina. HILLSIDE THORN. A small tree with spreading branches, forming a symmetrical oval head. Grows naturally in the mountains from Virginia to Georgia and Tennessee. Leaves broadest above the middle, with serrate borders, bright green, fading with yellow tones. Flowers white, borne in large clusters in early spring. Fruit dull red.

C. cordata. WASHINGTON THORN. A small tree with upright branches, forming a round-topped head. Occurs from Virginia to Georgia, westward to Illinois and Missouri. Leaves heart-shaped, serrate and incised, dark shining green, turning orange and scarlet in autumn. Flowers white, the anthers rose-color, borne in compact floriferous corymbs. Fruit scarlet, very lustrous, persisting until the following spring.

Crataegus crus-galli. COCKSPUR THORN. A small tree with very spiny branches and a broad round-topped head. Distributed from Quebec to North Carolina, westward to Michigan. Leaves obovate, dark green and shining, fading with tones of orange and scarlet. Flowers white, in large, compound corymbs. Fruit dull red, persisting until the following spring. Valuable as a specimen tree.

C. monogyna. ENGLISH HAWTHORN. A shrub or small tree with spreading, spiny branches, native of Europe. Leaves ovate, 3- to 7-lobed, bright glossy green. Flowers single, white, borne in compound, many-flowered corymbs. Fruit scarlet, long persistent. The double-flowered forms described below make handsome specimen plants.

C. monogyna alba plena. DOUBLE WHITE HAWTHORN. A shrub or small tree with spreading branches and beautiful double white flowers disposed in branched corymbs. Leaves lustrous green, similar to the species. A most beautiful flowering Thorn.

C. monogyna pauli. PAUL'S DOUBLE SCARLET THORN. The most showy of the double-flowering Thorns. A small tree or large shrub with spreading branches. Flowers bright scarlet, large, full and very double. Leaves as in the type.

C. monogyna punicea. SINGLE PINK HAWTHORN. Resembling the species, but the flowers single, deep red. A vigorous grower, forming a beautiful small tree.

C. oxyacantha. MAY THORN. A shrub or small tree with spreading branches, forming a symmetrical round head. Native of Europe. Leaves broadly ovate, lobed and incisely serrate, deep lustrous green, fading with tones of yellow and red. Flowers single white, disposed in 5- to 10-flowered corymbs. Fruit scarlet, long

For grades and prices of above, see page 139

Cratægus, continued

persistent. This is the May Thorn of England. The beautiful garden Thorns with double flowers will be found under *Cratægus monogyna,* with which this species is often confounded.

C. punctata. LARGE-FRUITED THORN. A tree with stout spreading branches, forming a round or flat-topped head. Grows naturally from Quebec to Georgia, and westward to Illinois and Michigan. Leaves obovate, dull green, turning orange and yellow in autumn. Flowers white, large, borne in compound many-flowered corymbs. Fruit very large, dull red or bright yellow.

C. spathulata. SMALL-LEAVED THORN. A shrub or small tree with spreading branches and a broad head. Distributed from Virginia to Florida, westward to Arkansas and Texas. Leaves wedge-shaped, toothed or lobed, dark shining green. Flowers white, in many-flowered corymbs, the anthers rose-colored. Fruit small, bright scarlet.

C. tomentosa. PEAR HAW. A tree with spreading branches forming a broad flat-topped head. Distributed from New York to North Carolina, Michigan and Missouri. Leaves ovate, serrate and incised, permanently pubescent, turning orange and scarlet in autumn. Flowers white, in broad compound corymbs, the anthers pale rose-color. Fruit pear-shaped or oval, dull red.

Diospyros · The Persimmon Tree

An ornamental tree with handsome shining foliage, thriving in almost any kind of soil. While relatively hardy, it should be afforded protection from piercing winds in the colder sections. A desirable specimen tree for the lawn.

Diospyros virginiana. PERSIMMON. A shapely tree with spreading branches, forming a round-topped crown. Occurs from New England to Florida, westward to Iowa, Missouri and Texas. Leaves oval, dark green and lustrous, the borders entire. Fruit an inch or more in diameter, pale orange-yellow, with a bright cheek when ripe. The flesh is astringent when green, sweet and luscious when fully ripe or frosted.

Fagus · The Beeches

Majestic large trees of extreme hardiness. They are grand and imposing as shade trees for lawn or landscape. Both species thrive in almost any soils, but attain larger proportions when planted in rich sandy loam. The handsome foliage is singularly free from the attacks of insects or fungous diseases.

Fagus americana. AMERICAN BEECH. A large stately tree with smooth gray bark and a broad, compact round-topped head. Distributed from Canada to Florida, and westward to Missouri and Texas. Leaves oblong-ovate, coarsely serrate, dark green, turning bright yellow in autumn. Staminate flowers in globose pendent heads, opening when the leaves are nearly grown. Nuts sweet and rich. Unexcelled for lawn or landscape.

F. sylvatica. EUROPEAN BEECH. A large and beautiful tree with ovate or elliptic, dark green and glossy leaves. Native of Europe. Resembles the foregoing species, but is rather more compact in habit and of slower growth. A grand lawn tree. There are many forms in cultivation, the following being among the best.

F. sylvatica asplenifolia. CUT-LEAVED BEECH. Leaves deeply divided, cut almost to the midrib into numerous narrow segments. A graceful variety, forming a dense low tree.

F. sylvatica macrophylla. BROAD-LEAVED BEECH. Leaves very large, bright green. A splendid, large tree for lawn or landscape.

Fagus sylvatica pendula. WEEPING BEECH. Branches long and pendulous. Foliage deep green. Very picturesque.

F. sylvatica purpurea. PURPLE BEECH. A large tree with purple leaves, lending a strong contrast with the greenery of other vegetation. Makes a fine specimen tree for lawn or garden.

F. sylvatica purpurea pendula. WEEPING PURPLE BEECH. A form with purple leaves and pendulous branches. A favorite with many planters.

F. sylvatica riversi. RIVERS' PURPLE BEECH. Leaves very dark purple, perhaps the most intensely colored form. Makes a large, compact specimen tree.

Fraxinus · The Ash Trees

Hardy trees that thrive in almost any moist, fertile soils. They are valuable for park and landscape planting, and in many localities are satisfactory as street trees. Very rapid-growing, with remarkably straight trunks.

Fraxinus americana. WHITE ASH. A lofty tree with upright or spreading branches, forming a pyramidal or round-topped crown. Distributed from Nova Scotia and Minnesota, southward to Florida and Texas. Leaves compound, with five ovate leaflets, dark green and lustrous above, whitened beneath, fading in autumn with tones of purple and yellow. A beautiful and desirable shade tree.

F. biltmoreana. BILTMORE ASH. A stately tree of medium size with stout ascending or spreading branches, forming a symmetrical round-topped head. Indigenous to the Appalachian region from Virginia and Tennessee to Georgia and Alabama. Leaves compound: leaflets 7 to 9, ovate or lanceolate, dark green and glossy on the upper surface, pale beneath, turning in autumn to various tints of purple and yellow. Twigs velvety on older trees. A distinct and vigorous-growing species, suitable for lawn or landscape.

F. excelsior. EUROPEAN ASH. A tall and handsome tree, native of Europe. Leaves compound: leaflets 9 to 13, ovate or lanceolate, dark green on the upper surface, paler beneath, remaining green until killed by frosts. Makes an attractive specimen tree.

F. excelsior pendula. WEEPING ASH. A form with pendulous branches, grafted on a straight, upright stem. One of the best of the weeping trees.

F. lanceolata (*F. viridis*). GREEN ASH. A tree of medium size with slender, spreading branches forming a shapely round-topped head. Distributed from New

Cratægus crus-galli (see page 26)

For grades and prices of above, see pages 139 and 140

Fraxinus, continued

England and the Rocky Mountains to the Gulf States. Leaves compound, with 7 to 9 leaflets, bright green, fading in autumn with tones of yellow and brown. Often planted in the Middle West for shade and ornament.

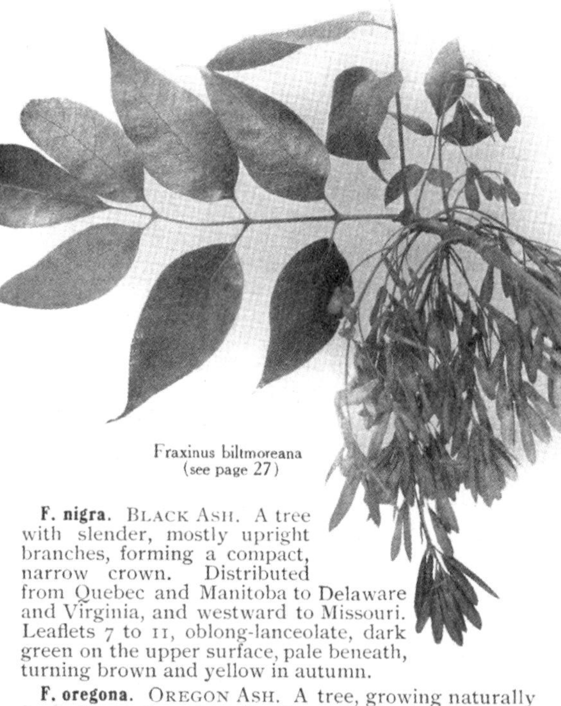

Fraxinus biltmoreana (see page 27)

F. nigra. BLACK ASH. A tree with slender, mostly upright branches, forming a compact, narrow crown. Distributed from Quebec and Manitoba to Delaware and Virginia, and westward to Missouri. Leaflets 7 to 11, oblong-lanceolate, dark green on the upper surface, pale beneath, turning brown and yellow in autumn.

F. oregona. OREGON ASH. A tree, growing naturally from Puget Sound to Southern California, the stout spreading branches forming a broad, symmetrical crown. Leaflets 5 to 7, oval, light green on the upper surface, paler beneath, turning yellow and brown in autumn.

F. ornus. FLOWERING ASH. A small tree, producing dense terminal panicles of fragrant white flowers in May or June. Leaves compound, the leaflets mostly 7, dark green. Very showy.

F. pennsylvanica (*F. pubescens*). RED ASH. A tree forty or fifty feet tall, with stout ascending branches and a compact pyramidal head. Distributed from New Brunswick, Ontario and Dakota, southward to the Gulf States. Leaflets 7 to 9, lanceolate, light green above, pale and pubescent beneath, fading in autumn with tones of yellow and brown. Twigs velvety.

F. quadrangulata. BLUE ASH. A large tree with stout four-angled branchlets. Occurs from Michigan to Missouri, southward to Tennessee and Alabama. Leaves compound: leaflets 5 to 9, lanceolate, bright green, turning to yellow in autumn. An attractive tree.

Gleditsia · The Honey Locusts

Hardy ornamental trees, thriving in almost any kind of soil. They are valuable as individual specimens and as street trees. Planted closely and severely trimmed to formal lines, the American Honey Locust makes an impenetrable hedge.

Gleditsia aquatica. WATER LOCUST. A spiny tree of medium size with a short trunk and spreading branches, forming a flat-topped head. Distributed from Kentucky and Missouri southward to the Gulf. Leaves compound, the leaflets deep green and shining. Pods pendent, in graceful racemes, 1 to 2 inches long, usually one-seeded. Thrives in moist soil.

Gleditsia japonica. JAPANESE LOCUST. A medium-sized tree bearing numerous spiny branches. Native of China and Japan. Leaves compound, the leaflets oblong, dark lustrous green. Pods flat, 10 to 12 inches long, twisted, containing several seeds. A valuable lawn tree.

G. triacanthos. HONEY LOCUST. A large spiny tree with spreading, somewhat pendulous branches forming a broad flat-topped crown. Distributed from Ontario and Minnesota southward to the Gulf States. Leaves compound, the leaflets dark green and glossy, fading pale yellow in autumn. Pods flat, 12 to 18 inches long, pendent, dark brown. A beautiful ornamental tree. Forms an almost impenetrable hedge if closely planted and severely clipped.

G. triacanthos bujoti (*G. bujoti pendula*). WEEPING HONEY LOCUST. A form with slender pendulous branches.

G. triacanthos inermis. THORNLESS HONEY LOCUST. A form of the above of more slender habit, with few if any thorns.

Gymnocladus · The Coffee Tree

The species described below is a stout hardy shade tree that thrives best in a deep loamy soil. Sometimes used as a street tree. The clusters of unopened seed-pods which hang on the trees all winter are both interesting and attractive.

Gymnocladus dioicus (*G. canadensis*). KENTUCKY COFFEE TREE. A large tree with stout, slightly spreading branches, forming a narrow round head. Distributed from Southern Ontario and New York to Michigan, Kansas and Tennessee. Leaves compound, the leaflets ovate, dark green at maturity, turning bright yellow in autumn. Flowers in terminal racemes, nearly white; pods 6 to 10 inches long, reddish brown with a glaucous bloom. An interesting and beautiful tree.

Hicoria · The Hickories

Handsome and hardy trees that are not so extensively planted as their grace and beauty justly warrants. They thrive in almost any kind of soil, but reach their greatest development in moist rich loam. Without doubt among the most handsome trees, with straight tall trunks, crowned with a wealth of lustrous foliage.

Hicoria alba (*Carya tomentosa*). MOCKERNUT, OR BIG BUD HICKORY. A tall tree, the spreading branches forming a round-topped crown. Occurs from Ontario to Florida, westward to Texas and Kansas. Leaves compound, fragrant when bruised, the 5 to 7 leaflets bright green and lustrous, turning golden yellow in autumn. Nuts with thick hard shells and sweet, edible kernels. Very beautiful as the large buds expand in the spring.

Hicoria alba

For grades and prices of above, see page 140

Hicoria, continued

Hicoria glabra (*Carya porcina*). PIGNUT. A tall tree with spreading branches, forming a narrow round-topped head. Distributed from Maine and Ontario to Florida, westward to Texas and Missouri. Leaves compound, the bright green leaflets turning yellow in autumn. Nuts with bitter kernels. Handsome lawn tree.

H. minima (*Carya amara*). BITTERNUT. A large and stately tree with spreading branches, forming a broad crown. Grows naturally from New England, Ontario and Minnesota, southward to Florida and Texas. Leaves compound, with 5 to 9 lanceolate leaflets, dark yellow-green, fading in autumn with tones of yellow and gold. Nuts with a thin shell, the kernel extremely bitter and astringent. A superb tree for the lawn, requiring moist soil.

H. ovata (*Carya alba*). SHAGBARK HICKORY. A tree with a tall, straight trunk and shaggy bark. Branches stout and spreading, forming a narrow round-topped crown. Distributed from Ontario and Quebec to Florida and Texas. Leaves compound, with 5 to 7 leaflets, fragrant when bruised, bright green, turning yellow in autumn. Next to the pecan, the most delicious of the Hickory Nuts. Makes a grand, picturesque shade tree.

H. pecan (*Carya olivæformis*). PECAN. A large tree with spreading branches, forming a broad round-topped head. Grows naturally in the Mississippi basin from Iowa to the Gulf. Leaves compound, with 9 to 15 leaflets, bright green, fading in autumn with tones of yellow. A beautiful tree, cultivated largely for its nuts. Several large-fruited varieties are extensively planted in the South. These forms are all budded on seedling Pecans. The following are among the most desirable:

Bolton. A prolific tree, bearing annual crops of large oval nuts which average about 40 to the pound.

Frotscher's Egg-Shell. A remarkable variety, producing large nuts with very thin shells, averaging about 45 to the pound. Quality unsurpassed.

Pride of the Coast. Very popular and meritorious, producing extremely large nuts.

Stuart. A heavy cropping variety, producing nuts running about 45 to the pound. Valuable.

Van Deman. Nuts large, cracking well, averaging about 45 to the pound. Excellent quality.

Hovenia · The Honey Tree

A genus of but a single species. In addition to the handsome foliage this noteworthy tree is interesting on account of the fleshy, edible fruit-stalks. A rich, loamy soil is best adapted to its requirements.

Hovenia dulcis. HONEY TREE. A very attractive small tree with a symmetrical round head, native of China and Japan. Leaves heart-shaped, bright green and shining, the borders serrate. A desirable tree for lawn or garden in the South.

Ilex · The Deciduous Holly

The chief value of this interesting tree is centered in the bright red berries which literally cover the branches in early winter. It is known as the Bead Tree in the Carolina Mountains, on account of the similarity of its berries to coral beads. Thrives in a moist, loamy soil. The Deciduous Holly is seen at its best in colonies of six to ten trees, where both the pistillate and staminate forms may be closely associated. Other arborescent species will be found described under "Broad-leaved Evergreen Trees."

Ilex monticola. DECIDUOUS HOLLY. A deciduous tree with slender spreading branches, forming a narrow pyramidal crown. Grows naturally from New York to Alabama, along the mountains. Leaves ovate, bright green, fading in autumn with tones of yellow. Berries scarlet.

Juglans · The Walnuts and Butternut

All of the species are valuable objects for lawn or landscape, and, in addition, for their toothsome nuts. The fruits of the Japanese Walnuts are considered superior to those of the native species, and, in localities where the English Walnut is not hardy, are commended to the attention of orchardists. These hardy and ornamental trees thrive in moist, fertile soils.

Juglans cinerea. BUTTERNUT. A large tree with a low round-topped crown. Distributed from New Brunswick and Georgia, west to Dakota and Arkansas. Leaves compound, consisting of 11 to 17 leaflets, bright yellow-green, fading and falling in autumn with tones of yellow and brown. Nuts borne in 3- to 5-fruited drooping clusters, the kernels sweet and edible. An attractive tree for lawn or landscape, or for orchard planting.

Kœlreuteria paniculata (see page 30)

J. cordiformis. HEART-SHAPED JAPANESE WALNUT. A tree with a broad round head, native of Japan. Leaves compound, with 11 to 17 leaflets, bright green, fading with yellow tones. Fruit in pendent clusters, the nuts heart-shaped, much flattened, with thin smooth shells and sweet, edible kernels. A valuable nut tree, and an attractive ornamental.

J. nigra. BLACK WALNUT. A noble tree with a symmetrical round-topped crown. Grows naturally from New England, Ontario and Minnesota, southward to the Gulf States. Leaves compound, with 15 to 23 leaflets, bright yellow-green, turning yellow in autumn. Nuts solitary or in pairs, the kernels sweet and edible. One of the most shapely and beautiful trees, very adaptable and desirable for lawn or landscape, or for orchard planting.

For grades and prices of above, see pages 140 and 141

Juglans, continued

Juglans regia. English Walnut. A tree with a symmetrical round head, native of Europe. Leaves compound, bright green, the 9 to 13 leaflets oblong-ovate. The delicious nuts are everywhere known. Extensively grown in California. Hardy and often productive in the Middle and Southern States. An early-bearing variety, often fruiting when four or five years old, is frequently planted. It is a very much smaller tree than the typical form.

J. sieboldiana. Japanese Walnut. A tree, in habit and foliage similar to *J. cordiformis*. Native of Japan. Nuts somewhat thicker-shelled, not conspicuously flattened, the kernels sweet and edible. Deserves to be widely cultivated, both for nuts and ornament. Perfectly hardy.

Liriodendron tulipifera

Kœlreuteria · The Varnish Tree

Few ornamental trees afford more pleasing combinations with shrub plantations than the beautiful Koelreuteria. Thrives best in rich loamy soil, and is hardy even in the colder regions of the country.

Koelreuteria paniculata. Varnish Tree. A small tree with a handsome round head, twenty or thirty feet tall. Native of China and Japan. Leaves compound, with 8 to 14 ovate, toothed leaflets, reddish purple at the time of unfolding, at maturity bright lustrous green, fading with exquisite tones of yellow, crimson and bronze. Flowers yellow, borne in large terminal panicles, soon followed by clusters of inflated triangular pods. Arranged in groups of three, five or more, most beautiful effects may be obtained, especially with an underplanting of early-flowering shrubs. We recommend the Kœlreuteria with extreme confidence.

Laburnum · The Golden Chain Trees

Ornamental trees with handsome pea-shaped flowers, borne in long, drooping racemes, and described by Cowper as "rich in streaming gold." They thrive best in moist fertile soil, and are more luxuriant in the North than in the South.

Laburnum alpinum. Scotch Laburnum. A small tree or large shrub of irregular outline, generally regarded as the hardiest of the Laburnums. Native of the mountains of Southern Europe. Branches erect, clothed with pale green compound leaves. Flowers showy, yellow, borne in slender drooping racemes. Blossoms about a fortnight later than the common Golden Chain, and is, on this account, a desirable adjunct to the list of flowering trees.

L. vulgare (*Cytisus laburnum*). Golden Chain. A small tree with erect or ascending branches, forming a narrow head. Native of Southern Europe. Leaves compound, consisting of three leaflets of a beautiful green color. Flowers yellow, borne in silky drooping racemes. This is the Bean Tree of European gardens. Very few indeed of the flowering trees can surpass in splendor the Golden Chain, when, in late spring, it is a mass of graceful pendent blossoms—the attraction of busy bees and butterflies.

L. watereri (*L. parksi*). Parks' Golden Chain. An interesting small tree of garden origin, nearly as hardy as the Scotch Laburnum. Leaves compound, consisting of three leaflets, bright green and lustrous. Flowers yellow, borne in long and slender racemes in great profusion in early summer. A distinct and valuable addition to the list of ornamentals.

Liquidambar · The Sweet Gum

A picturesque tree thriving in almost any soil, but reaching its greatest development in moist rich loam. Of inestimable value to the planter in the Middle and Southern States. Farther North it should be planted in protected situations.

Liquidambar styraciflua. Sweet Gum. A shapely tree with slender corky-ridged branches, forming a pyramidal head. Distributed in nature from Connecticut to Missouri, southward to the Gulf States. Leaves deeply 5- to 7-lobed, with pointed serrate divisions, of starry aspect. They are bright green and lustrous at maturity, in autumn fading with tones of crimson, unsurpassed in brilliancy by any other tree. The remarkably straight trunks and symmetrical outlines of this beautiful species have won many admirers, especially when clothed in the glowing colors of autumn.

Liriodendron · The Tulip Tree

A hardy, rapid-growing tree of great adaptability. For lawns and avenues this tree is unsurpassed, both on account of its handsome foliage and the large tulip-like flowers. Grows best in deep rich soil, and succeeds best when transplanted in the spring.

Liriodendron tulipifera. Tulip Tree. A large and stately rapid-growing tree with a narrow pyramidal crown. Occurs from New England and the southern region of the Great Lakes, westward to Missouri and southward to the Gulf. Leaves 4-lobed, bright green and lustrous, turning yellow in autumn. Flowers cup-shaped, resembling a Tulip, greenish yellow blotched with orange. A handsome tree, and one that is deserving of the highest esteem of planters. The lumber that is made from this tree is known as whitewood in the Middle West, and as poplar and yellow poplar in the East and South.

For grades and prices of above, see page 141

Magnolia · The Magnolias

No group of trees contains such a wealth of floral treasures. Every species is characterized by large and showy flowers; some blossoming in earliest spring before the leaves appear, others when the foliage is almost fully grown. The Asiatic species are perhaps the showiest of all flowering trees. Hardy and durable, thriving in rich loamy soil. The evergreen species will be found under "Broad-leaved Evergreen Trees."

Magnolia acuminata. CUCUMBER TREE. A pyramidal tree with spreading or ascending branches. Distributed from New York to Georgia, westward to Illinois and Arkansas. Leaves deciduous, oblong, bright green, turning yellow in autumn. Flowers expanding in May or June, greenish yellow, 2 to 3 inches long, with upright petals. Fruit rosy red, 2 to 3 inches long, the seeds scarlet. A most valuable hardy shade tree.

M. conspicua. YULAN. A very showy tree literally covered with flowers in early spring. Native of China and Japan. Leaves obovate, bright green, 4 to 7 inches long, appearing after the flowers. Flowers sweet-scented, pure white, about 6 inches across. A grand lawn or garden tree. Usually branched very low.

M. fraseri. FRASER'S MAGNOLIA. A handsome tree with spreading or ascending branches, forming a pyramidal crown. Grows naturally in the mountains from Virginia and Tennessee to Georgia and Alabama. Leaves deciduous, obovate, auriculed at the base, bright green. Flowers creamy white, sweet-scented, 6 to 8 inches in diameter. Fruit 3 to 4 inches long, rose-red. A hardy tree of great merit.

M. glauca. SWEET, OR WHITE BAY. A slender tree or large shrub, evergreen in the South. Distributed from Massachusetts to Florida, near the coast, and westward to Texas. Leaves oblong or oval, green and lustrous on the upper surface, pale or nearly white beneath. Flowers creamy white, fragrant, cup-shaped, 2 to 3 inches across, blossoming for several weeks in spring or early summer. Fruit dark red, with scarlet seeds.

M. kobus. JAPANESE MAGNOLIA. A narrow, pyramidal tree with short and slender branches. Native of Japan. Leaves obovate, deep green, 3 to 5 inches long. Flowers pure white, appearing before the leaves, 4 to 5 inches across. One of the hardiest of the early-flowering species. Our strain is from an unusually floriferous type.

M. macrophylla. GREAT-LEAVED MAGNOLIA. A symmetrical tree with stout, widespreading branches forming a wide-topped head. Distributed from Kentucky to Florida, westward to Arkansas and Louisiana. Leaves very large, 20 to 30 inches long, 9 to 10 inches wide, bright green above, silvery gray beneath. Flowers creamy white, fragrant, 10 to 12 inches across. Fruit 2 to 3 inches long, rose-color. A beautiful and distinct hardy tree.

M. obovata (*M. purpurea and M. discolor*). PURPLE MAGNOLIA. In cultivation usually a large shrub with erect branches. Native of China and Japan. Leaves obovate, dark green, expanding after the flowers have fallen. Flowers large, cup-shaped, purple outside, nearly white within. One of the latest to bloom.

M. soulangeana. SOULANGE'S MAGNOLIA. A large shrub or small tree of garden origin and regarded as a hybrid between *M. obovata* and *M. conspicua.* Leaves obovate, dark green, expanding after the flowers have fallen. Flowers large, cup-shaped, white, more or less suffused with rose or pink, fragrant. Very hardy and showy. The following forms are all distinct and desirable.

M. soulangeana lennei. LENNE'S MAGNOLIA. Flowers deep crimson on the outside, very large; later than the foregoing.

M. soulangeana nigra. DARK-FLOWERED MAGNOLIA. Flowers dark purple on the outside.

M. soulangeana norbertiana. NORBERT'S MAGNOLIA. Flowers more deeply tinted and much later than *M. soulangeana.*

Magnolia soulangeana speciosa. SHOWY-FLOWERED MAGNOLIA. Almost identical in color with *M. soulangeana,* but blossoms later.

M. stellata. STARRY MAGNOLIA. A large shrub or small tree with spreading branches. Native of Japan. Leaves obovate, dark green, expanding after the flowers have fallen. Flowers very numerous, white, about three inches across, sweet-scented, the petals eventually reflexed. A hardy free-flowering plant with a wonderful wealth of starry flowers in earliest spring. Very highly recommended.

Magnolia acuminata

M. thompsoniana. THOMPSON'S SWEET BAY. A shrub or small tree of garden origin, resembling *M. glauca.* Leaves oblong or oval, bright green above, whitened beneath. Flowers fragrant, white, 5 to 6 inches across. A favorite garden plant, and quite hardy.

M. tripetala. UMBRELLA TREE. A tree with stout, irregular branches, sometimes 30 to 40 feet tall. Grows naturally from Pennsylvania to Alabama, westward to Arkansas. Leaves 10 to 20 inches long, 6 to 8 inches wide, bright green, or the younger with ruddy tints. Flowers creamy white, 8 to 10 inches across, expanding in late spring. Fruit rose-color, 3 to 4 inches long. Very attractive.

For grades and prices of above, see page 141

Malus · The Flowering Crab Apples

Handsome small trees, literally covered in spring with showy, sweet-scented flowers. They are very hardy, and thrive in almost any kind of soil. As specimen trees for garden and lawn they are both ornamental and desirable.

Malus angustifolia. NARROW-LEAVED CRAB. A small tree with a short trunk and rigid, spiny, spreading branches, forming a broad and usually symmetrical head. Occurs naturally from Pennsylvania to Florida, westward to Louisiana and Tennessee. Leaves oblong or lanceolate, dark glossy green, fading with tones of yellow and bronze. Flowers very fragrant, pink or rose, borne in numerous small clusters. Fruit globose, an inch or less in diameter, often used for preserves. Very beautiful and floriferous. Rarely cultivated, but one of the very best.

M. baccata. SIBERIAN FLOWERING CRAB. A small tree with spreading branches, forming a symmetrical, close head. Distributed from Siberia and Manchuria to the Himalayas. Leaves ovate, bright green, turning yellow in autumn. Flowers appearing with the leaves, on long and slender pedicels, white or slightly pink, fragrant. Fruit about the size of a cherry, yellow or ruddy. Hardy and beautiful.

M. coronaria. WILD CRAB-APPLE. A small tree with spreading spiny branches, forming a symmetrical round head. Distributed from Ontario to Alabama, and from New York to Missouri. Leaves ovate or heart-shaped, incisely serrate, ruddy bronze at the time of unfolding, at maturity bright green, turning yellow or bronze in autumn. Flowers very fragrant, pink or rose-color, produced in 5- to 6-flowered clusters. Fruit yellow-green, fragrant, waxy and translucent at maturity. Frequently used for making preserves. A handsome free-flowering tree.

M. floribunda. FLOWERING CRAB. A shrub or small tree with a symmetrical crown. Native of Japan. Leaves ovate, appearing with the flowers, bright green and lustrous, fading with tones of yellow and bronze. Flowers rose or rose-red, produced in great profusion; fragrant. Fruit red, about the size of a pea, on long, slender pedicels. A grand specimen plant and one of the best of the spring-flowering trees. Should be included in every collection.

M. floribunda parkmani (*M. halleana*). PARKMAN'S CRAB. A form with beautiful semi-double rose-colored flowers.

M. floribunda schiedeckeri. DOUBLE-FLOWERING CRAB. Flowers double, bright rose, of great substance and durability. Splendid for cut-flowers.

M. ioensis bechteli. BECHTEL'S DOUBLE-FLOWERING CRAB. A shrub or small tree with spreading or ascending branches, forming a wide head. Leaves ovate or oval, dark green and lustrous on the upper surface, paler and pubescent beneath, turning yellow in autumn. Flowers large and very double, resembling small roses, of a delicate pink or blush color; fragrant. One of the most remarkable of Double-flowering Crabs, and worthy of a place in any garden.

M. spectabilis. CHINESE FLOWERING CRAB. A small tree with a symmetrical, broad crown, native of China. Leaves oval or oblong, bright green and smooth at maturity, turning yellow in autumn. Flowers coral-red in the bud; when fully expanded, lighter in color. Fruit reddish yellow. A hardy and handsome early-flowering tree.

M. spectabilis riversi. DOUBLE-FLOWERING CHINESE CRAB. Flowers very large, semi-double, bright rose-red. A grand flowering tree.

M. toringo. TORINGO, OR DWARF CRAB. A dwarf tree with white or pinkish flowers. Native of Japan. Leaves bright green, fading in autumn with tones of yellow and orange. Fruit small, about the size of a pea. Very attractive in spring and literally covered with flowers of surpassing beauty.

Melia · The China Tree

Extensively cultivated in the South and, indeed, inseparably associated with the garden aspects of that region. These rapid-growing trees thrive in almost any soil and may be safely planted as far north as Washington and Memphis.

Melia azederach. PRIDE OF INDIA. CHINA TREE. A rapid-growing tree widely naturalized in the South, originally introduced from Persia and India. Leaves compound, deciduous, the leaflets bright green, retained until late in autumn. Flowers in large, graceful panicles, fragrant, lilac-colored, opening usually in April. Berries yellowish, translucent, largely sought by birds. A beautiful shade tree.

M. azederach umbraculiformis. TEXAS UMBRELLA TREE. A distinct form of the China Tree with a dense, spreading, umbrella-like head. Very formal and symmetrical in outline, and of rapid growth. Highly prized as a shade tree.

Mespilus · The Medlar

A hardy tree thriving in almost any kind of soil. In many respects the Medlar resembles the Quince, but is more ornamental. It is an interesting subject for the garden, commanding attention and comment wherever seen.

Mespilus germanica. MEDLAR, OR MESPIL. A small bushy tree, often grown in the Old World for its acid fruits. Native of Europe. Flowers large, white, expanding in late spring and after the leaves are fully grown. An interesting object, but rarely seen in cultivation.

Mohrodendron · The Silver Bell Trees

Trees with showy flowers in early spring, thriving in rich moist loam. The Silver Bell is hardy in the North, but the Snowdrop Tree needs protection from cold winds north of Philadelphia or Memphis. Splendid for planting in proximity to water or as specimen plants for the lawn.

Mohrodendron carolinum (*Halesia tetraptera*). SILVER BELL. A tree with a narrow crown, the short, stout branches bearing a wealth of drooping white flowers in early spring. Grows naturally from West Virginia and Illinois, southward to Florida and Texas, attaining its maximum development in the high mountains of North Carolina. Leaves oval, finely serrate, bright green, turning pale yellow in autumn. A beautiful flowering tree. Fruit with four papery wings.

M. dipterum (*Halesia diptera*). SNOWDROP TREE. A small tree or large shrub with spreading branches, forming a low wide head. Distributed from South Carolina and Florida to Arkansas and Texas. Leaves ovate, slightly serrate, bright green, turning pale yellow in autumn. Flowers white, about an inch long, opening in early spring. Fruit with two papery wings. Commonly cultivated in the South.

Morus · The Mulberries

Hardy ornamental trees thriving in almost any soil. The sweet fleshy fruits are a great attraction to birds, and on this account they have been extensively planted in many house-grounds and gardens.

Morus alba. WHITE MULBERRY. A rapid-growing tree with spreading and ascending branches, forming a broad and dense round-topped crown. Native of China. Leaves ovate, bright green and lustrous, variously lobed and divided. Fruit 1 to 2 inches long, white or violet, sweet and edible. Has been cultivated from time immemorial, chiefly for feeding silkworms.

For grades and prices of above, see pages 141 and 142

Morus, continued

Morus alba pendula. TEA'S WEEPING MULBERRY. A weeping form grafted on straight stems. The branches are long and slender, drooping to the ground. One of the most vigorous and hardy of weeping trees.

M. alba tatarica. RUSSIAN MULBERRY. A very hardy type of *M. alba* introduced into the Western States by the Russian Mennonites. A low-growing tree with an intricately branched crown. The leaves are small and much lobed. Extensively planted in the West.

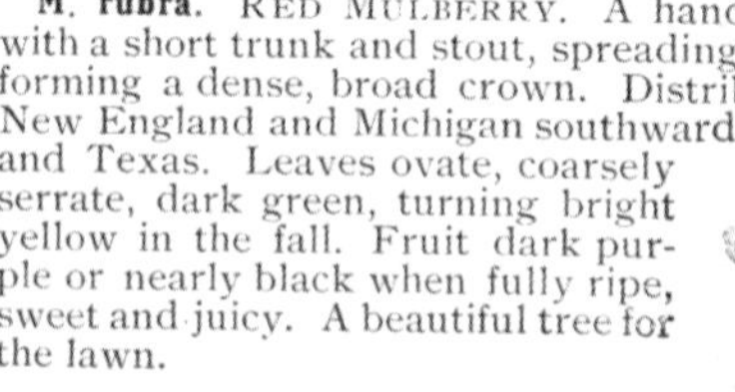

M. rubra. RED MULBERRY. A handsome tree with a short trunk and stout, spreading branches, forming a dense, broad crown. Distributed from New England and Michigan southward to Florida and Texas. Leaves ovate, coarsely serrate, dark green, turning bright yellow in the fall. Fruit dark purple or nearly black when fully ripe, sweet and juicy. A beautiful tree for the lawn.

Nyssa

The Tupelo and Gum Trees

Hardy picturesque trees chiefly valued for the flaming tones of their autumn foliage. They thrive best in proximity to water or in moist loamy soil. The drooping habit of the Sour Gum is greatly admired.

Nyssa aquatica. COTTON GUM. A tall tree with relatively small spreading branches, forming a pyramidal crown. Occurs from Virginia to Florida, westward to Illinois and Texas. Leaves dark green and lustrous above, downy pubescent beneath, turning orange and red in autumn.

N. sylvatica. TUPELO, OR SOUR GUM. A tree with slender, more or less pendulous branches, forming a round-topped crown. Grows naturally from Maine to Florida, westward to Missouri and Texas. Leaves oval or obovate, the margins entire, dark green and shining, fading in autumn with gorgeous tones of red and scarlet. Fruit dark blue. The autumnal coloring of this shapely tree commends it to many planters.

Oxydendrum arboreum

Oxydendrum · The Sourwood

A handsome hardy tree of inestimable value. As a specimen tree for the lawn, or with an undergrowth of shrubs, the beautiful Sourwood is always an object of admiration. Thrives in any soil.

Oxydendrum arboreum. SOURWOOD. A small tree with slender spreading branches, forming a narrow crown. Grows naturally from Pennsylvania and Indiana to Florida and Louisiana. Leaves lanceolate, bright green, fading in autumn with dazzling tones of scarlet. Flowers borne in panicles of spreading racemes, resembling Lily-of-the-valley flowers, pure white and slightly fragrant. Beautiful in floral aspect but of greater charm in autumn by reason of the intense coloring of the foliage. One of the really fine ornamentals.

Parrotia

The Persian Ironwood

This charming little tree is seldom seen in cultivation, although relatively hardy and adapted to any well-drained soil. Especially attractive in autumn by reason of the intense coloring of the foliage.

Parrotia persica. PERSIAN IRONWOOD. A small tree or large shrub with spreading branches. Native of Persia. Leaves oval or obovate, coarsely toothed, dark green, fading in autumn with brilliant tones of yellow, orange and scarlet. Flowers in dense heads in early spring, with pendulous purple anthers.

Ostrya · The Ironwood

In cultivation an attractive small tree with peculiar furrowed and scaly bark, thriving in rich loamy soils. The hop-like fruits, which are borne in profusion, are both noteworthy and interesting.

Ostrya virginiana. HOP HORNBEAM, OR IRONWOOD. A slender tree with long branches drooping at the tips and forming a round-topped crown. Occurs naturally from Quebec to Dakota, southward to Florida and Texas. Leaves oval, bright green, turning yellow in autumn. Fruiting clusters resembling hops. An interesting tree.

Paulownia

The Empress Tree

A remarkable tree, both on account of its handsome flowers and exceedingly large leaves. During the winter the clusters of flower-buds for the ensuing year, together with the seed-pods of the past season, hang side by side, and impart a peculiar aspect. Thrives best in a moist rich loam, and in the North should be protected from cold winds.

Paulownia imperialis. EMPRESS TREE. A tree with stout spreading branches, forming a round-topped crown. Native of China and Japan. Leaves very large, heart-shaped, the margins usually entire. Flowers pale violet, disposed in large, erect panicles. One of the showiest of flowering trees, but not entirely hardy north of Massachusetts and Missouri. It has been successfully used in the South as a street tree, where it withstands admirably the effects of smoke and dust.

For grades and prices of above, see page 142

Persica · The Flowering Peach

No garden is complete without one or more trees of the beautiful double-flowered forms of the Peach. They thrive in almost any soil and may be grown wherever the typical form is hardy.

Persica vulgaris alba plena. DOUBLE WHITE-FLOWERING PEACH. A double white-flowering form of the common Peach. Not only do the Flowering Peaches make beautiful garden objects, but they are very valuable as cut-flowers.

P. vulgaris rosea plena. DOUBLE ROSE-FLOWERING PEACH. A form of the Peach with beautiful double rose-colored flowers. A charming spring-flowering tree.

Phellodendron · The Chinese Cork Tree

A hardy rapid-growing tree thriving in any well-drained soil. It has been successfully used as a street tree in the Southwest, where it resists both heat and drought.

Phellodendron amurense. CHINESE CORK TREE. A tree with corky bark and spreading branches, forming a round-topped crown. Native of China and Japan. Leaves compound, odd-pinnate, with 7 to 17 dark green leaflets. Fruit black, emitting a strong odor like turpentine when crushed. Of rapid growth and very hardy.

Platanus · The Plane Trees

Rapid-growing hardy trees of great adaptability, but thriving best in moist loam. The two species described are very much alike to the casual observer, but the American species may be recognized by the single "buttons" drooping on their long stalks.

Platanus occidentalis

Platanus occidentalis. BUTTONWOOD, OR AMERICAN PLANE. A large and lofty tree with massive branches, forming a wide head. Distributed from New England and Ontario to Kansas, southward to Florida and Texas. Leaves shallowly lobed, the borders toothed, bright green at maturity, borne on stout petioles which encase the winter buds at their bases. Flowers and fruit pendulous, the latter about an inch in diameter. A rapid-growing and very beautiful tree, with picturesque white or gray bark.

P. orientalis. ORIENTAL PLANE. A large and massive tree with a very wide round-topped head. Native of Europe and India. Bark whitened, exfoliating, lending a picturesque aspect, especially in winter. Leaves 5- to 7-lobed, bright green, the petioles encasing the winter buds. Fruiting heads 2 to 4, on long pendent stalks. Cultivated from time immemorial, and today one of the best street trees known. Very hardy.

Populus · The Poplars and Aspens

Rapid-growing trees of great hardiness, extensively used for windbreaks, street trees and ornamental planting. They thrive in almost any soil, but attain their greatest proportions in moist rich loam. They are beautiful objects in spring, with long, drooping catkins, and also attractive throughout the growing season by reason of their trembling leaves.

Populus alba. WHITE POPLAR. ABELE. A large and intricately branched tree with whitish bark. Native of Europe and Asia. Leaves broadly ovate, the margins toothed, green above, white woolly beneath. Flowers in pendent catkins in early spring.

P. alba bolleana. BOLLE'S SILVER POPLAR. A tall columnar tree of formal aspect, the leaves deeply 3- to 5-lobed, silvery white beneath. Resembles the Lombardy Poplar, and, like it, is useful for formal gardens or architectural effects.

P. alba nivea. SILVER POPLAR. A form of the White Poplar with 3- to 5-lobed leaves, the under surface being snow-white.

P. balsamifera. BALSAM POPLAR. A tall tree with stout, erect branches forming a narrow pyramidal head. Distributed from Labrador to Alaska, southward to New England, New York, Minnesota and Nevada. Leaves ovate-lanceolate, finely serrate, dark green and shining above, pale green or dull white beneath, borne on slender round petioles. Flowers in catkins in early spring. Often planted for the delightful resinous odor of the buds.

P. candicans. BALM OF GILEAD. A handsome tall tree with spreading branches, forming a comparatively broad crown. Of uncertain origin, but probably native of the region of Lake Michigan. Frequently planted for its hardiness and rapidity of growth and the resinous fragrance of its buds. Leaves ovate, coarsely serrate, dark green above, white or rusty white beneath, borne on pubescent, round petioles. Flowers in catkins in early spring.

P. carolinensis. CAROLINA POPLAR. A symmetrical and very rapid-growing tree, making an upright or pyramidal head. Closely related to and resembling *P. deltoidea*, but the leaves are more tapering at the apex, and the habit of growth is quite distinct. The most popular and widely planted species.

P. deltoidea. COTTONWOOD. A large, much-branched tree with a graceful broad crown. Distributed from Quebec to the Rockies, southward to Florida. Leaves large, triangular, coarsely toothed, bright green and lustrous, borne on slender flattened petioles. Flowers in early spring, disposed in pendulous catkins. One of the best for ornamental planting.

For grades and prices of above, see pages 142 and 143

Populus, continued

Populus deltoidea vangeerti. VAN GEERT'S GOLDEN POPLAR. A form with yellow foliage. One of the best of yellow-leaved trees, generally holding its color throughout the growing season.

P. grandidentata. LARGE-TOOTHED ASPEN. A tree with stiff but slender branches, forming a round-topped crown. Distributed from Nova Scotia to Minnesota, southward to Delaware and Iowa, and in the Alleghany Mountains to North Carolina and Tennessee. Leaves ovate, coarsely toothed, dark green, borne on slender flattened petioles. Flowers in drooping catkins in early spring.

P. nigra fastigiata. LOMBARDY POPLAR. A tall columnar tree of picturesque and very formal aspect. One of the characteristic trees of Lombardy and other parts of Italy. Widely planted; a very rapid-growing and hardy tree. Leaves triangular, the borders serrate, dark green, borne on flattened petioles, moving freely in the wind.

P. tremula. EUROPEAN ASPEN. A tree with ascending or spreading branches, forming an open pyramidal head. Widely distributed in Europe and Asia. Leaves oval or nearly round, dark green above, whitened beneath, the margins toothed, borne on slender flattened petioles, moving or trembling with the slightest current of air. Flowers in great profusion in early spring, borne in long pendent catkins. Blossoms before other varieties of the Poplars and on this account, when growth is anxiously looked for, is much esteemed.

P. tremula pendula. WEEPING EUROPEAN ASPEN. The best weeping tree among the Poplars. Branches long and very pendulous, making a tree of much grace. Grafted on straight, erect stems.

P. tremuloides. AMERICAN ASPEN. A tree with slender, somewhat pendulous branches, forming a narrow round head. Distributed from Labrador to Alaska, southward to Pennsylvania, Missouri, New Mexico and California. Leaves ovate, serrate, dark green, borne on slender flattened petioles, moving with the slightest currents of air. Flowers in drooping catkins in early spring.

Prunus · The Plums

Hardy trees of great beauty, thriving in almost any soil. The Wild Plum is successfully used in groups or colonies in conjunction with shrubs, and occasionally is seen as a specimen tree on the lawn. The Purple-leaved Plum is especially adapted for use in formal gardens and in producing striking foliage effects.

Prunus americana. WILD PLUM. A small tree with an intricately branched broad head. Distributed from New York to Florida, westward to Montana and Texas. Leaves oval or obovate, finely serrate, dark green and rugose, turning yellow and bronze in autumn. Flowers appearing in early spring, white, produced in great profusion. Fruit nearly round, three-quarters of an inch wide, reddish. Very showy when in flower, and frequently cultivated as an ornamental.

P. pissardi. PURPLE-LEAVED PLUM. A handsome small tree of garden origin, with purple foliage. Very hardy and retaining its color throughout the summer. In spring the blush-pink flowers are borne in great profusion, harmonizing with the color tone of the unfolding leaves. One of the best of purple-leaved trees, the hot sun not affecting the leaves.

Ptelea · The Hop Trees

Small hardy trees thriving in any well-drained soil. They are interesting objects on account of the clusters of wafer-like seeds. Most effective when planted in groups or colonies.

Ptelea trifoliata. HOP TREE, OR WAFER ASH. A small round-headed tree, or more frequently a large shrub, with short spreading or erect branches. Occurs naturally from Ontario to Florida, and westward to Minnesota and Texas. Leaves compound, the three ovate or oblong leaflets dark green and lustrous, turning yellow in autumn. Flowers greenish white, in compound cymes, appearing in spring. Fruit wafer-like, the seed surrounded by a papery marginal wing. Frequently planted in parks and gardens.

P. trifoliata aurea. GOLDEN HOP TREE. Foliage golden yellow, the bright color retained throughout the summer.

Pods and buds of Paulownia imperialis (see page 33)

Pterocarya · The False Walnut

A rapid-growing tree with large compound leaves and long pendulous racemes of curious winged fruits. It thrives best in rich, moist soil, and is hardy as far north as Missouri and Massachusetts.

Pterocarya fraxinifolia. FALSE WALNUT A handsome tree with spreading branches, frequently with several stems from the base, native of Western Asia. Leaves rich dark green, consisting of 11 to 25 leaflets. Fruits light green, drooping in graceful racemes 12 to 15 inches long. Rare and interesting.

Pterostyrax · The Japanese Silver Bell

A handsome ornamental tree closely related to the Halesias. It thrives best in moist sandy loam, and needs protection from cold winds in the North. In the Middle and Southern States, where it is quite hardy, it is justly prized for its wealth of showy flowers.

Pterostyrax hispida (*Halesia hispida*). JAPANESE SILVER BELL. A small tree with graceful spreading branches, forming a narrow head. Native of Japan. Leaves oblong, light green above, pale beneath, turning yellow in autumn. Flowers fragrant, creamy white, resembling the Deutzias, borne in drooping panicles early in summer. Fruit covered with bristly hairs.

For grades and prices of above, see page 143

Quercus · The Oak Trees

These hardy long-lived trees are among the most majestic and picturesque of all arborescent species. No lawn or landscape is complete without them, and, fortunately, there are species adapted to every quarter of the country. Oaks thrive in any soil, but, in common with other trees, attain their greatest proportions in a fertile substratum.

Quercus alba. WHITE OAK. A tall majestic tree with a broad round-topped crown. Distributed from Maine to Minnesota, southward to Florida and Texas. Leaves mostly divided into seven lobes, the larger segments usually shallowy lobed. They are highly colored with red at the time of unfolding, soon becoming silvery white, at maturity bright green above, pale or glaucous beneath, fading in autumn with rich tones of purple and vinous red and tardily separating from the branches, sometimes not until spring. One of the finest Oaks for lawn or landscape, attaining great age.

Q. cerris. TURKEY OAK. A handsome tall tree with short spreading branches, forming a broad pyramidal head. Native of Europe and Asia. Leaves divided, with 3 to 8 pairs of entire or few-toothed lobes, dark green, fading in autumn without bright color effects, and persisting on the branches sometimes until spring. Acorn brown, embraced for half of its length by the large mossy cup. Winter buds surrounded by thread-like scales. Of rapid, vigorous growth.

Q coccinea. SCARLET OAK. A beautiful tree with spreading branches forming a conical or comparatively narrow crown. Occurs in nature from New England and Minnesota to North Carolina and Nebraska. Leaves mostly 7-lobed, the divisions toothed near their apices. They are bright red at the time of unfolding, at maturity bright green and very lustrous, turning brilliant scarlet in the autumn. A tree valued chiefly for its gorgeous autumn tints. Very symmetrical in outline.

Q. digitata (*Q. falcata*). SPANISH OAK. A handsome tree with stout spreading branches, forming a very broad round-topped crown. Distributed from New Jersey to Florida, westward to Missouri and Texas. Leaves 3- to 7-lobed, the terminal lobe usually elongated, dark green and shining on the upper surface, rusty pubescent beneath, turning orange or brown in autumn. Acorn yellow-brown, enclosed only at the base in the thin cup. A superb lawn tree.

Quercus alba

Q. imbricaria. SHINGLE OAK. A symmetrical tree with horizontal somewhat drooping branches, forming a round-topped crown. Occurs naturally from Pennsylvania to Georgia, westward to Wisconsin and Arkansas. Leaves oblong, broadest above the middle, dark green and shining, turning in autumn to tones of orange, red and yellow. Acorn dark brown, slightly enclosed in the thin cup. An interesting and beautiful tree.

Q. lyrata. OVERCUP OAK. A tree with somewhat pendulous branches, forming a shapely round-topped crown. Grows naturally from Maryland to Florida, westward to Illinois and Texas. Leaves deeply divided into 5 to 9 lobes, dark green, silvery whitened beneath, fading in autumn with brilliant tones of scarlet and orange. Acorn nearly covered by the deep cup. A handsome and symmetrical tree.

Q. michauxi. BASKET OAK. A large and stately tree with a dense round-topped crown. Distributed from Delaware to Florida, westward to Illinois and Texas. Leaves obovate, regularly toothed with coarse blunt teeth. They are dark green and shining on the upper surface, pale or silvery beneath, turning deep red or crimson in the autumn. Acorn brown, about one-third enclosed in the thick cup.

Q. macrocarpa. BUR, OR MOSSY CUP OAK. A majestic tree with massive spreading branches, forming a broad head. Distributed from Nova Scotia to the Rocky Mountains, southward to Pennsylvania and Texas. Leaves are

Oak leaves

Quercus coccinea

For grades and prices of above, see page 143

Quercus, continued

broadest above the middle, the lower portion deeply lobed, the upper with large rounded teeth. They are silvery white on the upper surface when very young, eventually dark green and shining, pale or whitened beneath, turning yellow and brown in autumn. Acorn deeply enclosed in the mossy cup.

Q. nigra (*Q. aquatica.*). WATER OAK. A tree with a symmetrical round-topped crown. Occurs naturally from Delaware to Florida, westward to Kentucky and Texas. Leaves dilated upwards, broadest near the apex, the margins mostly entire. They are dull green on the upper surface, pale beneath, falling in late autumn or early winter. Acorn light brown, enclosed only at the base in the shallow cup. Commonly planted as a shade tree in the South.

Q. palustris. PIN OAK. A handsome tree with drooping branches, forming a broad, shapely, pyramidal crown. Distributed from New England to Missouri, southward to Virginia and Arkansas. Leaves deeply 5- to 7-lobed, the divisions toothed toward the apex with bristle-tipped teeth. They are ruddy green at the time of unfolding, dark green and glossy at maturity, fading in autumn with tones of deep and brilliant scarlet. Acorn light brown, enclosed only at the base in the thin cup. Makes one of the most shapely and graceful of trees, the branches sweeping the ground.

Quercus digitata

Q. pedunculata (*Q. robur*). ENGLISH OAK. A large tree with spreading tortuous branches, forming a broad round-topped head. Native of Europe and Asia. Leaves dilated upwards, with 3 to 7 rounded lobes on each side, dark green above, pale bluish green beneath, fading with tones of yellow and russet-brown. Acorn brown, about one-third enclosed in the cup. A picturesque, hardy tree.

Q. pedunculata concordia. GOLDEN OAK. A form of the above with leaves of a beautiful bright yellow color.

Q. pedunculata fastigiata. PYRAMIDAL ENGLISH OAK. A handsome tree resembling in outline the Lombardy Poplar. Desirable for formal effects.

Q. pedunculata pendula. DAUVESSE'S WEEPING OAK. A form with slender drooping branches. Very graceful.

Q. phellos. WILLOW OAK. A graceful tree with a conical head. Grows naturally from New York to Florida, and westward to Missouri and Texas. Leaves lanceolate, very narrow and resembling a willow leaf, the borders entire, bright green, turning yellow in autumn. Acorn yellow-brown, enclosed only at the base in the thin, small cup. A remarkable and beautiful tree.

Q. platanoides (*Q. bicolor*). SWAMP WHITE OAK. A stately tree with a narrow round-topped crown. Distributed from Maine to Missouri, southward to Georgia and Arkansas. Leaves oblong-obovate, the margins regularly broken by small blunt lobes. They are bright yellow-green at the time of unfolding, at maturity dark green and lustrous above, silvery white on the lower surface, turning dark crimson in autumn. Acorn bright brown, enclosed about one-third its length in the cup. A beautiful tree.

Q. prinus. CHESTNUT OAK. A tall tree with a broad open crown. Distributed from Maine to Georgia, westward to Kentucky and Tennessee. Leaves oblong or obovate, the borders bluntly and coarsely toothed. They are bronze-green at the time of unfolding, yellow-green at maturity, turning orange or brown in autumn. Acorn chestnut-brown, less than half submerged in the top-shaped cup. A very distinct species.

Q. rubra. RED OAK. A large and handsome tree with a symmetrical round-topped crown. Grows naturally from Nova Scotia to Lake Huron, southward to Georgia and Kansas. Leaves 7- to 9-lobed, the divisions bearing bristle-tipped teeth. They are rosy pink at the time of unfolding, at maturity dark dull green, turning orange and brown

Quercus palustris

Oak leaves

 For grades and prices of above, see pages 143 and 144

Quercus, continued

in autumn. Acorn very large, but slightly enclosed in the shallow cup. A grand specimen or street tree and one of the most rapid-growing Oaks.

Q. velutina. Black Oak. A tall and shapely tree with a comparatively narrow round-topped head. Occurs naturally from Maine to Minnesota, southward to Florida and Texas. Leaves mostly 7-lobed, the divisions bearing several bristle-tipped teeth. They are bright red when they unfold, becoming pale and silvery; at maturity dark green and shining, fading in autumn with tones of orange and dull red. Acorn brown, often striped with dark lines, enclosed for about half its length in the top-shaped cup. A handsome tree.

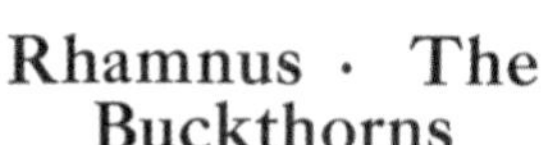

Rhamnus · The Buckthorns

Attractive small trees thriving in almost any soil. They are relatively hardy, but in the extreme North should be protected from cold winds. When loaded with berries they are remarkably beautiful objects. Other species of Buckthorn will be found under "Deciduous Shrubs."

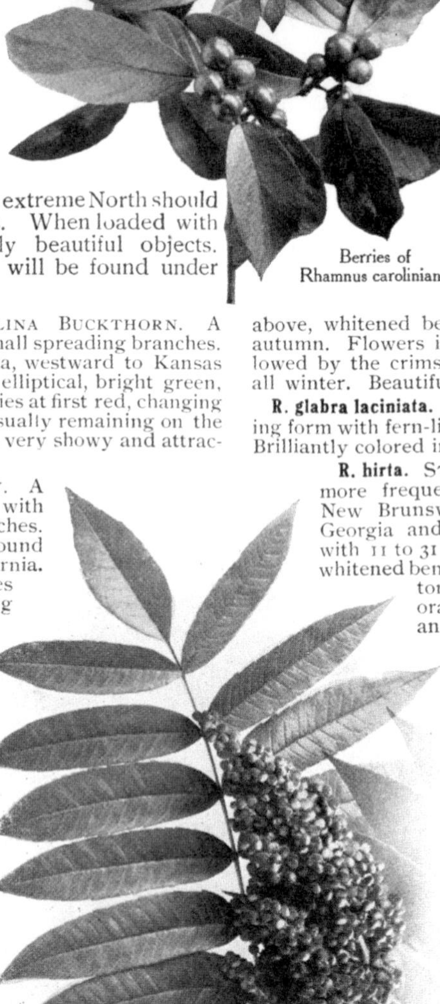

Berries of Rhamnus caroliniana

Rhamnus caroliniana. Carolina Buckthorn. A small tree or large shrub with small spreading branches. Grows from Virginia to Florida, westward to Kansas and Texas. Leaves oblong or elliptical, bright green, turning yellow in autumn. Berries at first red, changing to black, in great profusion, usually remaining on the branches until early winter. A very showy and attractive little tree.

R. purshiana. Coffee-Berry. A small tree or large shrub with ascending or spreading branches. Grows naturally from Puget Sound to Montana, southward to California. Hardy in New England. Leaves elliptical, dark green, turning pale yellow in late autumn. Berries changing from red to black.

Rhus

The Sumac Trees

These beautiful ornamentals have not been planted as extensively as they should be, in view of their brilliant color tones and graceful outlines. They thrive in any well-drained soil and are very hardy.

Rhus copallina. Upland Sumac. A small tree, or more frequently a shrub. Distributed from New England to Florida, westward to Kansas and Texas. Leaves compound, with 9 to 19 leaflets, the main stalk winged between the leaflets, dark green and lustrous, fading in autumn with tones of ruddy brown. Fruiting panicles fully grown and bright red by early autumn, often persisting until the following spring. A valuable ornamental.

R. cotinoides. Chittam-wood. A small and widely branched tree with a short trunk, usually divided near the base into several erect stems, forming an open crown. Distributed from Alabama and Tennessee to Missouri and Texas. Leaves simple, oval or obovate, light purple when very young, at maturity dark green, fading in autumn with brilliant tones of scarlet and orange. Flowers greenish yellow, in compound panicles, soon followed by the feathery fruiting stage. A hardy and interesting tree.

R. cotinus. Smoke Tree. A small tree or large shrub with obovate leaves. Native of Europe and Asia. Flowers pale purple, borne in loose panicles, the pedicels of which soon lengthen and become plumose, lending the smoky aspect which gave to the plant its common name. A highly ornamental object. In autumn the foliage assumes brilliant tones of red and yellow.

R. glabra. Smooth Sumac. A shrub or low tree with an open crown. Distributed over the United States and Canada. Leaves compound, with 11 to 31 lanceolate leaflets, dark green above, whitened beneath, turning brilliant scarlet in autumn. Flowers in large terminal panicles, soon followed by the crimson fruiting clusters, which persist all winter. Beautiful for massive effects.

R. glabra laciniata. Cut-leaved Sumac. A low-growing form with fern-like leaves. Very beautiful in effect. Brilliantly colored in autumn.

R. hirta. Staghorn Sumac. A small tree, or more frequently a large shrub. Occurs from New Brunswick to Minnesota, southward to Georgia and Mississippi. Leaves compound, with 11 to 31 leaflets, dark green above, pale or whitened beneath, fading in autumn with brilliant tones of scarlet, crimson, purple and orange. Fruiting panicles fully grown and brilliantly colored with crimson in late summer, persisting until the following spring. Very showy.

R. semialata (*R. osbecki*). Japanese Sumac. A shrub or low tree, under favorable conditions growing to a height of 15 or 20 feet. Native of Japan. Leaves compound, with 9 to 13 leaflets, the main stalk winged between the leaflets, dark glossy green, turning brilliant orange and red in autumn. Flowers creamy white, borne in large terminal panicles.

Robinia

The Locust Trees

Rapid-growing trees with showy flowers, thriving in any well-drained soil. They are hardy, graceful objects with feathery foliage, adapted to sunny situations in the

Rhus glabra

For grades and prices of above, see page 144

Robinia, continued

shrub borders. The Black Locust makes a beautiful specimen tree when planted in rich loam.

Robinia neo-mexicana. WESTERN LOCUST. A small tree or low shrub from the Rocky Mountains. Leaves compound, with 15 to 21 leaflets, bluish green, turning yellow in autumn. Flowers pale rose, borne in short hispid racemes. Very showy in flower.

R. pseudacacia. BLACK LOCUST. A tree with a comparatively narrow crown. Widely distributed in the United States east of the Rocky Mountains. Leaves compound, with 7 to 19 leaflets, bright green, turning pale yellow in autumn. Flowers white, very fragrant, borne in drooping racemes, expanding in May or June. Has been largely planted as an ornamental.

R. viscosa. CLAMMY LOCUST. A small tree with clammy, viscid twigs. Native of the Mountains of North and South Carolina. Leaves compound, with 13 to 21 leaflets, dark green, turning yellow in autumn. Flowers pale rose, borne in dense glandular racemes. Pods hispid. The flowers are very handsome.

Salix · The Willow Trees

Rapid-growing hardy trees thriving in any moist soil. The Willows are valuable and interesting subjects, both on account of their graceful aspect, showy catkins and bright bark. The Babylonian Weeping Willow is everywhere associated with waterside planting, and is without doubt one of the most remarkable of trees. Wonderful effects may be obtained by grouping or massing the bright-barked varieties, especially when they are contrasted against evergreens or other strong backgrounds. Other species will be found under "Deciduous Shrubs."

Salix alba (*S. regalis*). WHITE WILLOW. A large tree with yellowish brown bark. Native of Europe. Leaves broadly lanceolate, silvery gray, silky on both surfaces, the margins serrate. Often planted for the silvery aspect of its foliage.

S. amygdaloides. PEACH-LEAVED WILLOW. A tree with reddish brown bark and ascending branches. Distributed from New York to the Rocky Mountains, and from Ohio to Texas. Leaves lanceolate, the margins serrate, light green and lustrous, glaucous beneath.

S. babylonica. WEEPING WILLOW. A large tree with slender pendent branches. Native of Asia. Leaves narrow, tapering to a long point, bright green, the margins serrate. A very picturesque tree, universally known and cultivated for several centuries in the Old World.

S. babylonica annularis. RING-LEAVED WILLOW. A form of the last with curiously curled or twisted leaves. An interesting tree, attracting attention wherever seen.

S. babylonica dolorosa. WISCONSIN WEEPING WILLOW. A very hardy variety, withstanding the winters of the far North. The leaves are whitened on the lower surface.

S. caprea. GOAT, OR PUSSY WILLOW. A small tree with upright or ascending branches. Native of Europe and Asia. Leaves relatively large and broad, green and rugose above, whitened beneath. Catkins very numerous, appearing in early spring before the leaves appear. Very handsome in flower and greatly esteemed by reason of its extreme earliness. Very many of us can associate sweet memories with the Pussy Willow.

S. caprea pendula. KILMARNOCK WEEPING WILLOW. A form with drooping branches grafted on an upright straight stem. Forms an umbrella-like canopy, the branches eventually sweeping the ground.

S. elegantissima. THURLOW'S WEEPING WILLOW. Similar to *S. babylonica*, but of more spreading habit and of greater hardiness. Native of Japan. Branches long and pendulous, clothed with yellow-green bark. A large tree with a massive, symmetrical crown.

Salix fragilis. BRITTLE WILLOW. A rapid-growing tree with brittle branches, clothed with lustrous brown bark. Native of Europe and Asia. Leaves lanceolate, relatively large, bright green on both surfaces. Has been widely cultivated for hedges and for holding banks of streams from erosion.

S. incana (*S. rosmarinifolia*). ROSEMARY WILLOW. A shrub or small tree with a symmetrical round top and long slender branches. Native of Europe. Leaves narrow, bright green above, silvery white beneath.

S. lucida. SHINING WILLOW. A large shrub or short-trunked tree with a symmetrical round-topped crown. Very abundant from New England to Alberta, southward to Pennsylvania and Nebraska. Leaves large, lanceolate, with long tapering points, dark green and very lustrous. Bark orange-brown.

S. nigra. BLACK WILLOW. A large tree usually with several stems, forming an irregular open crown. Grows throughout the United States. The largest native American Willow. Leaves narrowly lanceolate, bright green and lustrous, the margins serrate. Bark reddish brown.

Rhus cotinus (see page 38)

S. pentandra. BAY- OR LAUREL-LEAVED WILLOW. A small tree or large shrub of compact habit. Native of Europe and Asia. Leaves very large, ovate-lanceolate or elliptic, dark green and shining, fragrant when bruised, the odor resembling that of the Bay Tree. One of the best of the Willows for ornamental planting and foliage effects. Bark light chestnut-brown.

S. purpurea. PURPLE OSIER. A shrub or small tree with long slender branches. Native of Europe. Leaves oblanceolate, the margins shallowly serrate, of a rich green color. Bark rich shining purple, somewhat glaucous. Much esteemed for basketry.

S. vitellina. YELLOW WILLOW. A large tree with bright yellow bark. Native of Europe. Leaves lanceolate, silky when young, bright green and smooth on the upper surface at maturity, glaucous beneath. The conspicuous yellow color of the bark is very attractive in winter, especially when contrasted with evergreens or masses of white- or red-barked trees.

S. vitellina aurea. GOLD-BARKED WILLOW. Bark of the branches golden yellow, especially intense in color in the spring, before the leaves appear.

S. vitellina britzensis. BRONZE-BARKED WILLOW. Bark of the branches red or bronze in early spring.

For grades and prices of above, see page 144

Sassafras · The Sassafras Tree

A hardy ornamental tree thriving in any well-drained soil, seemingly preferring a sunny exposure. In rich loam the Sassafras attains a relatively large size and is a desirable shade tree.

S. officinalis. SASSAFRAS. An aromatic tree with spreading branches, forming a flat-topped head. Grows from Maine to Michigan, southward to the Gulf. Leaves entire, mitten-shaped or three-lobed, bright green, turning in autumn to soft shades of orange, yellow and red. Flowers yellow-green; the dark blue fruits ripe in autumn. The roots are often highly esteemed as a mild aromatic stimulant, and many of us are familiar with them.

Sophora · The Pagoda Tree

Remarkably graceful hardy trees with dark green bark and a wealth of flowers. They thrive best in well-drained sandy loam, and in the colder sections of the country should be protected from cold piercing winds.

Sophora japonica. JAPANESE SOPHORA. A medium-sized tree with spreading branches forming a symmetrical compact head. Native of China and Japan. Leaves compound, with 5 to 13 leaflets, dark green and glossy, fading with soft tones of yellow. Flowers creamy white, borne in large loose panicles, expanding in midsummer. A handsome tree with green-barked twigs.

S. japonica pendula. WEEPING SOPHORA. One of the most beautiful of pendulous trees. The wavy curves of the long, drooping branches are factors of grace and beauty.

Sorbus · The Mountain Ash Trees

Hardy ornamental trees with handsome foliage and showy red fruit. They thrive in moist loamy soils and are particularly valuable as specimen trees for the lawn. The fruits are eagerly sought by birds, and a few trees near the house will give bird-lovers much pleasure in early autumn.

Sorbus americana. AMERICAN MOUNTAIN ASH. A small tree with spreading branches, forming a round-topped crown. Grows from the Maritime Provinces of Canada to Minnesota, and southward in the mountains to North Carolina. Leaves compound, the leaflets 11 to 17, dark green, turning yellow in autumn. Flowers white, in flat cymes, followed later in the season by showy clusters of bright scarlet fruit. A beautiful object in the North, but does not thrive long in Southern gardens.

S. aria. WHITE BEAM TREE. A small tree with a compact oval head. Native of Europe and Asia. Leaves simple, ovate, deep green on the upper surface, white-woolly beneath, turning yellow in autumn. Flowers white, in tomentose, broad corymbs. Fruit orange-red, nearly globose. When the foliage is ruffled by the winds the contrasting colors of the leaf-surfaces are very effective.

S. aucuparia. EUROPEAN MOUNTAIN ASH, OR ROWAN TREE. A small tree with a symmetrical round-topped crown. Native of Europe and Asia. Leaves compound, with 9 to 15 leaflets, dark green, turning yellow in autumn. Flowers white, borne in broad, flat corymbs, expanding in late spring or early summer, followed in fall by large clusters of bright red berries. Very showy.

S. aucuparia pendula. WEEPING MOUNTAIN ASH. A form with large and slender drooping branches, grafted on straight upright stems. The bright red berries are borne in profusion.

Sterculia · The Parasol Tree

A valuable tree for lawn and street planting in the South. It thrives best in rich loamy soils. The dull red and scarlet, rarely greenish flowers, which are borne in profusion, add greatly to its beauty. In sheltered places it may be grown as far north as Memphis and Washington.

Sterculia platanifolia. CHINESE, OR JAPANESE PARASOL TREE. A medium-sized tree with a round-topped head. Native of China and Japan. Leaves very large, 3- to 5-lobed, Maple-like, bright green, turning yellow in autumn. Flowers in terminal panicles, soon followed by the curious fruits, with the seeds attached to the margins of the carpels. A splendid, strong-growing tree.

Tilia americana as a street tree

Syringa · The Tree Lilac

A beautiful free-flowering tree thriving best in rich loam. As specimen plants, or in groups or masses, this handsome species attracts attention and comment wherever seen.

Syringa japonica. JAPANESE LILAC. A small pyramidal tree, very floriferous and hardy, from Japan. Leaves ovate or heart-shaped, dark green, pale beneath, turning yellow in the fall. Flowers creamy white, in panicles often a foot long, produced in great abundance in early summer.

Tilia · The Lindens

Handsome hardy trees thriving best in deep loamy soils. Valuable as shade trees for the lawn or street. The Lindens are of rapid growth and among the best of ornamentals.

Tilia americana. AMERICAN LINDEN, OR BASSWOOD. A large tree forming a broad round-topped crown.

For grades and prices of above, see page 145

Tilia, continued

Distributed from Canada to Georgia, westward to Dakota and Texas. Leaves broadly oval or heart-shaped, dark green above, pale green beneath, turning yellow in autumn. Flowers creamy white, opening in summer. A grand tree, suitable for streets, lawns or parks.

T. dasystyla. CRIMEAN LINDEN. A handsome tree with a pyramidal head. Native of Europe and Asia. Bark of the young branches bright green. Leaves heart-shaped, dark lustrous green on the upper surface, pale beneath, turning yellow and brown in autumn. A distinct and valuable Linden.

A branch of Ulmus alata

T. europaea. EUROPEAN LINDEN, OR LIME TREE. A large tree with spreading branches, forming a symmetrical round-topped crown. Native of Europe. Leaves obliquely heart-shaped, bright green, fading in autumn with tones of yellow and brown. Flowers creamy white, fragrant. A handsome tree, valuable for street planting.

T. heterophylla. WHITE BASSWOOD. A tree with slender branches and a narrow pyramidal head. Distributed from New York and Alabama to Illinois and Tennessee. Leaves broadly ovate, oblique at the base, bright green above, silvery white beneath, turning yellow in autumn. Flowers creamy white in early summer. A beautiful tree.

T. petiolaris (*T. argentea pendula*). WEEPING LINDEN. A beautiful medium-sized tree with slender, somewhat pendulous branches. Native of Europe. Leaves heart-shaped, rich green on the upper surface, silvery white beneath, fading with yellow tones in fall. Flowers yellowish white, very fragrant. The snowy whiteness of the undersurface of the leaves when ruffled by the wind lends striking contrasts.

T. platyphyllos. LARGE-LEAVED LINDEN. A large and stately tree with a handsome pyramidal crown, or, in age, round-topped and massive. Native of Europe. Leaves heart-shaped, relatively large, dark green, turning yellow in autumn. Flowers large, yellowish white, fragrant. The largest European Lime Tree.

T. tomentosa (*T. alba* and *T. argentea*). WHITE, OR SILVER LINDEN. A shapely tree with a dense pyramidal crown. Native of Europe. Leaves heart-shaped, dark green on the upper surface, silvery white beneath, turning yellow and brown in autumn. The contrast of the leaf-surfaces is very effective.

Toxylon · The Osage Orange

A hardy tree widely planted for hedges. Stands clipping remarkably well and forms an almost impenetrable barrier when properly cared for. The Osage Orange makes a beautiful tree when planted in rich loamy soil, and is peculiarly attractive in the autumn when loaded with the large round fruits.

Toxylon pomiferum (*Maclura aurantiaca*). OSAGE ORANGE. A handsome hardy tree with a short trunk. The ascending, or, in age, spreading branches form a narrow round-topped crown. Grows naturally from Arkansas to Texas. Leaves broadly lanceolate, bright glossy green, turning clear yellow in autumn. Fruit globose, 4 to 5 inches in diameter, light yellow-green.

Ulmus · The Elms

Stately trees combining grace of habit and beauty of outline. They are hardy and of extremely rapid growth when planted in moist loam. No lawn or landscape is complete without them. Several of the species are most satisfactorily used as street trees both in the North and in the South.

Ulmus alata. WAHOO, OR WINGED ELM. A medium-sized tree with corky-winged branches. Grows naturally from Virginia to Florida, westward to Illinois and Texas. Often planted in the South as a shade tree. Leaves ovate, coarsely serrate, dark green at maturity, turning yellow in autumn. An attractive tree with a narrow round-topped crown.

U. americana. AMERICAN ELM. A large and stately tree with long and graceful branches. Distributed from Newfoundland to the foothills of the Rocky Mountains, southward to the Gulf. Leaves oblong, sharply serrate, dark green, turning pale yellow in autumn. Very picturesque in age, and desirable for lawn or landscape.

U. campestris. ENGLISH ELM. A large tree with spreading branches forming a round-topped crown. Native of Europe. Leaves broadly ovate, with serrate and incised borders, deep rich green, persisting and holding their color longer than any other species. Extensively planted as a shade tree in both lawns and avenues.

U. campestris corylifolia purpurea. PURPLE-LEAVED ENGLISH ELM. A form with large purplish leaves, of brightest color in early spring, changing to greener tones as the season progresses.

U. campestris major (*U. latifolia*). BROAD-LEAVED ENGLISH ELM. A very robust form with large leaves. One of the best shade trees; its handsome foliage retained until late autumn.

U. scabra (*U. montana*). SCOTCH, OR WYCH ELM. A large handsome tree with wide-spreading, somewhat drooping branches, forming a broad round-topped crown. Native of Europe. Leaves broadly obovate,

Fruit of Toxylon pomiferum

For grades and prices of above, see page 145

Ulmus, continued

sharply serrate and somewhat incised, very rough, of a deep green color, remaining bright and fresh until late in the season.

U. scabra pendula. CAMPERDOWN WEEPING ELM. A very picturesque and graceful form with drooping branches, grafted on an erect straight stem. One of the best of the weeping trees. The branches of the umbrella-like canopy eventually sweep the ground, and enclose a shady place as effectively as an arbor.

Viburnum · The Black Haws

Handsome little trees, thriving in moist loam. They are hardy and very ornamental, both on account of their showy flowers and conspicuous fruits. They are seen at their best, perhaps, in groups or colonies, in conjunction with shrubs. Other species are described under "Deciduous Shrubs."

Viburnum lentago. SHEEPBERRY, OR NANNYBERRY. A small tree or large shrub with a compact round-topped head. Distributed from Saskatchewan to Georgia and Nebraska. Leaves ovate, bronze-green in earliest spring, at maturity bright shining green, turning red and orange in autumn. Flowers creamy white, opening in spring, followed in autumn by red-stemmed clusters of black or dark blue berries. A remarkably symmetrical and decorative plant.

V. prunifolium. BLACK HAW, OR STAG BUSH. A bushy tree with stiff, spreading branches. Occurs in a wild state from New England to Georgia and Missouri. Leaves ovate, pale yellow-green in spring, at maturity dark green, turning brilliant scarlet or vinous red in autumn. Flowers white or creamy, expanding in spring, very showy, succeeded in autumn by red-stemmed clusters of glaucous blue berries. Very ornamental.

Vitex agnus-castus

V. rufidulum. SOUTHERN BLACK HAW. A small tree, with short, stout branches. Grows naturally from Southern Illinois and Virginia to Florida and Texas. Leaves elliptical, dark green and shining, bearing patches, more or less conspicuous, of rusty brown hairs on the veins or leaf-stalks. Flowers creamy white, disposed in flat-topped clusters, expanding with the leaves. Berries glaucous blue, in drooping red-stemmed clusters. A distinct and beautiful species.

Vitex · The Chaste Tree

An extremely showy shrub or small tree with wide-spreading branches. It thrives best in a well-drained, loamy soil, and is hardy as far north as Kentucky and Pennsylvania, or with protection from cold winds it may be grown in colder localities.

Vitex agnus-castus. CHASTE TREE. Leaves compound, consisting of 5 to 7 narrow leaflets, dark green above, grayish downy beneath, with a strong aromatic odor when bruised. Flowers lilac or violet-purple, disposed in dense terminal racemes during late summer. Native of Europe and Asia.

Xanthoceras · Chinese Flowering Chestnut

A handsome free-flowering tree thriving in a loamy well-drained soil fully exposed to sun and air. While relatively hardy, it is best to afford protection from cold winds when planted in the colder sections of the North. One of the most beautiful ornamentals, rarely seen in cultivation.

Xanthoceras sorbifolia. CHINESE FLOWERING CHESTNUT. A small tree or large shrub with a wealth of floral beauty. Native of Northern China. Leaves compound, consisting of 9 to 17 dark green leaflets, strongly resembling those of the Mountain Ash. Flowers in long racemes, pure white, with an orange blotch at the base of each petal. Fruit green, about two inches long, borne in clusters.

Xanthoxylum · The Prickly Ash Tree

Small trees with handsome shining foliage. They thrive in porous loamy soils, and are relatively hardy.

Xanthoxylum americanum. PRICKLY ASH. A large shrub or small tree with prickly branches. Grows naturally from Quebec to Virginia and Nebraska. Leaves compound, consisting of from 5 to 7 dark green leaflets. The hardiest species.

X. piperitum. CHINESE, OR JAPANESE PEPPER TREE. A shrub or small bushy tree armed with slender prickles. Native of China and Japan. Leaves compound, consisting of 11 to 13 dark green shining leaflets. The fruits are used as a substitute for black pepper in Japan. Should be planted in a protected place in the North.

Concerning Biltmore Plants

There are many of our patrons, some of them more or less remote from quick-transportation facilities, who will greet with delight our attempt to provide both mailing, express and freight sizes of almost all of the items of our long list of ornamentals. It affords opportunity to secure accessions to their gardens, as may meet the exigencies of their locations, in a manner that has not heretofore been anticipated by many nurserymen.

For grades and prices of above, see page 145

BROAD-LEAVED EVERGREEN TREES

THESE beautiful trees add wonderfully to the attractiveness and winter aspect of lawn and garden. Wherever it is possible to grow them they should be freely planted. Several of the species are ordinarily difficult to transplant, but our trees are so carefully prepared and frequently transplanted that success is practically insured. In some instances we pick off the leaves before shipping, in order to prevent unnecessary evaporation of the sap during transit and the time necessary for the trees to become reëstablished.

Buxus · The Box Tree

This hardy tree thrives in almost any well-drained soil. A position in partial shade is advantageous, as under such conditions the foliage assumes a more verdant and glossy lustre. In the extreme North, protection from cold winds and direct sun rays in winter is desirable.

Buxus arborescens. TREE BOX. A small intricately branched tree of great beauty. Native of Europe and the Orient. Universally used in the Middle and Southern states as an ornament to the home grounds. Splendid colonial results are possible by the free use of this evergreen.

Eriobotrya · The Loquat Tree

A handsome little tree extensively cultivated in the South, both for ornament and utility. It thrives best in moist loamy soil and in its northern range of usefulness should be afforded protection from cold winds.

Eriobotrya japonica. LOQUAT, OR JAPANESE MEDLAR. A small tree with thick evergreen leaves, glossy green above, rusty pubescent beneath. Flowers white, in terminal rusty-woolly clusters, large and fragrant, produced in late summer and autumn and frequently until the approach of winter. Fruit pear-shaped, about the size of a plum, bright yellow, of an agreeable acid flavor, ripening from the end of February until April. Fruitful only in the South, but otherwise hardy as far north as Washington and Tennessee. A large-fruited variety known as the Giant Medlar has fruits about four times as large as the typical form, and is highly prized in the South.

Ilex · The Holly Trees

Hollies are seen at their best only when planted in groups or colonies, where both the pistillate and staminate forms may be closely associated. They thrive in most soils, but reach their largest proportions in moist rich loam. A situation in partial shade is desirable, by reason of the added lustre and brilliancy attained by the foliage under such conditions. Other species will be found under "Broad-leaved Evergreen Shrubs," "Deciduous Shrubs" and "Deciduous Trees."

I. aquifolium. ENGLISH, OR EUROPEAN HOLLY. A small tree or shrub of pyramidal outline, native of Europe and Asia. Leaves persistent, deep green and shining, the margins wavy and bearing spine-tipped teeth. Fruit scarlet, glossy. A very beautiful object, especially in winter, when the glossy green leaves contrast with the fiery-colored berries. Excellent for the South but needs protection in the Middle and Northern States.

I. aquifolium aureo-regina. VARIEGATED HOLLY. Leaves ovate, spiny-toothed, mottled with gray and green and with a broad yellow border. Very striking.

I. aquifolium ferox. HEDGEHOG HOLLY. Leaves with spine-toothed borders, and numerous small spines growing from the upper surface. Curious and interesting.

I. aquifolium laurifolia. ENTIRE-LEAVED HOLLY. Leaves ovate, glossy green, without spines. Of strange aspect.

I. aquifolium myrtifolia. MYRTLE-LEAVED HOLLY. Leaves small and narrow, sometimes without spines. A remarkably distinct form.

I. cornuta. CHINESE HOLLY. A broad-leaved evergreen shrub or small tree with spreading branches. Native of Northern China. Leaves oblong, dark glossy green, the margins bearing several strong spines. Berries in clusters, bright scarlet. A beautiful object for Southern gardens.

I. crenata. JAPANESE HOLLY. An intricately branched evergreen shrub or small tree. Native of Japan. Leaves small, in size and shape similar to those of the Boxwood, deep lustrous green. Berries black. Excellent for hedge plants or specimens. Withstands temperatures of ten degrees below zero.

I. opaca. AMERICAN HOLLY. A handsome broad-leaved evergreen tree, familiar to the majority of Americans as Christmas Holly. Distributed from New England to Florida, westward to Missouri and Texas.

For grades and prices of above, see page 146

Ilex, continued

The spiny green leaves and bright scarlet berries bring back Christmas memories and associations that dearly commend this beautiful hardy tree. Of easy culture, thriving in almost any soil.

I. vomitoria. CASSENA, OR YAUPON. A small much-branched tree or large shrub with many stems, forming an open irregular crown. Grows naturally from Virginia to Florida, westward to Arkansas and Texas. Leaves small, persistent until late winter or early spring, usually falling with the appearance of new growth. Berries scarlet.

Laurocerasus · The Laurel Trees

Small bushy trees with glossy evergreen foliage. They thrive in ordinary garden soils and in their northern range of usefulness should be afforded protection from cold winds. A location in partial shade where the full rays of the sun in winter may be diverted, will add greatly to the color and lustre of the foliage. Very valuable as tub plants for decorating.

Laurocerasus caroliniana (*Prunus caroliniana*). WILD ORANGE. A small evergreen tree with dark green lustrous foliage. Grows naturally from North Carolina to Florida and Texas. Flowers white, in earliest spring, disposed in short dense racemes. Fruit black and lustrous, ripening in autumn, and remaining on the branches until the following spring. Often cultivated in the Southern States as an ornamental plant and for hedges.

L. laurocerasus. ENGLISH, OR CHERRY LAUREL. A small tree or bush with handsome shining foliage. Native of Europe. Flowers white, in numerous short racemes, expanding in April or May. Justly popular in Europe and destined to be widely planted in the Southern and Pacific States. Requires protection north of Washington and Memphis.

L. laurocerasus schipkanensis. HARDY ENGLISH LAUREL. A form of the above, noted for its hardiness. It is reported to stand the winters in Central New York. This variety is recommended where hardiness is a desideratum.

L. lusitanica. PORTUGAL LAUREL. A small, intricately branched tree with glossy leaves. Native of Spain and Portugal. Flowers white, disposed in slender racemes, appearing in late spring or early summer. A promising and valuable plant for Southern gardens. Not quite so hardy as the English Laurel.

Laurus · The Bay Tree

This beautiful tree is commonly cultivated as a tub plant, and is used universally for decorating. It will stand considerable frost without injury, but is hardy out-of-doors only in the warmer sections of the country. A rich porous soil with good drainage and ample water makes a congenial medium, whether the plants are confined in tubs or set out in the open ground.

Laurus nobilis. BAY TREE. Handsome ornamental trees usually trained to formal lines. Native of Southern Europe. We offer select plants in standards and pyramids, in several sizes.

Magnolia · The Evergreen Magnolias

Noble trees, and without doubt the grandest in their class. They thrive in moist, porous soils, demanding for their best development an abundance of fertility. Will withstand considerable cold, but should be protected from piercing winds in the colder sections. Not altogether trustworthy north of Philadelphia and Memphis, except on the Pacific Coast. Other species will be found under "Deciduous Trees."

Magnolia glauca. SWEET, OR WHITE BAY. A slender tree or large shrub, evergreen in the South, tardily deciduous in the North. Distributed from Massachusetts to Florida, near the coast, and westward to Texas. Leaves oblong or oval, green and lustrous on the upper surface, pale or nearly white beneath. Flowers creamy white, fragrant, cup-shaped, 2 to 3 inches across, blossoming for several weeks in spring and early summer. Fruit dark red, with scarlet seeds.

M. grandiflora. SOUTHERN MAGNOLIA. A stately pyramidal tree with short, spreading or ascending branches. Occurs naturally from North Carolina and Florida to Texas and Arkansas. Leaves evergreen, oblong or ovate, thick and firm, bright green and glossy on the upper surface, coated below with rusty hairs. Flowers fragrant, opening in spring and summer, 6 to 8 inches across, pure waxy white. Fruit rusty brown, 3 to 4 inches long; the seeds scarlet. One of the most beautiful trees, and widely cultivated in the South.

M. grandiflora exoniensis. EXMOUTH MAGNOLIA. The most distinct variety, characterized by a rather fastigiate habit and broad leaves densely coated with rusty hairs on the lower surface. Flowers when only a few feet high.

M. grandiflora galissoniensis. GALISSON MAGNOLIA. The hardiest form of the Southern Magnolia and the one likely to be most satisfactory in the North.

M. grandiflora gloriosa. LARGE-FLOWERED MAGNOLIA. A form with extremely large flowers, often measuring 15 inches in diameter. Leaves large and relatively broad, clothed beneath with felt-like brown hairs.

M. thompsoniana. THOMPSON'S SWEET BAY. A shrub or small tree of garden origin, resembling *M. glauca*, and like it, evergreen in the South, tardily deciduous in the North. Leaves oblong or oval, bright green above, whitened beneath. Flowers fragrant, white, 5 to 6 inches across. A favorite garden plant; quite hardy.

Magnolia grandiflora

For grades and prices of above, see page 146

BROAD-LEAVED EVERGREEN SHRUBS

THESE beautiful plants afford a wide range of selection in producing some of the most pleasing results in ornamental planting. No garden or plantation is altogether satisfactory without some provision for results and effects that may be had continuously throughout the winter. Groups of evergreen shrubs add wonderfully in brightening the winter aspect of our gardens. In choosing the planting site, due preference should be given to a northern exposure, where the direct rays of the sun are seldom felt, or, failing in this, a situation in partial shade should be substituted. Under such conditions the verdure and lustre of the foliage is greatly enhanced. A cool, moist soil with a porous substratum is best adapted to them, and it is recommended that a mulch of forest leaves, pine needles or spent tan bark, be spread over the soil to a depth of 2 or 3 inches. This prevents the rapid evaporation of moisture from the soil and is a potent factor in keeping the earth and growing roots cool and free from sudden variations of temperature. With due regard to these simple requirements, it is possible, even for the amateur, to successfully cultivate the Rhododendrons, Laurels, Andromedas and many others of these enchanting plants.

Abelia · The Free-flowering Abelias

Handsome floriferous shrubs worthy of extensive cultivation. They thrive best in sandy loam, either exposed to the sun or in partial shade. *Abelia grandiflora* is the hardiest variety and may be successfully cultivated as far north as Southern New York and Missouri, if planted in sheltered situations.

Abelia floribunda. MEXICAN ABELIA. An evergreen shrub with small deep green leaves. Native of Mexico. Flowers pale pink or rosy purple, about 2 inches long, borne in 1- to 3-flowered clusters. The blossoms begin to open in early summer and continue until autumn. Not hardy in the North.

A. grandiflora (*A. rupestris*). HYBRID ABELIA. One of the most beautiful shrubs in cultivation. The graceful arching stems are clothed with dark glossy leaves, which are evergreen in the South and tardily deciduous in the North. Flowers white, tinged with pink, about an inch long, borne in profuse clusters from early summer until checked by frost. Probably of garden origin.

Andromeda · The Wild Rosemary

A low evergreen shrub of extreme hardiness. Although a native of swampy situations, it takes kindly to garden treatment, thriving in any moist, loamy or sandy soil. It is very effective in masses or colonies, especially when very closely planted.

Andromeda polifolia. WILD ROSEMARY. An attractive little shrub with narrow leaves, green or grayish green above, white beneath. Grows wild from Newfoundland to Alaska, southward to Pennsylvania and Michigan. Flowers nodding, white or pink, borne in little clusters near the ends of the branches, blooming in spring.

Abelia grandiflora

For grades and prices of above, see page 147

Aucuba · The Japanese Laurel

Shrubs with glossy evergreen leaves, thriving in ordinary garden soil. They are well adapted to Southern and Pacific regions, and are especially luxuriant when afforded partial shade and ample moisture. Aucubas are always seen at their best when planted in groups or colonies, where the pistillate and staminate forms are in close proximity, thereby insuring a wealth of bright scarlet berries. They are beautiful subjects for growing in tubs or jardinières.

Aucuba japonica. JAPANESE LAUREL. A medium-sized shrub with dark glossy leaves, unaffected by smoke and dust. Excellent for city planting. Berries scarlet, in showy contrast with the foliage.

A. japonica aureo-maculata. GOLD-DUST LAUREL. A form with yellow-spotted leaves. A strikingly attractive plant and one that is much used for jardinières and window-boxes.

Azalea · The Indian Azaleas

Free-flowering evergreen shrubs, thriving in woods earth or other fibrous rich soils. They require for their best development partial shade and ample moisture. The varieties of *Azalea indica* are hardy in the Southern and Pacific States. *Azalea amœna* is hardy as far north as Missouri and New York.

Azalea amoena. HARDY EVERGREEN AZALEA. A low bushy shrub with small green leaves which change in winter to a rich bronze or coppery brown. Native of China and Japan. In spring the whole plant is covered by a wealth of claret-purple flowers which continue to open for a period of two or three weeks. Very attractive low hedges may be made by planting in single line, or bolder results may be obtained by massing or grouping in front of Rhododendrons and Kalmias.

A. indica. INDIAN AZALEA. Without doubt one of the most handsome and showy of flowering shrubs, thriving without protection in the Southern and Pacific States. The colors of the flowers range from pure white and shades of purple, crimson and salmon, to mottled, blotched and striped forms, both in single and double-flowered varieties. The following are among the best:

Berberis japonica

Apollo. Semi-double, vermilion. Early.

Bernard Andre. Double, dark violet-purple. A large and showy variety of unusual merit and attractiveness.

Comtesse de Beaufort. Single, rich rose, blotched with crimson.

Deutsche Perle. Double, pure white. Early.

Dr. Moore. Double, deep rose, shaded white and violet. Very fine.

Le Flambeau. Single, glowing crimson. Very rich.

Mme. Van der Cruyssen. Double pink. Of exquisite form and substance.

Theo. Reimers. Double lilac. Very fine.

Vervaeneana. Double, rose bordered with white and often striped with salmon.

Berberis · The Mahonias and Evergreen Barberries

Attractive shrubs with yellow inner-bark and wood, and evergreen, usually spiny toothed leaves. They thrive in almost any soil, but a sandy fibrous loam is best. Partial shade and ample moisture result in brighter and glossier foliage.

Berberis aquifolium (*Mahonia aquifolium*). OREGON GRAPE, or MAHONIA. A handsome ornamental shrub with compound leaves, the 5 to 9 leaflets dark lustrous green, spiny toothed. In winter the foliage assumes a bronze or coppery hue. Flowers yellow, in dense clusters, appearing in spring. Berries blue or nearly black. Distributed naturally from British Columbia to Oregon. Hardy throughout most of the country, but requires some protection in the colder sections.

B. buxifolia (*B. dulcis*). BOX-LEAVED BARBERRY. A small shrub with spiny branches. Native of Chili and Patagonia. Leaves simple, about an inch long, dark green. Flowers orange-yellow, solitary, on long stalks. Fruit nearly round, dark purple, or nearly black. A graceful and free-flowering shrub, and one of the hardiest of the evergreen species.

B. congestiflora. CHILIAN BARBERRY. A handsome shrub with erect or curving branches. Native of Chili. Leaves simple, oval or nearly round, spiny toothed, glaucous green. Flowers yellow, in dense round clusters, appearing in early spring. Apparently quite hardy.

B. darwini. DARWIN'S BARBERRY. A small shrub with silky brown branches. Native of Chili and Patagonia. Leaves usually with three spiny points at the tip, dark glossy green. Flowers orange-yellow, often tinged with red, borne in many-flowered pendulous racemes. Berries dark purple.

B. fascicularis. FASCICLED BARBERRY. An erect shrub with compound leaves and 5 to 15 spiny toothed, dark green leaflets. Grows in California and New Mexico. Flowers greenish yellow, in short racemes, appearing in early spring. Berries blue or nearly black. Valuable in the Southern and Pacific States.

B. fortunei. FORTUNE'S MAHONIA. A low shrub with compound leaves. Native of China. Leaflets 5 to 9, small and relatively narrow, with numerous spiny teeth. Flowers yellow, in erect clustered racemes. A very pretty variety.

B. ilicifolia. HOLLY-LEAVED BARBERRY. A charming shrub with holly-like, dark lustrous-green leaves, which persist until midwinter or spring. Native of Terra del Fuego. Flowers orange-yellow, in short-stalked clusters. Of value in the milder sections of the country.

B. japonica (*Mahonia japonica*). JAPANESE MAHONIA. Perhaps the most effective of the Mahonias. Leaves large, compound, with 9 to 13 spiny toothed leaflets,

For grades and prices of above, see page 147

Berberis, continued

bright shining green. Flowers yellow, in long racemes, opening in early spring. Fruit bluish black, with a bloom. Native of China and Japan.

B. nepalensis. NEPAULESE MAHONIA. An effective evergreen shrub with large, compound leaves. Native of Asia. Leaflets 5 to 25, bright glossy green, with few spiny teeth on each border. Hardy as far north as Washington in sheltered positions.

B. newberti. NEWBERT'S MAHONIA. A hardy shrub with spineless branches. Of garden origin. Leaves simple, dark grayish green, often tinged with purple, with spiny teeth. Quite evergreen in the South, but only partially so in the North.

B. repens (*Mahonia repens*). CREEPING MAHONIA. Resembling the Oregon grape, but of smaller size. A low shrub, seldom more than a foot tall, with creeping rootstalks. In the mountains from British Columbia to Colorado. Leaves compound, consisting of from 3 to 7 glaucous green, spiny toothed leaflets. Flowers yellow, in short-clustered racemes. Berries blue or nearly black.

B. stenophylla. SMALL-LEAVED BARBERRY. A handsome shrub of garden origin. The slender arching branches vary from 1 to 3 feet in length, and bear numerous, narrow, spiny-pointed, dark green leaves. Flowers yellow, in small drooping clusters. Hardy as far north as Washington and Memphis.

Buxus

The Boxwoods

These beautiful shrubs have been extensively used for hedges in formal gardens, and as specimen plants for lawn and landscape. They are justly popular, hardy evergreens that thrive in all save the extreme northern portions of the country. A well-drained loamy soil is best adapted to their requirements, and for specimen plants it is advisable to select a situation in partial shade.

Buxus sempervirens. BOXWOOD. Large shrubs of dense habit and symmetrical outline. Native of Europe. This species is used for single specimen plants, and is often trimmed into architectural or fantastic shapes. Our stock embraces both clipped and unclipped plants, the former trained as pyramids, standards or low-headed bushes.

B. sempervirens handsworthi. HANDSWORTH'S BOX. A distinct form of the Boxwood, of stiff upright habit, bearing large, dark green, oval leaves; very hardy.

B. suffruticosa. DWARF BOX. A dwarf compact shrub with evergreen foliage, extensively used for low hedges. Our strain is exceptionally hardy, of a pleasing bright lustrous green color, and is carefully selected from noteworthy old gardens. The low Box borders of many gardens, especially the old-time gardens, lend a sense of dignity and beauty that is difficult to surpass. The remarkably fine effect of Box hedges in Washington's garden at Mount Vernon is known to thousands.

Calluna vulgaris

Calluna · The Scotch Heather

This, the famous Heather of literature, is a dwarf evergreen shrub much resembling a small cedar. It thrives in almost any well-drained soil and is relatively hardy, thriving even in New England. Effective results are obtained by grouping or massing and especially in front of coniferous or other evergreens.

Calluna vulgaris. SCOTCH HEATHER. A low, compact shrub densely covered with minute green leaves. Native of Northern Europe. Flowers in great profusion, pink or rosy pink. Very handsome and invariably admired.

C. vulgaris alba. WHITE-FLOWERED SCOTCH HEATHER. A form with white flowers. Planted along with the typical variety the color contrast is very pleasing.

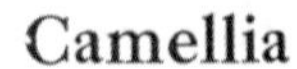

Camellia

The Camellia and Tea Plant

Evergreen shrubs with handsome foliage and showy flowers. Cultivated in the open air in the Southern States and California, and as pot-plants in the North. They thrive in fertile porous soils, either in sun or partial shade.

Camellia japonica. CAMELLIA. A shrub with shining dark green leaves and beautiful waxy flowers of great substance and durability. Native of China and Japan. We offer a choice assortment of varieties embracing double-flowered forms, white, pink and variegated.

C. thea (*Thea bohea* and *T. viridis*). TEA PLANT. A shrub with dark green elliptic leaves and white fragrant flowers. Native of China. This is the true tea plant from which the tea of commerce is obtained. It is hardy in the South and is successfully grown in South Carolina, where many thousands of pounds of tea are annually harvested and sent to market.

Chamædaphne · The Leather-leaf

A hardy dwarf shrub, chiefly valuable for the extreme earliness of its pretty white flowers. A sandy moist loam is best for garden conditions, although the plant thrives in wet boggy land and is a good subject for waterside planting.

Chamaedaphne calyculata (*Cassandra calyculata*). LEATHER-LEAF. A small evergreen shrub widely distributed over the Northern Hemisphere. Leaves dull green above, with minute rusty scales beneath. Flowers white, nodding, in leafy racemes, opening at the first approach of spring.

For grades and prices of above, see pages 147 and 149

Cleyera · The Japanese Cleyera

A very pretty shrub that is frequently cultivated in the Southern and Pacific States as a garden plant. It thrives in rich loamy soil, either in sun or partial shade.

Cleyera japonica. JAPANESE CLEYERA. A charming evergreen shrub, attaining a height of about six feet. Leaves rich glossy green, thick and leathery. Flowers creamy white, fragrant, borne in profusion in early summer. Berries red, persisting all winter.

Cotoneaster · The Evergreen Cotoneasters

Handsome evergreen shrubs of great value for planting in rock-gardens. They thrive in any well-drained soil, either in full sun or partial shade. They are relatively hardy except in the colder sections of the North.

Cotoneaster buxifolia. BOX-LEAVED COTONEASTER. A low spreading shrub with small persistent leaves resembling those of the Boxwood. Native of the Himalayas. Flowers white, in small clusters, appearing in spring or early summer, soon followed by bright red fruit. Very attractive.

Cotoneaster microphylla

C. horizontalis. PROSTRATE COTONEASTER. A low shrub with almost horizontal branches. Native of China. Leaves dark green, persistent or nearly so, about half an inch long. Flowers pinkish white, solitary or in pairs. Fruit bright red. Very attractive in rockeries.

C. microphylla. SMALL-LEAVED COTONEASTER. A smaller shrub than the last, with minute glossy persistent leaves. Native of the Himalayas. Flowers white, usually solitary, expanding in late spring. Fruit bright red, persisting until midwinter. The effect of this pretty species, closely hugging the rocks among which it is often planted, is very unique.

C. simoni. SHINING-LEAVED ROSE BOX. An attractive shrub with spreading branches. Native of the Himalayas. Leaves about three-quarters of an inch long, deep lustrous green, semi-persistent or wholly evergreen. Flowers white, in 2- to 5-flowered clusters, followed by bright red berries. Very showy.

C. thymifolia. THYME-LEAVED COTONEASTER. Similar in many respects to *C. microphylla*, but smaller and of more spreading habit. Native of the Himalayas. Foliage bright shining green, whitened beneath, persistent. Flowers white, in late spring, followed by a wealth of scarlet berries. One of the most attractive species.

Daphne · The Evergreen Garland Flowers

Charming shrubs with evergreen foliage and showy, sweet-scented flowers. They thrive in light, well-drained soils, either fully exposed to the sun or in partial shade. A top-dressing of thoroughly decomposed manure or a mulch of fine leaves is very beneficial. The species *cneorum* and *blagayana* are hardy in the North, and while the others thrive in Tennessee and Southern New York, they should be afforded protection.

Daphne blagayana. WHITE GARLAND FLOWER. An attractive little shrub with relatively broad, lustrous green leaves, from the mountains of Southeastern Europe. Flowers white or creamy white, fragrant, about an inch long, produced in compact, many-flowered heads. Very beautiful.

D. cneorum. GARLAND FLOWER. A dwarf shrub of trailing habit, with numerous heads of small pink, delightfully fragrant flowers. From the mountains of Middle Europe. Leaves crowded, dark green and glossy above, glaucous beneath. One of the daintiest of flowering shrubs.

D. hybrida (*D. dauphini*). HYBRID GARLAND FLOWER. A garden hybrid similar to *D. odora*, but much hardier. An erect shrub with dark green shining leaves, 2 to 3 inches long. Flowers fragrant, ruddy purple, relatively large. A splendid shrub for the warmer portions of the country.

D. laureola. SPURGE LAUREL. A bushy evergreen shrub with thick glossy leaves. Native of Europe and Asia. Flowers yellowish green, in short racemes, slightly if at all odorous. Commonly planted in shade.

Dendrium · The Sand Myrtle

A hardy evergreen shrub with intricate branches. It thrives in sandy or loamy soils, either in sunny or partly shaded situations. Very effective in rockeries or in front of other evergreens. The best results are obtained by planting in masses or colonies.

Dendrium buxifolium (*Leiophyllum buxifolium*). SAND MYRTLE. A low shrub, densely clothed with small dark green leaves, resembling somewhat those of the Dwarf Boxwood. Occurs naturally from New Jersey to Florida. Flowers white or pinkish, borne in profusion in spring. Very neat and attractive.

Elæagnus · The Evergreen Oleasters

Graceful shrubs with handsome foliage and showy fruit. The evergreen species are hardy as far north as Memphis and Washington. They grow in almost any porous soil, either in sun or partial shade.

Elaeagnus macrophylla. BROAD-LEAVED OLEASTER. An interesting shrub with silvery white branches. Native of Japan. Leaves broadly ovate, green above, silvery white beneath. Flowers creamy white, with brown and silvery scales on the outside. Planted in close proximity to the next species, a beautiful and striking contrast is obtained.

E. reflexa (*E. pungens*). BRONZE OLEASTER. A spreading shrub with bronze-brown branches. Native of Japan. Leaves 2 to 4 inches long, dark green above, coated beneath with lustrous silvery and brown scales. Flowers in axillary clusters, creamy white, very fragrant.

E. reflexa variegata. VARIEGATED OLEASTER. A form with the leaves beautifully marked with yellow.

Ephedra · The Shrubby Horsetail

A low shrub, evergreen in effect (from the color of the branches), thriving in sandy soils. Perfectly hardy at Biltmore and likely to thrive as far north as New England and Missouri. A strange and curious plant, attracting attention wherever seen.

Ephedra distachya. TWO-SPIKED EPHEDRA. A much-branched, spreading or procumbent shrub. Native of Europe and Asia. Branches green, wand-like, resembling the Wild Horsetail. Flowers inconspicuous.

For grades and prices of above, see page 148

Plantation of Kalmias against Hemlocks

Erica · The Heaths

Small evergreen shrubs with numerous short branches, densely clothed with small needle-like leaves. They are very showy plants, thriving in porous, fertile soils. The species described are the hardiest, and thrive in sheltered situations, even in the North.

Erica carnea. MOOR HEATH. A low shrub indigenous to Switzerland and the Balkans. Flowers bright rose, drooping, borne on short pedicels, opening in earliest spring. A charming little plant, excellent for shrub- or rock-gardens.

E. stricta. CORSICAN HEATH. A larger shrub than the preceding one, with erect and rigid branches. Native of Corsica. Flowers in summer and early autumn, rosy purple, disposed in terminal clusters. A very showy species.

E. tetralix. CROSS-LEAVED HEATH. An attractive dwarf shrub with grayish green foliage. Native of Europe. Flowers rosy pink, in summer and early autumn, freely borne at the tips of the branches. The leaves are delicately fringed with short white hairs. This species was used as the insignia of the Scotch clan of Macdonald.

E. vagans. CORNISH HEATH. A free-flowering shrub with the leaves in whorls of fours and fives. Native of Western Europe. Flowers purplish red, borne on one side of the branches and expanding in summer and early autumn. A charming plant.

Euonymus · The Evergreen Euonymus

Ornamental shrubs with glossy evergreen foliage, thriving in any porous, fertile soil. Hardy as far north as New Jersey and Tennessee. *Euonymus japonicus* is largely used in the South as a hedge plant. It stands clipping remarkably well and forms a dense evergreen hedge of great beauty. The variety *microphyllus* may be used in the same manner as the Dwarf Box, as a low edging or border plant.

Euonymus japonicus. EVERGREEN EUONYMUS. A handsome evergreen shrub of dense upright habit. Native of Japan. Leaves dark lustrous green, holding their brilliancy and attractiveness throughout the winter. A grand plant for single specimens on the lawn, either in sun or in partial shade, or as tub plants for decorating cool rooms or corridors.

E. japonicus aureo-variegatus. VARIEGATED EUONYMUS. Leaves beautifully variegated with golden yellow. Valuable where lively effects are desired, or for jardinières.

E. japonicus microphyllus (*E. pulchellus*). SMALL-LEAVED EUONYMUS. A dwarf form of the above with small and narrow foliage. Valuable for low hedges.

Gardenia · The Cape Jasmines

Evergreen shrubs with large fragrant flowers, blossoming from spring until autumn in the South, where they are frequently planted. Hardy as far north as Tennessee and Virginia. Thrive in fertile loamy soil. They make splendid house plants on account of the durability of the flowers.

Gardenia jasminoides (*G. florida*). CAPE JASMINE. This beautiful flowering shrub is again becoming very popular. The double wax-like flowers, which are exquisitely fragrant, are greatly in demand for buttonhole bouquets.

G. jasminoides fortunei. LARGE-FLOWERED CAPE JASMINE. Flowers larger than those of the preceding. A splendid plant for jardinières.

Erica vagans

For grades and prices of above, see page 148

Ilex · The Inkberry, or Winterberry

An evergreen shrub of great hardiness and adaptability. It thrives in sandy soil, either in sun or partial shade, and is admirably adapted for rockeries or border planting.

Ilex glabra. INKBERRY, OR WINTERBERRY. An upright, much-branched shrub, seldom attaining in cultivation more than 2 to 4 feet in height. Occurs naturally from Massachusetts to the Gulf. Leaves dark green and shining above, pale beneath, retaining their brilliancy throughout the winter. Berries black.

Illicium · The Anise Tree

A handsome broad-leaved evergreen with aromatic twigs and foliage. It is frequently planted in California and the South, and thrives in porous loamy soils.

Illicium anisatum (*I. religiosum*). ANISE TREE. Leaves thick and leathery, bright green, emitting an anise-like fragrance when bruised. Flowers with numerous narrow petals, yellowish. Native of Japan.

Kalmia · The American Laurels

Beautiful evergreen shrubs with showy flowers. The Mountain Laurel is one of the most ornamental shrubs in cultivation, and its liberal use makes possible some of the most enchanting results. Kalmias thrive in porous or loamy soils, especially those containing leaf-mould or woods earth. A mulch of forest leaves or pine needles is beneficial, preventing the rapid evaporation of moisture and sudden changes of temperature from affecting the roots. Either massed, in groups, or as single specimens, the floral effects are most beautiful, and we confidently recommend these valuable hardy plants.

Kalmia angustifolia. NARROW-LEAVED LAUREL. A dwarf shrub somewhat resembling the better known broad-leaved variety. Grows naturally from Hudson's Bay to Georgia. Flowers wheel-shaped, rosy purple with crimson marks, borne in great profusion.

K. latifolia. MOUNTAIN LAUREL, OR CALICO BUSH. One of the most attractive of broad-leaved evergreens, both on account of its wide, dark green and glossy leaves, and for its masses of showy pink or rose-colored flowers which appear in greatest profusion in early summer. It is found growing from Nova Scotia to Florida, and seems to endure all conditions of climate.

Leucothoë · The Evergreen Leucothoës

Graceful and desirable shrubs with brilliant evergreen foliage and showy flowers. They thrive in moist porous soils, especially those containing leaf-mould or woods earth. A mulch of forest leaves or similar material adds greatly to their comfort and development. In the selection of a site, a northern exposure should be chosen, but failing in

Kalmia latifolia

For grades and prices of above, see page 148

Leucothoë, continued

this, with sufficient moisture and partial shade, excellent results may be obtained.

Leucothoë acuminata. PIPEWOOD. A shrub with leathery evergreen leaves and spreading hollow branches. Grows naturally in the South Atlantic States, but with slight protection is hardy as far north as Washington and Tennessee. Flowers white, appearing in early summer. This is the "Ti-ti" of South Carolina and Florida, extensively collected for pipe stems.

L. catesbaei. CATESBY'S LEUCOTHOE. A hardy, graceful shrub with spreading, recurved branches. Grows naturally from Virginia to Georgia, in the mountains. Leaves dark shining green, borne in fern-like regularity on the arching stems, and assuming in winter brilliant shades of bronze and vinous red. Flowers creamy white, in axillary racemes, fragrant and showy. The leaf-sprays are extensively used for Christmas greens.

Leucothoe catesbæi

Ligustrum

The Evergreen Privets

Very attractive shrubs with handsome foliage and showy flowers. They are of inestimable value in the Southern and Pacific States for grouping or massing in border plantations, or as specimen plants for the lawn. They make handsome hedges when closely planted in single rows and stand clipping to sharp and formal lines without detriment. The Chinese Ligustrum is an admirable hedge plant, which we confidently recommend. The Amoor Privet, described under "Deciduous Shrubs," is also an excellent hedge plant, but is not altogether evergreen at Biltmore.

Ligustrum japonicum. JAPANESE PRIVET. A handsome evergreen shrub of dense and symmetrical outline. Native of Japan. Leaves thick, dark lustrous green, often with a reddish margin and midrib. Flowers creamy white, disposed in loose panicles. The berries are bluish black, with a bloom.

Berries of Ligustrum sinense

L. quihoui. LATE-FLOWERING PRIVET. An attractive shrub of spreading habit. Native of China. Leaves dark lustrous green, persistent in the South, half evergreen in the North. Flowers creamy white, in large panicles, opening after the flowers of the other species have fallen. Berries blue-black with a bloom. The showiest and latest flowering species.

Ligustrum sinense. CHINESE PRIVET. A tall shrub of graceful habit, with dark green glossy leaves, which are persistent in the South, semi-evergreen in the North. Flowers in great profusion in late spring or early summer, creamy white, disposed in numerous panicles. Berries blue-black, with a bloom, on older specimens literally covering the branches. Very handsome.

Myrtus · The Myrtle

This classic shrub, with handsome aromatic foliage, is extensively cultivated as a pot-plant in the North, or in the open air in California and the South. It is easily cultivated, requiring only a fertile soil and an abundance of water during the growing season.

Myrtus communis. TRUE MYRTLE. A noteworthy shrub with strongly scented lustrous green leaves. Flowers pure white, deliciously fragrant, either single or double. We can furnish both forms.

Nandina

An interesting shrub closely related to the Barberries. It is often planted in the South and in California, and is hardy as far north as Washington and Tennessee. Has withstood temperatures below zero at Biltmore. It thrives in any well-drained loamy soil.

Nandina domestica. JAPANESE NANDINA. Of stiff upright habit, occasionally reaching a height of six or eight feet. Native of China and Japan. Leaves compound, with numerous small leaflets, rich red when young, at maturity dark green, assuming beautiful coppery tones in winter. Flowers white, in panicles, very numerous.

Nerium

The Oleander

This old-fashioned, yet popular shrub is extensively cultivated as a house plant in the North, and as a garden plant in the Southern States and California. There are both single- and double-flowered forms, the popular colors ranging from white to shades of rose and pink.

Flowers of Ligustrum sinense

For grades and prices of above, see pages 148 and 149

Nerium, continued

All of the varieties are of easy culture, thriving in almost any kind of soil. They are adapted to city conditions, withstanding smoke and dust without apparent detriment.

Nerium oleander. OLEANDER. A free-flowering shrub with narrow dark green leaves. Native of Southern Europe and the Orient. We can supply the following distinct varieties, Single or Double: White, Pink, Rose.

Osmanthus · The Fragrant Olives

In the South and in California, these handsome shrubs are desirable garden objects, both on account of their attractive foliage and very fragrant flowers. The Holly-leaved Olive is hardy as far north as Memphis and Philadelphia.

Osmanthus aquifolium. HOLLY-LEAVED OLIVE. An evergreen shrub with spiny-toothed leaves resembling those of the Holly. Native of Japan. In the autumn it produces short axillary clusters of deliciously fragrant white flowers. Very attractive and the hardiest of the genus.

O. fragrans. FRAGRANT OLIVE. A shrub with thick glossy evergreen leaves. Native of Asia. Flowers white, in spreading clusters, exquisitely fragrant. In the North often used as a pot-plant.

Phillyrea · The Filarias

Ornamental evergreen shrubs thriving in sheltered positions as far north as Missouri and New York. A porous, loamy soil, in sun or partial shade, is adapted to their requirements.

Phillyrea angustifolia. NARROW-LEAVED FILARIA. A graceful shrub with spreading branches, and narrow, dull green leaves. Native of Southern Europe. In early summer it bears numerous small white, fragrant flowers which are soon followed by small dark fruits.

P. decora (*P. vilmoriniana*). BROAD-LEAVED FILARIA. A handsome shrub with stout, spreading branches. Native of Western Asia. Leaves dark green and shining above, yellowish beneath. Flowers white, in axillary clusters, in early summer. Berries purplish black.

Photinia · The Evergreen Photinia

A highly ornamental evergreen shrub of easy culture. Hardy as far north as Washington and Memphis, but needs protection from cold winds. It thrives best in a moist, sandy loam, either in full sun or partial shade.

Photinia serrulata. EVERGREEN PHOTINIA. A tall shrub with handsome shining foliage. Native of China. Leaves 5 to 7 inches long, dark green, often with ruddy margins and footstalks. Flowers in broad panicles, white, soon followed by a wealth of bright red berries.

Pieris · The Fetter Bushes

The beautiful white flowers of these valuable shrubs expand with the first breath of early spring. They thrive in partial shade or in situations with northern exposure, in any porous, fertile soil, especially one containing leaf-mould. The American species is extremely hardy, the Japanese requiring protection from cold winds in Missouri and Massachusetts.

Pieris floribunda (*Andromeda floribunda*). MOUNTAIN FETTER BUSH. A dense evergreen shrub attaining in cultivation a height of 2 to 4 feet. Native of the high mountains from Virginia to Georgia. Leaves dark green above, black-dotted beneath, densely clothing the short stiff branches. Flowers showy, produced in terminal panicles well above the foliage. One of the most desirable ornamentals.

P. japonica (*Andromeda japonica*). JAPANESE FETTER BUSH. Of larger size and looser habit than the last. Leaves bright green, assuming in winter rich tones of red and bronze. Flowers in drooping panicles, more or less associated with the leaves. A very graceful shrub of Japanese origin.

Pittosporum · The Japanese Pittosporum

A winter-flowering evergreen shrub, often grown in the South and in California in the open air, and in the North as a house plant. It withstands some degrees of frost. Thrives in a porous, fertile soil in sun or partial shade.

Pittosporum tobira. TOBIRA, OR JAPANESE PITTOSPORUM. Leaves dark green, clustered at the tips of the branches. Flowers pure white, fragrant, produced in short dense clusters. Makes a splendid specimen plant.

Pyracantha · The Evergreen Thorn

When loaded with bright scarlet berries in autumn and early winter, the Pyracantha Thorn is one of the showiest of ornamental shrubs. It thrives in any porous soil, either in full sun or partial shade, the former situation being more conducive to highly colored fruit. Often used as a hedge plant. Hardy as far north as Missouri and New England, but should be afforded protection from cold winds.

Pyracantha coccinea (*Cratægus pyracantha*). EVERGREEN, OR PYRACANTHA THORN. A compact, much-branched evergreen shrub of low, spreading habit. Native of Southern Europe. Flowers white, in flat-topped clusters in spring, soon followed by a wealth of scarlet berries. Should be in every collection.

P. coccinea lalandi. LALAND'S PYRACANTHA. A variety of the above of more vigorous and hardy constitution, being especially adapted for training against walls or lattice. Perhaps more fruitful and decorative than the typical form, but of straggly outline.

Berries of Pyracantha coccinea

For grades and prices of above, see page 149

Rhododendron maximum

Rhododendron
The Rosebay and Laurels

These, the showiest of all ornamentals, are justly popular hardy evergreen shrubs. They are very effective as single specimens on the lawn, or in groups or masses in front of coniferous or other evergreens. Their handsome foliage and showy flowers make possible some of the most enchanting results, and add a zest and interest that cannot be obtained by any other plants. They thrive in porous, fertile soils, preferring a northern exposure with partial shade. When in the open, it is advisable to shelter the plantations against drying winds and hot sun by a belt of tall, coniferous evergreens. After planting, the surface of the ground should be liberally covered with forest leaves or pine needles to protect the roots from sudden changes of temperature. The dwarf varieties are more effective if planted by themselves, as their smaller leaves and flowers do not harmonize with those of larger species. The Great Laurel is the largest and hardiest, while the Catawba Rhododendron and its numerous garden forms ranks second.

Rhododendron arbutifolium (*R. wilsonianum*). DWARF RHODODENDRON. A beautiful dwarf shrub of compact habit. Of garden origin. Leaves 2 to 3 inches long, dark green, densely clothing the short branches. Flowers pink or very light rose, expanding during the summer. This variety is very hardy and among the best of the dwarf Rhododendrons.

R. catawbiense. CATAWBA RHODODENDRON. A highly ornamental species indigenous to the mountains from Virginia to Georgia. Leaves oval or oblong, bright green above, glaucous beneath, clustered at the ends of the branches. Flowers very large, rose-purple, freely produced in late spring. A magnificent hardy flowering shrub. The following varieties, known as Catawba Hybrid Rhododendrons, are among the best and hardiest in cultivation:

A. Lincoln. Crimson, of a rich and brilliant shade.

Album elegans. Blush, changing to white; large flowers.

Album grandiflorum. Blush-white; very large truss and flowers.

Anna Parsons. Soft red.

Atrosanguineum. Deep blood-red; of great substance.

Betsy Parsons. Reddish purple.

Caractacus. Rich purplish crimson; grand truss.

Catawbiense album. White. One of the best, and very floriferous.

Charles Bagley. Cherry-red; large truss.

Charles Dickens. Dark scarlet. Handsome.

Delicatissimum. Blush-white, tinted pink. A handsome and extremely desirable variety.

Everestianum. Rosy lilac, spotted and fringed. The best hardy Rhododendron.

General Grant. Bright red. One of the best of the bright-colored forms.

Giganteum. Light rose; large truss and flowers.

H. H. Hunnewell. Dark rich crimson. Splendid.

Lady Armstrong. Pale rose, beautifully spotted.

Lee's Purple. Dark purple; free-flowering.

Parsons' gloriosum. Soft rose, of a most delightful shade.

Parsons' grandiflorum. Clear rose; free flowering and unusually effective.

President Lincoln. Soft rose.

Purpureum elegans. Fine purple; large truss and flowers.

Roseum elegans. Rose.

Roseum superbum. Light rose.

Rhododendron arbutifolium

For grades and prices of above, see page 149

Specimen plant of Rhododendron arbutifolium

Rhododendrons, continued

Rhododendron maximum. Rose Bay, or Great Laurel. A magnificent large shrub with narrowly oblong dark green leaves which vary from 6 to 10 inches in length. Occurs naturally from Canada to Georgia. Flowers pinkish white, in profuse large clusters in early summer. This is the grandest species for massing. We are prepared to furnish splendid plants in any quantity. For carload lots please write for quotations.

R. myrtifolium. Myrtle-leaved Rhododendron. A low dense shrub of garden origin. Leaves dark green, assuming in winter a rich shade of bronze. Flowers pink or rose-color. A charming plant.

R. punctatum. Small, or Early-flowering Rhododendron. A distinct hardy species from the high mountains of North Carolina and Georgia. Leaves dark green, dotted beneath. Flowers in spring, pale rose, spotted with yellow-green within. The earliest-flowering species.

Viburnum · The Evergreen Viburnum and Laurustinus

Beautiful free-flowering shrubs, frequently grown in the open air in the Southern States and California, or as pot-plants in the North. They thrive in almost any well-drained fertile soil.

Viburnum sandankwa (*V. suspensa*). Evergreen Viburnum. A shrub with slender warty branches, attaining a height of 4 to 5 feet. Native of the Loochoo Islands. Leaves dark shining green, 3 to 4 inches long. Flowers white, or tinted with pink, in dense clusters, resembling those of the Trailing Arbutus, expanding in early spring.

V. tinus. Laurustinus. An evergreen shrub with dark green shining leaves. Native of Southern Europe. Flowers white or flesh-colored, fragrant, borne in numerous terminal clusters. Berries black at maturity.

Catawba hybrid Rhododendrons

For grades and prices of above, see page 149

DECIDUOUS SHRUBS

THE judicious planting of shrubs adds greatly to the beauty and value of property, and contributes a wealth of pleasure and interest to the home. There are a few hard and fast principles, yet simple ones, governing the artistic arrangement of these beautiful ornamentals, that should be more strictly observed. In general, individual specimens, those grown wholly for the characteristic grace or attractiveness of the specific subject, should rarely be isolated from the body of the design. Irregular groups or masses arranged against buildings, fences or property lines, or as border plantations along walks or drives, are much more effective. A good arrangement of shrubs invariably provides wide open stretches near the center of the lawn. From the comprehensive list of shrubs which follows, it is possible to select plants adapted to a wide range of conditions and requirements. Our collection is extensive but extremely practical, carefully grown and the plants vigorous and healthy. In propagating, it is our practice, so far as it is possible to perfect the selection, to handle only the offspring of desirable and noteworthy specimens.

Acanthopanax · The Five-leaved Angelica

A hardy ornamental shrub with prickly branches, in habit much resembling an Aralia. It is excellent for planting on rocky banks or slopes, thriving in almost any well-drained soil.

Acanthopanax pentaphyllum (*Aralia pentaphylla*). FIVE-LEAVED ANGELICA. Of compact, graceful outline, usually attaining a height of 5 to 8 feet. Native of Japan. Leaves compound, consisting of 5 to 7 leaflets, bright green and shining. Flowers greenish, borne in long-stalked clusters. The effect of the luxuriant glossy foliage crowning the arching branches is very beautiful.

Adelia · The Adelias or American Privets

Hardy shrubs with handsome dark green foliage, thriving best in moist loamy soil. Very attractive hedges may be made by planting the pointed-leaved Adelia in single rows, keeping it clipped to formal outline.

Adelia acuminata (*Forestiera acuminata*). POINTED-LEAVED ADELIA. A twiggy, almost spiny shrub, attaining a height of 6 to 8 feet. Occurs naturally from Illinois to Georgia and Texas. Leaves 2 to 3 inches long, pointed at the apex, rich dark green. Flowers small, nearly yellow, appearing in early spring before the leaves.

A. ligustrina (*Forestiera ligustrina*). PRIVET-LEAVED ADELIA. A spreading shrub of irregular outline, reaching a height of about 6 feet. Distributed naturally from Tennessee to Florida. Leaves obtuse at the tips, dark green, about an inch long. Flowers small, in tiny clusters, expanding before the leaves unfold.

Æsculus · The Dwarf Horse-chestnut

A singularly attractive hardy shrub, producing long spikes of showy flowers. Planted in groups on the lawn, or in connection with other shrubbery, magnificent floral results may be obtained. It thrives best in porous, loamy soil. Other species are described under "Deciduous Trees."

AEsculus parviflora (*Æ. macrostachya*). DWARF HORSE CHESTNUT. A free-flowering shrub usually attaining a height of 5 to 8 feet. Native of the Southern States. Leaves compound, consisting of 5 to 7 dark green leaflets. Flowers creamy white, often suffused with pink, produced in narrow spikes 10 to 16 inches long. One of the handsomest of ornamentals.

Alnus · The Shrubby Alders

Small hardy shrubs with handsome foliage, adapted to waterside planting, especially on the banks of rocky brooks. They thrive in any moist soil.

Alnus alnobetula (*A. viridis*). GREEN, OR MOUNTAIN ALDER. Seldom exceeds 4 or 5 feet in height. Widely distributed in the Northern Hemisphere. Leaves broadly oval, rich lustrous green above, pale beneath. Catkins drooping, long and slender, flowering in early spring. Very pleasing.

A. rugosa. SMOOTH ALDER. A shrub or small tree occurring from Maine to Minnesota, Florida and Texas. Leaves green on both sides, oval in outline, minutely toothed. Flowers in earliest spring or late winter, the staminate ones drooping in long, slender catkins. Very attractive in spring. Grows 10 to 15 feet high.

For grades and prices of above, see page 150

Amelanchier · The Dwarf Juneberries

Free-flowering hardy shrubs of great adaptability. The blossoms expand very early in spring and are soon followed by a bountiful crop of blue-black edible berries. They thrive in almost any well-drained soil. Other species are described under "Deciduous Trees."

Amelanchier alnifolia. ALDER-LEAVED, OR WESTERN JUNEBERRY. A shrub with oval or nearly orbicular leaves, widely distributed in the Western States. Flowers white, in short racemes, relatively large and showy. Fruit purplish, or when fully ripe, blue-black with a bloom, sweet and juicy. Grows 3 to 6 feet tall. Often grown in gardens, in the same manner as currants and gooseberries, for the abundant crop of luscious berries, which ripen in June and July.

A. rotundifolia. ROUND-LEAVED JUNEBERRY. A remarkably floriferous shrub of irregular outline, growing naturally from New Brunswick and Minnesota to North Carolina. Leaves rounded, coarsely but shallowly toothed, bright rich green. Flowers white, in drooping racemes, very showy; the petals unusually long and broad. Fruit blue-black, sweet and succulent. Attains a height of 4 to 6 feet.

A. spicata. DWARF JUNEBERRY. A low shrub 1 to 3 feet tall, occurring in a wild state from Pennsylvania to North Carolina. Leaves elliptical, woolly when young, eventually bright green. Flowers white, in long dense racemes. Splendid for rockeries.

A. vulgaris. EUROPEAN SERVICEBERRY, OR JUNEBERRY. An attractive shrub, though rarely seen in American gardens. Native of Central Europe. Leaves rounded, coarsely but shallowly toothed, bright green above, woolly beneath when young. Flowers white, disposed in short racemes; the petals long and narrow. Fruit blue-black, sweet and juicy.

Amorpha · The Lead Plant and Indigo Bushes

Hardy free-flowering shrubs with feathery foliage, thriving in sunny situations in well-drained soils. They are very valuable for border plantations, or for massing on rocky slopes or banks. The unusual color of the flowers invariably attracts attention.

Amorpha canescens. LEAD PLANT. A low dense shrub of silvery aspect. Native of the Middle West. Leaves compound, consisting of 15 to 47 crowded leaflets. Flowers light blue, in dense clustered racemes. Splendid for rock-gardens.

A. fruticosa. FALSE INDIGO. A branching shrub, usually 6 to 10 feet tall, growing naturally from North Carolina to the Gulf. Leaves compound, consisting of 11 to 25 bright green leaflets. Flowers violet-purple, disposed in clustered racemes, 3 to 6 inches long.

A. herbacea. DWARF INDIGO. A low shrub with all its parts grayish green. Distributed naturally from North Carolina to Florida. Leaves compound, consisting of 11 to 37 small leaflets which are distinctly dotted with dark glands. Flowers in long clustered racemes, violet-purple. Desirable for rock-gardens or sandy soils.

A. montana. Mountain Indigo. A smooth, much-branched shrub 4 to 6 feet high, indigenous to the high mountains of North Carolina and Tennessee. Leaves compound, consisting of 9 to 19 bright green leaflets which have a decided purplish tone and glaucous bloom when young. Flowers violet-purple, in clustered racemes, 4 to 6 inches long. This is the handsomest of the taller-growing species.

A. tennesseensis. TENNESSEE INDIGO. A very distinct ornamental shrub, usually growing 6 to 10 feet high. A native of Middle Tennessee. Leaves compound, consisting of 21 to 55 small bright green leaflets. Flowers violet-purple, in clustered racemes, 4 to 6 inches long.

Aronia · The Chokeberries

Small hardy shrubs with handsome foliage, thriving best in moist loamy soil. They are very valuable plants for massing, both on account of the early white flowers and the profuse clusters of showy berries.

A good example of shrub planting

For grades and prices of above, see page 150

Azalea arborescens

Aronia, continued

Aronia arbutifolia (*Pyrus arbutifolia*). RED CHOKEBERRY. A very ornamental shrub, usually attaining a height of 3 to 5 feet. Grows naturally from Nova Scotia to the Gulf. Leaves bright green above, woolly beneath, fading in autumn with tones of yellow, orange and red. Flowers white, disposed in profuse terminal clusters. Berries bright red, persisting until late winter.

A. nigra (*Pyrus nigra*). BLACK CHOKEBERRY. Similar to the preceding species, except that the berries are black and the leaves quite smooth on the under surface. Very effective results may be obtained by planting small groups of each species sufficiently close to contrast the colors of the showy berries.

Azalea • The Deciduous Azaleas

These beautiful shrubs are among the showiest of ornamentals and should have a prominent place in every garden. They thrive in moist well-drained soils, preferring those containing leaf-mould or woods earth, either in full sun or partial shade. A liberal mulch of forest leaves held in place by a light sprinkling of earth, is advantageous, and while ordinarily quite hardy, a protection from cold piercing winds in bleak situations should be provided.

Azalea arborescens. FRAGRANT AZALEA. A large deciduous shrub with bright green foliage which assumes a rich shade of crimson in autumn. Native of the Alleghany Mountains. Flowers sweet-scented, white, tinged with rose, and with long exserted red style and stamens. One of the easiest Azaleas to cultivate, thriving in almost any situation. Very showy and desirable.

A. gandavensis. GHENT AZALEA. Of the deciduous hardy Azaleas those known as the Ghent Hybrids are among the most floriferous and produce the largest flowers. The blossoms appear in profuse clusters in spring, literally covering the branches with their varied and gorgeous hues. The following are the best and hardiest varieties:

Arethusa. Double; creamy white, tinged with yellow. A very beautiful, free-flowering variety.

Daviesi. Single; pure white. Remarkable on account of the delightful fragrance.

Geant des Batailles. Single; deep crimson. Superb.

Guelder Roos. Single; bright orange. Free flowering.

Louis A. Van Houtte. Double; vermilion-red. Very rich and warm in effect.

Mina Van Houtte. Double; rosy pink. The color-tone is unusually soft and beautiful.

Azalea lutea (*A. calendulacea*). FLAME-COLORED AZALEA. One of the most gorgeous of flowering shrubs, producing in late spring profuse clusters of large flowers, ranging from flame-color through shades of red and yellow. Grows naturally from New York and Pennsylvania to Georgia. A most valuable plant, remaining in bloom for several weeks. Usually grows from 6 to 8 feet tall in cultivation.

A. mollis. JAPANESE AZALEA. A hardy deciduous shrub with flowers rivaling in size and substance those of the Indian Azalea. Besides the named varieties, which are often known as Mollis Hybrids, we offer a fine lot of seedlings embracing a wide range of colors which will be found very satisfactory for mass planting. Like the Ghent Azaleas, these beautiful shrubs are literally covered with flowers in spring:

Anthony Koster. Single; yellow, shaded with orange.

For grades and prices of above, see page 150

Azalea mollis, continued

Byron. Double; pure white.

Charles Rogier. Single; bright rose, margined with white. Remarkably effective and attractive. Produces quantities of handsome flowers.

Frederic de Merode. Single; scarlet. A bright and richly colored variety.

Murillo. Double; rosy purple. Excellent. A form that is highly recommended.

Virgille. Double; clear yellow.

A. nudiflora. PINKSTER FLOWER. A handsome free-flowering shrub, usually growing 3 to 5 feet in height. Flowers in early spring, before the leaves appear; deep pink, profuse and very showy. The extreme earliness and beauty of the flowers commend this shrub to the planter.

A. vaseyi (*Rhododendron vaseyi*). CAROLINA AZALEA. A distinct and remarkably free-flowering shrub. Native of the mountains of North Carolina. Flowers profuse, pink or rose, expanding in early spring before the leaves appear. In autumn the foliage assumes a deep rich tone of vinous red or crimson. In cultivation it usually attains a height of 4 to 6 feet.

A. viscosa. SMALL WHITE AZALEA. Usually a small shrub 2 to 4 feet tall, blossoming profusely at an early age. Grows naturally from Maine and Ohio to Florida. Flowers white, fragrant, very profuse. This species is the latest to flower.

Berries of Berberis thunbergi

Baccharis · The Groundsel Bush

A hardy species, cultivated for the beauty of the snowy white feathery appendages of the seeds, which lend to the fertile plants a very showy appearance. It thrives in almost any porous soil, preferring a situation in full sun. The most effective results are obtained by planting in groups or masses, thereby bringing the pistillate and staminate forms in close proximity.

Baccharis halimifolia. GROUNDSEL BUSH. A large shrub of spreading, bushy habit. Grows naturally from New England, southward to Florida and Texas. Foliage dark green and lustrous, remaining on the branches quite late in the season. The fruiting heads are very showy, consisting of large clusters of cottony white down. It is the only hardy member of the thistle family of shrub-like aspect. A remarkable plant, possessing a wonderful range of adaptability, thriving in proximity to salt water and in contact with its spray, or even in inland regions or high altitudes in the mountains.

Benzoin · The Spice Bush

A hardy ornamental shrub thriving best in moist, loamy soil. Very attractive as a specimen plant and for massing on the banks of streams or margins of ponds.

Benzoin benzoin (*Lindera benzoin*). SPICE BUSH. An early-flowering shrub, growing naturally from Canada to Georgia, westward to Kansas. Leaves bright green, fading in autumn with intense tones of yellow. Flowers yellow, in early spring, appearing before the leaves. Berries scarlet, in late summer or early autumn. Attains a height of 6 to 10 feet under ordinary conditions.

Berberis · The Deciduous Barberries

Hardy shrubs with thorny branches, thriving in almost any kind of soil. They are of inestimable value in the plantations, both on account of the profuse and highly colored fruits, and the gorgeous colors of the autumn foliage. Thunberg's Barberry is justly popular as a hedge plant, forming without clipping a low dense hedge of surpassing grace and beauty, or by the free use of the shears, a formal hedge of great density and durability.

Berberis canadensis. CANADIAN BARBERRY. A low shrub, seldom exceeding three feet in height. It is the only species indigenous to Eastern America, occurring in the Mountains of Virginia and Carolina. Leaves bristly-serrate, bright green, fading with rich tones of orange, red and bronze. Very ornamental.

B. heteropoda. TURKESTAN BARBERRY. A very handsome and distinct species, usually growing 3 to 5 feet in height. Leaves pale bluish green, assuming brilliant tones in autumn. Flowers in long-stalked racemes, orange-yellow, slightly fragrant.

B. thunbergi. THUNBERG'S BARBERRY. A graceful shrub of low dense habit. Native of Japan. Leaves entire, bright green, assuming in autumn dazzling tones of orange, scarlet and crimson. Berries brilliant red, borne in great profusion, and persisting throughout the winter. One of the most beautiful shrubs in cultivation.

B. vulgaris. COMMON EUROPEAN BARBERRY. A sturdy shrub, usually growing 5 to 8 feet tall. Native of Europe. Branches upright or arching, bearing a wealth of bristly-toothed dark green leaves. Flowers golden yellow, in profuse clusters in early spring; very showy. Berries bright scarlet, remaining on the branches throughout the winter.

B. vulgaris atropurpurea. PURPLE-LEAVED BARBERRY. A form of the last, with purple foliage. Very unique, and a striking contrast with the greenery of other shrubs.

For grades and prices of above, see pages 150 and 151

Buddleia · The Hardy Buddleias

These interesting free-flowering shrubs require light porous soils and sunny exposures for their best development. In the North, where they are not altogether hardy, sheltered situations should be selected. The handsome flowers are produced throughout the summer season.

Buddleia intermedia. HYBRID BUDDLEIA. A graceful and attractive shrub of garden origin, usually growing 4 to 6 feet in height. Leaves dark green, about 4 to 5 inches long. Flowers violet, disposed in slender drooping racemes 10 to 20 inches long. Invites comment wherever seen.

B. japonica (*B. curviflora*). JAPANESE BUDDLEIA. A curious shrub with four-sided, wing-margined branches, which attains a height of 4 to 6 feet. Native of Japan. Leaves dark green, 4 to 5 inches long. Flowers lilac, produced in dense, pendulous racemes 6 to 8 inches long. Very showy.

B. lindleyana. CHINESE BUDDLEIA. This has proved to be the hardiest of the Buddleias at Biltmore, and retains its foliage later in the season than the other species. A shrub with very dark green leaves, usually attaining a height of 5 to 8 feet. Native of China. Flowers violet-purple, in dense arching racemes 4 to 8 inches long.

B. variabilis. SWEET-SCENTED BUDDLEIA. Although recently introduced, this shrub has gained many admirers by reason of its profuse handsome flowers. Native of China. Flowers lilac, with an orange-yellow spot in the throat, produced in dense, terminal panicles 4 to 6 inches long. Very ornamental and desirable.

Butneria · The Carolina Allspice and Sweet Shrubs

Aromatic shrubs with deliciously fragrant flowers and handsome foliage. Most of the species are hardy and thrive in rich, loamy soil, either in sun or partial shade. They are popular favorites wherever grown.

Butneria fertilis (*Calycanthus lævigatus* and *glaucus*). CAROLINA ALLSPICE, OR SWEET SHRUB. A vigorous free-flowering shrub with upright, rigid branches. Native of the mountains from Virginia to Georgia. Leaves smooth, bright green, turning yellow in early autumn. Flowers chocolate-colored, very fragrant, produced in late spring and early summer. Grows 4 to 6 feet high.

B. florida (*Calycanthus floridus*). STRAWBERRY SHRUB. A desirable and very ornamental shrub, widely cultivated for its large fragrant flowers. Grows naturally from Virginia to Florida. Leaves broad, dark green above, downy beneath. Flowers reddish brown, sweet-scented, profusely borne in late spring and early summer. Grows 4 to 6 feet high.

B. occidentalis (*Calycanthus occidentalis*). WESTERN SWEET SHRUB. A larger shrub than the preceding species, usually attaining a height of 6 to 10 feet. Native of California. Flowers light brown, slightly fragrant, 2 to 3 inches wide. Not so hardy as the eastern forms.

Callicarpa · The So-called French Mulberries

The grace and exquisite beauty of the fruiting sprays of these superb plants are almost without parallel in the ranks of garden shrubs. A moist, loamy soil is best suited to their requirements.

Callicarpa americana. FRENCH MULBERRY. One of the handsomest species, but unfortunately not the hardiest. It will thrive as far north as Tennessee and Washington. A shrub 3 to 4 feet tall, with dark green, downy leaves. Fruit violet-purple, borne in great profusion. Very showy. Grows naturally from Virginia to Texas.

C. japonica. JAPANESE CALLICARPA. An upright shrub usually growing 3 to 4 feet tall. Native of Japan. Leaves dark green, long-pointed, with serrate borders. Flowers bright pink, followed in early autumn by a wealth of bright violet-colored berries. Relatively hardy and likely to thrive as far north as Missouri and Southern New York.

C. purpurea. PURPLE-FRUITED CALLICARPA, OR BEAUTY FRUIT. This is the hardiest species and the one most commonly cultivated. Leaves dark green, serrate above the middle, 2 to 3 inches long. Flowers pink, expanding in midsummer. Fruit violet-purple, produced in great profusion. Extremely ornamental.

Buddleia lindleyana

For grades and prices of above, see page 151

Caragana · The Pea Shrubs

Hardy shrubs with showy yellow flowers, thriving in almost any well-drained soil. They are valuable additions to shrub borders, providing a wealth of blossoms in spring or early summer.

Caragana arborescens. SIBERIAN PEA SHRUB. A large shrub with compound leaves, consisting of 8 to 12 bright green leaflets. Native of Siberia. Flowers yellow, in numerous small clusters, in late spring. Grows 10 to 12 feet tall.

C. chamlagu. MONGOLIAN PEA SHRUB. A small shrub, usually 3 to 4 feet high, with spiny branches. Native of Mongolia. Leaves compound, consisting of 2 to 4 dark green leaflets. Flowers large and showy, yellow, with an orange shade, opening in April and May. Very handsome.

Caryopteris · The Blue Spiræa

A very floriferous shrub with lavender-blue flowers in summer and early autumn. Not quite hardy in the colder sections. It requires a well-drained loamy soil and sunny situation.

Caryopteris mastacanthus. BLUE SPIRAEA, OR CHINESE BEARD-WORT. A compact shrub usually 3 to 4 feet high. Native of China. Leaves coarsely toothed, grayish green, 2 to 3 inches long. Flowers showy, very profuse. One of the best of the newer introductions.

Ceanothus · The New Jersey Tea

Attractive free-flowering shrubs, admirably adapted for planting in rockeries or shrub gardens. They thrive in almost any well-drained soil.

Ceanothus americanus. NEW JERSEY TEA. A low spreading shrub, usually about two feet tall. Grows naturally from Canada to Texas. Leaves bright green, very strongly nerved. Flowers white, in dense clustered panicles, blossoming in midsummer. The great profusion of delicate foam-like flowers has won many admirers. Very hardy.

C. hybridus Gloire de Versailles. HYBRID CEANOTHUS. A handsome late-flowering shrub of garden origin. The erect or spreading branches reach a height of 4 to 8 feet and are furnished with dark green rugose leaves. Flowers light blue, in large showy panicles. Hardy as far north as Memphis and Washington.

Buddleia variabilis (see page 59)

Cephalanthus · The Button Bush

A hardy vigorous shrub with large glossy foliage and attractive flowers. Thrives best in moist loamy soil. Very valuable for water-side planting, especially when fully exposed to the sun.

Cephalanthus occidentalis. BUTTON BUSH. In cultivation usually 4 to 6 feet tall. Flowers in dense round heads, creamy white, fragrant, appearing in midsummer. Grows naturally from Canada to Florida.

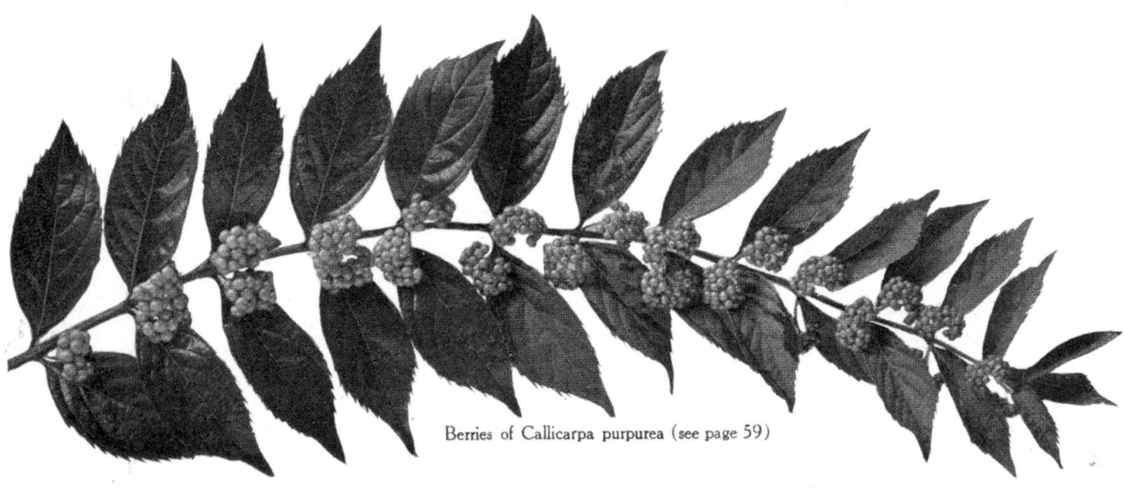

Berries of Callicarpa purpurea (see page 59)

Chimonanthus · The Oriental Sweet Shrub

An early-flowering shrub with a wealth of fragrant flowers, closely related to the American Sweet Shrubs. It thrives in moist loamy soils in sunny situations. Very desirable for the milder portions of the country.

Chimonanthus fragrans. ORIENTAL SWEET SHRUB. A shrub with dark green, lustrous foliage. Native of China and Japan. Flowers exquisitely fragrant, produced in great abundance in earliest spring and before the leaves appear, yellow, or with the inner sepals tinged with purplish brown. Not hardy north of Memphis and Washington.

Clethra · The Sweet Pepper Bushes, or White Alders

Hardy free-flowering shrubs with showy spikes of fragrant creamy white flowers. They thrive in moist loamy soil. The Clethras are justly classed among the most ornamental and desirable of garden shrubs.

Clethra acuminata. MOUNTAIN PEPPER BUSH. A tall shrub with dark green, long-pointed leaves. Native of the mountains from Virginia to Georgia. Flowers creamy white, fragrant, in nodding racemes. A showy plant, but quite rare in cultivation.

C. alnifolia. SWEET PEPPER BUSH. A sturdy compact shrub, usually attaining a height of 3 to 5 feet, widely distributed from Maine to Florida. Leaves dark green and lustrous, fading with yellow tones. Flowers creamy white, fragrant, in erect or panicled racemes. A grand flowering shrub and worthy of a prominent place in any garden.

Clethra alnifolia

Colutea · The Bladder Senna

Rapid-growing floriferous shrubs with curious inflated seed-pods. They are relatively hardy, but require protection from cold winds in the North. A well-drained soil and sunny exposure are best adapted to their requirements.

Ceanothus americanus (see page 60)

Colutea arborescens. BLADDER SENNA. A tall shrub with compound leaves, consisting of 9 to 13 dull green leaflets. Native of Europe. Flowers yellow, more or less tinged with reddish brown, soon followed by large inflated, often highly colored seed-pods. Very attractive and ornamental.

C. orientalis (*C. cruenta*). ORIENTAL BLADDER SENNA. A shrub, usually 4 to 6 feet tall. Native of Southern Europe and the Orient. Leaves compound, consisting of 7 to 11 glaucous green leaflets. Flowers orange-yellow, often tinged with reddish brown. Pods inflated, usually mottled with brown and red.

Comptonia · The Sweet Fern

A low shrub with fern-like fragrant foliage, well adapted for massing on rocky banks and sandy stretches. Very hardy and ornamental.

Comptonia peregrina (*Myrica asplenifolia*). SWEET FERN. A much-branched shrub with brown bark, usually growing about 2 feet tall. Grows naturally from Canada to North Carolina. Very effective.

Coriaria · The Coriarias

Remarkably graceful shrubs with arching branches and showy berries. They are relatively hardy, but require some

For grades and prices of above, see pages 151 and 152

Coriaria, continued

protection from cold winds in the North. A sunny location in well-drained loamy soil is best suited to their demands.

Coriaria japonica. Japanese Coriaria. A graceful shrub with drooping, quadrangular branches. Native of Japan. Leaves bright green, with three prominent veins. Berries red in summer, changing to violet-black. The leafy branches have a decided frond-like aspect. This is the hardier species.

C. myrtifolia. Myrtle-leaved Coriaria. An ornamental under-shrub with handsome myrtle-like leaves. Height 2 to 3 feet. Berries black, very showy. Leaves arranged in frond-like regularity along the graceful, arching branches. Native of Southern Europe.

Corylus americana (see page 63)

Coronilla · The Scorpion Senna

While rarely seen in cultivation, this free-flowering shrub possesses many attractive features. Hardy as far north as Tennessee and Southern New York. It thrives in porous, loamy soil.

Coronilla emerus. Scorpion Senna. A dense and shapely shrub with compound leaves. Native of Europe. Leaflets 5 to 7, dark, glossy green. Flowers yellow, tipped with red, large and showy, expanding in late spring and early summer. Nearly evergreen in the South.

Cornus

The Osier Dogwoods, or Cornels

Hardy and vigorous shrubs, thriving best in moist, fertile soils. In addition to the showy flowers and fruits which characterize most of the species, they are very attractive objects in winter on account of the brilliant color of the bark of the young shoots and twigs. Valuable for shrub borders and for waterside planting. Other species are described under "Deciduous Trees."

Cornus alba (*C. sibirica*). Siberian Red Osier. An upright shrub with bright blood-red branches. Native of Siberia. Leaves dark green, pale beneath, 2 to 3 inches long. Flowers creamy white, in numerous small flat-topped clusters. Fruit light blue or bluish white. Usually 6 to 10 feet tall. Very brilliant, especially in early spring, when the bark is intensely colored.

Colutea arborescens (see page 61)

Cornus alba spaethi. Yellow-leaved Dogwood. A form of the above with the leaves broadly bordered with golden yellow. A very striking plant.

C. amomum (*C. sericea*). Silky Dogwood. A spreading shrub with reddish purple twigs, distributed from New Brunswick to Florida. Leaves dark green above, pale or whitened beneath. Flowers creamy white, in flat-topped clusters, opening in early summer. Fruit blue or bluish white. Grows 6 to 10 feet tall.

C. candidissima (*C. paniculata*). Panicled Dogwood. A handsome free-flowering shrub with gray branches. Grows naturally from Maine and Minnesota, southward to North Carolina and Nebraska. Leaves dull green, whitened beneath. Flowers white, in short panicle-like clusters. Fruit white, borne on deep red stems. Grows 6 to 10 feet tall.

C. circinata. Round-leaved Dogwood. A spreading shrub with purplish branches. Grows naturally from Canada, southward to Iowa and Virginia. Leaves very broad and large, dark green above, pale and downy beneath. Flowers creamy white, in dense flat-topped clusters. Fruit light blue.

C. mas (*C. mascula*). Cornelian Cherry. A large dense shrub with handsome glossy foliage. Native of Europe. Flowers yellow, in small dense heads, appearing before the leaves in early spring. Fruit bright scarlet, very showy. Height 10 to 12 feet.

C. sanguinea. European Red Osier. A spreading shrub with deep red or purplish branches. Leaves ovate, dark green, paler beneath, 2 to 3 inches long. Flowers greenish white, in dense flat-topped clusters. Berries black. Grows 8 to 10 feet tall.

C. stolonifera. Red Osier Cornel. A spreading shrub with bright reddish purple branches, attaining a height of from 4 to 6 feet. Widely distributed over the Northern United States and Canada. Leaves dark green above, whitened beneath. Flowers creamy white, in dense flat-topped clusters. Berries white. Remarkably showy.

C. stolonifera flaviramea. Golden-twigged Osier. A form of the above with yellow branches. Planted with the red-branched species, very effective and striking contrast may be secured. It is quite as hardy as the normal species.

Corylopsis

The Flowering Hazel

Interesting shrubs, with handsome bluish green foliage and showy yellow flowers in early spring. They are hardy as far north as Missouri and New York when protected

Cornus amomum (see page 62)

Corylopsis, continued

from cold winds. A moist sandy loam is best adapted to their requirements.

Corylopsis pauciflora. FLOWERING HAZEL. A small shrub, usually 2 to 3 feet tall, with numerous branches. Native of Japan. Leaves heart-shaped, coarsely toothed, pale bluish green above, glaucous beneath. Flowers pale yellow, fragrant, borne in short racemes.

C. spicata. LARGE-LEAVED FLOWERING HAZEL. An attractive small shrub, usually 3 to 4 feet high, with handsome foliage and showy flowers. Native of Japan. Flowers bright yellow, fragrant, in many-flowered racemes. Both leaves and flowers are larger than those of the preceding species, but it is not quite so hardy.

Corylus · The Hazels

Hardy shrubs possessing many attractive and ornamental qualities. The long drooping catkins expand with the first breath of spring, just at the time when flowers are most highly prized. Again in summer and autumn, the fringed or fluted fruit-husks add beauty and interest to the heavy-laden plants. The nuts of all the species, known as Hazelnuts and Filberts, are sweet and toothsome. They thrive in almost any well-drained soil.

Corylus americana. HAZELNUT. A vigorous shrub with numerous upright branches, attaining a height of 4 to 8 feet. Grows naturally from Florida to Canada. Leaves heart-shaped, dark green, more or less downy on both surfaces. Nuts large, enclosed in ruffled husks, with sweet and edible kernels. Very prolific.

C. avellana. FILBERT. A large shrub 10 to 12 feet tall with heart-shaped deep green leaves. Native of Europe and Asia. Nuts large, embraced in a short, fringed husk, with sweet edible kernels.

C. avellana laciniata. CUT-LEAVED HAZEL. A very ornamental variety with deeply cut leaves.

C. maxima purpurea. PURPLE-LEAVED FILBERT. A large shrub with dark bronzy purple leaves. The rich color of the foliage is retained throughout the growing season. Very showy.

C. rostrata. BEAKED HAZELNUT. A showy shrub, 2 to 4 feet tall, with dark green oval leaves. Widely distributed across the United States and Canada. Nuts small, enclosed in a long beak-like husk. Effective results are obtained by planting in small groups or masses.

Cotoneaster · The Deciduous Cotoneasters

Hardy shrubs with erect stems and spreading branches. They are very effective in the shrub borders, both on account of the profuse white flowers and the bright red autumnal berries. They thrive best in a porous, loamy soil.

Cotoneaster multiflora. CHINESE COTONEASTER. A large spreading shrub with slender curving branches. Native of Asia. Leaves broadly ovate, dark green, pale and slightly downy beneath. Flowers white, in numerous flat-topped clusters, expanding in spring; very showy. Berries red. Grows 5 to 8 feet tall. Very rapid-growing and attractive.

C. nummularia. BROAD-LEAVED COTONEASTER. An upright shrub with spreading branches, usually attaining a height of 3 to 4 feet. Native of the Himalayas. Leaves roundish, dark green above, coated on the lower surface with pale white hairs. Flowers white, in short flat-topped clusters, blossoming in late spring. Fruit red, persisting until midwinter, often borne in such profusion as to lend striking color effect, and affording a great attraction to birds.

Cratægus · The Shrubby Hawthorns

Beautiful hardy shrubs with glossy foliage, white flowers and showy fruits. They are well adapted for groups or specimen plants, and when closely planted in single rows make excellent low hedges, either clipped or unclipped. They thrive in almost any well-drained soil.

Crataegus uniflora. ONE-FLOWERED THORN. A low shrub with glossy, wedge-shaped leaves. Occurs from New York to Florida and Louisiana. Flowers mostly solitary, white, with cream-colored anthers. Fruit yellow or greenish. A neat little bush, seldom growing more than 2 feet high.

C. vailiae. MISS VAIL'S THORN. A shrub with ovate or oval deep green lustrous leaves. Occurs from Virginia to North Carolina. Flowers white, in 2- to 6-flowered corymbs, the anthers creamy white. Fruit red. Makes a remarkably beautiful and unique hedge plant.

Corylus rostrata

For grades and prices of above, see page 152

Deutzia crenata candidissima (see page 65)

Cydonia · The Japanese Quince, or Japonica

Hardy shrubs with handsome showy flowers in early spring. They are invaluable for border or garden planting, and make beautiful informal or clipped hedges. The fragrant fruits are often used for making a tart, delicious jelly. They thrive in almost any well-drained soil.

Cydonia japonica (*Pyrus japonica*). JAPANESE, OR FLOWERING QUINCE. Spiny shrubs with bright green glossy leaves. Native of China and Japan. Flowers scarlet, large and showy. Fruits about 2 inches in diameter, yellowish green, aromatic-fragrant. There are several forms with double and single flowers in various shades of color. The following are among the best:

Atrosanguinea. Double; deep scarlet.
Candida. Single; pure white.
Mallardi. Single; rose, bordered with white.
Rosea plena. Semi-double; rose.
Rubra grandiflora. Single; deep crimson.
Umbilicata. Single; rose-red.

Cydonia maulei (*Pyrus maulei*). DWARF FLOWERING QUINCE. A low shrub with spiny branches, growing 1 to 3 feet high. Leaves dark green and lustrous, 1 to 2 inches long. Flowers bright orange-scarlet, large and showy. Fruit nearly round, yellow. Very free-flowering. An exceptionally good subject with distinct habit and flowers of a peculiar color-tone.

Cytisus · The Broom

A strange and interesting shrub with long and slender green branches. It thrives in almost any well-drained soil, preferring sunny situations. Of European origin, but has become naturalized in waste places from Nova Scotia to Virginia.

Cytisus scoparius (*Genista scoparia*). SCOTCH BROOM. A rapid-growing shrub, usually attaining a height of 6 to 8 feet. Leaves small, consisting of 1 to 3 dark green leaflets. Flowers in great profusion, bright yellow, very handsome.

Daphne · The Deciduous Daphnes

These beautiful hardy shrubs deserve a prominent place in the plantations, as they are among the most attractive of ornamentals. The showy flowers are borne in great profusion in early spring. A porous loamy soil is well adapted to their requirements.

Cytisus scoparius

For grades and prices of above, see page 152

Daphne, continued

Daphne genkwa. JAPANESE DAPHNE. A low shrub with slender branches, usually about 2 feet tall. Native of Japan. Flowers lilac, borne in profuse, short-stalked clusters, expanding before the leaves appear. A handsome shrub; but rarely seen in cultivation.

D. mezereum. MEZEREON DAPHNE. A shrub with stout, upright branches, usually growing 3 to 4 feet tall. Native of Europe. Flowers lilac-purple, very fragrant, appearing before the leaves and almost hiding the naked branches. A grand shrub, and fortunately, the hardiest species.

Deutzia · The Deutzias

Hardy, vigorous shrubs with showy flowers. They are extremely floriferous and ornamental, and make possible many striking effects in garden or border plantations. Of easy culture, thriving in almost any well-drained soil.

Deutzia crenata candidissima. DOUBLE WHITE DEUTZIA. A tall shrub, usually 6 to 8 feet high, with numerous upright branches. Leaves dull green, rough on both sides, 2 to 3 inches long. Flowers double, pure white, in erect panicles 2 to 4 inches long. A handsome free-flowering shrub of garden origin.

D. crenata flore roseo plena. DOUBLE PINK DEUTZIA. Similar to the preceding, but with one or more of the outer rows of petals rosy purple. Very showy.

D. crenata Pride of Rochester. LARGE-FLOWERED DEUTZIA. A vigorous form with very large double white flowers. A distinct and valuable variety.

D. gracilis. SLENDER DEUTZIA. A small shrub, usually about 2 feet tall, with slender, often arching branches. Native of Japan. Leaves bright green, 1 to 2 inches long, slightly rough on the upper surface. Flowers white, in graceful nodding racemes. Very showy.

D. gracilis rosea. SLENDER PINK DEUTZIA. A pleasing shrub of hybrid origin, strongly resembling the Slender Deutzia, which is one of its parents. Flowers light rose, in profuse clusters. A valuable acquisition.

D. lemoinei. LEMOINE'S DEUTZIA. A small shrub with spreading branches, usually about 3 feet tall; of garden origin. Leaves bright green, 2 to 3 inches long. Flowers white, in large compound clusters or panicles. Very vigorous and floriferous.

Deutzia scabra

D. parviflora. SMALL-FLOWERED DEUTZIA. A compact shrub with upright branches, attaining a height of 4 to 6 feet. Native of China. Leaves bright green, 2 to 3 inches long, rather rough on both surfaces. Flowers pure white, profuse, disposed in numerous compound clusters. One of the hardiest species.

D. scabra. ROUGH-LEAVED DEUTZIA. A tall shrub, usually 6 to 8 feet high, with dull green scabrous leaves. Native of China and Japan. Flowers in upright racemes, pure white, profuse and showy.

Deutzia gracilis

For grades and prices of above, see page 153

Diervillas · The Weigelias and Bush Honeysuckles

Hardy free-flowering shrubs of spreading habit, thriving best in moist loamy soil. The Asiatic species are justly classed among the showiest of garden shrubs, presenting in late spring or early summer great masses of showy flowers.

Diervilla floribunda. FLORIFEROUS WEIGELIA. A large shrub with numerous upright branches, growing 6 to 8 feet high. Native of Japan. Leaves dark green, more or less downy, especially on the lower surface. Flowers trumpet-shaped, brownish crimson in the bud, changing to rich bright crimson when fully expanded. Very floriferous.

D. florida (*Weigelia amabilis* and *W. rosea*). ROSE-COLORED WEIGELIA. A free-flowering shrub, usually about six feet tall, with numerous spreading branches. Leaves dark green, smooth except on the midrib and veins. Flowers rose-colored, large and showy, produced in great profusion. The following are among the best varieties of this species:

Candida. Large, pure white flowers. The very best white Weigelia, possessing every good quality.

Isoline. White or flesh-colored outside, a yellowish spot in the throat.

Kosteriana variegata. A dwarf form with the leaves bordered with yellow; flowers deep rose-color.

Nana variegata. A dwarf form with the leaves variegated with white; flowers white or slightly suffused with rose.

Diervilla diervilla (*D. trifida*). BUSH HONEYSUCKLE. A small shrub, spreading rapidly by underground shoots, distributed naturally from Canada to North Carolina. Leaves bright green, 3 to 4 inches long, fading in autumn with tones of red and yellow. Flowers yellow, borne in flat-topped clusters. Very effective in groups or masses. Grows 2 to 3 feet tall.

D. hybrida. HYBRID WEIGELIA. Tall growing, with numerous spreading branches, usually attaining a height of 6 to 8 feet. Flowers trumpet-shaped, large and showy, embracing a wide range of colors. Of garden origin. The following are among the most distinct and best varieties:

Abel Carriere. Rose-carmine, changing to red, with yellow spot in the throat. Forms a very symmetrical, large shrub of great vigor.

Conquete. Deep pink; the flowers very large. A grand, showy kind, of great merit.

Edouard Andre. Dark purple, with a shade of brown. An unusual and exceedingly attractive variety.

Eva Rathke. Flowers deep carmine-red. Very floriferous. A universal favorite.

Gustav Mallet. Light pink, margined with white. Delicate and dainty—a form much admired.

Steltzneri. Dark rose. Very floriferous.

Diervilla rivularis. GATTINGER'S BUSH HONEYSUCKLE. A spreading shrub 4 to 5 feet tall, with soft downy twigs and foliage. Native of the Southern Alleghany Mountains. Leaves broadly lanceolate, bright green, 3 to 4 inches long, borne on short footstalks. Flowers lemon-yellow, produced in terminal clusters. Rare in cultivation.

D. sessilifolia. HIGH BUSH HONEYSUCKLE. A shrub 4 to 5 feet tall with spreading branches. Native of the Southern Alleghany region. Leaves without foot-stalks, bright lustrous green, 3 to 5 inches long. Flowers yellow, in terminal clusters.

Elæagnus angustifolia

Dirca · The Leatherwood

A hardy much-branched shrub with tough pliant branches. Very symmetrical in outline when given ample space, sometimes looking like a miniature tree. Grows 3 to 5 feet high. It thrives best in a moist loamy soil.

Dirca palustris. LEATHERWOOD. An attractive shrub with light, almost yellow-green twigs and foliage, widely distributed from Canada to Florida. Flowers yellowish, appearing before the leaves, soon followed by numerous red fruits.

Elæagnus · The Deciduous Oleasters

Hardy shrubs with handsome foliage and showy fruits. The young branches and leaves are covered with silvery or brownish scales, which impart a singular lustre and aspect. They thrive in almost any well-drained soil, preferring sunny situations.

Elaeagnus angustifolia (*E. hortensis*). RUSSIAN OLIVE. A large shrub with silvery, often spiny branches. Native of Europe and Asia. Leaves light green above, silvery white beneath, lanceolate, 2 to 3 inches long. Flowers yellow within, silvery on the outside, fragrant. Berries yellow, coated with silvery scales. Height 8 to 12 feet.

E. argentea. SILVER BERRY. A large shrub with spreading branches, the younger twigs of which are clothed with silvery scales. Grows naturally from Canada to Minnesota and Utah. Leaves ovate, silvery on both sides, about 2 inches long. Flowers yellowish within, silvery without, fragrant, very profuse. Berries silvery. Grows 6 to 10 feet tall.

E. longipes. THE "GOUMI" OF JAPAN. A large shrub with reddish brown scaly branches. Native of China and Japan. Leaves oval, dark green above, with scattered brown scales beneath. Flowers yellowish white, fragrant, more or less covered with brownish scales without. Fruit red, drooping on long slender stalks, ripening in summer. Height 5 to 8 feet. The acid and slightly astringent fruit is often used in making delicious jellies and jams.

E. parvifolia. SMALL-LEAVED SILVER THORN. A large shrub, usually 8 to 12 feet tall, with erect or spreading spiny branches. Native of Japan. Leaves 2 to 3 inches long, dark green above, silvery white beneath. Flowers whitish within, silvery on the outside, fragrant. Berries pink, more or less coated with silvery scales, ripening in late summer or early autumn.

E. umbellatus. JAPANESE OLEASTER. A large shrub with spreading, often spiny branches, clothed with yellowish brown scales. Native of Japan. Leaves silvery white beneath, more or less coated on the upper surface. Flowers fragrant, yellowish white. Berries scarlet when ripe, silvery when young, ripening in autumn.

Euonymus · The Strawberry, or Burning Bushes

Hardy shrubs with showy fruits, noted for the intense coloring of the autumnal foliage. They are

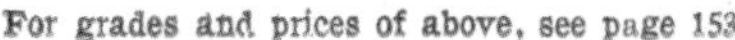
For grades and prices of above, see page 153

Euonymus, continued

well adapted for specimen plants or for massing in the shrub borders. A moist, loamy soil meets their requirements.

Euonymus alatus WINGED BURNING BUSH. A handsome shrub 6 to 8 feet tall, with corky-winged branches. Native of China and Japan. Leaves oval, bright green, fading in autumn with gorgeous tones of red and crimson. A capital shrub for an isolated specimen plant, attracting attention wherever seen.

E. americanus. STRAWBERRY BUSH. An erect shrub with slender green branches, 5 to 8 feet tall. Grows naturally from New York to the Gulf States. Leaves broadly lanceolate, bright green, 2 to 3 inches long. Fruit warty, rose-color, with scarlet seed-coats. Very showy.

E. atropurpureus. BURNING BUSH. A large shrub, usually 8 to 12 feet tall, with upright branches. Grows naturally from Canada to Florida, and westward to the Rocky Mountains. Leaves bright green, 2 to 4 inches long, turning pale yellow in autumn. Flowers purple, in slender nodding clusters. Fruit deeply lobed, bright red, disclosing the scarlet arils, usually persisting on the branches until midwinter.

E. europaeus. EUROPEAN SPINDLE-TREE. A large, erect shrub or low tree, usually 10 to 15 feet tall. Native of Europe. Leaves broadly lanceolate, about 2 inches long, dark green. Flowers yellowish, in nodding clusters, expanding in spring. Fruits lobed, rose-pink, the seeds invested with orange-colored arils.

E. hamiltonianus. HAMILTON'S SPINDLE-TREE. A large shrub with upright branches, growing 12 to 20 feet tall. Native of Asia, Leaves broadly lanceolate, 3 to 5 inches long, bright green, unfolding very early in spring. Flowers yellowish, in forked cymes. Fruit deeply lobed, bright pink.

E. nanus. NARROW-LEAVED BURNING BUSH. A low shrub, 1 to 2 feet tall, with slender, often arching, branches. Native of Asia. Leaves narrow, almost linear, about an inch long. Flowers purplish, in nodding cymes. Pods four-lobed, rose-pink, with orange arils. A handsome little shrub for rock-gardens. The fruit ripens in summer.

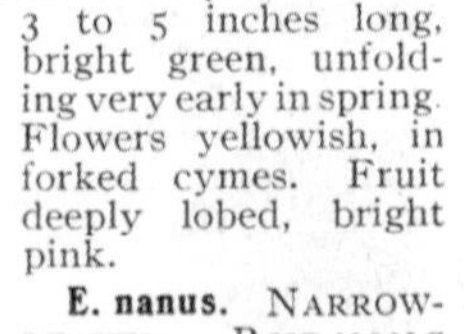

Euonymus americanus

Euonymus patens

E. obovatus. RUNNING STRAWBERRY BUSH. A low, procumbent shrub, the stems rooting wherever they come in contact with the ground. Grows naturally from Canada to Indiana and Kentucky. Leaves bright green, 1 to 2 inches long, broadest above the middle. Flowers purplish. Pods usually three-lobed, warty, rose-colored, with scarlet arils.

E. patens. LATE-FLOWERING SPINDLE-TREE. A large shrub, 6 to 10 feet tall, with green branches. Probably a native of China. Leaves rich green, nearly evergreen in the North, probably evergreen in the South. Flowers greenish yellow, in profuse, forked cymes. Fruit pink, the arils bright orange-red. A meritorious, but little-known ornamental.

Exochorda · The Pearl Bush

A hardy free-flowering shrub with a wealth of showy blossoms in early spring. Unquestionably one of the floral gems. Thrives best in a moist fertile soil.

Exochorda grandiflora. PEARL BUSH. A large shrub, 8 to 10 feet tall. Native of China. Leaves bright green, pale or whitened beneath, fading with yellow tones. Flowers dazzling white, produced in numerous terminal racemes. Very showy.

Forsythia · The Golden Bells

Few, if any, of the spring-flowering hardy shrubs can surpass the splendor and brilliancy of the Forsythias. Both grace and beauty are combined in all their attributes and give them rank for any station in the shrub plantations. They thrive in almost any fertile soil.

Forsythia intermedia. HYBRID GOLDEN BELL. A tall shrub with slender arching branches, of garden origin. Leaves simple or three-parted, dark green and lustrous. Flowers golden yellow, borne in great profusion Grows 8 to 10 feet high. Very floriferous.

 For grades and prices of above, see pages 153 and 154

Genista tinctoria

Forsythia, continued

Forsythia suspensa. DROOPING GOLDEN BELL. A graceful shrub with long and slender drooping branches. Native of China. Leaves dark green and lustrous, persisting until frost. Flowers in great profusion, golden yellow, very showy. Grows about 8 feet tall. One of the showiest shrubs in cultivation.

F. suspensa fortunei (*F. fortunei*). FORTUNE'S GOLDEN BELL. Similar to the preceding, but of more vigorous upright growth. Branches arching, bearing dark lustrous green leaves, either simple or three-parted. Flowers golden yellow, often with twisted petals. A grand shrub, often growing 8 to 10 feet high.

F. viridissima. DARK GREEN FORSYTHIA. A large shrub with erect green-barked branches. Native of China. Leaves simple, very dark green, relatively narrow. Flowers golden yellow, with somewhat reflexed, often twisted petals. A handsome shrub, but perhaps not quite so hardy as the foregoing species.

Fothergilla · The Fothergillas

Hardy shrubs with showy creamy white flowers in early spring. They are admirably adapted for planting in the foreground of shrub borders, and although rarely seen in cultivation, are most attractive subjects. A moist loamy soil is best adapted to their requirements.

Fothergilla carolina (*F. gardeni* and *F. alnifolia*). DWARF FOTHERGILLA. A low shrub, usually about two feet tall, growing naturally from Virginia to Georgia. Leaves dark green, coarsely toothed, fading with yellow or ruddy tones. Flowers in dense terminal heads or spikes, soft and fluffy. Very neat and attractive.

F. major. LARGE FOTHERGILLA. An upright bushy shrub with dark green, coarsely and remotely toothed leaves. Native of the Southern Alleghanies. Flower-spikes plume-like, very large and showy. Grows 4 to 5 feet high. A beautiful and desirable plant.

Genista · The Dyers' Green-weed

A hardy free-flowering shrub with small leaves and slender green branches. Very valuable for massing in well-drained soils, in sunny situations.

Genista tinctoria. DYERS' GREENWEED. A low spreading shrub with slender green branches. Native of Europe. Flowers yellow, in upright floriferous racemes, panicled at the ends of the branches. Splendid for rock-gardens or in groups or masses in the foreground of larger shrubs.

Halimodendron · The Salt Bush

A very hardy shrub with showy rose-purple flowers which appear in late spring or early summer. Thrives best in sandy soils, and is able to endure the extremes of drought and cold peculiar to many sections of the West, and soils highly impregnated with alkali or other saline compounds.

Halimodendron argenteum. SALT BUSH. A shrub 5 to 8 feet tall, with whitish prickly branches. Native of Siberia. Leaves compound, terminating in sharp spiny points, and composed of 1 to 2 pairs of blue-green leaflets. Flowers large and showy, rosy purple, disposed in clusters at the base of the season's growth.

Hamamelis · The Witch Hazel

A hardy shrub with singular bright yellow flowers in late autumn, often after the leaves have been killed by frost. Thrives best in moist, loamy soil, either in full sun or partial shade.

Hamamelis virginiana. WITCH HAZEL. A large shrub, usually 10 to 15 feet tall, with spreading, often numer-

Hibiscus syriacus (see page 69)

For grades and prices of above, see page 154

Hamamelis, continued

ous stems. Grows naturally from Canada to the Gulf, and westward to Nebraska and Texas. Leaves obliquely heart-shaped, with wavy borders, turning bright yellow, orange or purple in autumn. Petals bright yellow, narrow, often twisted. Flowers in autumn at a time when other shrubs are dormant.

Hibiscus · The Althæa, or Rose of Sharon

A hardy shrub with handsome large flowers, extensively cultivated in American gardens. Thrives in any fertile soil. The flowers appear in great profusion in late summer, at a time when few other shrubs are in blossom.

Hibiscus syriacus (*Althæa frutex*). ROSE OF SHARON. A tall shrub with upright or slightly spreading branches. There are both double- and single-flowered forms, with a wide range of colors. The following are among the best varieties:

Amaranth. Reddish purple.

Ardens. Bluish purple.

Boule de Feu. Double; red.

Carneo-plenus. Double; flesh-color.

Coelestis. Single; blue. A very attractive and unusually free-flowering variety.

Jeanne d'Arc. Double; white.

Paeoniflorus. Double; rosy purple.

Rubis. The deepest red of the single-flowering forms, and one of the best.

Totus albus. Single; white. A lovely and likeable flower, and a variety much sought by planters.

Variegatus. Leaves variegated with creamy white; flowers lavender with a purple blotch at the base of the petals.

Hydrangea radiata (see page 70)

Hydrangea Otaksa (see page 70)

Hippophaë · The Sea Buckthorn

A hardy shrub with gray or silvery foliage. It thrives in sandy or loamy soils. The most effective results are secured by planting in groups or masses, thereby bringing the pistillate and staminate forms into close proximity and insuring a bountiful crop of berries.

Hippophaë rhamnoides. SEA BUCKTHORN. A large shrub with spine-tipped branches. Native of Europe and Asia. Height 8 to 12 feet. Flowers yellowish, produced in short clusters in spring. Berries orange or bright orange-red, maturing in early autumn; very showy.

Hydrangea · The Hydrangeas

Grand, free-flowering shrubs with large clusters or panicles of showy flowers. They are admirably adapted for border planting, either as specimen plants or in masses. A moist fertile soil, with full or partial exposure to sun, is best adapted to their requirements.

Hydrangea arborescens. WILD HYDRANGEA. An upright shrub, usually 4 to 8 feet tall, with bright green leaves. Grows naturally from New Jersey and Iowa, southward to Florida. Flowers creamy white, generally with a few sterile rays, borne in numerous flat-topped clusters in early summer. Hardy and attractive.

H. arborescens sterilis. HILLS OF SNOW. A form of the last with all of the flowers ray-like and sterile, resembling a Snowball. A handsome floriferous hardy shrub, literally loaded with dazzling white flowers, and continuing to blossom for a large part of the summer.

H. hortensis. JAPANESE, OR GARDEN HYDRANGEAS. Beautiful shrubs with dark glossy green foliage and very showy flowers. They are not hardy North, unless afforded a great deal of protection,

For grades and prices of above, see page 154

Hydrangea, continued

but extensively grown as pot or tub plants and frequently used for decorating piazzas and formal gardens. The color of the flowers seemingly varies in different soils, ranging from white to shades of blue and pink. The following are among the best varieties:

With flat-topped clusters of flowers, several of the marginal ones ray-like and sterile:

Belzoni. Usually with white or blue rays.

Japonica. With large pink rays.

Rosalba. Rays deeply toothed, white or rose-color.

With globular clusters of flowers, all of them ray-like and sterile:

Hortensia. Large showy heads of flowers, usually pink.

Otaksa. Handsome clusters of pink or blue flowers.

Ramulis pictis. Branches dark purple; flowers pink or blue.

Thos. Hogg. Huge clusters of white flowers.

Hydrangea paniculata. PANICLED HYDRANGEA. A very hardy tall shrub with handsome dark green foliage. Native of Japan. Flowers creamy white with numerous white rays, borne in large panicles 6 to 12 inches long, the sterile flowers changing in age to tones of rose and purple. Very ornamental and graceful, producing charming effects when massed.

H. paniculata grandiflora. LARGE-FLOWERED HYDRANGEA. Undoubtedly the most popular variety and one of the showiest shrubs in cultivation. The flowers are almost all ray-like and sterile, and are produced in very large panicles. When fully expanded the flowers are white, but soon assume tones of rose and bronze on the exposed sides. This shrub requires severe pruning in early spring to insure the largest trusses.

Hydrangea quercifolia

H. paniculata praecox. EARLY-FLOWERING HYDRANGEA. Similar to *H. paniculata*, but blossoms 4 to 6 weeks earlier. By the judicious use of this shrub in connection with the typical form, the floral duration of the Hydrangeas may be considerably extended.

H. quercifolia. OAK-LEAVED HYDRANGEA. A distinct and handsome shrub with spreading branches. Occurs naturally from Kentucky to Florida. Young branches densely clothed with rusty brown felt-like hairs. Leaves large, deeply lobed, dark green above, whitened and downy beneath. Flowers disposed in large panicles, creamy white with numerous white or pinkish white rays. A beautiful ornamental. Height 4 to 6 feet.

H. radiata. SILVER-LEAVED HYDRANGEA. An erect shrub 4 to 6 feet tall, indigenous to the Southern Appalachian region. Leaves narrowly heart-shaped, rich green on the upper surface, silvery white beneath. Flowers creamy white, in numerous flat-topped clusters, with several large ray-flowers on the outer margin. Splendid for rocky banks and rock-gardens.

Hypericum calycinum (see page 72)

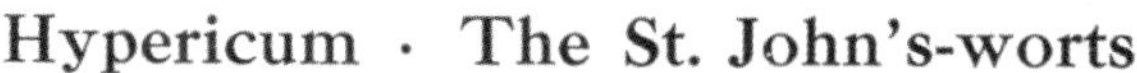

Hypericum · The St. John's-worts

Very ornamental free-flowering shrubs with yellow flowers, blossoming in summer. They thrive in almost any well-drained soil, either in full sun or partial shade.

Hypericum aureum. GOLDEN HYPERICUM. LARGE-FLOWERED ST. JOHN'S-WORT. A hardy shrub, attaining a height of about three

For grades and prices of above, see pages 154 and 155

Hydrangea paniculata (see page 70)

Hypericum, continued

feet. Grows naturally from Tennessee to Georgia. Leaves oblong, bluish green above, pale beneath, persisting until cold weather. Flowers golden yellow, nearly two inches across. Very showy.

H. buckleyi. BUCKLEY'S HYPERICUM. BUCKLEY'S ST. JOHN'S-WORT. A low dense shrub forming little tufts or colonies, usually less than a foot high. Native of the high mountains from North Carolina to Georgia. Leaves bluish green, 1 to 2 inches long, turning scarlet in autumn. Flowers about an inch in diameter, bright yellow. Splendid for rockeries and as a ground cover. Quite hardy.

Hypericum lobocarpum

H. calycinum. AARON'S BEARD. A low shrub, usually less than a foot high, spreading by root-stocks and completely covering the soil. Native of Greece and Asia Minor. Leaves dark green and leathery, evergreen in the South, but usually browned and seared in the North by severe freezing. Flowers large and showy, 2 to 3 inches in diameter. A capital ground cover. Thrives best in partial shade. Not quite hardy in the colder sections.

H. densiflorum. DENSE-FLOWERED ST. JOHN'S-WORT. A handsome shrub with numerous branches, attaining a height of 3 to 5 feet. Occurs in a wild state from New Jersey and Missouri, southward to the Gulf. Leaves narrow, dark green, usually with clusters of smaller leaves in their axils. Flowers very numerous, in compound clusters, bright yellow. Very pleasing.

H. glomeratum. MOUNTAIN ST. JOHN'S-WORT. A hardy spreading shrub, usually 1 to 2 feet tall. Native of the high mountains of North Carolina. Leaves narrowly oblong, dark green above, pale beneath, with clusters of smaller leaves in their axils. Flowers in dense terminal clusters, bright yellow. Very compact and attractive. Splendid for rockeries and for foreground planting.

H. kalmianum. KALM'S ST. JOHN'S-WORT. A very hardy shrub, growing 2 to 3 feet in height. Native of the Niagara and Great Lake region. Leaves blue-green above, glaucous beneath, about 2 inches long. Flowers bright yellow, in several-flowered clusters. Very distinct and attractive, and the best species for the colder sections.

H. lobocarpum. GATTINGER'S ST. JOHN'S-WORT. A remarkably floriferous, hardy shrub, with an open, somewhat irregular crown. Grows naturally in Middle Tennessee. Leaves narrow, about 2 inches long, dark green, with clusters of smaller leaves in their axils. Flowers very profuse, bright yellow, disposed in compound terminal clusters. Height 3 to 5 feet.

H. moserianum. GOLD FLOWER. A small shrub 1 to 2 feet high, of garden origin. The numerous nodding branches are densely furnished with dark green ovate leaves, which persist until seared by severe frost. Flowers golden yellow, 2 inches across, very showy. Most effective in groups or masses.

H. prolificum. SHRUBBY ST. JOHN'S-WORT. A vigorous hardy shrub with numerous compact branches. Occurs naturally from New Jersey to Georgia, westward to Iowa. Leaves dark lustrous green, narrowly oblong, with clusters of smaller leaves in their axils. Flowers bright yellow, profusely borne in terminal branching clusters. One of the best.

Ilex · The Deciduous Holly

A hardy shrub with showy bright red berries, which persist on the naked branches until mid-winter. It thrives in almost any moist soil. The best results are obtained by planting in groups or masses, thereby bringing into close proximity the pistillate and staminate forms, and insuring a bountiful display of berries.

Ilex verticillata. BLACK ALDER, OR WINTERBERRY. The handsome sprays of brilliant berries, which are often used for decorating, justly proclaim the high rank of this grand shrub. It is widely distributed, extending from Canada to Florida, westward to Missouri and Wisconsin. Grows 6 to 10 feet tall.

Itea · The Virginian Willow

An upright shrub, 3 to 4 feet tall, with brilliant autumn foliage. Thrives in almost any moist soil. Very effective in groups or masses in the shrub borders, or for waterside planting.

Itea virginica. VIRGINIAN WILLOW. A vigorous free-flowering shrub, distributed naturally from New Jersey and Pennsylvania to the Gulf. Leaves bright lustrous green, changing in autumn to brilliant shades of red. Flowers white, fragrant, borne in erect terminal racemes 3 to 6 inches long.

Jasminum · The Jasmines

Graceful shrubs with numerous arching branches and showy flowers. They thrive best in moist loamy soils. In sections where the climate is too severe, they are often treated as house plants.

Jasminum humile. ITALIAN YELLOW JASMINE. A much-branched shrub with angled branches. Native of Asia. Leaves compound, consisting of 3 to 7 glossy dark green leaflets; evergreen in the South. Flowers bright yellow, in small clusters. Hardy as far north as Tennessee and Maryland, and on the Pacific Coast.

For grades and prices of above, see page 155

Jasminum, continued

Jasminum nudiflorum. NAKED-FLOWERED JASMINE. A graceful shrub with quadrangular drooping branches. Native of China. Leaves compound, consisting of three leaflets, dark green, falling in late autumn. Flowers bright yellow, opening very early in spring, or on warm days in winter. Hardy as far north as Washington, or with protection from bleak cold winds, to Missouri and New York.

J. officinale. TRUE JASMINE, OR JESSAMINE. This is the classic species and the Jessamine of literature. A graceful shrub with numerous long branches. Native of Persia and India. Leaves compound, with 3 to 7 glossy dark green leaflets. Flowers white, deliciously fragrant, produced in terminal leafy clusters. Hardy South, and as far North, with protection, as Tennessee and Maryland.

Kerria · The Globe Flower, or Japanese Rose

An attractive shrub with slender green branches and showy yellow flowers. It thrives in almost any well-drained soil. Hardy, but benefited by protection from cold winds in severe climates.

Kerria japonica (*Corchorus japonica*). GLOBE FLOWER, OR JAPANESE ROSE. A shrub 4 to 6 feet tall. Native of Japan. Leaves bright green, sharply toothed, fading in autumn with tones of yellow. Flowers numerous, bright yellow, large and showy. A charming old-fashioned plant, and one worthy of a place in any garden.

K. japonica argenteo-variegata. VARIEGATED-LEAVED KERRIA. A dwarf form, usually growing 2 to 3 feet high, with small leaves bordered with white.

K. japonica flore pleno. DOUBLE-FLOWERED KERRIA. A variety with showy double flowers, of vigorous growth. More often seen in gardens than the typical form.

K. japonica ramulis variegatis. STRIPED-BARKED KERRIA. A low-growing form with the branches striped with yellow and green. Very unique.

Lagerstroemia · The Crape Myrtle

A handsome free-flowering shrub, extensively planted in the South. It thrives in almost any good soil with ample drainage. Hardy as far north as Memphis and Baltimore, with slight protection.

Lagerstroemia indica. CRAPE MYRTLE. A large shrub, 10 to 20 feet tall, with brown bark. Native of Asia. Leaves ovate, dark lustrous green. Flowers crinkled and ruffled, produced in profuse panicles in summer and continuing for two or three months. There are forms with crimson, pink, white and purple flowers. It makes a splendid house plant.

Lespedeza · The Shrubby Bush Clover

An interesting shrub of considerable hardiness, thriving as far north as Missouri and Massachusetts. Thrives in almost any well-drained soil. The flowers appear in midsummer. Other species are described under "Herbaceous Plants."

Lespedeza bicolor. SHRUBBY BUSH CLOVER. A shrub, 3 to 6 feet tall, with graceful slender branches. Native of Japan. Leaves compound, consisting of three dark green leaflets. Flowers purple, produced in nodding racemes, profuse and showy. Rare in cultivation.

Leucothoë · The Deciduous Leucothoës

Hardy deciduous shrubs, producing numerous one-sided racemes of white flowers in spring. They thrive in moist loamy soils, especially those containing leaf-mould or woods earth. In autumn the leaves assume brilliant tones of red and scarlet. The evergreen species will be found under "Evergreen Shrubs."

Leucothoë racemosa (*Andromeda racemosa*). SWAMP LEUCOTHOE. A rigid shrub with upright branches, usually growing 3 to 4 feet tall. Grows naturally from Massachusetts to Florida. Leaves bright green, about 2 inches long, fading with bright colors in autumn. Flowers numerous, in erect racemes 2 to 3 inches long.

L. recurva. MOUNTAIN LEUCOTHOE. A shrub with stiff branches, much resembling the foregoing species. Native of the mountain region from Virginia to Alabama. The flowers are produced in arching racemes at the tips of the shoots of the preceding season. Rarely seen in cultivation.

Hypericum prolificum (see page 72)

Ligustrum · The Deciduous Privets

These grand shrubs are extensively used for hedges and screens and are occasionally given space in the shrub plantations for the beauty of their flowers and berries. They are hardy and vigorous, thriving in almost any fertile soil and stand clipping admirably. Other species are described under "Broad-leaved Evergreen Shrubs."

Ligustrum amurense. AMOOR RIVER PRIVET. A large shrub with upright branches, growing 8 to 12 feet tall. Native of China. Leaves dark green and lustrous, tardily deciduous, or in the South nearly evergreen. Flowers white, in erect panicles. Splendid for hedges.

For grades and prices of above, see page 155

Berries of Lonicera tatarica

Ligustrum, continued

Ligustrum ciliatum. BRIGHT-FRUITED PRIVET. A comparatively small shrub with spreading branches, attaining a height of 4 to 6 feet. Native of Japan. Leaves dark green, 1 to 2 inches long. Flowers white, in erect, compact clusters. Berries black, shining.

L. ibota. IBOTA PRIVET. A large shrub with graceful arching branches. Native of China and Japan. Leaves dark green and lustrous, 1 to 2 inches long, persisting until the advent of cold weather. Flowers white, in numerous nodding clusters. Berries black with a bloom. A handsome shrub, valuable for specimen plants, mass planting or hedges.

L. ibota regelianum (*L. regelianum*). REGEL'S PRIVET. A form of the last with spreading, often horizontal branches. It is a smaller plant and much more dense in habit. Very picturesque and valuable for informal hedges or as single specimens.

L. ovalifolium. CALIFORNIA PRIVET. A large shrub of compact upright habit. Native of Japan. Leaves dark green and glossy, broad and firm, about 2 inches long. Flowers white, in dense, upright panicles 2 to 3 inches long. This is the most popular hedge plant. Nearly evergreen in the South. Height 8 to 12 feet.

L. vulgare. COMMON, OR EUROPEAN PRIVET, OR PRIM. A tall shrub, usually growing 8 to 12 feet high, with spreading or upright branches. Native of Europe. Leaves dark green and lustrous, half-evergreen. Flowers white, in dense upright panicles 2 inches long. Berries black, shining. A good old-fashioned shrub.

Lonicera · The Honeysuckles

Handsome upright shrubs, often with showy flowers and bright berries. Most of the species are very hardy. They thrive in almost any fertile soil, and in most instances prefer sunny situations. Invaluable for border or mass planting. Other species are described under "Vines"

Lonicera fragrantissima. EARLY FRAGRANT HONEYSUCKLE. A large shrub with numerous spreading branches. Native of China and Japan. Leaves broadly ovate, bright green, persistent until midwinter. Flowers creamy white or light yellow, expanding with the first breath of spring, deliciously fragrant. Height 6 to 8 feet. A grand shrub.

L. involucrata. WESTERN FLY HONEYSUCKLE. A shrub 3 to 5 feet tall, with upright branches. Grows naturally from Ontario and Alaska to the Rocky Mountains and California. Leaves broadly lanceolate, bright green, 3 to 4 inches long. Flowers yellow, tinged with red, opening in early summer. Berries black, shining, enveloped partially by large purple bracts.

L. morrowi. JAPANESE BUSH HONEYSUCKLE. A shrub with widespreading branches 4 to 6 feet tall. Native of Japan. Leaves oval, dark green above, downy-gray beneath, 1 to 2 inches long. Flowers pure white, changing to yellow, freely produced in early spring. Berries bright red, very profuse, ripening in summer.

L. ruprechtiana. MANCHURIAN HONEYSUCKLE. A large shrub 8 to 12 feet tall, with broadly lanceolate, dark green leaves, which are whitened beneath with fine down. Native of Manchuria. Flowers pure white, changing to yellow, opening in late spring. Berries red or yellow. Very showy.

L. spinosa (*L. alberti*). LARGE-FRUITED HONEYSUCKLE. A low shrub with slender graceful branches. Native of Turkestan. Leaves narrow, glaucous or bluish green, about an inch long. Flowers rosy pink, fragrant, in late spring or early summer. Berries very large, vinous-red, with a glaucous bloom. Height 1 to 2 feet. Well adapted for rock-gardens.

L. standishi. STANDISH'S BUSH HONEYSUCKLE. A half-evergreen shrub, 5 to 7 feet tall, resembling *Lonicera fragrantissima*. Native of China. Flowers blush white or cream-colored, very fragrant, opening in late winter and early spring.

L. tatarica. TARTARIAN HONEYSUCKLE. A large shrub with numerous upright or spreading branches. Native of Europe and Asia. Leaves ovate, bright green, about 2 inches long. Flowers white or pink, borne in great profusion in late spring. Fruit red or orange, ripening in summer and persisting until autumn. Height 8 to 10 feet.

L. xylosteum. FLY HONEYSUCKLE. A large shrub 8 to 10 feet tall, with dull green leaves. Native of Europe and Asia. Flowers yellowish white, often tinged with red, hairy on the outside, blossoming in late spring. Berries dark red or scarlet.

Ligustrum vulgare

For grades and prices of above, see pages 155 and 156

Opulaster opulifolius
(see page 76)

Neviusia · The Snow Wreath

A rare and graceful shrub with slender, wand-like branches, producing a profusion of feathery flowers in summer. It is hardy in Missouri and Massachusetts, and thrives in almost any fertile well-drained soil.

Neviusia alabamensis. SNOW WREATH. Leaves ovate, bright green, with serrate borders, turning golden yellow in autumn. Flowers fringe-like from the numerous white filaments of the stamens, borne in great profusion along the arching branches. Height 5 to 8 feet. Grows naturally on rocky cliffs in Alabama.

Lycium · The Matrimony Vine

An old-fashioned hardy shrub with a wealth of bright red or scarlet berries. It thrives in almost any fertile soil. The long branches may be trained over fences or trellises, but more effective results may be obtained by planting at the top of retaining walls or steep banks and allowing the graceful stems to fall over.

Lycium vulgare. MATRIMONY VINE, OR BOX THORN. A shrub with long and slender, usually spiny branches. Native of Europe and Asia. Leaves grayish green, 1 to 2 inches long. Flowers pale violet or purple, soon followed by coral-red or scarlet berries, which are borne in great profusion. Very showy.

Myrica · The Wax-Berries and Sweet Gale

Hardy shrubs with waxy berries and rich green foliage. They thrive in moist sandy loam in sunny exposures.

Myrica caroliniensis. WAX-BERRY, OR BAY-BERRY. A branching shrub, 4 to 6 feet high, widely distributed from Nova Scotia to Florida. Leaves broadest above the middle, dark green and lustrous, fragrant when bruised. Berries bluish white, very waxy, persisting throughout the winter. The Bay-Berry "tallow" of New England is made from the waxy berries.

M. cerifera. WAX-MYRTLE. Similar to the preceding, but of larger size, occasionally reaching the proportions of a small tree. Grows naturally from New Jersey to Florida and westward to Texas. In cultivation 5 to 8 feet tall, with bright green leaves. Berries bluish white, coated with wax.

M. gale. SWEET GALE. A low shrub with dark brown twigs. Grows naturally from Newfoundland to Alaska, southward to Michigan and Virginia. Leaves dark green above, pale beneath, unfolding after the flowers appear. An interesting shrub for planting in the foreground of taller shrubs.

Opulaster · The Ninebark

A hardy shrub with showy flowers and clusters of bright red pods. It makes a beautiful specimen plant, and is also effective in groups or masses in

Philadelphus falconeri (see p. 76)

For grades and prices of above, see page 156

Opulaster, continued

the plantations. Thrives in almost any moist soil and is remarkably attractive either in fruit or flower.

Opulaster opulifolius (*Physocarpus opulifolius* and *Spiræa opulifolia*). NINEBARK. A tall shrub with spreading, often arching branches, growing 8 to 10 feet high. Grows naturally from Canada to Georgia, westward to Kansas. Leaves ovate, deeply lobed, bright green and lustrous. Flowers whitish, in early summer, disposed in numerous clusters along the branches, very showy. The pods assume a bright red color, contrasting strongly with the foliage.

O. opulifolius aureus. GOLDEN NINEBARK. A striking variety with bright yellow leaves, changing in summer to a beautiful golden bronzy yellow. Splendid for producing bright effects.

Philadelphus · The Mock Oranges

Hardy free-flowering shrubs with showy, mostly fragrant flowers, which appear in late spring or early summer. They are justly classed among the "grand shrubs" that add beauty, grace and perfume to our gardens. Any well-drained soil with average fertility is suited to their requirements.

Philadelphus coronarius. COMMON MOCK ORANGE. A hardy shrub with upright, often arching branches, attaining a height of 8 to 10 feet. Native of Europe. Leaves ovate, bright green, 2 to 4 inches long. Flowers creamy white, deliciously fragrant, borne in great profusion. Very showy and desirable.

P. coronarius aureus. GOLDEN MOCK ORANGE. A form with yellow foliage, much prized for its bright effect.

Philadelphus grandiflorus

Philadelphus latifolius

P. coronarius dianthiflorus. DOUBLE-FLOWERED MOCK ORANGE. The flowers of this variety are double, of exquisite form and substance.

P. falconeri. FALCONER'S MOCK ORANGE. A graceful shrub with wide-spreading, arching branches. Probably of garden origin. Leaves broadly lanceolate, 2 to 3 inches long, bright green. Flowers pure white, of starry aspect, borne in great profusion. Very attractive.

P. gordonianus. GORDON'S MOCK ORANGE. A large shrub with spreading branches, 8 to 10 feet tall. Occurs naturally from Washington to Oregon. Leaves broadly ovate, bright green, 2 to 3 inches long. Flowers pure white, produced in dense racemes. Blossoms later than most of the species.

P. grandiflorus. LARGE-FLOWERED MOCK ORANGE. A tall shrub with spreading, often arching branches, clothed with brown exfoliating bark. Distributed from Virginia to Florida, mainly along the mountains. Leaves broadly lanceolate, bright green, 2 to 4 inches long. Flowers very large, pure white, very showy.

P. hirsutus. HAIRY MOCK ORANGE. A spreading shrub 4 to 6 feet tall, with slender, often drooping branches. Distributed from North Carolina and Tennessee to Georgia. Leaves ovate, green above, downy gray beneath, 1 to 2 inches long. Flowers pure white, produced in late spring. Splendid for planting on rocky banks.

P. inodorus. SCENTLESS MOCK ORANGE. A shrub with upright or spreading branches, coated with brown exfoliating bark. Grows naturally from North Carolina and Tennessee to the Gulf. Leaves ovate, deep green, 2 to 3 inches long. Flowers pure white, large and showy.

P. latifolius. BROAD-LEAVED MOCK ORANGE. The tallest species and one of the showiest. Known in a wild state only in Tennessee. A large shrub with upright or spreading branches, clothed with persistent gray bark. Leaves broadly ovate, downy beneath, 2 to

For grades and prices of above, see page 156

Philadelphus, continued

4 inches long. Blossoms creamy white, in many-flowered racemes, produced in great profusion.

P. lemoinei. HYBRID MOCK ORANGE. A very showy and floriferous shrub of garden origin. Leaves bright green, broadly lanceolate or ovate in outline, downy beneath, 1 to 2 inches long. Flowers white, in short racemes, very fragrant, literally covering the branches. Height 4 to 6 feet. The following are some of the best forms:

Avalanche. Very graceful, the slender arching branches almost covered with showy white flowers.

Boule d'Argent. Flowers double, pure white, of remarkable substance and durability.

Mont Blanc. Large and showy white flowers, borne in great profusion.

Philadelphus lewisi. WESTERN MOCK ORANGE. An upright shrub with brown twigs, attaining a height of 6 to 8 feet. Distributed from British Columbia to California. Leaves deep green, broadly ovate, nearly smooth, 2 to 3 inches long. Flowers white, in short dense racemes, about an inch across.

P. microphyllus. SMALL-LEAVED SYRINGA. A small shrub 2 to 3 feet tall, with slender rigid branches. Native of the Rocky Mountains. Leaves oblong, more or less coated with grayish down, ½ to 1 inch long. Flowers white, exquisitely fragrant. Splendid for rock-gardens.

P. pekinensis. CHINESE SYRINGA. A dense upright shrub 3 to 5 feet tall. Native of China. Leaves broadly lanceolate, 2 to 3 inches long, borne on purplish foot-stalks. Flowers white, fragrant, very freely produced in late spring.

P. zeyheri. ZEYHER'S MOCK ORANGE. A profuse-flowering shrub with spreading, often arching branches, of garden origin. Leaves bright green, ovate in outline, somewhat downy beneath. Flowers pure white, borne in great profusion, fully an inch and a half across. A very showy species.

Pieris · The Stagger-Bush

A deciduous shrub growing 2 to 4 feet tall, with showy nodding flowers. It is both hardy and desirable, thriving in moist, porous soils.

Pieris mariana (*Andromeda mariana*). STAGGER-BUSH. Leaves oval, dark green, 2 to 3 inches long. Flowers nodding, white or pinkish, produced in clusters on the naked shoots of the previous season and expanding in late spring. Grows naturally from Rhode Island to Florida, westward to Tennessee and Arkansas.

Polycodium · The Deerberry

A hardy shrub 2 to 4 feet tall, with numerous nodding flowers and a profusion of globular berries. Thrives in almost any well-drained soil. An interesting subject for rock-gardens.

Polycodium stamineum (*Vaccineum stamineum*). DEERBERRY. A branching shrub with green or blue-green foliage, widely distributed from Canada to the Gulf. Flowers in late spring, white, produced in numerous bracted racemes, showy. Berries green, yellow-green or purplish, borne in great profusion.

Potentilla · The Shrubby Cinquefoil

A remarkably distinct and handsome hardy shrub, flowering throughout the summer. It thrives in moist soils, preferring sunny situations. A splendid border plant.

Potentilla fruticosa. SHRUBBY CINQUEFOIL. An erect, much-branched shrub with shreddy bark, widely distributed in the Northern Hemisphere. Leaves compound, consisting of 3 to 7 dark green silky leaflets. Flowers numerous, bright yellow, produced all summer. Highly recommended.

Prunus

The Flowering Plums, Dwarf Almonds and Sand Cherries

Hardy free-flowering shrubs with showy flowers in early spring. They are splendid garden subjects, thriving in almost any well-drained soil. The Beach Plum and Sand Cherries are excellent for waterside planting.

Prunus besseyi. WESTERN SAND CHERRY. A shrub with spreading, sometimes prostrate branches, 2 to 4 feet high. Grows naturally from Manitoba to Kansas

Pieris mariana

and Utah. Leaves oval, bluish green, fading with yellow and orange tones. Flowers white, in clusters, expanding with the leaves. Fruit black, sometimes mottled. Often grown for its fruit under the name of Rocky Mountain Dwarf Cherry.

P. japonica (*P. nana* and *sinensis. Amygdalus pumila*). DWARF, OR FLOWERING ALMOND. A branching shrub, 2 to 4 feet tall, with broadly lanceolate bright green leaves. Native of China and Japan. Flowers double, rose-color and white, borne in great profusion in early spring. One of the best of flowering shrubs and highly recommended.

P. maritima. BEACH PLUM. A decumbent, usually spiny shrub with warty branches. Grows naturally from New Brunswick and the Great Lakes to Virginia. Leaves dark green, usually broadest above the middle, fading with yellow and orange tones. Flowers white, produced in early spring before the leaves appear. Fruit purple, with a bloom, sweet and juicy.

For grades and prices of above, see pages 156 and 157

Prunus, continued

Prunus pumila. SAND CHERRY. A shrub with upright branches, 3 to 5 feet tall, growing naturally from Maine and Manitoba, southward to Virginia. Leaves narrow, dull green above, whitened beneath, fading with tones of orange, yellow and red. Flowers white, in numerous clusters, produced in early spring. Fruit dark purple.

P. triloba. FLOWERING PLUM. A small shrub with downy, broadly ovate and often 3-lobed leaves. Native of China. Flowers double, pink or rose-color, appearing just before the leaves unfold, very profuse and showy. Very hardy and desirable.

Rhamnus • The Buckthorns

Hardy vigorous shrubs with handsome foliage and showy berries. The larger-growing species are well adapted and often used for hedges, both informal and clipped. They thrive in moist, loamy soils, and are not averse to partial shade.

Rhamnus alnifolia. DWARF ALDER. A small shrub with wide-spreading branches, attaining a height of 3 to 4 feet. Grows naturally from New Brunswick to British Columbia, southward to New Jersey and California. Leaves oval, of a pleasing deep green color, 2 to 3 inches long. Berries black.

R. alpina. MOUNTAIN BUCKTHORN. A shrub with stout ascending branches, usually growing 3 to 5 feet tall. Native of the mountains of Europe. Leaves oval, dark lustrous green, 3 to 5 inches long. Berries large, jet-black. One of the handsomest species.

R. catharticus. COMMON BUCKTHORN. A large shrub with spiny branches, usually attaining a height of 6 to 10 feet. Native of Europe. Leaves oval, dark green and lustrous, 2 to 3 inches long, fading in autumn with yellow tones. Berries black, borne in great profusion. A valuable hedge plant on account of its extreme hardiness and vigorous constitution.

R. frangula. ALDER BUCKTHORN. A large shrub with numerous leafy branches. Native of Europe and Asia. Leaves dark green on the upper surface, paler beneath, fading with tones of yellow, orange and red. Berries changing from red to black, ripening in September.

Rhodora • The Rhodora

A hardy shrub with showy rose-colored or purple flowers. It thrives well in moist, loamy soils, and on account of its showy, abundant and early bloom, is worthy of a prominent place in the shrub borders.

Rhodora canadensis. RHODORA. A low deciduous shrub usually 1 to 2 feet tall. Grows naturally from Canada to Pennsylvania and New Jersey. Leaves dark green on the upper surface, pale and glaucous beneath. Flowers in various shades of rose and purple, profusely borne in clusters before the leaves appear. A very pretty plant.

Rhodotypos • The White Kerria

A hardy ornamental shrub with showy white flowers and shining black berries. It thrives in any well-drained fertile soil.

Rhodotypos kerrioides. WHITE KERRIA. A handsome and distinct shrub, usually 4 to 5 feet tall. Native of Japan. Leaves ovate, with a long slender point, bright green and lustrous. Flowers pure white, an inch or more across, appearing in late spring. Berries retained throughout the winter.

Rhus • The Shrubby Sumacs

For convenience, the larger-growing species have been included under "Deciduous Trees." Both the shrubby forms and those that attain tree-like proportions under favorable conditions, are remarkably attractive objects, on account of the showy autumn tints and bright clusters of berries. They thrive in almost any well-drained soil, and are very hardy.

Rhus aromatica (*R. canadensis*). SWEET-SCENTED SUMAC. A much-branched spreading shrub, usually 2 to 4 feet tall, widely distributed in North America. Leaves compound, consisting of three bright green leaflets. Flowers yellow, disposed in short spikes or clusters along the branches. Fruit bright red, clothed with short silky hairs. Splendid for rock-gardens.

R. michauxi (*R. pumila*). DWARF SUMAC. A low downy shrub, creeping by underground rootstocks, distributed from North Carolina to Georgia. Stems 1 to 2 feet tall, bearing numerous compound leaves with 9 to 15 dark green leaflets, which assume brilliant tones in autumn. Flower-spikes 4 to 6 inches long, followed by deep red showy berries. A rare plant.

Ribes • The Flowering Currants and Gooseberries

Hardy ornamental shrubs thriving in almost any well-drained soil. The Gooseberries have spiny and often prickly branches, but those of the Currants are unarmed. They are attractive and interesting objects and worthy of more universal attention.

Ribes aureum. MISSOURI, OR FLOWERING CURRANT. A vigorous shrub with upright branches, attaining a height of 5 to 8 feet. Grows naturally from Missouri to the Rocky Mountains. Leaves bright lustrous green, usually 3-lobed, densely covered with yellowish resinous dots when young. Flowers yellow, large and showy, produced in leafy-bracted clusters in early spring. Berries dark brown or black, edible.

R. curvatum. SOUTHERN GOOSEBERRY. A diffusely branched shrub, with spiny, recurved or drooping branchlets. Grows naturally in Georgia and Alabama. Leaves 3-lobed, bright lustrous green, an inch or less in length. Flowers whitish, profusely borne on drooping pedicels in spring. Splendid for rock-gardens.

R. floridum. WILD BLACK CURRANT. A vigorous shrub with upright branches, usually 3 to 5 feet tall. Grows naturally from Nova Scotia and Minnesota, southward to Virginia and Nebraska. Leaves sharply 3- to 5-lobed, resinous dotted, especially on the lower surface. Flowers greenish white or yellow, in long pendulous racemes. Fruit black, resembling in flavor that of the Black Currant of the gardens.

R. gordonianum. PINK-FLOWERED CURRANT. A large shrub with several strong, upright branches, of garden origin. Leaves bright green, 3- to 5-lobed, fading with tones of yellow and orange. Flowers rose-colored, produced in long pendulous racemes, profuse and showy.

R. sanguineum. RED-FLOWERED CURRANT. A large shrub with upright branches and red-barked twigs, distributed from British Columbia to Mexico. Leaves broadly cordate, 3- to 5-lobed, dark green, with conspicuous veins. Flowers rose or ruddy purple, in long pendulous racemes in early spring. Fruit bluish black with gland-tipped hairs. Very ornamental.

Robinia • The Rose Acacia

A hardy shrub with bristly branches, spreading by underground rootstocks. The showy flowers appear in late spring or early summer. Thrives in almost any well-drained soil.

Robinia hispida. ROSE ACACIA. A small shrub, usually 2 to 3 feet tall, more or less bristly-hairy. Grows naturally from Virginia to Georgia, in the mountains. Leaves compound, consisting of 9 to 13 bright green leaflets. Flowers rose-color, very showy, in loose nodding racemes.

For grades and prices of above, see page 157

Rosa · The Roses

ROSES—the mere name is an inspiration to garden lovers—are justly classed among the showiest and best plants for decorating the home grounds. No garden is complete without them, no arrangements satisfactory that neglect them—in fact, they are indispensable. Fortunately, it is possible to select from the numerous species and garden forms, varieties that are adapted to almost every requirement. They thrive in a wide range of soils, but amply repay any effort made to afford them fertile and congenial surroundings. For convenience, the various groups are described separately, and the more noteworthy and desirable varieties assembled under their respective positions.

The Wild Roses, or Rose Species

Hardy, vigorous-growing shrubs or climbers that require very little attention or pruning. They are very valuable for planting in the shrub borders, producing showy single flowers in great profusion, together with a wealth of bright-colored fruits that prolong the period of beauty throughout the season, and, in instances, well into the winter months. The climbing species are well adapted for covering trellises, fences and similar supports, or they may be permitted to assume informal outlines by the unrestricted development of their branches.

Rosa alba. WHITE ROSE. An upright shrub with prickly branches, of uncertain origin. This is the single form of the Old White Cottage Garden Rose, with the beautiful fragrant white flowers which are used for the manufacture of "Attar of Roses." Very showy throughout the winter on account of the wealth of bright scarlet fruits. Height 4 to 6 feet. The delightful perfume of this Rose and its derivatives is renowned.

R. alpina. ALPINE ROSE. A handsome free-flowering shrub, with slender, upright branches 2 to 3 feet high. Native of the mountains of Europe. Flowers bright rose or pink, 2 inches across. Fruit nodding, bright scarlet, very showy. Splendid for rockeries.

R. arvensis (*R. repens*). EUROPEAN RUNNING ROSE. A creeping shrub with long slender stems. Native of Europe. Leaves deciduous,

Wild Roses

For grades and prices of above, see page 157

Wild Roses, continued

dull green, consisting of about seven leaflets. Flowers white, about 2 inches across, produced in numerous clusters in early summer. A very pleasing ground-cover.

R. blanda. MEADOW ROSE. An erect shrub, 3 to 5 feet tall, with reddish purple, often glaucous branches, armed with slender prickles. Grows naturally from Canada to New York and Wisconsin. Leaves dull or bluish green, with 5 to 7 leaflets. Flowers pink, large and showy. Fruit red, with a bloom.

R. bracteata. MACARTNEY ROSE. A handsome climbing shrub with glossy bright green foliage. Native of China. Stems stout and very thorny, covered with close silky hairs. Flowers very large, pure white, with numerous golden yellow stamens. Not hardy north of Memphis and Washington. Nearly evergreen in the Southern and Pacific States, where it is freely planted.

R. carolina. CAROLINA ROSE. An upright shrub with numerous branches, armed with hooked spines. Grows naturally from Canada to the Gulf. Leaves bright green, usually with seven leaflets. Flowers pink, in flat-topped clusters in summer. Fruit red, profuse and showy. Splendid for massing and for waterside planting.

R. gallica. PROVENCE ROSE. A low upright shrub, usually 2 to 3 feet tall, with dark green glandular leaflets. Native of Europe. Flowers pink, very large and showy, individual flowers often 2 to 3 inches across. Fruit brick-red, persisting until late fall. One of the grandest single Roses in cultivation.

R. humilis. LOW, OR PASTURE ROSE. An upright shrub, 2 to 3 feet high, with numerous prickly branches. Grows naturally from Maine to Georgia, westward to Wisconsin and Missouri. Flowers pink, in early summer. A capital little plant for massing or ground-cover.

R. laevigata. CHEROKEE ROSE. A climbing shrub with slender prickly branches. Native of China and Japan, and naturalized in the Southern States. Leaves dark green and shining. Flowers white, 2 to 3 inches across, fragrant and very showy. Not hardy in the North.

R. multiflora. JAPANESE CLIMBING ROSE. A vigorous shrub with long, recurved or climbing branches. Native of China and Japan. Leaves bright green and lustrous, consisting of 7 to 9 leaflets. Flowers white, borne in great profusion in pyramidal clusters, covering almost the entire length of the arching branches. Handsome and showy.

R. rubiginosa. EGLANTINE, OR SWEET BRIER. An upright shrub with numerous prickly branches. Native of Europe, and naturalized in the Eastern States.

Fruit of Rosa rugosa

Leaves bright green, emitting an agreeable aromatic odor when bruised. Flowers bright pink, on hispid glandular pedicels. Fruit orange-red or scarlet.

R. rubrifolia. RED-LEAVED ROSE. An upright shrub with slender purplish branches, covered with a glaucous bloom. Native of Europe. Leaves blue-green, deeply tinged with purplish red, consisting of 7 to 9 leaflets. Flowers pink, an inch and a half in diameter, borne on hispid pedicels. Fruit scarlet. A remarkable plant.

R. rugosa. WRINKLED JAPANESE ROSE. An upright shrub with spreading branches, densely beset with spines and prickles. Native of China and Japan. Leaves wrinkled, dark lustrous green above, pale beneath, consisting of 5 to 9 leaflets. Flowers purple or white, 3 inches or more across, very showy. Fruits bright red, very large and effective. A grand Rose.

R. setigera. PRAIRIE ROSE. A handsome shrub, with long and slender, recurved or climbing branches. Grows naturally from Canada to Florida, westward to Wisconsin and Texas. Flowers deep rose, produced in great profusion in many-flowered corymbs, in early summer. Fruits bright red, long persistent. Very ornamental and desirable. One of the hardiest Roses.

Rosa multiflora

For grades and prices of above, see page 157

Wild Roses, continued

Rosa spinosissima. SCOTCH ROSE. A low shrub with upright and densely prickly branches. Native of Europe and Asia. Leaves bright green, consisting of 5 to 11 small leaflets. Flowers very numerous along the branches, pink, white or creamy white, about 2 inches across. Fruit black. A remarkably attractive and hardy shrub.

R. watsoni. WATSON'S ROSE. A curious Rose of unknown origin, with numerous arching branches. Height 2 to 3 feet. Leaves compound, with 3 to 5 narrow, undulate leaflets. Flowers small, white, in dense-flowered pyramidal corymbs. Makes an attractive low hedge for a rose-garden.

R. wichuraiana. MEMORIAL ROSE. A hardy half-evergreen shrub with long and slender creeping branches. Native of Japan. Leaves dark green and shining, consisting of 5 to 9 leaflets. Flowers pure white, fragrant, about 2 inches across, borne in many-flowered pyramidal clusters. A handsome and desirable Rose for covering banks and rockeries or for training on fences and trellises.

Bourbon Roses

Very floriferous compact shrubs with bright glossy foliage. The flowers are most profuse in late summer and autumn, and are noted for their exquisite form and color. They require close pruning in early spring.

Appolline. Rosy pink; flowers large and cupped. One of the best varieties.

Champion of the World. Deep rosy pink, large and double, very fragrant. A vigorous, free-flowering variety, valuable for bedding.

Hermosa. Bright rose, very double and fragrant; a constant bloomer.

Souv. de la Malmaison. Delicate flesh, tinted with fawn; large and very double, deliciously fragrant. A grand Rose.

Brier Roses

Handsome flowering shrubs, perhaps more useful as garden plants than for cut-flowers. They require very little in the way of pruning, and the shoots should be shortened only a few inches. If severely trimmed, they will not blossom until another season's growth has been produced. It is common practice to grow several plants, severely pruning a part of them in alternate years.

Austrian Copper. Flowers single, bright coppery red, the reverse of the petals golden yellow. Very effective.

Austrian Yellow. Flowers single, bright golden yellow. Handsome and showy.

Harrison's Yellow. Golden yellow semi-double flowers. Very free-flowering.

Persian Yellow. Bright yellow, nearly double flowers, of exquisite form. An old-time favorite.

Lord Penzance Sweet Briers

Beautiful and interesting hybrids between the Common Sweet Brier and other Roses. The foliage is deliciously fragrant when bruised. The flowers are single and of exquisite tones of color. Very valuable for specimen plants or hedges. The following are desirable varieties:

Amy Robsart. Bright satiny rose.
Anne of Geierstein. Dark velvety crimson.
Brenda. Blush, or peach-color.
Catherine Seyton. Soft rosy pink.
Flora McIvor. Pure white, flushed with rose.
Lady Penzance. Soft copper, shaded with rose.
Lord Penzance. Fawn and lemon-color.
Lucy Ashton. White with pink edges.
Meg Merrilies. Rosy crimson.
Rose Bradwardine. Beautiful clear rose.

Climbing Tea and Noisette Roses

Free-flowering climbing Roses with an almost continuous succession of handsome fragrant flowers. They are especially valuable for trailing over porches, pillars or other supports, and require very little pruning. They are partial to fertile, moist soils, with a sunny exposure, and it is recommended that so far as possible, positions should be chosen that are protected from the coldest winds.

Climbing Clothilde Soupert. White shaded with silvery rose. Flowers throughout the summer. Very hardy. A favorite in many localities.

Climbing Wootton. Deep crimson; richly perfumed. Flowers large and double, blossoming throughout the summer.

Gloire de Dijon. Creamy white with a blush tint, large and very double. Needs protection in the North.

Keystone. Deep lemon-yellow; flowers double, of exquisite form and fragrance. Perfectly hardy and blossoms with remarkable freedom. We commend this Rose to the attention of planters.

Rosa wichuraiana

Lamarque. Pure white with a lemon-yellow center; beautiful large buds; flowers very double and sweet. Hardy in the Southern and Pacific States.

Marechal Niel. Golden yellow; flowers large and very double, very sweetly scented, produced in great profusion. A great favorite in California and the South. Not hardy in the colder sections.

Mary Washington. Pure white, with double, sweet-scented flowers, produced in great profusion, in large showy clusters. Relatively hardy.

Mrs. Robert Peary. Pure white; with large double flowers of exquisite form and substance; very fragrant. A grand hardy Rose.

Reine Marie Henriette. Glowing crimson, the flowers large and very double, produced in profuse clusters. Relatively hardy.

 For grades and prices of above, see pages 157 and 158

Hardy Climbing Roses

Remarkably hardy climbing Roses which are much esteemed for training over arbors, porches, fences and other objects. They blossom profusely once in each season, the wealth of flowers almost covering the branches. Very little in the way of pruning is necessary, and the plants require no protection.

Baltimore Belle. Blush-white; flowers very double, profusely borne in large showy clusters. Very hardy.

Queen of the Prairies. Bright pink; flowers full and compact, produced in profuse showy clusters. Very hardy.

Tennessee Belle. Blush rose; flowers large and double, very sweet-scented. Floriferous and hardy.

Hybrid Perpetual Roses

Shrubs of vigorous, upright growth, with large double flowers which sometimes measure 4 to 5 inches across. They are very hardy plants, and thrive in almost all localities. It is recommended that a protection of leaves or straw litter be afforded in the colder portions of the country. They are among the most valuable and beautiful of all the Roses. As to pruning, they should be cut back moderately, or if very long stems are wanted at the sacrifice of numbers of flowers, more severe pruning is necessary. The following are among the most noteworthy and desirable varieties:

Paul Neyron Rose

Abel Carriere. Dark velvety crimson with fiery center; large and very double, of fine form and fragrance.

Alfred Colomb. Bright cherry-red to deep rich crimson; large and extremely fragrant, of good form and substance. A grand Rose.

American Beauty. Rich rosy crimson; remarkably fragrant; large and deep-petaled. A universal favorite.

Anne de Diesbach. Brilliant carmine; very large and double, delightfully fragrant. A very desirable Rose.

Clio. Flesh-color with rosy pink center; large globular form, fragrant. A splendid Rose in every way.

Dinsmore. Glowing crimson, large and showy; flowers very double, delightfully fragrant. A popular variety.

Duke of Edinburgh. Bright crimson, large and full; foliage vigorous and attractive.

Fisher Holmes. Deep velvety crimson with brilliant scarlet center; of good form and substance.

Francois Levet. One of the grand Roses. Cherry-rose; very floriferous and fragrant.

Frau Karl Druschki. Pure white; flowers large and full, of exquisite form and substance.

Gen. Jacqueminot. Glowing crimson, very soft and velvety. Perhaps the most popular garden Rose.

Giant of Battles. Deep fiery crimson, very brilliant; flowers of good form and substance, delightfully fragrant.

Gloire de Lyonnaise. A rare shade of salmon-yellow, and the nearest approach to yellow in the Hybrid Perpetual Roses. Flowers full and sweet.

John Hopper. Bright rose with carmine center; flowers large and full, with exquisite perfume. A grand old stand-by.

Mme. Charles Wood. Bright scarlet, passing to rosy crimson; flowers large and full, sweetly fragrant. Very free-flowering.

Mme. Gabriel Luizet. Pink or coral-rose, large and very double; of good form and substance. A splendid variety.

Mme. Masson. Bright rose; large and full, with exquisite fragrance. A splendid free-flowering variety.

Mme. Plantier. A grand hardy Rose; and one of the best white varieties in the Hybrid Perpetual class. Pure white, large and very double, sweetly fragrant.

Magna Charta. Pink suffused with carmine, large and very double; of fine form and substance. One of the very best.

Margaret Dickson. A magnificent white Rose. Very large, of excellent form and substance, delightfully fragrant. A vigorous and free-flowering variety.

Marshall P. Wilder. Bright crimson, shaded with maroon, very fragrant; flowers large and full; freely produced.

Mrs. John Laing. A very free-flowering, sweetly fragrant Rose. Bright pink, exquisitely shaded; flowers very large, full and double.

Paul Neyron. Probably the largest flower of any Rose. Deep rose to bright pink, very full and double; exquisitely scented. One of the very best. Often blooms with considerable freedom in the autumn.

Prince Camille de Rohan. Deep velvety crimson, almost shaded with black; flowers large and handsome, delightfully fragrant. The darkest-colored Rose. Should be in every collection.

Ulrich Brunner. Cherry-red, flamed with scarlet; flowers large and full, of exquisite form and substance. The buds are perfection in outline and color.

For grades and prices of above, see pages 158 and 159

Hybrid Tea Roses

Vigorous shrubby Roses producing a profusion of handsome fragrant flowers, many of them unsurpassed in brilliancy of color and grace of outline. They are hardy as far north as Memphis and Washington, but require protection in colder climates. They should be moderately or even severely pruned in the spring, by eliminating all of the weaker shoots, and by heading back the stronger ones. They thrive in any fertile garden soil.

Belle Siebrecht. Deep pink; flowers large, full and double, with long-pointed buds. Very free-flowering.

Kaiserin Augusta Victoria. Creamy white; flowers full and double, sweetly fragrant, with large pointed buds. Remarkably hardy and floriferous. A grand Rose, continuing in flower from spring until autumn.

La France. A beautiful shade of silvery pink; flowers large and full, exquisitely fragrant. One of the most beautiful and popular Roses in this class.

Magnafrano. Deep rose; flowers large and very double, with the fragrance of a Tea Rose. Blossoms profusely and constantly from early summer until autumn.

Meteor. Rich velvety crimson, with wonderfully bright high-lights; flowers large and very double. Splendid for cutting on account of the long stems.

Mme. Abel Chatenay. Rosy carmine, with deeper shades; flowers large, full and double, freely produced throughout the summer.

Mme. Caroline Testout. Satiny rose, deepening to red at the center; flowers large and full, with revolute petals exquisitely bordered with silvery rose.

Pierre Guillot. Brilliant crimson shading to carmine; flowers large and very double, sweetly scented; very floriferous and remarkable for the dazzling color of the flowers.

Souv. du President Carnot. Blush-rose, with deeper shade at the center; flowers large and double, of extremely graceful outline. Buds long and pointed, very handsome.

Japanese Roses

A comparatively new class of Roses of great hardiness and beauty. They are vigorous growing shrubs, usually 4 to 5 feet tall, with deep green, more or less rugose foliage. They require very little pruning and thrive in almost any soil.

Chedane Guinnoseaux. Reddish crimson; flowers double, sweetly scented, continuously borne throughout the summer; berries bright coral-red, very showy.

Conrad F. Meyer. Silvery rose; flowers double, deliciously fragrant, freely produced throughout the season.

Mme. Charles F. Worth. Reddish carmine; flowers full and double, produced in large clusters, very sweet-scented.

Mme. Georges Bruant. Pure white; flowers loosely double, very fragrant, freely produced throughout the summer.

Monthly, or China Roses

Remarkably free-flowering, and without doubt the most continuous-blooming of the Roses. They are hardy throughout the Southern and Pacific States, but require some protection in the North, such as a covering of straw or loose litter. Splendid for bedding or for grouping in front of taller varieties. They require moderate pruning and thrive in almost any garden soil.

Antoinette Cuillerat. White with yellowish center, the reverse of the outer petals carmine-tinted; flowers large, loosely double, borne in great profusion.

Polyantha Rose (see page 84)

Fellenberg. Deep rosy red; flowers loosely double, very showy, borne in large clusters throughout the season.

Gloire de Rosomanes. Glowing crimson; flowers semi-double, produced in large clusters at the ends of the branches. Very vigorous and free-flowering.

Lemesie. Clear rose, gradually changing to red; flowers large and full, borne profusely throughout the season. A beautiful and distinct variety.

Serratipetala. Bright rose, gradually deepening to crimson. A curious old-fashioned variety, with five broad petals and a cluster of numerous narrow petals in the center. Very attractive, exciting comment wherever seen.

Viridiflora. Deep green. A curiosity with numerous double, deep green flowers.

Moss Roses

Hardy vigorous-growing shrubs, thriving in a wide range of soil and climate. They require moderate pruning, or, if longer stems are required at the sacrifice of many flowers, they may be more severely cut back. Most of the varieties flower but once during the season.

Blanche Moreau. Pure white; flowers large and sweet, produced in clusters, both flowers and buds invested with a wealth of deep green moss.

Common Moss. Pink or pale rose; flowers large and full, beautifully crested. A strong grower.

Crimson Globe. Crimson; flowers large and very double, of globular outline, very sweet, beautifully mossed.

Crested Moss. Rose or rosy pink; flowers large and full, of exquisite form and substance. One of the most popular varieties.

Salet. Light rose; flowers flattened, very freely produced. Both flowers and buds are crested with moss.

White Perpetual. White; flowers in profuse clusters; very mossy. An old favorite.

For grades and prices of above, see page 159

Old-Fashioned Roses

These grand Roses are hardy and very adaptable, thriving in almost any garden soil. They require comparatively little pruning and attention.

Cabbage, or **Provence.** There are both white and red forms. Flowers large, full and double, deliciously fragrant.

Celestial. The old-fashioned Celestial Rose, white and fragrant. No sweeter Rose in cultivation.

Damask. Deep rose, flowers large and double, very fragrant. Forms a round compact shrub with handsome deep green foliage which is retained until late autumn.

Maiden's Blush. Blush-white; flowers full and double, very sweet.

Perpetual. Delicate blush; very fragrant, blossoming throughout the season.

Tuscany. Dark velvety crimson. One of the richest colored of all the Old-Fashioned Roses.

Polyantha Roses

Dwarf bushy shrubs with very double fragrant flowers produced in large and profuse clusters. They are often and most successfully used as hedge plants or for bordering garden beds. They require rather severe pruning in order to perpetuate a leafy, floriferous growth. They are relatively hardy, but require protection in very cold climates.

Baby Rambler. Crimson-red; flowers borne in great profusion, in broad clusters throughout the season. Forms a compact bush about 2 feet high.

Clothilde Soupert. Ivory-white, shading towards the center to silvery rose; flowers freely produced in clusters throughout the season. A grand free-flowering variety.

Clothilde Soupert Rose

Etoile d'Or. Pale yellow, changing to rosy red at the center; flowers full and very double, borne in large clusters.

Marie Pavie. Creamy white, flushed with rose, full and double, borne in great profusion in broad clusters, delightfully perfumed.

Rambler Roses

Remarkably vigorous and rapid-growing Roses, often producing shoots 10 to 20 feet in length in a single season. They are well adapted for training against pillars or other supports, and produce a brilliant effect by the wonderful profusion of their flowers, which appear in early summer. They are very hardy and thrive in any fertile soil.

Crimson Rambler. Glowing crimson; flowers produced in great profusion, in large pyramidal trusses. A grand Rose for porches or arbors, or for training on fences. One of the most popular Roses of the period.

Philadelphia Rambler. A variety of the Crimson Rambler with brighter and more deeply colored, perfectly double flowers. Of exquisite form and substance, and lacking the faded appearance sometimes seen in the typical form.

Pink Rambler (Psyche). Light pink, suffused with salmon-rose and deeper pink, the base of the petals pale yellow. Very vigorous.

Yellow Rambler (Aglaia). Light yellow, changing to straw-color. Very floriferous. The very double flowers are produced in large clusters, and continue to appear for three or four weeks.

White Rambler (Thalia). White, sometimes with faint blush; flowers profuse and very fragrant, borne in large compact clusters.

Striped Roses

Hardy shrubs with quaint and very pretty flowers that command attention wherever seen. They thrive in almost any garden soil, and require very little pruning.

Cottage Maid. White, striped with rose. Very dainty.

York and Lancaster. White, striped with red. A legend associated with this Rose proclaims the blending of the warring clans of York and Lancaster, who fought in the historic Wars of the Roses under the insignia of white and red Roses.

Tea Roses

Handsome free-flowering shrubs with showy and delightfully fragrant flowers. They are well adapted for bedding in the open ground, and thrive in any good garden soil. They require protection in cold climates during the winter, such as would be afforded by litter, straw or evergreen boughs.

Aline Sisley. Reddish purple, toned with crimson and maroon; flowers large and double, of exquisite form and fragrance. Highly recommended.

Bon Silene. Deep rose, or rosy crimson; flowers full and fragrant. The buds are very large and of superb outline. One of the best.

Bridesmaid. Clear rich pink; flowers large and fragrant, especially beautiful in the bud. A grand bedding Rose.

Cornelia Cook. Creamy white, faintly tinged with lemon-yellow; flowers very double, produced in great profusion, of exquisite form and substance. Splendid for bedding.

Devoniensis. This is the Magnolia Rose of the South. Creamy white with rosy center; flowers large and double, deliciously fragrant. A universal favorite.

Etoile de Lyon. Golden yellow; flowers very deep and full, sweet-perfumed. One of the best Roses in its class.

For grades and prices of above, see pages 159 and 160

Tea Roses, continued

Maman Cochet. Clear pink, changing to silvery rose; flowers large and double, of graceful outline and delicate fragrance. A superb bedding Rose.

Marie Guillot. White, faintly tinged with pale yellow; flowers large, full and double, very fragrant and showy. One of the best white Roses for outdoor culture of its class.

Papa Gontier. Cherry-red, changing to glowing crimson, very fragrant; buds very large, of exquisite outline. Highly recommended.

Perle des Jardins. Golden yellow; flowers large, of a distinct globular form, richly perfumed. An old-time favorite.

Safrano. Apricot-yellow, changing to deeper tones of orange, rose and fawn.

The Bride. Pure white; flowers large and very double, richly perfumed. Very beautiful in bud. In the open ground the flowers are often tinged with pink.

Tea Roses

Wichuraiana Hybrid Roses

A comparatively new race of hardy Roses, adapted for training on pillars, fences or trellises, or as a ground cover where other Roses would be unlikely to thrive. They thrive in almost any kind of soil, but of course amply repay the planter for providing fertile and congenial surroundings. The flowers are borne in great profusion in late spring or early summer, and continue for a period of three or four weeks. The foliage is remarkably lustrous and remains green until midwinter.

Debutante. Soft pink; flowers double, in clusters, very fragrant, with the delicate odor of the Sweet Brier. Foliage dark glossy green. Splendid for training on trellises or trailing on the ground.

Dorothy Perkins. Clear shell-pink; flowers profusely borne in numerous clusters, full and double, with crinkled petals. Leaves bright green and lustrous, persisting until early winter. A grand Rose for training or for ground cover.

Pink Roamer Bright pink with a white center, often flushed with red; flowers profuse, large and showy, with the fragrance of the Sweet Brier. Foliage rich green and lustrous, persistent until early winter.

Sweetheart. Bright pink in bud, changing to white when fully expanded; flowers large and showy, deliciously fragrant. Foliage dark glossy green, persisting until early winter.

Wm. C. Egan. Rosy pink; flowers large and very double, sweetly fragrant, borne in great profusion in late spring or early summer. Foliage bright green and lustrous, persisting until early winter. A grand Rose.

Rubus · The Brambles

Ornamental shrubs of diverse habit with showy flowers, thriving in almost any soil. They are attractive objects for the shrub borders, several of the species having a flowering period of considerable duration, while others are chiefly attractive for their foliage.

Rubus crataegifolius. HAWTHORN-LEAVED BRAMBLE. A shrub with upright spiny stems, spreading from underground root-stocks. Native of Japan. Leaves simple, 3- to 5-lobed, bright green, fading in autumn with tones of deep red. Flowers white, produced in terminal clusters on the slender branchlets. Berries orange-red. Very hardy and well adapted for covering banks and sterile places.

R. deliciosus. ROCKY MOUNTAIN FLOWERING RASPBERRY. A compact spineless shrub with numerous branches, attaining a height of 3 to 5 feet. Native of the Rocky Mountains. Leaves simple, shallowly 3- to 5-lobed, bright green. Flowers white, very profuse, expanding in early summer and continuing for several weeks. Berries purplish. A hardy and very showy ornamental.

R. dumetorum. EUROPEAN DEWBERRY. A spiny trailing shrub with long and slender prostrate stems. Native of Europe. Leaves dark green, consisting of three leaflets, turning in autumn to beautiful tones of bronze and brown. Flowers small, white, produced at the ends of the short leafy branchlets. Fruit black. Splendid for a ground cover for banks and rocky exposures. Quite hardy.

R. laciniatus. CUT-LEAVED BLACKBERRY. A tall shrub with recurved spiny branches, of uncertain origin. Leaves more or less evergreen in mild climates, usually with three deeply incised dark green leaflets. Flowers white or tinged with pink, produced in large terminal panicles. Berries thimble-shaped, black. Very ornamental.

R. odoratus. FLOWERING RASPBERRY. A vigorous upright shrub, with numerous spineless stems, clothed with shreddy bark. Grows naturally from Nova Scotia and Michigan, southward to Georgia. Leaves simple, very large, 3- to 5-lobed, resembling a Maple leaf in outline. Flowers rose-purple, large and showy, blossoming for several weeks. Berries light red. One of the showiest species and a remarkably attractive plant. Height 3 to 5 feet.

R. parviflorus (*R. nutkanus*). WESTERN FLOWERING RASPBERRY. An upright shrub with numerous spineless branches, clothed with shreddy bark. Grows naturally from Michigan to the Pacific Coast and southward in the Rocky Mountains. Leaves simple, shallowly 3- to 5-lobed, bright green. Flowers white, very showy,

For grades and prices of above, see page 160

Rubus, continued

expanding in early summer. A splendid companion for the Flowering Raspberry. Grows 3 to 5 feet tall.

R. phoenicolasius. WINEBERRY. A graceful shrub with long arching branches, furnished with numerous prickles and reddish glandular hairs. Native of China and Japan. Leaves bright green, woolly white beneath, consisting of about three leaflets. Flowers in dense hairy clusters, the long bristly calyx lobes investing the growing fruits. Berries red. A very showy and extremely ornamental plant. Height 4 to 6 feet.

R. rosaeflorus. STRAWBERRY-RASPBERRY. An upright tall-growing shrub with arching spiny branches. Native of Asia. Leaves compound, strongly veined, consisting of 5 to 15 bright green leaflets. Flowers white, large and showy, often blooming throughout the summer. Berries thimble-shaped, bright red, an inch or more in length. A handsome plant.

R. rosaeflorus coronarius (*R. grandiflorus*). BRAMBLE ROSE. A form with showy, double white flowers, worthy of more general culture.

Rubus odoratus (see page 85)

Salix · The Bush Willows

The shrubby species of Willow are valuable for waterside planting, or, in the instance of *Salix tristis* and *S. humilis*, for rock-gardens and dry situations. They are hardy and rapid-growing, and the showy catkins add life and interest in early spring just at a time when flowers are most highly prized. Other species will be found under "Deciduous Trees."

Salix humilis. PRAIRIE WILLOW. An upright shrub, usually 3 to 5 feet tall, with brown twigs. Grows naturally from Canada to Nebraska and North Carolina. Leaves elliptic, bright green above, whitish beneath. Catkins expanding in early spring, before the leaves appear, yellow and gray. Thrives in dry soil.

S. incana (*S. rosmarinifolia*). ROSEMARY WILLOW. An upright shrub, usually 5 to 8 feet tall, with slender branches. Native of Europe. Leaves very narrow, green on the upper surface, white woolly beneath. Catkins long and slender, appearing with the leaves.

S. sericea. SILKY WILLOW. A diffuse shrub, usually 4 to 8 feet tall, with gray-green or reddish twigs; widely distributed in the Northeastern States. Leaves densely silky beneath, bright green above. Catkins appearing with the leaves, yellow or orange-yellow.

S. tristis. DWARF GRAY WILLOW. A low, diffuse and very leafy shrub, usually 1 to 2 feet high, with gray branches. Grows naturally from Maine and Minnesota to the Gulf. Leaves narrowly oblong, hoary white on both sides, or in age becoming greenish above. Catkins expanding before the leaves, nearly globular.

Sambucus · The Elders

Hardy vigorous-growing shrubs with showy flowers and a profusion of berries. They thrive best in moist loamy soils, and are well adapted for waterside and border planting.

Sambucus canadensis. AMERICAN ELDER. A tall shrub with stout stems filled with white pith. Widely distributed from Canada and Florida to the Rocky Mountains. Leaves compound, consisting of 5 to 11 bright green leaflets. Flowers white, in large flat-topped cymes, fragrant, opening in early summer. Fruit black, very profuse, ripening in August and September. Very showy and deserving of more extended cultivation. Grows 6 to 10 feet tall.

S. nigra. EUROPEAN ELDER. A large shrub, usually attaining a height of 10 to 15 feet, native of Europe. Leaves compound, consisting of 5 to 9 dark green leaflets. Flowers white, produced in flat-topped clusters in late spring or early summer. Fruit black, quite showy. A very vigorous plant.

S. nigra aurea. GOLDEN ELDER. A form with bright yellow foliage, much used for producing lively effects.

S. nigra laciniata. CUT-LEAVED ELDER. The foliage is deeply cut and incised, lending an airy fern-like aspect. Very attractive.

S. pubens. RED-BERRIED ELDER. A shrub with warty branches and brown pith, widely distributed in Canada and the United States. Leaves dark green, consisting of 5 to 7 leaflets. Flowers white, in large pyramidal cymes, blossoming in late spring. Berries red, very showy, ripening in early summer. A splendid companion for the American Elder, and often with ripe fruit when the latter is in bloom. Height 5 to 7 feet.

Schizonotus · The White Beam-leaved Spirea

A hardy free-flowering shrub with showy flowers. It thrives in almost any well-drained soil, preferring a sunny exposure.

Schizonotus discolor. WHITE BEAM-LEAVED SPIREA. A graceful shrub with handsome deeply lobed leaves. Native of the Rocky Mountains. Flowers creamy white, in large feathery drooping panicles, opening in midsummer. Height 5 to 10 feet.

Spartium · The Spanish Broom

A handsome shrub with long and slender green branches. It is hardy as far north as Memphis and Washington. Especially valuable for the Southern and Pacific States. Thrives in almost any well-drained soil, and is valuable for sandy and rocky exposures.

Spartium junceum. SPANISH BROOM. An upright shrub, usually 4 to 8 feet tall, with rush-like branches. Native of Southwestern Europe. Leaves small, bluish green, sparsely produced. Flowers yellow, in terminal showy racemes, about an inch long, blossoming for long periods, or, in the South, almost the whole year.

For grades and prices of above, see page 160

Spiræa · The Spireas

Spiræa cantonensis fl. pl.

A large group of showy free-flowering shrubs of inestimable garden value. Among the species may be found those that produce a profusion of flowers in earliest spring, others that blossom at later intervals, and even varieties that continue to produce flowers from midsummer until autumn. In general, they are graceful, compact bushes, many of them of great hardiness. They thrive best in moist, fertile soils, preferring sunny exposures. For convenience, the varieties are arranged in two groups, early- and late-flowering.

EARLY-FLOWERING SPIREAS

Spiraea arguta. HYBRID SNOW-GARLAND. A remarkably floriferous and showy shrub of garden origin. Leaves narrow, bright green, fading with tones of yellow and orange. Flowers pure white, borne in great profusion in early spring. Height 3 to 5 feet. Quite hardy and one of the best of the very early Spireas.

S. bracteata. ROUND-LEAVED SPIREA. A hardy shrub 5 to 8 feet tall, with numerous upright or spreading branches. Native of Japan. Leaves nearly round, dark green on the upper surface, bluish green beneath, persisting until late autumn. Flowers pure white, produced in numerous showy umbels in late spring. A vigorous and desirable species.

S. cantonensis. LANCE-LEAVED SPIREA. A graceful shrub with slender, arching branches, attaining a height of 3 to 5 feet. Native of China and Japan. Leaves lanceolate, with incised borders, dark green on the upper surface, pale bluish green beneath. Flowers pure white, in numerous densely flowered umbels in late spring. Needs protection from piercing winds in the colder sections.

S. cantonensis flore pleno (*S. reevesiana*). LANCE-LEAVED DOUBLE SPIREA. A handsome variety of the foregoing species with very double white flowers, possessing remarkable texture and durability.

S. chamaedryfolia. GERMANDER-LEAVED SPIREA. A hardy shrub with upright or spreading branches, 3 to 5 feet tall. Native of Europe and Asia. Leaves ovate or broadly lanceolate, dark green above, blue-green beneath, with sharply serrate borders. Flowers pure white, disposed in numerous densely-flowered umbels, appearing in late spring. A distinct and desirable species.

Spiræa vanhouttei (see page 88)

 For grades and prices of above, see pages 160 and 161

Spiræa, continued

Spiraea hypericifolia. HYPERICUM-LEAVED SPIREA. A sturdy, graceful shrub with upright, often arching branches. Distributed from Eastern Europe to Siberia. Leaves bright green, broadest above the middle, with tapering or wedge-shaped base. Flowers white, borne in numerous clusters along the branches and opening in early spring. Height 3 to 5 feet.

Spiræa alba

S. pikowiensis (*S. nicoudierti*). PIKOW SPIREA. An erect shrub with numerous stout branches, found in a wild state in Poland. Leaves oblong, bright green, fading with yellow tones in autumn. Flowers white, disposed in numerous dense-flowered umbels in spring. Very floriferous. Grows 3 to 5 feet tall.

S. prunifolia. PLUM-LEAVED SPIREA. A graceful tall-growing species with upright slender, often arching branches. Native of China and Japan. Leaves bright green, ovate or oblong, fading with yellow tones in autumn. Flowers pure white in early spring, disposed in numerous small clusters along the branches. Quite hardy. Grows 5 to 7 feet high.

S. prunifolia flore pleno. BRIDAL WREATH. A handsome form with very double showy white flowers, produced in great profusion in early spring. The leaves are very dark green and glossy and assume brilliant orange tones in autumn. One of the grandest garden shrubs.

S. thunbergi. SNOW GARLAND. A beautiful shrub with numerous slender branches, forming a dense feathery bush 3 to 4 feet tall. Native of China and Japan. Leaves narrow, bright green, fading in autumn with brilliant tones of orange and scarlet. Flowers pure white, appearing in great profusion in earliest spring and covering the plant as with a mantle of snow.

S. vanhouttei. VAN HOUTTE'S BRIDAL WREATH. A grand and graceful shrub with numerous arching branches, of garden origin. Leaves dark green, with incised borders, pale bluish green beneath, persisting until late autumn. Flowers white, in numerous dense-flowered umbels in late spring, Quite hardy and attaining a height of 5 to 6 feet. Highly recommended.

SUMMER-FLOWERING SPIREAS

Spiraea alba. MEADOW SWEET. An upright shrub with reddish brown branches, 3 to 5 feet tall. Distributed naturally from New York to the Rockies, southward to Georgia. Leaves willow-like, bright green, fading with yellow tones. Flowers white, in large pyramidal clusters, expanding in summer. Hardy and floriferous.

S. albiflora (S. *japonica alba*). DWARF WHITE SPIREA. A low dense shrub with stiff upright branches. Native of Japan. Leaves lanceolate, bright green, with incised or serrate borders. Flowers white, in numerous flat-topped clusters in summer. Neat and attractive.

S. billardi. BILLARD'S SPIREA. A hardy upright shrub with brownish branches, growing 4 to 5 feet tall. Of garden origin. Leaves oblong or lanceolate, bright green above, pale or grayish beneath. Flowers bright pink, produced in long dense panicles in summer. Very showy and attractive, and splendid for cut-flowers.

S. bumalda. EVERBLOOMING SPIREA. A remarkably free-flowering shrub with upright branches. attaining a height of about 2 feet. Of garden origin. Leaves bright green, often with variegations of yellow, with incised and serrate borders. Flowers deep pink, produced in large flat-topped clusters, blossoming throughout the summer and autumn.

S. bumalda Anthony Waterer. CRIMSON SPIREA. A form of the preceding with bright rosy crimson flowers, disposed in dense corymbs. Very floriferous, continuing to bloom until fall.

S. douglasi. DOUGLAS' SPIREA. An upright shrub, 5 to 7 feet tall, with reddish brown branches. Naturally distributed from British Columbia to California. Leaves narrowly oblong, green above, white woolly beneath. Flowers deep pink, in long dense panicles. Very showy and quite hardy.

S. japonica. JAPANESE SPIREA. A compact shrub with upright branches, 3 to 4 feet tall. Native of China and Japan. Leaves ovate or broadly lanceolate, bright green above, pale or bluish green beneath, persisting until frost. Flowers pink or rosy pink, in flat-topped clusters. Very floriferous.

S. latifolia. MEADOW QUEEN. An upright shrub with reddish brown branches, attaining a height of 3 to 4 feet. Grows naturally from Canada to North Carolina. Leaves oval or oblong, bright green, with serrate borders. Flowers white or blush pink, in large pyramidal panicles, blossoming in summer.

S. margaritae. PINK HYBRID SPIREA. A very floriferous shrub, with spreading branches, of garden origin. Leaves elliptical, bright green, often tinged with purple, with serrate and incised borders. Flowers bright pink, in broad flat-topped clusters, blossoming in midsummer. Handsome and showy. Grows 3 to 4 feet tall.

S. menziesi. MENZIES' SPIREA. A hardy upright shrub with brown branches, attaining a height of 3 to 4 feet. Grows naturally from Alaska to Oregon. Leaves oblong, bright green above, pale beneath, with serrate borders. Flowers pink, in large narrow panicles, opening in summer. Fine for cut-flowers.

S. tomentosa. STEEPLE-BUSH; HARDHACK. An upright shrub with brown felty branches, 3 to 4 feet tall. Grows naturally from Canada southward to Kansas and Georgia. Leaves ovate or oblong, dark green, densely coated on the lower surface with yellowish or gray down. Flowers deep pink, in narrow dense spikes 3 to 8 inches long. Hardy and distinct.

S. virginiana. VIRGINIA SPIREA. A hardy shrub with spreading, often wand-like branches, about 2 feet tall. Grows naturally in the mountains from Virginia to North Carolina. Leaves broadest above the middle, bright green above, pale beneath, fading with yellow tones. Flowers white, disposed in terminal flat-topped or globular clusters in early summer. Rare in cultivation.

Spiræa billardi

For grades and prices of above, see page 161

Staphylea · The Bladder-Nuts

Hardy shrubs with showy flowers and peculiar inflated seed-pods. They thrive best in moist loamy soil, either in sun or partial shade.

Staphylea bumalda. JAPANESE BLADDER-NUT. A sturdy shrub with upright or spreading branches, attaining a height of about 6 feet. Native of Japan. Leaves light green, consisting of three oval or ovate leaflets. Flowers white, in loose upright panicles in early summer. Pods usually 2-lobed, inflated, slightly flattened. Splendid for a specimen plant.

S. colchica. COLCHICAN BLADDER-NUT. A tall upright shrub, usually 10 to 12 feet tall. Native of the Caucasus. Leaves bright green, consisting of 3 to 5 leaflets. Flowers white, disposed in broad, often nodding panicles, very showy. Pods large and much inflated. Very ornamental.

S. pinnata. EUROPEAN BLADDER-NUT. A large upright shrub 12 to 15 feet tall. Native of Europe. Leaves bright green, consisting of 5 to 7 long-pointed leaflets. Flowers white, produced in long raceme-like clusters in late spring. Pods 2- to 3-lobed, widely inflated.

S. trifolia. AMERICAN BLADDER-NUT. A vigorous shrub with stout upright branches, growing naturally from Canada southward to Missouri and Georgia. Leaves bright green, composed of three ovate leaflets. Flowers white, in nodding raceme-like clusters in spring. Pods 3-lobed, much inflated.

Stephanandra · The Stephanandra

A graceful, fairly hardy shrub with handsome foliage and showy flowers. It thrives in a moist fertile soil, preferring sunny exposures. Worthy of a prominent place in the shrub border.

Stephanandra flexuosa. STEPHANANDRA. A beautiful shrub with drooping or arching branches, usually 3 to 4 feet high. Native of Japan. Leaves ovate, with incisely lobed and serrate borders; they are tinged with red at the time of unfolding, at maturity deep glossy green, fading with brilliant tones of yellow, red and purple. Flowers white, in soft feathery panicled racemes.

Stuartia · The Stuartias

Handsome relatively hardy shrubs with Camellia-like flowers and bright green foliage, which assumes brilliant shades of orange, red and scarlet in autumn. They thrive in rich porous soils with moderate moisture, especially those containing woods earth. A warm sunny exposure is preferable.

Stuartia pentagyna. ALLEGHANY STUARTIA. A shrub with spreading branches, usually 5 to 10 feet tall. Grows naturally from Tennessee and North Carolina to Georgia. Leaves bright green, ovate in outline, fading with glowing colors. Flowers white, large and showy, with wavy erose-bordered petals and golden anthers, opening in summer.

S. pseudo-camellia. JAPANESE STUARTIA. A large shrub with upright branches, native of Japan. Leaves elliptical, bright green, coloring brightly in autumn. Flowers showy, about 2 inches across, pure white, with silky petals and orange stamens, blossoming in summer. In cultivation usually 8 to 10 feet tall.

Spiræa margaritæ (see page 88).

Styrax · The Storax Shrubs

Attractive free-flowering shrubs with showy flowers, well adapted for outstanding specimen plants or grouping in the shrub borders. They thrive in well-drained loamy soils. With protection from cold winds they are successfully grown in Missouri and Massachusetts.

Styrax americana. AMERICAN STORAX. A spreading shrub, 4 to 6 feet tall, with bright green leaves. Distributed naturally from Virginia and Florida, westward to Arkansas and Louisiana. Flowers white, nodding, produced in numerous small clusters along the branches.

S. japonica. JAPANESE STORAX. A graceful shrub with spreading branches and pleasing bright green foliage. Native of Japan. Flowers white, in numerous drooping racemes, fragrant and showy, appearing in early summer. In cultivation usually 8 to 12 feet tall, or in favorable situations, even taller. Splendid for specimen plants.

S. obassia. BROAD-LEAVED STORAX. A vigorous tall shrub with large, broad leaves. Native of Japan. Flowers white, fragrant, freely produced in long graceful racemes 4 to 6 inches long. A very showy and distinct species.

Symphoricarpos

The Coral-Berry and Snowberries

Handsome hardy shrubs with very showy berries. They are unexcelled for massing and grouping, either under trees or in the foreground of larger shrubs. Almost any kind of soil meets their requirements.

Symphoricarpos occidentalis. WESTERN SNOWBERRY, OR WOLFBERRY. A shrub usually 3 to 5 feet tall with numerous spreading branches. Widely distributed in the Western States. Leaves ovate, green or bluish green. Flowers white or rose-colored, produced in numerous spikes in summer. Berries white, persisting until winter.

S. racemosus. SNOWBERRY. A graceful shrub, 3 to 5 feet tall, with slender branches. Distributed naturally from Canada to North Carolina. Leaves elliptic or broadly ovate, sometimes lobed on the shoots. Flowers white or pinkish, in loose, often leafy racemes, in summer. Berries white, long persistent, produced in showy profuse clusters, the branches bending under their weight. Very ornamental, and a capital companion for the next species.

S. symphoricarpos (*S. vulgaris*). CORAL-BERRY, OR INDIAN CURRANT. A grand shrub, producing a wealth of red or purplish berries which remain on the branches all winter. Grows naturally from New York and Dakota southward to Georgia and Texas. Leaves ovate, bright green, often tinged with reddish purple when young, persisting until early winter. Flowers greenish red, in summer. Berries coloring in early autumn, very showy.

Syringa · The Lilacs

Hardy free-flowering shrubs with showy fragrant flowers in spring and early summer. They are among the most popular and beautiful of flowering plants, and thrive in almost any fertile soil with

For grades and prices of above, see page 161

Syringa, continued

moderate moisture. One other species, the Japanese or Tree Lilac, will be found under "Deciduous Trees."

Syringa chinensis (*S. rothomagensis*). ROUEN LILAC. A graceful shrub with slender, often arching branches. Of garden origin. Leaves broadly lanceolate, bright green. Flowers lilac-purple, in showy broad panicles in mid-spring. Very handsome and free-flowering. Height 8 to 10 feet.

S. josikea. HUNGARIAN LILAC. A sturdy, vigorous shrub with stout upright branches. Native of Hungary. Leaves broadly oblong, pointed at the apex, dark green and shining. Flowers violet, in long narrow panicles, expanding in late spring or early summer. Height 8 to 10 feet.

S. pekinensis. CHINESE LILAC. A large shrub 10 to 12 feet tall, with slender spreading branches. Native of China. Leaves ovate or broadly lanceolate, long-pointed, dark green. Flowers creamy white, disposed in large terminal panicles, usually in pairs. Very floriferous when old and well established.

S. persica. PERSIAN LILAC. A graceful shrub with slender branches, attaining a height of 6 to 8 feet. Native of Persia. Leaves broadly lanceolate, of a rich green color. Flowers pale lilac, in broad panicles 3 to 4 inches long, opening in late spring.

S. persica alba. WHITE PERSIAN LILAC. Like the last, but with white flowers.

Symphoricarpos symphoricarpos (see page 89)

S. villosa. HIMALAYAN LILAC. An upright shrub with stout warty branches, attaining a height of 5 to 8 feet. Native of the Himalayas. Leaves broadly oblong, pointed at the apex, bright green, but without lustre. Flowers pinkish, in broad panicles 3 to 6 inches long, expanding in late spring.

S. vulgaris. COMMON LILAC. A large upright shrub with heart-shaped, bright green leaves. Native of Europe. Flowers deliciously fragrant, varying from white to shades of lilac, blue and purple. The varieties listed below embrace some of the best and most desirable forms in cultivation.

SINGLE LILACS

Ambroise Verschaffelt. Light pink. Showy.
Charles X. Dark lilac-red. One of the best.
Dr. Lindley. Pinkish lilac. A dainty color.
Marie Legraye. White. A beautiful variety.
Frau Bertha Dammann. White. Charming.
Geant des Batailles. Bluish lilac. Very showy.
Gloire des Moulins. Light pink. Delicate and dainty.
Ludwig Spath. Dark blue.

DOUBLE LILACS

Alphonse Lavalle. Bluish lilac.
Belle de Nancy. Pink with white center.
Condorcet. Blue.
La Tour d'Auvergne. Violet-purple.
Mme. Abel Chatenay. White.
Mme. Casimir Perier. White.
Mme. Lemoine. White.
Maxime Cornu. Pinkish lilac.
Michael Buchner. Pale lilac.
Pres. Carnot. Pale blue.

Tamarix · The Tamarisks

Graceful shrubs with feathery foliage and large panicles of showy flowers. They are relatively hardy, thriving as far north as Missouri and Massachusetts. A moist loamy or sandy soil is best adapted to them. They are also well adapted for seaside planting, or for saline or alkaline soils.

Tamarix gallica (*T. pentandra*). FRENCH TAMARISK. A tall shrub with slender spreading branches and bluish green scale-like leaves. Native of Europe. Flowers pinkish, in slender panicled racemes in spring or early summer. Showy and distinct.

T. gallica indica (*T. indica*). INDIAN TAMARISK. A variety of the foregoing species from the Himalayas, characterized by its upright growth, longer racemes of pink flowers and dull green foliage.

T. juniperina (*T. plumosa and T. japonica*). JAPANESE TAMARISK. A shrub, usually 10 to 12 feet tall, with slender spreading branches and bright green foliage. Native of Japan. Flowers pinkish, in numerous slender racemes, produced on the branches of the previous year and expanding in spring.

T. odessana. CASPIAN TAMARISK. An upright shrub, 4 to 6 feet tall, with bright green foliage. Native of the Caspian region. Flowers pink, disposed in loose panicled racemes, blossoming in late summer. Very valuable on account of its late-appearing flowers.

T. parviflora. EARLY-FLOWERING TAMARISK. A shrub with spreading branches, clothed with reddish brown bark. Native of Europe. Leaves small and scale-like, bright green. Flowers pink, disposed in slender racemes along the branches of the previous year, opening in early spring. A remarkably showy plant.

Ulex · The Furze

A much-branched shrub with green spiny branches and showy flowers. It thrives in sandy or very porous soils, preferring sunny exposures. Well adapted for seaside or rockery planting or for covering gravelly banks. Hardy with slight protection from cold winds as far north as Missouri and Massachusetts.

Ulex europaeus. FURZE, GORSE OR WHIN. A rigid and very spiny shrub with small or scale-like leaves. Native of Europe. Flowers bright yellow, very showy, fragrant, produced at or near the tips of the branches. Blossoms usually both in spring and fall, or, in California, almost throughout the season.

Viburnum · The Arrow-woods and Snowballs

Handsome hardy shrubs with showy flowers and foliage. They are not only attractive when in flower, but many species produce large and profuse clusters of bright or glistening berries, and the foliage frequently assumes brilliant and intense color tones in autumn. As specimen plants, the showier forms, like the Snowballs, have few rivals, and for grouping or massing, the humbler members of the genus make possible many charming effects. The

For grades and prices of above, see pages 161 and 162

Viburnum, continued

species described below thrive best in moist soils in sunny situations, except the Hobble-bush, which requires shade and cool, moist soil. Other species are described under "Broad-leaved Evergreen Shrubs" and "Deciduous Trees."

Viburnum acerifolium. Maple-leaved Viburnum. A shrub with slender, spreading or upright branches, 3 to 5 feet tall. Grows naturally from New Brunswick and Minnesota southward to North Carolina. Leaves 3-lobed, Maple-like, bright green, fading with handsome purple tones in autumn. Flowers creamy or yellowish white, in flat-topped clusters in late spring or early summer. Berries black. Splendid for massing.

V. alnifolium (*V. lantanoides*). Hobble-bush. A shrub with wide-spreading branches, usually 5 to 8 feet tall. Distributed naturally from New Brunswick and Michigan southward to North Carolina. Leaves heart-shaped, very large, rich green above, scurfy beneath, fading with beautiful tones of vinous red. Flowers white, in broad, flat-topped clusters, with several large showy white rays. Berries dark purple. Should be planted in shade in moist, porous soil. Very handsome.

V. cassinoides. Withe-rod. A very hardy free-flowering shrub with upright branches. Naturally distributed from Newfoundland and Manitoba to North Carolina. Leaves oval, dull green, fading with rich tones of purple and red. Flowers creamy or yellowish white, in broad flat-topped clusters in early summer. Berries pink, changing to dark blue. Splendid for waterside planting or for grouping in the shrub borders. In cultivation usually 4 to 8 feet tall.

V. dentatum. Arrow-wood. A bushy shrub with upright branches, growing naturally from New Brunswick to Minnesota southward to Georgia. Leaves heart-shaped, bright green, with coarsely toothed borders, fading with rich tones of purple and red. Flowers creamy white, in profuse flat-topped clusters in late spring or early summer. Berries blue-black. Height 8 to 12 feet. A handsome symmetrical species.

V. dilatatum. Japanese Bush Cranberry. A handsome floriferous shrub with upright branches, attaining a height of 8 to 10 feet. Native of Japan. Leaves broadly ovate, with coarsely toothed margins, bright green. Flowers pure white, in broad flat-topped clusters in late spring or early summer. Berries scarlet, persisting a long time on the branches. Showy and desirable.

V. lantana. Wayfaring Tree. A large shrub with scurfy branches, usually growing 10 to 15 feet tall. Native of Europe. Leaves heart-shaped, wrinkled, dark green above, downy beneath. Flowers white, disposed in dense flat-topped clusters, usually with seven showy white ray-flowers on the margins. Berries bright red, changing to black. Splendid for specimen plants.

V. macrocephalum. Chinese Viburnum. An attractive large shrub with spreading branches, attaining a height of 10 to 12 feet. Native of China. Leaves oval, dark green on the upper surface, coated with starry hairs beneath, persisting until early winter. Flowers yellowish white, in broad cymes, with many of the marginal flowers ray-like, appearing in late spring or early summer. Hardy as far north as Missouri and Massachusetts.

V. macrocephalum sterile. Chinese Snowball. A form of the preceding with all of the flowers ray-like and enlarged, produced in large globular clusters 7 to 8 inches across. A grand plant for the Southern and Pacific States, but not hardy in the North.

V. nudum. Larger Withe-rod. A tall upright shrub with slender branches, usually growing 10 to 12 feet tall. Grows naturally from Long Island to Florida, and westward to Kentucky and Louisiana. Leaves oval, bright green, persisting until late autumn. Flowers creamy or yellowish white, in broad cymes in summer. Berries pink, changing to blue. Apparently not hardy much north of its natural range, although withstanding twenty degrees below zero in the mountains of North Carolina.

V. opulus. High Bush Cranberry. A tall shrub with upright spreading branches, 8 to 10 feet tall, widely distributed in the Northern Hemisphere. Leaves broadly ovate, 3-lobed, bright green. Flowers white, disposed in flat-topped clusters in late spring and early summer. Berries scarlet, persisting all winter, very showy.

V. opulus nanum. Dwarf Cranberry Bush. A very dwarf compact shrub, well adapted for edging beds, and a good substitute for the Dwarf Boxwood where that plant is not hardy.

V. opulus sterile. Snowball, or Guelder Rose. A grand hardy shrub with handsome showy flowers produced in large globular clusters. All of the flowers are sterile and radiant, and appear in numerous compact balls in spring. An old-time favorite, and without doubt one of the best of flowering shrubs.

V. tomentosum. Single-flowered Japanese Snowball. A vigorous shrub with spreading branches, native of Japan. Leaves dark grëen with bronzy margins, broadly ovate in outline, very handsome. Flowers white, prôduced in flat-topped clusters, with the marginal ones sterile and radiant. Berries red, changing to bluish black. Height 6 to 8 feet. Hardy in Missouri and Massachusetts.

V. tomentosum plicatum (*V. plicatum*). Japanese Snowball. A handsome shrub with showy flowers and beautiful foliage. The large globose flower-clusters are 3 to 4 inches across, and consist wholly of sterile radiant flowers of purest white. Very highly recommended. Hardy in Missouri and Massachusetts, but should be protected from piercing winds in colder sections.

V. sieboldi (*V. japonicum*). Siebold's Viburnum. A vigorous hardy shrub with stout spreading branches. Native of Japan. Leaves large, dark green and shining above, starry pubescent beneath. Flowers white, disposed in broad pyramidal clusters 3 to 4 inches across. Berries pink, changing to bluish black. Height 8 to 10 feet. Very distinct.

Viburnum opulus sterile

For grades and prices of above, see page 163

Zenobia cassinifolia

Xanthorrhiza · The Yellow-root

A low shrub with handsome airy foliage that assumes a beautiful golden color in autumn. Splendid for massing as a ground cover. Thrives in almost any moist fertile soil.

Xanthorrhiza apiifolia. YELLOW-ROOT, OR BROOK-FEATHER. An attractive shrub, usually 1 to 2 feet tall, with bright yellow wood and roots. Grows naturally from New York to the Gulf. Leaves compound, consisting of about five deeply incised or lobed, bright lustrous green leaflets. Flowers brownish purple, in drooping compound racemes in early spring. Very ornamental. Every year it is being more extensively used as an underplanting and ground cover, giving a soft Fern-like aspect of singular beauty, and seemingly does not detract from the vigor and thriftiness of stronger-growing plants.

Xolisma · The Privet Andromeda

A hardy shrub with white flowers and highly colored autumnal foliage. It thrives in almost any moist soil and is well adapted for rockeries or border planting.

Xolisma ligustrina (*Andromeda ligustrina*). PRIVET ANDROMEDA. A branching shrub usually 2 to 3 feet tall. Grows naturally from Canada to Florida and Arkansas. Leaves oblong, bright green, fading with rich tones of purple and red. Flowers white, produced in elongated clusters in late spring or early summer. Rare in cultivation.

Zenobia · The Zenobia

A low shrub with upright or arching stems and numerous showy flowers in dense elongated clusters. It is hardy as far north as Missouri and Massachusetts, and thrives in almost any loamy soil, especially one containing leaf-mould or woods earth.

Zenobia cassinifolia (*Andromeda speciosa*). ZENOBIA. Leaves oval, more or less covered with a glaucous bloom, fading in autumn with beautiful shades of crimson. Flowers white, nodding, freely produced along the tips of the previous season's branches. Splendid for planting in the foreground of the shrub borders. Height 2 to 4 feet. Grows naturally from North Carolina to Florida. The dainty wax-like flowers are remarkably beautiful, resembling huge dense clusters of the flowers of the Lily-of-the-Valley.

An arbor of Wistaria (See page 102)

VINES

THE wonderful grace and beauty of well-placed vines add untold value and charm to the home and garden. The enchanting pergola, shady arbor and veranda, or clinging wall-cover gives that soft artistic effect that no other treatment can produce. We offer a comprehensive collection of the hardiest and best vines—those that have real merit and sterling worth. All vines delight in a deep, fertile soil with ample moisture, and the ground for them should be thoroughly prepared and trenched. Too often this is neglected and the plants set out in a mixture of subsoil and brick-bats from the foundation excavations and building refuse. In general, evergreen vines prefer shade and cool exposures, and should be planted on the northerly sides of buildings or trellis structures. Deciduous vines, on the other hand, thrive best in sunny positions. It is a good plan to carefully work into the surface soil at the base of the vines a quantity of well-rotted compost in late autumn or early spring, thereby supplying an ample amount of fertility and insuring a strong, vigorous growth, without which these charming plants are both disappointing and commonplace.

Actinidia · The Silver Vines

Vigorous climbing vines with handsome foliage, well adapted for training against pillars or for covering arbors or trellises. They are hardy and thrive best in moist loamy soils.

Actinidia arguta (*A. polygama*). DARK-LEAVED SILVER VINE. A strong-growing vine with dark green and lustrous heart-shaped leaves. Native of Japan. Flowers white, with dark purple anthers, produced in nodding clusters in early summer. Berries yellow. A distinct and handsome climber, and one that we confidently recommend.

A. kolomikta. BRIGHT-LEAVED SILVER VINE. A hardy climber with bright green, heart-shaped leaves 4 to 5 inches long. Native of Japan. Flowers white, very fragrant, blossoming in summer. Berries yellow. The leaves are often beautifully marked on the upper surface.

Akebia · The Akebia

A graceful hardy climber with twining stems, especially recommended for places where very dense shade is not required. It thrives best in moist, loamy soil with sunny exposure.

Akebia quinata. FIVE-LEAVED AKEBIA. A very ornamental vine of Japanese origin. The leaves are compound, consisting of five dark green, almost evergreen, leaflets. Flowers rosy purple, produced in axillary racemes in late spring or early summer. Fruit very showy, but unfortunately rarely produced, 3 to 5 inches long, dark purple. Very dainty and desirable.

Ampelopsis · The Deciduous Creepers

Hardy ornamental vines, climbing by tendrils. They are well adapted for arbors and trellises, and thrive in almost any moist, fertile soil.

Ampelopsis arborea (*Vitis bipinnata* and *Cissus stans*). PEPPER VINE. A stout climber with handsome foliage, growing naturally from Virginia and Missouri to Florida and Texas. Leaves compound, with several bluish green, incisely lobed leaflets. Berries dark purple, ripening in the fall.

A. cordata. SIMPLE-LEAVED AMPELOPSIS. A high-climbing vine with warty bark. Widely distributed from Virginia and Illinois southward to Florida and Texas. Leaves heart-shaped, with serrate borders, bright green, usually unchanged in color until killed by frost. Berries blue or bluish, very showy.

For grades and prices of above, see page 164

Ampelopsis, continued

Ampelopsis heterophylla. ASIATIC CREEPER. A handsome vine and one well adapted for covering low parapets and rocks. Native of Asia. Leaves heart-shaped, deeply 3- to 5-lobed, bright green and lustrous. Berries light blue, freely produced in autumn.

A. heterophylla elegans (*A. tricolor*). VARIEGATED ASIATIC CREEPER. A variegated form with the leaves blotched with white, and when young, softly flushed with pink.

A. quinquefolia. VIRGINIA CREEPER. A high-climbing vine clinging to walls or trunks of trees by means of disk-bearing tendrils. Grows naturally from Quebec and Manitoba, southward to Florida and Texas. Leaves compound, consisting of five bright green toothed leaflets, fading in autumn with gorgeous tones of red and scarlet. Berries blue, produced in ample panicles. A handsome and graceful species.

A. veitchi. JAPANESE OR BOSTON IVY. A graceful vine closely clinging to walls by means of disk-bearing tendrils. Native of China and Japan. Leaves 3-lobed, or often with three distinct leaflets, glossy green, coloring brilliantly in autumn. Berries blue, profusely borne in compound clusters. One of the most beautiful and perhaps one of the most popular of hardy vines.

Berries of Ampelopsis heterophylla

Aristolochia · The Dutchman's Pipe

A tall twining vine with very large leaves and curious flowers, well adapted for porches and arbors. It thrives best in a deep fertile soil, fully exposed to the sun.

Aristolochia macrophylla (*A. sipho*). DUTCHMAN'S PIPE. A grand hardy vine, producing a splendid dense shade. Grows in a wild state from Minnesota and Pennsylvania, southward to Kansas and Georgia. Leaves very broad and large, bright green. Flowers purplish and yellow-green, solitary or 2 to 3 together, from the axils of the leaves, resembling a Dutch tobacco pipe.

Berchemia · The Supple Jack

An attractive climbing vine with handsome foliage and large showy clusters of berries. It thrives in almost any soil, preferring sunny situations, and is hardy as far north as Missouri and Massachusetts. It is well adapted for covering trellis work or for planting against rocks or low walls.

Berchemia racemosa. JAPANESE SUPPLE JACK. A graceful shrubby vine with more or less glaucous, dark purple shoots. Native of Japan. Leaves ovate, dark green. Flowers nearly white, in terminal, leafy panicles, opening in summer. Berries in dense clusters, changing from red to nearly black, very showy.

Berries of Berchemia racemosa

Bignonia · The Cross-Vine

A handsome hardy vine, often climbing fifty feet high, with evergreen leaves and large showy flowers. It thrives in moist rich soils and is well adapted for climbing on walls or trunks of trees, or for training on arbors or trellises.

Bignonia crucigera (*B. capreolata*). CROSS VINE. A lofty vine with compound tendril-bearing leaves. Grows naturally from Illinois and Virginia, southward to the Gulf. Flowers trumpet-shaped, about two inches long, reddish orange without, yellow within, produced in axillary clusters in late spring and early summer. Very showy.

Celastrus The Bittersweet Vines

Twining shrubby vines with remarkably showy fruits, of extreme hardiness. They are very effective for covering walls, rocks or trellis work, or for climbing trees and lattice. Almost any kind of soil is suitable for them, either in sun or partial shade.

Celastrus orbiculatus (*C. articulatus*). JAPANESE BITTERSWEET. A tall and vigorous climber with bright green almost circular leaves. Native of Japan. Berries or capsules orange-yellow, splitting open in autumn and disclosing the crimson arils which envelop the seeds. Splendid for decorating.

C. scandens. AMERICAN BITTERSWEET. A high climbing vine with broadly lanceolate bright green leaves. Distributed naturally from Canada and Dakota, southward to Georgia and New Mexico. Capsules orange-yellow, with crimson arils, persisting throughout the winter. The unopened mature capsules will quickly open when cut and partially dried.

Clematis The Clematis Vines

Graceful free-flowering vines with showy flowers. They are well adapted for training on porches, balconies and trellises, or for covering walls, fences or arbors. A loamy fertile soil is well adapted to their requirements, and to secure the best results, the earth should be frequently enriched. In early spring all weak or crowded branches should be cut away, and the vines carefully tied and trained against their supports.

Clematis apiifolia. PARSLEY-LEAVED CLEMATIS. A handsome hardy vine well adapted for covering low walls or fences, or for training against pillars or other supports. Native of Japan. Leaves compound, consisting of several deep green, incisely lobed leaflets. Flowers white, produced in numerous broad

For grades and prices of above, see page 164

Clematis, continued

panicles. An exceedingly graceful and attractive species.

C. coccinea. SCARLET CLEMATIS. A small, but graceful vine, climbing 8 to 10 feet, with broad green leaflets. Native of Texas. Flowers scarlet, or purplish red, nodding, freely produced in late spring or summer. Fruiting heads globose, with plumose appendages.

C. crispa. MARSH CLEMATIS. A graceful slender vine, usually 3 to 5 feet tall. Grows naturally from Virginia to Texas. Leaves compound, consisting of several lobed or undivided leaflets. Flowers purple, nodding from the summit of stout stems. Fruiting heads globular, the spreading styles plumose.

C. flammula. SWEET CLEMATIS. A vigorous climber with slender stems attaining a height of 10 to 15 feet. Native of Europe. Leaves compound, dark green, persisting until early winter. Flowers white, in numerous showy panicles, in late summer or early autumn. Fruiting heads white and plumose. A very handsome vine, requiring a sunny position.

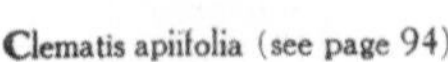
Clematis apiifolia (see page 94)

C. hybrida. THE LARGE-FLOWERING CLEMATIS. We offer a superb collection of named varieties embracing only the showiest and most vigorous forms that are well adapted for training against pillars or trellis work. The magnificent large flowers are freely produced in summer, and are justly prized on account of their beauty and splendor. In view of many failures in growing this type of Clematis, we add special cultural directions. A good depth of rich, loamy soil should be provided, into which a moderate amount of well-rotted manure has been incorporated. The plants are very susceptible to injury by drought, and it is essential to secure moist, yet porous and well-drained situations.

Duchess of Edinburgh. Double white, strongly imbricated.

Henryi. Creamy white. A robust, free-flowering variety.

Jackmanni. Velvety purple, with a ribbed bar in the middle of each sepal. Free flowering, and without doubt the most popular variety.

Mme. Baron Veillard. Rose, with a tone of lilac softly blended; very beautiful, and possessing the happy traits of flowering freely and growing vigorously.

Mme. Edouard Andre. Violet-red, of an intense but brilliant color, both rich and pleasing.

Ramona. Light blue, of a delicate and lovely shade. In every respect a worthy and meritorious vine, combining the hardiness and vigor so essential to success.

Clematis montana. MOUNTAIN CLEMATIS. A vigorous climber with numerous stems often 15 to 20 feet long. Native of the Himalayas. Leaves compound, with several deeply toothed bright green leaflets. Flowers white, resembling those of the Anemone, sweet-scented, produced in clusters from the axils of the leaves in late spring.

C. orientalis (*C. graveolens*). YELLOW-FLOWERED CLEMATIS. A vigorous and rapid-growing vine with stems often 10 to 12 feet long. Native of the Himalayas. Leaves compound, consisting of several shining glaucous-green leaflets. Flowers yellow, with reflexed sepals. Very showy. Fruiting clusters with plumose styles.

C. paniculata. JAPANESE CLEMATIS. A vigorous, hardy climber with long stems, well adapted for covering porches, arbors or trellis work, or for training against walls or the sides of buildings. Native of Japan. Leaves compound, consisting of several bright green leaflets which persist until early winter. Flowers white, fragrant, profusely borne in axillary and terminal panicles, literally covering the upper portions of the vine in late summer and early autumn. A grand plant.

C. viorna. LEATHER FLOWER. A hardy vine, climbing to a height of 8 to 10 feet. Grows naturally from Pennsylvania and Ohio, southward to Georgia and Alabama. Leaves compound, with bright green, often deeply lobed leaflets. Flowers nodding, on long stems, reddish purple, the sepals thick and leathery, with recurved tips. Fruiting clusters with plumose styles.

Bignonia crucigera (see page 94)

C. virginiana. VIRGIN'S BOWER. A hardy graceful climber with stems 10 to 12 feet long. Grows naturally from Canada, southward to Georgia and Kansas. Leaves compound, consisting of several toothed or incisely lobed bright green leaflets. Flowers white, in numerous pani-

Berries of Celastrus scandens (see page 94)

For grades and prices of above, see pages 164 and 165

Clematis paniculata (see page 95)

Clematis, continued

cles, expanding in late summer or early autumn. Fruiting clusters with plumose styles.

C. vitalba. TRAVELLER'S JOY. A remarkably vigorous vine with stems 20 to 30 feet long. Native of Europe. Leaves compound, with several toothed or incisely lobed bright green leaflets. Flowers white, in numerous axillary panicles, profusely borne in late summer. Fruiting clusters with long feathery styles.

Decumaria · The American Climbing Hydrangea

A showy vine, climbing by aërial rootlets, often ascending to the tops of tall trees. It thrives in almost any moist loamy soil, and is well adapted for covering walls, rocks, trellis work or trunks of trees. It is hardy as far north as Washington and Memphis, but requires protection in colder localities.

Decumaria barbara. AMERICAN CLIMBING HYDRANGEA. Leaves ovate, bright glossy green, fading with tones of orange and yellow. Flowers white, fragrant, freely produced in large terminal fluffy corymbs. Grows naturally from Virginia to Florida and Louisiana. A handsome and very distinct vine.

Euonymus · The Climbing Euonymus

An evergreen vine climbing by aërial rootlets and frequently ascending to a height of 15 to 20 feet. It is hardy and well adapted for covering walls, rocks or trunks of trees. Thrives in almost any soil but is perhaps a little more satisfactory when planted in shady situations.

An informal treatment of English Ivy

For grades and prices of above, see page 165

Euonymus, continued

Euonymus radicans. CLIMBING EUONYMUS. A graceful clinging vine with small rich green persistent foliage. Native of Japan. Fruits pink, the cells separating and exposing the scarlet arils which cover the seeds. A very attractive vine.

E. radicans variegata. VARIEGATED CLIMBING EUONYMUS. A form of the foregoing with the leaves variegated with silvery white.

Gelsemium · The Carolina Yellow Jessamine

A handsome evergreen vine, bearing a wealth of glossy foliage and bright yellow flowers. Thrives in almost any soil and is hardy as far north as Tennessee and the District of Columbia.

Gelsemium sempervirens. CAROLINA YELLOW JESSAMINE. A high-twining vine with dark green and lustrous persistent leaves. Grows naturally from Virginia, southward to Florida and Texas. Flowers bright yellow, very fragrant, profusely borne in axillary clusters in early spring.

G. sempervirens flore pleno. DOUBLE-FLOWERED CAROLINA JESSAMINE. A form of the above with double flowers. Very floriferous and showy.

Hedera · The Ivies

Handsome evergreen vines, closely clinging to walls or trunks of trees and often attaining great height. They thrive best in a moist rich soil, and preferably should be planted on the northerly sides of buildings or in other shady places. Very valuable for covering masonry and pillars, or as a ground cover or carpet in the shade of tall shrubs or trees. They are splendid house plants, and are very attractive when trained as screens in the living rooms, or in vases or hanging-baskets. Not quite hardy north of the Middle States.

Hedera colchica (*H. roegneriana*). COLCHICAN IVY. A remarkably vigorous and distinct species with high-climbing stems. Native of Asia. Leaves large and broad, ovate in outline, bright green when young, eventually dark green, firm and leathery. A grand companion to the English Ivy or its varieties, producing a bold and striking contrast. The leaves of the fruiting branches, which are produced when the plants are quite old, are nearly ovate. Berries black.

H. helix. ENGLISH IVY. A grand high-climbing vine with dark green, usually 3- to 5-lobed leaves of exquisite outline and beauty. Native of Europe and Asia. The climbing or creeping branches do not blossom or bear fruit, but in age, bushy spur-like branches with entire ovate leaves are produced, upon which the yellow-green flowers and black berries are borne. A number of forms, differing chiefly in the outline or marking of the leaves, are frequently cultivated, among which the following are both noteworthy and desirable:

Various forms of leaves of English Ivy

Forms with Green Leaves

Algeriensis. Leaves broadly ovate, entire or slightly 3-lobed.

Arborescens. This is the fruiting form of the English Ivy, and ordinarily forms a bushy shrub or vine. Leaves ovate, with entire borders.

Donerailensis. Leaves 3-lobed, with rather short, spreading lateral lobes; dark green with light-colored veins.

Formal treatment of English Ivy

For grades and prices of above, see page 165

Lonicera japonica (see page 99)

Hedera, continued

Digitata. Leaves deeply lobed, the middle division much prolonged; dark green with prominent light-colored veins.

Palmata. Leaves deeply 5- to 7-lobed, the middle division not much prolonged; deep green with light-colored veins.

Forms with Variegated Leaves

Argenteo-variegata. Leaves beautifully variegated with silvery white.

Aureo-variegata. Leaves variously blotched and bordered with golden yellow.

Hydrangea · The Creeping Hydrangea

A vigorous, tall-growing vine, the stems ascending by means of aërial rootlets to the tops of tall trees. It is very valuable for covering walls and trunks of trees, and is hardy as far north as Tennessee and New Jersey. In colder regions it should be afforded protection from cold winds. It thrives in any good garden soil, either in sun or partial shade.

Hydrangea petiolaris (*H. scandens*). CREEPING HYDRANGEA. Leaves broadly heart-shaped or nearly round, bright green, with shallowly serrate borders. Flowers creamy white, in loose, flat topped clusters 8 to 10 inches across, a few of the marginal flowers ray-like and sterile. Native of Japan.

Lonicera · The Climbing Honeysuckles

Hardy vines with showy and usually very sweet-scented flowers. They thrive in almost any kind of soil and are very valuable for covering walls and trellis work, and as a ground cover, where they should be allowed to ramble without support of any kind.

Lonicera caprifolium. ITALIAN HONEYSUCKLE. A free-flowering vine with stems 6 to 10 feet long. Native of Europe. Leaves oval or oblong, the uppermost joined together at the base and forming a cup through which the stem passes. Flowers yellowish white, purplish on the outside, borne in whorls in the axil of the cup-like leaves in summer.

L. chinensis. CHINESE HONEYSUCKLE. A showy vine with purplish evergreen foliage. Native of China. Leaves ovate, purple when young, changing to greener tones at maturity. Flowers white, changing to yellow, sweetly fragrant, freely produced in summer.

L. dioica (*L. parviflora*). SMALL-FLOWERED HONEYSUCKLE. A very hardy bush-like vine with short, sometimes twining branches. Grows naturally from Quebec and Manitoba, southward to Ohio and North Carolina. Leaves very glaucous beneath, the uppermost joined together at the base and surrounding the flower clusters. Flowers yellow, tinged with purple, appearing in late spring or early summer.

L. etrusca. ETRUSCAN HONEYSUCKLE. A low climber with stems seldom more than 6 to 8 feet long. Native of Southern Europe. Leaves broadly oval or broadest above the middle, the upper ones united at the base. Flowers about 2 inches long, yellowish white, tinged with red on the outside, very fragrant, freely produced in late spring and early summer.

L. flava. YELLOW HONEYSUCKLE. A handsome climber with stems 6 to 10 feet long. Occurs in a wild state from North Carolina and Kentucky, southward to Georgia and Alabama. Leaves green above, almost white beneath, the uppermost joined together at the base and surrounding the bright yellow fragrant flowers. Blossoms in spring.

L. glaucescens. DOUGLAS' HONEYSUCKLE. A very hardy free-flowering vine with stems 6 to 10 feet long. Grows naturally from Ontaria and the Saskatchewan

For grades and prices of above, see page 165

Lonicera, continued

region, southward to Pennsylvania and Nebraska. Leaves glaucous green, the uppermost united at their bases and subtending the flower clusters. Flowers yellow, tinged with red outside, opening in late spring and early summer.

L. heckrotti. HECKROTT'S HONEYSUCKLE. A shrubby vine with short, sometimes twining stems, of unknown origin. Leaves green above, whitened beneath, the uppermost united at their bases. Flowers purple, fragrant, about two inches long. Splendid for massing.

L. japonica (*L. halleana*). JAPANESE HONEYSUCKLE. A rampant evergreen climber with stems 10 to 15 feet long. Native of Japan. Leaves ovate, dark green, densely covering the vines and branches. Flowers white, changing to yellow, deliciously fragrant, borne in great profusion in the summer, and occasionally in the autumn. Grand for trellises and ground cover. One of the best.

L. japonica aureo-reticulata. GOLDEN-LEAVED HONEYSUCKLE. A form of the preceding species with the leaves beautifully netted with yellow.

L. periclymenum. WOODBINE. A low climber with stems 5 to 8 feet long. Native of Europe. Leaves ovate or oblong, dark green above, glaucous beneath, often fading in autumn with beautiful tones of yellow and purple. Flowers in dense terminal heads, yellowish white within, purple or carmine outside, very fragrant and showy. Blooms in summer.

L. periclymenum belgica (*L. belgica*). MONTHLY FRAGRANT HONEYSUCKLE. A form of the last of more vigorous habit, with bright red flowers freely produced throughout the summer. A grand plant.

L. sempervirens. TRUMPET, OR CORAL HONEYSUCKLE. A high climbing vine with stems 10 to 15 feet long. Occurs naturally from Connecticut and Nebraska, southward to Florida and Texas. Leaves oval or oblong, green or bluish green above, glaucous beneath, the uppermost united at their bases. Flowers scarlet, about 2 inches long, profuse and very showy. Splendid for porches.

L. sempervirens minor. NARROW-LEAVED CORAL HONEYSUCKLE. A variety of the above with narrow leaves and more slender orange-red flowers. Not quite so hardy as the typical form.

L. sullivanti. GLAUCOUS HONEYSUCKLE. A low climber with stems 4 to 6 feet long. Occurs in a wild state from Manitoba and Ontario, southward to Tennessee. Leaves oval, or broadest above the middle, silvery blue, the upper ones united at their bases. Flowers pale yellow, sometimes tinged with purple on the outside. Very handsome, not only on account of the remarkably glaucous foliage, but for the abundant scarlet berries.

Menispermum · The Moonseed

A graceful twining vine with more or less woody stems and handsome foliage, well adapted for training on trellises. It is very hardy and thrives in almost any good garden soil, either in full sun or partial shade.

Menispermum canadense. MOONSEED. Stems slender, usually attaining a height of 8 to 10 feet, rather densely clothed with bright green, mostly 3-lobed leaves. Flowers greenish white, in loose panicles, opening in summer. Fruit bluish black, resembling a bunch of small grapes, each berry containing a flattened crescent-shaped seed. Grows naturally from Quebec and Manitoba, southward to Georgia.

Passiflora · The Passion Flowers

Slender, but vigorous-growing vines, climbing by tendrils, with strange and curious flowers which were supposed by the early Spanish travelers in South America to be symbolic of the passion of our Lord. They thrive in almost any good garden soil, and are hardy in the Southern States and California. Frequently cultivated in greenhouses in the North.

Passiflora caerulea. PASSION FLOWER. Leaves deeply 5-lobed, bright or glaucous green. Flowers fragrant, 3 to 4 inches across, greenish white, the numerous rays of the crown blue at the tip, white in the middle and purple at the base. Native of Brazil.

P. caerulea Constance Elliott. WHITE PASSION FLOWER. A form of the foregoing species with remarkably fragrant white flowers. A very thrifty plant and one that invariably attracts attention.

Lonicera sempervirens

For grades and prices of above, see pages 165 and 166

Tecoma radicans (see page 101)

Periploca · The Silk Vine

A vigorous high-climbing vine with handsome foliage and fragrant flowers, well adapted for covering arbors or for training on trellis work. It thrives in almost any well-drained fertile soil, preferring sunny exposures. Hardy as far north as Missouri and New York, and, with protection, may be grown in colder climates.

Periploca graeca. SILK VINE. Stems twining, 20 to 30 feet long, clothed with numerous dark green and glossy leaves of broadly lanceolate outline. Flowers brownish purple inside, the margins and reverse side greenish, an inch or less across, borne in loose, long-stemmed cymes. Native of Southern Europe.

Pueraria · The Kudzu Vine

A hardy and remarkably vigorous vine, frequently producing stems 40 to 60 feet long in a single season—a veritable Jack-and-the-Bean-stalk. In the North the plant dies down to or near the ground in winter, but in the South the vines are woody and often of considerable diameter. Well adapted for covering arbors or verandas, especially where rampant vines and large bold leaves are required. Thrives in almost any well-drained soil, preferring sunny situations.

Pueraria thunbergiana (*Dolichos japonicus*). KUDZU VINE. Stems twining, hairy when young, very long and flexible. Leaves compound, consisting of three bright green ovate leaflets. Flowers pea-shaped, purple, produced in axillary racemes from the older woody stems in late summer. Native of China and Japan.

Schizophragma · The Climbing Hydrangea

A tall vine climbing by means of aërial rootlets, with large handsome leaves and showy clusters of white flowers. It is well adapted for covering walls and trunks of trees and is hardy as far north as Kentucky and Southern New York. It thrives best in moist, rich loam, either in full sun or partial shade.

Schizophragma hydrangeoides. CLIMBING HYDRANGEA. Stems climbing to a height of 20 to 30 feet, or even more. Leaves bright green, broadly ovate, or nearly round, 2 to 4 inches long, with toothed borders. Flowers produced in broad terminal flat-topped clusters, with the marginal flowers radiate, very showy. Native of Japan.

Smilax · The Greenbriers

Prickly vines with greenish flowers, climbing by means of coiling appendages borne on the leaf-stalks. They are hardy interesting subjects for trellises or wild gardens, and thrive in almost any kind of soil.

Smilax bona-nox. BRISTLY GREENBRIER. A high-climbing vine with angled branches. Grows naturally from Massachusetts and Kansas, southward to Florida and Texas. Leaves dark lustrous green, thick and leathery, nearly evergreen. Berries black.

S. glauca. GLAUCOUS-LEAVED GREENBRIER. A slender, often high-climbing vine with spiny stems. Occurs naturally from Massachusetts and Kansas to Florida and Texas. Leaves broadly ovate, glaucous green, persisting sometimes all winter, and often coloring deeply with purple and crimson. Berries bluish black, lustrous under the glaucous coating.

S. hispida. HISPID GREENBRIER. A vigorous tall climber with the stems thickly armed with dark-colored bristle-like spines. Grows naturally from Ontario and Minnesota, southward to North Carolina and Texas. Leaves broadly ovate, thinnish, bright green, fading with yellow tones in late autumn. Berries black or bluish black. Remarkably vigorous and perhaps the most responsive to cultivation of the species listed.

S. rotundifolia. CATBRIER. A strong spiny vine with green, usually angled stems 6 to 20 feet long. Grows naturally from Ontario and Minnesota, southward to Florida and Texas. Leaves ovate or nearly round, bright green and leathery, persisting until early winter Berries bluish black.

Wistaria chinensis alba (see page 102)

Pergola with Wistaria and Ivy

Tecoma · The Trumpet Vines

Vigorous-climbing vines with stout stems, clinging to walls and trunks of trees by means of aërial rootlets. They are very showy plants and blossom profusely for several weeks in summer. They thrive in almost any soil, preferring deep moist loam and sunny situations.

Tecoma grandiflora. CHINESE TRUMPET VINE. A high-climbing vine with numerous stout and spreading branches. Native of China. Leaves compound, consisting of 7 to 9 ovate bright green leaflets, which persist until killed by frost. Flowers in terminal clusters, bright scarlet, about two inches across, profuse and showy. Hardy as far north as Tennessee and the District of Columbia. Will need protection in colder climates.

T. radicans. AMERICAN TRUMPET VINE. A high-climbing vigorous vine with stout spreading branches, growing naturally from Pennsylvania to Illinois, southward to Florida and Texas. Leaves compound, consisting of 9 to 11 oval dark green leaflets. Flowers in large terminal clusters, orange-red within, scarlet without, 2 to 3 inches long. Hardy as far north as Missouri and Massachusetts.

Vitis · The Grape Vines

Several species of Wild Grapes are frequently grown for covering arbors, porches or trees, both on account of their rampant habit and dense foliage. The following forms are hardy and desirable, and thrive in almost any good soil.

Vitis aestivalis. SUMMER GRAPE. A vigorous tall-climbing vine, occurring naturally from New York and Missouri, southward to the Gulf States. Leaves angularly or deeply lobed, bright green above, coated beneath with rusty or brown felt-like down. Berries black, with a bloom.

V. baileyanus. 'POSSUM GRAPE. A high-climbing vine with short internodes, distributed naturally from the Virginias to Georgia and Alabama. Leaves broadly ovate, usually 3-lobed, bright green above, paler beneath. Berries black, in compact bunches.

V. coignetiae. CRIMSON GLORY VINE. A tall-climbing vine of great beauty, producing a very dense shade. Native of Japan. Leaves broadly heart-shaped, with 3 to 5 lobe-like points, rich green above, coated below with grayish down, turning brilliant scarlet in autumn. Berries black. A splendid strong-growing climber with remarkably handsome foliage.

V. cordifolia. FROST GRAPE. A very vigorous high-climbing vine, ascending to the tops of tall trees. Grows naturally from New York and Kansas, southward to the Gulf States. Leaves broadly ovate, sometimes angularly 3-lobed, deep green and lustrous on both surfaces. Berries black, with a faint bloom, long persistent.

V. labrusca. FOX GRAPE. A strong high-climbing vine with large and fragrant fruits. Distributed naturally from New England to Minnesota, southward to Georgia and Mississippi. Leaves large and thick, angularly 3-lobed, rich green above, densely clothed on the lower surface with a tawny or rufous felt-like down. Berries large, purple-black, or reddish brown, often gathered for making a delicious highly flavored jam or jelly.

Wistaria · The Wistarias

Grand free-flowering vines with handsome showy flowers. They are among the best and hardiest of ornamental vines, and are well adapted for training on porches, arbors or trellises. For their best development a deep rich loamy soil should be provided by trenching and enriching, for they amply repay for any favors of this kind. When well established, a greater profusion of blossoms may be

For grades and prices of above, see page 166

Wistaria, continued

secured by rather severe pruning, cutting back the lateral shoots to short spurs, but the gain in flowers is perhaps at the sacrifice of picturesque and natural grace and beauty.

Wistaria chinensis. CHINESE WISTARIA. A rapid-growing tall vine with handsome foliage and flowers. Native of China. Leaves compound, consisting of about eleven pale green leaflets. Flowers pea-shaped, purplish, profusely borne in dense drooping clusters 7 to 12 inches long, opening in mid-spring. Very showy and desirable.

W. chinensis alba. WHITE WISTARIA. A form of the above with pure white flowers.

W. chinensis flore pleno. DOUBLE-FLOWERED WISTARIA. A free-flowering variety with very double purple flowers.

W. frutescens. AMERICAN WISTARIA. A tall and slender vine with dark green foliage, growing naturally from Virginia to Florida. Leaves compound, consisting of 9 to 15 leaflets, producing an airy light shade. Flowers lilac-purple, in numerous dense short racemes, blossoming about three weeks later than the Chinese Wistaria.

W. macrostachys. LARGE-FLOWERED AMERICAN WISTARIA. A stout climbing vine with stems 20 to 30 feet long, distributed from Missouri and Arkansas eastward to Tennessee. Leaves compound, consisting of about nine bright green leaflets. Flowers in drooping racemes, 6 to 8 inches long, lilac-purple or light blue, very showy.

W. multijuga. JAPANESE WISTARIA. A vigorous tall-growing vine with bright green foliage, widely cultivated in Japan and long supposed to be a native of that country, but probably of Chinese origin. Leaves compound, consisting of 17 to 21 leaflets. Flowers light purple, in loose drooping racemes 1 to 3 feet long. A remarkably distinct and showy species. The long clusters of flowers at the top of the pergola picture shown on the preceding page, some of them 3 feet long, are of this superb vine.

Wistaria chinensis flora plena

Wistaria chinensis

ORNAMENTAL GRASSES AND BAMBOOS

VERY effective and artistic results may be obtained by the use of these graceful and attractive plants, either informally, as with clumps or masses in connection with other planting, or in formal beds or borders, where low varieties often stand in symmetrical arrangement in the foreground of tall-growing species. Hedges of the *Miscanthus* grasses are very showy and pleasing, especially in the garden, where, for example, it is often desirable to divide one part from another during the growing season. Bamboos are noble subjects, and make possible within their range of hardiness some of the most enchanting results. They are extremely graceful and picturesque planted above streams or pools of water, or in clumps on the borders of moist woodlands, where sufficient space may be allowed for the spreading of their rampant subterranean root-stocks, which, when the plants become thoroughly established, spread rapidly over a considerable area of ground.

Arundo · The Giant Reed

A tall leafy species with stout stems and showy plumes, well adapted for lawn decoration or for massing in formal beds. It is also valuable for waterside planting, producing striking results, especially in connection with *Typha* and *Phragmites*, which, unlike the *Arundo*, thrive in wet ground or shallow water. A deep loamy soil, well enriched, is best adapted to its welfare.

Arundo donax. GIANT REED. A hardy, vigorous perennial, attaining a height of 10 to 15 feet. Native of Europe and Asia. Leaves very long and broad, glaucous green, produced from the base almost to the top of the stems. Plumes reddish brown, changing to silvery gray, a foot or more in length, long persistent, quite showy.

A. donax variegata. VARIEGATED GIANT REED. Not so tall or so hardy as the typical form, requiring some protection in cold climates. Leaves longitudinally striped with green and creamy white. Very striking.

Bamboos

Including the genera Arundinaria, Bambusa and Phyllostachys

Giant grasses with woody stems and usually evergreen foliage, thriving in deep, loamy soils. While quite hardy in the Southern States and California, many of the species, when grown in positions sheltered from piercing winds, either in sun or partial shade, will withstand depressions of temperature to the zero mark, or occasionally even more, without injury to the vitality of their roots. These admirable plants are truly objects of grace and beauty. The arching stems and dainty branches, bending with a wealth of handsome foliage, produce an enchanting effect. It is well to allow ample space for the spread of the plants, as they are rampant growers when fully established. In the early stages of their development a liberal mulching with leaves and manure is very beneficial, preventing the penetration of heat and cold to the roots, and conserving the moisture. It usually requires a couple of years to establish a clump and realize the vigor and hardiness which they possess. They are very decorative when confined in tubs or pots, and valuable for furnishing living-rooms or porches.

Bambusa palmata
(see page 104)

For grades and prices of above, see page 167

Phyllostachys as a tub-plant

Bamboos, continued

Arundinaria auricoma. Golden Variegated Cane. Stems 2 to 3 feet tall, usually with several ascending branches. Of Japanese origin. Leaves 4 to 6 inches long, about one inch wide, brilliantly variegated with yellow.

A. japonica (*Bambusa metake*). Japanese Cane. Stems 6 to 10 feet tall, with numerous short ascending branches. Native of Japan. Leaves 6 to 12 inches long, 1 to 2 inches wide, rich lustrous green above, pale and somewhat whitened beneath. Perhaps the most commonly cultivated of the hardy Canes.

A. macrosperma. Large American Cane. Stems 10 to 18 feet, with numerous short divergent branches. Grows naturally from North Carolina to Florida, often forming large thickets known as cane-brakes. Leaves 3 to 6 inches long, densely clothing the branches, bright lustrous green, persistent.

A. simoni. Tall Chinese Cane. This, the tallest of the Canes, frequently reaches a height of 12 to 20 feet. Native of China. Leaves 8 to 12 inches long, about an inch wide, rich lustrous green, the apex very long and slender.

A. tecta. Deciduous Cane. Stems 2 to 6 feet tall, with numerous upright branches. Leaves 3 to 6 inches long, bright green, deciduous, fading in autumn with bright yellow tones. The botanical standing of this remarkable species is somewhat in doubt. Grows naturally in the Southern Alleghany Mountains.

Bambusa disticha (*B. nana*). Dwarf Bamboo. A low shrubby species of uncertain origin. Stems 2 to 3 feet tall, branched, densely leafy. Leaves about two inches long, half-inch wide, rich green, produced in two vertical ranks. A very distinct species and extremely valuable as a ground-cover.

B. palmata. Palmate-leaved Bamboo. One of the showiest and handsomest members of the genus.

A clump of Bamboos

For grades and prices of above, see page 167

Bamboos, continued

Native of Japan. Stems 2 to 5 feet tall, with ascending branches, producing a wealth of handsome foliage. Leaves 10 to 15 inches long, 2 to 3 inches wide, bright green and lustrous on the upper surface, pale beneath. Very attractive.

B. tessellata. LARGE-LEAVED BAMBOO. This grand species produces the largest leaves of any of the cultivated varieties. Native of China and Japan. Stems 2 to 3 feet tall, bearing near the summit several large bright green and lustrous leaves, 12 to 18 inches long and 3 to 4 inches wide.

B. veitchi. VEITCH'S BAMBOO. Stems 1 to 2 feet tall, simple or branched, bearing near the tips 5 to 7 broad leaves 4 to 6 inches long, bright green on the upper surface, pale beneath. In the winter the edges of the leaves wither, giving the foliage a variegated appearance.

Phyllostachys aurea. GOLDEN BAMBOO. A graceful species with numerous yellowish stems 10 to 15 feet tall. Native of Japan. Leaves soft green, spreading or drooping from the numerous dainty branches. One of the hardiest of its genus, and easily recognized by the numerous short internodes at the base of the stems.

P. mitis. TALL BAMBOO. A tall species with wand-like arching stems 15 to 20 feet tall, or even more in favorable situations. Native of Japan. Leaves light green, gracefully disposed along the yellow-green stems and branches. This is the tallest of the Bamboos, but is not so hardy as many of the other species.

P. nigra. BLACK-STEMMED BAMBOO. A remarkably attractive species with stems 10 to 15 feet tall, which are green in their first year, but change to black during the second year. Native of China and Japan. Leaves 3 to 5 inches long, less than an inch broad, pale green.

P. ruscifolia (*Bambusa viminalis*). RUSCUS-LEAVED BAMBOO. A dwarf species with slender zig-zag stems, about 2 feet tall. Native of Japan. Leaves 2 to 3 inches long, about an inch wide, rather densely produced on the numerous short branches.

Carex · The Evergreen Sedge

A grass-like plant with stiff evergreen leaves and numerous small feathery spikes in early spring. It is perfectly hardy and thrives in almost any soil. Valuable as a border plant and also attractive and ornamental when grown in pots as a house plant.

A bed of Ornamental Grasses

Carex morrowi (*C. japonica*). EVERGREEN SEDGE. Leaves narrow, dark green, with revolute white margins. Staminate spikes very showy, freely produced on stiff stems about a foot long. Native of Japan.

Erianthus · The Plume Grass

A highly ornamental Grass with large silky plumes, very valuable for producing bold effects. It is quite hardy, and thrives in almost any good soil, preferring sunny situations. Frequently used for waterside planting and in formal beds, either alone or associated with other species.

Erianthus ravennae. PLUME GRASS. Stems 5 to 7 feet tall, bearing numerous long, narrow leaves, rich deep green, often tinged with purple, and with a prominent whitened midrib. Native of Southern Europe. Plumes long and showy, rising well above the graceful drooping foliage.

Phyllostachys aurea

Gynerium The Pampas Grass

A remarkably showy and ornamental species with large and feathery plumes. Hardy in the Southern States and California, but requires protection in the North, such as may be afforded by a liberal covering of leaves or straw. It thrives in almost any garden soil, and prefers a sunny location.

Gynerium argenteum. PAMPAS GRASS. Stems 5 to 8 feet tall, forming a dense clump. Leaves long and narrow, chiefly from the base, gracefully spreading and drooping. Plumes silvery white, very showy, sometimes 2 feet or more in length. Native of South America. The following varieties, characterized by the color of the leaves or plumes, are very effective:

Carmineum. Plumes soft deep rose.
Roi des Roses. A handsome rosy plumed variety.
Wesserlingi variegatum. With golden variegated foliage.

Miscanthus · The Eulalias

Beautiful hardy Grasses with handsome foliage and numerous fan-shaped feathery panicles. They are among the best and most popular species for bedding or hedges, and thrive in almost any kind of soil.

Miscanthus japonica. JAPANESE EULALIA. Very vigorous and graceful, the numerous culms attaining a height of 6 to 9 feet. Leaves long and narrow, drooping, rich green, with prominent whitened midrib. Panicles 6 to 10 inches long, freely produced in early autumn.

M. japonica variegata. STRIPED EULALIA. Leaves longitudinally striped with green and silvery white. Very ornamental.

For grades and prices of above, see page 167

Miscanthus, continued

M. japonica zebrina. ZEBRA GRASS. Leaves banded crosswise with green and pale yellow. Remarkably brilliant and effective.

M. sinensis (*Eulalia gracillima univittata*). NARROW-LEAVED EULALIA. Culms densely tufted, 3 to 6 feet tall, with numerous very narrow drooping leaves arising mainly from near the base. Panicles 4 to 6 inches long, freely produced towards the end of the growing season.

Phragmites · The Common Reed

A tall hardy Grass with running rootstocks, thriving in shallow water or on the margins of ponds. Very effective results may be secured, especially in combination with a shore planting of terrestrial grasses.

Phragmites communis. COMMON REED. Stems 6 to 10 feet tall, bearing numerous broad, flat leaves and ample feathery plumes. Widely distributed in the Northern Hemisphere.

Phalaris · The Ribbon Grass

A tall, hardy Grass with variegated foliage, and a common plant in old-fashioned gardens. It thrives in almost any kind of soil or exposure.

Phalaris arundinacea variegata. RIBBON GRASS. Leaves longitudinally striped with white and green. Stems tufted, 3 to 5 feet tall, with graceful drooping foliage. A garden form of the native Reed Canary Grass.

Uniola · The Spike Grass

A handsome hardy Grass often cultivated for the ornamental panicles which are valuable for dry bouquets. It thrives in almost any soil, preferring rich loam and sunny situations.

Uniola latifolia. SPIKE GRASS. Stems 2 to 4 feet tall, tufted, at maturity bearing ample graceful panicles of large flattened spikelets which droop from slender pedicels. Grows naturally from Pennsylvania and Kansas, southward. Very ornamental, and highly prized as a border plant.

HARDY FERNS

THESE graceful and universally popular plants are of easy culture, and afford a wide range of possibilities. A shady nook, where the soil is moist and the drainage good, will prove an ideal location, especially if a liberal amount of leaf-mould or woods earth is available; and better still if rocks or stumps may unite in breaking the monotony of the ground's surface. Under such conditions Ferns require very little attention and amply repay in satisfaction and genuine pleasure. There are many places more or less shut out from the sunlight that may be converted into veritable beauty spots by clumps of Ferns of various kinds, and their intrinsic ornamental qualities are well worthy of our attention.

Adiantum pedatum. MAIDEN-HAIR FERN. A graceful species with large deciduous leaves, widely distributed in Canada and the United States. The dark chestnut-brown stipes are smooth and shining, radially forked at the summit and bearing numerous soft green pinnules. Height 9 to 18 inches. One of the most distinct and beautiful of the native Ferns.

Asplenium filix-foemina. LADY FERN. A large Fern with deciduous leaves 1 to 3 feet long, distributed almost throughout the Northern Hemisphere. Stipes tufted, straw-colored or brownish red, bearing numerous bright green incised divisions. A showy and thrifty species.

A. platyneuron. EBONY SPLEENWORT. A dainty little Fern with tufted ebony-colored stipes. Distributed naturally from Maine to Florida and westward to Colorado. Leaves deep green, simply pinnate, persistent. Very valuable for planting in clefts and crevices of rocks.

Camptosorus rhizophyllus. WALKING FERN. A singular species with simple, very long pointed evergreen leaves. Grows on rocks and occurs naturally from Quebec to Minnesota, southward to North Carolina and Kansas. The tips of the leaves take root and form new plants and several individuals are often found connected in this manner.

Dicksonia punctilobula. HAY-SCENTED FERN. A handsome large Fern with thin and delicate leaves 1 to 3 feet long. Grows naturally from New Brunswick and Minnesota, southward to Tennessee and Alabama. Stipes clustered, pale green and sweet-scented, bearing many soft green pinnatifid divisions. A very handsome deciduous species.

For grades and prices of above, see pages 167 and 168

Dryopteris goldieana. GOLDIE'S FERN. A grand vigorous Fern with broad deciduous leaves 2 to 4 feet long. Occurs naturally from New Brunswick and Minnesota to North Carolina and Tennessee. Stipes chaffy at the base, bearing numerous dark green pinnately parted divisions.

D. marginalis. EVERGREEN WOOD-FERN. A handsome evergreen species with a stout, densely chaffy rootstock. Grows naturally from the Dominion of Canada, southward to Georgia and Arkansas. Leaves borne in a crown, rich green, with numerous pinnate segments. Stipes chaffy, with many brownish lustrous scales.

D. noveboracensis. NEW YORK FERN. A graceful and dainty Fern with slender creeping rootstocks. Grows naturally from Newfoundland and Minnesota, southward to North Carolina and Arkansas. Leaves soft green, deciduous, sweet-scented in drying, with deeply pinnatifid segments.

Osmunda cinnamomea

D. spinulosa. SHIELD FERN. A remarkably beautiful evergreen Fern with stout chaffy rootstocks. Distributed from Labrador to Alaska, southward to North Carolina and Missouri. Leaves 1 to 3 feet long, dark lustrous green, with intricately divided and incised spinulose segments. Very handsome.

Lygodium palmatum. CLIMBING, OR HARTFORD FERN. A distinct and graceful species with flexible and twining stems 2 to 3 feet long. Rare and local, with a natural distribution from Massachusetts and Pennsylvania, southward to Florida and Tennessee. Leaves Maple-like, 4- to 7-lobed, bright green, persistent, the fruiitng pinnules several times forked and disposed in a terminal panicle.

Onoclea sensibilis. SENSITIVE FERN. Leaves usually 1 to 3 feet high, with bold lanceolate, either entire or undulately toothed segments. Distributed from Newfoundland and the Northwest Territory to Kansas and Florida. Fronds very sensitive to early frosts.

Types of Hardy Ferns

O. struthiopteris. OSTRICH FERN. A very vigorous stout Fern with a large rootstock, bearing an outer circle of sterile leaves and several fertile ones within. Extends across the continent from Nova Scotia and New Jersey to British Columbia, also in Europe and Asia. Leaves deciduous, 3 to 5 feet high, bright green, with numerous pinnate segments. Fruiting leaves simply pinnate, with necklace-like divisions. A splendid bold species.

Osmunda cinnamomea. CINNAMON FERN. A stately large Fern with very large creeping rootstocks. Grows naturally from Nova Scotia and Minnesota, southward to Florida and Texas. Leaves deciduous, produced in a circular cluster, subtending one or more fruiting ones, 3 to 5 feet tall, bright green, with numerous pinnatifid divisions. Fertile fronds eventually cinnamon brown, soon withering. Very ornamental and impressive.

O. claytoniana. CLAYTON'S FERN. A large and robust species with a stout rootstock, bearing a circle of bold leaves 2 to 4 feet tall. Fronds deciduous, bright green, with numerous deeply cleft divisions, frequently contracted in the middle and bearing several pairs of fruiting, early deciduous pinnæ. Very bold and attractive.

O. regalis. ROYAL FERN. A vigorous tall Fern with stout rootstocks, bearing a cluster of large broad leaves. Distributed from New Brunswick and the Northwest Territory, southward to Florida and Mississippi; also in Europe and Asia. Fronds 2 to 5 feet tall and a foot or more wide, with numerous oblong pinnules; the fruiting portions panicled at the summit.

Polypodium vulgare. COMMON POLYPODY. A charming little Fern with slender creeping rootstocks, widely distributed in the Northern Hemisphere. Leaves evergreen, deep green, simply pinnate, with very large fruiting dots on the lower surface. Splendid for planting in crevices of rocks.

Polystichum acrostichoides. CHRISTMAS FERN. A beautiful evergreen Fern with stout rootstocks and densely chaffy stipes. Distributed from Nova Scotia and Wisconsin, southward to Florida and Mississippi. Leaves deep green with numerous lanceolate pinnæ, 1 to 2 feet long, the fertile portions contracted near the summit.

Pteris aquilina. BRACKEN. A large rampant species growing either in full sun or partial shade. Widely distributed in the Northern Hemisphere. Leaves deciduous, 2 to 4 feet long, and 1 to 3 feet wide, bright green, borne on stout straw-colored or brownish stipes. Splendid for naturalizing among shrubs or in woodlands.

For grades and prices of above, see page 168

AQUATIC AND BOG PLANTS

THE pleasures and superb results attained in water gardens by the introduction of many rare and beautiful plants have awakened new interest among amateur and professional gardeners. Few plants indeed can surpass in splendor the stately Lotus or dainty Water Lily—and they are so hardy and easy to grow! Ponds, either natural or artificial, or slow-flowing streams, can be made focal points of attraction and beauty by careful planting, or perhaps one of the features of the home grounds. Where such conditions or opportunities are lacking, fountain basins or formal pools form good places for many of these grand plants, and even sunken tubs have been successfully used. The soil in natural ponds is usually all that is needed, but in artificial ones should consist of turfy loam well enriched, and for water plants, covered with varying depths of water in order to provide for the requirements of the plants and to prevent the freezing of their roots or tubers in winter. Shore plants thrive in sandy or mucky soils, and may be diversified, often advantageously, by rocks and boulders.

Acorus calamus. SWEET FLAG. A hardy waterside plant with sword-shaped, bright green leaves, attaining a height of 2 to 3 feet. The long branching rootstocks are pleasantly aromatic, and form the basis of a popular confection in certain parts of the country. The species is widely distributed in the Northern Hemisphere.

A. gramineus variegatus. VARIEGATED SWEET FLAG. A smaller plant than the foregoing, of Japanese origin, forming compact grass-like tufts. Leaves beautifully striped with green and white. Often grown as a pot-plant indoors, and thrives in either wet or moist garden soil.

Brasenia purpurea. WATER SHIELD. An interesting aquatic plant with floating leaves, widely distributed in both hemispheres. Stems long and slender, bearing numerous oval leaves which are bright green and shining on the upper surface, often purple beneath. Flowers borne on long pedicels, purple, blossoming in summer. Very hardy and useful.

Caltha palustris. MARSH MARIGOLD. A beautiful marsh plant flourishing in wet places near running water. Grows naturally from Newfoundland to South Carolina, westward to Nebraska. Leaves bright green, broadly heart-shaped. Flowers bright yellow, very showy, freely produced in spring.

C. palustris flore pleno. DOUBLE-FLOWERED MARSH MARIGOLD. A very beautiful variety of the preceding, with full and double flowers of exquisite form and substance.

Limnanthemum nymphaeoides. FLOATING HEART. An aquatic plant with submerged stems and floating leaves. Native of Europe and Asia. Leaves heart-shaped or nearly orbicular, 2 to 4 inches broad. Flowers about an inch across, bright yellow, freely produced almost throughout the season. Should be kept within bounds, as it spreads rapidly.

Myriophyllum proserpinacoides. PARROT'S FEATHER. This graceful aquatic plant is much admired on account of its delicate feathery foliage. It is very valuable for lily ponds and fountain basins, and is also grown indoors in vases and aquaria. Hardy in the Southern and Pacific States, and usually withstanding the winters as far north as Southern Ohio and New Jersey.

Myosotis palustris. TRUE FORGET-ME-NOT. A dainty plant with much sentimental interest associated with it. It is of easy culture and thrives admirably in wet places near running water, or in damp shady ground. Flowers freely produced from spring until fall, bright blue with a yellow eye, disposed in loose-flowered racemes. Native of Europe and Asia. We offer only the true perennial species.

Nelumbium · The Lotus Plants

Of all the hardy aquatic plants, none are more deserving of our attention and admiration than the stately Nelumbiums. The handsome circular leaves are often of very large size, soft bluish green, the stronger ones boldly and gracefully held above the surface of the water from 2 to 4 feet. Towards the end of June, and continuing for many weeks, the magnificent large fragrant flowers are freely produced, displaying both in form and color the highest type of grace and beauty. All of the Lotus plants are perfectly hardy, provided they are planted in a sufficient depth of water to keep the tubers from freezing. They should not be planted before the advent of the growing season, as the tubers cannot be safely handled much in advance of that period.

Nelumbium luteum. AMERICAN LOTUS, OR WATER CHINQUAPIN. A noble species with large glaucous green leaves 1 to 2 feet across. Grows naturally from Ontario and Michigan, southward to Florida and Louisiana; usually rare and local. Flowers sulphur-yellow, 6 to 10 inches in diameter when fully expanded. Very handsome.

N. speciosum. INDIAN LOTUS. This is the so-called Egyptian Lotus, and while it may not be historically

For grades and prices of above, see page 169

Nelumbium, continued

true, the name is everywhere associated with this beautiful plant. Native of Asia. Leaves very large, glaucous green, cupped in the center, 1 to 2 feet across. Flowers exquisitely tinted with rose, creamy white at the base of the petals. There are several varieties differing mainly in the color and substance of the flowers, of which the following are both beautiful and desirable:

Album. Flowers white, very large and showy.

Album plenum. Flowers double white. Very vigorous and floriferous.

Roseum. A grand variety with the flowers of a uniform deep rose-pink.

Roseum plenum. Double bright rose, very full.

Nuphar advena. SPATTER-DOCK. A hardy aquatic plant with stout creeping rootstocks, growing in 2 to 3 feet of water in the manner of a Water-Lily. Occurs naturally from New Brunswick and Georgia, westward to the Rocky Mountains. Leaves about a foot long, either floating or erect, deep green. Flowers yellow, 2 to 3 inches across, somewhat globular, usually held above the surface of the water.

Nymphæa · The Water-, or Pond-Lilies

The beautiful Water-Lilies are universally admired, and justly rank among the very best of hardy aquatic plants. The various forms produce a succession of flowers from spring until the close of the season—dainty, glorious flowers of exquisite form and fragrance. They are of the easiest culture, requiring only water, sun and fertile soil. When planting, it is best to set the tubers in soil that is submerged about a foot and a half or two feet deep, allowing them to spread naturally into deeper water.

Nelumbium speciosum

Nymphaea alba. EUROPEAN WATER-LILY. A robust species with large floating leaves 4 to 12 inches across. Native of Europe. Flowers white, 4 to 5 inches wide, with large concave waxy petals and numerous golden yellow stamens.

N. alba candidissima. LARGE EUROPEAN WATER-LILY. A form of the preceding species of very robust habit, requiring ample space. Flowers pure white, large and very showy, profusely borne from spring until frost. A most desirable variety.

N. flava. YELLOW WATER-LILY. A distinct and beautiful species indigenous to Florida, but hardy as far north as Missouri and Southern New York. Leaves dark green, beautifully blotched with brown, 3 to 5 inches across. Flowers pale yellow, usually raised 3 to 4 inches above the surface of the water. Very beautiful.

N. hybrida. HYBRID WATER-LILIES. A number of very showy and floriferous forms of garden origin have recently been introduced. The popular hybrids, which are the results of blending the American and European species, are the most desirable of hardy Water-Lilies, and produce wonderfully large and brilliant flowers in great profusion. The following are among the best:

Laydekeri lilacea. Soft rosy lilac, shaded with carmine, with numerous golden yellow stamens, delightfully fragrant, the odor resemblihg that of the Tea Rose. Remarkably floriferous.

Laydekeri purpurata. Rosy crimson, more intensely colored in the center, and with the outer petals light rose; stamens orange-red. A beautiful variety.

Marliacea albida. Flowers large, dazzling white, with numerous yellow stamens flushed with pink, fragrant. Blossoms continuously throughout the season.

Marliacea carnea. Soft flesh-pink with deeper tones towards the base of the numerous petals, with the fragrance of Vanilla.

Marliacea chromatilla. Bright yellow, with deep golden yellow stamens. The deep green leaves are blotched with brown in the manner of the yellow Water-Lily. A very vigorous plant, blooming continuously throughout the season.

Nymphaea odorata. SWEET-SCENTED WATER-LILY. A very beautiful species with orbicular leaves, widely distributed from Canada, southward to Florida and Texas. Flowers white, 3 to 5 inches across, very fragrant, with numerous golden yellow stamens. One of the best.

N. odorata gigantea. RICE-FIELD WATER-LILY. A form of the preceding species with large leaves often 12 to 15 inches across. Grows naturally from Delaware, southward to Florida and Louisiana. Flowers pure white, 4 to 7 inches wide, with numerous yellow stamens.

N. tetragona (*N. pygmæa*). SMALL WHITE WATER-LILY. This is the smallest of the Water-Lilies and is very desirable for tubs or small pools. Leaves oval, dark green above, purplish beneath, 3 to 4 inches across. Flowers white, the petals faintly striped with purple; stamens yellow. Very free-flowering. Widely distributed in the Northern Hemisphere.

N. tuberosa. TUBEROUS WHITE WATER-LILY. A very rampant species requiring ample space, otherwise it is likely to crowd out more delicate varieties. Grows naturally from the region of the Great Lakes to Delaware and Arkansas. Flowers pure white, 5 to 9 inches across, with numerous yellow stamens. Moderately floriferous. There are two garden varieties of this species, perhaps hybrids with other forms, that are among the most desirable of hardy Water-Lilies.

Richardsoni. Flowers pure white, full and double, borne well above the surface of the water. Universally admired and one of the largest and best.

Rosea. Flowers pink, of a beautiful soft shade, rising several inches above the surface of the

For grades and prices of above, see pages 169 and 170

Nymphæa tuberosa rosea, continued
water. A hardy, vigorous variety, but without the rampant character of its parent. In cultivation it is more desirable than the Cape Cod Pink Pond-Lily, which it closely resembles.

Orontium aquaticum. GOLDEN CLUB. A waterside plant with beautiful velvety dark green foliage. Grows naturally from Massachusetts to Florida and Louisiana. Leaves 6 to 12 inches long, with numerous parallel veins, either floating on the surface of the water or standing erect. The inflorescence is club-like, golden yellow, borne on a white stalk in early spring. Very curious and attractive.

Sagittaria sagittaefolia flore pleno. DOUBLE-FLOWERED ARROWHEAD. A bold floriferous variety, producing a wealth of showy double white flowers of wonderful form and substance. A garden form of the European and Asiatic Arrowhead. Very showy and desirable.

Sarracenia flava. YELLOW PITCHER-PLANT, OR YELLOW TRUMPET-LEAF. An interesting bog plant with curious trumpet-like leaves 1 to 2 feet long. Grows naturally from Virginia to Florida. Leaves yellowish green, reticulated with reddish or purple veins, and crowned by an apiculate hood. Flowers nodding, with an umbrella-like covering which conceals the attachment of the five large yellow petals.

Nymphæa marliacea carnea (see page 109)

S. purpurea. SIDE-SADDLE FLOWER. A very hardy plant growing in mossy bogs from Labrador and the Rocky Mountains, southward to Florida and Alabama. Leaves 6 to 10 inches long, dilated upwards, marked with purple veins, with a large, broad wing on one side and a hairy hood at the summit. Flowers similar in form to those of the preceding species, but with lurid purple petals.

S. rubra. RED TRUMPET-LEAF. An attractive bog plant growing naturally from the high mountains of North Carolina southward to the Gulf. Leaves trumpet-shaped, slender, reticulated with deep red or purple. Flowers reddish purple.

Saururus cernuus LIZARD'S TAIL. A hardy and very free-flowering plant, usually attaining a height of 2 to 3 feet. Grows naturally from Canada, southward to Florida and Texas. Leaves deep green, heart-shaped, borne on winged petioles. Flowers creamy white, in long and slender, drooping racemes, in summer. Excellent for massing at the water's edge.

Scirpus lacustris. BULRUSH. A very hardy plant growing in shallow water; widely distributed in the Northern Hemisphere. Culms round, 3 to 6 feet tall, quite erect, bearing at the summit a light brown inflorescence. Splendid for naturalizing in large ponds, where it is sometimes used to prevent erosion of the banks.

Typha angustifolia. NARROW-LEAVED CAT-TAIL. A hardy aquatic plant growing in shallow water. Widely distributed in the Northern Hemisphere. Attains a height of about 4 to 6 feet. Leaves long and remarkably narrow, bright green, scarcely overtopped by the brown spikes.

T. latifolia. CAT-TAIL. Usually attains a height of 4 to 8 feet, and is common in shallow water almost throughout North America, also in Europe and Asia. Leaves about an inch wide, bright green, overtopping the large brown spikes. Very picturesque and pleasing.

Peltandra sagittaefolia. ARROW ARUM. An upright waterside plant with deep green arrow-shaped leaves. Occurs naturally from Virginia southward to Florida and Alabama. Flowers white, resembling a Calla Lily, blooming in late spring and early summer. Very attractive, adding both interest and variety to aquatic gardens.

Piaropus crassipes. WATER HYACINTH. A curious and beautiful floating plant with showy flowers. Native of South America, but naturalized in many places in the Southern States. Leaves in clusters, with peculiar inflated petioles which enable the plant to float on the surface of the water. Flowers in a loose spike, produced well above the foliage, pale violet with the upper lobe marked with blue and bright yellow; very showy. Hardy in the Southern States and commonly wintered indoors in the North. It makes a very attractive house-plant for vase or aquarium.

Pontederia cordata PICKEREL-WEED. A strong, vigorous waterside plant with handsome foliage and showy flowers. Occurs naturally from Nova Scotia and Minnesota southward to Florida and Texas. Leaves erect, ovate in outline, with a heart-shaped base, dark green and lustrous, borne on stout elongated petioles. Flowers blue, in a dense spike, showy, freely produced in summer. An excellent plant for water gardens and shores of ponds or streams.

Sagittaria latifolia. ARROWHEAD. A valuable plant for colonizing on the borders of ponds and lily pools, widely distributed in North America. Leaves arrow-shaped, bright green, somewhat surpassed in height by the inflorescence. Flowers white, produced in successive whorls of threes in an elongated spike.

For grades and prices of above, see page 170

HERBACEOUS PERENNIALS

A GARDEN of hardy perennial herbs is an important adjunct to the home and its enjoyment. These grand plants increase in size and beauty year by year, and unlike the tender bedding plants, burst into growth with the advent of spring and welcome the return of the growing season with a wealth of flowers and foliage. The showy Peonies, Irises, Phloxes, Foxgloves and the like, add a charm and interest that should not be ignored. We offer a choice assortment of the best and showiest varieties that we confidently recommend. They are of easy culture and thrive in almost any good garden soil. It is, however, desirable to thoroughly prepare and fertilize the soil before planting, by deep spading and enriching, in order that a vigorous and luxuriant growth may be insured, for without these attributes the garden and its flowers will be lacking their essential qualities.

Acanthus

Acanthus mollis. BEAR'S BREECH. A hardy and exceedingly decorative plant with handsome foliage and showy flowers. Native of Europe. Leaves about 2 feet long and a foot wide, with deeply incised and toothed segments. Flowers rosy purple, in tall spikes during late summer. The Acanthus leaf has been widely copied in Art and appears in more or less conventionalized form in many classic designs.

Achillea

Achillea ptarmica flore pleno, The Pearl. DOUBLE-FLOWERED WHITE TANSY. A free-flowering herb with a profusion of small double white flowers almost throughout the season. It is a garden form of the European White Tansy and grows 1 to 2 feet tall. It is very valuable for cut flowers and on account of its remarkably floriferous character is one of the most popular of hardy perennials.

Aconitum

Aconitum autumnale. AUTUMN ACONITE. A tall free-flowering plant with spikes of showy blue or lilac flowers, opening in autumn. Stems clustered, 3 to 4 feet tall, bearing numerous dark green, 3- to 5-lobed leaves. Native of China.

A. napellus. MONK'S HOOD. Stems upright, 3 to 4 feet tall, with deeply lobed and cleft leaves. Flowers deep blue, in terminal racemes, opening in summer. Native of Europe. A very showy plant with flowers of a peculiar intense blue color.

Adonis

Adonis vernalis. PHEASANT'S EYE. A dainty little plant growing in tufts 8 to 12 inches high. Native of Europe. Leaves finely divided, densely clothing the stems to the very base of the flowers. The bright yellow blossoms, 2 to 3 inches wide, are produced in early spring. Splendid for rock-gardens and sunny borders.

Anemone

Anemone canadensis (*A. pennsylvanica*). CANADIAN WINDFLOWER. A very hardy, showy species, spreading rapidly by underground rootstocks. Grows naturally from Canada, southward to Maryland and Colorado. Leaves rich green, borne on long petioles, with 3 to 5 cleft and toothed divisions. Flowers white, profusely borne in early summer. Splendid for a ground

Anemone canadensis

For grades and prices of above, see page 171

Anemone, continued

cover in the shrub border or for colonizing in open moist woods. Height 1 to 2 feet.

A. japonica. Japanese Windflower. A grand subject both on account of the long blossoming period and the value of the handsome flowers for cutting. Native of Japan. Leaves dark green with three variously toothed or incised lobes. Stems clustered, 3 to 5 feet tall, bearing a great wealth of large and very beautiful flowers from late summer until the plants are killed by frost in late autumn. There are several forms in cultivation, differing chiefly by differences in color or substance of the flower. A number of the best varieties are listed below. The Japanese Anemones are hardy in the colder sections of the country with a protection of leaves or litter during the winter. A deep and loamy soil with good drainage and sunny exposure is adapted to the requirements of all the forms.

Anemone japonica alba

Alba. Showy white flowers with golden yellow stamens.

Loreley. Flowers semi-double; bright mauve-pink; symmetrical in outline and possessing the charm of opening in a manner that displays the full surface of the petals.

Prince Henry. A free-flowering form with very large, full and double flowers of a deep and rich pink color.

Queen Charlotte. Flowers very large, semi-double, of a soft silvery pink color. A charming variety.

Rosea purpurea. A remarkably floriferous form with semi-double rosy purple flowers.

Whirlwind. Flowers very large, semi-double, pure white, borne in great profusion.

Anthemis

Anthemis tinctoria. Golden Marguerite. A bushy plant, usually 2 to 3 feet tall, with dissected foliage. Native of Europe. Flowers golden yellow, 1 to 2 inches across, blossoming for a long period in summer. Splendid for cut-flowers and a most satisfactory border plant.

Aquilegia · The Columbines

Graceful hardy herbs with branched stems terminated by showy, mostly nodding flowers. They are delightful plants with compound glaucous-green leaves. They thrive best in moist, loamy soils, fully exposed to the sun. The following species are among the most desirable:

Aquilegia caerulea. Rocky Mountain Columbine. Stems 12 to 18 inches tall, either simple or branched, bearing several large flowers about 2 inches across, variously tinted with blue and light yellow. Common in the Rocky Mountain region. One of the most distinct and attractive species.

A. canadense. American Columbine. Stems 1 to 2 feet high, usually much branched, bearing numerous nodding flowers, yellow within, deep red on the outer surfaces. A very showy form, widely distributed from Canada to North Carolina and Kansas.

A. chrysantha. Golden-spurred Columbine. A tall and vigorous species with stems 3 to 4 feet high. Grows naturally in the high mountains of New Mexico and Arizona. Flowers very numerous, 2 to 3 inches across, yellow with claret-tinted sepals. A noble plant.

A. vulgaris. European Columbine. Stems 18 to 24 inches tall with numerous branches and flowers. Native of Europe. Flowers nodding, variously shaded with violet tones. An excellent free-flowering perennial.

Armeria

Armeria maritima. Sea Thrift. A very pretty dwarf plant with narrow evergreen leaves, forming dense tufts or mats which completely carpet the ground. Widely distributed in the Northern Hemisphere. Flowers bright rose-color, very freely produced in dense heads which are borne on upright stems about 9 inches high. Blossoms almost throughout the season and is very valuable for border planting.

Aruncus

Aruncus aruncus (*Spiræa aruncus*). Goat's Beard. A stately herb with large compound leaves consisting of numerous bright green incised leaflets. Widely distributed in the Northern Hemisphere. Stems 3 to 5 feet high, bearing clusters of slender racemes of small white flowers in plume-like panicles.

A. astilboides (*Spiræa astilboides*). Japanese Goat's Beard. Stems clustered, about 2 feet tall, bearing large feathery panicles of white flowers. Leaves compound, consisting of several soft green toothed leaflets. Native of Japan. A very graceful free-flowering herb.

Asclepias

Asclepias tuberosa. Butterfly Weed. A remarkably showy plant with several erect or spreading stems, rather densely clothed with narrow dark green leaves. Grows naturally from Canada and Minnesota, southward to Florida and Texas. Flowers disposed in numerous umbel-like clusters, bright orange, freely produced in summer.

Aster · The Michaelmas Daisies

The showy perennial Asters are becoming more and more popular as garden plants, both on account of their beauty and the wealth of blossoms which are produced so late in season, when other flowers are often past. They are of easy culture in ordinary soil and conditions, and are hardy and desirable. We list a number of the showiest forms, as follows:

Aster curtisi. Stems 2 to 4 feet tall with narrowly lanceolate leaves. Flowers large and showy, violet

For grades and prices of above, see page 171

Aster, continued

purple, often quite brilliant. A handsome slender species indigenous to the mountains of North Carolina and Tennessee.

A. lowrieanus. Stems 2 to 3 feet tall, usually clustered, bearing ovate or broadly lanceolate leaves which are contracted into winged petioles. Flowers very numerous, disposed in broad loose panicles, light blue. A very showy and floriferous species. Distributed from New England to Iowa, southward to South Carolina and Kentucky.

A. novae-angliae. Stems 3 to 4 feet high, densely clothed with narrowly lanceolate leaves. Flowers violet-purple, very large and showy. One of the best of the native Asters. Distributed from Canada, southward to North Carolina and Arkansas.

A. patens. Stems 2 to 3 feet tall, bearing oval or oblong, clasping leaves. Flowers deep violet or bluish purple. Very bright and attractive.

A. puniceus. Stems 3 to 5 feet tall, much branched above, bearing numerous lanceolate or narrowly lanceolate leaves. Flowers light violet, sometimes pale or purplish, very profuse. A robust species widely distributed from Nova Scotia to Minnesota, southward to North Carolina and Alabama.

A. undulatus. Stems 2 to 3 feet high, with ovate or heart-shaped leaves. Flowers numerous, racemosely disposed on the spreading branches, pale violet. Grows naturally from New Brunswick and Ontario, southward to the Gulf States.

Astilbe

Astilbe japonica. JAPANESE ASTILBE. A hardy border plant with clustered stems 1 to 3 feet tall. Native of Japan. Leaves compound, consisting of several bright green serrate leaflets. Flowers white, disposed in a broad racemose panicle. A charming and graceful perennial, perhaps most familiar to us as a greenhouse plant.

Baptisia

Baptisia australis. BLUE INDIGO. A remarkably showy plant with compound bluish green leaves, consisting of three oval leaflets. Stems usually 3 to 4 feet tall, bearing at the summit long racemes of pea-shaped indigo-blue flowers. Distributed naturally from Pennsylvania to Kansas, southward to Alabama and Texas.

Aster puniceus

Aster lowrieanus

Bellis

Bellis perennis. ENGLISH DAISY. A dainty border plant with numerous showy double flowers which appear for a period of several weeks in the spring. Native of Europe and naturalized in various places in the United States. Leaves clustered at the roots in rosettes. Flowering stems about 6 inches high, each bearing a large flower variously tinged with pink or rose. Very hardy and floriferous. Frequently grown in cold-frames for the dainty flowers which, under such treatment, are abundantly produced during late winter and early spring.

Bocconia

Bocconia cordata. PLUME POPPY. A stately plant with numerous spreading stems 5 to 8 feet high. Native of China and Japan. Leaves large, glaucous green, with the borders variously and deeply lobed. Flowers pinkish, borne in great plumy masses in terminal panicles. Splendid for producing bold and striking effects.

Brauneria

Brauneria purpurea (*Echinacea purpurea*). PURPLE CONE-FLOWER. A bushy plant 2 to 3 feet tall, blossoming profusely from midsummer until autumn. Grows naturally from Virginia and Illinois, southward to the Gulf. Flowers reddish purple, with a large conical brown center. Leaves ovate or broadly lanceolate, dark green, the borders commonly toothed.

Callirrhoë

Callirhoë involucrata. POPPY MALLOW. A handsome plant 9 to 12 inches tall with procumbent stems, widely distributed from Minnesota to Texas. Leaves 5- to 7-cleft or divided, with wedge-shaped incised lobes. Flowers reddish purple, very showy, produced throughout the summer. Thrives in any well-drained soil in sunny situations.

 For grades and prices of above, see pages 171 and 172

Campanula

Campanula carpatica. CARPATHIAN HAREBELL. A charming little plant growing in dense tufts about 6 to 12 inches high. Native of the Carpathian Mountains of Austria. Leaves dark green, ovate or heart-shaped, with coarsely toothed margins. Flowers large, often an inch or more across, varying from white to deep blue. Very free-flowering, producing blossoms almost throughout the summer.

C. persicifolia. PEACH BELLS. Stems 2 to 3 feet high, bearing numerous narrow dark green leaves. Flowers blue or white, nodding, from the axils of the upper leaves, very large and showy. Native of Europe.

C. persicifolia alba plena. DOUBLE PEACH BELLS. A form of the preceding species with large double flowers 2 inches or more in diameter. Splendid for cut-flowers.

C. pyramidalis. CHIMNEY BELLFLOWER. A tall and very floriferous species with clustered stems 4 to 5 feet tall. Native of Austria. Leaves ovate or broadly lanceolate, dark green, gradually diminishing in size up to the inflorescence. Flowers blue, in dense pyramidal racemes. One of the most beautiful and conspicuous of the Campanulas.

Cerastium

Cerastium tomentosum. SNOW-IN-SUMMER. An attractive low and creeping plant with silvery leaves much used for edgings and for rockeries. Native of Europe. Flowers white, freely produced in spring and early summer.

Ceratostigma

Ceratostigma plumbaginoides (*Plumbago larpentæ*). LEADWORT. A dainty little herb with wiry stems 6 to 12 inches tall. Native of China. Leaves dark green, with entire ciliate margins. Flowers intense blue, profusely borne in dense clusters above the foliage in late summer and early autumn. The unique color of the flowers gives added interest and value to this handsome plant.

Ceratostigma plumbaginoides

Chrysanthemum · The Hardy Pompon Chrysanthemums

The lateness of the blossoming period of these hardy plants (which occurs when other subjects of the garden have been destroyed by frost) commends them and accounts for their universal popularity. The earliest frosts of autumn do not materially affect the blossoms, and even in late fall or early winter their bright and showy flowers lend a cheerful aspect. They thrive in almost any garden soil, and although quite hardy, are benefitted by a light covering of litter or leaves in winter. The following varieties are among the showiest:

Autumn Glow. Rose-crimson, a shade both warm and bright.

Golden Queen. A grand, rich yellow, the flowers free and full, lavishly produced.

Indian. A fine Indian-red, very floriferous and excellent in habit and growth.

Old Homestead. This splendid variety has pink flowers of a delightful soft shade. The blooms are large and borne on long stems, making them splendid for cutting.

Victory. Pure white, producing a wealth of flowers that last until the approach of winter.

Chrysanthemum hybridum. SHASTA DAISY. A very free-flowering plant with large and showy daisy-like flowers 3 to 4 inches across, blossoming profusely throughout the summer and autumn. Flowers white, with golden center; petals in two or more rows.

Bocconia cordata (see page 113)

Cimicifuga

Cimicifuga racemosa. BLACK SNAKEROOT. A tall and very showy plant with long racemes of white feathery flowers. Distributed naturally from Canada, southward to Georgia and Missouri. Leaves compound, with numerous incisely toothed or divided leaflets. Flowering racemes often 2 feet long, bearing numerous flowers, all parts of which are white.

For grades and prices of above, see page 172

Clematis · The Herbaceous Clematis

This type of Clematis, although not common in gardens, deserves our recognition on account of the great profusion of flowers produced in summer and the unique herbaceous character of the stems, which are usually only 2 to 4 feet tall. They thrive in almost any good garden soil in sunny situations.

Clematis davidiana. Leaves dark green, larger than in any form of the cultivated Clematis, consisting of three-toothed leaflets. Flowers fragrant, lavender-blue, tubular, with four spreading or reflexed lobes, disposed in clustered heads. Native of China. Very showy and floriferous.

C. integrifolia. Stems erect, attaining a height of about 2 feet. Leaves broadly lanceolate, bright green, with entire margins. Flowers large, 1 to 2 inches long, solitary, nodding, deep blue, produced in great profusion. Native of Europe and Asia.

C. recta. Stems tufted, 2 to 3 feet tall, bearing numerous compound leaves, consisting of ovate long-pointed leaflets with entire margins. Flowers white, sweet-scented, about an inch across, disposed in large terminal corymbs. Native of Europe.

Convallaria

Convallaria majalis. LILY-OF-THE-VALLEY. A dainty little plant and a great favorite wherever grown. It is very hardy and thrives in any good garden soil, preferring partially shaded situations. Widely distributed in the Northern Hemisphere. The fragrant white flowers, nodding in a slender raceme and accompanied by the large soft green leaves, are freely produced in spring. To secure the best and largest flowers the beds should be replanted every few years.

Coreopsis

Coreopsis lanceolata. LANCE-LEAVED TICKSEED. A grand free-flowering species with large and very showy flowers. Grows naturally from Ontario to Florida. Stems 1 to 2 feet tall, usually clustered, leafy at the base, bearing long-stemmed golden yellow flowers about 2 inches across. Very showy and desirable for cutting.

C. rosea. PINK TICKSEED. A diffusely branched herb, spreading by creeping rootstocks, thriving in moist soil. Distributed naturally from Massachusetts to Georgia. Leaves very narrow, rather densely disposed on the slender stems. Flowers pink or rose, an inch or less across, appearing for several weeks in summer. Splendid for rock-gardens. Height 1 to 1½ feet.

C. tripteris. TALL TICKSEED. A tall and stout perennial with leafy stems 4 to 8 feet tall. Grows naturally from Pennsylvania to the Gulf States. Leaves divided into three lanceolate segments, bright green. Flowers numerous, large and showy, bright yellow.

Delphinium · The Larkspurs

Very beautiful hardy plants with lobed or divided rich green leaves and showy flowers in large racemes or panicles. They are universally admired and of easy culture. A deep, rich loamy soil, with sunny exposure, is best adapted to their requirements. The following species are very desirable:

Delphinium cashmerianum. HIMALAYAN LARKSPUR. Stems slender, 12 to 18 inches high, with the majority of the bright green leaves near the base. Native of the Himalayas. Flowers large, about 2 inches long, deep azure-blue, profusely produced in summer. A very handsome species.

D. formosum. SHOWY LARKSPUR. Stems stout, 2 to 3 feet tall, rather densely leafy. Probably a native of Asia Minor. Flowers blue, with deeper margins and violet spurs, disposed in dense racemes. A most durable and dependable plant.

D. grandiflorum. CHINESE LARKSPUR. Stems slender, usually clustered, 2 to 3 feet high. Native of Siberia. Flowers single or double, varying from white to blue, with long and tapering spurs, disposed in dense panicles. Leaves deeply parted into numerous narrow lobes. A splendid garden plant and a favorite wherever grown.

D. nudicaule. CALIFORNIA LARKSPUR. Stems 12 to 18 inches tall, usually clustered, with the leaves mostly at the base. Native of Northern California. Flowers panicled, bright orange-red, with yellow petals, opening in spring and early summer. Remarkably distinct and attractive.

Coreopsis tripteris

Dianthus · The Sweet William and Garden Pinks

These charming old-fashioned gems are not only favorites in our gardens, but they combine so many attributes of merit, such as hardiness, beauty and free-flowering qualities, that we confidently recommend them to all planters. They thrive in warm loamy soils, preferring sunny exposures. They are very valuable for border planting and rockeries.

Dianthus barbatus. SWEET WILLIAM. Stems 10 to 18 inches tall, from a tufted, very leafy base. Leaves rich lustrous green, the basal ones relatively broad and dense. Flowers very numerous, disposed in compact round-topped clusters of various tints and shades and in both double- and single-flowered forms. Every garden should have this old-time favorite. Native of Europe and Asia.

D. chinensis. CHINA, OR INDIAN PINK. Stems about a foot tall, from a tufted or mat-like base. Leaves mostly basal, flat or nearly so. Flowers large and showy, pink or lilac, the petals variously marked with deeper colors and with lacerate or fringe-like borders. Native of China and Japan.

D. deltoides. MAIDEN PINK. Stems tufted, 6 to 10 inches tall, arising from a dense leafy base. Distributed naturally from Scotland across Northern Europe to China and Japan. Flowers deep red with a crimson eye. A dainty little plant, forming dense mats of foliage and producing a great profusion of flowers.

D. latifolius. EVERBLOOMING SWEET WILLIAM. A very free-flowering border plant with stems 6 to 12

For grades and prices of above, see page 172

Dianthus, continued

inches tall, of uncertain origin. Flowers large and very double, in dense clusters, fiery crimson, opening in early summer and continuing to appear almost throughout the remainder of the growing season.

D. plumarius. SCOTCH PINK. Stems tufted, about a foot tall, arising from a dense mat of silvery blue foliage. Native of Europe and Asia. Flowers very fragrant, varying from white to shades of pink and purple, with the petals deeply fringed. A great favorite and a charming plant for border planting or rock-garden.

Dicentra

Dicentra eximia. ALLEGHANY BLEEDING HEART. A very handsome plant with finely divided glaucous leaves, of graceful fern-like aspect. Grows naturally from Western New York, southward to Georgia. Flowers heart-shaped, deep rose, nodding in slender scape-like racemes. A charming dainty species attaining a height of 12 to 15 inches and blossoming at intervals from spring until autumn.

D. formosa. CALIFORNIA BLEEDING HEART. Similar to the foregoing species but with pale rose-colored flowers. Native of Northern California. The leaves are finely divided and very graceful, clustered at the base of the flowering scapes. The flowers are freely produced from spring until late summer.

D. spectabilis. BLEEDING HEART. An old-time favorite with clustered stems 1 to 2 feet tall. Native of Japan. Leaves compound, glaucous green, with numerous rather broad segments. Flowers large and heart-shaped, deep rosy red, nodding in graceful drooping racemes. A beautiful plant, rich in sentiment and associations with the old home gardens.

Dictamnus

Dictamnus albus (*D. fraxinella*). GAS PLANT. A remarkably vigorous and durable perennial forming dense clumps about 3 feet tall. All parts of the plant emit a strong lemon-like odor. Leaves compound, with glossy green ovate leaflets. Flowers white or rosy purple, fragrant, borne in large terminal racemes. Native of Europe and Asia. An old-time favorite.

Digitalis

Digitalis purpurea. FOXGLOVE. Stately and handsome, the Foxglove possesses the dignity and atmosphere of the old-time garden, and yet has lost nothing in the competition and progress of more modern garden plants, which in vain would rival it. The stems vary from 2 to 3 feet in height, densely leafy at the base, bearing long spire-like racemes of large drooping flowers which vary from white to purple, usually more or less spotted.

Dodecatheon

Dodecatheon meadia. SHOOTING STAR. A very pretty and distinct plant with numerous nodding flowers, disposed in an umbel at the top of the slender scape. Petals pink or white, with an orange spot at the base, strongly reflexed. Blossoms in spring or early summer. Leaves oblong, 4 to 8 inches long, bright green, tufted at the base of the flowering stem. Distributed naturally from Canada to Georgia and Texas.

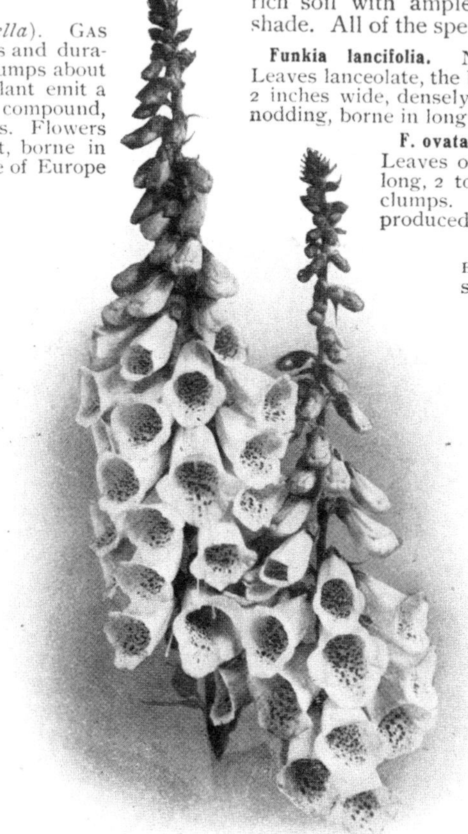

Digitalis purpurea

Doronicum

Doronicum caucasicum. LEOPARD'S BANE. An attractive perennial with stems 1 to 2 feet high, bearing showy yellow flowers 2 to 3 inches across, in spring. Leaves ovate or heart-shaped, at least the upper ones with a clasping base. A very effective plant, of value both for the herbaceous borders and for forcing, either in the conservatory or window garden in the late winter months. Native of Europe.

Epigaea

Epigaea repens. TRAILING ARBUTUS, OR MAYFLOWER. A charming little plant with creeping stems, forming mats or patches on the surface of the ground. Grows naturally from Canada to the Gulf States. Leaves oval, with entire margins, evergreen. Flowers white or pink, deliciously fragrant, opening in early spring. Difficult to transplant, but with proper environment and strong, vigorous plants, it can be successfully managed. Thrives in well-drained soils on shady slopes, especially those containing woods earth.

Funkia · The Day-Lilies, or Plantain Lilies

Hardy plants with Lily-like flowers, forming dense clumps of foliage. They thrive in almost any rich soil with ample moisture, either in sun or shade. All of the species are natives of Japan.

Funkia lancifolia. NARROW-LEAVED DAY-LILY. Leaves lanceolate, the blades 4 to 6 inches long and 1 to 2 inches wide, densely clustered. Flowers pale lilac, nodding, borne in long loose racemes.

F. ovata. BROAD-LEAVED DAY-LILY. Leaves ovate, the blades 5 to 10 inches long, 2 to 5 inches wide, forming dense clumps. Flowers deep blue, nodding, produced in long wand-like racemes.

F. subcordata. WHITE-FLOWERED DAY-LILY. Leaves heart-shaped, strongly many-ribbed. Flowers white, 4 to 6 inches long, erect or ascending, disposed in short leafy spikes.

Galax

Galax aphylla. GALAX. One of the most beautiful of the evergreen herbs. Leaves broadly heart-shaped, with shallowly toothed borders, evergreen, the exposed ones assuming brilliant shades of bronze and red at the approach of cold weather. Flowers creamy white, produced in slender spikes in summer. A splendid ground cover for beds of Kalmias and Rhododendrons, where the shade and cool surroundings are mutually favorable, and an admirable companion for the subjects of the Fern border. Native of Virginia and Georgia.

For grades and prices of above, see pages 172 and 173

Galium

Galium verum. BEDSTRAW. An attractive plant with elongated stems, densely clothed with whorls of tiny deep green leaves. Flowers yellow, disposed in graceful panicles in summer. Native of Europe. A capital ground-covering and rockery plant.

Gemmingia

Gemmingia chinensis (*Belemcanda* and *Pardanthus chinensis*). BLACKBERRY LILY. An old-time garden favorite with Iris-like leaves and showy flowers in terminal clusters. Native of China. Blossoms orange-red, spotted or mottled with crimson and purple. Seeds black, cohering in a globose cluster, closely resembling a blackberry.

Geranium

Geranium sanguineum. CRANESBILL. A showy species with erect or spreading stems 12 to 18 inches tall. Native of Europe. Leaves 5- to 7-parted, with incised or lobed segments. Flowers blood-red, large, profusely borne in summer. Valuable for border planting or rock-gardens.

Gypsophila

Gypsophila paniculata. BABY'S BREATH. A diffusely branched herb with stiff stems 2 to 3 feet tall, producing numerous small white flowers in summer. Leaves narrowly lanceolate, mostly basal. Native of Europe. An airy graceful plant that is greatly admired. Very valuable in an arrangement of cut-flowers to give a sense of softness and informality.

Helianthemum

Helianthemum chamaecistus (*H. vulgare*). ROCK ROSE. A spreading plant with slender stems forming tufts or mats on the surface of the ground. A grand plant for rock-gardens or sunny borders. Flowers yellow, red or copper-colored, rarely white, borne in loose, usually nodding racemes. Leaves small and very numerous, evergreen or nearly so. Native of Europe and Asia.

Helianthus

The Hardy Sunflowers

A very attractive class of plants producing striking and imposing results when planted in the herbaceous border or in the shrubbery. They thrive in almost any soil and produce with remarkable profusion, large and showy flowers that are very valuable for decorative purposes or cut-flowers. The following are among the best of both the single- and double-flowering forms :

Helianthus angustifolia. SWAMP SUNFLOWER. Stems 2 to 4 feet tall, branched above, bearing numerous narrow leaves with entire margins. Flowers yellow with a purple or brownish disk, borne in profusion in late summer or early autumn. Grows naturally from Southern New York to Kentucky, southward to the Gulf States. A charming free-flowering species, although rarely seen in cultivation.

Helianthus decapetalus maximus. LARGE-FLOWERED PERENNIAL SUNFLOWER. Stems 5 to 6 feet tall, branched, bearing very large single golden yellow flowers often 6 to 8 inches across, produced in late summer and early autumn. Leaves broadly lanceolate with toothed borders. A giant-flowered form of the Thin-leaved Wild Sunflower, and without doubt the largest flowered of the perennial forms.

H. mollis. HAIRY SUNFLOWER. Stems 3 to 4 feet tall, stout and very leafy, clothed with long white hairs. Leaves broadly lanceolate, white downy, with three prominent ribs. Flowers large, single, light yellow, expanding in late summer and early autumn. Grows naturally from Ohio to Georgia, westward to Iowa and Texas.

H. multiflorus flore plena. DOUBLE HARDY SUNFLOWER. Stems 3 to 5 feet tall, branched, with broadly lanceolate toothed leaves. Flowers large, full and very double, golden yellow, borne in great profusion towards the end of summer.

H. orgyalis. LINEAR-LEAVED SUNFLOWER. Stems 6 to 8 feet tall, branched near the summit, densely leafy. Grows naturally from Nebraska and Colorado, southward to Texas. Leaves drooping, linear or nearly lanceolate in outline. Flowers numerous, terminating slender branches, lemon-yellow, appearing in late summer or early autumn. One of the most showy species in cultivation, the inflorescence sometimes 3 to 4 feet long.

H. Soleil d'Or. DOUBLE GOLDEN SUNFLOWER. A remarkable garden form of the native Thin-leaved Sunflower with flowers resembling a Cactus Dahlia. Stems 4 to 5 feet tall, branched, bearing large very double golden yellow flowers with quilled petals, in late summer and early autumn.

Hardy Sunflowers

Hemerocallis · The Yellow Day-Lilies

These well-known favorites, so conspicuous and beautiful during their protracted flowering season, are among the hardiest and most satisfactory of the Herbaceous Plants. They thrive in almost any soil, preferring a moist rich loam. In the garden or borders, or on the banks of ponds, they lend bright pleasing effects, both in flower and foliage. All of the species have narrow grass-like leaves of a pleasing lively green color, and form large clumps.

Hemerocallis aurantiaca. FRAGRANT ORANGE LILY. Stems about 3 feet tall, very leafy at the base. Flowers large, bright orange, 5 to 6 inches across, opening in late summer. Leaves long and relatively broad. Native of Japan.

H. dumortieri. DWARF ORANGE LILY. Stems 1 to 2 feet high, with the leaves chiefly at the base. Flowers orange, marked with reddish brown on the outside. Native of Japan. The earliest species to blossom, the flowers appearing in late spring.

H. flava. LEMON LILY. Stems 2 to 3 feet tall, longer than the numerous gracefully arching leaves. Flowers fragrant, clear yellow, very freely produced in early summer. A grand plant. Native of Europe and Asia.

For grades and prices of above, see page 173

Hemerocallis, continued

Hemerocallis fulva. TAWNY DAY LILY. Stems 3 to 4 feet tall from a leafy base. Flowers tawny orange, with wavy-margined petals. Very floriferous and showy. Blossoms in late summer. Native of Europe and Asia.

H. fulva kwanso. DOUBLE ORANGE LILY. Similar to the preceding species, but with double flowers. The blossoms are produced for a longer period than any of the single-flowered forms.

H. thunbergi. LATE-FLOWERED LEMON LILY. Resembles the Lemon Lily very much, and differs mainly in producing a wealth of clear yellow flowers in midsummer.

Hibiscus · The Rose Mallows

Tall free-flowering perfectly hardy plants with remarkably large and showy flowers. They thrive in moist loamy soils and are very valuable border plants, producing throughout a long period numerous mammoth flowers, sometimes 6 to 8 inches across. They are also very effective when planted on the banks of pools, either in combination with shrubs or with other herbaceous plants.

Hibiscus militaris. HALBERT-LEAVED ROSE MALLOW. Stems stout, 4 to 6 feet high, bearing bright green leaves which are lobed near the base. Flowers 3 to 5 inches across, delicate pink or light rose, with a purple center. Grows naturally from Pennsylvania and Minnesota southward to the Gulf.

H. moscheutos. MARSH, OR ROSE MALLOW. Stems strong and vigorous, 3 to 5 feet tall, bearing numerous downy leaves which are whitened on the lower surface. Distributed from Massachusetts and the region of the Great Lakes, southward to Florida. Flowers very large, 5 to 8 inches across, light rose with a purple eye. One of the very best.

H. oculiroseus. CRIMSON EYE. Resembles the preceding species, but the flowers are creamy white with a large crimson center.

Iberis

Iberis sempervirens. EVERGREEN CANDYTUFT. Without doubt the hardiest and most satisfactory of the perennial species. A handsome plant with clustered stems, blossoming profusely in early spring. Native of Crete. Leaves oblong, broadest above the middle, persistent. Flowers dazzling white, disposed in terminal clusters. Splendid for border planting or rock-gardens.

Hemerocallis fulva kwanso

Hemerocallis fulva

Incarvillea

Incarvillea delavayi. HARDY GLOXINIA. A remarkably beautiful and free-flowering plant with handsome large flowers. Native of Asia. Leaves compound, all at the base of the flowering stems, consisting of 11 to 21 toothed leaflets. Flowers trumped-shaped, rosy purple, 2 to 3 inches long, borne in clusters on stems 1 to 2 feet high. Requires a protection of leaves or litter in winter in the colder sections.

Iris · The Irises

The grand and royal colors of the flowers of these superb hardy plants, so often softly blended or else intensified in various lines or marks, are not surpassed by those of any garden subject. They are invaluable in the herbaceous borders, both on account of their hardiness and easy culture, and for the lavish wealth of blossoms that crown their numerous stems. A sunny situation in moist, rich loam is best adapted to their requirements, and as the clumps increase in size, liberal enriching of the ground, or even replanting, is attended by a great gain in the size and number of the flowers.

Iris cristata. CRESTED IRIS. A dwarf plant with slender creeping rootstocks. Grows naturally from Maryland and Indiana, southward to Georgia and Missouri. Leaves bright green. Flowers blue, with an orange crest on the larger segments. A dainty little plant, blossoming in early spring.

I. florentina. ORRIS ROOT. Leaves 12 to 18 inches long from a creeping rootstock, which is, when dried,

For grades and prices of above, see page 173

Hibiscus oculiroseus (see page 118)

Iris, continued

the fragrant orris root of commerce. Flowers white, tinged with lavender. A handsome hardy species, flowering in early spring.

I. germanica. GERMAN IRIS, OR FLEUR-DE-LIS. A vigorous sturdy species with creeping rootstocks and broad bluish green leaves 12 to 18 inches long. Flowers large and very showy, white, blue or purple, often deeply veined with violet-blue, blossoming in spring. Native of Europe. We offer a superb strain of assorted colors as well as the following:

Amas. Inner segments sky-blue, the outer segments deep violet. A splendid variety.

Darius. Lilac-blue with a border of white, the upper petals canary-yellow.

Dr. Bernice. Standards coppery bronze; falls velvety crimson. Large and beautiful.

Innocenza. Ivory-white, rich and pure, with a golden crest.

Kharput. Rich violet-blue standards and deep purple falls. Tall and fine.

Mme. Chereau. White, with a broad frill-like border of clear blue. Superb.

Mandraliscoe. Lavender-purple; early flowering and very profuse.

Maori King. Standards golden, falls velvety crimson with gold margins.

Pallida Dalmatica. Lavender, rich and clear; tall, stately and superb.

Plicata. Standards bright violet-purple; falls violet-purple with lighter shadings.

Queen of May. The colors are a departure from the usual—soft lilac suffused with rosy pink.

Victorine. Standards white, mottled with blue; falls deep blue, mottled with white. Rare and very beautiful.

Iris laevigata. JAPANESE IRIS. Leaves 12 to 18 inches long, bright green, much overtopped by the strong stout stems which are 2 to 3 feet tall. Flowers very large and showy, 6 to 8 inches across, white and of various shades of blue, violet, lavender and purple. They are among the most beautiful of flowering plants, rivaling even the orchids in their rich tints and markings. Native of Japan. We offer a superb collection of mixed varieties, including a wide range of colors as well as the named forms which follow:

Double-flowered Forms

Geishoi. Bright crimson-purple, with white veinings. Six or more large petals.

Hana-Aoi. Yellow blotches surrounded by a blue halo, radiating blue lines to a grayish white border, overlaid with pale blue.

Kagarabi. White, traced and marbled ultra-marine-blue.

Kuma-Funjin. Petals silvery white in center, with broad border reddish lilac.

Manadzura. Flowers large, white, lined with blue.

Rish-no-Tama. Gray-violet petals, large and curled, with yellow blotches radiating into violet feathers.

Samidare. Large gray fluted petals, splashed with sky-blue and violet.

Sano-Watashi. Silvery white, center marked gold.

Senja-no-Hora. Vinous purple splashed with gray.

Taiheiraku. Rich purple, with golden blotches.

Waku-Hotei. White, veined throughout with purple.

Yoshimo. Creamy white, veined with pale blue; large.

Single-flowered forms

Date-Dogu. Three large falls of violet-blue; small center petals claret.

Kumoma-no-Sora. White, with strongly marked sky-blue zone in center; standards white, margined with soft blue; three immense falls. Very handsome.

Yomo-Zakuru. Light ground, suffused reddish purple.

Iris missouriensis. WESTERN BLUE FLAG. Leaves pale green, 12 to 18 inches long, delicately ribbed. Stems 1 to 2 feet high, surpassing the leaves. Flowers bright lilac with a yellow center.

I. pumila. EUROPEAN DWARF IRIS. A dwarf plant with narrow leaves 2 to 4 inches long. Flowers varying from white to lilac and velvety purple, opening in early spring. Native of Europe. The first Iris to blossom.

I. sibirica. SIBERIAN IRIS. Stems tufted, 2 to 3 feet tall, densely leafy at the base. Native of Siberia. Flowers rich violet-blue, very profuse. A favorite in cultivation, forming large compact clumps.

I. verna. AMERICAN DWARF IRIS. Leaves narrow, 4 to 8 inches long, longer than the flowering scapes. Flowers violet-blue, with a yellow center, blossoming

Double-flowered Japanese Iris

For grades and prices of above, see page 174

Iris, continued

in early spring. Distributed naturally from Pennsylvania and Kentucky, southward to Georgia.

I. versicolor. BLUE FLAG. Stems 2 to 3 feet tall, leafy, especially at the base, much overtopping the glaucous leaves. Flowers violet-blue, variegated with yellow and white, and veined with purple. Blossoms in late spring and early summer. Grows naturally from Canada to Florida and Arkansas.

Lathyrus

Lathyrus latifolius. EVERLASTING, OR HARDY SWEET PEA. A rampant plant with long winged stems and tendril-bearing glaucous green leaves. Native of Europe. Flowers varying from white to various shades of rose and purple, large and very showy, borne in clusters on slender stems. Very hardy and of the easiest culture, thriving in almost any soil. Needs lots of space. Splendid for covering rocks or stumps, and for planting above retaining walls.

Lavandula

Lavandula vera. TRUE LAVENDER. The sweet, fragrant Lavender is an old garden favorite of easy culture, producing numerous terminal spikes of "lavender" blue flowers of a soft and charming shade which originated the name of the color. It is a native of Southern Europe—a much-branched plant 2 to 3 feet tall, densely leafy. The narrow leaves, often with tufts of smaller ones in their axils, are silvery downy, with revolute entire borders, persistent or nearly so. Thrives best in a light well-drained soil, freely exposed to the sun. Needs the protection of coarse litter or pine boughs in the colder sections.

Lespedeza

Lespedeza japonica. WHITE-FLOWERED LESPEDEZA. A graceful and very floriferous plant with numerous clustered stems, literally loaded in autumn with pure white flowers in drooping racemes. Native of Japan. A very desirable hardy perennial, forming large specimens when well established. Leaves compound, bright green, consisting of three oblong leaflets.

L. sieboldi (*Desmodium penduliflorum*). SIEBOLD'S DESMODIUM. Stems clustered, gracefully arching, 2 to 4 feet tall, literally loaded in early autumn with drooping racemes of rose-purple flowers. Leaves rich green, compound, consisting of three elliptic leaflets. Native of Japan. A very showy hardy perennial, well adapted for planting in front of shrubs.

Lathyrus latifolius

Iberis sempervirens (see page 118)

Lilium · The Lilies

The glorious Lilies, arrayed in stately splendor, appeal more strongly to our sense of beauty than any other of our garden plants. Many of the best forms are among the grand old-fashioned plants that have made the home grounds a paradise, and reflect sweet memories and associations that we love to live again. Lilies delight in a light well-drained and fertile soil, with protection from severe winds, and are admirably adapted for planting in the herbaceous border or for scattering among rhododendrons and other shrubs. The bulbs should be deeply planted, a foot is not too much for the larger ones, and a top-dressing of well-rotted compost is advantageous.

Lilium auratum. GOLDEN-BANDED JAPANESE LILY. Stems 2 to 4 feet high, leafy up to the inflorescence. Native of Japan. Leaves scattered, bright lustrous green. Flowers spreading, with strongly reflexed and sometimes twisted segments, pure white, with crimson spots, and with a broad golden band running through the center of each of the six divisions. A superb Lily, but not as durable as many others.

L. canadense. WILD YELLOW LILY. Stems 2 to 4 feet high, slender, with leaves disposed in many

For grades and prices of above, see page 174

Lilium, continued

whorls. Flowers of various shades of orange, yellow and red, with numerous dark spots. Distributed from Canada and Minnesota, southward to Georgia and Missouri.

L. candidum. MADONNA LILY. Stems 3 to 4 feet high, with numerous glossy green scattered leaves. Native of Europe. Flowers numerous, 4 to 5 inches long, pure white, very fragrant. The best hardy white Lily.

L. carolinianum. CAROLINA LILY. Stems 2 to 3 feet tall, with the leaves verticillate or the uppermost scattered. Distributed naturally from Virginia to Florida and Louisiana. Flowers orange-red, nodding, with strongly reflexed, purple-spotted segments.

L. elegans (*L. umbellatum*). JAPANESE ORANGE LILY. Stems 2 to 3 feet high, stiff and boldly erect, more or less cobwebby, with numerous scattered leaves. Flowers several, mainly in some brilliant shade of yellow, orange or red. One of the most valuable of the hardy Lilies. Native of Japan.

L. speciosum. JAPANESE PINK LILY. Stems 2 to 4 feet high, bearing bright lustrous green, scattered leaves. Flowers several, or many, fragrant, white, more or less suffused with pink and rose, dotted with red, the segments strongly recurved. Native of Japan. A grand and desirable species of great durability and hardiness.

Lilium carolinianum

L. superbum. TURK'S CAP LILY. Stems 2 to 3 feet tall, with the leaves disposed in numerous whorls. Flowers several to many, bright reddish orange, conspicuously spotted with purple, the segments strongly recurved. Distributed from Maine to Ontario and Minnesota, southward to North Carolina and Tennessee.

L. tigrinum. TIGER LILY. Stems 3 to 5 feet high, more or less cobwebby, densely clothed with scattered rich green leaves. Native of China and Japan. Flowers several or numerous, nodding, orange-red spotted with black. We offer a superb strain (variety *splendens*), which is the most robust, free-flowering form.

L. tigrinum flore pleno. DOUBLE TIGER LILY. Similar to the preceding but with numerous double flowers of exquisite form and substance.

Liriope

Liriope graminifolia (*Ophiopogon spicatus*). PURPLE SNAKE-BEARD. A very pretty plant with grass-like foliage, growing in dense tufts. Native of China. Flowers lavender or violet-purple, borne in dense spikes in summer. Although ordinarily considered a greenhouse plant, it has withstood several degrees below zero on our nursery and we recommend it as a dainty acquisition to the herbaceous border.

Lychnis

Lychnis chalcedonica. MALTESE CROSS. A charming old-fashioned flower with the petals arranged in the form of a Maltese Cross. Stems tufted, from a leafy base, 2 to 3 feet tall, producing compact terminal heads of brilliant orange-scarlet flowers throughout the summer. Very free-flowering and desirable. Probably of Japanese origin.

Lysimachia

Lysimachia clethroides. LOOSESTRIFE. A showy vigorous species with leafy stems 2 to 3 feet high. Native of Japan. Flowers white, disposed in a long gracefully arching raceme, freely produced in summer. A splendid border plant and the flowers very valuable for cutting.

L. nummularia. MONEYWORT. Stems creeping, covering large patches of ground, bearing numerous nearly round leaves of a pleasing bright green color. Flowers golden yellow, very profuse. One of the best plants for carpeting the ground in moist or shady places. Native of Europe.

Mertensia

Mertensia virginica. BLUE BELLS. A beautiful early-flowering plant with handsome flowers. Grows naturally from Canada and Minnesota, southward to Kansas and Georgia. Stems clustered, bearing large glaucous green leaves up to the inflorescence. Flowers blue, large and showy, disposed in graceful nodding clusters. Thrives best in moist loamy soils.

Monarda

Monarda didyma. OSWEGO TEA. One of the most brilliant of our garden plants. Stems about 3 feet tall, sharply 4-angled, leafy up to the inflorescence. Flowers bright scarlet, disposed in numerous compact heads in late summer. Grows naturally from Canada to Georgia and Alabama.

Liriope graminifolia

For grades and prices of above, see pages 174 and 175

Nierembergia

Nierembergia rivularis. WHITE CUP. Stems creeping, forming a dense mat about 6 inches high, well adapted for borders or rock-gardens. Native of South America. Leaves oblong, usually broadest above the middle, bright green. Flowers 1½ to 2 inches across, creamy white, often tinged with rose or blue, with a golden yellow throat. Very showy.

Opuntia

Opuntia vulgaris. PRICKLY PEAR, OR HARDY CACTUS. A prostrate spiny plant with thick and fleshy jointed stems. Distributed from Massachusetts to the Gulf. Segments flattened, usually broadest above the middle, pale green, bearing large yellow flowers two inches across, in late spring and summer. Fruit red, pear-shaped, about an inch in diameter. Splendid for rock-gardens.

Pæonia festiva maxima

Pachysandra

Pachysandra procumbens. ALLEGHANY SPURGE. A low, evergreen plant with creeping matted rootstocks. Grows naturally from West Virginia to Florida and Louisiana. Leaves green, usually mottled in winter. Flowers white or tinged with purple, expanding with the first breath of spring. Very attractive when planted in the Fern border or in moist partially shaded situations. The early-appearing flowers are a great attraction to honey-bees, which literally fill the air with the music of their gauzy wings.

P. terminalis. JAPANESE SPURGE. A low dense evergreen plant with glossy foliage, forming large mats, well adapted for covering the ground, especially in moist or shaded situations. Native of Japan. Flowers white, disposed in small terminal spikes in mid-spring. Excellent for massing, in company with evergreen Ferns, above a spring of running water. This is the hardier species and the one most often cultivated.

Paeonia · The Peonies, or Pineys

These magnificent plants are among the showiest and choicest in our gardens. They are grand, and, like the Roses, are practically indispensable. The fragrance and delicate tints and shades of their beautiful flowers commend them, and, combined with all these noble traits, they are absolutely hardy and of the easiest culture. Peonies thrive best in a deep moist loam, well enriched, with full exposure to the sun. The plants should be set two or three inches below the surface of the ground, and are benefitted by an annual top-dressing of compost. We offer a superb collection of varieties in separate colors or mixtures in both single and double forms, also the following named varieties:

Double-flowered forms of Pæonia sinensis

Achille. Very delicate pink or flesh-color; nearly white.
Alba plena. A fine pure white.
Alexandrina. Beautiful lilac-rose; very large and full.
Ambroise Verschaffelt. Wine-red, the tips of the petals lighter colored.
Anemoneflora. Dark crimson, with center of small petals. Very early to bloom.
Bicolor. Light pink with a cream-colored center.
Bucchi. Delicate pink, changing to white.
Comte Neipperg. Brilliant reddish crimson.
Duc de Cazes. Dark rose, shading to salmon.
Duchesse de Nemours. Sulphur-white; extra large and fine. One of the very best varieties.
Duchesse d'Orleans. Dark rose, with shades of salmon in the center.
Duke of Wellington. Yellowish white; very soft. Flowers symmetrical and unusually fragrant.
Edulis superba. Rose, tinted with violet. One of the best for early cutting.
Festiva alba. Pure white; large and fine.
Festiva maxima. White, with some of the central petals flaked with red. A superb variety, conceded to be the finest white in cultivation.
Humei. Rich rose; late-flowering. A magnificent, free-flowering variety.
Jeanne d'Arc. Light rose, with creamy center. Extra good and desirable.
Lamartine. Beautiful violet-rose.
L'Esperance. Pink, striped with carmine.
Louis Van Houtte. Bright satiny crimson. Flowers of extra-good size and substance.
Ne Plus Ultra. Delicate shell-pink. A solid, clear color. Fragrant and floriferous.
Poiteau. Flesh-white.
Princess Mathilde. Violet-rose.
Queen Victoria. White; very free-flowering and one of the earliest to bloom.
Reevesi. Large; light pink.
Rosea elegans. Soft rose, with light center.
Sydonie. Delicate rose.
Whitleyi. A fine early-flowering white variety.

Double-flowered forms of Pæonia officinalis

Blossoming ten days or a fortnight earlier than the forms of *Pæonia sinensis*. These are the old-fashioned Peonies with very full, double fragrant flowers:

Alba. Blush-white.
Rosea. Bright rosy pink.
Rubra. Glowing crimson.

Cut-leaved Peony

Paeonia tenuifolia. Flowers single or double, rich crimson. Leaves deeply cut into numerous linear segments. A handsome and very ornamental plant.

Single-flowered forms of Pæonia sinensis

Abidan. Purple.
Abora. Rosy lilac.
Abyla. Carmine.
Gabreta. Dark crimson.
Iphis. Maroon.
Josephine. Dark red.
Libon. Rose-pink.
The Bride. White.

For grades and prices of above, see page 175

Tree Peonies. Pæonia moutan

These interesting plants differ widely from the foregoing forms, in their shrubby stems and branches, which attain eventually a height of 3 to 6 feet. Native of China. The following are among the most desirable forms in cultivation:

Comte de Flandres. Dark rose.
Elizabeth. Rosy red.
Gloire des Belgiques. Rose.
Guillaume Tell. White.
Regina belgica. Rose.
Semperflorens alba. White.
Van Houttei. Lilac-rose.

Papaver

Papaver orientale. ORIENTAL POPPY. A glorious plant, producing large satiny flowers 6 inches or more across. Stems 3 to 4 feet tall, leafy, especially at the base, hispid with long white hairs. Leaves deeply cut and parted, rich green, with numerous pale hairs. Flowers brilliant red or scarlet, exceedingly showy.

Phlox · The Perennial Phloxes

The beautiful Phloxes are universal favorites and rank among the showiest of garden plants. The great profusion of the showy flowers and the huge size of the panicles of the tall-growing forms are features that few perennials can parallel. They are very hardy and of easy culture, thriving best in moist, fertile loam. There are numerous species and varieties, differing in habit, time of blossoming and color of flowers, among which the following are highly recommended:

Phlox amoena. HAIRY PHLOX. Stems 6 to 12 inches high, from a decumbent base. Leaves numerous, narrowly lanceolate, mostly at the base. Flowers very showy, profuse, rose-pink, opening in late spring. Distributed naturally from Virginia to Tennessee and Florida.

Papaver orientale

Old-fashioned Peony

Phlox glaberrima. SMOOTH PHLOX. Stems 1 to 2 feet tall, usually tufted. Leaves narrowly lanceolate, more densely disposed at the base. Flowers rosy purple or pink, appearing in late spring and early summer. Grows naturally from Wisconsin and Virginia, southward to Florida and Alabama. The following forms are distinct and desirable, blossoming much in advance of the varieties of *Phlox paniculata*:

Lady Musgrove. White, with a band of ruddy purple on each petal.
Nettie Stewart. Soft rose.
Perfection. White, with a carmine eye; a charming and altogether desirable free-flowering variety.
Snowdon. Pure white.

Phlox ovata. MOUNTAIN PHLOX. Stems 1 to 2 feet tall, bearing many ovate or broadly lanceolate rich green leaves. Flowers bright rosy purple, large and handsome. Distributed from Pennsylvania and North Carolina to Tennessee and Alabama.

P. paniculata. GARDEN PHLOX. Stems 2 to 4 feet tall, leafy up to the inflorescence. Distributed from Pennsylvania and Illinois, southward to Florida and Louisiana. Leaves broadly lanceolate, bright rich green. Flowers rosy purple, or in the various Garden Phloxes, which are derivatives of this noble species, of a wide range of tints, shades and markings. We offer a superb collection of varieties, embracing the best forms in cultivation, as follows:

Athis. Tall; salmon-pink.
Beranger. Ground-color white, delicately suffused with rosy pink, distinct amaranth-red eye. Dwarf habit.
Bridesmaid. White, with a large, crimson-carmine eye. Tall and stately.
Brilliant. Scarlet, shaded salmon, darker eye.
Champs Elysees. A very bright rosy magenta, of an effective shade.
Coquelicot. A fine, pure scarlet, with crimson-red eye. Dwarf habit.
Eclaireur. Brilliant rosy magenta, with lighter halo.

 For grades and prices of above, see pages 175 and 176

Phlox paniculata, continued

Etna. Crimson-scarlet; the flowers conspicuously large and brilliant.
Flora Hornung. White, with brilliant crimson eye. Dwarf.
Independence. Pure white, tall and extra good.
Jeanne d'Arc. Tall growing; a grand late white.
La Vague. Pure mauve, with aniline-red eye.
Pantheon. Tall and robust. Bright carmine-rose, large and showy.
Peach Blossom. A beautiful peach-blossom-pink.
Von Goethe. Tyrian-rose, suffused with carmine-lake, with conspicuous carmine eye.

Phlox reptans. CREEPING PHLOX. Stems 6 to 12 inches tall, from a creeping base. Leaves ovate, short and broad, rich green. Flowers purple, often tinged with violet, freely produced in spring. Splendid for moist partially shaded places. Grows naturally from Pennsylvania to Kentucky, southward to Georgia and Alabama.

P. subulata. MOSS PINK. Stems tufted or matted, often carpeting large patches of ground. Leaves evergreen, small, densely crowded, sharp and rigid. Flowers very profuse, literally covering the plants as with a mantle, the colors varying from white to pink, purple and rose. Grows naturally from New York to Michigan, southward to Kentucky and Georgia. One of the grandest and showiest of the spring blossoming species, and unexcelled as a ground cover or rock-garden subject. Delights in well-drained sunny exposures. A number of garden forms, characterized by the color of the flowers, are as follows:

Alba. White.
Atropurpurea. Rosy purple.
Lilacina. Light lilac.
Rosea. Bright rose.

Physostegia

Physostegia virginiana. FALSE DRAGONHEAD. A very showy plant with large terminal spike-like racemes of rosy pink flowers in summer. Stems 3 to 4 feet high, bearing many narrow, deeply serrate leaves. Flowers an inch long, very profuse. Widely distributed from Canada to the Gulf.

Garden Phlox

Rudbeckia laciniata, Golden Glow (see page 125)

Platycodon

Platycodon grandiflorum. CHINESE BELLFLOWER, OR BALLOON FLOWER. Very hardy and floriferous, and one of the extra good perennials. Stems 1 to 2 feet high, much branched, of dense habit. Leaves lanceolate, sharply and irregularly toothed. Flowers blue or white. Native of China and Japan.

P. grandiflorum mariesi. GLAUCOUS CHINESE BELLFLOWER. A form of the above with very glaucous foliage. Stems about a foot tall, very stout and compact. Flowers blue or lavender.

Polemonium

Polemonium caeruleum. JACOB'S LADDER. A charming old-fashioned plant of easy culture. Stems 1 to 3 feet tall, bearing numerous compound leaves of a pleasing rich green color. Flowers blue, very profuse, produced in late spring and early summer. Widely distributed.

P. caeruleum album. WHITE-FLOWERED JACOB'S LADDER. Similar to the preceding, but with white flowers.

Polygonum

Polygonum cuspidatum. JAPANESE POLYGONUM. A bold, handsome plant 4 to 6 feet tall, with stout clustered stems. Native of Japan. Leaves broadly ovate or heart-shaped, bright green. Flowers white, small but very numerous, the great clouds of bloom giving a very soft and pleasing effect. Very hardy and desirable.

Potentilla

Potentilla tridentata. EVERGREEN CINQUEFOIL. A low evergreen plant only a few inches high, well adapted for rockeries and as a ground cover. Grows naturally from Labrador to Manitoba, southward along the mountains to Georgia. Leaves dark green, clustered, consisting of three leaflets, assuming rich red and bronze tones in winter. Flowers white, very small, opening in summer.

Rudbeckia

Rudbeckia laciniata, Golden Glow. A very showy hardy perennial with double golden yellow flowers. Stems 4 to 6 feet tall, leafy up to the inflorescence. Leaves bright green, deeply 3- to 5-lobed. Flowers very full and double, borne in great masses in late summer. A very popular free-flowering plant.

R. speciosa. SHOWY CONE-FLOWER. Stems branched, 2 to 3 feet tall, with many lanceolate, deeply incised leaves. Flowers numerous, bright yellow, with a brown-purple conical disk ; the ray petals usually deep orange at the base. Grows naturally from New Jersey and Michigan, southward to Alabama and Arkansas. Very handsome.

Santolina

Santolina chamaecyparissus. LAVENDER COTTON. A hardy much-branched plant 12 to 18 inches high, with evergreen silvery white foliage. Native of Europe. Flowers yellow, borne in globular heads in summer. A very pretty rock- or border-plant.

Sedum • The Stone-Crops

An interesting group of fleshy-leaved hardy plants, well adapted for planting in the herbaceous border or rock-garden. Many of the species produce very showy flowers, and all of them possess attractive foliage. They are of easy culture, thriving best in sandy, well-drained soils or in rocky situations.

Sedum acre. MOSSY STONE-CROP, OR WALL-PEPPER. A low spreading plant of moss-like aspect, 2 to 3 inches high, extensively used for carpeting bare spots or for planting in pockets of rockeries. Native of Europe and Asia. Leaves densely crowded, short and fleshy. Flowers yellow, starry, opening in early summer. Very charming.

S. album. WHITE STONE-CROP. A very pretty plant, 4 to 6 inches high, with many bright green leaves about half an inch long. Flowers white, with reddish anthers, about half an inch across, freely produced in forking cymes. Native of Europe and Asia.

S. maximum. LARGE STONE-CROP. A robust plant with clustered stems 15 to 20 inches tall. Native of Europe and Asia. Leaves large and fleshy, densely disposed. Flowers waxy white, with light pink centers.

S. maximum atropurpureum. PURPLE STONE-CROP. A form of the preceding species with dark bronzy purple foliage. Very attractive.

S. pulchellum. WIDOW'S CROSS. A beautiful little plant 3 to 6 inches high, gracefully spreading over the surface of the ground. Leaves minute, bright green, changing to rich tones of red and purple. Flowers pink, rarely white, disposed in a branched cyme, the divisions of which are gracefully arched. Grows naturally from Virginia, southward to Georgia and Alabama.

S. sexangulare. DARK GREEN STONE-CROP. A slender spreading plant of moss-like aspect, resembling the Mossy Stone-crop. The short fleshy leaves, which are crowded on the branches, are dark green. Flowers yellow, freely produced in early summer. Grows 3 to 6 inches high, and is an excellent subject for covering the ground. Native of Europe.

S. spectabile. BRILLIANT STONE-CROP. A remarkably handsome bold species with clustered stems, attaining a height of 18 to 24 inches. The thick fleshy leaves, which densely clothe the lower portions of the stems, are glaucous green. Flowers rose-colored, produced in very large cymes 4 to 6 inches in diameter. Probably of Japanese origin. Worthy of a place in every garden.

S. spectabile atropurpureum. DARK-FLOWERED STONE-CROP. A form of the preceding species with very large clusters of showy flowers of a deep rosy crimson color.

Sedum spurium. SPREADING STONE-CROP. A vigorous plant with long trailing stems, rooting at the joints. Leaves glaucous green, coarsely toothed. Flowers pink, with reddish anthers, opening in late summer. Native of Asia Minor and Persia.

S. spurium coccineum. CRIMSON-FLOWERED STONE-CROP. A variety of the foregoing species with beautiful crimson flowers.

S. ternatum. WILD STONE-CROP. A handsome tufted species with creeping stems. Leaves spatulate, disposed in tufted rosettes at the tips of the branches. Flowers white, in forked cymes. Grows naturally from New York and Indiana, southward to North Carolina and Tennessee.

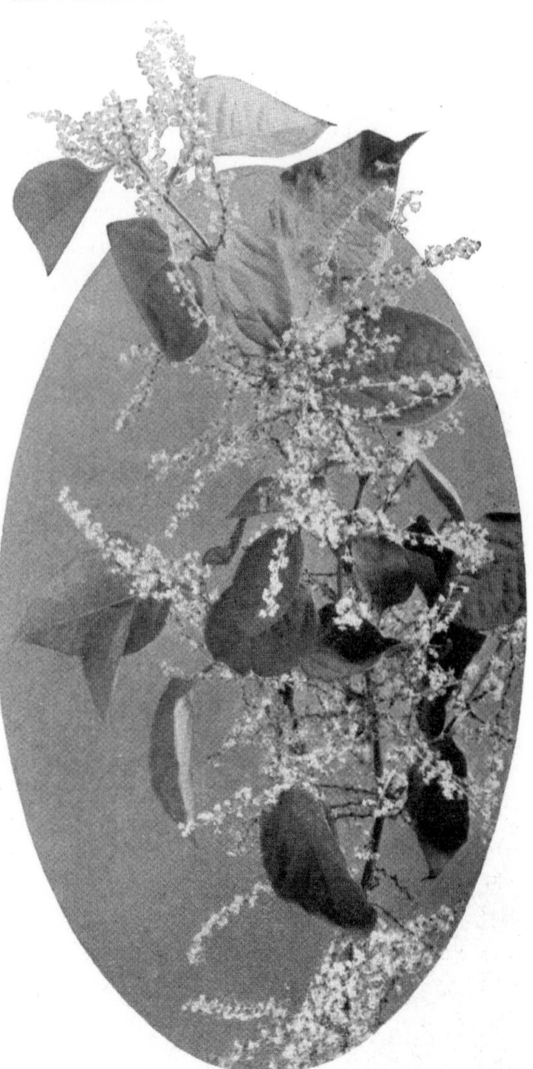

Polygonum cuspidatum (see page 124)

Shortia

Shortia galaxifolia. SHORTIA. A beautiful shade-loving plant with evergreen foliage, occurring in a secluded mountain valley in South Carolina. Leaves orbicular or oblong, bright green, resembling those of the Galax, Flowers white, nodding, borne on slender stems 3 to 6 inches tall, opening in early spring. Requires a moist shady situation, with woods earth or leaf-mould in the soil. One of the most local and historic American plants. Quite hardy, even in cold sections.

For grades and prices of above, see page 176

Tradescantia reflexa

Stokesia

Stokesia cyanea. STOKES' ASTER. A rare hardy plant of surpassing beauty. Stems branched, 1 to 2 feet high, very leafy at the base. Flowers blue or purplish blue, 3 to 4 inches across, resembling a China Aster. The leaves are of a rich green color, gradually diminishing in size up the stem, the uppermost almost clasping. Grows naturally in South Carolina and Georgia.

Tanasetum

Tanasetum vulgare crispum. CURLY-LEAVED TANSY. An old-time garden plant of robust habit, producing a wealth of handsome fern-like leaves. Native of Europe. Stems 2 to 3 feet tall, bearing numerous heads of yellow flowers. All parts of the plant emit a strong aromatic odor when bruised.

Thymus

Thymus citriodorus. LEMON THYME. An attractive little plant, especially useful for borders and rock-gardens. The numerous little leaves, seldom over half an inch long, are evergreen, and surpass in length the small axillary whorls of lilac-colored flowers and are often used for seasoning. Native of Europe and Asia.

T. lanuginosus. DOWNY THYME. A handsome little plant with small downy leaves, well adapted for dainty edgings. Native of Europe. Flowers minute, disposed in whorls in the axils of the leaves.

T. serpyllum. MOTHER OF THYME. Stems very slender, creeping on the surface of the ground. Leaves hardly half an inch long, oval or oblong, persistent. Flowers mauve, in axillary whorls. A common plant in old gardens.

T. vulgaris. COMMON THYME. Stems erect or ascending, 12 to 18 inches high, stiff and wiry. Flowers lilac or purplish, disposed in terminal spikes. Leaves numerous, with revolute borders. Native of Europe. An old garden plant, the leaves of which are often used for seasoning.

Tradescantia

Tradescantia montana. MOUNTAIN SPIDERWORT. A vigorous hardy plant with delicate bluish purple flowers in early summer. Leaves long and narrow, rich green, gracefully disposed on the clustered stems. Native of the Southern Alleghany Mountains. Height 12 to 18 inches.

T. reflexa. GLAUCOUS SPIDERWORT. Strong and robust, with clustered stems about 2 feet tall. Leaves very long and slender, bluish green, drooping. Flowers blue, the delicate petals a mere film of color, continuing to blossom for several weeks during summer. One of the most vigorous and desirable species. Grows naturally from North Carolina and Oklahoma to the Gulf.

T. virginica. COMMON SPIDERWORT. Stems about 2 feet tall, clustered, bearing long narrow leaves of a rich green color. Flowers violet-blue, an inch or more across, very showy, produced almost throughout the summer. Distributed from New York and Illinois to North Carolina and Arkansas.

Ulmaria

Ulmaria filapendula (*Spiræa filapendula*). HERBACEOUS MEADOW SWEET. A handsome plant with deeply cut fern-like leaves. Stems several, 2 to 3 feet tall, bearing numerous white flowers in showy terminal clusters in early summer. Native of Europe, Asia and Siberia.

U. pentapetala (*Spiræa ulmaria*). QUEEN OF THE MEADOWS. Stems clustered, 3 to 4 feet tall, bearing handsome compound leaves with variously lobed and incised leaflets. Flowers white, in dense clusters in late summer. Native of Europe and Asia. A splendid garden plant. The variety described below is perhaps even more popular than the single-flowered form and is more often cultivated.

U. pentapetala flore pleno. DOUBLE-FLOWERED ULMARIA. Flowers very full and double, pure white.

U. purpurea (*Spiræa palmata*). JAPANESE MEADOW SWEET. Stems 2 to 4 feet tall, with numerous compound leaves consisting of deeply lobed and serrate leaflets. Flowers deep pink or crimson-purple, very freely produced in summer. A very showy plant, and one of the best of the group. The stems and branches are deep reddish purple, contrasting sharply with the rich green foliage. Native of Japan.

U. rubra. QUEEN OF THE PRAIRIE. A beautiful hardy species with tall stems, sometimes 6 feet high. Leaves dark green, compound, the leaflets lobed and incised. Flowers pink, in large terminal clusters in summer; very showy. Grows naturally from Pennsylvania to Georgia, westward to Michigan and Iowa. Of easiest culture in any good soil.

Veronica

Veronica longifolia subsessilis. JAPANESE SPEEDWELL. A grand free-flowering plant, producing long spikes of showy flowers. Stems upright, 2 to 3 feet tall, leafy up to the inflorescence. Leaves dark green, lanceolate, with sharply toothed borders. Flowers intense blue, densely disposed in long terminal spikes in late summer and early autumn. Native of Japan. A very hardy and desirable border plant, producing handsome flowers that are valuable for cutting.

V. rupestris. ROCK SPEEDWELL. A dainty little plant growing in tufts or mats and covering large patches of ground. Stems 4 to 5 inches tall, bearing numerous showy racemes of blue flowers in spring. Leaves an inch or less in length, rich green. Splendid for rock-gardens and borders.

V. spicata. EUROPEAN SPEEDWELL. A handsome border-plant, with upright or ascending stems, 1½ to 2 feet tall. Native of Europe. Leaves rich green, an inch or two in length, densely disposed. Flowers bright blue, borne in long, dense racemes in summer. One of the best of the Veronicas, thriving best in sunny situations.

For grades and prices of above, see pages 176 and 177

Vinca

Vinca major. LARGER PERIWINKLE. A strong-growing plant with long trailing stems, producing large blue flowers in summer. Leaves broadly ovate or nearly orbicular, persistent, rich glossy green. Extensively used in hanging baskets and rockeries. A good border plant, but not so hardy as the next species, and requiring some protection in the colder sections. Native of Europe.

V. minor. COMMON PERIWINKLE, OR TRAILING MYRTLE. A hardy old-fashioned evergreen plant, well adapted for ground covering and rockeries. Delights in a cool shady place, often covering the ground with a dense mat of green. Leaves very dark green and glossy. Flowers blue, freely produced in summer. Native of Europe.

Yucca

Yucca filamentosa. ADAM'S NEEDLE, OR BEAR GRASS. A stately plant with stiff evergreen foliage. Flowering stems 4 to 6 feet tall, branched near the summit and bearing numerous drooping creamy white flowers in summer. The great profusion of the large showy blossoms, so majestically borne, lends a bold and imposing aspect. Every garden should have this grand hardy species. Grows naturally from North Carolina to Florida and Mississippi.

Y. filamentosa variegata. VARIEGATED YUCCA. A form of the preceding, with the leaves longitudinally striped with yellow and green. Very attractive and unique, and especially valuable where lively effects are desired. Apparently quite as hardy and vigorous as the typical form, with which it presents a striking contrast.

Yucca filamentosa

For grades and prices of above, see page 177

Express and Freight Rates on Trees and Shrubbery to Principal Cities of the United States, Canada, Mexico

FROM BILTMORE, N. C. TO	Rates per 100 pounds		
	Express	Freight	
		Boxed	Baled
Alabama, Birmingham	$2 00	$0 52	$0 79
Mobile	2 80	58	82
Montgomery	2 00	52	79
Arizona, Phœnix	11 40	3 48	4 57
Tucson	10 80	3 58	4 81
Arkansas, Ft. Smith	4 00	1 33	1 98
Little Rock	3 80	1 13	1 68
Texarkana	4 00	1 08	1 37
California, Los Angeles	10 60	2 75	3 72
Sacramento	11 20	2 75	3 72
San Francisco	12 00	2 75	3 72
Canada, Montreal	5 00	96	1 33
Toronto	4 10	1 01	1 45
Quebec	5 40	1 21½	1 73
Colorado, Denver	7 80	1 93	3 13
Durango	10 00	3 03	4 58
Grand Junction	9 20	3 03	4 58
Pueblo	7 80	1 93	3 13
Columbia, District of, Washington	1 80	71	1 00
Connecticut, Bridgeport	3 10	80	1 11
Hartford	3 20	80	1 11
New Haven	2 80	80	1 11
Delaware, Wilmington	2 40	75	1 06
Florida, Jacksonville	2 45	62	84
Tallahassee	2 60	1 12	1 51
Tampa	2 80	94	1 27
Georgia, Atlanta	1 20	50	76
Macon	1 80	56	76
Savannah	1 50	57	76
Idaho, Boise	10 80	3 13	4 28
Illinois, Cairo	3 20	89	1 19
Chicago	3 60	88	1 43
Springfield	3 80	88	1 43
Indiana, Evansville	3 20	89	1 19
Fort Wayne	3 60	95	1 26
Indianapolis	3 20	93½	1 31
Indian Territory, Muskogee	5 40	1 48	2 13
Iowa, Des Moines	4 60	1 14½	1 53
Dubuque	5 00	1 14½	1 53
Sioux City	5 20	1 43	2 22
Kansas, Fort Scott	4 40	1 13	1 78
Topeka	5 20	1 32	2 70
Wichita	5 20	1 49	2 17½
Kentucky, Lexington	2 80	81	1 09
Louisville	2 60	81	1 09
Paducah	3 20	89	1 19
Louisiana, Baton Rouge	3 95	67	1 03
New Orleans	3 20	58	82
Shreveport	4 00	95	1 31
Maine, Augusta	3 60	1 00	1 35
Portland	3 40	80	1 11
Maryland, Annapolis	2 45	58	1 00
Baltimore	2 00	58	1 00
Massachusetts, Boston	3 20	68	1 11
Fall River	3 20	80	1 11
Springfield	3 00	80	1 11
Worcester	3 20	80	1 11
Mexico, Mexico City	9 00	2 33	3 05
Monterey	7 35	1 82	2 35
Michigan, Detroit	3 60	95	1 26
Grand Rapids	4 00	96	1 28
Marquette	5 00	1 36	1 84
Saginaw	4 00	95	1 26
Minnesota, Duluth	6 00	1 34	1 89
Minneapolis	5 20	1 33	1 89
Mississippi, Jackson	3 20	80	1 01
Natchez	3 80	58	82
Vicksburg	3 40	58	82
Missouri, Kansas City	4 40	1 13	1 78
St. Louis	3 20	98	1 42
Montana, Butte	9 60	3 08	4 52
Helena	10 00	3 08	4 52

FROM BILTMORE, N. C. TO	Rates per 100 pounds		
	Express	Freight	
		Boxed	Baled
Nebraska, Grand Island	$6 00	$1 51	$2 29
Lincoln	5 00	1 19	1 85
Omaha	4 80	1 15	1 80
Nevada, Carson City	13 00	4 02	5 26
New Hampshire, Concord	3 45	80	1 11
Manchester	3 40	80	1 11
Nashua	4 15	80	1 11
New Jersey, Atlantic City	2 90	75	1 06
Newark	2 60	75	1 06
Patterson	3 00	76	1 08
Trenton	2 80	75	1 06
New Mexico, Albuquerque	8 40	2 68	3 54
Deming	8 00	2 81	3 61
Santa Fé	8 80	2 68	3 54
New York, Albany	3 10	75	1 06
Buffalo	3 60	79	1 15
Elmira	3 00	75	1 06
New York	2 60	63	1 06
Ogdensburg	3 40	82	1 21
North Carolina, Charlotte	60	32	54
Raleigh	1 20	41	63
Wilmington	1 40	55	72
North Dakota, Bismarck	7 40	2 00	2 89
Fargo	6 40	1 65	2 60
Ohio, Cincinnati	2 40	81	1 09
Cleveland	3 20	95	1 26
Columbus	2 80	95	1 26
Toledo	3 60	95	1 26
Oklahoma, Guthrie	5 40	1 65	2 28
Oregon, Portland	12 00	2 75	3 72
Salem	12 40	2 85	3 82
Pennsylvania, Harrisburg	2 40	71	1 00
Philadelphia	2 40	63	1 06
Pittsburg	3 00	78	1 13
Reading	2 80	75	1 06
Scranton	3 00	75	1 06
Williamsport	2 80	75	1 06
Rhode Island, Newport	3 40	68	1 11
Providence	3 20	68	1 11
South Carolina, Charleston	1 30	54	72
Columbia	80	53	72
Greenville	75	48	65
Spartanburg	60	35	46
Tennessee, Chattanooga	1 40	52	76
Knoxville	1 00	47	56
Memphis	2 60	68	98
Nashville	2 20	42	73
Texas, Austin	5 60	1 16	1 57
Dallas	5 20	1 16	1 57
El Paso	7 00	1 34	1 69
Houston	4 80	1 16	1 57
Utah, Ogden	9 60	2 83	4 08
Salt Lake City	9 20	2 83	4 08
Vermont, Burlington	3 60	87	1 22
Montpelier	3 90	87	1 22
Rutland	3 40	80	1 11
Virginia, Danville	1 00	46	63
Norfolk	1 80	55	72
Richmond	1 60	55	72
Roanoke	1 60	55	72
Washington, Seattle	12 00	2 75	3 72
Spokane	11 60	3 23	4 58
Tacoma	12 80	2 75	3 72
West Virginia, Charleston	3 20	85½	1 25
Huntington	2 60	85½	1 25
Parkersburg	3 20	78	1 13
Wheeling	3 20	78	1 13
Wisconsin, Eau Claire	5 00	1 33	1 89
Madison	4 40	1 09	1 48
Milwaukee	3 80	98	1 31
Racine	3 80	98	1 31
Wyoming, Cheyenne	7 60	1 93	3 13

Price-List

Magnolia glauca

Cone-Bearers, or Evergreens

Botanical and Common Names	Mailing size (postpaid) Size	Each	Express and freight sizes (purchaser paying transportation) Size	Each	Doz.	100
Abies amabilis. Lovely Silver Fir	1 ft.	$1 25	1½ ft.	$1 25	$12 50	
			2 to 3 ft.	2 00		
apollinis. Parnassus Fir	1 ft.	1 25	1½ ft.	1 25	12 50	
			2 to 3 ft.	2 00		
arizonica. Silver Cork Fir	1 ft.	1 25	1½ ft.	2 00		
balsamea. Balsam Fir	1 ft.	40	1½ ft.	40	4 00	
			2 to 3 ft.	75		
cephalonica. Cephalonian Fir	1 ft.	1 25	1½ ft.	1 25	12 50	
			2 to 3 ft.	2 00		
cilicica. Cilician Fir	1 ft.	1 25	1½ ft.	1 25	12 50	
			2 to 3 ft.	2 00		
concolor. White Fir	1 ft.	1 25	1½ ft.	1 25	12 50	
			2 to 3 ft.	2 00		
concolor violacea. Purple-coned White Fir	1 ft.	1 25	1½ ft.	1 25	12 50	
			2 to 3 ft.	2 00		
firma. Japanese Silver Fir	1 ft.	1 25	1½ ft.	1 25	12 50	
			2 to 3 ft.	2 00		
fraseri. Fraser's Balsam Fir	1 ft.	40	1½ ft.	40	4 00	
			2 to 3 ft.	75		
grandis (*A. gordoniana*). Tall Silver Fir	1 ft.	1 25	1½ ft.	1 25	12 50	
			2 to 3 ft.	2 00		
homolepis (*A. brachyphylla*). Nikko Fir	1 ft.	1 25	1½ ft.	1 25	12 50	
			2 to 3 ft.	2 00		
lasiocarpa (*A. subalpina*). Western Balsam Fir	1 ft.	1 25	1½ ft.	1 25	12 50	
			2 to 3 ft.	2 00		
magnifica. Red Fir	1 ft.	1 25	1½ ft.	1 25	12 50	
			2 to 3 ft.	2 00		
magnifica glauca. Glaucous Red Fir	1 ft.	1 50	1½ ft.	1 50	15 00	
			2 to 3 ft.	2 50		
nobilis. Noble Fir	1 ft.	1 25	1½ ft.	1 25	12 50	
			2 to 3 ft.	2 00		
nobilis glauca. Glaucous Noble Fir	1 ft.	1 50	1½ ft.	1 50	15 00	
			2 to 3 ft.	2 50		
nordmanniana. Nordmann's Fir	1 ft.	1 25	1 to 1½ ft.	1 25	12 50	
			2 to 3 ft.	2 00		
numidica. Algerian Fir	1 ft.	1 25	1 to 1½ ft.	1 25	12 50	
			2 to 3 ft.	2 00		
pectinata. Silver Fir	1 ft.	40	1½ ft.	40	4 00	
			2 to 3 ft.	75		
pectinata pendula. Weeping Silver Fir	1 ft.	1 25	1½ ft.	1 25	12 50	
			2 tc 3 ft.	2 00		
pectinata pyramidalis. Pyramidal Silver Fir	1 ft.	1 25	1½ ft.	1 25	12 50	
			2 to 3 ft.	2 00		
pindrow. Himalayan Fir	1 ft.	1 25	1½ ft.	1 25	12 50	
			2 to 3 ft.	2 00		
pinsapo. Spanish Fir	1 ft.	1 25	1½ ft.	1 25	12 50	
			2 to 3 ft.	2 00		
pinsapo glauca. Glaucous Spanish Fir	1 ft.	1 50	1½ ft.	1 50	15 00	
			2 to 3 ft.	2 50		
sacchalinensis. Saghalien Fir	1 ft.	1 50	1½ ft.	1 50	15 00	
			2 to 3 ft.	2 50		
sibirica (*A. pichta*). Siberian Fir	1 ft.	1 50	1½ ft.	1 50	15 00	
			2 to 3 ft.	2 50		
veitchi. Veitch's Fir	1 ft.	1 50	1½ ft.	1 50	15 00	
			2 to 3 ft.	2 50		
venusta (*A. bracteata*). Santa Lucia Fir	1 ft.	1 25	1½ ft.	2 00		

CONE-BEARERS, or EVERGREENS, continued

Botanical and Common Names	Mailing size, postpaid: Size	Each	Express and freight sizes, purchaser paying transportation: Size	Each	Doz.	100
Araucaria imbricata. Chile Pine, Monkey Puzzle	1 ft.	$1 50	1½ ft.	$2 00	$20 00	
			2 to 3 ft.	4 50		
Cedrus atlantica. Mt. Atlas Cedar	1 ft.	60	2 to 3 ft.	1 50	15 00	
atlantica glauca. Mt. Atlas Silver Cedar	1 ft.	60	2 to 3 ft.	1 50	15 00	
deodara. Deodar, Indian Cedar	1 ft.	40	2 to 3 ft.	1 00	10 00	
libani. Cedar of Lebanon	1 ft.	60	2 to 3 ft.	1 50	15 00	
Chamaecyparis						
lawsoniana (*Cupressus lawsoniana*). Lawson's Cypress	1 ft.	40	2 to 3 ft.	1 00	10 00	
			4 to 5 ft.	2 50		
lawsoniana bowleri. Weeping Lawson's Cypress	1 ft.	50	2 to 3 ft.	1 25	12 50	
lawsoniana glauca. Blue Lawson's Cypress	1 ft.	50	2 to 3 ft.	1 25	12 50	
nutkænsis (*Cupressus nutkænsis ; Thuyopsis borealis*). Nootka Sound Cypress	1 ft.	50	2 to 3 ft.	1 25	12 50	
nutkænsis compacta. Compact Nootka Sound Cypress	1 ft.	50	2 to 3 ft.	1 25	12 50	
nutkænsis glauca. Nootka Sound Blue Cypress	1 ft.	50	2 to 3 ft.	1 25	12 50	
nutkænsis pendula. Nootka Sound Weeping Cypress	1 ft.	50	2 to 3 ft.	1 25	12 50	
obtusa (*Retinospora obtusa*). Japanese Cypress	1 ft.	75	2 to 3 ft.	1 75	17 50	
obtusa aurea. Golden Japanese Cypress	1 ft.	85	2 to 3 ft.	2 00	20 00	
obtusa nana. Dwarf Japanese Cypress	1 ft.	85	2 to 3 ft.	2 00	20 00	
obtusa nana aurea. Dwarf Golden Japanese Cypress	1 ft.	85	1½ ft.	1 75	17 50	
			2 to 3 ft.	2 00		
pisifera (*Retinospora pisifera*). Sawara, or Pea-fruited Cypress	1 ft.	75	2 to 3 ft.	1 75	17 50	
pisifera aurea. Golden Pea-fruited Cypress	1 ft.	85	2 to 3 ft.	2 00	20 00	
pisifera filifera. Thread-branched Cypress	1 ft.	85	2 to 3 ft.	2 00	20 00	
pisifera filifera aurea. Golden Thread-branched Cypress	1 ft.	85	2 to 3 ft.	2 00	20 00	
pisifera plumosa. Plume-like Cypress	1 ft.	60	2 to 3 ft.	1 50		
pisifera plumosa argentea. Silver-plumed Cypress	1 ft.	75	2 to 3 ft.	1 75		
pisifera plumosa aurea. Golden-plumed Cypress	1 ft.	60	1½ ft.	75	7 50	
			2 to 3 ft.	1 50	15 00	
pisifera squarrosa. Veitch's Silver Cypress	1 ft.	85	2 to 3 ft.	2 00	20 00	
thyoides (*Cupressus thyoides*). White Cedar	1 ft.	60	2 to 3 ft.	1 25	12 50	
thyoides andelyensis. Andely's White Cedar	1 ft.	85	2 to 3 ft.	2 00	20 00	
thyoides variegata. Variegated White Cedar	1 ft.	75	2 to 3 ft.	1 75	17 50	
Cryptomeria japonica. Japanese Cedar	1 ft.	60	2 to 3 ft.	1 50	15 00	
japonica elegans. Elegant Japanese Cedar	1 ft.	60	2 to 3 ft.	1 50	15 00	
Cunninghamia sinensis. Cunninghamia	1 ft.	1 25	2 to 3 ft.	2 00		
Cupressus arizonica. Arizona Cypress	1 ft.	1 25	2 to 3 ft.	2 00		
funebris. Funeral Cypress	1 ft.	65	2 to 3 ft.	1 00	10 00	
goveniana. Gowan's Cypress	1 ft.	65	2 to 3 ft.	1 00	10 00	
knightiana. Glaucous Cypress	1 ft.	65	2 to 3 ft.	1 00	10 00	
macnabiana. Mendocino Cypress	1 ft.	1 25	2 to 3 ft.	2 00		
macrocarpa. Monterey Cypress	1 ft.	65	2 to 3 ft.	1 00	10 00	
macrocarpa lutea. Golden Monterey Cypress	1 ft.	75	1½ to 2 ft.	1 25	12 50	
sempervirens (*C. fastigiata*). Pyramidal, or Roman Cypress	1 ft.	65	2 to 3 ft.	1 00	10 00	
torulosa (*C. majestica*). Majestic Cypress	1 ft.	65	2 to 3 ft.	1 00	10 00	
Fitzroya patagonica. Patagonian Fitzroya	2 yrs.	2 50	3 yrs.	2 50		
Juniperus chinensis. Chinese Juniper	1 ft.	1 00	2 to 3 ft.	2 00		
chinensis aurea. Golden Chinese Juniper	1 ft.	1 00	2 to 3 ft.	2 00		
chinensis procumbens. Procumbent Chinese Juniper	1 ft.	1 00	1½ to 2 ft.	1 50	15 00	
chinensis procumbens aurea. Golden Procumbent Chinese Juniper	1 ft.	1 00	1½ to 2 ft.	1 50	15 00	
communis. Common Juniper	1 ft.	50	1½ to 2 ft.	50	5 00	$40 00
communis aurea. Golden Common Juniper	1 ft.	75	1½ to 2 ft.	1 00	10 00	
communis hibernica. Irish Juniper	1 ft.	60	2 to 3 ft.	75	7 50	

CONE-BEARERS, or EVERGREENS, continued

Botanical and Common Names	Mailing size, postpaid: Size	Each	Express and freight sizes, purchaser paying transportation: Size	Each	Doz.	100
Juniperus communis oblongo-pendula. Graceful Juniper	1 ft.	$0 75	2 to 3 ft.	$1 00	$10 00	
communis suecica. Swedish Juniper	1 ft.	60	2 to 3 ft.	75	7 50	
drupacea. Syrian Juniper	1 ft.	1 00	2 to 3 ft.	2 00		
excelsa. Greek Juniper	1 ft.	1 00	2 to 3 ft.	2 00		
excelsa stricta. Slender Greek Juniper	1 ft.	1 00	2 to 3 ft.	2 00		
macrocarpa (*J. neaboriensis*). Large-fruited Juniper	1 ft.	1 00	2 to 2½ ft.	1 50	15 00	
nana. Prostrate Juniper	1 ft.	50	1½ to 2 ft.	50	5 00	$40 00
prostrata. Dwarf Savin	1 ft.	60	1½ ft.	75	7 50	
rigida. Stiff Juniper	1 ft.	1 00	1½ to 2 ft.	1 50	15 00	
sabina. Savin Juniper	1 ft.	50	1½ to 2 ft.	50	5 00	40 00
sabina tamariscifolia. Tamarix-leaved Savin	1 ft.	60	1½ to 2 ft.	75	7 50	
sabina variegata. Variegated Savin	1 ft.	60	1½ to 2 ft.	75	7 50	
sphærica (*J. fortunei*). Round-fruited Juniper	1 ft.	1 00	2 to 3 ft.	2 00		
squamata. Scaly-leaved Juniper	1 ft.	75	1½ to 2 ft.	1 00	10 00	
virginiana. Red Cedar	1 ft.	50	2 to 3 ft.	75	7 50	60 00
virginiana elegantissima. Lee's Golden Cedar	1 ft.	75	2 to 3 ft.	1 00	10 00	
virginiana glauca. Blue Virginia Cedar	1 ft.	75	2 to 3 ft.	1 00	10 00	
virginiana pendula. Weeping Red Cedar	1 ft.	75	2 to 3 ft.	1 00	10 00	
Libocedrus decurrens. Incense Cedar	1 ft.	75	2 to 3 ft.	1 00	10 00	
Picea ajanensis. Yesso Spruce	1 ft.	1 25	2 to 3 ft.	2 00	20 00	
alcockiana. Sir Alcock's Spruce	1 ft.	1 25	2 to 3 ft.	2 00	20 00	
canadensis (*P. alba*). White Spruce	1 ft.	40	1½ ft.	40	4 00	30 00
			2 to 3 ft.	75	7 50	
engelmanni. Engelmann's Spruce	1 ft.	1 00	1½ ft.	1 25	12 50	
			2 to 3 ft.	2 00		
excelsa. Norway Spruce	1 ft.	40	1½ to 2 ft.	40	4 00	30 00
			2 to 3 ft.	50	5 00	40 00
excelsa inversa. Weeping Norway Spruce	1 ft.	1 25	2 to 3 ft.	2 50		
excelsa pygmæa. Dwarf Norway Spruce	1 ft.	1 25	1½ to 2 ft.	2 00	20 00	
excelsa pyramidalis. Pyramidal Norway Spruce	1 ft.	1 00	2 to 3 ft.	1 50	15 00	
mariana (*P. nigra*). Black Spruce	1 ft.	40	1½ ft.	40	4 00	30 00
			2 to 3 ft.	75	7 50	
obovata. Siberian Spruce	1 ft.	1 50	2 to 3 ft.	2 50		
omorika. Servian Spruce	1 ft.	1 25	2 to 3 ft.	2 00	20 00	
orientalis. Oriental Spruce	1 ft.	1 25	1½ to 2 ft.	1 25	12 50	
			2 to 3 ft.	2 00		
polita. Tiger's Tail Spruce	1 ft.	1 25	1½ ft.	1 25	12 50	
			2 to 3 ft.	2 00		
pungens. Colorado Spruce	1 ft.	1 25	1½ ft.	1 25	12 50	
			2 to 3 ft.	2 00		
pungens glauca. Colorado, or Koster's Blue Spruce	1 ft.	1 50	1½ ft.	1 50	15 00	
			2 to 3 ft.	2 50	25 00	
pungens glauca pendula. Weeping Blue Spruce	1 ft.	1 75	1½ ft.	2 00		
			2 to 3 ft.	5 00		
rubra. Red Spruce	1 ft.	40	1½ ft.	40	4 00	30 00
			2 to 3 ft.	75	7 50	
sitchensis (*Abies menziesi*). Sitka Spruce	1 ft.	1 25	2 to 3 ft.	2 00		
Pinus austriaca. Austrian Pine	1 ft.	50	2 to 3 ft.	1 00	10 00	
cembra. Swiss Stone Pine	1 ft.	65	1½ ft.	1 00	10 00	
			2 to 3 ft.	1 75	17 50	
contorta. Oregon Pine	1 ft.	65	1½ ft.	1 00	10 00	
			2 to 3 ft.	1 75	17 50	
densiflora. Japanese Red Pine	1 ft.	75	1½ ft.	1 25	12 50	
			2 to 3 ft.	2 00		
echinata. Yellow Pine	1 ft.	40	1½ ft.	40	4 00	30 00
			2 to 3 ft.	75	7 50	
excelsa. Bhotan Pine	1 ft.	50	1½ ft.	50	5 00	40 00
			2 to 3 ft.	1 25	12 50	
flexilis. Limber Pine	1 ft.	1 25	1½ ft.	1 25	12 50	
			2 to 3 ft.	2 00		
jeffreyi. Jeffrey's Pine	1 ft.	1 25	1½ ft.	1 25	12 50	
			2 to 3 ft.	2 00		

CONE-BEARERS, or EVERGREENS, continued

Botanical and Common Names	Mailing size, postpaid: Size	Each	Express and freight sizes, purchaser paying transportation: Size	Each	Doz.	100
Pinus koraiensis. Corean Pine	1 ft.	$1 25	1½ ft.	$1 25	$12 50	
			2 to 3 ft.	2 00		
lambertiana. Sugar Pine	1 ft.	1 25	1½ ft.	1 25	12 50	
			2 to 3 ft.	2 00		
laricio. Corsican Pine	1 ft.	1 25	1½ ft.	1 25	12 50	
			2 to 3 ft.	2 00	20 00	
montana. Swiss Mountain Pine	1 ft.	1 25	1 to 1½ ft.	1 25	12 50	
			1½ to 2 ft.	2 00		
monticola. Mountain White Pine	1 ft.	1 25	1 to 1½ ft.	1 25	12 50	
			1½ to 2 ft.	2 00		
mughus. Dwarf Pine	1 ft.	1 25	1 to 1½ ft.	1 25	12 50	
			1½ to 2 ft.	2 00		
parviflora. Japanese Short-leaved Pine	1 ft.	1 25	1½ ft.	1 25	12 50	
			2 to 3 ft.	2 00		
peuce. Macedonian Pine	1 ft.	1 25	1½ ft.	1 25	12 50	
			2 to 3 ft.	2 00		
pinaster. Cluster Pine	1 ft.	1 25	1½ ft.	1 25	12 50	
			2 to 3 ft.	2 00		
ponderosa. Bull Pine	1 ft.	1 00	1½ ft.	1 00	10 00	
			2 to 3 ft.	1 75	17 50	
pungens. Table Mountain Pine	1 ft.	1 00	2 to 3 ft.	1 00	10 00	
resinosa. Red, or Norway Pine	1 ft.	50	1½ to 2 ft.	50	5 00	
			2 to 3 ft.	1 00	10 00	
rigida. Pitch Pine	1 ft.	40	1½ to 2 ft.	40	4 00	
			2 to 3 ft.	75	7 50	
strobus. White Pine	1 ft.	40	1½ to 2 ft.	40	4 00	$30 00
			2 to 3 ft.	75	7 50	60 00
			3 to 4 ft.	1 00	10 00	80 00
			4 to 5 ft.	1 50	15 00	
			6 to 8 ft.	3 00	30 00	
sylvestris. Scotch Pine	1 ft.	50	1½ to 2 ft.	50	5 00	40 00
			2 to 3 ft.	1 00	10 00	
thunbergi. Japanese Black Pine	1 ft.	1 25	1½ to 2 ft.	1 25	12 50	
			2 to 3 ft.	2 00		
virginiana (*P. inops*). Jersey Pine	1 ft.	40	1½ to 2 ft.	40	4 00	
			2 to 3 ft.	75		
Pseudotsuga mucronata (*Abies douglasi*). Douglas Spruce	1 ft.	1 00	1½ to 2 ft.	1 00	10 00	
			2 to 3 ft.	1 50	15 00	
			3 to 4 ft.	2 00		
mucronata glauca. Blue Douglas Spruce	1 ft.	1 25	1½ to 2 ft.	1 25	12 50	
			2 to 3 ft.	2 00		
mucronata pendula. Weeping Douglas Spruce	1 ft.	1 50	1½ to 2 ft.	1 50	15 00	
			2 to 3 ft.	2 50		
Sciadopitys verticillata. Umbrella Pine	1 ft.	1 75	1½ ft.	1 75	17 50	
			2 to 3 ft.	3 00		
Sequoia gigantea. Big Tree, or Mammoth Tree	1 ft.	1 25	1½ ft.	1 25	12 50	
			2 ft.	2 00		
gigantea pendula. Weeping Big Tree	1 ft.	1 50	1½ ft.	1 50	15 00	
			2 ft.	2 50		
sempervirens. California Redwood	1 ft.	1 25	1½ ft.	1 25	12 50	
			2 ft.	2 00		
Thuya gigantea (*T. plicata; T. lobbi*). Western Arborvitæ	1 ft.	1 00	1½ ft.	1 00	10 00	
			2 to 3 ft.	1 50		
japonica (*Thuyopsis standishi*). Japanese Arborvitæ	1 ft.	1 00	1½ ft.	1 00	10 00	
			2 to 3 ft.	1 50		
occidentalis. American Arborvitæ	1 ft.	40	1½ to 2 ft.	40	4 00	30 00
			2 to 3 ft.	50	5 00	40 00
			3 to 4 ft.	1 00	10 00	
			4 to 6 ft.	2 00		
occidentalis alba. White-tipped Arborvitæ	1 ft.	75	1½ ft.	75	7 50	
			2 to 3 ft.	1 50	15 00	
occidentalis aurea. Geo. Peabody's Golden Arborvitæ	1 ft.	75	1½ ft.	75	7 50	
			2 to 3 ft.	1 50	15 00	
occidentalis filicoides. Fern-like Arborvitæ	1 ft.	75	1½ to 2 ft.	75	7 50	
			2 to 3 ft.	1 50	15 00	
			3 to 4 ft.	2 00		
occidentalis globosa. Globe Arborvitæ	1 ft.	75	1½ ft.	75	7 50	
			2 to 2½ ft.	1 75	17 50	
occidentalis plicata. Siberian Arborvitæ	1 ft.	75	1½ ft.	75	7 50	60 00
			2 to 3 ft.	1 50	15 00	
occidentalis pyramidalis. Pyramidal Arborvitæ	1 ft.	75	1½ to 2 ft.	75	7 50	60 00
			2 to 3 ft.	1 25	12 50	
occidentalis spaethi. Spath's Arborvitæ	1 ft.	75	1½ ft.	75	7 50	
orientalis (*Biota orientalis*). Oriental Arborvitæ	1 ft.	40	1½ to 2 ft.	40	4 00	30 00
			2 to 3 ft.	50	5 00	
			3 to 4 ft.	1 00	10 00	

CONE-BEARERS, or EVERGREENS, continued

Botanical and Common Names	Mailing size postpaid Size	Each	Express and freight sizes purchaser paying transportation Size	Each	Doz.	100
Thuya orientalis aurea. Golden Oriental Arborvitæ	1 ft.	$0 75	1½ to 2 ft.	$0 75	$7 50	
			2 to 3 ft.	1 25	12 50	
orientalis aurea nana. Berckman's Golden Arborvitæ	1 ft.	75	1½ ft.	75	7 50	$60 00
			2 to 2½ ft.	1 25	12 50	
orientalis compacta. Compact Oriental Arborvitæ	1 ft.	75	1½ ft.	75	7 50	
			2 to 3 ft.	1 25	12 50	
orientalis pendula (*T. filiformis*). Weeping, or Thread-branched Oriental Arborvitæ	1 ft.	75	1½ ft.	75	7 50	
			2 to 3 ft.	1 50	15 00	
orientalis pyramidalis. Pyramidal Oriental Arborvitæ	1 ft.	75	1½ to 2 ft.	75	7 50	
			2 to 3 ft.	1 50	15 00	
orientalis semperaurescens. Ever-golden Oriental Arborvitæ	1 ft.	75	1½ to 2 ft.	75	7 50	
			2 to 3 ft.	1 50	15 00	
Thuyopsis dolobrata. Japanese Thuya	1 ft.	1 00	1½ ft.	1 00	10 00	
			2 to 2½ ft.	1 50		
Tsuga canadensis. Canadian Hemlock	1 ft.	50	1½ to 2 ft.	50	5 00	40 00
			2 to 3 ft.	1 00	10 00	80 00
			3 to 4 ft.	1 25	12 50	100 00
			4 to 5 ft.	2 00	20 00	
			6 to 8 ft.	3 50		
canadensis compacta. Compact Canadian Hemlock	1 ft.	1 25	1½ ft.	1 25	12 50	
			2 to 3 ft.	2 00		
canadensis pendula. Weeping Hemlock	1 ft.	1 25	1½ ft.	1 25	12 50	
			2 to 3 ft.	2 00		
caroliniana. Carolina Hemlock	1 ft.	75	1½ ft.	75	7 50	60 00
			2 to 3 ft.	1 25	12 50	100 00
			3 to 4 ft.	3 50	35 00	
hookeriana. Western Hemlock	1 ft.	1 25	1½ ft.	1 25	12 50	
			2 to 3 ft.	2 00		
mertensiana. Western Mountain Hemlock	1 ft.	1 25	1½ ft.	1 25	12 50	
			2 to 3 ft.	2 00		
sieboldi. Japanese Hemlock	1 ft.	1 25	1½ ft.	1 25	12 50	
			2 to 3 ft.	2 00		

Drupe-Fruited Evergreens and the Ginkgo

Botanical and Common Names	Mailing size postpaid Size	Each	Express and freight sizes purchaser paying transportation Size	Each	Doz.	100
Cephalotaxus drupacea. Large-fruited Yew	1 ft.	$1 25	1½ ft.	$1 25	$12 50	
			2 to 3 ft.	2 00		
fortunei. Fortune's Yew	1 ft.	1 25	1½ ft.	1 25	12 50	
			2 to 3 ft.	2 00		
pedunculata. Stem-fruited Yew	1 ft.	1 25	1½ ft.	1 25	12 50	
			2 to 3 ft.	2 00		
pedunculata fastigiata (*Podocarpus koraiana*). Korean Yew	1 ft.	1 25	1½ ft.	1 25	12 50	
			2 to 3 ft.	2 00		
Ginkgo biloba (*Salisburia adiantifolia*). Maidenhair Tree	1 ft.	40	2 to 3 ft.	40	4 00	$30 00
			4 to 5 ft.	65	6 50	50 00
			6 to 8 ft.	1 00	10 00	
Taxus baccata. English Yew	1 ft.	1 00	1½ ft.	1 00	10 00	
			2 to 3 ft.	2 00	20 00	
baccata fastigiata. Irish Yew	1 ft.	1 00	1½ ft.	1 00	10 00	
			2 to 3 ft.	2 00	20 00	
canadensis. Canadian Yew	1 ft.	1 00	1½ ft.	1 00	10 00	
			2 to 3 ft.	1 50	15 00	
cuspidata. Japanese Yew	1 ft.	1 25	1½ ft.	1 25	12 50	
			2 to 3 ft.	2 00		
Torreya californica (*T. myristica*). California Nutmeg	1 ft.	1 50	1½ ft.	1 50		
			2 ft.	2 50		
nucifera. Japanese Nutmeg Cedar	1 ft.	1 50	1½ ft.	1 50		
			2 ft.	2 50		

Deciduous Cone-Bearers

Botanical and Common Names	Mailing size postpaid Size	Each	Express and freight sizes purchaser paying transportation Size	Each	Doz.	100
Larix americana. Tamarack	1 ft.	$0 40	2 to 3 ft.	$0 40	$4 00	$30 00
			4 to 5 ft.	75	7 50	
europæa. European Larch	1 ft.	40	2 to 3 ft.	40	4 00	30 00
			4 to 5 ft.	75	7 50	
leptolepis. Japanese Larch	1 ft.	75	2 to 3 ft.	75	7 50	
			4 to 5 ft.	1 00		
Taxodium distichum. Bald Cypress	1 ft.	50	2 to 3 ft.	50	5 00	40 00
			3 to 4 ft.	75	7 50	
Pseudolarix kæmpferi. Golden Larch	1 ft.	75	1½ ft.	75	7 50	
			2 to 3 ft.	1 00		

Deciduous Trees

Botanical and Common Names	Mailing size, postpaid: Size	Each	Express and freight sizes, purchaser paying transportation: Size	Each	Doz.	100
Acer campestre. European Cork Maple	1 ft.	$0 25	2 to 3 ft.	$0 25	$2 50	$20 00
			4 to 5 ft.	50	5 00	40 00
circinatum. Vine Maple	1 ft.	50	2 to 3 ft.	50	5 00	
			3 to 4 ft.	1 00		
ginnala. Siberian Maple	1 ft.	50	2 to 3 ft.	50	5 00	40 00
			4 to 5 ft.	75	7 50	
japonicum. Japanese Maple	1 ft.	1 25	1½ ft.	1 25	12 50	
			2 ft.	1 75		
japonicum aureum. Golden Japanese Maple	1 ft.	1 50	1½ ft.	1 50	15 00	
			2 ft.	2 00		
japonicum filicifolium. Fern-leaved Japanese Maple	1 ft.	1 50	1½ ft.	1 50	15 00	
			2 ft.	2 00		
japonicum purpureum. Purple Japanese Maple	1 ft.	1 50	1½ ft.	1 50	15 00	
			2 ft.	2 00		
laetum. Colchicum Maple	1 ft.	50	2 to 3 ft.	50	5 00	
			4 to 5 ft.	1 00	10 00	
laetum rubrum (*A. colchicum rubrum*). Red Colchicum Maple	1 ft.	50	2 to 3 ft.	50	5 00	
			4 to 5 ft.	1 00	10 00	
			6 to 8 ft.	1 50		
macrophyllum. Oregon Maple	1 ft.	50	2 to 3 ft.	50	5 00	
			4 to 5 ft.	1 00	10 00	
			6 to 8 ft.	1 50		
monspessulanum. Montpelier Maple	1 ft.	25	2 to 3 ft.	25	2 50	20 00
			4 to 5 ft.	50	5 00	40 00
negundo (*Negundo aceroides*). Ash-leaved Maple, or Box Elder	1 ft.	25	2 to 3 ft.	25	2 50	20 00
			4 to 5 ft.	35	3 50	25 00
			6 to 8 ft.	50	5 00	40 00
nigrum. Black Sugar Maple	1 ft.	25	2 to 3 ft.	25	2 50	20 00
			4 to 5 ft.	50	5 00	40 00
			6 to 8 ft.	75	7 50	60 00
palmatum. Japanese Maple	1 ft.	1 25	1½ ft.	1 25	12 50	
			2 ft.	1 75		
palmatum atropurpureum. Blood-leaved Japanese Maple	1 ft.	1 50	1½ ft.	1 50	15 00	
			2 ft.	2 00		
palmatum aureum. Golden Japanese Maple	1 ft.	1 50	1½ ft.	1 50	15 00	
			2 ft.	2 00		
palmatum dissectum. Cut-leaved Japanese Maple	1 ft.	1 50	1½ ft.	1 50	15 00	
			2 ft.	2 00		
palmatum ornatum. Dissected Blood-leaved Japanese Maple	1 ft.	1 50	1½ ft.	1 50	15 00	
			2 ft.	2 00		
palmatum septemlobum. Seven-lobed Japanese Maple	1 ft.	1 50	1½ ft.	1 50	15 00	
			2 ft.	2 00		
pennsylvanicum. Moosewood, or Striped Maple	1 ft.	25	1½ to 2 ft.	25	2 50	20 00
			3 to 4 ft.	50	5 00	40 00
platanoides. Norway Maple	1 ft.	25	2 to 3 ft.	25	2 50	20 00
			4 to 5 ft.	50	5 00	40 00
			6 to 8 ft.	75	7 50	60 00
platanoides cucullatum. Crimped-leaved Norway Maple			6 to 8 ft.	1 50	15 00	120 00
platanoides globosum. Round-headed Norway Maple			6 to 8 ft.	2 00		

DECIDUOUS TREES, continued

Botanical and Common Names	Mailing size, postpaid: Size	Each	Express and freight sizes, purchaser paying transportation: Size	Each	Doz.	100
Acer platanoides reitenbachi. Reitenbach's Purple Maple	1 ft.	50	2 to 3 ft.	$0 50	$5 00	$40 00
			4 to 5 ft.	75	7 50	60 00
			6 to 8 ft.	1 50	15 00	120 00
platanoides schwedleri. Schwedler's Purple Maple	1 ft.	50	2 to 3 ft.	50	5 00	40 00
			4 to 5 ft.	75	7 50	60 00
			6 to 8 ft.	1 50	15 00	120 00
pseudoplatanus. Sycamore Maple	1 ft.	25	2 to 3 ft.	25	2 50	20 00
			4 to 5 ft.	50	5 00	40 00
			6 to 8 ft.	75	7 50	60 00
pseudoplatanus purpurascens. Purple Sycamore Maple	1 ft.	50	2 to 3 ft.	50	5 00	40 00
			4 to 5 ft.	75	7 50	60 00
			6 to 8 ft.	1 50	15 00	120 00
rubrum., Red, or Scarlet Maple	1 ft.	25	2 to 3 ft.	25	2 50	20 00
			4 to 5 ft.	65	6 50	50 00
			6 to 8 ft.	1 00	10 00	80 00
rubrum tridens. Small-fruited Red Maple	1 ft.	50	2 to 3 ft.	50	5 00	
			4 to 5 ft.	75	7 50	
			6 to 8 ft.	1 50		
saccharinum (*A. dasycarpum*). Silver Maple	1 ft.	25	2 to 3 ft.	25	2 50	20 00
			4 to 5 ft.	50	5 00	40 00
			6 to 8 ft.	75	7 50	60 00
saccharinum wieri. Wier's Cut-leaved Maple	1 ft.	25	2 to 3 ft.	25	2 50	20 00
			4 to 5 ft.	65	6 50	50 00
			6 to 8 ft.	1 00	10 00	80 00
saccharum. Sugar, or Rock Maple	1 ft.	25	2 to 3 ft.	25	2 50	20 00
			4 to 5 ft.	50	5 00	40 00
			6 to 8 ft.	75	7 50	60 00
spicatum. Mountain Maple	1 ft.	25	1½ to 2 ft.	25	2 50	20 00
			2 to 3 ft.	50	5 00	40 00
tataricum. Tartarian Maple	1 ft.	25	1½ to 2 ft.	25	2 50	20 00
			2 to 3 ft.	50	5 00	40 00
velutinum. Velvety-leaved Maple			6 to 8 ft.	1 50	15 00	120 00
Æsculus glabra. Ohio Buckeye	1 ft.	25	2 to 3 ft.	25	2 50	
			4 to 5 ft.	50	5 00	
hippocastanum. European, or Common Horse-Chestnut	1 ft.	25	2 to 3 ft.	25	2 50	20 00
			4 to 5 ft.	65	6 50	50 00
			6 to 8 ft.	1 00	10 00	80 00
hippocastanum flore pleno. Double-flowered Horse-Chestnut	1 ft.	40	2 to 3 ft.	40	4 00	30 00
			4 to 5 ft.	75	7 50	60 00
			6 to 8 ft.	1 50	15 00	120 00
octandra. Yellow Buckeye	1 ft.	40	2 to 3 ft.	40	4 00	
			4 to 5 ft.	75	7 50	
parviflora (*Æ. macrostachya*). Long-racemed Horse-Chestnut	1 ft.	50	2 to 3 ft.	50	5 00	40 00
			3 to 4 ft.	75	7 50	60 00
pavia. Smooth-fruited Buckeye	1 ft.	40	2 to 3 ft.	40	4 00	
			4 to 5 ft.	75		
rubicunda. Red-flowering Horse-Chestnut	1 ft.	40	2 to 3 ft.	40	4 00	30 00
			4 to 5 ft.	75	7 50	60 00
			6 to 8 ft.	1 50	15 00	120 00
Ailanthus glandulosa. Tree of Heaven	1 ft.	25	2 to 3 ft.	25	2 50	20 00
			4 to 5 ft.	50	5 00	40 00
			6 to 8 ft.	75	7 50	60 00
Albizzia julibrissin (*Acacia nemu*). Mimosa Tree	1 ft.	25	2 to 3 ft.	25	2 50	
			4 to 5 ft.	50	5 00	
Alnus glutinosa. European, or Black Alder	1 ft.	25	2 to 3 ft.	25	2 50	
			4 to 5 ft.	50	5 00	
glutinosa imperialis. Cut-leaved Alder	1 ft.	40	2 to 3 ft.	40	4 00	
			4 to 5 ft.	75	7 50	
incana. Speckled, or Hoary Alder	1 ft.	25	2 to 3 ft.	25	2 50	
			4 to 5 ft.	50	5 00	
rugosa. Smooth Alder	1 ft.	25	2 to 3 ft.	25	2 50	20 00
			4 to 5 ft.	50	5 00	
Amelanchier botryapium. Service Berry	1 ft.	25	2 to 3 ft.	25	2 50	20 00
			4 to 5 ft.	50	5 00	
canadensis. Shad-bush	1 ft.	25	2 to 3 ft.	25	2 50	20 00
			4 to 5 ft.	50	5 00	
Aralia chinensis (*A. mandchurica; A. japonica*). Chinese Angelica Tree	1 ft.	40	2 to 3 ft.	40	4 00	30 00
			4 to 5 ft.	60	6 00	
spinosa. Angelica Tree, or Hercules' Club	1 ft.	40	2 to 3 ft.	40	4 00	30 00
			4 to 5 ft.	60	6 00	

DECIDUOUS TREES, continued

Botanical and Common Names	Mailing size, postpaid: Size	Mailing size, postpaid: Each	Express and freight sizes (purchaser paying transportation): Size	Each	Doz.	100
Asimina triloba. Pawpaw	1 ft.	$0 50	2 to 3 ft.	$0 50	$5 00	
Betula alba. European White Birch	1 ft.	25	2 to 3 ft.	25	2 50	$20 00
			4 to 5 ft.	50	5 00	40 00
			6 to 8 ft.	75	7 50	60 00
alba atropurpurea. Purple Birch	1 ft.	50	2 to 3 ft.	50	5 00	
			4 to 5 ft.	1 00	10 00	
alba fastigiata. Pyramidal White Birch	1 ft.	50	2 to 3 ft.	50	5 00	
			4 to 5 ft.	1 00	10 00	
			6 to 8 ft.	1 50		
alba laciniata pendula. Cut-leaved Weeping Birch	1 ft.	50	2 to 3 ft.	50	5 00	
			4 to 5 ft.	1 00	10 00	
			6 to 8 ft.	1 50		
alba youngi. Young's Weeping Birch	1 ft.	75	2 to 3 ft.	75	7 50	
			4 to 5 ft.	1 00	10 00	
			6 to 8 ft.	2 00	20 00	
lenta. Cherry, Sweet, or Black Birch	1 ft.	25	2 to 3 ft.	25	2 50	20 00
			4 to 5 ft.	50	5 00	40 00
			6 to 8 ft.	75	7 50	60 00
lutea. Yellow Birch	1 ft.	25	2 to 3 ft.	25	2 50	20 00
			4 to 5 ft.	50	5 00	40 00
			6 to 8 ft.	75	7 50	60 00
nigra. River, or Red Birch	1 ft	25	2 to 3 ft.	25	2 50	20 00
			4 to 5 ft.	50	5 00	40 00
			6 to 8 ft.	75	7 50	60 00
papyrifera. Paper, or Canoe Birch	1 ft.	25	2 to 3 ft.	25	2 50	20 00
			4 to 5 ft.	50	5 00	40 00
			6 to 8 ft.	75	7 50	60 00
populifolia. American White Birch	1 ft.	25	2 to 3 ft.	25	2 50	20 00
			4 to 5 ft.	50	5 00	40 00
Broussonetia papyrifera. Paper Mulberry	1 ft.	25	2 to 3 ft.	25	2 50	
			4 to 5 ft.	50	5 00	
Carpinus betulus. European Hornbeam	1 ft.	40	2 to 3 ft.	40	4 00	30 00
			4 to 5 ft.	75	7 50	
caroliniana. American Hornbeam, or Blue Beech	1 ft.	50	2 to 3 ft.	50	5 00	40 00
			4 to 5 ft.	75	7 50	
Castanea dentata (*C. americana*). American Chestnut	1 ft.	25	2 to 3 ft.	25	2 50	20 00
			4 to 5 ft.	50	5 00	40 00
			6 to 8 ft.	75	7 50	60 00
japonica. Japanese Chestnut	1 ft.	50	2 to 3 ft.	50	5 00	40 00
			3 to 4 ft.	1 00	10 00	80 00
pumila. Chinquapin	1 ft.	25	2 to 3 ft.	25	2 50	20 00
sativa. Spanish Chestnut	1 ft.	25	2 to 3 ft.	50	5 00	40 00
			4 to 5 ft.	1 00	10 00	80 00
Paragon			3 to 4 ft.	1 00	10 00	80 00
Ridgley			3 to 4 ft.	1 00	10 00	80 00
Catalpa bignonioides. Catalpa, or Indian Bean	1 ft.	25	2 to 3 ft.	25	2 50	20 00
			4 to 5 ft.	50	5 00	40 00
			6 to 8 ft.	75	7 50	
bignonioides aurea. Golden Catalpa	1 ft.	50	2 to 3 ft.	50	5 00	
			4 to 5 ft.	1 00	10 00	
			6 to 8 ft.	1 50	15 00	
bignonioides nana (*C. bungei*). Round-headed Catalpa			6 to 8 ft.	1 75	17 50	
ovata (*C. kæmpferi*). Japanese Catalpa	1 ft.	25	2 to 3 ft.	25	2 50	20 00
			4 to 5 ft.	65	6 50	
			6 to 8 ft.	1 00	10 00	
speciosa. Western Catalpa	1 ft.	25	2 to 3 ft.	25	2 50	20 00
			4 to 5 ft.	40	4 00	30 00
			6 to 8 ft.	50	5 00	40 00
Cedrela sinensis. Chinese Cedrela	1 ft.	25	2 to 3 ft.	25	2 50	20 00
			4 to 5 ft.	65	6 50	50 00
			6 to 8 ft.	1 00	10 00	
Celtis crassifolia. Hackberry	1 ft.	25	2 to 3 ft.	25	2 50	
			4 to 5 ft.	50	5 00	
mississippiensis. Southern Hackberry	1 ft.	25	2 to 3 ft.	25	2 50	
			4 to 5 ft.	50	5 00	
occidentalis. Nettle Tree, or Sugarberry	1 ft.	25	2 to 3 ft.	25	2 50	
			4 to 5 ft.	50	5 00	
Cerasus avium flore pleno. European Double-flowering Cherry	1 ft.	50	2 to 3 ft.	50	5 00	
			4 to 5 ft.	75	7 50	
			5 to 6 ft.	1 00	10 00	
hortensis. Japanese Flowering Cherry	1 ft.	50	2 to 3 ft.	50	5 00	
			4 to 5 ft.	75	7 50	
			5 to 6 ft.	1 00	10 00	

DECIDUOUS TREES, continued

Botanical and Common Names	Mailing size, postpaid: Size	Each	Express and freight sizes, purchaser paying transportation: Size	Each	Doz.	100
Cerasus hortensis flore pleno. Japanese Double-flowering Cherry	1 ft.	$0 50	2 to 3 ft.	$0 50	$ 5 00	
			4 to 5 ft.	75	7 50	
			5 to 6 ft.	1 00	10 00	
padus. European Bird Cherry	1 ft.	25	2 to 3 ft.	25	2 50	$20 00
			4 to 5 ft.	50	5 00	40 00
pendula. Japanese Weeping, or Rose-bud Cherry	1 ft.	75	2 to 3 ft.	75	7 50	
			4 to 5 ft.	1 50	15 00	
			5 to 6 ft.	2 00		
pennsylvanica. Wild Red Cherry	1 ft.	25	1½ to 2 ft.	25	2 50	20 00
			3 to 4 ft.	50	5 00	40 00
			5 to 6 ft.	75		
serotina. Wild Black Cherry	1 ft.	25	2 to 3 ft.	25	2 50	20 00
			4 to 5 ft.	50	5 00	40 00
			6 to 8 ft.	75	7 50	
virginiana. Choke Cherry	1 ft.	25	2 to 3 ft.	25	2 50	20 00
			4 to 5 ft.	50	5 00	40 00
Cercidiphyllum japonicum. Kadsura Tree	1 ft.	50	1½ to 2 ft.	50	5 00	
			3 to 4 ft.	75	7 50	
			5 to 6 ft.	1 00	10 00	
Cercis canadensis. Red Bud, or Judas Tree	1 ft.	25	2 to 4 ft.	25	2 50	20 00
			5 to 6 ft	50	5 00	40 00
chinensis (*C. japonica*). Oriental Judas Tree	1 ft.	50	1½ to 2 ft.	50	5 00	40 00
			3 to 4 ft.	75	7 50	
siliquastrum. European Judas Tree	1 ft.	50	1½ to 2 ft.	50	5 00	40 00
			3 to 4 ft.	75	7 50	
siliquastrum album. White-flowered Judas Tree	1 ft.	50	1½ to 2 ft.	50	5 00	40 00
			3 to 4 ft.	75	7 50	
Chionanthus virginica. White Fringe	1 ft.	50	2 to 3 ft.	50	5 00	40 00
			4 to 5 ft.	75	7 50	60 00
Citrus trifoliata. Trifoliate Orange	1 ft.	25	2 to 3 ft.	25	2 50	20 00
			3 to 4 ft.	50	5 00	40 00
Cladrastis amurense (*Maackia amurensis*). Manchurian Yellowwood	1 ft.	75	1½ to 2 ft.	75	7 50	
			2 to 3 ft.	1 00		
lutea (*Virgilia lutea*). Yellowwood	1 ft.	25	2 to 3 ft.	25	2 50	
			3 to 4 ft.	50	5 00	
			4 to 5 ft.	1 00		
Cornus alternifolia. Alternate-leaved Dogwood	1 ft.	25	2 to 3 ft.	25	2 50	20 00
			3 to 4 ft.	50	5 00	
florida. White-flowering Dogwood	1 ft.	25	1½ to 2 ft.	25	2 50	20 00
			2 to 3 ft.	50	5 00	40 00
			3 to 4 ft.	75	7 50	60 00
florida pendula. Weeping Dogwood	1 ft.	1 50	2 to 3 ft.	1 50	15 00	
			3 to 4 ft.	2 00		
florida rubra. Red-flowering Dogwood	1 ft.	1 00	2 to 3 ft.	1 00	10 00	
			3 to 4 ft.	1 50	15 00	
Crataegus apiifolia. Parsley-leaved Thorn	1 ft.	25	1½ to 2 ft.	25	2 50	
			3 to 4 ft.	50	5 00	
boyntoni. Boynton's Thorn	1 ft	25	1½ to 2 ft.	25	2 50	
			3 to 4 ft.	50	5 00	
buckleyi. Buckley's Thorn	1 ft.	25	1½ to 2 ft.	25	2 50	
			3 to 4 ft.	50	5 00	
collina. Hillside Thorn	1 ft.	25	1½ to 2 ft.	25	2 50	
			3 to 4 ft.	50	5 00	
cordata. Washington Thorn	1 ft.	25	1½ to 2 ft.	25	2 50	20 00
			3 to 4 ft.	50	5 00	40 00
crus-galli. Cockspur Thorn	1 ft.	25	1½ to 2 ft.	25	2 50	20 00
			3 to 4 ft.	50	5 00	40 00
monogyna. English Hawthorn	1 ft.	25	1½ to 2 ft.	25	2 50	20 00
			3 to 4 ft.	50	5 00	40 00
monogyna alba plena. Double White Hawthorn	1 ft.	50	1½ to 2 ft.	50	5 00	40 00
			3 to 4 ft.	75	7 50	
monogyna pauli. Paul's Double Scarlet Thorn	1 ft.	50	1½ to 2 ft.	50	5 00	40 00
			3 to 4 ft.	75	7 50	
monogyna punicea. Single Pink Hawthorn	1 ft.	50	1½ to 2 ft.	50	5 00	40 00
			3 to 4 ft.	75	7 50	
oxyacantha. May Thorn	1 ft.	25	1½ to 2 ft.	25	2 50	20 00
			3 to 4 ft.	50	5 00	40 00
punctata. Large-fruited Thorn	1 ft.	25	1½ to 2 ft.	25	2 50	20 00
			3 to 4 ft.	50	5 00	40 00
spathulata. Small-leaved Thorn	1 ft.	25	1½ to 2 ft.	25	2 50	
			2 to 3 ft.	50	5 00	

DECIDUOUS TREES, continued

Botanical and Common Names	Mailing size, postpaid: Size	Each	Express and freight sizes, purchaser paying transportation: Size	Each	Doz.	100
Crataegus tomentosa. Pear Haw	1 ft.	$0 25	1½ to 2 ft.	$0 25	$2 50	
			3 to 4 ft.	50	5 00	
Diospyros virginiana. Persimmon	1 ft.	25	1½ to 2 ft.	25	2 50	$20 00
			3 to 4 ft.	50	5 00	
Fagus americana. American Beech	1 ft.	25	1½ to 2 ft.	25	2 50	20 00
			3 to 4 ft.	1 00	10 00	80 00
			4 to 5 ft.	1 50	15 00	
sylvatica. European Beech	1 ft.	25	1½ to 2 ft.	25	2 50	20 00
			3 to 4 ft.	1 00	10 00	80 00
			4 to 5 ft.	1 50	15 00	
sylvatica asplenifolia. Cut-leaved Beech	1 ft.	50	1½ to 2 ft.	50	5 00	
			2 to 3 ft.	1 00	10 00	
			3 to 4 ft.	1 50	15 00	
sylvatica macrophylla. Broad-leaved Beech	1 ft.	50	1½ to 2 ft.	50	5 00	
			2 to 3 ft.	1 00	10 00	
			4 to 5 ft.	1 50	15 00	
sylvatica pendula. Weeping Beech	1 ft.	75	1½ to 2 ft.	75	7 50	
			2 to 3 ft.	1 00	10 00	
			4 to 5 ft.	2 00	20 00	
sylvatica purpurea. Purple Beech	1 ft.	50	1½ to 2 ft.	50	5 00	40 00
			3 to 4 ft.	75	7 50	60 00
			4 to 5 ft.	1 00	10 00	
sylvatica purpurea pendula. Weeping Purple Beech			3 to 4 ft.	1 50	15 00	
sylvatica riversi. Rivers' Purple Beech	1 ft.	75	1½ to 2 ft.	75	7 50	
			2 to 3 ft.	1 00	10 00	
			3 to 4 ft.	1 50	15 00	
Fraxinus americana. White Ash	1 ft.	25	2 to 3 ft.	25	2 50	20 00
			4 to 5 ft.	50	5 00	40 00
			6 to 8 ft.	75	7 50	60 00
biltmoreana. Biltmore Ash	1 ft.	50	2 to 3 ft.	50	5 00	
			4 to 5 ft.	1 00	10 00	
excelsior. European Ash	1 ft.	25	2 to 3 ft.	25	2 50	20 00
			4 to 5 ft.	50	5 00	40 00
			6 to 8 ft.	75	7 50	60 00
excelsior pendula. Weeping Ash			8 ft.	2 00		
lanceolata (*F. viridis*). Green Ash	1 ft.	25	2 to 3 ft.	25	2 50	20 00
			4 to 5 ft.	50	5 00	40 00
			6 to 8 ft.	75	7 50	60 00
nigra. Black Ash	1 ft.	25	2 to 3 ft.	25	2 50	
			4 to 5 ft.	50	5 00	
			6 to 8 ft.	75	7 50	
oregona. Oregon Ash	1 ft.	25	2 to 3 ft.	25	2 50	
			4 to 5 ft.	50	5 00	
ornus. Flowering Ash	1 ft.	25	2 to 3 ft.	25	2 50	
			4 to 5 ft.	50	5 00	
pennsylvanica (*F. pubescens*). Red Ash	1 ft.	25	2 to 3 ft.	25	2 50	
			4 to 5 ft.	50	5 00	
			6 to 8 ft.	75	7 50	
quadrangulata. Blue Ash	1 ft.	50	2 to 3 ft.	50	5 00	
			4 to 5 ft.	75	7 50	
			6 to 8 ft.	1 00	10 00	
Gleditsia aquatica. Water Locust	1 ft.	50	2 to 3 ft.	50	5 00	
			4 to 5 ft.	75	7 50	
japonica. Japanese Locust	1 ft.	50	2 to 3 ft.	50	5 00	
			4 to 5 ft.	75	7 50	
triacanthos. Honey Locust	1 ft.	25	2 to 3 ft.	25	2 50	20 00
			4 to 5 ft.	50	5 00	40 00
			6 to 8 ft.	1 00	10 00	
triacanthos bujoti (*G. bujoti pendula*). Weeping Honey Locust			6 to 8 ft.	2 00		
triacanthos inermis. Thornless Honey Locust	1 ft.	50	2 to 3 ft.	50	5 00	
			4 to 5 ft.	75	7 50	
			6 to 8 ft.	1 50	15 00	
Gymnocladus dioicus (*G. canadensis*). Kentucky Coffee Tree	1 ft.	50	2 to 3 ft.	50	5 00	40 00
			4 to 5 ft.	75	7 50	60 00
			6 to 8 ft.	1 00	10 00	80 00
Hicoria alba (*Carya tomentosa*). Mockernut, or Big Bud Hickory	1 ft.	25	1½ to 2 ft.	25	2 50	
			3 to 4 ft.	75	7 50	
glabra (*Carya porcina*). Pignut	1 ft.	25	1½ to 2 ft.	25	2 50	
			3 to 4 ft.	75	7 50	
minima (*Carya amara*). Bitternut	1 ft.	25	1½ to 2 ft.	25	2 50	
			3 to 4 ft.	75	7 50	
ovata (*Carya alba*). Shagbark Hickory	1 ft.	25	1½ to 2 ft.	25	2 50	20 00
			3 to 4 ft.	75	7 50	60 00

DECIDUOUS TREES, continued

Botanical and Common Names	Mailing size, postpaid: Size	Mailing size, postpaid: Each	Express and freight sizes, purchaser paying transportation: Size	Each	Doz.	100
Hicoria pecan (*Carya olivæformis*). Pecan	1 ft.	$0 25	1½ to 2 ft.	$0 25	$2 50	$20 00
			3 to 4 ft.	50	5 00	40 00
Any of the following varieties: Bolton, Frotscher's Egg-shell, Pride of the Coast, Stuart, Van Deman			2 ft.	1 00	10 00	80 00
			3 ft.	1 25	12 50	100 00
Hovenia dulcis. Honey Tree	1 ft.	50	3 to 4 ft.	50	5 00	
			5 to 6 ft.	1 00	10 00	
Ilex monticola. Deciduous Holly	1 ft.	25	1½ to 2 ft.	25	2 50	
			3 to 4 ft.	50	5 00	
Juglans cinerea. Butternut	1 ft.	25	1½ to 2 ft.	25	2 50	20 00
			3 to 4 ft.	50	5 00	40 00
cordiformis. Heart-shaped Japanese Walnut	1 ft.	25	1½ to 2 ft.	25	2 50	20 00
			3 to 4 ft.	50	5 00	40 00
nigra. Black Walnut	1 ft.	25	1½ to 2 ft.	25	2 50	20 00
			3 to 4 ft.	50	5 00	40 00
			6 to 8 ft.	75	7 50	60 00
regia. English Walnut	1 ft.	25	1½ to 2 ft.	25	2 50	20 00
			3 to 4 ft.	50	5 00	40 00
sieboldianus. Japanese Walnut	1 ft.	25	1½ to 2 ft.	25	2 50	20 00
			3 to 4 ft.	50	5 00	40 00
Koelreuteria paniculata. Varnish Tree	1 ft.	25	1½ to 2 ft.	25	2 50	20 00
			3 to 4 ft.	75	7 50	60 00
			6 to 8 ft.	1 00	10 00	80 00
Laburnum alpinum. Scotch Laburnum	1 ft.	25	1½ to 2 ft.	25	2 50	
			3 to 4 ft.	50	5 00	
vulgare (*Cytisus laburnum*). Golden Chain	1 ft.	25	1½ to 2 ft.	25	2 50	
			3 to 4 ft.	50	5 00	
			6 to 8 ft.	1 00	10 00	
watereri (*L. parksi*). Park's Golden Chain			5 to 6 ft.	1 50		
Liquidamber styraciflua. Sweet Gum	1 ft.	25	1½ to 2 ft.	25	2 50	20 00
			3 to 4 ft.	50	5 00	40 00
			6 to 8 ft.	1 00	10 00	80 00
Liriodendron tulipifera. Tulip Tree	1 ft.	25	1½ to 2 ft.	25	2 50	20 00
			3 to 4 ft.	50	5 00	40 00
			6 to 8 ft.	75	7 50	60 00
Magnolia acuminata. Cucumber Tree	1 ft.	25	1½ to 2 ft.	25	2 50	20 00
			3 to 4 ft.	50	5 00	40 00
			6 to 8 ft.	75	7 50	60 00
conspicua. Yulan	1 ft.	1 00	1½ to 2 ft.	1 00	10 00	
			3 to 4 ft.	2 00	20 00	
fraseri. Fraser's Magnolia	1 ft.	50	1½ to 2 ft.	50	5 00	
			3 to 4 ft.	1 00	10 00	
glauca. Sweet, or White Bay	1 ft.	50	1½ to 2 ft.	50	5 00	
			3 to 4 ft.	1 00	10 00	
kobus. Japanese Magnolia	1 ft.	1 00	1½ to 2 ft.	1 00	10 00	
			3 to 4 ft.	2 00	20 00	
			5 to 6 ft.	2 50	25 00	
macrophylla. Great-leaved Magnolia	1 ft.	1 00	1½ to 2 ft.	1 00	10 00	
			3 to 4 ft.	1 50	15 00	
			4 to 5 ft	2 00		
obovata (*M. purpurea; M. discolor*). Purple Magnolia	1 ft.	50	1½ to 2 ft.	50	5 00	
			3 to 4 ft.	1 00	10 00	
soulangeana. Soulange's Magnolia	1 ft.	1 00	1½ to 2 ft.	1 00	10 00	
			3 to 4 ft.	2 00	20 00	
soulangeana lennei. Lenne's Magnolia	1 ft.	1 00	1½ to 2 ft.	1 00	10 00	
			3 to 4 ft.	2 00	20 00	
soulangeana nigra. Dark-flowered Magnolia	1 ft.	1 00	1½ to 2 ft.	1 00	10 00	
			2 to 3 ft.	2 00	20 00	
soulangeana norbertiana. Norbert's Magnolia	1 ft.	1 00	1½ to 2 ft.	1 00	10 00	
			2 to 3 ft.	2 00	20 00	
soulangeana speciosa. Showy-flowered Magnolia	1 ft.	1 00	1½ to 2 ft.	1 00	10 00	
			3 to 4 ft.	2 00	20 00	
stellata. Starry Magnolia	1 ft.	1 00	1½ to 2 ft.	1 00	10 00	
			2 to 3 ft.	2 00	20 00	
thompsoniana. Thompson's Sweet Bay	1 ft.	75	1½ to 2 ft.	75	7 50	
			2 to 3 ft.	1 25	12 50	
tripetala. Umbrella Tree	1 ft.	25	1½ to 2 ft.	25	2 50	
			3 to 4 ft.	50	5 00	
Malus angustifolia. Narrow-leaved Crab	1 ft.	25	1½ to 2 ft.	25	2 50	20 00
			3 to 4 ft.	50	5 00	40 00
baccata. Siberian Flowering Crab	1 ft.	25	1½ to 2 ft.	25	2 50	
			3 to 4 ft.	50	5 00	
coronaria. Wild Crab Apple	1 ft.	25	1½ to 2 ft.	25	2 50	
			3 to 4 ft.	50	5 00	

DECIDUOUS TREES, continued

Botanical and Common Names	Mailing size, postpaid: Size	Mailing size, postpaid: Each	Express and freight sizes, purchaser paying transportation: Size	Each	Doz.	100
Malus floribunda. Flowering Crab	1 ft.	$0 25	1½ to 2 ft.	$0 25	$2 50	
			3 to 4 ft.	50	5 00	
floribunda parkmani (*M. halleana*). Parkman's Crab	1 ft.	25	1½ to 2 ft.	25	2 50	
			3 to 4 ft.	50	5 00	
floribunda scheideckeri. Double-flowering Crab	1 ft.	75	1½ to 2 ft.	75	7 50	
			3 to 4 ft.	1 50		
ioensis bechteli. Bechtel's Double-flowering Crab	1 ft.	25	1½ to 2 ft.	25	2 50	
			3 to 4 ft.	50	5 00	
spectabilis. Chinese Flowering Crab	1 ft.	25	1½ to 2 ft.	25	2 50	
			3 to 4 ft.	50	5 00	
spectabilis riversi. Double-flowering Chinese Crab	1 ft.	75	1½ to 2 ft.	75	7 50	
			3 to 4 ft.	1 50		
toringo. Toringo, or Dwarf Crab	1 ft.	25	1½ to 2 ft.	25	2 50	
			3 to 4 ft.	50	5 00	
Melia azederach. Pride of India, or China Tree	1 ft.	25	2 to 3 ft.	25	2 50	
			4 to 5 ft.	50	5 00	
			6 to 8 ft.	75		
azederach umbraculiformis. Texas Umbrella Tree	1 ft.	25	2 to 3 ft.	25	2 50	$20 00
			4 to 5 ft.	50	5 00	40 00
			6 to 8 ft.	1 00	10 00	80 00
Mespilus germanica. Medlar, or Mespil	1 ft.	75	2 to 3 ft.	75	7 50	
			3 to 4 ft.	1 00		
Mohrodendron carolinum (*Halesia tetraptera*). Silver Bell	1 ft.	25	1½ to 2 ft.	25	2 50	20 00
			3 to 4 ft.	50	5 00	40 00
dipterum (*Halesia diptera*). Snowdrop Tree	1 ft.	25	1½ to 2 ft.	25	2 50	
			3 to 4 ft.	50	5 00	
Morus alba. White Mulberry	1 ft.	25	2 to 3 ft.	25	2 50	20 00
			4 to 5 ft.	50	5 00	40 00
alba pendula. Teas' Weeping Mulberry			6 to 8 ft.	2 00		
alba tatarica. Russian Mulberry	1 ft.	25	2 to 3 ft.	25	2 50	20 00
			4 to 5 ft.	50	5 00	40 00
rubra. Red Mulberry	1 ft.	25	2 to 3 ft.	25	2 50	
			4 to 5 ft.	50	5 00	
Nyssa aquatica. Cotton Gum	1 ft.	25	1½ to 2 ft.	25	2 50	
			3 to 4 ft.	50	5 00	
sylvatica. Tupelo, or Sour Gum	1 ft.	25	1½ to 2 ft.	25	2 50	
			3 to 4 ft.	50	5 00	
Ostrya virginiana. Hop Hornbeam, or Ironwood	1 ft.	25	1½ to 2 ft.	25	2 50	
			3 to 4 ft.	50	5 00	
Oxydendron arboreum. Sourwood	1 ft.	25	1½ to 2 ft.	25	2 50	20 00
			3 to 4 ft.	50	5 00	40 00
			5 to 6 ft.	75	7 50	60 00
Parrotia persica. Persian Ironwood	1 ft.	75	1½ to 2 ft.	75	7 50	
			2 to 3 ft.	1 00		
Paulownia imperialis. Empress Tree	1 ft.	25	2 to 3 ft.	25	2 50	20 00
			4 to 5 ft.	50	5 00	40 00
			6 to 8 ft.	1 00	10 00	
Persica vulgaris alba plena. Double White-flowered Peach	1 ft.	50	3 to 4 ft.	50	5 00	
vulgaris rosea plena. Double Rose-flowered Peach	1 ft.	50	3 to 4 ft.	50	5 00	
Phellodendron amurense. Chinese Cork Tree	1 ft.	50	2 to 3 ft.	50	5 00	
			4 to 5 ft.	75	7 50	
			6 to 8 ft.	1 00	10 00	
Platanus occidentalis. Buttonwood, or American Plane	1 ft.	25	2 to 3 ft.	25	2 50	20 00
			4 to 5 ft.	50	5 00	40 00
			6 to 8 ft.	75	7 50	60 00
orientalis. Oriental Plane	1 ft.	25	2 to 3 ft.	25	2 50	20 00
			4 to 5 ft.	50	5 00	40 00
			6 to 8 ft.	75	7 50	60 00
Populus alba. White Poplar, or Abele	1 ft.	25	2 to 3 ft.	25	2 50	20 00
			4 to 5 ft.	50	5 00	40 00
			6 to 8 ft.	75	7 50	60 00
alba bolleana. Bolle's Silver Poplar	1 ft.	25	2 to 3 ft.	25	2 50	20 00
			4 to 5 ft.	50	5 00	40 00
			6 to 8 ft.	75	7 50	60 00
alba nivea. Silver Poplar	1 ft.	25	2 to 3 ft.	25	2 50	20 00
			4 to 5 ft.	50	5 00	40 00
			6 to 8 ft.	75	7 50	60 00
balsamifera. Balsam Poplar	1 ft.	25	2 to 3 ft.	25	2 50	20 00
			4 to 5 ft.	50	5 00	40 00
			6 to 8 ft.	75	7 50	60 00
candicans. Balm of Gilead	1 ft.	25	2 to 3 ft.	25	2 50	20 00
			4 to 5 ft.	50	5 00	40 00
			6 to 8 ft.	75	7 50	60 00

DECIDUOUS TREES, continued

Botanical and Common Names	Mailing size postpaid Size	Each	Express and freight sizes purchaser paying transportation Size	Each	Doz.	100
Populus carolinensis. Carolina Poplar	1 ft.	$ 25	2 to 3 ft.	$0 25	$02 50	$20 00
			4 to 5 ft.	50	5 00	40 00
			6 to 8 ft.	75	7 50	60 00
deltoidea. Cottonwood	1 ft.	25	2 to 3 ft.	25	2 50	20 00
			4 to 5 ft.	50	5 00	40 00
			6 to 8 ft.	75	7 50	60 00
deltoidea vangeerti. Van Geert's Golden Poplar	1 ft.	25	2 to 3 ft.	25	2 50	20 00
			4 to 5 ft.	50	5 00	40 00
			6 to 8 ft.	75	7 50	60 00
grandidentata. Large-toothed Aspen	1 ft.	25	2 to 3 ft.	25	2 50	20 00
			4 to 5 ft.	50	5 00	40 00
			6 to 8 ft.	75	7 50	60 00
nigra fastigiata. Lombardy Poplar	1 ft.	25	2 to 3 ft.	25	2 50	20 00
			4 to 5 ft.	50	5 00	40 00
			6 to 8 ft.	75	7 50	60 00
tremula. European Aspen	1 ft.	25	2 to 3 ft.	25	2 50	20 00
			4 to 5 ft.	50	5 00	40 00
			6 to 8 ft.	75	7 50	60 00
tremula pendula. Weeping European Aspen			8 ft.	2 00		
tremuloides. American Aspen	1 ft.	25	2 to 3 ft.	25	2 50	20 00
			4 to 5 ft.	50	5 00	40 00
			6 to 8 ft.	75	7 50	60 00
Prunus americana. Wild Plum	1 ft.	25	2 to 3 ft.	25	2 50	20 00
			4 to 5 ft.	50	5 00	40 00
pissardi. Purple-leaved Plum	1 ft.	25	2 to 3 ft.	25	2 50	20 00
			3 to 4 ft.	50	5 00	40 00
Ptelea trifoliata. Hop-Tree, or Wafer Ash	1 ft.	25	2 to 3 ft.	25	2 50	20 00
			4 to 5 ft.	50	5 00	40 00
trifoliata aurea. Golden Hop-Tree	1 ft.	25	2 to 3 ft.	25	2 50	20 00
			4 to 5 ft.	50	5 00	40 00
Pterocarya fraxinifolia. False Walnut	1 ft.	50	1½ to 2 ft.	50	5 00	
			3 to 4 ft.	1 00	10 00	
Pterostyrax hispida (*Halesia hispida*). Japanese Silver Bell	1 ft.	50	2 to 3 ft.	50	5 00	
			4 to 5 ft.	1 00		
Quercus alba. White Oak	1 ft.	25	2 to 3 ft.	25	2 50	20 00
			4 to 5 ft.	1 00	10 00	80 00
			6 to 8 ft.	1 50	15 00	
cerris. Turkey Oak	1 ft.	25	2 to 3 ft.	25	2 50	20 00
			4 to 5 ft.	75	7 50	60 00
			6 to 8 ft.	1 00	10 00	80 00
coccinea. Scarlet Oak	1 ft.	25	2 to 3 ft.	25	2 50	20 00
			4 to 5 ft.	75	7 50	60 00
			6 to 8 ft.	1 50	15 00	
digitata (*Q. falcata*). Spanish Oak	1 ft.	25	2 to 3 ft.	25	2 50	
			4 to 5 ft.	1 00	10 00	
imbricaria. Shingle Oak	1 ft.	25	2 to 3 ft.	25	2 50	
			4 to 5 ft.	1 00	10 00	
lyrata. Overcup Oak	1 ft.	25	2 to 3 ft.	25	2 50	
			4 to 5 ft.	1 00	10 00	
michauxi. Basket Oak	1 ft.	25	2 to 3 ft.	25	2 50	
			4 to 5 ft.	1 00	10 00	
macrocarpa. Bur, or Mossy Cup Oak	1 ft.	25	2 to 3 ft.	25	2 50	
			5 to 6 ft.	1 00	10 00	
nigra (*Q. aquatica*). Water Oak	1 ft.	25	2 to 3 ft.	25	2 50	
palustris. Pin Oak	1 ft.	25	2 to 3 ft.	25	2 50	20 00
			4 to 5 ft.	75	7 50	60 00
			6 to 8 ft.	1 00	10 00	80 00
pedunculata (*Q. robur*). English Oak	1 ft.	25	2 to 3 ft.	25	2 50	20 00
			4 to 5 ft.	75	7 50	60 00
			6 to 8 ft.	1 00	10 00	80 00
pedunculata concordia. Golden Oak			6 to 8 ft.	2 00		
pedunculata fastigiata. Pyramidal English Oak	1 ft.	25	2 to 3 ft.	25	2 50	20 00
			4 to 5 ft.	1 00	10 00	80 00
			6 to 8 ft.	1 50	15 00	
pedunculata pendula. Dauvesse's Weeping Oak			6 to 8 ft.	2 00		
phellos. Willow Oak	1 ft.	25	2 to 3 ft.	25	2 50	20 00
			4 to 5 ft.	1 00	10 00	80 00
			6 to 8 ft.	1 50	15 00	
platanoides (*Q. bicolor*). Swamp White Oak	1 ft.	25	2 to 3 ft.	25	2 50	
			4 to 5 ft.	1 00	10 00	
			6 to 8 ft.	1 50	15 00	
prinus. Chestnut Oak	1 ft.	25	2 to 3 ft.	25	2 50	20 00
			4 to 5 ft.	75	7 50	
			6 to 8 ft.	1 00	10 00	

DECIDUOUS TREES, continued

Botanical and Common Names	Mailing size postpaid: Size	Each	Express and freight sizes, purchaser paying transportation: Size	Each	Doz.	100
Quercus rubra. Red Oak	1 ft.	$0 25	2 to 3 ft.	$0 25	$2 50	$20 00
			4 to 5 ft.	75	7 50	60 00
			6 to 8 ft.	1 25	12 50	100 00
velutina. Black Oak	1 ft.	25	2 to 3 ft.	25	2 50	20 00
			4 to 5 ft.	1 00	10 00	
			6 to 8 ft.	1 50	15 00	
Rhamnus caroliniana. Carolina Buckthorn	1 ft.	25	2 to 3 ft.	25	2 50	20 00
			3 to 4 ft.	50	5 00	40 00
			5 to 6 ft.	75	7 50	
purshiana. Coffee-berry	1 ft.	50	1½ to 2 ft.	50	5 00	
			3 to 4 ft.	75		
Rhus copallina. Upland Sumac	1 ft.	25	1½ to 2 ft.	25	2 50	20 00
			2 to 3 ft.	35	3 50	25 00
cotinoides. Chittam-wood	1 ft.	50	2 to 3 ft.	50	5 00	
			3 to 4 ft.	75	7 50	
cotinus. Smoke Tree	1 ft.	25	2 to 3 ft.	25	2 50	20 00
			3 to 4 ft.	50	5 00	40 00
glabra. Smooth Sumac	1 ft.	25	2 to 3 ft.	25	2 50	20 00
			4 to 5 ft.	35	3 50	25 00
glabra laciniata. Cut-leaved Sumac	1 ft.	25	2 to 3 ft.	25	2 50	20 00
			4 to 5 ft.	50	5 00	40 00
hirta. Staghorn Sumac	1 ft.	25	2 to 3 ft.	25	2 50	20 00
			4 to 5 ft.	35	3 50	25 00
semialata (*R. osbecki*). Japanese Sumac	1 ft.	25	2 to 3 ft.	25	2 50	
			4 to 5 ft.	50	5 00	
Robinia neo-mexicana. Western Locust	1 ft.	25	2 to 3 ft.	25	2 50	
			4 to 5 ft.	50	5 00	
pseudacacia. Black Locust	1 ft.	25	2 to 3 ft.	25	2 50	
			4 to 5 ft.	35	3 50	
			6 to 8 ft.	50	5 00	
viscosa. Clammy Locust	1 ft.	25	2 to 3 ft.	25	2 50	
			4 to 5 ft.	50	5 00	
Salix alba (*S. regalis*). White Willow	1 ft.	25	2 to 3 ft.	25	2 50	20 00
			4 to 5 ft.	50	5 00	40 00
			6 to 8 ft.	75	7 50	60 00
amygdaloides. Peach-leaved Willow	1 ft.	25	2 to 3 ft.	25	2 50	
			4 to 5 ft.	50	5 00	
babylonica. Weeping Willow	1 ft.	25	2 to 3 ft.	25	2 50	20 00
			4 to 5 ft.	50	5 00	40 00
			6 to 8 ft.	75	7 50	60 00
babylonica annularis. Ring-leaved Willow	1 ft.	25	2 to 3 ft.	25	2 50	
			4 to 5 ft.	50	5 00	
			6 to 8 ft.	75	7 50	
babylonica dolorosa. Wisconsin Weeping Willow	1 ft.	25	2 to 3 ft.	25	2 50	20 00
			4 to 5 ft.	50	5 00	40 00
			6 to 8 ft.	75	7 50	60 00
caprea. Goat, or Pussy Willow	1 ft.	25	2 to 3 ft.	25	2 50	20 00
			4 to 5 ft.	50	5 00	40 00
			6 to 8 ft.	75	7 50	60 00
caprea pendula. Kilmarnock Weeping Willow			6 to 8 ft.	1 50	15 00	
elegantissima. Thurlow's Weeping Willow	1 ft.	25	2 to 3 ft.	25	2 50	
			4 to 5 ft.	50	5 00	
			6 to 8 ft.	75	7 50	
fragilis. Brittle Willow	1 ft.	25	2 to 3 ft.	25	2 50	
			4 to 5 ft.	50	5 00	
			6 to 8 ft.	75	7 50	
incana (*S. rosmarinifolia*). Rosemary Willow	1 ft.	25	2 to 3 ft.	25	2 50	
			4 to 5 ft.	50	5 00	
lucida. Shining Willow	1 ft.	25	2 to 3 ft.	25	2 50	
			4 to 5 ft.	50	5 00	
nigra. Black Willow	1 ft.	25	2 to 3 ft.	25	2 50	
			4 to 5 ft.	50	5 00	
pentandra. Bay, or Laurel-leaved Willow	1 ft.	25	2 to 3 ft.	25	2 50	
			4 to 5 ft.	50	5 00	
purpurea. Purple Osier	1 ft.	25	2 to 3 ft.	25	2 50	
			4 to 5 ft.	50	5 00	
vitellina. Yellow Willow	1 ft.	25	2 to 3 ft.	25	2 50	20 00
			4 to 5 ft.	50	5 00	40 00
			6 to 8 ft.	75	7 50	60 00
vitellina aurea. Golden-barked Willow	1 ft.	25	2 to 3 ft.	25	2 50	20 00
			4 to 5 ft.	50	5 00	40 00
			6 to 8 ft.	75	7 50	60 00
vitellina britzensis. Bronze-barked Willow	1 ft.	25	2 to 3 ft.	25	2 50	20 00
			4 to 5 ft.	50	5 00	40 00
			6 to 8 ft.	75	7 50	60 00

DECIDUOUS TREES, continued

Botanical and Common Names	Mailing size, postpaid: Size	Each	Express and freight sizes, purchaser paying transportation: Size	Each	Doz.	100
Sassafras officinalis. Sassafras	1 ft.	$0 25	1½ to 2 ft.	$0 25	$2 50	
			3 to 4 ft.	50	5 00	
Sophora japonica. Japanese Sophora	1 ft.	75	1½ to 2 ft.	75	7 50	
			3 to 4 ft.	1 25	12 50	
			4 to 5 ft.	1 50	15 00	
			6 to 8 ft.	2 00		
japonica pendula. Weeping Sophora			6 to 8 ft.	2 50		
Sorbus americana. American Mountain Ash	1 ft.	25	2 to 3 ft.	25	2 50	
			4 to 5 ft.	50	5 00	
aria. White Beam Tree	1 ft.	50	2 to 3 ft.	50	5 00	
			4 to 5 ft.	75		
aucuparia. European Mountain Ash, or Rowan Tree	1 ft.	25	2 to 3 ft.	25	2 50	
			4 to 5 ft.	5c	5 00	
			6 to 8 ft.	75	7 50	
aucuparia pendula. Weeping Mountain Ash			6 to 8 ft.	1 25	12 50	
Sterculia platanifolia. Chinese, or Japanese Parasol Tree	1 ft.	25	2 to 3 ft.	25	2 50	
			4 to 5 ft.	50	5 00	
			6 to 8 ft.	75	7 50	
Syringa japonica. Japanese Lilac	1 ft.	25	2 to 3 ft.	25	2 50	
			3 to 4 ft.	50	5 00	
Tilia americana. American Linden, or Basswood	1 ft.	25	2 to 3 ft.	25	2 50	$20 00
			4 to 5 ft.	50	5 00	40 00
			6 to 8 ft.	75	7 50	60 00
dasystyla. Crimean Linden	1 ft.	25	2 to 3 ft.	25	2 50	20 00
			4 to 5 ft.	50	5 00	40 00
			6 to 8 ft.	75	7 50	60 00
europæa. European Linden, or Lime Tree	1 ft.	25	2 to 3 ft.	25	2 50	20 00
			4 to 5 ft.	50	5 00	40 00
			6 to 8 ft.	75	7 50	60 00
heterophylla. White Basswood	1 ft.	25	2 to 3 ft.	25	2 50	20 00
			4 to 5 ft.	50	5 00	40 00
			6 to 8 ft.	75	7 50	60 00
petiolaris (*T. argentea pendula*). Weeping Linden			6 to 8 ft.	2 00		
platyphyllos. Large-leaved Linden	1 ft.	25	2 to 3 ft.	25	2 50	20 00
			4 to 5 ft.	50	5 00	40 00
			6 to 8 ft.	75	7 50	60 00
tomentosa (*T. alba* and *T. argentea*). White, or Silver Linden	1 ft.	25	2 to 3 ft.	25	2 50	20 00
			4 to 5 ft.	50	5 00	40 00
			6 to 8 ft.	75	7 50	60 00
Toxylon pomiferum (*Maclura aurantiaca*). Osage Orange	1 ft.	25	2 to 3 ft.	25	2 50	20 00
			4 to 5 ft.	35	3 50	25 00
Ulmus alata. Wahoo, or Winged Elm	1 ft.	25	2 to 3 ft.	25	2 50	
			4 to 5 ft.	50	5 00	
			6 to 8 ft.	75	7 50	
americana. American Elm	1 ft.	25	2 to 3 ft.	25	2 50	20 00
			4 to 5 ft.	50	5 00	40 00
			6 to 8 ft.	75	7 50	60 00
campestris. English Elm	1 ft.	25	2 to 3 ft.	25	2 50	20 00
			4 to 5 ft.	50	5 00	40 00
			6 to 8 ft.	75	7 50	60 00
campestris corylifolia purpurea. Purple-leaved English Elm	1 ft.	50	2 to 3 ft.	50	5 00	
			3 to 5 ft.	75	7 50	
			6 to 8 ft.	1 25	12 50	
campestris major (*U. latifolia*). Broad-leaved English Elm	1 ft.	25	2 to 3 ft.	25	2 50	20 00
			4 to 5 ft.	50	5 00	40 00
			6 to 8 ft.	75	7 50	60 00
scabra (*U. montana*). Scotch, or Wych Elm	1 ft.	25	2 to 3 ft.	25	2 50	
			4 to 5 ft.	50	5 00	
			6 to 8 ft.	75	7 50	
scabra pendula. Camperdown Weeping Elm			6 to 8 ft.	2 00		
Viburnum lentago. Sheepberry, or Nannyberry	1 ft.	25	2 to 3 ft.	25	2 50	20 00
			3 to 4 ft.	50	5 00	40 00
prunifolium. Black Haw, or Stag Bush	1 ft.	25	2 to 3 ft.	25	2 50	20 00
			3 to 4 ft.	50	5 00	40 00
rufidulum. Southern Black Haw	1 ft.	25	2 to 3 ft.	25	2 50	
			3 to 4 ft.	50	5 00	
Vitex agnus-castus. Chaste Tree	1 ft.	25	2 to 3 ft.	25	2 50	
			3 to 4 ft.	50	5 00	
Xanthocerus sorbifolia. Chinese Flowering Chestnut	1 ft.	25	2 to 3 ft.	25	2 50	
			3 to 4 ft.	50	5 00	
Xanthoxylum americanum. Prickly Ash	1 ft.	25	2 to 3 ft.	25	2 50	
			3 to 4 ft.	50	5 00	
piperitum. Chinese, or Japanese Pepper Tree	1 ft.	25	2 to 3 ft.	25	2 50	
			3 to 4 ft.	50	5 00	

Broad-Leaved Evergreen Trees

Botanical and Common Names	Mailing size, postpaid: Size	Mailing size, postpaid: Each	Express and freight sizes, purchaser paying transportation: Size	Each	Doz.	100
Buxus arborescens. Tree Box	1 ft.	$0 50	1½ ft.	$0 50	$5 00	$40 00
			2 ft.	1 00	10 00	80 00
			3 ft.	2 00	20 00	
Eriobotrya japonica. Loquat, or Japanese Medlar	1 ft.	1 00	1½ to 2 ft.	1 00		
Ilex aquifolium. English, or European Holly	1 ft.	50	1½ ft.	50	5 00	
			2½ to 3 ft.	1 00	10 00	
aquifolium aurea-regina. Variegated Holly	1 ft.	1 00	1½ ft.	1 00		
			2 to 2½ ft.	2 00		
aquifolium ferox. Hedgehog Holly	1 ft.	1 00	1½ ft.	1 00		
			2 to 2½ ft.	2 00		
aquifolium laurifolia. Entire-leaved Holly	1 ft.	1 00	1½ ft.	1 00		
			2 to 2½ ft.	2 00		
aquifolium myrtifolia. Myrtle-leaved Holly	1 ft.	1 00	1½ ft.	1 00		
			2 to 2½ ft.	2 00		
cornuta. Chinese Holly	1 ft.	1 00	1½ ft.	1 00		
			2 ft.	2 00		
crenata. Japanese Holly	1 ft.	50	1½ ft.	50	5 00	40 00
			2 ft.	1 00	10 00	80 00
opaca. American Holly	1 ft.	50	1½ to 2 ft.	50	5 00	40 00
			2 to 3 ft.	1 00	10 00	80 00
vomitoria. Cassena, or Yaupon	1 ft.	50	1½ ft.	50	5 00	
			2 ft.	1 00		
Laurocerasus caroliniana (*Prunus caroliniana*). Wild Orange	1 ft.	50	1½ ft.	50		
			2 to 3 ft.	1 00		
laurocerasus. English, or Cherry Laurel	1 ft.	75	1½ ft.	75		
			2 to 3 ft.	1 50		
laurocerasus schipkanensis. Hardy English Laurel	1 ft.	1 00	1½ ft.	1 00		
			2 to 3 ft.	2 00		
lusitanica. Portugal Laurel	1 ft.	75	1½ ft.	75		
			2 to 3 ft.	1 50		
Laurus nobilis. Bay Tree	1 ft.	25				
Pyramids in tubs, 28 inches in diameter at base			5 ft.	10 00	100 00	
" " " 32 " " " " "			6 ft.	12 50	125 00	
" " " 34 " " " " "			6 ft.	15 00	150 00	
" " " 40 " " " " "			7 ft.	20 00	200 00	
Standards in tubs 28 inch crown, stems 45 inches			6 ft.	10 00	100 00	
" " " 32 " " " 45 "			6½ ft.	12 50	125 00	
" " " 36 " " " 45 "			6½ ft.	15 00	150 00	
" " " 40 " " " 45 "			7 ft.	20 00	200 00	
Magnolia glauca. Sweet, or White Bay	1 ft.	50	1½ to 2 ft.	50	5 00	
			3 to 4 ft.	1 00	10 00	
grandiflora. Southern Magnolia	1 ft.	75	1½ to 2 ft.	75	7 50	
			2½ to 3 ft.	1 00	10 00	
			4 to 5 ft.	2 00	20 00	
grandiflora exoniensis. Exmouth Magnolia	1 ft.	1 25	1½ to 2 ft.	1 25		
			2½ to 3 ft.	2 50		
grandiflora galissoniensis. Galisson Magnolia	1 ft.	1 25	1½ to 2 ft.	1 25		
			2½ to 3 ft.	2 50		
grandiflora gloriosa. Large-flowered Magnolia	1 ft.	1 50	1½ to 2 ft.	1 50		
			2½ to 3 ft.	3 00		
thompsoniana. Thompson's Sweet Bay	1 ft.	75	1½ to 2 ft.	75	7 50	
			2 to 3 ft.	1 25	12 50	

Broad-Leaved Evergreen Shrubs

Botanical and Common Names	Mailing size, postpaid: Size	Each	Express and freight sizes, purchaser paying transportation: Size	Each	Doz.	100
Abelia floribunda. Mexican Abelia	1 ft.	$0 50	1½ ft.	$0 50	$5 00	
			2 to 2½ ft.	75	7 50	
grandiflora (*A. rupestris*). Hybrid Abelia	1 ft.	25	1½ ft.	25	2 50	$20 00
			2 to 3 ft.	50	5 00	40 00
Andromeda polifolia. Wild Rosemary	1 ft.	25	1½ ft.	25	2 50	
			2 ft.	50	5 00	
Aucuba japonica. Japanese Laurel	1 ft.	50	1½ ft.	50	5 00	
			2 ft.	75	7 50	
japonica aureo-maculata. Gold-dust Laurel	1 ft.	50	1½ ft.	50	5 00	
			2 ft.	75	7 50	
Azalea amœna. Hardy Evergreen Azalea	10 ins.	60	12 to 15 ins.	60	6 00	50 00
			15 to 18 ins.	1 00	10 00	80 00
indica. Indian Azalea	10 ins.	60	12 to 15 ins.	60	6 00	50 00
			15 to 18 ins.	1 00	10 00	80 00
Any of the following forms of Indian Azaleas, with crowns 36 to 45 inches in circumference				1 50		
Apollo Bernard Andre Comtesse de Beaufort Deutsche Perle Dr. Moore Le Flambeau Mme. Van der Cruyssen Theo. Reimers Vervæneana						
Berberis aquifolium (*Mahonia aquifolium*). Oregon Grape, or Mahonia	1 ft.	50	1½ to 2 ft.	50	5 00	40 00
			2 to 3 ft.	75	7 50	60 00
buxifolia (*B. dulcis*). Box-leaved Barberry	10 ins.	50	12 to 15 ins.	50	5 00	40 00
congestiflora. Chilian Barberry	1 ft.	50	1½ to 2 ft.	50	5 00	
			2 to 3 ft.	75	7 50	
darwini. Darwin's Barberry	1 ft.	50	1½ to 2 ft.	50	5 00	
fascicularis. Fascicled Barberry	1 ft.	50	1½ to 2 ft.	50	5 00	
fortunei. Fortune's Mahonia	1 ft.	75	1½ ft.	75	7 50	
			2 to 3 ft.	1 25	12 50	
ilicifolia. Holly-leaved Barberry	1 ft.	50	1½ ft.	50	5 00	
			2 to 3 ft.	75	7 50	
japonica (*Mahonia japonica*). Japanese Mahonia	1 ft.	50	1½ ft.	50	5 00	40 00
			2 to 3 ft.	1 00	10 00	80 00
nepalensis. Nepaulese Mahonia	1 ft.	75	1½ ft.	75	7 50	
			2 to 3 ft.	1 25	12 50	
newberti. Newbert's Barberry	1 ft.	50	1½ to 2 ft.	50	5 00	
			2 to 3 ft.	75	7 50	
repens (*Mahonia repens*). Creeping Mahonia	1 ft.	50	1½ ft.	50	5 00	
stenophylla. Small-leaved Barberry	1 ft.	50	1½ ft.	50	5 00	
			2 to 3 ft.	75	7 50	
Buxus sempervirens. Boxwood. Bushes	1 ft.	50	1½ ft.	50	5 00	40 00
			2 ft.	1 00	10 00	80 00
			3 ft.	2 50	25 00	200 00
			4 ft.	4 00	40 00	
sempervirens, Pyramids	1 ft.	1 00	1½ ft.	1 00	10 00	80 00
			2 ft.	1 50	15 00	120 00
			3 ft.	2 50	25 00	200 00
			4 ft.	4 00	40 00	
sempervirens, Standards. Crowns 18 ins. in diam., stems 2 to 2½ ft.			3½ to 4 ft.	2 50	25 00	
Crowns 24 ins. in diam., stems 2½ to 3 ft.			4 to 4½ ft.	5 00	50 00	
sempervirens handsworthi. Handsworth's Box	1 ft.	75	1½ ft.	75	7 50	
			2 ft.	1 50	15 00	
suffruticosa. Dwarf Box. (4 to 6 ins., per 1,000, $45)	6 to 8 ins.	15	4 to 6 ins.		60	5 00
(6 to 8 ins., per 1,000, $90)			6 to 8 ins.	15	1 50	10 00
Calluna vulgaris. Scotch Heather	6 to 8 ins.	25	1 ft.	25	2 50	20 00
			1½ ft.	50	5 00	40 00
vulgaris alba. White-flowered Scotch Heather	6 to 8 ins.	25	1 ft.	25	2 50	20 00
			1½ ft.	50	5 00	40 00

BROAD-LEAVED EVERGREEN SHRUBS, continued

Botanical and Common Names	Mailing size, postpaid: Size	Each	Express and freight sizes, purchaser paying transportation: Size	Each	Doz.	100
Camellia japonica. Camellia	1 ft.	$0 75	15 to 18 ins.	$0 75	$7 50	
			20 to 24 ins.	1 50	15 00	
Named varieties						
thea (*Thea bohea* and *T. viridis*). Tea Plant	10 ins.	25	1 ft.	25	2 50	
Chamaedaphne calyculata (*Cassandra calyculata*). Leather-leaf	1 ft.	25	1½ ft.	25	2 50	$20 00
			2 ft.	50	5 00	40 00
Cleyera japonica. Japanese Cleyera	10 ins.	25	1 ft.	25	2 50	
Cotoneaster buxifolia. Box-leaved Cotoneaster	10 ins.	25	1 ft.	25	2 50	20 00
			1½ ft.	50	5 00	40 00
horizontalis. Prostrate Cotoneaster	10 ins.	25	1 ft.	25	2 50	20 00
			1½ ft.	50	5 00	40 00
microphylla. Small-leaved Cotoneaster	10 ins.	25	1 ft.	25	2 50	20 00
			1½ ft.	50	5 00	40 00
simoni. Shining-leaved Rose Box	10 ins.	25	1 ft.	25	2 50	20 00
			1½ ft.	50	5 00	40 00
thymifolia. Thyme-leaved Cotoneaster	10 ins.	25	1 ft.	25	2 50	20 00
			1½ ft.	50	5 00	40 00
Daphne blagayana. White Garland Flower	6 ins.	1 00	8 to 10 ins.	1 00	10 00	
			12 to 15 ins.	1 50	15 00	
cneorum. Garland Flower	8 to 10 ins.	50	10 ins.	50	5 00	40 00
			12 to 15 ins.	1 00	10 00	80 00
hybrida (*D. dauphini*). Hybrid Garland Flower	2 yrs.	1 00	3 yrs.	1 00	10 00	
laureola. Spurge Laurel	2 yrs.	75	3 yrs.	75	7 50	
Dendrium buxifolium (*Leiophyllum buxifolium*). Sand Myrtle	6 to 8 ins.	25	10 to 12 ins.	25	2 50	20 00
			12 to 15 ins.	50	5 00	40 00
Elaeagnus macrophylla. Broad-leaved Oleaster	1 ft.	50	1½ ft.	50	5 00	
			2 to 3 ft.	1 00	10 00	
reflexa (*E. pungens*). Bronze Oleaster	1 ft.	50	1½ ft.	50	5 00	
			2 to 3 ft.	1 00	10 00	
reflexa variegata. Variegated Oleaster	1 ft.	50	1½ ft.	50	5 00	
			2 to 3 ft.	1 00	10 00	
Ephedra distachya. Two-spiked Ephedra	8 to 10 ins.	50	1 ft.	50	5 00	
			1½ ft.	1 00	10 00	
Erica carnea. Moor Heath	2 yrs.	25	3 yrs.	25	2 50	20 00
			4 yrs.	50	5 00	40 00
stricta. Corsican Heath	2 yrs.	25	3 yrs.	25	2 50	
			4 yrs.	50	5 00	
tetralix. Cross-leaved Heath	2 yrs.	25	3 yrs.	25	2 50	
			4 yrs.	50	5 00	
vagans. Cornish Heath	2 yrs.	25	3 yrs.	25	2 50	20 00
			4 yrs.	50	5 00	40 00
Euonymus japonicus. Evergreen Euonymus	1 ft.	25	1½ ft.	25	2 50	20 00
			2 to 2½ ft.	50	5 00	40 00
japonicus aureo-variegatus. Variegated Euonymus	1 ft.	50	15 to 18 ins.	50	5 00	
			1½ to 2 ft.	75	7 50	
japonicus microphyllus (*E. pulchellus*). Small-leaved Euonymus	6 to 8 ins.	25	10 to 12 ins.	25	2 50	20 00
			12 to 15 ins.	35	3 50	25 00
Gardenia jasminoides (*G. florida*). Cape Jasmine	10 to 12 ins.	25	12 to 15 ins.	25	2 50	20 00
			1½ to 2 ft.	50	5 00	
jasminoides fortunei. Large-flowered Cape Jasmine	10 to 12 ins.	25	12 to 15 ins.	25	2 50	20 00
			1½ to 2 ft.	50	5 00	
Ilex glabra. Inkberry, or Winterberry	10 to 12 ins.	25	12 to 15 ins.	25	2 50	20 00
			1½ to 2 ft.	50	5 00	
Illicium anisatum (*I. religiosum*). Anise Tree	10 to 12 ins.	25	12 to 15 ins.	25	2 50	
			1½ ft.	50	5 00	
Kalmia angustifolia. Narrow-leaved Laurel	8 to 10 ins.	25	1 ft.	25	2 50	
			1½ ft.	50	5 00	
latifolia. Mountain Laurel, or Calico Bush	8 to 10 ins.	50	12 ins.	50	5 00	40 00
			15 to 18 ins.	75	7 50	60 00
			2 to 2½ ft.	1 00	10 00	80 00
			2½ to 3 ft.	2 00	20 00	150 00
Leucothoë acuminata. Pipe-wood	8 to 10 ins.	50	1 ft.	50	5 00	
catesbæi. Catesby's Leucothoë	8 to 10 ins.	25	1 ft.	25	2 50	20 00
			1½ ft.	35	3 50	25 00
Ligustrum japonicum. Japanese Privet	10 to 12 ins.	25	1 to 1½ ft.	25	2 50	20 00
			2 to 3 ft.	50	5 00	
quihoui. Late-flowering Privet	1 ft.	25	1½ to 2 ft.	25	2 50	20 00
			3 to 4 ft.	50	5 00	40 00
sinense. Chinese Privet	1 ft.	25	1½ to 2 ft.	25	2 50	20 00
			3 to 4 ft.	50	5 00	40 00

BROAD-LEAVED EVERGREEN SHRUBS, continued

Botanical and Common Names	Mailing size, postpaid: Size	Mailing size, postpaid: Each	Express and freight sizes, purchaser paying transportation: Size	Each	Doz.	100
Myrtus communis. True Myrtle	2 yrs.	$0 25	3 yrs.	$0 25	$2 50	
Nandina domestica. Japanese Nandina	1 ft.	50	1½ to 2 ft.	50	5 00	
			2½ to 3 ft.	75	7 50	
Nerium oleander. Oleander	10 to 12 ins.	25	1 to 1½ ft.	25	2 50	
Osmanthus aquifolium. Holly-leaved Olive	1 ft.	50	1 to 1½ ft.	50	5 00	
fragrans. Fragrant Olive	1 ft.	50	1 to 1½ ft.	50	5 00	
Phillyrea angustifolia. Narrow-leaved Filaria	1 ft.	50	1 to 1½ ft.	50	5 00	
			2 to 3 ft.	75	7 50	
decora (*P. vilmoriniana*). Broad-leaved Filaria	1 ft.	50	1 to 1½ ft.	50	5 00	
			1½ to 2 ft.	1 00	10 00	
Photinia serrulata. Evergreen Photinia	1 ft.	50	1 to 1½ ft.	50	5 00	
Pieris floribunda (*Andromeda floribunda*). Mountain Fetter Bush	6 to 8 ins.	1 00	12 ins.	1 00	10 00	
			15 ins.	1 25	12 50	
			18 ins.	1 75	17 50	
			24 ins.	2 50	25 00	
japonica (*Andromeda japonica*). Japanese Fetter Bush	6 to 8 ins.	75	12 ins.	75	7 50	
			15 ins.	1 00	10 00	
			18 ins.	1 50	15 00	
			24 ins.	2 00	20 00	
Pittosporum tobira. Tobira, or Japanese Pittosporum	10 to 12 ins.	50	1 to 1½ ft.	50	5 00	
Pyracantha coccinea (*Cratægus pyracantha*). Evergreen, or Pyracantha Thorn	8 to 10 ins.	25	1 ft.	25	2 50	$20 00
			1½ ft.	50	5 00	
coccinea lalandi. Laland's Pyracantha	1 ft.	50	1 to 1½ ft.	50	5 00	
			2 ft.	75	7 50	
Rhododendron arbutifolium (*R. wilsonianum*). Dwarf Rhododendron	6 to 8 ins.	1 00	10 to 12 ins.	1 00	10 00	80 00
			12 to 15 ins.	1 25	12 50	100 00
			1½ ft.	1 50	15 00	
catawbiense. Catawba Rhododendron	10 to 12 ins.	1 00	1 to 1½ ft.	1 00	10 00	80 00
			1½ to 2 ft.	1 50	15 00	120 00
			2 to 2½ ft.	2 00	20 00	150 00
			2½ to 3 ft.	2 50	25 00	200 00
catawbiense hybrids. Catawba Hybrid Rhododendrons. Any of the following varieties			1½ to 2 ft.	2 00	20 00	
			2 to 2½ ft.	2 50	25 00	
Those marked * can be furnished in mailing size	10 to 12 ins.	1 00				

- *A. Lincoln
- *Album elegans
- *Album grandiflorum
- *Anna Parsons
- Atrosanguineum
- *Betsy Parsons
- Caractacus
- *Catawbiense album
- Charles Bagley
- Charles Dickens
- *Delicatissimum
- *Everestianum
- *General Grant
- Giganteum
- H. H. Hunnewell
- Lady Armstrong
- Lee's Purple
- *Parsons' gloriosum
- *Parsons' grandiflorum
- *President Lincoln
- *Purpureum elegans
- *Roseum elegans
- *Roseum superbum

Botanical and Common Names	Mailing size, postpaid: Size	Mailing size, postpaid: Each	Express and freight sizes, purchaser paying transportation: Size	Each	Doz.	100
maximum. Rose Bay, or Great Laurel	10 to 12 ins.	1 00	1 to 1½ ft.	1 00	10 00	80 00
			1½ to 2 ft.	1 25	12 50	100 00
			2 to 2½ ft.	1 50	15 00	120 00
			2½ to 3 ft.	1 75	17 50	140 00
			3 to 4 ft.	2 00	20 00	150 00
myrtifolium. Myrtle-leaved Rhododendron	6 to 8 ins.	1 00	10 to 12 ins.	1 00	10 00	80 00
			12 to 15 ins.	1 25	12 50	100 00
			1½ ft.	1 50	15 00	
punctatum. Small, or Early-flowering Rhododendron	10 to 12 ins.	1 00	12 to 15 ins.	1 00	10 00	80 00
			15 to 18 ins.	1 50	15 00	
			1½ to 2 ft.	1 75	17 50	
Viburnum sandankwa (*V. suspensa*). Evergreen Viburnum	10 to 12 ins.	25	12 to 15 ins.	25	2 50	
			1½ ft.	50	5 00	
tinus. Laurustinus	10 to 12 ins.	25	12 to 15 ins.	25	2 50	
			1½ ft.	50	5 00	

Deciduous Shrubs

Botanical and Common Names	Mailing size, postpaid: Size	Mailing size, postpaid: Each	Express and freight sizes, purchaser paying transportation: Size	Each	Doz.	100
Acanthopanax pentaphyllum (*Aralia pentaphylla*). Five-leaved Angelica	1 ft.	$0 25	1½ to 2 ft.	$0 25	$2 50	$20 00
			3 to 4 ft.	50	5 00	40 00
Adelia acuminata (*Forestiera acuminata*). Pointed-leaved Adelia	1 ft.	25	2 to 3 ft.	25	2 50	20 00
			4 to 5 ft.	50	5 00	40 00
ligustrina (*Forestiera ligustrina*). Privet-leaved Adelia	1 ft.	25	1½ to 2 ft.	25	2 50	
			2 to 3 ft.	50	5 00	
Æsculus parviflora (*Æ. macrostachya*). Dwarf Horse-chestnut	1 ft.	50	1½ to 2 ft.	50	5 00	
			2 to 3 ft.	75	7 50	
Alnus alnobetula (*A. viridis*). Green, or Mountain Alder	1 ft.	25	1½ to 2 ft.	25	2 50	
			2 to 3 ft.	50	5 00	
rugosa. Smooth Alder	1 ft.	25	2 to 3 ft.	25	2 50	
			4 to 5 ft.	50	5 00	
Amelanchier alnifolia. Alder-leaved, or Western Juneberry	1 ft.	25	1½ to 2 ft.	25	2 50	
			2 to 3 ft.	50	5 00	
rotundifolia. Round-leaved Juneberry	1 ft.	25	1½ to 2 ft.	25	2 50	
			2 to 3 ft.	50	5 00	
spicata. Dwarf Juneberry	1 ft.	25	1½ to 2 ft.	25	2 50	
			2 to 3 ft.	50	5 00	
vulgaris. European Serviceberry, or Juneberry	1 ft.	25	1½ to 2 ft.	25	2 50	
			2 to 3 ft.	50	5 00	
Amorpha canescens. Lead Plant	1 ft.	25	1½ ft.	25	2 50	
			2 to 3 ft.	50	5 00	
fruticosa. False Indigo	1 ft.	25	1½ to 2 ft.	25	2 50	20 00
			2 to 3 ft.	50	5 00	40 00
herbacea. Dwarf Indigo	1 ft.	25	1½ ft.	25	2 50	
			1½ to 2 ft.	50	5 00	
montana. Mountain Indigo	1 ft.	25	1½ ft.	25	2 50	
			2 to 3 ft.	50	5 00	
tennesseensis. Tennessee Indigo	1 ft.	25	1½ to 2 ft.	25	2 50	20 00
			3 to 4 ft.	50	5 00	40 00
Aronia arbutifolia (*Pyrus arbutifolia*). Red Chokeberry	1 ft.	25	1½ ft.	25	2 50	20 00
			2 to 3 ft.	35	3 50	25 00
			3 to 4 ft.	50	5 00	40 00
nigra (*Pyrus nigra*). Black Chokeberry	1 ft.	25	1½ ft.	25	2 50	20 00
			2 to 3 ft.	50	5 00	40 00
Azalea arborescens. Fragrant Azalea	10 to 12 ins.	75	12 to 15 ins.	75	7 50	60 00
			15 to 18 ins.	1 00	10 00	80 00
gandavensis Ghent Azalea	10 to 12 ins.	75	1 to 1½ ft.	75	7 50	60 00
			1½ to 2 ft.	1 00	10 00	80 00
Any of the following varieties of Azalea gandavensis			1 to 1½ ft.	1 00		
			1½ to 2 ft.	1 50		

Arethusa
Daviesi
Geant des Batailles
Guelder Roos
Louis Aime Van Houtte
Mina Van Houtte

Botanical and Common Names	Mailing Size	Mailing Each	Express Size	Each	Doz.	100
lutea (*A. calendulacea*). Flame-colored Azalea	10 to 12 ins.	75	12 to 15 ins.	75	7 50	60 00
			15 to 18 ins.	1 00	10 00	80 00
mollis. Japanese Azalea	10 to 12 ins.	75	1 to 1½ ft.	75	7 50	60 00
			1½ to 2 ft.	1 00	10 00	80 00
Any of the following named varieties of Azalea mollis			1 to 1½ ft.	1 00		
			1½ to 2 ft.	1 50		

Anthony Koster
Byron
Charles Rogier
Frederic de Merode
Murillo
Virgille

DECIDUOUS SHRUBS, contiuued

Botanical and Common Names	Mailing size, postpaid: Size	Each	Express and freight sizes, purchaser paying transportation: Size	Each	Doz.	100
Azalea nudiflora. Pinkster Flower	10 to 12 ins.	$0 75	12 to 15 ins.	$0 75	$7 50	$60 00
			15 to 18 ins.	1 00	10 00	80 00
vaseyi (*Rhododendron vaseyi*). Carolina Azalea	10 to 12 ins.	75	12 to 15 ins.	75	7 50	60 00
			15 to 18 ins.	1 00	10 00	80 00
viscosa. Small White Azalea	10 to 12 ins.	50	12 to 15 ins.	50	5 00	40 00
			15 to 18 ins.	75	7 50	60 00
Baccharis halimifolia. Groundsel Bush	1 ft.	25	1½ to 2 ft.	25	2 50	20 00
			2 to 3 ft.	50	5 00	40 00
Benzoin benzoin (*Lindera benzoin*). Spice Bush	1 ft.	25	1½ to 2 ft.	25	2 50	20 00
			2 to 3 ft.	50	5 00	40 00
Berberis canadensis. Canadian Barberry	1 ft.	25	1½ ft.	25	2 50	20 00
			2 to 3 ft.	50	5 00	40 00
heteropoda. Turkestan Barberry	1 ft.	25	1½ ft.	25	2 50	20 00
			2 to 3 ft.	50	5 00	40 00
thunbergi. Thunberg's Barberry	1 ft.	15	1½ ft.	15	1 50	10 00
			1½ to 2 ft.	25	2 50	20 00
			2 to 2½ ft.	35	3 50	25 00
			2½ to 3 ft.	50	5 00	40 00
vulgaris. Common European Barberry	1 ft.	15	1½ ft.	15	1 50	10 00
			1½ to 2 ft.	25	2 50	20 00
			2 to 3 ft.	35	3 50	25 00
			3 to 4 ft.	50	5 00	40 00
vulgaris atropurpurea. Purple-leaved Barberry	1 ft.	15	1½ ft.	15	1 50	10 00
			1½ to 2 ft.	25	2 50	20 00
			2 to 3 ft.	40	4 00	30 00
Buddleia intermedia. Hybrid Buddleia	1 ft.	25	1½ to 2 ft.	25	2 50	
			2 to 3 ft.	50	5 00	
japonica (*B. curviflora*). Japanese Buddleia	1 ft.	25	1½ to 2 ft.	25	2 50	
			2 to 3 ft.	50	5 00	
lindleyana. Chinese Buddleia	1 ft.	25	1½ to 2 ft.	25	2 50	
			2 to 3 ft.	50	5 00	
variabilis. Sweet-scented Buddleia	1 ft.	25	1½ to 2 ft.	25	2 50	
			2 to 3 ft.	50	5 00	
Butneria fertilis (*Calycanthus lævigatus* and *glaucus*). Carolina Allspice, or Sweet Shrub	1 ft.	15	1½ to 2 ft.	15	1 50	10 00
			2 to 3 ft.	25	2 50	20 00
			3 to 4 ft.	35	3 50	25 00
florida (*Calycanthus floridus*). Strawberry Shrub	1 ft.	15	1½ to 2 ft.	15	1 50	10 00
			2 to 3 ft.	25	2 50	20 00
occidentalis (*Calycanthus occidentalis*). Western Sweet Shrub	1 ft.	25	1½ to 2 ft.	25	2 50	
			2 to 3 ft.	50	5 00	
Callicarpa americana. French Mulberry	1 ft.	25	1½ to 2 ft.	25	2 50	
			2 to 3 ft.	50	5 00	
japonica. Japanese Callicarpa	1 ft.	25	1½ to 2 ft.	25	2 50	
			2 to 3 ft.	50	5 00	
purpurea. Purple-fruited Callicarpa, or Beauty Fruit	1 ft.	25	1½ to 2 ft.	25	2 50	
			2 to 3 ft.	50	5 00	
Caragana arborescens. Siberian Pea Shrub	1 ft.	25	1½ to 2 ft.	25	2 50	20 00
			2 to 3 ft.	50	5 00	40 00
chamlagu. Mongolian Pea Shrub	1 ft.	25	1½ to 2 ft.	25	2 50	20 00
			2 to 3 ft.	50	5 00	40 00
Caryopteris mastacanthus. Blue Spirea, or Chinese Beard-wort	1 ft.	15	1 to 1½ ft.	15	1 50	10 00
			1½ to 2 ft.	25	2 50	20 00
Ceanothus americanus. New Jersey Tea	1 ft.	25	1 to 1½ ft.	25	2 50	20 00
			1½ to 2 ft.	35	3 50	25 00
Ceanothus hybridus Gloire de Versailles. Hybrid Ceanothus	1 ft.	25	1 to 1½ ft.	25	2 50	
			2 to 3 ft.	50	5 00	
Cephalanthus occidentalis. Button Bush	1 ft.	25	1½ to 2 ft.	25	2 50	20 00
			2 to 3 ft.	35	3 50	25 00
Chimonanthus fragrans. Oriental Sweet Shrub	1 ft.	25	1 to 1½ ft.	25	2 50	
			2 to 3 ft.	50	5 00	
Clethra acuminata. Mountain Pepper Bush	1 ft.	25	1 to 1½ ft.	25	2 50	
			2 to 3 ft.	35	3 50	
			4 to 5 ft.	50	5 00	
alnifolia. Sweet Pepper Bush	1 ft.	15	1 to 1½ ft.	15	1 50	10 00
			1½ to 2 ft.	25	2 50	20 00
			2 to 3 ft.	50	5 00	40 00
Colutea arborescens. Bladder Senna	1 ft.	25	1 to 1½ ft.	25	2 50	
			2 to 3 ft.	50	5 00	
orientalis (*C. cruenta*). Oriental Bladder Senna	1 ft.	25	1 to 1½ ft.	25	2 50	
			2 to 3 ft.	50	5 00	

DECIDUOUS SHRUBS, continued

Botanical and Common Names	Mailing size postpaid Size	Each	Express and freight sizes purchaser paying transportation Size	Each	Doz.	100
Comptonia peregrina (*Myrica asplenifolia*). Sweet Fern	1 ft.	$0 25	1 to 1½ ft.	$0 25	$2 50	$20 00
			1½ to 2 ft.	50	5 00	
Coriaria japonica. Japanese Coriaria	1 ft.	25	1 to 1½ ft.	25	2 50	
			1½ to 2 ft.	50	5 00	
myrtifolia. Myrtle-leaved Coriaria	1 ft.	25	1 to 1½ ft.	25	2 50	
			1½ to 2 ft.	50	5 00	
Cornus alba (*C. sibirica*). Siberian Red Osier	1 ft.	15	1 to 1½ ft.	15	1 50	10 00
			1½ to 2 ft.	25	2 50	20 00
			2 to 3 ft.	35	3 50	25 00
alba spæthi. Yellow-leaved Dogwood	1 ft.	25	1 to 1½ ft.	25	2 50	
			1½ to 2 ft.	35	3 50	
			2 to 3 ft.	50	5 00	
amomum (*C. sericea*). Silky Dogwood	1 ft.	15	1 to 1½ ft.	15	1 50	10 00
			1½ to 2 ft.	25	2 50	20 00
			2 to 3 ft.	35	3 50	25 00
candidissima (*C. paniculata*). Panicled Dogwood	1 ft.	25	1 to 1½ ft.	25	2 50	20 00
			1½ to 2 ft.	35	3 50	25 00
			2 to 3 ft.	50	5 00	40 00
circinata. Round-leaved Dogwood	1 ft.	25	1 to 1½ ft.	25	2 50	20 00
			1½ to 2 ft.	35	3 50	25 00
			2 to 3 ft.	50	5 00	
mas (*C. mascula*). Cornelian Cherry	1 ft.	25	1 to 1½ ft.	25	2 50	20 00
			1½ to 2 ft.	35	3 50	25 00
			2 to 3 ft.	50	5 00	40 00
sanguinea. European Red Osier	1 ft.	15	1 to 1½ ft.	15	1 50	10 00
			1½ to 2 ft.	25	2 50	20 00
			2 to 3 ft.	35	3 50	25 00
stolonifera. Red Osier Cornel	1 ft.	15	1 to 1½ ft.	15	1 50	10 00
			1½ to 2 ft.	25	2 50	20 00
			2 to 3 ft.	35	3 50	25 00
stolonifera flaviramea. Golden-twigged Osier	1 ft	25	1 to 1½ ft.	25	2 50	20 00
			1½ to 2 ft.	35	3 50	25 00
			2 to 3 ft.	50	5 00	40 00
Coronilla emerus. Scorpion Senna	1 ft.	25	1 to 1½ ft.	25	2 50	
			1½ to 2 ft.	50	5 00	
Corylopsis pauciflora. Flowering Hazel	1 ft.	1 00	1 to 1½ ft.	1 00	10 00	
			1½ to 2 ft.	1 25	12 50	
			2 to 3 ft.	1 50		
spicata. Large-leaved Flowering Hazel	1 ft.	1 00	1 to 1½ ft.	1 00	10 00	
			1½ to 2 ft.	1 25	12 50	
			2 to 3 ft.	1 50		
Corylus americana. Hazelnut	1 ft.	25	1½ to 2 ft.	25	2 50	20 00
			2 to 3 ft.	50	5 00	40 00
avellana. Filbert	1 ft.	25	1½ to 2 ft.	25	2 50	20 00
			2 to 3 ft.	50	5 00	40 00
avellana laciniata. Cut-leaved Hazel	1 ft.	25	1½ to 2 ft.	25	2 50	20 00
			2 to 3 ft.	50	5 00	40 00
maxima purpurea. Purple-leaved Filbert	1 ft.	25	1½ to 2 ft.	25	2 50	20 00
			2 to 3 ft.	50	5 00	40 00
rostrata. Beaked Hazelnut	1 ft.	25	1½ to 2 ft.	25	2 50	20 00
			2 to 2½ ft.	50	5 00	40 00
Cotoneaster multiflora. Chinese Cotoneaster	1 ft.	25	1 to 1½ ft.	25	2 50	20 00
			2 to 3 ft.	50	5 00	40 00
nummularia. Broad-leaved Cotoneaster	1 ft.	25	1 to 1½ ft.	25	2 50	20 00
			2 to 3 ft.	50	5 00	40 00
Crataegus uniflora. One-flowered Thorn	1 ft.	25	1 to 1½ ft.	25	2 50	20 00
			1½ to 2 ft.	50	5 00	40 00
vailiæ. Miss Vail's Thorn	1 ft.	25	1 to 1½ ft.	25	2 50	20 00
			1½ to 2 f..	50	5 00	40 00
Cydonia japonica (*Pyrus japonica*). Japanese, or Flowering Quince	1 ft.	15	1 to 1½ ft.	15	1 50	10 00
			1½ to 2 ft.	25	2 50	20 00
			2 to 2½ ft.	35		
Any of the following named varieties of Cydonia japonica	1 ft.	25	1 to 1½ ft.	25	2 50	
Atrosanguinea — Rosea plena						
Candida — Rubra grandiflora						
Mallardi — Umbilicata						
maulei (*Pyrus maulei*). Dwarf Flowering Quince	1 ft.	25	1 to 1½ ft.	25	2 50	
Cytisus scoparius (*Genista scoparia*). Scotch Broom	1 ft.	25	1 to 1½ ft.	25	2 50	20 00
			2 to 3 ft.	50	5 00	40 00
Daphne genkwa. Japanese Daphne	1 ft.	1 00	1 to 1½ ft.	1 00	10 00	
			1½ to 2 ft.	1 50		

DECIDUOUS SHRUBS, continued

Botanical and Common Names	Mailing size, postpaid: Size	Each	Express and freight sizes, purchaser paying transportation: Size	Each	Doz.	100
Daphne mezereum. Mezereon Daphne	1 ft.	$0 25	1 to 1½ ft.	$0 25	$2 50	$20 00
			1½ to 2 ft.	50	5 00	40 00
			2 to 3 ft.	75	7 50	
Deutzia crenata candidissima. Double White Deutzia	1 ft.	15	1½ to 2 ft.	15	1 50	10 00
			2 to 3 ft.	25	2 50	20 00
			3 to 4 ft.	35	3 50	25 00
crenata flore roseo plena. Double Pink Deutzia	1 ft.	15	1½ to 2 ft.	15	1 50	10 00
			2 to 3 ft.	25	2 50	20 00
			3 to 4 ft.	35	3 50	25 00
crenata, Pride of Rochester. Large-flowered Deutzia	1 ft.	15	1½ to 2 ft.	15	1 50	10 00
			2 to 3 ft.	25	2 50	20 00
			3 to 4 ft.	35	3 50	25 00
gracilis. Slender Deutzia	1 ft.	15	1 to 1½ ft.	15	1 50	10 00
			1½ to 2 ft.	25	2 50	20 00
gracilis rosea. Slender Pink Deutzia	1 ft.	15	1 to 1½ ft.	15	1 50	10 00
			1½ to 2 ft.	25	2 50	20 00
lemoinei. Lemoine's Deutzia	1 ft.	15	1 to 1½ ft.	15	1 50	10 00
			1½ to 2 ft.	25	2 50	20 00
			2 to 3 ft.	35	3 50	25 00
parviflora. Small-flowered Deutzia	1 ft.	15	1 to 1½ ft.	15	1 50	10 00
			1½ to 2 ft.	25	2 50	20 00
			2 to 3 ft.	35	3 50	25 00
scabra. Rough-leaved Deutzia	1 ft.	15	1 to 1½ ft.	15	1 50	10 00
			1½ to 2 ft.	25	2 50	20 00
			2 to 3 ft.	35	3 50	25 00
Diervilla diervilla (*D. trifida*). Bush Honeysuckle	1 ft.	15	1 to 1½ ft.	15	1 50	10 00
			1½ to 2 ft.	25	2 50	20 00
floribunda. Floriferous Weigelia	1 ft.	15	1 to 1½ ft.	15	1 50	10 00
			2 to 3 ft.	25	2 50	20 00
			3 to 4 ft.	35	3 50	25 00
florida (*Weigelia amabilis; Weigelia rosea*). Rose-colored Weigelia	1 ft.	15	1 to 1½ ft.	15	1 50	10 00
			2 to 3 ft.	25	2 50	20 00
			3 to 4 ft.	35	3 50	25 00
Any of the following forms of Diervilla florida	1 ft.	15	1 to 1½ ft.	15	1 50	
			2 to 3 ft.	25	2 50	
			3 to 4 ft.	35	3 50	
Candida; Isolene; Kosteriana variegata; Nana variegata						
hybrida. Hybrid Weigelia	1 ft.	15	1 to 1½ ft.	15	1 50	10 00
			2 to 3 ft.	25	2 50	20 00
			3 to 4 ft.	35	3 50	25 00
Any of the following varieties of Diervilla hybrida	1 ft.	15	1 to 1½ ft.	15	1 50	
			2 to 3 ft.	25	2 50	
			3 to 4 ft.	35	3 50	
Abel Carriere; Conquete; Edouard Andre; Eva Rathke; Gustav Mallet; Steltzneri						
rivularis. Gattinger's Bush Honeysuckle	1 ft.	15	1 to 1½ ft.	15	1 50	10 00
			2 to 3 ft.	25	2 50	20 00
sessilifolia. High Bush Honeysuckle	1 ft.	15	1 to 1½ ft.	15	1 50	10 00
			2 to 3 ft.	25	2 50	20 00
			3 to 4 ft.	35	3 50	25 00
Dirca palustris. Leatherwood	1 ft.	25	1 to 1½ ft.	25	2 50	
			1½ to 2 ft.	50	5 00	
Elaeagnus angustifolia (*E. hortensis*). Russian Olive	1 ft.	15	1 to 1½ ft.	15	1 50	10 00
			2 to 3 ft.	25	2 50	20 00
argentea. Silver Berry	1 ft.	25	1 to 1½ ft.	25	2 50	
			1½ to 2 ft.	50	5 00	
longipes. The "Goumi" of Japan	1 ft.	25	1½ to 2 ft.	25	2 50	20 00
			2 to 3 ft.	50	5 00	40 00
parvifolia. Small-leaved Silver Thorn	1 ft.	25	1½ to 2 ft.	25	2 50	20 00
			2 to 3 ft.	50	5 00	40 00
umbellatus. Japanese Oleaster	1 ft.	25	1½ to 2 ft.	25	2 50	20 00
			2 to 3 ft.	50	5 00	40 00
Euonymus alatus. Winged Burning Bush	1 ft.	50	1 to 1½ ft.	50	5 00	40 00
			1½ to 2 ft.	75	7 50	60 00
americanus. Strawberry Bush	1 ft.	15	1 to 1½ ft.	15	1 50	10 00
			2 to 3 ft.	25	2 50	20 00
atropurpureus. Burning Bush	1 ft.	25	1 to 1½ ft.	25	2 50	
			2 to 3 ft.	50	5 00	

DECIDUOUS SHRUBS, continued

Botanical and Common Names	Mailing size (postpaid) Size	Each	Express and freight sizes (purchaser paying transportation) Size	Each	Doz.	100
Euonymus europæus. European Spindle-Tree	1 ft.	$0 15	1 to 1½ ft.	$0 15	$1 50	$10 00
			2 to 3 ft.	25	2 50	20 00
			3 to 4 ft.	35	3 50	25 00
hamiltonianus. Hamilton's Spindle-Tree	1 ft.	25	1 to 1½ ft.	25	2 50	
			2 to 3 ft.	50	5 00	
			3 to 4 ft.	75	7 50	
nanus. Narrow-leaved Burning Bush	1 ft.	25	1 to 1½ ft.	25	2 50	
			1½ to 2 ft.	50	5 00	
obovatus. Running Strawberry Bush	1 ft.	25	1 to 1½ ft.	25	2 50	
			1½ to 2 ft.	50	5 00	
patens. Late-Flowering Spindle-Tree	1 ft.	25	1 to 1½ ft.	25	2 50	
			2 to 3 ft.	50	5 00	
Exochorda grandiflora. Pearl Bush	1 ft.	25	1 to 1½ ft.	25	2 50	20 00
			2 to 3 ft.	50	5 00	40 00
Forsythia intermedia. Hybrid Golden Bell	1 ft.	15	1 to 1½ ft.	15	1 50	10 00
			2 to 3 ft.	25	2 50	20 00
			3 to 4 ft.	35	3 50	25 00
suspensa. Drooping Golden Bell	1 ft.	15	1 to 1½ ft.	15	1 50	10 00
			2 to 3 ft.	25	2 50	20 00
			3 to 4 ft.	35	3 50	25 00
suspensa fortunei (*F. fortunei*). Fortune's Golden Bell	1 ft.	15	1 to 1½ ft.	15	1 50	10 00
			2 to 3 ft.	25	2 50	20 00
			3 to 4 ft.	35	3 50	25 00
viridissima. Dark Green Forsythia	1 ft.	15	1 to 1½ ft.	15	1 50	10 00
			2 to 3 ft.	25	2 50	20 00
			3 to 4 ft.	35	3 50	25 00
Fothergilla carolina (*F. gardeni*; *F. alnifolia*). Dwarf Fothergilla	10 ins.	50	10 to 12 ins.	50	5 00	
			12 to 14 ins.	75	7 50	
major. Large Fothergilla	1 ft.	50	1 to 1½ ft.	50	5 00	40 00
			2 to 3 ft.	75	7 50	60 00
Genista tinctoria. Dyer's Greenweed	1 ft.	25	1 to 1½ ft.	25	2 50	20 00
			1½ to 2 ft.	50	5 00	
Halimodendron argenteum. Salt Bush	1 ft.	25	1 to 1½ ft.	25	2 50	20 00
			2 to 3 ft.	50	5 00	
Hamamelis virginiana. Witch Hazel	1 ft.	15	1 to 1½ ft.	15	1 50	10 00
			2 to 3 ft.	25	2 50	20 00
			3 to 4 ft.	50	5 00	40 00
Hibiscus syriacus (*Althæa frutex*). Rose of Sharon	1 ft.	15	1 to 1½ ft.	15	1 50	10 00
			2 to 3 ft.	25	2 50	20 00
Any of the following varieties of Hibiscus syriacus	1 ft.	25	1 to 1½ ft.	25	2 50	
			2 to 3 ft.	50	5 00	

Amaranth
Ardens
Boule de Feu
Carneo-plenus
Cœlestis
Jeanne d'Arc
Pæoniflorus
Rubis
Totus albus
Variegatus

Botanical and Common Names	Size	Each	Size	Each	Doz.	100
Hippophaë rhamnoides. Sea Buckthorn	1 ft.	25	1 to 1½ ft.	25	2 50	20 00
			2 to 3 ft.	50	5 00	40 00
Hydrangea arborescens. Wild Hydrangea	1 ft.	15	1 to 1½ ft.	15	1 50	10 00
			2 to 3 ft.	25	2 50	20 00
arborescens sterilis. Hills of Snow	1 yr.	75	2 yrs.	75	7 50	
hortensis. Japanese, or Garden Hydrangeas	1 yr.	15	2 yrs.	15	1 50	10 00
			3 yrs.	25	2 50	20 00
Any of the following varieties of Hydrangea hortensis	1 yr.	25	2 yrs.	25	2 50	20 00
			3 yrs.	50	5 00	40 00

Fertile forms:
Belzoni
Japonica
Rosalba

Sterile forms:
Hortensis
Otaksa
Ramulis picta
Thos. Hogg

Botanical and Common Names	Size	Each	Size	Each	Doz.	100
paniculata. Panicled Hydrangea	1 ft.	15	1 to 1½ ft.	15	1 50	10 00
			2 to 3 ft.	25	2 50	20 00
paniculata grandiflora. Large-flowered Hydrangea	1 ft.	15	1 to 1½ ft.	15	1 50	10 00
			1½ to 2 ft.	25	2 50	20 00
			2 to 3 ft.	35	3 50	25 00
			3 to 4 ft.	50	5 00	40 00
paniculata præcox. Early-flowering Hydrangea	1 ft.	15	1 to 1½ ft.	15	1 50	10 00
			2 to 3 ft.	25	2 50	20 00
quercifolia. Oak-leaved Hydrangea	1 ft.	25	1 to 1½ ft.	25	2 50	20 00
			1½ to 2 ft.	50	5 00	40 00
			2 to 3 ft.	75	7 50	60 00
radiata. Silver-leaved Hydrangea	1 ft.	15	1 to 1½ ft.	15	1 50	10 00
			1½ to 2 ft.	25	2 50	20 00

DECIDUOUS SHRUBS, contiuued

Botanical and Common Names	Mailing size postpaid: Size	Mailing size postpaid: Each	Express and freight sizes purchaser paying transportation: Size	Each	Doz.	100
Hypericum aureum. Golden Hypericum, or Large-flowered St. John's Wort	1 ft.	$0 25	1 to 1½ ft.	$0 25	$2 50	$20 00
			1½ to 2 ft.	35	3 50	25 00
buckleyi. Buckley's Hypericum, or Buckley's St. John's Wort	3 to 4 ins.	25	4 to 6 ins.	25	2 50	20 00
			6 to 8 ins.	35	3 50	25 00
calycinum. Aaron's Beard	1 yr.	15	2 yrs.	15	1 50	10 00
			3 yrs.	25	2 50	20 00
densiflorum. Dense-flowered St. John's Wort	1 ft.	15	1 to 1½ ft.	15	1 50	10 00
			2 to 3 ft.	25	2 50	20 00
glomeratum. Mountain St. John's Wort	1 ft.	15	1 to 1½ ft.	15	1 50	10 00
			1½ to 2 ft.	25	2 50	20 00
kalmianum. Kalm's St. John's Wort	1 ft.	15	1 to 1½ ft.	15	1 50	10 00
			1½ to 2 ft.	25	2 50	20 00
lobocarpum. Gattinger's St. John's Wort	1 ft.	15	1 to 1½ ft.	15	1 50	10 00
			2 to 3 ft.	25	2 50	20 00
moserianum. Gold Flower	1 yr.	15	2 yrs.	15	1 50	10 00
			3 yrs.	25	2 50	20 00
prolificum. Shrubby St. John's Wort	1 ft.	15	1 to 1½ ft.	15	1 50	10 00
			2 to 3 ft.	25	2 50	20 00
Ilex verticillata. Black Alder, or Winterberry	1 ft.	25	1 to 1½ ft.	25	2 50	20 00
			2 to 3 ft.	50	5 00	40 00
Itea virginica. Virginian Willow	1 ft.	15	1 to 1½ ft.	15	1 50	10 00
			2 to 3 ft.	25	2 50	20 00
			3 to 4 ft.	35	3 50	25 00
Jasminum humile. Italian Yellow Jasmine	1 ft.	15	1 to 1½ ft.	15	1 50	10 00
			2 to 3 ft.	25	2 50	20 00
nudiflorum. Naked-flowered Jasmine	1 ft.	15	1 to 1½ ft.	15	1 50	10 00
			2 to 3 ft.	25	2 50	20 00
officinale. True Jasmine, or Jessamine	1 ft.	15	1 to 1½ ft.	15	1 50	10 00
			2 to 3 ft.	25	2 50	20 00
Kerria japonica (*Corchorus japonica*). Globe Flower, or Japanese Rose	1 ft.	15	1 to 1½ ft.	15	1 50	10 00
			1½ to 2 ft.	25	2 50	20 00
japonica argenteo-variegata. Variegated-leaved Kerria	1 ft.	15	1 to 1½ ft.	15	1 50	10 00
			1½ to 2 ft.	25	2 50	20 00
japonica flore pleno. Double-flowered Kerria	1 ft.	15	1 to 1½ ft.	15	1 50	10 00
			1½ to 2 ft.	25	2 50	20 00
japonica ramulis variegatis. Striped-barked Kerria	1 ft.	15	1 to 1½ ft.	15	1 50	10 00
			1½ to 2 ft.	25	2 50	20 00
Lagerstroemia indica. Crape Myrtle	1 ft.	15	1 to 1½ ft.	15	1 50	10 00
			1½ to 2 ft.	25	2 50	20 00
			2 to 3 ft.	35	3 50	25 00
Lespedeza bicolor. Shrubby Bush Clover	1 yr.	25	2 yrs.	25	2 50	
			3 yrs.	35	3 50	
Leucothoë racemosa (*Andromeda racemosa*). Swamp Leucothoë	1 ft.	25	1 to 1½ ft.	25	2 50	20 00
			2 to 3 ft.	35	3 50	25 00
			3 to 4 ft.	50	5 00	40 00
recurva. Mountain Leucothoë	1 ft.	25	1 to 1½ ft.	25	2 50	20 00
			2 to 3 ft.	50	5 00	40 00
Ligustrum amurense. Amoor River Privet	1 ft.	15	1 to 1½ ft.	15	1 50	10 00
1 to 1½ ft., per 1,000, $75			2 to 3 ft.	25	2 50	20 00
			3 to 4 ft.	35	3 50	25 00
ciliatum. Bright-fruited Privet	1 ft.	15	1 to 1½ ft.	15	1 50	10 00
			2 to 3 ft.	25	2 50	20 00
			3 to 4 ft.	35	3 50	25 00
ibota. Ibota Privet	1 ft.	15	1 to 1½ ft.	15	1 50	10 00
1 to 1½ ft., per 1,000, $75			2 to 3 ft.	25	2 50	20 00
			3 to 4 ft.	35	3 50	25 00
ibota regelianum (*L. regelianum*). Regel's Privet	1 ft.	15	1 to 1½ ft.	15	1 50	10 00
1 to 1½ ft., per 1,000, $75			1½ to 2 ft.	25	2 50	20 00
			2 to 3 ft.	35	3 50	25 00
ovalifolium. California Privet	1 ft.	15	1 to 1½ ft.	15	1 50	10 00
1 to 1½ ft., per 1,000, $75			2 to 3 ft.	25	2 50	20 00
			3 to 4 ft.	35	3 50	25 00
vulgare. Common, or European Privet or Prim	1 ft.	15	1 to 1½ ft.	15	1 50	10 00
1 to 1½ ft., per 1,000, $75			2 to 3 ft.	25	2 50	20 00
			3 to 4 ft.	35	3 50	25 00
Lonicera fragrantissima. Early Fragrant Honeysuckle	1 ft.	15	1 to 1½ ft.	15	1 50	10 00
			2 to 3 ft.	25	2 50	20 00
			3 to 4 ft.	35	3 50	25 00
involucrata. Western Fly Honeysuckle	1 ft.	25	1 to 1½ ft.	25	2 50	20 00
			2 to 3 ft.	50	5 00	40 00

DECIDUOUS SHRUBS, continued

Botanical and Common Names	Mailing size, postpaid: Size	Each	Express and freight sizes, purchaser paying transportation: Size	Each	Doz.	100
Lonicera morrowi. Japanese Bush Honeysuckle	1 ft.	$0 15	1 to 1½ ft.	$0 15	$1 50	$10 00
			2 to 3 ft.	25	2 50	20 00
ruprechtiana. Manchurian Honeysuckle	1 ft.	15	1 to 1½ ft.	15	1 50	10 00
			2 to 3 ft.	25	2 50	20 00
spinosa (*L. alberti*). Large-fruited Honeysuckle	1 ft.	15	1 to 1½ ft.	15	1 50	10 00
			1½ to 2 ft.	25	2 50	20 00
standishi. Standish's Bush Honeysuckle	1 ft.	25	1 to 1½ ft.	25	2 50	
			1½ to 2 ft.	35	3 50	
tatarica. Tartarian Honeysuckle	1 ft.	15	1 to 1½ ft.	15	1 50	10 00
			2 to 3 ft.	25	2 50	20 00
			3 to 4 ft.	35		
xylosteum. Fly Honeysuckle	1 ft.	15	1 to 1½ ft.	15	1 50	10 00
			2 to 3 ft.	25	2 50	20 00
Lycium vulgare. Matrimony Vine, or Box Thorn	1 ft.	15	1 to 1½ ft.	15	1 50	10 00
			2 to 3 ft.	25	2 50	20 00
Myrica caroliniensis. Waxberry, or Bayberry	1 ft.	25	1 to 1½ ft.	25	2 50	20 00
			1½ to 2 ft.	35	3 50	25 00
cerifera. Wax Myrtle	1 ft.	25	1 to 1½ ft.	25	2 50	20 00
			1½ to 2 ft.	35	3 50	25 00
gale. Sweet Gale	1 ft.	25	1 to 1½ ft.	25	2 50	20 00
			1½ to 2 ft.	35	3 50	25 00
Neviusia alabamensis. Snow Wreath	1 ft.	25	1 to 1½ ft.	25	2 50	20 00
			2 to 3 ft.	50	5 00	40 00
Opulaster opulifolius (*Physocarpus opulifolius; Spiræa opulifolia*). Ninebark	1 ft.	15	1 to 1½ ft.	15	1 50	10 00
			2 to 3 ft.	25	2 50	20 00
			3 to 4 ft.	35	3 50	25 00
opulifolius aurea. Golden Ninebark	1 ft.	25	1 to 1½ ft.	25	2 50	20 00
			2 to 3 ft.	35	3 50	25 00
			3 to 4 ft.	50	5 00	
Philadelphus coronarius. Common Mock Orange	1 ft.	15	1 to 1½ ft.	15	1 50	10 00
			2 to 3 ft.	25	2 50	20 00
			3 to 4 ft.	35	3 50	25 00
coronarius aureus. Golden Mock Orange	1 ft.	25	1 to 1½ ft.	25	2 50	20 00
			1½ to 2 ft.	35	3 50	25 00
			2 to 3 ft.	50	5 00	
coronarius dianthiflorus. Double-flowered Mock Orange	1 ft.	25	1 to 1½ ft.	25	2 50	20 00
			1½ to 2 ft.	35	3 50	25 00
			2 to 3 ft.	50	5 00	
falconeri. Falconer's Mock Orange	1 ft.	25	1 to 1½ ft.	25	2 50	20 00
			1½ to 2 ft.	35	3 50	25 00
			2 to 3 ft.	50	5 00	
gordonianus. Gordon's Mock Orange	1 ft.	25	1 to 1½ ft.	25	2 50	20 00
			1½ to 2 ft.	35	3 50	25 00
			2 to 3 ft.	50	5 00	
grandiflorus. Large-flowered Mock Orange	1 ft.	15	1 to 1½ ft.	15	1 50	10 00
			1½ to 2 ft.	25	2 50	20 00
			2 to 3 ft.	35	3 50	25 00
hirsutus. Hairy Mock Orange	1 ft.	15	1 to 1½ ft.	15	1 50	10 00
			1½ to 2 ft.	25	2 50	20 00
			2 to 3 ft.	35	3 50	25 00
inodorus. Scentless Mock Orange	1 ft.	15	1 to 1½ ft.	15	1 50	10 00
			1½ to 2 ft.	25	2 50	20 00
			2 to 3 ft.	35	3 50	25 00
latifolius. Broad-leaved Mock Orange	1 ft.	15	1 to 1½ ft.	15	1 50	10 00
			2 to 3 ft.	25	2 50	20 00
			3 to 4 ft.	35	3 50	25 00
lemoinei. Hybrid Mock Orange	1 ft.	15	1 to 1½ ft.	15	1 50	10 00
			2 to 3 ft.	25	2 50	20 00
Any of the following varieties of Philadelphus lemoinei	1 ft.	25	1 to 1½ ft.	25	2 50	20 00
Avalanche; Boule d'Argent; Mont Blanc			1½ to 2 ft.	50	5 00	40 00
lewisi. Western Mock Orange	1 ft.	25	1 to 1½ ft.	25	2 50	
			2 to 3 ft.	50	5 00	
microphyllus. Small-leaved Syringa	1 ft.	25	1 to 1½ ft.	25	2 50	
			1½ to 2 ft.	50	5 00	
pekinensis. Chinese Syringa	1 ft.	15	1 to 1½ ft.	15	1 50	10 00
			1½ to 2 ft.	25	2 50	20 00
			2 to 3 ft.	35	3 50	25 00
zeyheri. Zeyher's Mock Orange	1 ft.	15	1 to 1½ ft.	15	1 50	10 00
			1½ to 2 ft.	25	2 50	20 00
			2 to 3 ft.	35	3 50	25 00

DECIDUOUS SHRUBS, continued

Botanical and Common Names	Mailing size (postpaid) Size	Each	Express and freight sizes (purchaser paying transportation) Size	Each	Doz.	100
Pieris mariana (*Andromeda mariana*). Stagger-bush	1 ft.	$0 50	1 to 1½ ft.	$0 50	$5 00	$40 00
			1½ to 2 ft.	75	7 50	60 00
Polycodium stamineum (*Vaccineum stamineum*). Deerberry	1 ft.	25	1 to 1½ ft.	25	2 50	20 00
			1½ to 2 ft.	50	5 00	40 00
Potentilla fruticosa. Shrubby Cinquefoil	1 ft.	15	1 to 1½ ft.	15	1 50	10 00
			1½ to 2 ft.	25	2 50	20 00
			2 to 3 ft.	35	3 50	25 00
Prunus besseyi. Western Sand Cherry	1 ft.	25	1 to 1½ ft.	25	2 50	20 00
			1½ to 2 ft.	35	3 50	25 00
japonica (*P. nana* and *sinensis; Amygdalus pumila*). Dwarf, or Flowering Almond	1 ft.	25	1 to 1½ ft.	25	2 50	20 00
			1½ to 2 ft.	35	3 50	25 00
maritima. Beach Plum	1 ft.	25	1 to 1½ ft.	25	2 50	20 00
			1½ to 2 ft.	35	3 50	25 00
pumila. Sand Cherry	1 ft.	25	1 to 1½ ft.	25	2 50	20 00
			1½ to 2 ft.	35	3 50	25 00
triloba. Flowering Plum	1 ft.	25	1 to 1½ ft.	25	2 50	20 00
			2 to 3 ft.	50	5 00	40 00
Rhamnus alnifolia. Dwarf Alder	1 ft.	25	1 to 1½ ft.	25	2 50	20 00
			2 to 3 ft.	50	5 00	40 00
alpina. Mountain Buckthorn	1 ft.	25	1 to 1½ ft.	25	2 50	
			2 to 3 ft.	50	5 00	
catharticus. Common Buckthorn	1 ft.	25	1 to 1½ ft.	25	2 50	20 00
			2 to 3 ft.	35	3 50	25 00
frangula. Alder Buckthorn	1 ft.	25	1 to 1½ ft.	25	2 50	20 00
			2 to 3 ft.	35	3 50	25 00
Rhodora canadensis. Rhodora	1 ft.	50	1 to 1½ ft.	50	5 00	40 00
			1½ to 2 ft.	75	7 50	
Rhodotypos kerrioides. White Kerria	1 ft.	15	1 to 1½ ft.	15	1 50	10 00
			1½ to 2 ft.	25	2 50	20 00
			2 to 3 ft.	35	3 50	25 00
Rhus aromatica (*R. canadensis*). Sweet-scented Sumac	1 ft.	25	1 to 1½ ft.	25	2 50	20 00
			1½ to 2 ft.	50	5 00	40 00
michauxi (*R. pumila*). Dwarf Sumac	6 to 10 ins.	1 00	10 to 12 ins.	1 00	10 00	
			12 to 15 ins.	1 25	12 50	
Ribes aureum. Missouri, or Flowering Currant	1 ft.	25	1 to 1½ ft.	25	2 50	20 00
			2 to 3 ft.	35	3 50	25 00
curvatum. Southern Gooseberry	1 ft.	25	1 to 1½ ft.	25	2 50	20 00
			2 to 3 ft.	35	3 50	25 00
floridum. Wild Black Currant	1 ft.	25	1 to 1½ ft.	25	2 50	20 00
			2 to 3 ft.	35	3 50	25 00
gordonianum. Pink-flowered Currant	1 ft.	25	1 to 1½ ft.	25	2 50	20 00
			2 to 3 ft.	35	3 50	25 00
sanguineum. Red-flowered Currant	1 ft.	25	1 to 1½ ft.	25	2 50	20 00
			2 to 3 ft.	35	3 50	25 00
Robinia hispida. Rose Acacia	1 ft.	25	1 to 1½ ft.	25	2 50	20 00
			2 to 3 ft.	35	3 50	25 00
Rosa alba. White Rose	1 ft.	25	1 to 1½ ft.	25	2 50	20 00
			2 to 3 ft.	50	5 00	40 00
alpina. Alpine Rose	1 ft.	25	1 to 1½ ft.	25	2 50	20 00
			1½ to 2 ft.	50	5 00	40 00
arvensis (*R. repens*). European Running Rose	1 ft.	25	1 to 2 ft.	25	2 50	20 00
			2 to 3 ft.	50	5 00	40 00
blanda. Meadow Rose	1 ft.	15	1 to 1½ ft.	15	1 50	10 00
			2 to 3 ft.	25	2 50	20 00
bracteata. Macartney Rose	1 ft.	25	1 to 1½ ft.	25	2 50	20 00
			1½ to 2 ft.	50	5 00	40 00
carolina. Carolina Rose	1 ft.	15	1 to 1½ ft.	15	1 50	10 00
			2 to 3 ft.	25	2 50	20 00
gallica. Provence Rose	1 ft.	25	1 to 1½ ft.	25	2 50	20 00
			2 to 3 ft.	50	5 00	40 00
humilis. Low, or Pasture Rose	1 ft.	15	1 to 1½ ft.	15	1 50	10 00
			1½ to 2 ft.	25	2 50	20 00
lævigata. Cherokee Rose	1 ft.	25	1 to 1½ ft.	25	2 50	20 00
			1½ to 2 ft.	50	5 00	40 00
multiflora. Japanese Climbing Rose	1 ft.	15	1 to 1½ ft.	15	1 50	10 00
			2 to 3 ft.	25	2 50	20 00
			3 to 4 ft.	35	3 50	25 00
rubiginosa. Eglantine, or Sweet Brier	1 ft.	15	1 to 1½ ft.	15	1 50	10 00
			2 to 3 ft.	25	2 50	20 00
rubrifolia. Red-leaved Rose	1 ft.	25	1 to 1½ ft.	25	2 50	20 00
			2 to 3 ft.	50	5 00	40 00

DECIDUOUS SHRUBS, continued

Botanical and Common Names	Mailing size, postpaid: Size	Mailing size, postpaid: Each	Express and freight sizes, purchaser paying transportation: Size	Each	Doz.	100
Rosa rugosa. Wrinkled Japanese Rose	1 ft.	$0 15	1 to 1½ ft.	$0 15	$1 50	$10 00
			1½ to 2 ft.	25	2 50	20 00
			2 to 3 ft.	35	3 50	25 00
setigera. Prairie Rose	1 ft.	15	1 to 1½ ft.	15	1 50	10 00
			2 to 3 ft.	25	2 50	20 00
			3 to 4 ft.	35	3 50	25 00
spinosissima. Scotch Rose	1 ft.	25	1 to 1½ ft.	25	2 50	20 00
			1½ to 2 ft.	50	5 00	40 00
watsoni. Watson's Rose	1 ft.	25	1 to 1½ ft.	25	2 50	20 00
			1½ to 2 ft.	50	5 00	40 00
wichuraiana. Memorial Rose	1 ft.	15	2 to 3 ft.	15	1 50	10 00
			3 to 4 ft.	25	2 50	20 00
Bourbon Roses						
Appolline	2 yrs.	30	field-grown	30	3 00	
Champion of the World	2 yrs.	30	field-grown	30	3 00	
Hermosa	2 yrs.	30	field-grown	30	3 00	
Souv. de la Malmaison	2 yrs.	30	field-grown	30	3 00	
Brier Roses						
Austrian Copper	2 yrs.	35	3 yrs.	35	3 50	25 00
Austrian Yellow	2 yrs.	35	3 yrs.	35	3 50	25 00
Harrison's Yellow	2 yrs.	35	3 yrs.	35	3 50	25 00
Persian Yellow	2 yrs.	35	3 yrs.	35	3 50	25 00
Lord Penzance Sweet Briers						
Amy Robsart	1 yr.	40	2 yrs.	40	4 00	30 00
Anne of Geierstein	1 yr.	40	2 yrs.	40	4 00	30 00
Brenda	1 yr.	40	2 yrs.	40	4 00	30 00
Catherine Seyton	1 yr.	40	2 yrs.	40	4 00	30 00
Flora McIvor	1 yr.	40	2 yrs.	40	4 00	30 00
Lady Penzance	1 yr.	40	2 yrs.	40	4 00	30 00
Lord Penzance	1 yr.	40	2 yrs.	40	4 00	30 00
Lucy Ashton	1 yr.	40	2 yrs.	40	4 00	30 00
Meg Merrilies	1 yr.	40	2 yrs.	40	4 00	30 00
Rose Bradwardine	1 yr.	40	2 yrs.	40	4 00	30 00
Climbing Tea and Noisette Roses						
Climbing Clothilde Soupert	2 yrs.	35	field-grown	35	3 50	
Climbing Wootton	2 yrs.	35	field-grown	35	3 50	
Gloire de Dijon	2 yrs.	30	field-grown	30	3 00	
Keystone	2 yrs.	35	field-grown	35	3 50	
Lamarque	2 yrs.	30	field-grown	30	3 00	
Marechal Niel	2 yrs.	30	field-grown	30	3 00	
Mary Washington	2 yrs.	30	field-grown	30	3 00	
Mrs. Robert Peary	2 yrs.	40	field-grown	40	4 00	
Reine Marie Henriette	2 yrs.	30	field-grown	30	3 00	
Hardy Climbing Roses						
Baltimore Belle	1 yr.	25	field-grown	25	2 50	
Queen of the Prairies	1 yr.	25	field-grown	25	2 50	
Tennessee Belle	1 yr.	25	field-grown	25	2 50	
Hybrid Perpetual Roses						
Abel Carriere	2 yrs.	35	field-grown	35	3 50	25 00
Alfred Colomb	2 yrs.	35	field-grown	35	3 50	25 00
American Beauty	2 yrs.	40	field-grown	40	4 00	30 00
Anne de Diesbach	2 yrs.	35	field-grown	35	3 50	25 00
Clio	2 yrs.	40	field-grown	40	4 00	30 00
Dinsmore	2 yrs.	35	field-grown	35	3 50	25 00
Duke of Edinburgh	2 yrs.	35	field-grown	35	3 50	25 00
Fisher Holmes	2 yrs.	35	field-grown	35	3 50	25 00
Francois Levet	2 yrs.	35	field-grown	35	3 50	25 00
Frau Karl Druschki	2 yrs.	50	field-grown	50	5 00	40 00
Gen. Jacqueminot	2 yrs.	35	field-grown	35	3 50	25 00
Giant of Battles	2 yrs.	35	field-grown	35	3 50	25 00
Gloire de Lyonnaise	2 yrs.	35	field-grown	35	3 50	25 00
John Hopper	2 yrs.	35	field-grown	35	3 50	25 00
Mme. Charles Wood	2 yrs.	35	field-grown	35	3 50	25 00
Mme. Gabriel Luizet	2 yrs.	40	field-grown	40	4 00	30 00

HYBRID PERPETUAL ROSES, continued

Botanical and Common Names	Mailing size postpaid Size	Each	Express and freight sizes purchaser paying transportation Size	Each	Doz.	100
Mme. Masson	2 yrs.	$0 35	field-grown	$0 35	$3 50	$25 00
Mme. Plantier	2 yrs.	35	field-grown	35	3 50	25 00
Magna Charta	2 yrs.	35	field-grown	35	3 50	25 00
Margaret Dickson	2 yrs.	50	field-grown	50	5 00	40 00
Marshall P. Wilder	2 yrs.	35	field-grown	35	3 50	25 00
Mrs. John Laing	2 yrs.	35	field-grown	35	3 50	25 00
Paul Neyron	2 yrs.	35	field-grown	35	3 50	25 00
Prince Camille de Rohan	2 yrs.	35	field-grown	35	3 50	25 00
Ulrich Brunner	2 yrs.	35	field-grown	35	3 50	25 00
Hybrid Tea Roses						
Belle Siebrecht	2 yrs.	35	field-grown	35	3 50	
Kaiserin Augusta Victoria	2 yrs.	35	field-grown	35	3 50	
La France	2 yrs.	35	field-grown	35	3 50	
Magnafrano	2 yrs.	35	field-grown	35	3 50	
Meteor	2 yrs.	35	field-grown	35	3 50	
Mme. Abel Chatenay	2 yrs.	35	field-grown	35	3 50	
Mme. Caroline Testout	2 yrs.	35	field-grown	35	3 50	
Mme. Pierre Guillot	2 yrs.	35	field-grown	35	3 50	
Souv. du President Carnot	2 yrs.	35	field-grown	35	3 50	
Japanese Roses						
Chedane Guinnoseaux	1 yr.	50	2 yrs.	50	5 00	
Conrad F. Meyer	1 yr.	50	2 yrs.	50	5 00	
Mme. Charles F. Worth	1 yr.	50	2 yrs.	50	5 00	
Mme. Georges Bruant	1 yr.	50	2 yrs.	50	5 00	
Monthly, or China Roses						
Antoinette Cuillerat	1 yr.	35	2 yrs.	35	3 50	
Fellenburg	1 yr.	30	2 yrs.	30	3 00	
Gloire de Rosomanes	1 yr.	35	2 yrs.	35	3 50	
Lemesie	1 yr.	30	2 yrs.	30	3 00	
Serratipetala	1 yr.	40	2 yrs.	40	4 00	
Viridiflora	1 yr.	30	2 yrs.	30	3 00	
Moss Roses						
Blanche Moreau	2 yrs.	35	field-grown	35	3 50	25 00
Common Moss	2 yrs.	35	field-grown	35	3 50	25 00
Crested Moss	2 yrs.	35	field-grown	35	3 50	25 00
Crimson Globe	2 yrs.	35	field-grown	35	3 50	25 00
Salet	2 yrs.	35	field-grown	35	3 50	25 00
White Perpetual	2 yrs.	35	field-grown	35	3 50	25 00
Old-fashioned Roses						
Cabbage, or Provence	2 yrs.	35	field-grown	35	3 50	
Celestial	2 yrs.	35	field-grown	35	3 50	
Damask	2 yrs.	35	field-grown	35	3 50	
Maiden's Blush	2 yrs.	35	field-grown	35	3 50	
Perpetual	2 yrs.	35	field-grown	35	3 50	
Tuscany	2 yrs.	35	field-grown	35	3 50	
Polyantha Roses						
Baby Rambler	2 yrs.	35	field-grown	35	3 50	25 00
Clothilde Soupert	2 yrs.	30	field-grown	30	3 00	20 00
Etoile d' Or	2 yrs.	30	field-grown	30	3 00	20 00
Marie Pavie	2 yrs.	30	field-grown	30	3 00	20 00
Rambler Roses						
Crimson Rambler	1 yr.	30	2 yrs.	30	3 00	20 00
Philadelphia Rambler	1 yr.	35	2 yrs.	35	3 50	25 00
Pink Rambler (Psyche)	1 yr.	30	2 yrs.	30	3 00	20 00
Yellow Rambler (Aglaia)	1 yr.	30	2 yrs.	30	3 00	20 00
White Rambler (Thalia)	1 yr.	30	2 yrs.	30	3 00	20 00
Striped Roses						
Cottage Maid	2 yrs.	50	field-grown	50	5 00	
York and Lancaster	2 yrs.	50	field-grown	50	5 00	

DECIDUOUS SHRUBS, continued

Botanical and Common Names	Mailing size postpaid Size	Each	Express and freight sizes purchaser paying transportation Size	Each	Doz.	100
Tea Roses						
Aline Sisley	2 yrs.	$0 30	field-grown	$0 30	$3 00	
Bon Silene	2 yrs.	30	field-grown	30	3 00	
Bridesmaid	2 yrs.	30	field-grown	30	3 00	
Cornelia Cook	2 yrs.	30	field-grown	30	3 00	
Devoniensis	2 yrs.	30	field-grown	30	3 00	
Etoile de Lyon	2 yrs.	30	field-grown	30	3 00	
Maman Cochet	2 yrs.	30	field-grown	30	3 00	
Marie Guillot	2 yrs.	30	field-grown	30	3 00	
Papa Gontier	2 yrs.	30	field-grown	30	3 00	
Perle des Jardins	2 yrs.	30	field-grown	30	3 00	
Safrano	2 yrs.	30	field-grown	30	3 00	
The Bride	2 yrs.	30	field-grown	30	3 00	
Wichuraiana Hybrid Roses						
Debutante	1 yr.	30	2 yrs.	30	3 00	$20 00
Dorothy Perkins	1 yr.	30	2 yrs.	30	3 00	20 00
Pink Roamer	1 yr.	30	2 yrs.	30	3 00	20 00
Sweetheart	1 yr.	30	2 yrs.	30	3 00	20 00
Wm. C. Egan	1 yr.	30	2 yrs.	30	3 00	20 00
Rubus cratægifolius. Hawthorn-leaved Bramble	1 ft.	25	1 to 1½ ft.	25	2 50	20 00
			2 to 3 ft.	35	3 50	25 00
deliciosus. Rocky Mountain Flowering Raspberry	1 ft.	25	1 to 1½ ft.	25	2 50	
			1½ to 2 ft.	35	3 50	
dumetorum. European Dewberry	1 ft.	15	1 to 1½ ft.	15	1 50	10 00
			1½ to 2 ft.	25	2 50	20 00
laciniatus. Cut-leaved Blackberry	1 ft.	25	1 to 1½ ft.	25	2 50	
			2 to 3 ft.	35	3 50	
odoratus. Flowering Raspberry	1 ft.	15	1 to 1½ ft.	15	1 50	10 00
			2 to 3 ft.	25	2 50	20 00
parviflorus (*R. nutkanus*). Western Flowering Raspberry	1 ft.	25	1 to 1½ ft.	25	2 50	
			1½ to 2 ft.	35	3 50	
phœnicolasius. Wineberry	1 ft.	15	1 to 1½ ft.	15	1 50	10 00
			2 to 3 ft.	25	2 50	20 00
rosæflorus. Strawberry-Raspberry	1 ft.	25	1 to 1½ ft.	25	2 50	
			1½ to 2 ft.	35	3 50	
rosæflorus coronarius (*R. grandiflorus*). Bramble Rose	1 ft.	35	1 to 1½ ft.	35	3 50	
			1½ to 2 ft.	50	5 00	
Salix humilis. Prairie Willow	1 ft.	25	1½ to 2 ft.	25	2 50	20 00
			2 to 3 ft.	50	5 00	40 00
incana (*S. rosmarinifolia*). Rosemary Willow	1 ft.	25	2 to 3 ft.	25	2 50	20 00
			4 to 5 ft.	50	5 00	20 00
sericea. Silky Willow	1 ft.	25	2 to 3 ft.	25	2 50	20 00
			4 to 5 ft.	50	5 00	40 00
tristis. Dwarf Gray Willow	1 ft.	25	1 to 1½ ft.	25	2 50	20 00
			1½ to 2 ft.	50	5 00	40 00
Sambucus canadensis. American Elder	1 ft.	25	2 to 3 ft.	25	2 50	20 00
			3 to 4 ft.	35	3 50	25 00
nigra. European Elder	1 ft.	25	2 to 3 ft.	25	2 50	20 00
			3 to 4 ft.	35	3 50	25 00
nigra aurea. Golden Elder	1 ft.	25	2 to 3 ft.	25	2 50	20 00
			3 to 4 ft.	35	3 50	25 00
nigra laciniata. Cut-leaved Elder	1 ft.	25	2 to 3 ft.	25	2 50	20 00
			3 to 4 ft.	35	3 50	25 00
pubens. Red-berried Elder	1 ft.	25	2 to 3 ft.	25	2 50	20 00
			3 to 4 ft.	35	3 50	25 00
Schizonotus discolor. White Beam-leaved Spirea	1 ft.	25	1 to 1½ ft.	25	2 50	20 00
			1½ to 2 ft.	50	5 00	
Spartium junceum. Spanish Broom	1 ft.	25	1 to 1½ ft.	25	2 50	20 00
			1½ to 2 ft.	50	5 00	
Spiraea. EARLY-FLOWERING FORMS						
arguta. Hybrid Snow Garland	1 ft.	25	1 to 1½ ft.	25	2 50	20 00
			1½ to 2 ft.	35	3 50	25 00
bracteata. Round-leaved Spirea	1 ft.	25	1 to 1½ ft.	25	2 50	20 00
			1½ to 2 ft.	35	3 50	25 00
cantonensis. Lance-leaved Spirea	1 ft.	15	1½ to 2 ft.	15	1 50	10 00
			2 to 3 ft.	25	2 50	20 00
cantonensis flore pleno (*S. reevesiana*). Lance-leaved Double Spirea	1 ft.	15	1½ to 2 ft.	15	1 50	10 00
			2 to 3 ft.	25	2 50	20 00

DECIDUOUS SHRUBS, continued

Botanical and Common Names	Mailing size postpaid Size	Each	Express and freight sizes purchaser paying transportation Size	Each	Doz.	100
Spiraea chamædrifolia. Germander-leaved Spirea	1 ft.	$0 25	1 to 1½ ft.	$0 25	$2 50	$20 00
			1½ to 2 ft.	35	3 50	25 00
hypericifolia. Hypericum-leaved Spirea	1 ft.	25	1 to 1½ ft.	25	2 50	20 00
			1½ to 2 ft.	35	3 50	25 00
pikowiensis (*S. nicoudierti*). Pikow Spirea	1 ft.	25	1 to 1½ ft.	25	2 50	20 00
			1½ to 2 ft.	35	3 50	25 00
prunifolia. Plum-leaved Spirea	1 ft.	15	1 to 1½ ft.	15	1 50	10 00
			2 to 3 ft.	25	2 50	20 00
prunifolia flore pleno. Bridal Wreath	1 ft.	15	1 to 1½ ft.	15	1 50	10 00
			2 to 3 ft.	25	2 50	20 00
thunbergi. Snow Garland	8 to 10 ins.	15	1 ft.	15	1 50	10 00
			1½ to 2 ft.	25	2 50	20 00
vanhouttei. Van Houtte's Bridal Wreath	1 ft.	15	1 to 1½ ft.	15	1 50	10 00
			2 to 3 ft.	25	2 50	20 00
Spiraea. Summer-flowering Forms						
alba. Meadow Sweet	1 ft.	15	1½ to 2 ft.	15	1 50	10 00
			2 to 3 ft.	25	2 50	20 00
albiflora (*S. japonica alba*). Dwarf White Spirea	8 to 10 ins.	15	1 ft.	15	1 50	10 00
			1 to 1½ ft.	25	2 50	20 00
billardi. Billard's Spirea	1 ft.	15	1 to 1½ ft.	15	1 50	10 00
			2 to 3 ft.	25	2 50	20 00
bumalda. Everblooming Spirea	6 to 8 ins.	15	1 ft.	15	1 50	10 00
			1 to 1½ ft.	25	2 50	20 00
bumalda Anthony Waterer. Crimson Spirea	6 to 8 ins.	15	1 ft.	15	1 50	10 00
			1 to 1½ ft.	25	2 50	20 00
douglasi. Douglas' Spirea	1 ft.	15	1 to 1½ ft.	15	1 50	10 00
			2 to 3 ft.	25	2 50	20 00
japonica. Japanese Spirea	6 to 8 ins.	15	1 ft.	15	1 50	10 00
			1 to 1½ ft.	25	2 50	20 00
latifolia. Meadow Queen	1 ft.	15	1½ to 2 ft.	15	1 50	10 00
			2 to 3 ft.	25	2 50	20 00
margaritæ. Pink Hybrid Spirea	1 ft.	15	1 to 1½ ft.	15	1 50	10 00
			1½ to 2 ft.	25	2 50	20 00
menziesi. Menzies' Spirea	1 ft.	15	1½ to 2 ft.	15	1 50	10 00
			2 to 3 ft.	25	2 50	20 00
tomentosa. Steeple-bush. Hardhack	1 ft.	15	1½ to 2 ft.	15	1 50	10 00
			2 to 3 ft.	25	2 50	20 00
virginiana. Virginia Spirea	1 ft.	25	1 to 1½ ft.	25	2 50	20 00
			1½ to 2 ft.	35	3 50	25 00
Staphylea bumalda. Japanese Bladder-nut	1 ft.	25	1½ to 2 ft.	25	2 50	20 00
			2 to 3 ft.	50	5 00	
colchica. Colchican Bladder-nut	1 ft.	25	1½ to 2 ft.	25	2 50	20 00
			2 to 3 ft.	50	5 00	
pinnata. European Bladder-nut	1 ft.	25	1½ to 2 ft.	25	2 50	20 00
			2 to 3 ft.	50	5 00	
trifolia. American Bladder-nut	1 ft.	25	1½ to 2 ft.	25	2 50	20 00
			2 to 3 ft.	35	3 50	25 00
			3 to 4 ft.	50	5 00	40 00
Stephanandra flexuosa. Stephanandra	1 ft.	15	1 to 1½ ft.	15	1 50	10 00
			1½ to 2 ft.	25	2 50	20 00
Stuartia pentagyna. Alleghany Stuartia	1 ft.	25	1 to 1½ ft.	25	2 50	20 00
			1½ to 2 ft.	50	5 00	40 00
pseudo-camellia. Japanese Stuartia	1 ft.	50	1 to 1½ ft.	50	5 00	
			1½ to 2 ft.	75	7 50	
Styrax americana. American Storax	1 ft.	50	1 to 1½ ft.	50	5 00	
			2 to 3 ft.	75	7 50	
japonica. Japanese Storax	1 ft.	50	1 to 1½ ft.	50	5 00	
			2 to 3 ft.	75	7 50	
obassia. Broad-leaved Storax	1 ft.	75	1 to 1½ ft.	75	7 50	
			2 to 3 ft.	1 50	15 00	
Symphoricarpos occidentalis. Western Snowberry, or Wolfberry	1 ft.	15	1 to 1½ ft.	15	1 50	10 00
			2 to 3 ft.	25	2 50	20 00
racemosus. Snowberry	1 ft.	15	1 to 1½ ft.	15	1 50	10 00
			2 to 3 ft.	25	2 50	20 00
symphoricarpos (*S. vulgaris*). Coral-berry, or Indian Currant	1 ft.	15	1 to 1½ ft.	15	1 50	10 00
			2 to 3 ft.	25	2 50	20 00
Syringa chinensis (*S. rothomagensis*). Rouen Lilac	1 ft.	15	1 to 1½ ft.	15	1 50	10 00
			2 to 3 ft.	25	2 50	20 00
			3 to 4 ft.	50	5 00	40 00

DECIDUOUS SHRUBS, continued

Botanical and Common Names	Mailing size, postpaid: Size	Mailing size, postpaid: Each	Express and freight sizes, purchaser paying transportation: Size	Each	Doz.	100
Syringa josikea. Hungarian Lilac	1 ft.	$0 25	1 to 1½ ft.	$0 25	$2 50	$20 00
			1½ to 2 ft.	35	3 50	25 00
pekinensis. Chinese Lilac	1 ft.	15	1 to 1½ ft.	15	1 50	10 00
			1½ to 2 ft.	25	2 50	20 00
persica. Persian Lilac	1 ft.	15	1 to 1½ ft.	15	1 50	10 00
			1½ to 2 ft.	25	2 50	20 00
			2 to 3 ft.	35	3 50	25 00
persica alba. White Persian Lilac	1 ft.	15	1 to 1½ ft.	15	1 50	10 00
			1½ to 2 ft.	25	2 50	20 00
			2 to 3 ft.	35	3 50	25 00
villosa. Himalayan Lilac	1 ft.	25	1 to 1½ ft.	25	2 50	20 00
			1½ to 2 ft.	35	3 50	25 00
vulgaris. Common Lilac	1 ft.	15	1 to 1½ ft.	15	1 50	10 00
			1½ to 2 ft.	25	2 50	20 00
			2 to 3 ft.	35	3 50	25 00
VARIETIES WITH SINGLE FLOWERS:						
Ambroise Verschaffelt	1 ft.	25	1 to 1½ ft.	25	2 50	
			2 to 3 ft.	50	5 00	
Charles X	1 ft.	25	1 to 1½ ft.	25	2 50	
			1½ to 2 ft.	35	3 50	30 00
			2 to 3 ft.	50	5 00	
Dr. Lindley	1 ft.	25	1 to 1½ ft.	25	2 50	
			2 to 3 ft.	50	5 00	
Frau Bertha Dammann	1 ft.	25	1 to 1½ ft.	25	2 50	
			1½ to 2 ft.	35	3 50	30 00
			2 to 3 ft.	50	5 00	
Geant des Batailles	1 ft.	25	1 to 1½ ft.	25	2 50	
			2 to 3 ft.	50	5 00	
Gloire des Moulins	1 ft.	25	1 to 1½ ft.	25	2 50	
			2 to 3 ft.	50	5 00	
Ludwig Spath	1 ft.	25	1 to 1½ ft.	25	2 50	
			2 to 3 ft.	50	5 00	
Marie Legraye	1 ft.	25	1 to 1½ ft.	25	2 50	
			1½ to 2 ft.	35	3 50	30 00
			2 to 3 ft.	50	5 00	
VARIETIES WITH DOUBLE FLOWERS:						
Alphonse Lavalle	1 ft.	25	1 to 1½ ft.	25	2 50	
			2 to 3 ft.	50	5 00	
Belle de Nancy	1 ft.	25	1 to 1½ ft.	25	2 50	
			2 to 3 ft.	50	5 00	
Condorcet	1 ft.	25	1 to 1½ ft.	25	2 50	
			2 to 3 ft.	50	5 00	
La Tour d'Auvergne	1 ft.	25	1 to 1½ ft.	25	2 50	
			1½ to 2 ft.	35	3 50	30 00
			2 to 3 ft.	50	5 00	
Mme. Abel Chatenay	1 ft.	25	1 to 1½ ft.	25	2 50	
			1½ to 2 ft.	35	3 50	30 00
			2 to 3 ft.	50	5 00	
Mme. Casimir Perier	1 ft.	25	1 to 1½ ft.	25	2 50	
			2 to 3 ft.	50	5 00	
Mme. Lemoine	1 ft.	25	1 to 1½ ft.	25	2 50	
			2 to 3 ft.	50	5 00	
Maxime Cornu	1 ft.	25	1 to 1½ ft.	25	2 50	
			2 to 3 ft.	50	5 00	
Michael Buchner	1 ft.	25	1 to 1½ ft.	25	2 50	
			2 to 3 ft.	50	5 00	
Pres. Carnot	1 ft.	25	1 to 1½ ft.	25	2 50	
			2 to 3 ft.	50	5 00	
Tamarix gallica (*T. pentandra*). French Tamarisk	1 ft.	25	1½ to 2 ft.	25	2 50	20 00
			2 to 3 ft.	35	3 50	25 00
gallica indica (*T. indica*). Indian Tamarisk	1 ft.	25	2 to 3 ft.	25	2 50	20 00
			3 to 4 ft.	35	3 50	25 00
juniperina (*T. plumosa* and *T. japonica*). Japanese Tamarisk	1 ft.	25	1½ to 2 ft.	25	2 50	20 00
			2 to 3 ft.	35	3 50	25 00
odessana. Caspian Tamarisk	1 ft.	25	1½ to 2 ft.	25	2 50	20 00
			2 to 3 ft.	35	3 50	25 00
parviflora. Early-flowering Tamarisk	1 ft.	25	1½ to 2 ft.	25	2 50	20 00
			2 to 3 ft.	35	3 50	25 00
Ulex europæus. Furze, Gorse or Whin	1 ft.	25	1½ to 2 ft.	25	2 50	20 00
			2 to 3 ft.	35	3 50	25 00

DECIDUOUS SHRUBS, continued

Botanical and Common Names	Mailing size (postpaid) Size	Each	Express and freight sizes (purchaser paying transportation) Size	Each	Doz.	100
Viburnum acerifolium. Maple-leaved Viburnum	1 ft.	$0 25	1½ to 2 ft.	$0 25	$2 50	$20 00
			2 to 3 ft.	35	3 50	25 00
			3 to 4 ft.	50	5 00	40 00
alnifolium (*V. lantanoides*). Hobble-bush	1 ft.	25	1 to 1½ ft.	25	2 50	20 00
			1½ to 2 ft.	35	3 50	25 00
cassinoides. Withe-rod	1 ft.	25	1 to 1½ ft.	25	2 50	20 00
			1½ to 2 ft.	35	3 50	25 00
dentatum. Arrow-wood	1 ft.	25	1½ to 2 ft.	25	2 50	20 00
			2 to 3 ft.	35	3 50	25 00
			3 to 4 ft.	50	5 00	40 00
dilatatum. Japanese Bush Cranberry	1 ft.	25	1½ to 2 ft.	25	2 50	
			2 to 3 ft.	35	3 50	
lantana. Wayfaring Tree	1 ft.	25	1½ to 2 ft.	25	2 50	20 00
			2 to 3 ft.	35	3 50	25 00
			3 to 4 ft.	50	5 00	
macrocephalum. Chinese Viburnum	1 ft.	50	1 to 1½ ft.	50	5 00	
			1½ to 2 ft.	1 00		
macrocephalum sterile. Chinese Snowball	1 ft.	50	1 to 1½ ft.	50	5 00	
			1½ to 2 ft.	1 00		
nudum. Larger Withe-rod	1 ft.	25	1 to 1½ ft.	25	2 50	
			1½ to 2 ft.	35	3 50	
opulus. High Bush Cranberry	1 ft.	25	1 to 1½ ft.	25	2 50	
			1½ to 2 ft.	35	3 50	
opulus nanum. Dwarf Cranberry Bush	6 to 8 ins.	15	8 to 10 ins.	15	1 50	10 00
			10 to 12 ins.	25	2 50	20 00
opulus sterile. Snowball, or Guelder Rose	1 ft.	15	1 to 1½ ft.	15	1 50	10 00
			1½ to 2 ft.	25	2 50	20 00
			2 to 3 ft.	35	3 50	25 00
			3 to 4 ft.	50	5 00	40 00
tomentosum. Single-flowered Japanese Snowball	1 ft.	25	2 to 3 ft.	25	2 50	20 00
			3 to 4 ft.	50	5 00	40 00
tomentosum plicatum (*V. plicatum*). Japanese Snowball	1 ft.	25	2 to 3 ft.	25	2 50	20 00
			3 to 4 ft.	50	5 00	40 00
sieboldi (*V. japonicum*). Siebold's Viburnum	1 ft.	25	2 to 3 ft.	25	2 50	20 00
			3 to 4 ft.	50	5 00	40 00
Xanthorrhiza apiifolia. Yellow-root, or Brook-feather	1 yr.	15	2 yrs.	15	1 50	10 00
			3 yrs.	25	2 50	20 00
Xolisma ligustrina (*Andromeda ligustrina*). Privet Andromeda	1 ft.	25	1 to 1½ ft.	25	2 50	20 00
			1½ to 2 ft.	50	5 00	40 00
Zenobia cassinifolia (*Andromeda speciosa*). Zenobia	1 ft.	50	1 to 1½ ft.	50	5 00	
			1½ to 2 ft.	75	7 50	

Wild Roses

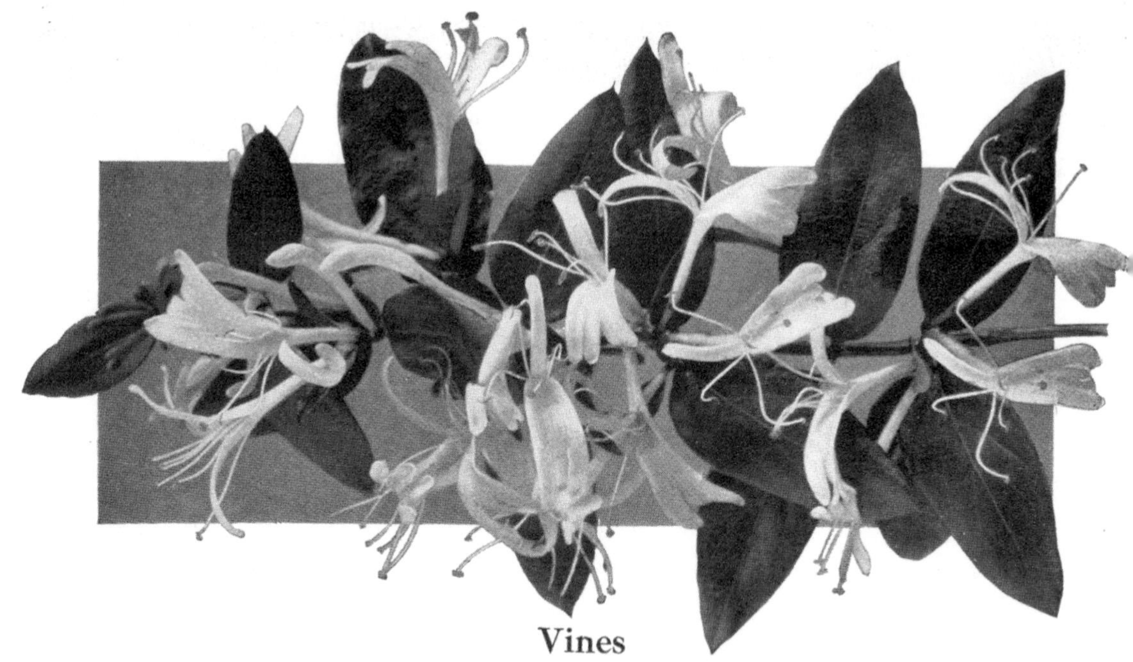

Vines

Botanical and Common Names	Mailing size (postpaid) Size	Each	Express and freight sizes (purchaser paying transportation) Size	Each	Doz.	100
Actinidia arguta (*A. polygama*). Dark-leaved Silver Vine	1 ft.	$0 25	1½ to 2 ft.	$0 25	$2 50	$20 00
			2 to 3 ft.	50	5 00	40 00
kolomikta. Bright-leaved Silver Vine	1 ft.	25	1½ to 2 ft.	25	2 50	20 00
			2 to 3 ft.	50	5 00	40 00
Akebia quinata. Five-leaved Akebia	1 ft.	25	1½ to 2 ft.	25	2 50	20 00
			2 to 3 ft.	50	5 00	40 00
Ampelopsis arborea (*Vitis bipinnata* and *Cissus stans*). Pepper Vine	1 ft.	25	1½ to 2 ft.	25	2 50	
			2 to 3 ft.	50	5 00	
cordata. Simple-leaved Ampelopsis	1 ft.	25	1½ to 2 ft.	25	2 50	
			2 to 3 ft.	50	5 00	
heterophylla. Asiatic Creeper	1 ft.	25	1½ to 2 ft.	25	2 50	
			2 to 3 ft.	50	5 00	
heterophylla elegans (*A. tricolor*). Variegated Asiatic Creeper	1 ft.	25	1½ to 2 ft.	25	2 50	
			2 to 3 ft.	50	5 00	
quinquefolia. Virginia Creeper	1 ft.	15	1½ to 2 ft.	15	1 50	10 00
			2 to 3 ft.	25	2 50	20 00
veitchi. Japanese, or Boston Ivy	1 ft.	15	1½ to 2 ft.	15	1 50	10 00
			2 to 3 ft.	25	2 50	20 00
Aristolochia macrophylla (*A. sipho*). Dutchman's Pipe	1 ft.	25	1½ to 2 ft.	25	2 50	20 00
			2 to 3 ft.	50	5 00	40 00
Berchemia racemosa. Japanese Supple Jack	1 ft.	50	1½ to 2 ft.	50	5 00	
			2 to 3 ft.	75	7 50	
Bignonia crucigera (*B. capreolata*). Cross Vine	1 ft.	25	1½ to 2 ft.	25	2 50	20 00
			2 to 3 ft.	50	5 00	40 00
Celastrus orbiculatus (*C. articulatus*). Japanese Bittersweet	1 ft.	15	1½ to 2 ft.	15	1 50	10 00
			2 to 2½ ft.	25	2 50	20 00
			3 to 4 ft.	35	3 50	25 00
scandens. American Bittersweet	1 ft.	15	1½ to 2 ft.	15	1 50	10 00
			2 to 2½ ft.	25	2 50	20 00
			3 to 4 ft.	35	3 50	25 00
Clematis apiifolia. Parsley-leaved Clematis	1 ft.	25	1½ to 2 ft.	25	2 50	20 00
			2 to 3 ft.	50	5 00	40 00
coccinea. Scarlet Clematis	2 yrs.	25	strong plants	25	2 50	
			extra strong	35	3 50	
crispa. Marsh Clematis	2 yrs.	25	strong plants	25	2 50	
			extra strong	35	3 50	
flammula. Sweet Clematis	2 yrs.	25	strong plants	25	2 50	20 00
			extra strong	35	3 50	25 00
hybrida. Large-flowering Clematis. Any of the following varieties of Clematis hybrida	2 yrs.	40	strong plants	40	4 00	
			extra strong	50	5 00	

Duchess of Edinburgh
Henryi
Jackmanni
Mme. Baron Veillard
Mme. Edouard Andre
Ramona

VINES, continued

Botanical and Common Names	Mailing size, postpaid: Size	Each	Express and freight sizes, purchaser paying transportation: Size	Each	Doz.	100
Clematis montana. Mountain Clematis	2 yrs.	$0 25	strong plants	$0 25	$2 50	
			extra strong	35	3 50	
orientalis (*C. graveolens*). Yellow-flowered Clematis	2 yrs.	25	strong plants	25	2 50	
			extra strong	35	3 50	
paniculata. Japanese Clematis	2 yrs.	25	strong plants	25	2 50	$20 00
			extra strong	35	3 50	25 00
viorna. Leather Flower	2 yrs.	25	strong plants	25	2 50	
			extra strong	35	3 50	
virginiana. Virgin's Bower	2 yrs.	25	strong plants	25	2 50	20 00
			extra strong	35	3 50	25 00
vitalba. Traveller's Joy	2 yrs.	25	strong plants	25	2 50	20 00
			extra strong	35	3 50	25 00
Decumaria barbara. American Climbing Hydrangea	2 yrs.	25	strong plants	25	2 50	
			extra strong	50	5 00	
Euonymus radicans. Climbing Euonymus	2 yrs.	25	strong plants	25	2 50	20 00
			extra strong	35	3 50	25 00
radicans variegata. Variegated Climbing Euonymus	2 yrs.	25	strong plants	25	2 50	
			extra strong	35	3 50	
Gelsemium sempervirens. Carolina Yellow Jessamine	2 yrs.	25	strong plants	25	2 50	
			extra strong	50	5 00	
sempervirens flore pleno. Double-flowered Carolina Jessamine	2 yrs.	25	strong plants	25	2 50	
			extra strong	50	5 00	
Hedera colchica (*H. roegneriana*). Colchican Ivy	2 yrs.	25	strong plants	25	2 50	
			extra strong	50	5 00	
helix. English Ivy	2 yrs.	15	strong plants	15	1 50	10 00
			extra strong	25	2 50	20 00
GREEN-LEAVED VARIETIES: Any of the following varieties of *Hedera helix*	2 yrs.	25	strong plants	25	2 50	
			extra strong	50	5 00	
Algeriensis, Arborescens, Digitata, Donerailensis, Palmata						
VARIEGATED VARIETIES: Any of the following forms of Variegated *Hedera helix*	2 yrs.	50	strong plants	50	5 00	
			extra strong	75	7 50	
Argenteo-variegata, Aureo-variegata						
Hydrangea petiolaris (*H. scandens*). Creeping Hydrangea	2 yrs.	50	strong plants	50	5 00	
			extra strong	75	7 50	
Lonicera caprifolium. Italian Honeysuckle	2 yrs.	25	strong plants	25	2 50	
			extra strong	35	3 50	
chinensis. Chinese Honeysuckle	2 yrs.	25	strong plants	25	2 50	20 00
			extra strong	35	3 50	25 00
dioica (*L. parviflora*). Small-flowered Honeysuckle	2 yrs.	25	strong plants	25	2 50	20 00
			extra strong	35	3 50	25 00
etrusca. Etruscan Honeysuckle	2 yrs.	25	strong plants	25	2 50	
			extra strong	35	3 50	
flava. Yellow Honeysuckle	2 yrs.	25	strong plants	25	2 50	
			extra strong	35	3 50	
glaucescens. Douglas' Honeysuckle	2 yrs.	25	strong plants	25	2 50	
			extra strong	35	3 50	
heckrotti. Heckrott's Honeysuckle	2 yrs.	25	strong plants	25	2 50	
			extra strong	35	3 50	
japonica (*L. halliana*). Japanese Honeysuckle	1 yr.	15	strong plants	15	1 50	10 00
			extra strong	25	2 50	20 00
japonica aureo-reticulata. Golden-leaved Honeysuckle	1 yr.	15	strong plants	15	1 50	10 00
			extra strong	25	2 50	20 00
periclymenum. Woodbine	2 yrs.	25	strong plants	25	2 50	
			extra strong	35	3 50	
periclymenum belgica (*L. belgica*). Monthly Fragrant Honeysuckle	2 yrs.	25	strong plants	25	2 50	20 00
			extra strong	35	3 50	25 00
sempervirens. Trumpet, or Coral Honeysuckle	2 yrs.	25	strong plants	25	2 50	20 00
			extra strong	35	3 50	25 00
sempervirens minor. Narrow-leaved Coral Honeysuckle	2 yrs.	25	strong plants	25	2 50	
			extra strong	35	3 50	
sullivanti. Glaucous Honeysuckle	2 yrs.	25	strong plants	25	2 50	20 00
			extra strong	35	3 50	25 00
Menispermum canadense. Moonseed	2 yrs.	25	strong plants	25	2 50	
			extra strong	50	5 00	

VINES, continued

Botanical and Common Names	Mailing size, postpaid: Size	Each	Express and freight sizes, purchaser paying transportation: Size	Each	Doz.	100
Passiflora cærulea. Passion Flower	1 ft.	$0 25	1½ to 2 ft.	$0 25	$2 50	
			2 to 3 ft.	50	5 00	
cærulea Constance Elliott. White Passion Flower	1 ft.	25	1½ to 2 ft.	25	2 50	
			2 to 3 ft.	50	5 00	
Periploca græca. Silk Vine	1 ft.	25	2 to 3 ft.	25	2 50	$20 00
			3 to 4 ft.	50	5 00	40 00
Pueraria thunbergiana (*Dolichos japonicus*). Kudzu Vine	1 yr.	25	2 yrs.	25	2 50	
			3 yrs.	50	5 00	
Schizophragma hydrangeoides. Creeping Hydrangea	2 yrs.	50	strong plants	50	5 00	
			extra strong	75	7 50	
Smilax bona-nox. Bristly Greenbrier	2 yrs.	25	strong plants	25	2 50	
			extra strong	50	5 00	
glauca. Glaucous-leaved Greenbrier	2 yrs.	25	strong plants	25	2 50	
			extra strong	50	5 00	
hispida. Hispid Greenbrier	2 yrs.	25	strong plants	25	2 50	
			extra strong	50	5 00	
rotundifolia. Catbrier	2 yrs.	25	strong plants	25	2 50	
			extra strong	50	5 00	
Tecoma grandiflora. Chinese Trumpet Vine	2 yrs.	25	strong plants	25	2 50	
			extra strong	50	5 00	
radicans. American Trumpet Vine	2 yrs.	25	strong plants	25	2 50	20 00
			extra strong	50	5 00	40 00
Vitis æstivalis. Summer Grape	2 yrs.	25	strong plants	25	2 50	20 00
			extra strong	50	5 00	40 00
baileyanus. 'Possum Grape	2 yrs.	25	strong plants	25	2 50	20 00
			extra strong	50	5 00	40 00
coignetiæ. Crimson Glory Vine	2 yrs.	25	strong plants	25	2 50	20 00
			extra strong	50	5 00	40 00
cordifolia. Frost Grape	2 yrs.	25	strong plants	25	2 50	20 00
			extra strong	50	5 00	40 00
labrusca. Fox Grape	2 yrs.	25	strong plants	25	2 50	20 00
			extra strong	50	5 00	40 00
Wistaria chinensis. Chinese Wistaria	2 yrs.	25	strong plants	25	2 50	20 00
			extra strong	50	5 00	40 00
chinensis alba. White Wistaria	2 yrs.	25	strong plants	25	2 50	20 00
			extra strong	50	5 00	40 00
chinensis flore pleno. Double-flowered Wistaria	2 yrs.	50	strong plants	50	5 00	
			extra strong	75	7 50	
frutescens. American Wistaria	2 yrs.	25	strong plants	25	2 50	20 00
			extra strong	50	5 00	40 00
macrostachys. Large-flowered American Wistaria	2 yrs.	25	strong plants	25	2 50	20 00
			extra strong	50	5 00	40 00
multijuga. Japanese Wistaria	2 yrs.	25	strong plants	25	2 50	20 00
			extra strong	50	5 00	40 00

An arbor of Wistaria

Ornamental Grasses and Bamboos

Botanical and Common Names	Mailing size, postpaid: Size	Each	Express and freight sizes, purchaser paying transportation: Size	Each	Doz.	100
Arundo donax. Giant Reed	1 yr.	$0 25	strong plants	$0 25	$2 50	$20 00
			extra strong	50	5 00	40 00
donax variegata. Variegated Giant Reed	1 yr.	25	strong plants	25	2 50	20 00
			extra strong	50	5 00	40 00
Arundinaria auricoma. Golden Variegated Cane			strong plants	50	5 00	40 00
			extra strong	1 00	10 00	80 00
japonica (*Bambusa metake*). Japanese Cane			strong plants	50	5 00	40 00
			extra strong	1 00	10 00	80 00
macrosperma. Large American Cane			strong plants	50	5 00	40 00
			extra strong	1 00	10 00	80 00
simoni. Tall Chinese Cane			strong plants	50	5 00	40 00
			extra strong	1 00	10 00	80 00
tecta. Deciduous Cane			strong plants	50	5 00	40 00
			extra strong	1 00	10 00	80 00
Bambusa disticha (*B nana*). Dwarf Bamboo			strong plants	50	5 00	40 00
			extra strong	1 00	10 00	80 00
palmata. Palmate-leaved Bamboo			strong plants	50	5 00	40 00
			extra strong	1 00	10 00	80 00
tessellata. Large-leaved Bamboo			strong plants	50	5 00	40 00
			extra strong	1 00	10 00	80 00
veitchi. Veitch's Bamboo			strong plants	50	5 00	40 00
			extra strong	1 00	10 00	80 00
Phyllostachys aurea. Golden Bamboo			strong plants	1 00	10 00	80 00
			extra strong	2 00	20 00	
mitis. Tall Bamboo			strong plants	2 00	20 00	160 00
			extra strong	3 00	30 00	
nigra. Black-stemmed Bamboo			strong plants	2 00	20 00	
			extra strong	3 00	30 00	
ruscifolia (*Bambusa viminalis*). Ruscus-leaved Bamboo			strong plants	75	7 50	
			extra strong	1 00	10 00	
Carex morrowi (*C. japonica*). Evergreen Sedge	1 yr.	25	strong plants	25	2 50	20 00
			extra strong	35	3 50	25 00
Erianthus ravennæ. Plume Grass	1 yr.	25	strong plants	25	2 50	20 00
			extra strong	35	3 50	25 00
Gynerium argenteum. Pampas Grass	1 yr.	25	strong plants	25	2 50	
			extra strong	35	3 50	
Any of the following forms of Gynericum argenteum: Carmineum, Wesserlingi variegatum, Roi des Roses			strong plants	75	7 50	
Miscanthus japonica. Japanese Eulalia	1 yr.	15	strong plants	15	1 50	10 00
			extra strong	25	2 50	20 00
japonica variegata. Striped Eulalia	1 yr.	15	strong plants	15	1 50	10 00
			extra strong	25	2 50	20 00
japonica zebrina. Zebra Grass	1 yr.	15	strong plants	15	1 50	10 00
			extra strong	25	2 50	20 00
sinensis (*Eulalia gracillima univittata*). Narrow-leaved Eulalia	1 yr.	15	strong plants	15	1 50	10 00
			extra strong	25	2 50	20 00

ORNAMENTAL GRASSES AND BAMBOOS, continued	Mailing size postpaid		Express and freight sizes purchaser paying transportation			
Botanical and Common Names	Size	Each	Size	Each	Doz.	100
Phalaris arundinacea variegata. Ribbon Grass	1 yr.	$0 15	strong plants	$0 15	$1 50	$10 00
			extra strong	25	2 50	20 00
Phragmites communis. Common Reed	1 yr.	25	strong plants	25	2 50	20 00
			extra strong	35	3 50	25 00
Uniola latifolia. Spike Grass	1 yr.	15	strong plants	15	1 50	10 00
			extra strong	25	2 50	20 00

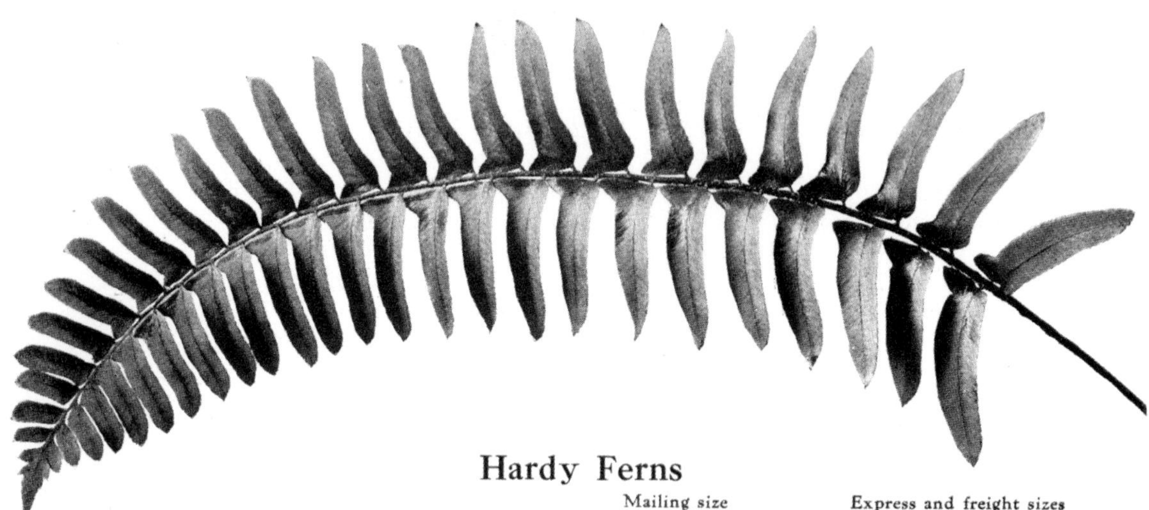

Hardy Ferns

Botanical and Common Names	Mailing size postpaid Size	Each	Express and freight sizes purchaser paying transportation Size	Each	Doz.	100
Adiantum pedatum. Maidenhair Fern	strong	$0 15	large plants	$0 15	$1 50	$10 00
			extra large	25	2 50	20 00
Asplenium filix-fœmina. Lady Fern	strong	15	large plants	15	1 50	10 00
			extra large	25	2 50	20 00
platyneuron. Ebony Spleenwort	strong	15	large plants	15	1 50	10 00
			extra large	25	2 50	20 00
Camptosorus rhizophyllus. Walking Fern	strong	15	large plants	15	1 50	10 00
			extra large	25	2 50	20 00
Dicksonia punctilobula. Hay-scented Fern	strong	15	large plants	15	1 50	10 00
			extra large	25	2 50	20 00
Dryopteris goldieana. Goldie's Fern	strong	25	large plants	25	2 50	20 00
			extra large	35	3 50	
marginalis. Evergreen Wood-fern	strong	15	large plants	15	1 50	10 00
			extra large	25	2 50	20 00
noveboracensis. New York Fern	strong	15	large plants	15	1 50	10 00
			extra large	25	2 50	20 00
spinulosa. Shield Fern	strong	15	large plants	15	1 50	10 00
			extra large	25	2 50	20 00
Lygodium palmatum. Climbing, or Hartford Fern	strong	25	large plants	25	2 50	
			extra large	50	5 00	
Onoclea sensibilis. Sensitive Fern	strong	15	large plants	15	1 50	10 00
			extra large	25	2 50	20 00
struthiopteris. Ostrich Fern	single crowns	25	large plants	25	2 50	20 00
			extra large	50	5 00	40 00
Osmunda cinnamomea. Cinnamon Fern	single crowns	25	large plants	25	2 50	20 00
			extra large	40	4 00	30 00
claytoniana. Clayton's Fern	single crowns	25	large plants	25	2 50	20 00
			extra large	40	4 00	30 00
regalis. Royal Fern	single crowns	25	large plants	25	2 50	20 00
			extra large	40	4 00	30 00
Polypodium vulgare. Common Polypody	strong	15	large plants	15	1 50	10 00
			extra large	25	2 50	20 00
Polystichum acrostichoides. Christmas Fern	strong	15	large plants	15	1 50	10 00
			extra large	25	2 50	20 00
Pteris aquilina. Bracken	strong	15	large plants	15	1 50	10 00
			extra large	25	2 50	20 00

Aquatic and Bog Plants

Botanical and Common Names	Mailing size, postpaid: Size	Each	Express and freight sizes, purchaser paying transportation: Size	Each	Doz.	100
Acorus calamus. Sweet Flag	strong	$0 15	large plants	$0 15	$1 50	$10 00
			extra large	25	2 50	20 00
gramineus variegatus. Variegated Sweet Flag	strong	15	large plants	15	1 50	
			extra large	25	2 50	
Brasenia purpurea. Water Shield	strong	15	large plants	15	1 50	
			extra large	25	2 50	
Caltha palustris. Marsh Marigold	strong	15	large plants	15	1 50	10 00
			extra large	25	2 50	20 00
palustris flore pleno. Double-flowered Marsh Marigold	strong	25	large plants	25	2 50	
			extra large	35	3 50	
Limnanthemum nymphæoides. Floating Heart	strong	15	large plants	15	1 50	10 00
			extra large	25	2 50	20 00
Myosotis palustris. True Forget-me-not	strong	15	large plants	15	1 50	10 00
			extra large	25	2 50	20 00
Myriophyllum proserpinacoides. Parrot's Feather	strong	15	large plants	15	1 50	10 00
			extra large	25	2 50	20 00
Nelumbium luteum. American Lotus, or Water Chinquapin	strong	75	large tubers	75	7 50	
			extra large	1 00	10 00	
speciosum. Indian Lotus	strong	75	large tubers	75	7 50	
			extra large	1 00	10 00	
VARIETIES OF INDIAN LOTUS:						
album	strong	1 50	large tubers	1 50	15 00	
			extra large	2 00	20 00	
album plenum	strong	3 00	large tubers	3 00	30 00	
			extra large	4 00	40 00	
roseum	strong	3 00	large tubers	3 00	30 00	
			extra large	4 00	40 00	
roseum plenum	strong	2 00	large tubers	2 00	20 00	
			extra large	3 00	30 00	
Nuphar advena. Spatter-dock	strong	35	large tubers	35	3 50	
			extra large	50	5 00	
Nymphaea alba. European Water-Lily	strong	50	large tubers	50	5 00	
			extra large	75	7 50	
alba candidissima. Large European Water-Lily	strong	50	large tubers	50	5 00	
			extra large	75	7 50	
flava. Yellow Water-Lily	strong	50	large tubers	50	5 00	
			extra large	75	7 50	
hybrida. Hybrid Water-Lilies						
VARIETIES OF NYMPHÆA HYBRIDA:						
laydeckeri lilacea	strong	1 00	large tubers	1 00	10 00	
laydeckeri purpurata	strong	1 00	large tubers	1 00	10 00	
marliacea albida	strong	50	large tubers	50	5 00	
marliacea carnea	strong	75	large tubers	75	7 50	
marliacea chromatilla	strong	75	large tubers	75	7 50	
odorata. Sweet-scented Water-Lily	strong	25	large tubers	25	2 50	20 00
			extra large	35	3 50	
odorata gigantea. Rice-field Water-Lily	strong	25	large tubers	25	2 50	20 00
			extra large	35	3 50	
tetragona (*N. pygmæa*). Small White Water-Lily	strong	75	large tubers	75	7 50	
			extra large	1 00	10 00	
tuberosa. Tuberous White Water-Lily	strong	25	large tubers	25	2 50	20 00
			extra large	35	3 50	

AQUATIC AND BOG PLANTS, continued

Botanical and Common Names	Mailing size postpaid Size	Each	Express and freight sizes purchaser paying transportation Size	Each	Doz.	100
Nymphaea tuberosa richardsoni	strong	$0 50	large tubers	$0 50	$5 00	
			extra large	75	7 50	
tuberosa rosea	strong	50	large tubers	50	5 00	$40 00
			extra large	75	7 50	
Orontium aquaticum. Golden Club	strong	25	large plants	25	2 50	
			extra large	35	3 50	
Peltandra sagittæfolia. Arrow Arum	strong	25	large plants	25	2 50	
			extra large	35	3 50	
Piaropus crassipes. Water Hyacinth	strong	15	large plants	15	1 50	
			extra large	25	2 50	
Pontederia cordata. Pickerel-weed	strong	15	large plants	15	1 50	
			extra large	25	2 50	
Sagittaria latifolia. Arrowhead	strong	15	large plants	15	1 50	10 00
			extra large	25	2 50	
sagittæfolia flore pleno. Double-flowered Arrowhead	strong	25	large plants	25	2 50	
			extra large	35	3 50	
Sarracenia flava. Yellow Pitcher-plant, or Yellow Trumpet-leaf	strong	25	large plants	25	2 50	
			extra large	35	3 50	
purpurea. Side-saddle Flower	strong	25	large plants	25	2 50	
			extra large	35	3 50	
rubra. Red Trumpet-leaf	strong	25	large plants	25	2 50	
			hxtra large	35	3 50	
Saururus cernuus. Lizard's Tail	strong	15	large plants	15	1 50	10 00
			extra large	25	2 50	
Scirpus lacustris. Bulrush	strong	15	large plants	15	1 50	
			extra large	25	2 50	
Typha angustifolia. Narrow-leaved Cat-tail	strong	15	large plants	15	1 50	10 00
			extra large	25	2 50	
latifolia. Cat-tail	strong	15	large plants	15	1 50	10 00
			extra large	25	2 50	

Nymphæa marliacea carnea

Herbaceous Perennials

Botanical and Common Names	Mailing size, postpaid: Size	Each	Express and freight sizes, purchaser paying transportation: Size	Each	Doz.	100
Acanthus mollis. Bear's Breech	strong	$0 25	large plants	$0 25	$2 50	
			extra large	35	3 50	
Achillea ptarmica flore pleno The Pearl. Double-flowered White Tansy	strong	15	large plants	15	1 50	$10 00
			extra large	25	2 50	
Aconitum autumnale. Autumn Aconite	strong	25	large plants	25	2 50	20 00
			extra large	35	3 50	
napellus. Monkshood	strong	25	large plants	25	2 50	20 00
			extra large	35	3 50	
Adonis vernalis. Pheasant's Eye	strong	25	large plants	25	2 50	
			extra large	35	3 50	
Anemone canadensis (*A. pennsylvanica*). Canadian Windflower	strong	15	large plants	15	1 50	10 00
			extra large	25	2 50	
japonica. Japanese Windflower	strong	15	large plants	15	1 50	10 00
			extra large	25	2 50	
Any of the following varieties of Anemone japonica	strong	25	large plants	25	2 50	20 00
			extra large	35	3 50	
Alba; Loreley; Prince Henry; Queen Charlotte; Rosea purpurea; Whirlwind						
Anthemis tinctoria. Golden Marguerite	strong	15	large plants	15	1 50	
			extra large	25	2 50	
Aquilegia cærulea. Rocky Mountain Columbine	strong	15	large plants	15	1 50	10 00
			extra large	25	2 50	
canadense. American Columbine	strong	15	large plants	15	1 50	
			extra large	25	2 50	
chrysantha. Golden-spurred Columbine	strong	15	large plants	15	1 50	10 00
			extra large	25	2 50	
vulgaris. European Columbine	strong	15	large plants	15	1 50	10 00
			extra large	25	2 50	
Armeria maritima. Sea Thrift	strong	15	large plants	15	1 50	10 00
			extra large	25	2 50	
Aruncus aruncus (*Spiræa aruncus*). Goat's Beard	strong	15	large plants	15	1 50	10 00
			extra large	25	2 50	
astilboides (*S. astilboides*). Japanese Goat's Beard	strong	15	large plants	15	1 50	10 00
			extra large	25	2 50	
Asclepias tuberosa. Butterfly Weed	strong	15	large plants	15	1 50	10 00
			extra large	25	2 50	
Aster. Michaelmas Daisies:—						
curtisi	strong	15	large plants	15	1 50	
			extra large	25	2 50	
lowrieanus	strong	15	large plants	15	1 50	
			extra large	25	2 50	
novæ-angliæ	strong	15	large plants	15	1 50	
			extra large	25	2 50	
patens	strong	15	large plants	15	1 50	
			extra large	25	2 50	
puniceus	strong	15	large plants	15	1 50	
			extra large	25	2 50	
undulatus	strong	15	large plants	15	1 50	
			extra large	25	2 50	
Astilbe japonica. Japanese Astilbe	strong	15	large plants	15	1 50	
			extra large	25	2 50	
Baptisia australis. Blue Indigo	strong	15	large plants	15	1 50	
			extra large	25	2 50	

HERBACEOUS PERENNIALS, continued

Botanical and Common Names	Mailing size, postpaid: Size	Each	Express and freight sizes, purchaser paying transportation: Size	Each	Doz.	100
Bellis perennis. English Daisy	strong	$0 15	large plants	$0 15	$1 50	$10 00
			extra large	25	2 50	
Bocconia cordata. Plume Poppy	strong	15	large plants	15	1 50	
			extra large	25	2 50	
Brauneria purpurea (*Echinacea purpurea*). Purple Cone-flower	strong	15	large plants	15	1 50	
			extra large	25	2 50	
Callirrhoe involucrata. Poppy Mallow	strong	15	large plants	15	1 50	
			extra large	25	2 50	
Campanula carpatica. Carpathian Harebell	strong	15	large plants	15	1 50	10 00
			extra large	25	2 50	
persicifolia. Peach Bells	strong	15	large plants	15	1 50	
			extra large	25	2 50	
persicifolia alba plena. Double Peach Bells	strong	25	large plants	25	2 50	
			extra large	35	3 50	
pyramidalis. Chimney Bellflower	strong	25	large plants	25	2 50	
			extra large	35	3 50	
Cerastium tomentosum. Snow-in-Summer	strong	15	large plants	15	1 50	10 00
			extra large	25	2 50	
Ceratostigma plumbaginoides (*Plumbago larpentæ*). Leadwort	strong	15	large plants	15	1 50	10 00
			extra large	25	2 50	
Chrysanthemum, Hardy Pompon Chrysanthemum. Any of the following varieties of Chrysanthemums: Autumn Glow, Golden Queen, Indian, Old Homestead, Victory	strong	15	large plants	15	1 50	10 00
			extra large	25	2 50	20 00
hybridum. Shasta Daisy	strong	15	large plants	15	1 50	10 00
			extra large	25	2 50	
Cimicifuga racemosa. Black Snakeroot	strong	25	large plants	25	2 50	20 00
			extra large	35	3 50	
Clematis, Herbaceous—						
davidiana	strong	25	large plants	25	2 50	
			extra large	35	3 50	
integrifolia	strong	25	large plants	25	2 50	
			extra large	35	3 50	
recta	strong	25	large plants	25	2 50	
			extra large	35	3 50	
Convallaria majalis. Lily-of-the-Valley	strong	15	clumps	15	1 50	10 00
			large clumps	25	2 50	20 00
Coreopsis lanceolata. Lance-leaved Tickseed	strong	15	large plants	15	1 50	10 00
			extra large	25	2 50	
rosea. Pink Tickseed	strong	15	large plants	15	1 50	10 00
			extra large	25	2 50	
tripteris. Tall Tickseed	strong	15	large plants	15	1 50	
			extra large	25	2 50	
Delphinium cashmerianum. Himalayan Larkspur	strong	25	large plants	25	2 50	
			extra large	35	3 50	
formosum. Showy Larkspur	strong	25	large plants	25	2 50	
			extra large	35	3 50	
grandiflorum. Chinese Larkspur	strong	25	large plants	25	2 50	
			extra large	35	3 50	
nudicaule. California Larkspur	strong	25	large plants	25	2 50	
			extra large	35	3 50	
Dianthus barbatus. Sweet William	strong	15	large plants	15	1 50	10 00
			extra large	25	2 50	
chinensis. China, or Indian Pink	strong	15	large plants	15	1 50	10 00
			extra large	25	2 50	
deltoides. Maiden Pink	strong	15	large plants	15	1 50	10 00
			extra large	25	2 50	
latifolius. Everblooming Sweet William	strong	15	large plants	15	1 50	
			extra large	25	2 50	
plumarius. Scotch Pink	strong	15	large plants	15	1 50	
			extra large	25	2 50	
Dicentra eximia. Alleghany Bleeding Heart	strong	15	large plants	15	1 50	
			extra large	25	2 50	
formosa. California Bleeding Heart	strong	15	large plants	15	1 50	
			extra large	25	2 50	
spectabilis. Bleeding Heart	strong	15	large plants	25	1 50	10 00
			extra large	25	2 50	

HERBACEOUS PERENNIALS, continued

Botanical and Common Names	Mailing size, postpaid: Size	Each	Express and freight sizes, purchaser paying transportation: Size	Each	Doz.	100
Dictamnus alba (*D. fraxinella*). Gas Plant	strong	$0 15	large plants	$0 15	$1 50	
			extra large	25	2 50	
Digitalis purpurea. Foxglove	strong	15	large plants	15	1 50	$10 00
			extra large	25	2 50	
Dodecatheon meadia. Shooting Star	strong	15	large plants	15	1 50	
			extra large	25	2 50	
Doronicium caucasicum. Leopard's Bane	strong	25	large plants	25	2 50	
			extra large	35	3 50	
Epigaea repens. Trailing Arbutus, or Mayflower	strong	25	large plants	25	2 50	20 00
			extra large	35	3 50	
Funkia lancifolia. Narrow-leaved Day Lily	strong	15	large plants	15	1 50	10 00
			extra large	25	2 50	
ovata. Broad-leaved Day Lily	strong	15	large plants	15	1 50	10 00
			extra large	25	2 50	
subcordata. White-flowered Day Lily	strong	15	large plants	15	1 50	10 00
			extra large	25	2 50	
Galax aphylla. Galax	strong	25	large plants	25	2 50	20 00
			extra large	35	3 50	
Galium verum. Bedstraw	strong	15	large plants	15	1 50	
			extra large	25	2 50	
Gemmingia chinensis (*Belemcanda* and *Pardanthus*). Blackberry Lily	strong	15	large plants	15	1 50	
			extra large	25	2 50	
Geranium sanguineum. Cranesbill	strong	15	large plants	15	1 50	
			extra large	25	2 50	
Gypsophila paniculata. Baby's Breath	strong	15	large plants	15	1 50	
			extra large	25	2 50	
Helianthemum chamæcistus (*H. vulgare*). Rock Rose	strong	15	large plants	15	1 50	
			extra large	25	2 50	
Helianthus angustifolius. Swamp Sunflower	strong	15	large plants	15	1 50	
			extra large	25	2 50	
decapetalus maximus. Large-flowered Perennial Sunflower	strong	15	large plants	15	1 50	
			extra large	25	2 50	
mollis. Hairy Sunflower	strong	15	large plants	15	1 50	
			extra large	25	2 50	
multiflorus flore plena. Double Hardy Sunflower	strong	15	large plants	15	1 50	
			extra large	25	2 50	
orgyalis. Linear-leaved Sunflower	strong	15	large plants	15	1 50	
			extra large	25	2 50	
Soleil d'Or. Double Golden Sunflower	strong	15	large plants	15	1 50	
			extra large	25	2 50	
Hemerocallis aurantiaca. Fragrant Orange Lily	strong	25	large plants	25	2 50	
			extra large	35	3 50	
dumortieri. Dwarf Orange Lily	strong	15	large plants	15	1 50	10 00
			extra large	25	2 50	
flava. Lemon Lily	strong	15	large plants	15	1 50	10 00
			extra large	25	2 50	
fulva. Tawny Day Lily	strong	15	large plants	15	1 50	10 00
			extra large	25	2 50	
fulva kwanso. Double Orange Lily	strong	15	large plants	15	1 50	10 00
			extra large	25	2 50	
thunbergi. Late-flowering Lemon Lily	strong	15	large plants	15	1 50	10 00
			extra large	25	2 50	
Hibiscus militaris. Halbert-leaved Rose Mallow	strong	25	large plants	25	2 50	
			extra large	35	3 50	
moscheutos. Marsh, or Rose Mallow	strong	25	large plants	25	2 50	
			extra large	35	3 50	
oculiroseus. Crimson Eye	strong	25	large plants	25	2 50	
			extra large	35	3 50	
Iberis sempervirens. Evergreen Candytuft	strong	15	large plants	15	1 50	10 00
			extra large	25	2 50	
Incarvillea delavayi. Hardy Gloxinia	strong	25	large plants	25	2 50	
			extra large	35	3 50	
Iris cristata. Crested Iris	strong	15	large plants	15	1 50	10 00
			extra large	25	2 50	20 00
florentina. Orris Root	strong	15	large plants	15	1 50	10 00
			extra large	25	2 50	20 00

HERBACEOUS PERENNIALS, continued

Botanical and Common Names	Mailing size, postpaid: Size	Each	Express and freight sizes, purchaser paying transportation: Size	Each	Doz.	100
Iris germanica. German Iris, or Fleur-de-Lis	strong	$0 15	large plants	$0 15	$1 50	$10 00
			extra large	25	2 50	20 00
Any of the following varieties of Iris germanica	strong	25	large plants	25	2 50	20 00
			extra large	35	3 50	25 00

Amas, Darius, Dr. Bernice, Innocenza, Kharput, Mme. Chereau, Mandraliscoe, Maori King, Pallida Dalmatica, Plicata, Queen of May, Victorine

Botanical and Common Names	Size	Each	Size	Each	Doz.	100
lævigata. Japanese Iris	strong	15	large plants	15	1 50	10 00
			extra large	25	2 50	20 00
Any of the following varieties of Iris lævigata	strong	25	large plants	25	2 50	20 00
			extra large	35	3 50	25 00

DOUBLE-FLOWERED FORMS:

Geishoi, Hana-Aoi, Kagarabi, Kuma-Funjin, Manadzura, Rish-no-Tama, Samidare, Sano-Watashi, Senja-no-Hora, Taiheiraku, Waku-Hotei, Yoshimo

SINGLE-FLOWERED FORMS:

Date-Dogu, Kumoma-no-Sora, Yomo-Zakuru

Botanical and Common Names	Size	Each	Size	Each	Doz.	100
missouriensis. Western Blue Flag	strong	15	large plants	15	1 50	10 00
			extra large	25	2 50	20 00
pumila. European Dwarf Iris	strong	15	large plants	15	1 50	10 00
			extra large	25	2 50	20 00
sibirica. Siberian Iris	strong	15	large plants	15	1 50	10 00
			extra large	25	2 50	20 00
verna. American Dwarf Iris	strong	15	large plants	15	1 50	10 00
			extra large	25	2 50	20 00
versicolor. Blue Flag	strong	15	large plants	15	1 50	10 00
			extra large	25	2 50	20 00
Lathyrus latifolius. Everlasting, or Hardy Sweet Pea	strong	15	large plants	15	1 50	
			extra large	25	2 50	
Lavandula vera. True Lavender	strong	15	large plants	15	1 50	
			extra large	25	2 50	
Lespedeza japonica. White-flowered Lespedeza	strong	15	large plants	15	1 50	10 00
			extra large	25	2 50	20 00
sieboldi (*Desmodium penduliflorum*). Siebold's Desmodium	strong	15	large plants	15	1 50	10 00
			extra large	25	2 50	20 00
Lilium auratum. Golden-banded Japanese Lily	bulbs	25	large bulbs	25	2 50	20 00
			extra large	35	3 50	
canadense. Wild Yellow Lily	bulbs	15	large bulbs	15	1 50	10 00
			extra large	25	2 50	
candidum. Madonna Lily	bulbs	25	large bulbs	25	2 50	20 00
			extra large	35	3 50	
carolinianum. Carolina Lily	bulbs	25	large bulbs	25	2 50	20 00
			extra large	35	3 50	
elegans (*L. umbellatum*). Japanese Orange Lily	bulbs	25	large bulbs	25	2 50	20 00
			extra large	35	3 50	
speciosum. Japanese Pink Lily	bulbs	25	large bulbs	25	2 50	20 00
			extra large	35	3 50	
superbum. Turk's Cap Lily	bulbs	25	large bulbs	25	2 50	20 00
			extra large	35	3 50	
tigrinum. Tiger Lily	bulbs	15	large bulbs	15	1 50	10 00
			extra large	25	2 50	
tigrinum flore pleno. Double Tiger Lily	bulbs	15	large bulbs	15	1 50	10 00
			extra large	25	2 50	
Liriope graminifolia (*Ophiopogon spicatus*). Purple Snakebeard	strong	15	large plants	15	1 50	10 00
			extra large	25	2 50	
Lychnis chalcedonica. Maltese Cross	strong	15	large plants	15	1 50	10 00
			extra large	25	2 50	

HERBACEOUS PERENNIALS, continued

Botanical and Common Names	Mailing size, postpaid: Size	Each	Express and freight sizes, purchaser paying transportation: Size	Each	Doz.	100
Lysimachia clethroides. Loosestrife	strong	$0 15	large plants	$0 15	$1 50	$10 00
			extra large	25	2 50	
nummularia. Moneywort	strong	15	clumps	15	1 50	10 00
			large clumps	25	2 50	
Mertensia virginica. Blue Bells	strong	15	large plants	15	1 50	
			extra large	25	2 50	
Monarda didyma. Oswego Tea	strong	15	large plants	15	1 50	10 00
			extra large	25	2 50	
Nierembergia rivularis. White Cup	strong	15	large plants	15	1 50	
			extra large	25	2 50	
Opuntia vulgaris. Prickly Pear, or Hardy Cactus	strong	15	large plants	15	1 50	
			extra large	25	2 50	
Pachysandra procumbens. Alleghany Spurge	strong	15	large plants	15	1 50	10 00
			extra large	25	2 50	
terminalis. Japanese Spurge	strong	15	large plants	15	1 50	10 00
			extra large	25	2 50	
Paeonia sinensis. Double-flowering Peony	strong	25	large plants	25	2 50	20 00
			extra large	35	3 50	25 00
Any of the following named varieties of Pæonia sinensis:	strong	35	large plants	35	3 50	25 00
			extra large	50	5 00	40 00

Achille, Alba plena, Alexandrina, Ambroise Verschaffelt, Anemoneflora, Bicolor, Bucchi, Comte Neipperg, Duc de Cazes, Duchesse de Nemours, Duchesse d'Orleans, Duke of Wellington, Edulis superba, Festiva alba, Festiva maxima, Humei, Jeanne d'Arc, Lamartine, L'Esperance, Louis Van Houtte, Ne Plus Ultra, Poiteau, Princess Mathilde, Queen Victoria, Reevesi, Rosea elegans, Sydonie, Whitleyi

Botanical and Common Names	Size	Each	Size	Each	Doz.	100
officinalis. Double-flowering Peony						
Any of the following named varieties of Pæonia officinalis:	strong	35	large plants	35	3 50	25 00
			extra large	50	5 00	40 00

Alba, Rosea, Rubra

Botanical and Common Names	Size	Each	Size	Each	Doz.	100
tenuifolia. Cut-leaved Peony	strong	35	large plants	35	3 50	25 00
			extra large	50	5 00	40 00
sinensis. Single-flowering Peony	strong	35	large plants	35	3 50	25 00
			extra large	50	5 00	40 00
Any of the following named varieties of Single-flowered Pæonia sinensis:	strong	50	large plants	50	5 00	40 00
			extra large	65	6 50	50 00

Abidan, Abora, Abyla, Gabreta, Iphis, Josephine, Libon, The Bride

Botanical and Common Names	Size	Each	Size	Each	Doz.	100
moutan. Tree Peony.						
Any of the following named varieties of Pæonia moutan:	2 yrs.	1 00	3 yrs.	1 00	10 00	
			4 yrs.	1 25	12 50	

Comte de Flanders, Elizabeth, Gloire des Belgiques, Guillaume Tell, Regina belgica, Semperflorens alba, Van Houttei

Botanical and Common Names	Size	Each	Size	Each	Doz.	100
Papaver orientale. Oriental Poppy	1 yr.	15	2 yrs.	15	1 50	10 00
			3 yrs.	25	2 50	
Phlox amœna. Hairy Phlox	strong	15	large plants	15	1 50	10 00
			extra large	25	2 50	
glaberrima. Smooth Phlox	strong	15	large plants	15	1 50	10 00
			extra large	25	2 50	
Any of the following named varieties of Phlox glaberrima:	strong	25	large plants	25	2 50	
			extra large	35	3 50	

Lady Musgrove, Nettie Stewart, Perfection, Snowdon

Botanical and Common Names	Size	Each	Size	Each	Doz.	100
ovata. Mountain Phlox	strong	15	large plants	15	1 50	10 00
			extra large	25	2 50	

HERBACEOUS PERENNIALS, continued

Botanical and Common Names	Mailing size, postpaid: Size	Each	Express and freight sizes, purchaser paying transportation: Size	Each	Doz.	100
Phlox paniculata. Garden Phlox.						
Any of the following named varieties of Phlox paniculata:	strong	$0 15	large plants	$0 15	$1 50	$10 00
			extra large	25	2 50	20 00

Athis
Beranger
Bridesmaid
Brilliant
Champs Elysees
Coquelicot
Eclaireur
Etna
Flora Hornung
Independence
Jeanne d'Arc
La Vogue
Pantheon
Peach Blossom
Von Goethe

Botanical and Common Names	Size	Each	Size	Each	Doz.	100
reptans. Creeping Phlox	strong	15	large plants	15	1 50	10 00
			extra large	25	2 50	20 00
subulata. Moss Pink	strong	15	large plants	15	1 50	10 00
			extra large	25	2 50	20 00
Any of the following named varieties of Phlox subulata	strong	15	large plants	15	1 50	
			extra large	25	2 50	

Alba
Atropurpurea
Lilacina
Rosea

Botanical and Common Names	Size	Each	Size	Each	Doz.	100
Physostegia virginiana. False Dragonhead	strong	15	large plants	15	1 50	10 00
			extra large	25	2 50	20 00
Platycodon grandiflorum. Chinese Bellflower, or Balloon Flower	strong	15	large plants	15	1 50	10 00
			extra large	25	2 50	20 00
grandiflorum mariesi. Glaucous Chinese Bellflower	strong	15	large plants	15	1 50	10 00
			extra large	25	2 50	20 00
Polemonium cæruleum. Jacob's Ladder	strong	15	large plants	15	1 50	10 00
			extra large	25	2 50	20 00
cæruleum album. White-flowered Jacob's Ladder	strong	15	large plants	15	1 50	10 00
			extra large	25	2 50	20 00
Polygonum cuspidatum. Japanese Polygonum	strong	15	large plants	15	1 50	10 00
			extra large	25	2 50	20 00
Potentilla tridentata. Evergreen Cinquefoil	strong	15	large plants	15	1 50	10 00
			extra large	25	2 50	20 00
Rudbeckia laciniata Golden Glow. Double-flowered Rudbeckia	strong	15	large plants	15	1 50	10 00
			extra large	25	2 50	
speciosa. Showy Cone-flower	strong	15	large plants	15	1 50	
			extra large	25	2 50	
Santolina chamæcyparissus. Lavender Cotton	strong	15	large plants	15	1 50	10 00
			extra large	25	2 50	
Sedum acre. Mossy Stone-crop, or Wall-pepper	strong	15	large plants	15	1 50	10 00
			extra large	25	2 50	
album. White Stone-crop	strong	15	large plants	15	1 50	10 00
			extra large	25	2 50	
maximum. Large Stone-crop	strong	15	large plants	15	1 50	10 00
			extra large	25	2 50	
maximum atropurpureum. Purple Stone-crop	strong	15	large plants	15	1 50	10 00
			extra large	25	2 50	
pulchellum. Widow's Cross	strong	15	large plants	15	1 50	10 00
			extra large	25	2 50	
sexangulare. Dark Green Stone-crop	strong	15	large plants	15	1 50	10 00
			extra large	25	2 50	
spectabile. Brilliant Stone-crop	strong	15	large plants	15	1 50	10 00
			extra large	25	2 50	20 00
spectabile atropurpureum. Dark-flowered Stone-crop	strong	15	large plants	15	1 50	
			extra large	25	2 50	
spurium. Trailing Stone-crop	strong	15	large plants	15	1 50	10 00
			extra large	25	2 50	
spurium coccineum. Crimson-flowered Stone-crop	strong	15	large plants	15	1 50	10 00
			extra large	25	2 50	
ternatum. Wild Stone-crop	strong	15	large plants	15	1 50	10 00
			extra large	25	2 50	20 00
Shortia galacifolia. Shortia	strong	25	large plants	25	2 50	20 00
			extra large	35	3 50	
Stokesia cyanea. Stokes' Aster	strong	15	large plants	15	1 50	10 00
			extra large	25	2 50	
Tanacetum vulgare crispum. Curly-leaved Tansy	strong	15	large plants	15	1 50	10 00
			extra large	25	2 50	

HERBACEOUS PERENNIALS, continued

Botanical and Common Names	Mailing size postpaid Size	Each	Express and freight sizes purchaser paying transportation Size	Each	Doz.	100
Thymus citriodorus. Lemon Thyme	strong	$0 15	large plants	$0 15	$1 50	
			extra large	25	2 50	
lanuginosus. Downy Thyme	strong	15	large plants	15	1 50	
			extra large	25	2 50	
serpyllum. Mother of Thyme	strong	15	large plants	15	1 50	
			extra large	25	2 50	
vulgaris. Common Thyme	strong	15	large plants	15	1 50	
			extra large	25	2 50	
Tradescantia montana. Mountain Spiderwort	strong	15	large plants	15	1 50	
			extra large	25	2 50	
reflexa. Glaucous Spiderwort	strong	15	large plants	15	1 50	
			extra large	25	2 50	
virginica. Common Spiderwort	strong	15	large plants	15	1 50	
			extra large	25	2 50	
Ulmaria filapendula (*Spiræa filapendula*). Herbaceous Meadow Sweet	strong	15	large plants	15	1 50	$10 00
			extra large	25	2 50	
pentapetala (*Spiræa ulmaria*). Queen of the Meadows	strong	15	large plants	15	1 50	10 00
			extra large	25	2 50	
pentapetala flore pleno. Double-flowered Queen of the Meadows	strong	15	large plants	15	1 50	10 00
			extra large	25	2 50	
purpurea (*Spiræa palmata*). Japanese Meadow Sweet	strong	15	large plants	15	1 50	10 00
			extra large	25	2 50	
rubra. Queen of the Prairie	strong	15	large plants	15	1 50	10 00
			extra large	25	2 50	
Veronica longifolia subsessilis. Japanese Speedwell	strong	25	large plants	25	2 50	20 00
			extra large	35	3 50	
rupestris. Rock Speedwell	strong	15	large plants	15	1 50	10 00
			extra large	25	2 50	
spicata. European Speedwell	strong	15	large plants	15	1 50	10 00
			extra large	25	2 50	
Vinca major. Larger Periwinkle	strong	15	large plants	15	1 50	10 00
			extra large	25	2 50	
minor. Common Periwinkle, or Trailing Myrtle	strong	15	large plants	15	1 50	10 00
			extra large	25	2 50	
Yucca filamentosa. Adam's Needle, or Bear Grass	1 yr.	15	2 yrs.	15	1 50	10 00
			3 yrs.	25	2 50	20 00
			4 yrs.	35	3 50	
filamentosa variegata. Variegated Yucca	1 yr.	25	2 yrs.	25	2 50	
			3 yrs.	35	3 50	

Berries of Berberis thunbergi

Rhododendron catawbiense

INDEX

Photographed, Designed, Engraved and Printed by
J. HORACE McFARLAND COMPANY
Mount Pleasant Press
HARRISBURG, PENNA.